HANDBOOK OF HUMAN RESOURCE MANAGEMENT IN THE TOURISM AND HOSPITALITY INDUSTRIES

Handbook of Human Resource Management in the Tourism and Hospitality Industries

Edited by

Ronald J. Burke

Emeritus Professor, Schulich School of Business, York University, Canada

Julia Christensen Hughes

Professor, College of Business and Economics, University of Guelph, Canada

 Edward Elgar
PUBLISHING

Cheltenham, UK • Northampton, MA, USA

Published by
Edward Elgar Publishing Limited
The Lypiatts
15 Lansdown Road
Cheltenham
Glos GL50 2JA
UK

Edward Elgar Publishing, Inc.
William Pratt House
9 Dewey Court
Northampton
Massachusetts 01060
USA

A catalogue record for this book
is available from the British Library

Library of Congress Control Number: 2017947102

This book is available electronically in the **Elgar**online
Business subject collection
DOI 10.4337/9781786431370

MIX
Paper from
responsible sources
FSC® C013056
www.fsc.org

ISBN 978 1 78643 136 3 (cased)
ISBN 978 1 78643 137 0 (eBook)

Typeset by Servis Filmsetting Ltd, Stockport, Cheshire
Printed and bound in Great Britain by TJ International Ltd, Padstow

Contents

Contributors

Tom Baum, PhD, is Professor and Head of Department of Human Resource Management at the University of Strathclyde, Glasgow, Scotland. His research interests focus on employment issues in the international hospitality and tourism industry, a sector that continues to fascinate and excite him despite over 30 years of engagement with it. He has authored twelve books and over 200 scientific papers and has supervised over 35 PhD students to completion.

Marie-Hélène Budworth is an Associate Professor of Human Resource Management within the School of Human Resource Management at York University, UK. She completed her PhD in Management at the Rotman School of Management, University of Toronto, Canada. Her research is focused on performance management, learning and motivation. Most recently she has been studying the effectiveness of various techniques for delivering feedback within performance management systems.

Ronald J. Burke (PhD University of Michigan) is Emeritus Professor of Organizational Studies, Schulich School of Business, York University in Toronto, Canada. His current research interests include women in management, violence and abuse in and around organizations, the sandwich generation, and creating psychologically healthy workplaces. He has also conducted research in the hospitality sector in Turkey and China.

Catherine Cheung, PhD, is Associate Professor and Associate Dean at the School of Hotel and Tourism Management of the Hong Kong Polytechnic University. Her research interests are in the area of hospitality human resources management, service quality and hotel branding. She has authored or co-authored over 70 research papers and supervised over 12 PhD students to completion. She has also served as a management consultant to hotels, airlines, hospitals and clubs in Asia.

Julia Christensen Hughes is Dean of the College of Business and Economics at the University of Guelph in Ontario, Canada where she is also a faculty member in the School of Hospitality, Food and Tourism Management. Her research interests include strategic HRM, employee empowerment, employee engagement and talent management. In 2012 Julia was recognized as Educator of the Year by the Ontario Hostelry Institute. In 2003 she received a Highly Commended Award by the International Journal of Contemporary Hospitality Management.

Andrew Jenkins is Subject Leader in Hospitality and Events Management at the University of Huddersfield, UK. He has written extensively on employment issues and his research has been published in *Employee Relations*; *Equality, Diversity and Inclusion*; *International Journal of Contemporary Hospitality Management*; *Journal of Human Resources in Hospitality and Tourism*; and *Tourism Management*. He is co-author of the textbook *Introducing Human Resource Management*, and is co-author of a chapter on International Assignments in *Human Resource Management in a Global Context: A Critical Approach*.

Camille E. Kapoor, MS, has extensive experience in the hospitality industry, including working as the Director of the Hospitality Industry Diversity Institute, as a consultant for PKF Consulting, and as a financial/marketing analyst for Boardwalk Pipeline Partners. She is the recipient of the 2013 Donald Greenaway Teaching Excellence Award. She has taught a variety of subjects including graduate research methods, human resources, marketing, business law, and hospitality finance. Camille is a PhD student at the Conrad N. Hilton College of Hotel and Restaurant Management at the University of Houston, USA.

Derya Kara is an Associate Professor in the Faculty of Economics and Administrative Sciences, Gazi University, Turkey. She received a PhD from the Department of Tourism Management Education, Gazi University, Turkey. She has extensive experience in the travel and tourism field, human resource management, and tourism management. Her current research interests are in the areas of human resource management with respect to gender in tourism and hospitality settings. She has published numerous articles in national and international journals. She has also received a number of awards for her research contributions.

Lindsey Lee, MS, is a PhD student at the Conrad N. Hilton College of Hotel and Restaurant Management at the University of Houston, USA. Her research focuses on emotional labour in service settings and on diversity management. She has worked at the Rosen Centre as a convention coordinator, assisting convention and catering service managers to deliver successful conventions and events. Lindsey Lee received her MS from the Rosen College of Hospitality Management at the University of Central Florida.

Juan M. Madera, PhD, is an Associate Professor at the Conrad N. Hilton College of Hotel and Restaurant Management at the University of Houston, USA. His research focuses on hospitality workforce diversity. His research has appeared in several top-tier hospitality-specific and general management journals such as *Journal of Applied Psychology*; *Journal of Business and Psychology*; *Journal of Contemporary Hospitality Management*; *International Journal of Hospitality Management*; *Cornell Quarterly*; and *Journal of Hospitality and Tourism Research*. He received his PhD in Industrial/Organizational Psychology from Rice University, USA.

Sara L. Mann is an Associate Professor of Organizational Behavior and Strategic Human Resource Management in the Department of Management at the University of Guelph, Canada. Sara completed her Bachelor of Commerce and MBA at McMaster University, and a PhD in Management at the Rotman School of Management, University of Toronto. Prior to going back to school to complete her PhD, Sara worked as a supply chain analyst for Kraft Foods and Stelco. Sara's expertise includes employment issues, performance management, selection and compensation.

Shelagh Mooney lectures on Organizational Behavior and Human Resources Management at Auckland University of Technology in New Zealand. She has presented at academic conferences and published in peer-reviewed international journals on women's career progression and how age, gender and/or ethnicity influence individual career experiences in hospitality. Prior to entering the academic environment, Shelagh held senior executive roles across Europe with companies such as the Savoy Group, IHG and Hilton, in addition to working with independent organizations. In Australia she has represented academic perspectives on gender equality in hospitality industry forums. Due to her extensive operational experience and contextual qualitative research focus, Shelagh continues to explore how organizations in the service sector can enhance employee performance and well-being through enlightened human resource management practices.

William C. Murray is an Assistant Professor with the School of Hospitality, Food and Tourism Management at the University of Guelph in Ontario, Canada, where he teaches both operational skills and management theory. His research interests focus around the human experience, examining the management of talent, what motivates people to act, and how people create meanings within their socially constructed world. He is co-author of the textbook *Snapshots: An Introduction to Tourism*, 6th Canadian edition. He holds a PhD in Management from Saint Mary's University, an MBA from the University of Guelph, a BA from Carleton University and a diploma in Hotel and Restaurant Management from Algonquin College.

Alfred Ogle, PhD, is a researcher and academic specializing in the areas of Hospitality and Tourism Management, and Marketing. A former hotelier, he runs a research consultancy in Perth, Australia and holds sessional academic positions at various tertiary institutions. His research interests include: guestology; facilities management and sustainability; servicescape and atmospherics; strategic marketing management; service innovation/hospitality service encounters; and the theory–practice nexus. He works closely with industry partners and fellow academics on applied research projects.

William J. Pallett is President of his own consulting firm specializing in the hotel industry. Much of his consulting work addresses management development and talent management and their role in improving organizational performance. He previously held senior management positions with the Delta Hotels and Resorts and the Four Seasons Hotels and Resorts chains. His work with Delta contributed to their various awards for human resource management excellence. Delta has consistently been voted one of the 50 best companies to work for in Canada, their highly engaging culture being cited. He has taught human resource management at various Canadian institutions, and is a frequent conference speaker at both hotel industry and other industry gatherings.

Ta-Wei Tang is Associate Professor of the Department of Leisure and Recreation Management at Asia University in Taiwan. He is also a consultant in the Department of Medical Research at China Medical University Hospital, Taiwan. His major research interests are high performance human resource management practices, service innovation, and hospitality management. His research papers have been published in the *International Journal of Hospitality Management*; *International Journal of Contemporary Hospitality Management*; *Asia Pacific Journal of Tourism Research*; *Service Business*; and *Total Quality Management & Business Excellence*.

Ya-Yun Tang is Associate Professor of the Department of Recreation Management at the Shih Chien University, Taiwan. She received a PhD from the Department of Business Administration, National Central University, Taiwan. Her research is primarily on human resource management and employee innovative behaviour in the hospitality industry, specifically focusing on enhancing service employees' service performance in the organizational environment and group affect. Her articles have appeared in the *International Journal of Hospitality Management*; *International Journal of Contemporary Hospitality Management*; and *Service Business*.

Muzaffer Uysal is Professor and Chair of the Department of Hospitality and Tourism Management at the University of Massachusetts – Amherst. He has extensive experience in the hospitality and tourism field; and he has worked on several funded tourism management and marketing projects and conducted tourism workshops and seminars in more than 25 countries. He is a member of International Academy for the Study of Tourism, the Academy of Leisure Sciences, and co-founder of *Tourism Analysis: An Interdisciplinary Journal.* He has also authored and co-authored a significant number of articles, book chapters, five monographs, and eleven books related to tourism and hospitality settings. Dr Uysal has also received a number of awards for Research, Excellence in International Education, Teaching Excellence, Lifetime Achievement Awards, and best paper awards. His current research interests centre on demand/supply interaction, tourism development and QOL research in tourism and hospitality.

Michael Chih-Hung Wang is Assistant Professor of the Department of Business Administration at the Feng Chia University, Taiwan. He received his PhD degree from the Department of Business Administration, National Central University, Taiwan. His research primarily focuses on branding and service innovation in hospitality and sports. His articles have appeared in journals such as *International Journal of Market Research*; *Sport Management Review*; *Managing Service Quality*; and *Service Business.*

Tsai-Chiao Wang is a postdoctoral research fellow of the Institute of Physical Education, Health and Leisure Studies at National Cheng Kung University, Taiwan. She received her PhD degree from the Department of International Business Studies, National Chi Nan University, Taiwan. Her major research interests are in the hospitality fields of service innovation, service science and marketing. Her research papers have been published in academic journals such as *International Journal of Hospitality Management*; and *International Journal of Contemporary Hospitality Management.*

Acknowledgements

I have been involved in human resource management research throughout my career. I first undertook research in the hospitality and tourism sector with colleagues in Turkey, who now unfortunately have been removed from their offices as a result of the recent government crackdown. I thank our international writers and researchers for their excellent contributions. Fran O'Sullivan and the staff at Edward Elgar have supported our efforts over a long period of time. My friend and colleague, Julia Christensen Hughes, Dean of Canada's premier programme in hospitality management, brought her vast knowledge and experience as well as her extensive network to this effort. Carla D'Agostino, as usual, provided outstanding administrative assistance in Toronto in linking with our authors and Edward Elgar. My participation was supported in part by York University.

Ronald Burke
Toronto

I am delighted to have had the opportunity to participate as co-editor and author in this important project. I am grateful for the leadership of Ron Burke who conceptualized the book and invited my participation. I am also thankful for the support of the University of Guelph, who provided me with sabbatical leave. I would also like to recognize the contributing researchers for their excellent work, as well as faculty in the University of Guelph's College of Business and Economics and School of Hospitality, Food and Tourism Management. They are inspiring and innovative educational leaders, committed to exploring important issues and developing future management and academic talent for this fascinating and essential industry.

Julia Christensen Hughes
Guelph

PART I

SETTING THE STAGE

1. Human resource management in the hospitality and tourism sector
Ronald J. Burke

The hospitality and tourism industry currently employs about ten percent of the worldwide workforce. As tourism is seen as continuing to grow, the number of travelers will also increase. About one billion people now travel each year with this figure reaching over 1.5 billion in 2015. This will produce a shortage of talented managers, coupled with the need to meet increasingly diverse future customer needs. Changes in technology, along with changes in the make-up of customers – fewer Baby boomers and more Gen Xers and Gen Ys – will increasingly challenge hospitality organizations. In addition, greater use will be made of social media and mobile technologies, requiring the training of staff. Retaining qualified staff at all levels who are now on board and recruiting and orienting new staff will be critical to success.

The hospitality and tourism sector represents a major contributor to the Gross Domestic Product of various countries and this sector is growing in importance. Perhaps every country in the world supports their hospitality and tourism industries (Baker, 2013). Growth in this sector has been particularly strong in South East Asia, with Macau now becoming the leading gambling center in the world. Several recent publications have documented the positive contribution of hospitality and tourism to the economies of various countries. These include Spain and Italy (Cortes-Jimenez and Paluna, 2010); Spain (Balaguer and Cantavella-Jorda, 2002); Germany (Brida and Risso, 2010); Turkey (Gunduz and Hatemi-J, 2008); Cyprus (Katircioglu, 2009); and China (Shan and Wilson, 2001). In addition, surveys of tourism and economic development in a number of countries considered simultaneously have shown the significant contribution made by hospitality and tourism (Sinclair, 1998; Hazari and Sgro, 1995; Sequeira and Nunes, 2008). Research on human resource management practices in this sector has also grown to reflect international practices and concerns.

SERVICE QUALITY

As a service industry, providing high quality service to all customers and clients is vital to customer and client satisfaction, loyalty, and positive word-of-mouth. Thus providing high quality of service is central to the success of hospitality and tourism organizations. But measuring service quality is complicated, as service quality is mainly a subjective assessment of an interpersonal experience between an individual providing a service and an individual receiving this service. As service is intangible, diverse, and simultaneously produced and consumed, quantitative measures of perceived service quality are important. Perceptions of service quality, and customer satisfaction with provided services, while related, are different concepts. Service quality is one aspect of customer satisfaction (Zeithaml and Bitner, 2003).

Parasuraman et al. (1985; 1989) developed a multidimensional scale for assessing perceptions of service quality. They view perceived service quality as a global assessment about the superiority of service provided. Customer satisfaction, however, only relates to a particular transaction between provider and consumer. Thus service quality includes several dimensions.

Parasuraman et al. (1989) offer five dimensions: reliability; responsiveness; assurance; empathy; and tangibles. Reliability involves the ability to perform the promised service dependably and accurately. Responsiveness involves a willingness to help customers and provide prompt service. Assurance involves knowledge and courtesy of employees and their ability to inspire trust and confidence. Empathy involves caring and individualized attention given to customers. Tangibles involve the appearance of physical facilities, equipment, personnel and written materials. Thus Zeithaml and Bitner (2003) require customers to assess quality of service in terms of these five dimensions.

Since service quality is basically a provider and consumer transaction, human resources are seen as the most important aspect of organizational success in hospitality organizations. Employees possess skills, knowledge, experience, ability, attitudes and values, behaviors, and relationships, both inside and outside their work area or organizations. Many of these qualities (for example, attitudes, values, knowledge, behaviors, skills) are affected by the human resource management policies and practices of their organization and the behaviors of their supervisors and managers.

Michel et al. (2012) considered the relationship of an organization's customer service climate/culture on ratings of employee service self-efficacy beliefs, job performance, and intentions to quit. Data were collected from both front-line employees and their supervisors. Their supportive service climate measure had three dimensions: HR support (rewards and incentives for providing high quality service); management support (managers had standards for high service quality); and job support (enough staff to deliver high quality service). Employee perceptions of climate for service quality predicted higher levels of staff motivation, less intention to quit and higher performance ratings by supervisors.

Service quality has received considerable and increasing research attention over the past 20 years (Kandampully et al., 2014). This research and writing has considered measuring service quality in hospitality organizations, the relationship of service quality and important outcomes such as customer satisfaction, customer loyalty, customer behavioral intentions, brand loyalty, customer expectations, front-line and managerial employee behaviors, human resource management policies and practices, organizational climate or culture, and business performance.

The central concept of developing a high quality service culture emerges as a focus for human resource management (Kandampully et al., 2014). The key then is the role played by human resource management policies and practices in the process of providing high quality service to customers and clients. How would you define a high service quality culture? What factors make up a high quality service culture? How would an organization measure their standing on these factors? How can organizations develop a high quality service culture? What human resource management policies and practices foster high levels of service quality? Studies have reported that service quality cultures are associated with higher levels of client satisfaction, more return business, more customer loyalty, and positive word-of-mouth to others (Batt, 2002).

Workplace culture is critical for organizational success (Davidson, 2003; Parasuraman, 1987). One can copy other organizations' physical facilities and products, their business strategies, and one can hire away their employees, but it is impossible to duplicate their culture easily. Culture is how things get done, the norms, and behavioral, attitudinal and value expectations of all the staff. Aligning your human resource management policies and practices to your desired workplace culture is important in achieving high levels of service excellence and financial performance. Chief executive leadership is key in starting this process. Human resource management policies and practices that shape recruitment, retention, performance through goal-setting, monitoring, appraising, discussing, recognizing and rewarding excellence in performance will heighten employee satisfaction, work engagement and organizational identification.

Human resource management issues emerge as the most difficult challenge facing hotel general managers and corporate executives (Enz, 2009a; 2001). Enz (2001) collected data from 170 hospitality managers from over

25 different countries, asking them to identify the "thorniest" issues that they encountered. At the top of the list was the use of their human capital – how to care for and get the best performance from their employees. This involved functions of attracting, retaining, training and developing and motivating staff. These concerns were expressed by managers at all levels. Enz (2009b) replicated her 2001 study, surveying 243 managers from over 60 countries. The most pressing concerns were attracting qualified staff, retaining successful staff, training employees, maintaining or improving staff morale, and creating career development opportunities. Employee benefits and compensation costs were of less concern.

Yet human resource management policies and practices play a central role for success in the hospitality and tourism sector (Zemke and Schaef, 1989; Schneider and Bowen, 1995; Schneider and White, 2004; Bowen and Lawler, 1995). Service workers become part of the product representing their hotels, and creating an image of their organizations. The personality, skills, knowledge, appearance, attitudes and behaviors of the service worker become critical; how they are managed becomes similarly vital. These factors produce high levels of service quality, customer satisfaction, customer loyalty, a source of competitive advantage for an organization, and high levels of organizational performance and success. Human resource management policies and practices, organizational culture, and the integration of human resource management and business strategies are all associated with valued customer and organizational outcomes.

The basic framework that guides much of the thinking, research and application of research findings linking human resource management practices with ultimate organizational outcomes proposes (1) antecedents including level of human capital talents, human resource management practices, and organizational culture leading to (2) employee attitudes and behaviors such as job satisfaction, work engagement, team contribution, exercising voice, loyalty and commitment to the organization, and commitment to service quality, which leads to (3) customer satisfaction and customer loyalty, which then contributes to (4) valued organizational outcomes such as productivity, profit and competitive advantage.

Human resource management in hospitality organizations emphasizes attracting an effective workforce, maintaining an effective workforce and continuously developing an effective workforce (Worsfold, 1999). Human resource policies and practices that apply to hospitality and tourism organizations would include: shaping the organizational culture; determination of the organization's labor and talent needs; recruitment and selection; employee orientation and socialization; training and development; performance management and performance appraisal; equal opportunity and managing diversity; rewards and recognition systems; supporting effective team functioning; internal and external branding challenges; employee relations; working with professional associations and labor unions; health and safety issues; and grievance and disciplinary processes.

CONSIDERING BOTH THE ORGANIZATION AND EMPLOYEES

A small but increasing body of research has examined organizational level and individual level factors in the delivery of high quality customer service. Liao and Chuang (2004) examined the influence of both individual and organizational factors on employee service performance and customer outcomes. They collected data in 25 restaurants from 44 managers, 257 employees and 1993 customers. Both employee conscientiousness and extraversion were associated with higher levels of employee service performance, and both restaurant service climate and levels of employee involvement were associated with higher levels of restaurant performance. Finally, employee service performance at the restaurant level predicted customer satisfaction and loyalty. In a second study, Liao and Chuang (2007) reported that managers' transformational leadership increased employee service performance in a sample of hair stylists in Taiwan, which in turn increased client loyalty and retention nine months later. Store-level transformational leadership increased store-level service climate, which in turn increased the relationship between individual transformational leadership and employee service performance. Thus while "the people make the place", the place matters.

   This introductory chapter sets the stage for the rest of the collection. The hospitality sector is a major contributor to the GDP of many countries, is a major source of jobs, and is growing. This industry today faces some important old and emerging challenges. This collection provides a practical view on how human resource management initiatives have been found to be useful in addressing these issues. It first considers the context including leadership and management, organizational culture and people, leadership competencies, and human resource practices more generally. It moves to a consideration of ongoing and new challenges facing hospitality organizations. It then offers a sample of human resource initiatives that address some of these challenges. Human resource initiatives are also included in the material on ongoing and new challenges, and in the chapters that follow.

LEADERSHIP COMPETENCIES FOR HOSPITALITY AND TOURISM MANAGEMENT

Given the importance of both the hospitality and tourism sector and service leadership, it is not surprising that research and writing attention is being paid to required leadership competences. These competencies are typically captured in competency models. Testa and Sipe (2012) undertook interviews with 110 individuals at high levels of management in four industry segments: hotels, tourism, restaurants and attractions. They identified 100 managerial behaviors which they then allocated into 20 competency areas. Many of these behaviors and areas had been noted earlier by others, while some were new. These 20 areas were then collapsed into three major areas of service leadership competencies: business savvy; people savvy; and self savvy. Business savvy included: planning; numberwise; continuous improvement; strategic decision making; systems thinking; technical service; and results oriented. People savvy included: interpersonal; communication; expressive service; team orientation; coaching and training; inspiration; cultural alignment; and networked. Finally, self savvy included: accountability; professionalism; self-development; time management; spirit of optimism; and change management.

But increasing these competencies in managers turns out to be difficult. Agut et al. (2003) interviewed 80 hotel and restaurant managers in Spain to identify competency needs and training demands. They distinguished between technical managerial competencies needed (economic-financial, computing, language, work organization, people and work team management) and generic managerial competencies needed (job performance, efficacy including time management and self-confidence, self-control including stress tolerance and listening to others, social relationships, and proactive behaviors such as having a positive vision and being committed to meeting targets). They also examined present and future training demands based on a gap between present and required levels of knowledge and skill in these two areas and found that managers reported strong needs for technical managerial competencies but significantly lower training needs for general managerial competencies. When training needs were identified, they were oriented towards the present rather than the future. These managers did not indicate that they required training in any of the general managerial competencies. Managers may have seen these skills as not particularly relevant to them in their jobs, or not a priority, or that training would not increase levels of these skills and knowledge.

There is a sense that many managers in the hospitality and tourism sector lack the skills necessary to perform managerial functions (Foster et al., 2010). They found in a study in the UK that half the managerial skills in their skills assessments were deficient. In addition, there appeared to be little demand for development. The largest skill deficiencies were in marketing, customer service and financial skills.

LEADERS AND MANAGERS

Leadership and management are both important but they are different (Nicolaides, 2006). Leadership involves possessing a vision of what the ideal workplace should look like, being inspiring to all levels of staff, having high levels of communication skills, being ethical, and possessing business knowledge vital to organizational success. Managing involves understanding and structuring work roles, processes and tasks, standardizing operating procedures, sharing performance expectations with staff, monitoring staff performance, developing staff, and meeting the needs of one's staff.

Thus Whitelaw (2013) studied leadership styles (transformational, transactional, laissez-faire) of 105 senior managers, 135 middle managers, and 42 line managers, most working in large international hotels in Australia. Respondents indicated not only the extent to which they used each of these leadership styles, but how they related to three areas of their job: their effectiveness, their satisfaction and their commitment of extra effort. Managers at higher levels tended to exhibit higher levels of contingent reward and more transformational behaviors such as idealized influence, inspirational motivation, intellectual stimulation, and individual consideration. Senior managers also tended to rate themselves higher on extra effort. In addition, there were differences between the three levels of managers in relationships of the various leadership behaviors with the three work outcomes.

ONGOING HRM CHALLENGES

Unfortunately, challenges facing hospitality and tourism organizations are compounded by relatively low historical interest in human resource management policies and practices in this sector and in people management more generally (Baum, 2007). The hospitality and tourism sector, as a result, has a negative image as far as working conditions, pay, and career development are concerned (Kuslavan et al., 2012). As a consequence, very high rates of employee turnover plague this sector (Davidson et al., 2010). Zopiatis and Constanti (2005) list human resource challenges facing the Cyprus hospitality industry involving managers, included low levels of motivation and high levels of both burnout and turnover.

In addition, studies of perceptions of students in hospitality and tourism management programs, a key source of staff, have typically found negative attitudes and views of this sector (Kuslavan and Kuslavan, 2000). Aksu and Koksal (2005) collected data from 689 tourism and hospitality management students in each of the four years of study. Students believed that workers in this industry were generally unmotivated and uneducated, industry managers did not expect much effort from their employees, managers failed to provide necessary training or promotional opportunities, and working hours interfered with having a regular life. Richardson (2009), in an Australian study of 320 tourism and hospitality students from eight university and college programs, reported that most students did not believe that tourism and hospitality as a career provided factors that they believed to be important: enjoyment, security, salary, promotion prospects, a reasonable workload, and a pleasant workplace environment. Zopiatis and Kyprianou (2006) reported generally negative attitudes towards the hospitality sector in a study of 227 secondary school students in Cyprus. Perceptions of the hospitality sector on 12 factors (for example, poor salary, boring work, negative working environment) ranged from neutral to negative. Richardson and Thomas (2012), in a study of US students enrolled in hospitality programs who had worked in the hospitality sector, who had generally favorable views about working in the sector and who had planned to work in the sector, almost always, however, rated the importance of particular factors higher than the extent to which they would be met in the hospitality and tourism sector.

Keep and Mayhew (1999) wrote that inadequate and limited human resource management practices in the hospitality and tourism industry were associated with a number of human resource issues. These included low wages, skill shortages, work hours and shift patterns that interfere with family functioning, limited career promotion options, high levels of employee turnover, and women holding lower status jobs while men held higher status jobs. This had been attributed to the underlying economics of the sector, an emphasis on short-term responses and quick fixes, an unwillingness of employing organizations to acknowledge their problems, a low skill base, and the presence of large numbers of small and medium-sized enterprises. But progress and changes have been observed here as well, particularly in the larger hospitality organizations and the international chains.

WORKPLACE STRESS AND ITS EFFECTS

Hospitality employees, particularly front-line service workers, experience workplace stress. Han et al. (2016) collected data from 228 front-line service workers working in 28 Florida-based restaurants, studying the relationship of customer incivility and both burnout and turnover intentions. Customer incivility (personally insulting, sexual comments, comments on appearance, verbal attacks) were associated with burnout, which in turn fully mediated the relationship of customer incivility and intent to quit. Both hospitality organization and supervisor support reduced the association of customer incivility and burnout.

Shani and Pizam (2009) found a modest but higher rate of depression among hospitality workers in a study carried out in Florida. Depression is associated with higher health-related costs, absenteeism, and lower productivity. Depression can be the result of job stress, burnout and low social support.

Hospitality organizations and their supervisors can work to reduce the association of customer incivility and adverse employee and organizational outcomes by using examples of customer incivility in training programs to help employees better handle and diffuse these instances. Employees can also share with each other what seemed to work for them. In addition, managers can also be more visible to both employees and customers to make readily available access to lower tension before a major incident occurs. Incivility from co-workers can have similar negative effects and be addressed in similar ways (Sakurai and Jex, 2012).

Zopiatis and Constanti (2005), based on questionnaire data from 75 managers in the hospitality sector in Cyprus, examined three burnout components: emotional exhaustion, depersonalization, and lack of personal accomplishment, using the Maslach Burnout Inventory. Managers scoring higher on these burnout components were younger, had less work experience, were more highly educated, and worked in five-star hotels. A worrying finding was the low level of personal accomplishment reported by a large proportion of respondents. The good news is that both alcohol abuse and depression, among other stress-related outcomes, can be treated.

EMOTIONAL LABOR

Considerable research attention has been given to the concept of emotional labor in service industries. Emotional labor involves managing one's emotions and their expression to fit organizational or occupational expectations about appropriate emotional expression (Pizam, 2004). These emotions need to be expressed even though they are at odds with the person's real feelings – a discrepancy or emotional dissonance. Emotional labor involves faking positive emotions as well as suppressing negative emotions. Individuals can also genuinely feel and express positive emotions. It is possible to genuinely express negative emotions but unlikely in a service or workplace interaction. That is, positive emotional displays are required while negative emotional displays are prohibited.

The positive display of emotions by front-line service workers has been found to be associated with higher levels of customer satisfaction and perceptions of service quality (Pugh, 2001) and customer retention and satisfaction (Ashkanazy et al., 2002). But emotional labor can be psychologically and physically harmful to service workers (Brotheridge and Grandey, 2002; Grandey, 2003).

Kim (2008) studied antecedents and consequences of emotional labor among 197 front-line workers in the US. Antecedents included job characteristics and personal attributes; consequences included job burnout. The measure of emotional labor considered both surface acting (faking, pretending) and deep acting (trying to feel these emotions). Two personality characteristics were measured: neuroticism and extraversion; three interaction characteristics: frequency, duration and variety; job characteristics included autonomy and control in one's work; and company display rules: negative and positive. Variety, duration and positive display rules predicted deep acting; negative display rules predicted surface acting. Workers higher on neuroticism reported more surface acting and workers higher on extraversion reported more deep acting. Surface actors reported higher levels of burnout than did deep actors.

Shani et al. (2014), in a qualitative study conducted in Israel, considered context factors associated with emotional labor. Interviews were conducted with 35 front-line workers, 26 female and 9 male. They identified four context factors: the manager–employee relationship, the manager's attitude towards employees and their degree of supervisor support; physical demands of the job – physical strains, job demands and stresses; training for emotional labor – training in dealing with emotional interactions and their de-escalation; and the frequency, duration and repetition of the employee–customer encounter – depending on whether the customer was a first time or repeat customer. They suggest that supervisors receive more training in soft skills, provide staff training in emotional labor causes and consequences, and improve the employee's physical work conditions.

WORK–FAMILY CONFLICT

Work and family are two important roles for most working women and men. Work–family conflict exists when the demands of one role make it hard to meet the demands of the other role (Greenhaus and Beutell, 1985). Work–family conflict is seen as having three types: time-based conflict – time devoted to one role makes it difficult to fill the second role; strain-based conflict – strain in one role interferes with successful performance of the other role; and behavior-based conflict – the behaviors required in one role are incompatible with behaviors required in the other role. Conflict can also occur from family to work as well. Work–family conflict is increasing due to more dual-worker/dual-career couples, more single parents, more workers caring both for children and ageing parents, and the need to earn more income.

Workers in the hospitality sector work long hours, workplaces are open 24/7, workers also work on days when most other women and men do not (for example, weekends and holidays), they have unsupportive supervisors, there is more absenteeism and a high labor turnover, resulting in labor shortages requiring some to work longer (Magnini, 2009). Magnini (2009) lists other costs to hospitality organizations resulting from work–family conflict. These include reduced job performance, increased recruiting, staffing and training costs, more absenteeism, and being "present": at work but not fully functioning. Thus integrating and balancing work and family roles becomes important.

Burke et al. (2014) collected data from 549 front-line service workers in Turkish hotels in a study of consequences of work–family and family–work conflict, their sample generally working long hours. Work–family conflict and family–work conflict were significantly and positively correlated, work–family conflict being greater, but levels of both were moderate. Respondents at higher organizational levels and those with responsibility for supervising others, these two personal demographics being positively correlated, reported higher levels of both work–family conflict and family–work conflict. Workers reporting higher levels of family–work conflict also indicated lower levels of job satisfaction and vigor; workers reporting higher levels of work–family conflict also reported more job satisfaction and absorption, likely reflecting their higher organizational levels. Neither work–family nor family–work conflict predicted intent to quit, which was at very low levels.

Wong and Ko (2009), using both quantitative and qualitative data from a large sample of hotel employees in Hong Kong, examined perceptions of work–life balance issues. Most respondents were front-line employees (food and beverage, front desk, housekeeping), with about 20 percent being managers or higher level employees. A 30-item measure of work–life balance was created for the study, measuring seven factors: life orientation; allegiance to work; workplace support of work–life balance; voluntary reduction of contracted working hours to cater to personal needs; upkeep of work and career; flexibility of work schedules; and enough time off from work. These factors were presented here from high to low in agreement. In general, respondents indicated low perceptions of work–life balance. They made the following recommendations: listen to employees and appreciate their differences and needs; provide more free time and increase flexibility of work schedules; provide workplace support on family matters; and initiate a wider organizational effort to address work–life balance issues and evaluate their effectiveness.

Magnini (2009) offers the following initiatives for reducing work–family conflict in hospitality organizations:

- Selection and hiring: clearly indicate to applicants the job requirements, work hours, and family support policies and programs of the organization.
- Training and education: offer training sessions on coping with work–family conflict, the importance of employees discussing their jobs with their families, training of supervisors in supporting work–family conflict.
- Job design: encourage employees to discuss their job stressors and ways of making their jobs less stressful; offer flexibility in worker breaks.
- Scheduling initiatives: allow more flexibility in scheduling; longer but fewer shifts; changes in start and finish times of shifts.
- Other initiatives: child care centers, adult day care, employee wellness and physical fitness facilities.

SEXUAL HARASSMENT

Kate Burnham, a pastry chef working in Toronto, reported unwanted sexual banter and sexual harassment by previous bosses, some of whom grabbed her breasts and crotch. Sexual harassment in hospitality has now become a topic of discussion and action. The Province of Ontario has committed $1.7 m to educate and equip hospitality workers to address sexual harassment (Ferguson, 2016). The training will include ways of intervening in a safe way, such as calling authorities or talking to an individual across the bar.

Poulston (2008) writes that sexual harassment is more prevalent in hospitality than elsewhere, and is acknowledged by managers. Sexual harassment is associated with higher levels of absenteeism, turnover, monetary damages and legal costs. Causes include high levels of interpersonal contact, flirting by staff for tips, provocative clothing (for example, uniform for waitresses at Hooters), satisfying customer expectations, low status of hospitality workers, and a hierarchical workplace structure. In her New Zealand study, Poulston (2008) found, in order of frequency, harassment was engaged in by co-workers, customers, peers, supervisors and juniors. Sexual harassment was generally tolerated, it being associated with enjoyment and the nature of the industry.

Sexual harassment in hospitality organizations is very common (Poulston, 2008), reflecting the hierarchical nature of hospitality organizations, the nature of hospitality work, characteristics of front-line workers, some front-line workers required to dress provocatively, an emphasis on meeting the needs of customers, and a low sense of responsibility of customers. Sexual harassment includes unwelcome sexual advances, requests for sexual favors and either verbal or physical contact of a sexual nature (Gilbert et al., 1998). Gilbert et al. (1998) list the costs of sexual harassment as higher turnover, poor working relationships with other staff and customers, and costs in lost productivity and turnover. There are also psychological and physical costs for victims. Some harassment remains unreported, particularly if historically such incidents were not dealt with promptly or appropriately or the perpetrator was a higher level manager or chef. The lack of sexual harassment training for managers, the lack of sexual harassment policies, and the non-response of managers to cases of sexual harassment are common.

Practical initiatives should start in hospitality management university programs then move on to hospitality organizations. Hospitality management students need to be exposed to diversity management concepts, discrimination and sexual harassment. Students on work placements should be alerted to instances of sexual discrimination and harassment, particularly for female students. Hospitality managers need to be educated in diversity management, issues of discrimination and harassment, they should be trained in how to deal with these, contribute to the development of appropriate organizational policies, and foster a culture that makes it possible to discuss such behaviors.

Gilbert et al. (1998) describe a three stage process for creating policies for sexual harassment. The first stage involves *research* – current policies, a review of court cases, soliciting input from all levels in the workplace; the second stage involves *policy development* – circulating draft policies to all employees, surveying their feedback, consulting policies of other organizations and associations; the third stage is *policy implementation* –

distributing policies to all employees and having them sign that they have read them, training of staff, and evaluation of effectiveness of all initiated policies and activities.

CUSTOMER MISBEHAVIOR

Customers can misbehave in a wide range of ways. Such behavior goes against accepted norms of conduct in such situations. Examples would include customers acting in abusive ways to staff or other customers, damaging property, theft, and being drunk or on drugs. Customer misbehavior creates problems for front-line employees, managers and hospitality organizations in general. Managers need to both proactively and actively address instances of customer misbehavior in order to prevent future occurrences and minimize their negative effects (Daunt and Harris, 2011). In addition, all employees should receive information and training in how to best respond.

EMPLOYEES BEHAVING BADLY

Pizam (2010) reviewed research studies of alcohol abuse among hospitality workers compared to other occupations, finding more alcohol abuse among hospitality workers. These findings raise potential employee health problems and risks to the industry. They attribute this heightened alcohol abuse to a drinking sub-culture, easy access to alcohol, and work conditions including stress and long work hours.

In an Israeli study, Belhassen and Shani (2012) found that hotel employees used more tobacco, alcohol and cannabis than the average in Israel society. Usage was highest among young, single male employees with low levels of education working in the front of house.

WORKFORCE DIVERSITY

Workforce diversity is expected to grow in hospitality organizations over the next decade, the workforce reflecting the overall population, which has become more diverse. Organizations that capitalize on diversity will reap financial gains (Singal, 2014). Gender and racial discrimination in this and other sectors has been documented. Durrani and Rajagopal (2016) collected data from 80 human resources managers on their views of workplace diversity, their definitions of ethical hiring, and on ethical hiring in their organizations. Respondents were mainly white (84 percent), 46–55 years of age (41 percent), spoke only one language (68 percent), had undergraduate degrees (50 percent), were Christian (55 percent), worked in organizations having 1000 or more employees (66 percent), and had been in human resources for 10 years (30 percent) or 29 years or more (29 percent). The sample had generally favorable attitudes towards workplace diversity (mean = 4.1 on a 5-point scale). Whites had more positive views on workplace diversity than non-whites. Most viewed their organization's hiring practices as ethical and fair (mean = 3.9 on a 5-point scale). Human resources managers from larger organizations viewed their hiring practices as more ethical and fair than did managers from smaller organizations. Most respondents gave similar definitions of ethical and fair hiring practices, sharing an understanding of the meaning of ethical hiring.

Madera (2013) reviewed diversity management practices in 14 top ranked companies. He identified some common categories of diversity practices: creating a corporate diversity council, offering diversity training programs, supplier diversity, employee networking and mentoring, creating cultural awareness, support for female, lesbian, gay, bisexual and transgender employees, and same-sex benefits.

Madera et al. (2011) developed and tested a diversity training program using perspective-taking and empathy towards non-English-speaking individuals. Participants were students in a hospitality management program in the US. Most had either full-time or part-time work in this sector. The group included several ethnicities. Some measures were taken before and after the training.

GENDER ISSUES

Three gender issues will be considered here. First is the slow progress that qualified women have made in advancing to senior executive levels in the hospitality and tourism sector. Second is the question of whether women and men function and behave differently in leadership roles. Third is the question of whether women and men in front-line service positions have similar or different work experiences.

Most research in the 1990s reported very few women in senior management positions (Crafts and Thompson, 1997; Diaz and Umbreit, 1995; Brownell, 1994). Woods and Viehland (2000), while noting slow progress, observed women and men provided similar competences for advancement, behavior and circumstances, contributing to women's and men's career development, but women more than men saw these as problems for women. Burrell et al. (1997), in a study of women's employment patterns in the hospitality industry in four countries (France, Italy, Spain, the UK), found that stereotyped attitudes existed as barriers in the kinds of jobs women and men had in hotels. Fleming (2005), based on a random sample of 112 990 women and men working in the hospitality sector in 2010, found women earned less money then men, controlling for several factors (education, hours worked), the pay gap being largest among managers. The good news was that the gender pay gap was smaller in the 2010 data than in an earlier 1989 study, indicating slow progress.

Marinakou (2014) interviewed 15 male and 15 female managers working in five-star hotels in Spain. Both males and females indicated that a glass ceiling existed for women. Barriers were long work hours, relocation, work–family and work–personal life issues, and having to work harder than men to prove themselves. Fewer women aspired to become General Managers and they believed discrimination existed. But both male and female managers thought the situation was getting better. Females described their leadership styles as more nurturing and team oriented than men did, interestingly. If this is indeed the case, women's leadership styles may actually be more in sync with the new realities of many workplaces (for example, more team-based, more participative and involving a greater emphasis on empowering front-line workers).

Purcell (1993), in a sample of three graduating cohorts of a hotel and catering management course (1985, 1986, 1987), found that even though women and men had similar credentials, women were less likely to be recruited, developed and rewarded as employees with senior management capabilities.

Thus one can consider both "push" factors in educated and qualified women's decisions to turnover including the glass ceiling, the old boys' network, a hostile, biased workplace environment, difficulties in relocating, a masculine culture, tokenism, limited mentoring and developmental opportunities and few promotional prospects, and "pull" factors such as work versus family, caregiving responsibilities for both children and ageing parents, and home responsibilities.

Let us now consider the work experiences of women and men in front-line service positions. In studies we have carried out involving several different areas of both work experience and work and well-being outcomes, we have found relatively few sex differences. Women and men tend to report similar levels of job satisfaction, work engagement, feelings of psychological empowerment, organizational identification and intent to quit, among other factors. This is the good news. Women do, however, report greater concerns with sexual harassment, discrimination, and work–family conflict (Blomme et al., 2010). This is the continuing bad news.

Women and men may respond to the same work experiences differently. Kim et al. (2009a) examined gender as a moderator of experienced job stress (role conflict and role ambiguity) and job satisfaction in a sample of 165 men and 153 women working in hotels in Korea. They found that though males reported higher levels of both role stressors than did females, these role stressors were more strongly related to job dissatisfaction for females than males. They attributed this to women's greater valuing of communal and social oriented behaviors in relationships with others who understand their roles. Women may also have coped with these stressors differently than men did.

Although some progress is being seen, senior executive positions in the hospitality sector still convey a "man's world". There are several reasons for this, including both subtle and obvious discrimination, long work hours required, the need for relocation, family responsibilities, and some women not being interested in senior level positions. The glass ceiling is alive and well, but showing a few cracks.

CROSS-CULTURAL DIFFERENCES

Pizam (2014), noting the increase in globalization and internationalization of hospitality organizations, makes the case for cross-cultural competence training in the hospitality and tourism sector. This refers to increasing one's ability to interact successfully with others of different cultures. This competence improves the interaction of service providers and customers, increasing customer satisfaction and ultimately organizational performance. Few, if any, hospitality and tourism programs offer courses to increase the cultural competence of students. Both college and university programs as well as hospitality and tourism organizations need to offer such training.

MIGRANT WORKERS

The hospitality industry relies on migrant workers for day-to-day functioning, increasing workforce diversity and making new demands on human resource management practices (Forde and MacKenzie, 2009). But managers lacked the training to capitalize on this source of labor. Managers were also not clear on what diversity initiatives would be helpful to them. Migrants will undertake work that the locals avoid. Migrants are highly motivated, seeking opportunities they cannot obtain at home. Thus migrant labor will continue to be an important source of employees in hospitality and tourism workplaces. The sector needs to understand why locals do not want to work in the hospitality sector. There is also a need to foster management interest in learning to improve the way they introduce and work with migrants in their workplaces.

Zopiatis et al. (2014) interviewed managers, local workers and migrant workers to understand the work experiences of migrants in Cyprus. Managers offered three reasons for hiring migrants: locals will not do the work; potential contribution of migrants given the seasonal nature of the industry; and lower pay for migrants. Migrants were willing to work for the pay, realizing that locals would not do their jobs for this pay, and believed that knowing other languages was an asset. Managers, however, saw language as a problem with migrants. Migrants were generally satisfied with their experiences with locals. Locals noted language barriers as problematic, but other than that, relationships with migrants were generally satisfactory. Some managers observed an exploitation of migrants and discrimination. There was disagreement on whether migrants provided good service to customers, however; some customers complained about the service provided to them by migrants. Some migrants had low skill levels and poor language ability, risking quality of service.

Recent research undertaken in Toronto involving 184 Chinese restaurant workers showed they were exploited in terms of low pay, unpaid overtime hours, being paid in cash or by check so as not to leave a paper trail, not receiving payroll slips from their employers, and their injuries at work not being reported (Mojtehedzadeh and Keung, 2016). Some had legal issues in terms of their working in Canada, others had limited English skills, and some were afraid of complaining for fear of losing their job.

GENERATIONAL DIFFERENCES

There have always been different generations in workplaces. Younger employees have always been different from older ones. But today the reality may be more complicated. There is considerable evidence that indicates that different employee generations (for example, Baby boomers, Generation Xers, Millennials) have somewhat different values, expectations and priorities. These differences can be a source of conflict and barriers between these generations, creating an "us versus them" mentality (Lub et al., 2012).

Chi et al. (2013) studied generational difference on perceptions of younger and older managers among hospitality employees. Data were collected from 677 front-line workers and 228 managers of a large US hotel organization. Baby boomers were born between 1946 and 1964,

Generation Xers were born between 1965 and 1980, and Millennials were born between 1981 and 2000. There were significant differences by generation in perceptions of younger and older managers, as well as differences by job position among these three generations. Millennials had a more negative view of managers than did respondents from the two other generations. Boomers and Generation Xers had more negative views on younger managers' competency than did Millennials.

Park and Gursoy (2012), in a study of 677 customer service employees, examined generational effects in work engagement and the association of work engagement with quit intentions. Three generational cohorts were considered: Baby boomers, Generation Xers and Millennials. Millennials tended to report lower levels of work engagement than the other two cohorts, and engagement was more strongly associated with quit intentions among Millennials as well. Millennials indicated the highest turnover intentions. Managers then need to spend more time with their Millennials, identifying their work preferences (meaningful work, fulfilling jobs) to retain them.

Organizations can use these differences for the better. Organizations first need to be sensitive to the potential effects of these differences across generational cohorts. Intergenerational blending of their workforce is important for performance. Executive leadership needs to understand the needs of each generation and meet them. Managers and supervisors need to communicate, communicate, communicate with Millennials; Millennials need to receive information and feedback from their managers. Organizations need to support Millennials in the use of the latest technologies. Millennials will need flexibility in order to integrate their work and personal lives. Managers and supervisors need training in how best to work with Millennials. Since Millennials value growth, training and development should be available to them. Employees of each generation should have meaningful opportunities to work together. Encouraging Baby boomers to mentor Millennials, and Millennials to offer their talents and strengths to complement Baby boomers supports cross-generational synergies. Cross-generational team building meetings also would serve a useful purpose here. Finally, having different generations serve on task forces and committee tasks allows across-generational contacts and interaction.

EMPLOYEES WITH DISABILITIES

Employees with disabilities still encounter difficulties gaining employment despite supportive legislation. Disabilities can be physical, intellectual or psychological. Given the importance of appearance and personality among front-line workers in the hospitality sector, this has presented a challenge. The principal reason for this is the negative attitudes of employers.

Barnes and Mercer (2006) and Jasper and Waldhart (2013) noted the following barriers facing the disabled: stereotypes about work they can and cannot perform; lack of management training and education in the hiring of the disabled; hiring the disabled increases costs of training, accommodation and supervision; both managers and the disabled lack information about government support for their hiring; concerns about their level of job performance; and the disabled need more supervision.

Chi and Qu (2003) examined attitudes in this area among food service employers in Oklahoma. They found a somewhat favorable attitude towards workers with disabilities, attitudes being more favorable among those having prior positive work experiences with people with disabilities. Those with more positive attitudes towards the disabled were also more likely to hire or commit to hire persons with disabilities. It should be noted that there is often a gap between organizations saying they are open to hiring the disabled and actually hiring the disabled. Larger organizations, and managers having higher levels of education, were more open to hiring the disabled. In addition there are various government programs offering financial support for disabled hiring.

Houtenville and Kalargyrou (2015) compared employers' perspectives regarding hiring the disabled in 263 hospitality and leisure companies with 3126 firms in other industries and found that service firms were more open to hiring the disabled than were goods-producing industries, which is potentially encouraging news. The vast majority of the disabled want to work. There is a looming labor shortage in the hospitality and tourism industry; many able-bodied people prefer not to work in this sector. And the societal costs of unemployment among the disabled are paid by the taxpayers.

While hiring the disabled is important, the disabled need more support to prevent accidents and injuries, employees with disabilities having higher rates of workplace accidents and injuries. Employees with disabilities need additional training as they have as much right to a safe workplace as anyone else. They need to know their rights to a safe and bias-free workplace, that they may have accidents, be injured, or killed on the job. They need to know that accidents can be prevented, understand the risks they may face, and how best to deal with these risks and hazards by identifying resources that can keep them safe. All employees need to inform their supervisors if they feel at risk and unsafe. Interested readers will find a document created by the Labor Occupational Health Program at the University of California at Berkeley and NIOSH (2016) invaluable here.

LOW PAY AND THE ROLE PLAYED BY TIPPING

Some countries (for example, Japan) do not allow tipping. Some people argue that tipping makes staff subservient to and of lower status than the customer. A few restaurants in Toronto have done away with tipping, probably incorporating an increase in the prices of their food; it is hoped that this money is allocated to staff. The minimum wage in Ontario is currently $11.25 an hour and will rise to $11.40 in the near future. It is difficult to have a life at this rate of pay. Thus individuals can increase their pay through receiving tips. I have asked waiting staff at a few restaurants if they receive the Ontario minimum wage and they have said no, but they share in the pooling of tips. An increasing number of Toronto restaurants no longer allocate the tips received to staff, but instead pay above the minimum wage, for example $13.25 an hour. However, this results in staff getting less money and the employer getting more. The practice of tipping and pay levels is becoming an increasingly important issue in the hospitality sector.

An increasing number of restaurant employees (chefs, servers) failed even to receive pay they were due when restaurants closed, or they failed to receive pay for extra shifts worked or after a contract termination (Henry and Wallace, 2016).

BUILDING A SAFETY CULTURE

Workplace accidents and injuries such as slips and falls, strain from lifting heavy objects and burns from hot substances are common in hospitality organizations, being both dangerous to employees and costly to workplaces. Employees sometimes fail to follow established safety practices as well. Workplace accidents and injuries can be significantly reduced by building a workplace safety culture. Zohar (1980) defined a safety culture as employee perceptions of the value and role of safety in organizations. Clarke et al. (2013), based on an extensive literature review, reported associations between the presence of a safety culture and safety work outcomes such as compliance with safety rules, undertaking safety audits, injury frequency and injury severity, and less accident under-reporting. Antecedent factors associated with a strong safety culture included the values of safety held by executives, the behaviors of managers and supervisors, safety-related communications, safety education and training, quality of co-worker relationships, safety supportive systems, and lower levels of workplace stress (Griffin and Neal, 2000; Taylor, 2010).

PHYSICAL SAFETY AND SECURITY OF HOTELS: ROOM FOR IMPROVEMENT?

Enz (2009a) developed two indexes of hotel safety and security (safety equipment and security equipment). Data were obtained from 5487 US hotels. The average safety index score was 70 and the average security index score was 64 out of possible score of 100. Each index had a large standard deviation, suggesting wide variance among hotels. Hotels scoring higher on these indices charged higher prices, were newer, in urban and airport locations or in the luxury market, and were larger. Although Enz doesn't say this, possible concerns might be raised about the physical safety and security among the lowest ranking properties.

TERRORIST ATTACKS ON HOTELS AND CAFES

We have witnessed a new challenge to hospitality organizations over the past decade. Al-Qaeda militants attacked three hotels in the Ivory Coast on Sunday 13 March 2016, killing at least 16; the six attackers were also killed (Corey-Boulet, 2016). Pizam (2016) cites the terrorist attacks in Paris, the Sinai and Mumbai, as well as attacks on tourist-carrying airlines and the Russian airliner shot down in Egypt, as occurring because these sites were unprotected and openly accessible, highly visible and having a high impact, and they represented activities (drinking alcohol, Western music) that were seen as decadent by Jihadists. He suggests a need to "harden" their targets, making it more difficult for terrorists to attack them. This is difficult to do because of the thousands of such organizations involved, the belief that the state should be responsible for this, lack of clarity on how to do this, and a lack of resources and manpower. There are training programs to increase employee awareness of security and terrorism issues, and efforts have been made to involve the public at large in identifying any potential terrorist activities. Some hospitality organizations have hired trained security staff, installed safety and security equipment, and posted policies of safety and security to all staff.

Baker (2014; 2015) provides a review of the effects of terrorism on tourism, with the literature spanning over 30 years. Terrorism has been associated with increased unemployment, homelessness and economic costs. It is linked with reductions to travel and tourism, with the financial and economic consequences. A key element is the perception of risk by potential travelers and tourists. Risk perceptions have certainly increased in 2016 from a rising number of terrorist attacks in more countries.

Terrorism also has other less dramatic effects on the hospitality sector. Bader and Berg (2014) consider the impact of terrorism on the job performance of expatriates using a stressor–strain framework. It is common for major hotel chains to move senior managers from one country to another. They consider two types of stressors: situation-related stressors including previous terrorist attacks, terrorist threat levels, one's working and living conditions, and threat levels of a particular host country; and interaction-related stressors such as relationships with host country staff and potential spouse and family conflicts. These comprise terrorist-related stressors and strains which influence an individual's work attitudes towards their colleagues, job and organization, and ultimately expatriate job performance.

Hospitality organizations can address some employee concerns about terrorism. Bader and Berg (2013) suggest an emphasis on the expatriate family, including greater preparation before entering the host country, greater family support once there, and more frequent trips home coupled with shorter foreign assignments. Howie (2007) proposes seminars tackling fear of flying, dealing with those who fit a terrorist profile, working in tall buildings, making greater use of technologies to minimize travel to high risk countries, and developing a security-oriented workplace climate, with senior managers making efforts to maintain or increase staff morale.

INCREASING TURBULENCE IN TOURIST DESTINATIONS

A recent report (Kivanc, 2016) noted that increasing levels of fear are causing tourism in Turkey to drop dramatically. They attribute this decline to increasing terrorism and ethnic tensions, decreasing numbers of Russian tourists after Turkey shot down a Russian warplane, and the attempted but failed coup against the country's President, Recep Erdogan, in July 2016. They estimate a $12 billion decline in tourism revenues in 2016, a 50 percent decline in European tourists and loss of 100 000 jobs in Antalya, a prime tourist region, as well (Arango and Yeginsu, 2016).

Egypt, another prime tourist destination, has experienced increasing instability over the past few years, also resulting in a drop in tourism. Former military dictator and President Hosni Mubarak, now imprisoned, maintained some semblance of stability during his regime. When he was overthrown in a citizen uprising beginning in Tahrir Square, a democratic election led to the leader of the Muslim Brotherhood becoming President. He in turn was later arrested in a coup led by the military and is still imprisoned. General al-Sisi is now the Egyptian president, but protests in the streets are still ongoing.

SEX TOURISM: A PROBLEM

There are many forms and reasons for tourism. In some countries sex tourism is seen as a means of economic development (Hall and Ryan, 2001; Jeffrey, 2003). Sex tourism involves prostitution, the payment for sexual services. Sex tourism destinations then are generally in developing countries. Mason (1999) reviews the historical development of large-scale prostitution in South East Asia as moving from local demand to tourist demand. Women are usually the prostitutes, with concerns being raised about their mental and physical health, marginal economic status, and the possibility of HIV/AIDS.

A new study found child-sex tourism has increased dramatically in the travel and tourism sector – a disturbing development (Lowrie, 2016). This growth raises ethical and moral issues for the industry. However, it is not clear what official stand the industry has taken and what efforts have been made to combat this activity.

ECPAT International (2016) conducted a global study on the sexual exploitation of children in travel and tourism (SECTT). SECTT has increased despite country efforts to reduce it. SECTT exists in all countries, though regional variations were found to exist. Child victims can suffer serious and life-long emotional, psychological and physical damage. ECPAT International calls for greater protection of potential and actual victims, for cultural and social norms of child sexual abuse and child marriages, and cultural views of masculinity to be addressed, and for stronger enforcement of laws currently in place. Coordinated efforts by government agencies, the hospitality and tourism sector, and country citizens are necessary for progress to be realized.

MEDICAL TOURISM: A CAUTION

Given the high and increasing costs of medical treatment in the developed world, a growing market has developed for patients needing treatment to seek it in the developing world where it is cheaper; hence the emerging field of medical tourism (Lunt et al., 2012; Cortez, 2008). Medical tourism involves consumers traveling across international borders to receive medical treatment. Medical treatment includes services such as dental care, cosmetic surgery, other elective surgeries, and fertility treatments. Individuals from wealthier, more developed countries travel to less well developed countries, seeking cheaper treatments. Top destinations include Costa Rica, India, Mexico, Singapore, Taiwan, Thailand and Turkey. Millions of people engage in medical tourism annually, with potential cost savings of 25 percent to 90 percent, depending on the destination chosen.

Medical tourism requires a first class tourism infrastructure in order to succeed. Medical tourism is enhanced by cheap airfares and reasonably priced hotel and vacation possibilities, so high levels of customer service become important selling features (Connell, 2006). National governments have developed strategies to support medical tourism in their countries (MacReady, 2007). But questions must be addressed about the quality and safety of medical treatment in other countries; there is always a risk in international patients traveling back home (Burkett, 2007). Much more research needs to be devoted to understanding the health outcomes from medical tourism and the impact of medical tourism on the health care systems of the treatment-providing countries.

HOSPITALITY AND TOURISM ORGANIZATIONS NEED TO ADDRESS THE FOLLOWING CHALLENGES

These challenges include: being selective in staffing and hiring; the need for staff orientation and training; the need to offer competitive and fair pay; more supportive, friendly and humane supervision; using job characteristics and job design to offer more variety, control and job enlargement; empowering staff, increasing job involvement; reducing levels of some job stressors; creating a customer service culture; and developing stronger and visionary leadership at senior and executive levels.

HUMAN RESOURCE MANAGEMENT INITIATIVES

Fortunately a range of human resource management initiatives have been undertaken to address some of these challenges. This section begins by offering ideas on what constitutes a high performance workplace culture and a high quality of working life; human resource practices that increase both internal and external branding and why these are important; creating fun at work, the use of service rewards, and the role of psychological capital in increasing staff resilience and performance.

High Performance Work Practices

High performance human resource management practices refers to a collection of separate human resource practices that suggest ways that managers and employees can interact to improve both individual and organizational functioning. Dhar (2015), in a study of 618 front-line employees and 31 managers/supervisors, considered the relationship of eight high performance human resource practices and organizational commitment and service innovative behaviors. The eight high performance human resource practices were: selective staffing; extensive training; internal mobility; employment security; clear job descriptions; results-oriented appraisal; incentive reward; and high staff participation. He reported that high performance human resource management practices increased employee organizational commitment, which in turn increased employee service innovative behaviors, the latter relationship mediated by the organizational climate for innovation.

What elements make up a high performance management system for hospitality organizations and perhaps elsewhere? Murphy and Murrmann (2009) used a two-step process, the first one involving interviews with industry experts at the Vice-President level and above to identify elements of a high performance management system; the second involving a Delphi study with restaurant experts, consultants and academics from the hospitality field. The first study identified 13 high performance work practices, and the second step added two more and eliminated three.

These were: Training and skill development; Employer of choice; Information sharing; Selectivity in recruiting; Measurement of the HR practices; Promotion from within; Quality of worklife; Diversity; Incentive pay based on performance appraisal; Participation and empowerment; Employee ownership; Self-managed teams; High wages. The three that were dropped were: Employment security; Job design; and Reduced status distinctions.

Kandasamy and Ancheri (2009) employed qualitative methods (interviews, focus groups) with both hospitality students and hotel employees to identify their views and expectations of a good work–life balance. Eight dimensions were identified:

- job characteristics: work that is challenging, interesting, satisfying and manageable;
- person–job fit: a match with qualifications and interests;
- company image: growing, good performance, a clean and safe working environment;
- human resource policies: adequate and fair pay, training and

development, fringe benefits, performance appraisals, orientation programs;
- work group relationships: cooperation, trust support, communication;
- physical working conditions: enough space, good lighting and air conditioning, ergonomically designed work stations;
- work–life balance: time for social and family life;
- interaction with customers: respect of customers, customer praise for doing a good job.

Human Resource Management Practices and Internal Branding

Internal branding within hospitality organizations has been proposed as a vehicle for increasing employee brand commitment. Brand-committed leaders increase employee brand commitment by serving as role models, championing the brand, and regularly communicating to staff in ways that develop and support the desired brand identity. Terglav et al. (2016), using a sample of 226 employees in a European hotel chain, considered the role of top management brand commitment. They found that leader brand commitment was associated with employee brand commitment through three mediating variables: employee brand knowledge; employee brand fit; and fulfillment of their psychological contract. Besides top management's commitment to service quality as a brand feature, and an internal brand, employees need to have brand-relevant information and knowledge, come to share features of the internal brand, and feel that they are engaged and committed in the process.

Kim et al. (2009b), in a study of 194 managers and 104 front-line service workers from ten Bangkok hotels, found that three measures of managerial commitment to service quality had positive associations with employee levels of job satisfaction, which in turn had positive relationships with both extra-role customer service behaviors and cooperation with co-workers. The three management commitment to service factors were organizational rewards, empowerment of employees, and levels of training provided.

Human Resource Management Practices and External Branding

Love and Singh (2011) show how human resource management practices contribute to organizational branding reflected in "Best employers" surveys. They identified eight common human resource practices in these surveys: inspired leadership; a strategic plan that promotes "best employer" human resource practices; employee communications; performance management; training and development; benefits based on best practices that meet the needs of employees (e.g, work–life balance, workplace flex-ibility, a safe and healthy work environment, feedback from employees); appealing physical workplaces; and strong corporate citizenship.

Are We Having Fun Yet?

Having fun at work has been shown to be associated with higher levels of job satisfaction, employee retention, job performance and customer satis-faction (Evans and Vernon, 2007; Fleming, 2005; Karl et al., 2005). Chan (2010) undertook an interview study to identify a typology of workplace fun in the hospitality sector using preliminary interviews, focus groups and then final interviews with 10 human resource managers. He identified four categories of fun:

- staff-oriented workplace fun: celebration of birthdays and special events, extra time off, employee appreciation days, flexible work schedules;
- supervisor-oriented workplace fun: lunch with one's supervisor, happy hours with supervisors;
- social-oriented workplace fun: annual dinners, picnics, Christmas parties, friendly competitions, charity events;
- strategy-oriented workplace fun: casual dress days, family-friendly policies, organization-provided food and refreshments, newsletters, emails, sharing sessions with the chief executives.

Maddeaux (2016) writes that all employees at some of the best rated restaurants eat a meal together before opening for dinner customers as a simple team building initiative. This allows the lunch shift and the dinner shift to both take part.

Tews et al. (2013) studied the influence of workplace fun on employee turnover and performance among front-line servers in a national US restaurant chain. Data were collected from 195 servers. Fun activities included productivity contests, social events, team building activities and celebration of work accomplishments and personal milestones. First, these fun events were positively associated with work performance; secondly, manager support for fun was negatively associated with performance. They suggest that managers should adopt a fun managerial style (using fun activities) along with implementing specific performance goals – creat-ing fun at work while maintaining higher levels of work performance.

Service Rewards and Prosocial Service Behaviors of Front-line Service Employees

As mentioned earlier, one important human resource management practice is the use of rewards for the provision of outstanding customer service by hospitality employees. Eren et al. (2014) undertook a study of levels of service rewards perceived by front-line service workers from four- and five-star Turkish hotels and their engaging in prosocial service behaviors. The latter included engaging in extra-role, role prescribed, and cooperative helpful behaviors. Data were collected from 241 employees working in 18 different hotels. Personal demographic characteristics were weak predictors of both perceptions of service rewards and levels of prosocial behaviors undertaken. However, service rewards were strong and consistent predictors of the three prosocial service behaviors. The two most common reward types offered by these properties were recognition and bonuses. It would seem to be easy to increase the types of available rewards for outstanding job performance.

Psychological Capital

Psychological capital is a positive psychological state involving four dimensions: self-efficacy, optimism, hope and resilience. It has been shown to be associated with a range of individual and organizational health, well-being and performance variables. It is a source of strength that can be developed in training programs (Luthans et al., 2006a; 2006b; 2007). Min et al. (2015), in a study of 232 hotel employees in South Korea, mostly front-line service workers from 10 middle to upscale hotels, 7 in Seoul, examined the role of psychological capital as a buffer between challenge and hindrance stressors and both burnout and work engagement. They found that psychological capital buffered the negative relationship of both challenge and hindrance stressors and burnout. Psychological capital also buffered the effects of challenge stressors and work engagement.

Paek et al. (2015), using data from 312 front-line workers from 15 five-star hotels in Seoul, found in a one-month longitudinal study that psychological capital increased employee work engagement, which in turn increased both job satisfaction and hotel affective commitment.

NEW EMPLOYEE ONBOARDING PRACTICES

Turnover, particularly among new employees, is very high in the hospitality sector. Employee onboarding has been shown to be an effective way to reduce turnover, increase employee satisfaction and ultimately customer loyalty (Bradt and Vonnegut, 2009; Sims, 2010; Stein and Christiansen, 2010; Watkins, 2013). Onboarding processes make employees feel valued, comfortable and assist them to succeed. Onboarding fits into the employee socialization literature (Klein and Heuser, 2008).

Onboarding of new hires helps them become productive employees. But onboarding takes time and resources. Supervisors/managers need to review the onboarding process with the new hirer as a way of getting feedback on their onboarding efforts. The supervisor/manager needs to spend up to three months helping new hires succeed. Onboarding can start even before the new hire begins work by describing the job expectations and organizational mission and culture in the interview process, developing email accounts and organizing work spaces. Onboarding can also take place outside of work at social and business events sponsored by the organization. Work teams are also a source of information during onboarding.

Graybill and her colleagues (2013) studied employee onboarding in 17 US university and college libraries. Onboarding practices involved a discussion of job expectations and evaluation criteria (100 percent), a discussion of mission, vision and values (59 percent), and organizational culture (29 percent). Onboarding programs ranged from one week to six months.

Grillo and Kim (2015) suggest three key onboarding processes: a survey of newly hired employees in the first 60 days; providing materials to managers and newly hired employees during the onboarding process; and paying special attention to diverse hires (women, racial minorities, ethnic minorities, the disabled). They offer practical examples and onboardng materials to address these three objectives.

UNIVERSITY AND COLLEGE INTERN PROGRAMS

Almost all university and college programs in hospitality management include an internship program for students. These programs typically fall short in meeting the needs of students and potential employers (Zopiatis and Constanti, 2012). Building on the concept of experiential learning, they suggest ways that universities and college programs, the hospitality industry and students can contribute to making internships a valuable learning experience.

HUMAN RESOURCE MANAGEMENT IMPLICATIONS FOR HOSPITALITY ORGANIZATIONS: SOME BOTTOM LINES

The hospitality industry is facing a number of old and new challenges. Executive leadership needs to identify the workplace culture that best meets the needs of the firm and its employees, then determine ways that human resource management practices can support this. Examples include:

- using realistic job previews in selection to reduce turnover;
- appreciating the importance of early socialization practices after new employees are hired;
- clearly articulating performance expectations, monitoring job performance, conducting performance appraisal reviews, recognizing and rewarding high levels of contribution;
- training supervisors and managers in supporting employees;
- educating employees on the causes and costs of emotional labor and job stress and failing to cope with these;
- offering flexibility to address work–family issues when it is practical to do so;
- training and development of supervisors to improve the quality of leadership and management;
- using teams where appropriate and offering training in team effectiveness.

REFERENCES

Agut, S., Grau, R. and Piero, J.M. (2003) Competency needs among managers from Spanish hotels and restaurants and their training demands. *Hospitality Management*, **22**, 281–95.

Aksu, A.A. and Koksal, C.D. (2005) Perceptions and attitudes of tourism students in Turkey. *International Journal of Contemporary Hospitality Management*, **17**, 436–47.

Arango, T. and Yeginsu, C. (2016) Turkey blames ISIL for attack. *Toronto Star*, 16 July, A1, A16.

Ashkanasy, N.M., Hartel, C.E.J. and Daus, C.S. (2002) Diversity and emotion: the new frontiers in organizational behavior research. *Journal of Management*, **28**, 307–38.

Bader, B. and Berg, N. (2013) An empirical investigation of terrorism-induced stress on expatriate attitudes and performance. *Journal of International Management*, **19**, 163–75.

Bader, B. and Berg, N. (2014) The influence of terrorism on expatriate performance: a conceptual approach. *International Journal of Human Resource Management*, **25**, 539–57.

Baker, D.Mc.A. (2013) Understanding the economic impact of tourism in the Asian Pacific Region using the Tourism Satellite Account. *Asian Journal of Hospitality and Tourism*, **12**, 1–15.

Baker, D.Mc.A. (2014) The effects of terrorism on the travel and tourism industry. *International Journal of Religious Tourism and Pilgrimage*, **2**, 58–67.

Baker, D.Mc.A. (2015) Tourism and terrorism: terrorists threats to commercial aviation safety and security. *International Journal of Safety and Security in Hospitality and Tourism*, **12**, 21–40.

Balaguer, J. and Cantavella-Jorda, M. (2002) Tourism as a long-run economic growth factor: the Spanish case. *Applied Economics*, **14**, 877–84.

Barnes, C. and Mercer, G. (2006) Disability, work, and welfare challenging the social exclusion of disabled people. *Work, Employment and Society*, **19**, 527–45.

Batt, R. (2002) Managing customer service: human resource practices, quit rates, and sales growth. *Academy of Management Journal*, **45**, 587–97.

Baum, T. (2007) Human resources in tourism: still waiting for change. *Tourism Management*, **28**, 1383–99.

Belhassen, Y. and Shani, A. (2012) Hotel workers' substance use and abuse. *International Journal of Hospitality Management*, **31**, 1292–302.

Blomme, R.J., Van Rheede, A. and Tromp, D.M. (2010) Work–family conflict as a cause of turnover intentions in the hospitality industry. *Tourism and Hospitality Research*, **10**, 269–85.

Bowen, D.E. and Lawler, E.E. (1995) The empowerment of service workers: what, why, how and when. *Sloan Management Review*, **33**, 31–40.

Bradt, G.B. and Vonnegut, M. (2009) *Onboarding: How to Get Your New Employees up to Speed in Half the Time*. New York: John Wiley.

Brida, J.G. and Risso, W.A. (2010) Tourism as a determinant of long-run economic growth. *Journal of Policy Research in Tourism, Leisure and Events*, **2**, 14–28.

Brotheridge, C.M. and Grandey, A. (2002) Emotional labor and burnout: comparing two perspectives of "people work". *Journal of Vocational Behavior*, **60**, 17–39.

Brownell, J. (1994) Women in hospitality management: general managers' perceptions of factors related to career development. *International Journal of Hospitality Management*, **13**, 101–17.

Burke, R.J., Koyuncu, M. and Fiksenbaum, L. (2014) Antecedents and consequences of work–family and family–work conflict among front line employees in Turkish hotels. *IUP Journal of Management Research*, **12**, 39–55.

Burkett, L. (2007) Medical tourism: concerns, benefits, and the American legal perspective. *Journal of Legal Medicine*, **28**, 223–45.

Burrell, J., Manfredi, S., Rollin, H., Price, L. and Stead, L. (1997) Equal opportunities for women employees in the hospitality industry: a comparison between France, Italy, Spain and the UK. *International Journal of Hospitality Management*, **18**, 161–79.

Chan, S.C.H. (2010) Does workplace fun matter? Developing a useable typology of workplace fun in a qualitative study. *International Journal of Hospitality Management*, **29**, 720–28.

Chi, C.G. and Qu, H. (2003) Integrating persons with disabilities into the work force: a study on employment of people with disabilities in foodservice industry. *International Journal of Hospitality and Tourism Administration*, **4**, 59–83.

Chi, C.G., Maier, T.A. and Gursoy, D. (2013) Employees' perceptions of younger and older managers by generation and job category. *International Journal of Hospitality Management*, **34**, 42–50.

Clarke, S., Guediri, S. and O'Connor, E. (2013) Creating a safe and healthy workplace. In R.J. Burke and C.L. Cooper (eds) *The Fulfilling Workplace: The Organization's Role in Achieving Individual and Organizational Health*. Farnham: Gower, pp. 265–85.

Connell, J. (2006) Medical tourism: sea, sun, sand and . . . surgery. *Tourism Management*, **27**, 1093–100.

Corey-Boulet, R. (2016) Assailants open fire at Ivory Coast beach resort. *Toronto Star*, 14 March, A3.

Cortes-Jimenez, I. and Paluna, M. (2010) Inbound tourism and long-run economic growth. *Current Issues in Tourism*, **13**, 61–74.

Cortez, N. (2008) Patients without borders: the emerging global market for patients and the evolution of modern health care. *Indiana Law Journal*, **83**, 71–131.

Crafts, D.S. and Thompson, M. (1997) Managers' perceptions of career advancement obstacles for women managers in the food service industry. *Journal of College and University Foodservice*, **3**, 41–56.

Daunt, K.L. and Harris, L.C. (2011) Customers acting badly: evidence from the hospitality industry. *Journal of Business Research*, **64**, 1034–42.

Davidson, M.C.G. (2003) Does organizational climate add to service quality in hotels? *International Journal of Contemporary Hospitality Management*, **1**, 206–13.

Davidson, M.C.G., Timo, N. and Wang, Y. (2010) How much does labor turnover cost? A study of four and five star hotels. *International Journal of Contemporary Hospitality Management*, **22**, 1–31.

Dhar, R.L. (2015) The effects of high performance human resource practices on service innovative behavior. *International Journal of Hospitality Management*, **51**, 67–75.

Diaz, P.E. and Umbreit, W.T. (1995) Women leaders – a new beginning. *Hospitality Research Journal*, **18**, 47–60.

Durrani, A.S. and Rajagopal, L. (2016) Restaurant human resource managers' attitudes towards workplace diversity, perceptions, and definition of ethical hiring. *International Journal of Hospitality Management*, **53**, 145–51.

ECPAT International (2016) *Global Study on Sexual Exploitation of Children in Travel and Tourism*. Bangkok: ECPAT International.

Enz, C.A. (2001) What keeps you up at night: key issues of concern for lodging managers. *Cornell Hotel and Restaurant Administration Quarterly*, **42**, 38–45.

Enz, C.A. (2009a) Human resource management: a troubling issue for the global hotel industry. *Cornell Hospitality Quarterly*, **50**, 578–83.

Enz, C.A. (2009b) The physical safety and security features of U.S. hotels. *Cornell Hospitality Quarterly*, **50**, 553–60.

Eren, D., Burke, R.J., Ashtakova, M., Koyuncu, M. and Cullu, N. (2014) Service rewards and prosocial behaviors among employees in four- and five-star hotels in Cappadocia, *Anatolia: An International Journal of Hospitality and Tourism*, **25**, 341–51.

Evans, A. and Vernon, K. (2007) Work–life balance in Hong Kong: case studies. *Community Business*, June, 12–27.

Ferguson, R. (2016) 1.7M for education to create safe spaces. *Toronto Star*, 8 September, A8.

Fleming, P. (2005) Workers' playtime? Boundaries and cynicism in a "culture of fun" program. *Journal of Applied Behavioral Science*, **41**, 285–303.

Forde, C. and MacKenzie, R. (2009) Employers' use of low skilled migrant workers: assessing the implications for human resource management. *International Journal of Manpower*, **30**, 437–52.

Foster, C., McCabe, S. and Dewhurst, H. (2010) Management development skills in the hospitality and tourism sector: needs and issues from a regional perspective. *Tourism and Hospitality Planning and Development*, **7**, 429–45.

Gilbert, D., Guerrier, Y. and Guy, J. (1998) Sexual harassment issues in the hospitality industry. *International Journal of Contemporary Hospitality Management*, **10**, 48–53.

Grandey, A. (2003) When the show must go on: surface acting and deep acting as determinants of emotional exhaustion and peer-related service delivery. *Academy of Management Journal*, **46**, 86–96.

Graybill, J.O., Carpenter, M.T.H., Offord, J., Piorun, M. and Shaffer, G. (2013) Employee onboarding: identification of best practices in ACRL libraries. *Library Management*, **34**, 200–18.

Greenhaus, J.H. and Beutell, N.J. (1985) Sources of conflict between work and family roles. *Academy of Management Review*, **10**, 76–88.

Griffin, M.A. and Neal, J.A. (2000) Perceptions of safety at work: a framework for linking safety climate to safety performance knowledge and motivation. *Journal of Occupational Health Psychology*, **5**, 347–58.

Grillo, M. and Kim, H.K. (2015) *A Strategic Approach to Onboarding Design: Surveys, Materials and Diverse Hires*. Ithaca, NY: ILR School Cornell University.

Gunduz, L. and Hatemi-J, A. (2008) Is the tourism-led growth hypothesis valid for Turkey? *Applied Economics Letters*, **12**, 499–504.

Hall, C.M. and Ryan, C. (2001) *Sex Tourism: Marginal People and Liminalities*. London: Routledge.

Han, S.J., Bonn, N.M.A. and Cho, M. (2016) The relationship between customer incivility, restaurant frontline service employee burnout, and turnover intention. *International Journal of Hospitality Management*, **52**, 97–106.

Hazari, B.R. and Sgro, P.M. (1995) Tourism and growth in a dynamic model of trade. *Journal of International Trade and Economic Development*, **4**, 243–52.

Henry, M. and Wallace, K. (2016) Thousands owed after five year fight. *Toronto Star*, 16 May, A3.

Houtenville, A. and Kalargyrou, V. (2015) Employers' perspectives about employing people with disabilities: a comparative study across industries. *Cornell Hospitality Quarterly*, **56**, 168–79.

Howie, L. (2007) The terrorist threat and managing workplaces. *Disaster Prevention and Management*, **16**, 70–78.

Jasper, C.R. and Waldhart, P. (2013) Employer attitudes on hiring employees with disabilities in the leisure and hospitality industry: practical and theoretical implications. *International Journal of Contemporary Hospitality Management*, **25**, 577–94.

Jeffrey, L.A. (2003) *Sex and Borders*. Vancouver: University of British Columbia Press.

Kandampully, J., Keating, B.W., Kim, B.C.P., Mattila, A.S. and Soinet, D. (2014) Service research in the hospitality literature: insights from a systematic review. *Cornell Hospitality Quarterly*, **55**, 287–99.

Kandasamy, I. and Ancheri, S. (2009) Hotel employees' expectations of QWL: a qualitative study. *International Journal of Hospitality Management*, **28**, 328–37.

Karl, K.A., Peluchette, J., Hall, L. and Harland, L. (2005) Attitudes toward workplace fun: a three sector comparison. *Journal of Leadership and Organizational Studies*, **12**, 1–17.

Katircioglu, S. (2009) Tourism, trade and growth: the case of Cyprus. *Applied Economics*, **41**, 2741–50.

Keep, E. and Mayhew, K. (1999) The assessment: knowledge, skills and competitiveness. *Oxford Review of Economic Policy*, **15**, 1–15.

Kim, B.P., Murrmann, S.K. and Lee, G. (2009a) Moderating effects of gender and organizational level between role stress and job satisfaction among hotel employees. *International Journal of Hospitality Management*, **28**, 612–19.

Kim, H.J. (2008) Hotel service providers' emotional labor: the antecedents and effects on burnout. *International Journal of Hospitality Management*, **27**, 151–61.

Kim, H.J., Tavitiyaman, P. and Kim, W.G. (2009b) The effect of management commitment to service on employee service behaviors: the mediating role of job satisfaction. *Journal of Hospitality and Tourism Research*, **33**, 369–90.

Kivanc, J. (2016) Violence worries Turkish Canadians. *Toronto Star*, 16 July, A16.

Klein, H.J. and Heuser, A.E. (2008) The learning of socialization content: a framework for researching orienting practices. In J.J. Martoccio (ed.) *Research in Personnel and Human Resources Management, Vol. 27*. Bingley: Emerald, pp. 279–336.

Kuslavan, S. and Kuslavan, Z. (2000) Perceptions and attitudes of undergraduate tourism students towards working in the tourism industry in Turkey. *Tourism Management*, **21**, 251–69.

Kusluvan, S., Kusluvan, Z., Ilhan, I. and Buyruk, L. (2012) A review of human resources management issues in the tourism and hospitality industry. *Cornell Hospitality Quarterly*, **51**, 171–214.

Labor Occupational Health Program and NIOSH (2016) *Staying Safe at Work: Teaching Workers with Intellectual and Developmental Difficulties about Health and Safety on the Job*. Berkeley, CA: Labor Occupational Health Program.

Liao, H. and Chuang, A. (2004) A multi-level investigation of factors influencing employee service performance and customer outcomes. *Academy of Management Journal*, **47**, 41–58.

Liao, H. and Chuang, A. (2007) Transforming service employees and climate: a multilevel, multisource examination of transformational leadership in building long-term service relationships. *Journal of Applied Psychology*, **92**, 1006–19.

Love, L.F. and Singh, P. (2011) Workplace branding: leveraging human resources management practices for competitive advantage through "Best Employer" surveys. *Journal of Business and Psychology*, **26**, 175–81.

Lowrie, M. (2016) Travel sector child sex abuse rising globally. *Toronto Star*, 13 May, A4.

Lub, X., Bijvank, M.N., Bal, P.M., Blomme, R. and Schalk, R. (2012) Different or alike? Exploring the psychological contract and commitment of different generations of hospitality workers. *International Journal of Contemporary Hospitality Management*, **24**, 553–73.

Lunt, N., Smith, R., Exworthy, M., Green, S.T., Horsfall, D. and Mannion, R. (2012) *Medical Tourism: Treatments, Markets and Health System Implications: A Scoping Review*. Paris: Organisation for Economic Co-operation and Development.

Luthans, F., Vogelgesang, G.R. and Lester, P.B. (2006a) Developing the psychological capital of resiliency. *Human Resource Development Review*, **5**, 25–44.

Luthans, F., Youssef, C.M. and Avolio, B.J. (2007) *Psychological Capital*. New York: Oxford University Press.

Luthans, F., Avey, J.B., Avolio, B.J., Norman, S.M. and Combs, G.M. (2006b) Psychological capital development: toward a micro-intervention. *Journal of Organizational Behavior*, **27**, 387–93.

MacReady, N. (2007) Developing countries court medical tourists. *The Lancet*, **369**, 1849–50.

Maddeaux, S. (2016) Eating to go: how staff meals bring a restaurant together. *National Post*, 2 June, B5.

Madera, J.M. (2013) Best practices in diversity management in customer service organizations: an investigation of top companies cited by Diversity Inc. *Cornell Hospitality Quarterly*, **54**, 124–35.

Madera, J.M., Neal, J.A. and Dawson, M. (2011) A strategy for diversity training: focusing on empathy in the workplace. *Journal of Hospitality and Tourism Research*, **35**, 469–87.

Magnini, V.P. (2009) Understanding and reducing work–family conflict in the hospitality industry. *Journal of Human Resources in Hospitality and Tourism*, **8**, 119–36.

Marinakou, E. (2014) Women in hotel management and leadership: diamond or glass? *Journal of Tourism and Hospitality Management*, **2**, 18–25.

Mason, A. (1999) Tourism and the sex trade in Southeast Asia. *Totem: The University of Western Ontario Journal of Anthropology*, **7**, 1–12.

Michel, J.W., Kavanagh, M.J. and Tracey, J.B. (2012) Got support? The impact of supportive work practices on the perceptions, motivation and behavior of customer-contact employees. *Cornell Hospitality Quarterly*, **54**, 161–73.

Min, H., Kim, H.J. and Lee, S-B. (2015) Extending the challenge–hindrance stressor framework: the role of psychological capital. *International Journal of Hospitality Management*, **50**, 105–14.

Mojtehedzadeh, S. and Keung, N. (2016) Chinese workers in restaurants endure "widespread" abuse. *Toronto Star*, 25 April, A1, A2.

Murphy, K.S. and Murrmann, S. (2009) The research design used to develop a high performance management system construct for US restaurant managers. *International Journal of Hospitality Management*, **38**, 547–55.

Nicolaides, A. (2006) Management versus leadership in the hospitality industry. *Journal of Travel and Tourism Research*, **6**, 29–38.

Paek, S., Schuckert, M., Kim, T.T. and Lee, G. (2015) Why is hospitality employees' psychological capital important? The effects of psychological capital on work engagement and employee morale. *International Journal of Hospitality Management*, **50**, 9–26.

Parasuraman, A. (1987) Customer-oriented corporate cultures are crucial to services marketing success. *Journal of Services Marketing*, **1**, 39–46.

Parasuraman, A., Zeithaml, V.A. and Berry, L.L. (1985) A conceptual model of service quality and its implications for future research. *Journal of Marketing*, **49**, 41–50.

Parasuraman, A., Zeithaml, V.A. and Berry, L.L. (1989) SERQUAL: a multiple item scale for measuring consumer perceptions of service quality. *Journal of Retailing*, **64**, 12–40.

Park, J. and Gursoy, D. (2012) Generation effects on work engagement among U.S. hotel employees. *International Journal of Hospitality Management*, **31**, 1195–202.

Pizam, A. (2004) Are hospitality employees supposed to hide their feelings? *International Journal of Hospitality Management*, **23**, 315–16.

Pizam, A. (2010) Alcoholism among hospitality employees: an editorial. *International Journal of Hospitality Management*, **29**, 547–8.

Pizam, A. (2014) The need for cross-cultural competence training. *International Journal of Hospitality Management*, **37**, A1, A2.

Pizam, A. (2016) The Jihadists' Holy War against the hospitality and tourism industries. *International Journal of Hospitality Management*, **53**, 173–4.

Poulston, J. (2008) Metamorphosis in hospitality: a tradition of sexual harassment. *International Journal of Hospitality Management*, **27**, 232–40.

Pugh, S.D. (2001) Service with a smile: emotional contagion in the service encounter. *Academy of Management Journal*, **22**, 1018–27.

Purcell, K. (1993) Equal opportunities in the hospitality industry: customs and credentials. *International Journal of Hospitality Management*, **12**, 127–40.

Richardson, S. (2009) Undergraduates' perceptions of tourism and hospitality as a career choice. *International Journal of Hospitality Management*, **28**, 382–8.

Richardson, S. and Thomas, N.J. (2012) Utilizing Generation Y: United States hospitality and tourism students' perceptions of careers in the industry. *Journal of Hospitality and Tourism Management*, **19**, 1–13.

Sakurai, K. and Jex, S.M. (2012) Coworker incivility and incivility targets' work effort and counter-productive work behaviors: the moderating effect of supervisor social support. *Journal of Occupational Health Psychology*, **17**, 150–61.

Schneider, B. and Bowen, D.E. (1995) *Winning the Service Game*. Boston, MA: Harvard Business School Press.

Schneider, B. and White, S.S. (2004) *Service Quality: Research Perspectives*. Thousand Oaks, CA: Sage Publications.

Sequeira, T.N. and Nunes, P.M. (2008) Does tourism influence economic growth? A dynamic panel data approach. *Applied Economics*, **40**, 2431–41.

Shan, J. and Wilson, K. (2001) Causality between trade and tourism: empirical evidence from China. *Applied Economics Letters*, **8**, 279–83.

Shani, A. and Pizam, A. (2009) Work-related depression among hotel employees. *Cornell Hospitality Quarterly*, **50**, 446–59.

Shani, A., Uriely, N., Reichel, A. and Ginsburg, L. (2014) Emotional labor in the hospitality industry: the influence of contextual factors. *International Journal of Hospitality Management*, **17**, 150–58.

Sims, D.M. (2010) *Creative Onboarding Programs: Tools for Energizing your Orientation Programs*. New York: McGraw-Hill.

Sinclair, M.T. (1998) Tourism and economic development: a survey. *Journal of Development Studies*, **34**, 1–51.

Singal, M. (2014) The business case for diversity management in the hospitality industry. *International Journal of Hospitality Management*, **40**, 10–19.

Stein, M.A. and Christiansen, L. (2010) *Successful Onboarding: A Strategy to Unlock Hidden Value in your Organization*. New York: McGraw-Hill.

Taylor, J. (2010) *Safety Culture: Assessing and Changing the Behavior of Organizations*. Farnham: Gower.

Terglav, K., Ruzzier, M.K. and Kase, R. (2016) Internal branding process. Exploring the role of mediators in top management's leadership–commitment relationship. *International Journal of Hospitality Management*, **54**, 1–11.

Testa, M.R. and Sipe, L. (2012) Service-leadership competencies for hospitality and tourism management. *International Journal of Hospitality Management*, **31**, 648–58.

Tews, M.J., Michel, J.W. and Stafford, K. (2013) Does fun pay? The impact of workplace fun on employee turnover and performance. *Cornell Hospitality Quarterly*, **54**, 370–82.

Watkins, M.D. (2013) *The First 90 Days: Proven Strategies for Getting up to Speed Faster and Smarter*. Boston, MA: Harvard Business School Press.

Whitelaw, P.A. (2013) Leadership up the ladder: the construction of leadership styles in the hospitality industry. *Contemporary Issues in Businesses and Government*, **19**, 65–79.

Wong, S.C. and Ko, A. (2009) Exploratory study of understanding hotel employees' perceptions on work–life balance issues. *International Journal of Hospitality Management*, **28**, 195–203.

Woods, R.H. and Viehland, D. (2000) Women in hotel management. *Cornell Hotel and Restaurant Administration Quarterly*, **41**, 51–69.

Worsfold, P. (1999) HRM performance, commitment and service quality in the hotel industry. *International Journal of Contemporary Hospitality Management*, **11**, 340–48.

Zeithaml, V. and Bitner, M. (2003) *Services Marketing: Integrating Customer Focus Across the Firm*, 3rd edn. New York: McGraw-Hill.

Zemke, R. and Schaef, D. (1989) *The Service Edge: 101 Companies that Profit from Customer Care*. New York: New American Library.

Zohar, D. (1980) Safety climate in industrial organizations: theoretical and applied implications. *Journal of Applied Psychology*, **65**, 96–101.

Zopiatis, A. and Constanti, P. (2005) A review and profile of managerial burnout in the hospitality industry in Cyprus. *Tourism Today*, Fall, 25–35.

Zopiatis, A. and Constanti, P. (2012) Managing hospitality internship practices: a conceptual framework. *Journal of Hospitality and Tourism Education*, **24**, 44–51.

Zopiatis, A. and Kyprianou, G. (2006) Perceptions and attitudes towards the hospitality professions in Cyprus. *Tourism Today*, Fall, 33–46.

Zopiatis, A., Constanti, P. and Theocharous, A.L. (2014) Job involvement, commitment, satisfaction and turnover: evidence from hotel employees in Cyprus. *Tourism Management*, **41**, 129–40.

2. The changing tourism and hospitality context: implications for human resource management in an age of disruption and growth
Julia Christensen Hughes

We are living in a time of profound disruption (Christensen, 2003; 2011; Schwab, 2016; Tapscott and Tapscott, 2016), with organizations – and even entire industries – encountering both the promise of new opportunities and the nagging fear of impending obsolescence. Driven by smartphones, digital currency, and the rising influence of Millennials, people from around the globe are more directly connected with information, and each other, than ever before. The domination of Amazon and other technology-enabled disruptors, such as PayPal, Airbnb and Uber, amongst others, has signaled the power of new entrants to challenge entire industries.

The commanding growth of these relative newcomers has both resulted from – and enabled – radical changes in consumer behavior including how, where and why people make purchase decisions. Demand for convenience has risen, alongside increased expectations for sustainable products and services, and authentic and meaningful experiences, both internationally and at home. In some cases, this has led to market dichotomization, with successful businesses providing either low-cost, highly convenient products, services and experiences on the one hand, or more expensive and luxurious products, services and experiences on the other, with little room for competitive success in the middle.

Within tourism and hospitality, these changes are resulting in considerable economic and employment growth throughout the world. Successful hotels and restaurants are providing an enhanced, increasingly differentiated customer value proposition at either end of the market. This dichotomy has significant implications for the human resource function within the hospitality industry, with businesses embracing technology and automation (in jobs where labor is relatively easily replaced) and seeking a more highly trained and engaged workforce (where it is not).

Arguably, given heightened expectations for the guest experience and the increasing complexity of some job functions (such as in data analytics and technology), effective human resource management will become increasingly essential – an acknowledged competitive advantage – to delivering the various value propositions on order. The hospitality industry has always been about people. The disruption that is occurring will only heighten this fundamental truth.

This chapter begins with an overview of some of the most significant trends occurring in the global tourism sector and hospitality – particularly with respect to the foodservice and accommodation industries. Areas of growth are highlighted as well as key sources of disruption, including digital technology, values-based consumption, the growing influence of Millennials, and the quest for authentic, meaningful guest experiences. Some of these trends are also explored from the perspective of the US hospitality industry. Given that human resource issues can be significantly impacted by national (and local) employment cultures and legislative issues, the US foodservice and accommodation industries are highlighted in order to illustrate one particular context. The chapter concludes by reflecting on the implications of these trends and disruptions for the human resource function within the hospitality industry. The case is made that effective human resource management practices are more critical now than they have ever been, and that the current disruption will inevitably cull those organizations that are unable to figure this out.

GLOBAL TRENDS IN TOURISM AND HOSPITALITY

According to the World Travel and Tourism Council (2016a), the travel and tourism sector – which includes tourist expenditures in a range of industries, including travel, hotels and restaurants – directly contributed US$2.2 trillion to GDP and 108 million jobs in 2015. When indirect factors are also taken into account, including capital investments and supply chain effects, the sector reportedly contributed more than US$7 trillion in 2015, or 9.8 percent of total GDP, employing 284 million people and providing almost 10 percent of jobs worldwide (World Travel and Tourism Council, 2016a).

In terms of growth, travel and tourism continues to outperform other significant sectors (such as manufacturing, retail, education and health care). In 2015, travel and tourism GDP grew by 3.1 percent, its 6th consecutive year of positive growth, creating 2.5 million new jobs (a growth rate of 2.6 percent) (World Travel and Tourism Council, 2016a). The sector is expected to continue on this trajectory, outperforming the global economy, with an expected average growth of 4 percent in GDP over the next decade.

All regions of the world economy are expected to participate in this growth, with the exception of South America (due to economic volatility in Brazil) (World Travel and Tourism Council, 2016a). Regions where growth has been particularly strong include Asia as well as destinations sought by Chinese travelers. In China, outbound travel and tourism expenditures grew by a remarkable 67 percent in 2015, predominantly benefiting Japan (where international arrivals grew by 47 percent), but also other countries such as the UK, Germany, Iceland, Australia and New Zealand (World Travel and Tourism Council, 2016a).

Growth in the Global Food Services Industry

Contributing to the travel and tourism sector is the global food service industry. This industry is comprised of full service restaurants (including family style, casual dining, upscale casual and fine dining), and limited service restaurants (including quick service/fast food, fast casual, and delivery/take away only) (CHD Expert, 2016). According to market research firm Euromonitor International (as cited in QSR Magazine, 2016), global consumer food service sales grew by 5.7 percent in 2015, up from 5.3 percent the year before. Geographically, China remained the largest consumer foodservices market, with sales of USD 617 billion and a growth rate of 9.5 percent (from 2014 to 2015). China is forecast to grow by an additional USD 235 billion in food service sales by 2020, with the US and India following, with forecasted additional sales growth of USD 48.8 billion and USD 35.7 billion respectively.

The most dominant players in global foodservices, based on total system-wide sales, remain quick service/fast food chains. The "top ten" global ranking, along with the number of non-US units, is as follows (QSR Magazine, 2017): McDonald's, 18 710; KFC, 11 798; Burger King, 4998; Pizza Hut, 5890; Subway, 10 109; Domino's Pizza, 4422; Starbucks Coffee Company, 5727; Wendy's, 693; Dunkin' Donuts, 3005; and Dairy Queen, 802. These chains play a significant role in the international franchise sector, which is expected to grow by USD 36 billion or 5.3 percent in 2017, to 744 437 locations (Maze, 2017b).

Suggesting some disruption within the quick service restaurant (QSR) segment, while market leader McDonald's experienced an average same-store sales increase of 3.8 percent in 2016, "the best year for the company since 2011", declines were experienced in its US units. McDonald's also reported a 1 percent reduction in Net Income (to USD 1.19 billion) along with a 5 percent decline in revenue (to USD 6 billion), due to "refranchising, general and administrative cuts and various one-time costs and revenue sources" (Maze, 2017a).

The fastest-growing market segment in food services globally is "fast-casual", which, while much smaller than QSR, led the industry with growth of 10.4 percent and an increase in sales of USD 3.4 billion in 2015. These results have been attributed to shifting consumer preferences: "Coffee shops, for example, saw a high increase in sales last year, which shows that the dining-out culture is continuing to evolve toward more modern, premium, casual, and social experiences" (QSR Magazine, 2016).

According to industry consultant Deloitte (2016), customers are increasingly expecting an "outstanding, personalized experience" and companies need to become more adept at crafting and delivering customized value propositions. At the other end of the market, home delivery is expected to become increasingly dominant: "since 2012, meal delivery and grocery delivery startups have raised more than $8.4 billion cumulatively. To put it in perspective, that's more than all of the restaurant IPOs of the last 16 years, combined" (Allen, 2016).

Growth in the Global Accommodation Industry

Another significant contributor to the travel and tourism sector is the global accommodation industry. This industry is segmented by bed and breakfasts/guest houses, youth hostels, budget, economy, midscale, upscale, upperscale, and luxury hotels. Within the accommodation industry, global revenue is forecast to reach USD 550 billion in 2016, a growth rate of over 20 percent since 2011 (Hospitality Net, 2015). The highest occupancy rates have been occurring in Europe and Asia Pacific, and the highest room rates in Africa and the Middle East.

These results suggest considerable opportunity for market-leading hotels and other accommodation providers and have fueled some industry consolidation; AccorHotels acquired Fairmont Raffles Hotels International in 2015 and Marriott International acquired Starwood Hotels & Resorts in 2016. As a result of this acquisition, Marriott is now the world's largest hotel operator, with 30 brands, 1.1 million rooms, and 5700 hotels in 110 countries (Ting, 2016a). This acquisition, which has brought together 300 000 Marriott employees and 200 000 Starwood employees, will require strong leadership in order to successfully integrate two very different cultures and operating systems. The merger is expected to provide increased bargaining power with suppliers, collaborators (including increasingly powerful online travel agencies (OTA) such as Expedia and Booking.com) and customers (Marriott will now control 60 percent of hotel rooms in New York, for example) (Skift Magazine, 2016, p. 17).

Digital Disruption

Digital-based disruption is having a profound impact on the hospitality industry. In foodservices, technology is providing customers with greater convenience (particularly in the home delivery market) and the opportunity for product customization. Online ordering, self-serve kiosks, digital menu boards (that can adjust product offerings based on a range of factors, including the weather), tablets, mobile payments and digital customer loyalty programs are becoming increasingly common, while 3-D printing pizza ovens, drone delivery and driverless cars are being tested. These disruptions are arguably fundamentally changing consumer behavior. In China, 26 percent of fast food sales were ordered online in 2015 (QSR Magazine, 2016).

Some of the disruption that is occurring can be attributed to leading global retailer Amazon, who has set the standard for online ordering, including choice, convenience and speed of home delivery. Amazon recently entered the foodservice industry, offering an online ordering portal and home delivery capability (in one hour or less) for participating restaurants. Foreshadowing things to come, Amazon is currently testing drone delivery. Other companies, such as "UberEATS, Google Express, Grub Hub, and SkipTheDishes are all offering food delivery from local restaurants – from fast food to upscale dining – in under an hour" (Duffy, 2016); consumers can now have "a hot, gourmet meal delivered to the door in less time than it might take to get seated at a restaurant". This presents an opportunity for restaurants not yet in the home delivery business, or for outsourcing, for those who are. Significant increases in home delivery have important operational implications, including greater need for kitchen staff and lost opportunity from beverage sales.

Underscoring the extent to which digital technology has supported the home delivery segment, Domino's, the global leader in pizza delivery, provides its customers with the opportunity to: place customized orders through multiple platforms (Facebook, Twitter, Apple TV), amass points for free pizza through an online customer loyalty program, use coupons delivered via Twitter, track their deliveries online (potentially soon by drone) and post their feedback through social media.

While foodservices has lagged behind other industries in the adoption of technology, this is beginning to change, with myriad potential benefits (Allen, 2016): "This continued emphasis on tech will inevitably lead to new foodservice careers in the future".

Digital disruption is also having a significant impact on the travel and accommodation industry, with online travel agents (OTA), bots and apps increasingly helping consumers plan their trips, read online reviews and make their bookings. More than 50 percent of hotel reservations are now being made online (Hospitality Net, 2015). "Technology [is]. . . shaping the way we want to travel, how travel agencies interact with us and the places we want to go" (Hospitality Net, 2017).

Digital platforms have also helped fuel the sharing economy. Airbnb, which doesn't own any physical hotel rooms (just as Amazon doesn't own any restaurants), currently lists over two million properties, in over 191 countries and over 34 000 cities (Airbnb, 2017). Underscoring its rapid growth and global reach, Airbnb reportedly accommodates "10–12% of travel demand in New York City, Paris, London and other major global metropolitan areas alone" (Starkov and Safer, 2017). Airbnb is now the top ranked hospitality company on the Fortune 100 list; valued at $30 billion, it out-ranks Hilton ($25 billion) and Marriott ($21 billion) (Ting, 2016b).

One of the reasons these digital disruptors have been so impactful has been their ability to enhance the customer value proposition. According to Alton (2016), Airbnb's success can be attributed to "connecting people to people. This peer-sharing aspect is what's allowed the company to grow so quickly." Uber, on the other hand, "disrupted the industry by offering something that's cheaper, easier and modernized . . . As Uber has shown, people like simplicity and personalization."

In order to remain competitive against Airbnb and other disruptors, traditional accommodation providers will need to provide a superior guest experience in areas that they are uniquely able to provide. According to Starkov and Safer (2017), this includes:

> 24/7 security; ADA compliance; baggage storage, room service, concierge, luxuries such as plush robes, and employees dedicated to customer service. This also includes amenities such as spa services, onsite dining, fitness center, inspiring communal spaces for guests to gather and socialize, including inviting lobbies, lobby bars and cafes, executive meeting rooms, etc. Guest Appreciation Programs/Loyalty Programs supported by a robust CRM Program.

They will also need to embrace technology: "Social media platforms are now the main battleground for hoteliers to strategically engage with their customers if they wish to grow their occupancy" (Hospitality Net, 2015). As an example, global accommodation leader Marriott International collaborated with the Massachusetts Institute of Technology (MIT) to develop an application for connecting guests with common interests. They also have a customer loyalty program, which enables them to collect customer data and personalize the guest experience, including providing preferred (and faster) check-in; tracking guest preferences for bed linens, pillows and room location; and providing access to enhanced services including private lounges, premium food and upgraded amenities for their most frequent guests.

Digital disruption is also automating many internal systems, including human resources, particularly within the larger chains. Recruitment and pre-screening can now be done largely online, with company websites providing detailed background information on the company and available positions, along with automated pre-screening tools. Prospective employees may be asked to upload a video from their phone, respond to questions online, or participate in something more interactive, such as Heineken's game-changing "go places" video and survey tool (Natividad, 2016). All of these approaches contribute to the employer brand, as do anonymous online employee comments, such as those recorded on Glassdoor (Glassdoor, 2017). The industry has also automated employee scheduling, with employees reporting shift preferences and availability online, and using a scheduler app to find a replacement, when conflicts do occur.

While technology is being used to enhance some internal and customer-facing processes, improving convenience and reducing the need for some positions (particularly front-line order taking and reservations), demand for other positions will inevitably increase. Organizations will increasingly require employees skilled in data analytics, artificial intelligence and information technology, and adept at responding to online comments. Restaurants and hotels in upscale markets will also need more highly skilled employees who are capable of interacting with digital-savvy guests and providing customized guest experiences. Some of the ways in which guest expectations are changing are outlined in the section that follows.

Changing Consumer Expectations: Values, Millennials and the Experience Economy

Changing consumer expectations are contributing to the disruption that is occurring within the hospitality industry. Associated factors include the growing influence of ethical consumption, Millennials and the growing desire for authentic, memorable experiences.

Ethical consumption
There has been a marked increase in consumer interest in businesses perceived as promoting ethical consumption, including local and organic foods and beverages; sustainable approaches to water and energy use; and integrity across the supply chain, including food authenticity, ethical sourcing, fair labor practices and the humane treatment of animals. This shift represents a growing trend in retail toward "sustainability, consumer desire to be more ethically conscious in purchase decisions, and a keen interest in supporting a 'strong sense of identity'" (Vend, 2017).

Within Canada, as an example, restaurants that are succeeding are increasingly offering a clear point of differentiation on the basis of "free-from" beef and poultry products – such as hormone free, antibiotic free, and preservative free (Bostock, 2016). Canadian fast food chain A&W was one of the first in the country to offer a "100% Pure Beef Guarantee" with their commitment to serving hormone- and steroid-free beef.

Some restaurants have gone beyond "free-from" products, incorporating sustainability throughout their operations, and seeking certification, such as through the B Corp certification (B Corp, 2017a) program, as evidence of their commitment to offering an authentic values-based consumer proposition. The B Corp certification process encourages continuous improvement in a number of domains, including paying a living wage, embracing sustainable energy practices, and making a social contribution beyond the business itself. There are now over 180 B Corp certified food and beverage providers in the world (B Corp, 2017b), but just eight travel and accommodation providers (B Corp, 2017c).

Reflecting this shift, globally dominating restaurant chains previously renowned for their ability to deliver a highly processed, consistent product and customer experience the world over are increasingly being challenged by local competitors. Within China, for example, "opportunities are strongest in local cuisines rather than in formerly dominant growth categories like chicken and burger fast food" (Euromonitor, 2015). As a result, foodservice chains will increasingly be exploring how to integrate "local" into their menus and business models, which will undoubtedly require more decentralized decision-making and empowered domestic business leaders.

Reflecting the growing influence of values on the customer value proposition, Almquist (2016) suggested a framework, using four hierarchical categories, much like Maslow's Hierarchy of Needs. In addition to "functional benefits" (such as reducing time, effort, or cost), which most companies focus on, Almquist proposed three other important layers of consumer benefit including "emotional benefits" (such as reducing anxiety or enhancing fun, attractiveness or wellness); "life changing benefits" (such as supporting affiliation or self-actualization); and "social impact benefits" (self-transcendence). All of these "higher order" values are reflected in changing consumer preferences, including the growth of ethical consumption.

As values play an increasing role in the customer value proposition, employee talent will be needed that is capable of sharing the company's "values story" with confidence, including providing information on product sourcing, for example. Companies competing in this space will also be able to take advantage of the growing desire of millennial employees to work for organizations where there is a values-alignment. More on the impact of millennials is shared in the section that follows.

The growing influence of Millennials

Millennials are an increasingly important market segment, having been described as "the fastest growing segment" within the US restaurant industry (Duffy, 2016). They are also expected to become the "dominant consumer group" within the travel and accommodation sector by 2017 (Hospitality Net, 2015). This is based on both their "immense travel spending potential" and "higher tendencies to travel" (Hospitality Net, 2017).

As digital natives, Millennials are fueling a lot of the digital disruption previously described. According to Duffy (2016), "A recent survey found that 33% of consumers aged 18–34 state that the availability of technology is an important factor in making a decision where to eat, compared to 20% of 45–54 year olds." In addition, Millennials are much more likely to consult "reviews from TripAdvisor, Facebook, and Yelp when deciding where to dine".

Millennials are also looking for different types of travel experiences; low-cost, with the opportunity to connect with others and have authentic, local experiences. Accordingly, the youth hostel concept is being reinvigorated in order to cater to the millennial market. Shared or dorm-style accommodation is being paired with enhanced facilities, such as innovative common areas, self-service kitchens and cafes, and enhanced services, such as salons, tattoo parlors, walking tours and bicycle rentals. According to Craggs (as cited in Holmes, 2017):

> This reimagined hostel meets the needs of the modern traveler. . .It offers flexibility on the room product, and, often, organized events that encourage guests to meet and mingle. . . [it] not only taps into some of the spending power at the younger end of the market, but is also, to some extent, a response to the influence of Airbnb and the challenges that disruptive business has had on the hotel industry.

AccorHotels has moved aggressively into the youth market with a radical new concept called Jo&Joe. According to AccorHotels (2016), Jo&Joe was "co-constructed with its future guests and disrupts traditional codes"; "blends the best of private-rental, hostel and hotel formats"; and is a "totally reinvented and disruptive experience in terms of design approach, catering, service and customer journey". Accor plans to open 50 Jo&Joe venues by 2020. Commenting on the project, Sébastien Bazin, Chairman and CEO, explained the company's intention to "break with tradition, forget old habits, be surprising, authentic, unexpected, bring a breath of fresh air to AccorHotels" (AccorHotels, 2016).

As well as their growing influence as consumers, Millennials also represent a significant employee group to the industry. Given their ability to relate to this growing customer segment, retention of Millennials is increasingly being recognized as an important concern. According to management consulting firm Deloitte (2016):

> Because Millennial-generation employees understand and identify with their influential customer counterparts, long-term retention of Millennial talent is essential for future success. However, in an industry where seasonality may contribute to a sense of "temporariness", Millennials often leave T&H organizations because they feel their input is not valued or they lack "skin in the game." To invest these and other employees with a sense of ownership, empower and engage them across all strategic pain points. Give employees the ability to deliver personalized customer experiences. Train and incentivize them to make independent decisions. Hold them accountable and reward them for the results of their decisions.

The experience economy
Arguably, what AccorHotels is tapping into is the "experience economy", which was first articulated by Pine and Gilmore (1999) as a "previously unarticulated genre of economic output" (p. ix). Consistent with this view, and as previously described, foodservice and accommodation guests are increasingly expecting authentic and personalized experiences.

Pine and Gilmore (1999) distinguished the "experience economy" from the "service economy", suggesting: "When a person buys a service, he purchases a set of intangible activities carried out on his behalf. But when he buys an experience, he pays to spend time enjoying a series of memorable events that a company stages – as in a theatrical play – to engage him in a personal way" (p. 2). Pine and Gilmore (1999, p. 70) argued that such experiences "stand apart from the routine transactions mass producers foist on their customers" and that "With theatre as the model, even mundane tasks engage customers in a memorable way" (p. 106).

Pine and Gilmore (1999) suggested that the experience economy can be understood as encompassing four dimensions, including: entertainment, education, estheticism and escapism, varying by the degree of active participation on the part of the guest and the extent of immersion. Entertainment, they suggested, results from a positive passive exchange that leads the guest to "smile, laugh, or otherwise enjoy themselves" (p. 31). Education is the opportunity to actively acquire new knowledge or physical skills (for example, learning about other cultures, learning to cook or to ski). Estheticism involves passively experiencing a new reality, such as touring a nature reserve. Finally, escapism involves full immersion and active participation of the guest in a new reality (whether staged or real), such as visiting a casino, mountain climbing or white-water kayaking.

Clearly, there are significant implications for effectively delivering a customer value proposition, based on one or more of these types of experiences. As just one example, when employees are viewed as actors, recruitment might be thought of as a casting call, complete with auditions, to ensure the right people are selected for the right roles. Similarly, onboarding and training might be thought of as a dress rehearsal. Another implication pertains to the emotional dissonance that can result when employees are required to display emotions that are incongruent with their actual feelings (Ashforth and Humphrey, 1993; Hochschild, 1983). Emotional dissonance can result in either surface acting (faking it) or deep acting (modifying emotions genuinely felt). Surface acting has been associated with increased employee stress and burnout. On the other hand, a strong service climate (the provision of direction, support, rewards and encouragement) can facilitate deep acting and employee well-being. As experience becomes an increasingly important factor in the customer value proposition, management's ability to hire and train the right people and to provide a positive service climate will become increasingly important.

In summary, the global travel, tourism and hospitality (food services and accommodation) sector is a significant contributor to GDP and employment around the world. Projected growth estimates suggest increased demand and competitiveness for employees, in both global foodservice and hotel chains, as well as within independents. The need for employees at all levels and across multiple concepts will undoubtedly increase over the coming years. The hospitality industry is undergoing significant disruption, with profound implications for the type of employee talent that will be most needed. This disruption includes the increasing influence of digital technology and changing consumer preferences for ethical consumption and authentic, meaningful experiences. While the adoption of technology will reduce the need for some types of jobs, changes in consumer preferences will increase demand in others. Employees will increasingly be needed in high-value-added activities, not easily replaced by automation. At the unit level, this will include empowering managers and service staff, in order to provide authentic local products and service experiences (requiring presence, knowledge, judgment and spontaneity). At a leadership level, there will be a growing need for more sophisticated expertise with respect to marketing analytics, new product and concept development, and information technology, as well as with respect to the delivery of a more sophisticated and customized guest experience.

Given that employment takes place within local cultures and local legislative contexts, a brief review of these issues within the US hospitality industry follows.

US TRAVEL, TOURISM AND HOSPITALITY INDUSTRY TRENDS

According to the World Travel and Tourism Council (2016b), the United States ranks first amongst all countries in terms of the importance of travel and tourism to GDP. In 2015, the industry directly contributed USD 488 billion (2.7 percent of total GDP), with an expected growth rate of 3.7 percent over the next decade, to USD 722 billion (3.2 percent of total GDP) by 2026. Total contribution to GDP (including indirect effects) was USD 1469.9 billion in 2015 (8.2 percent of GDP) and is forecast to grow to over USD 2118.6 billion (9.3 percent of GDP) by 2026.

This activity is comprised primarily of leisure travel (71.6 percent), with business travel accounting for 28.4 percent; and domestic travel (80.9 percent), with foreign visitors and international tourism receipts of 19.1 percent. International tourist arrivals are expected to grow from just over 76 million people (USD 189.7 billion) in 2016 to over 124 508 000 (USD 295.9 billion) by 2026 (World Travel and Tourism Council, 2016b).

The US ranks second behind only China in terms of the importance of travel and tourism for domestic employment (World Travel and Tourism Council, 2016b). Currently, travel and tourism in the US directly supports the employment of over 5 million people (3.8 percent of total employment), and is expected to grow to over 7 million (4.5 percent of total employment) by 2026. When indirect factors are taken into account, the industry supports over 14 million people (9.6 percent of total employment), and is forecast to provide over 18 million jobs (11.4 percent) by 2026.

The US Foodservice Industry

Contributing to the US travel and tourism sector is the food services industry. According to the US National Restaurant Association (NRA) (2017), the US restaurant industry is expected to account for USD 799 billion in sales in 2017, and employ almost 15 million people (representing 10 percent of the US workforce) in over 1 million locations. Over two-thirds (70 percent) of US restaurants are single unit operations and 90 percent of restaurants employ fewer than 50 people each, with many managers and owners having worked their way up from first jobs (National Restaurant Association, 2017); 90 percent of restaurant managers started in entry-level positions as did 80 percent of restaurant owners (National Restaurant Association, 2017).

Restaurants are a critical source of employment for American youth, employing 1.5 million teenagers between the ages of 16 and 19 (America Works Here, 2017). One half of Americans have worked in a restaurant, one in three people get their first paid job in a restaurant and one in four restaurant employees are students. Suggesting that restaurants provide opportunity for advancement, 71 percent of restaurant employees aged 18 to 24 are reportedly promoted (America Works Here, 2017). According to the NRA, the restaurant industry is also supportive of diversity, employing more Hispanic managers and more women owners and managers than any other industry (America Works Here, 2017).

With respect to US restaurant sales, same-store growth occurred in just three segments in 2016 – primarily quick service, which accounts for "about 80 percent of total visits industry-wide" (Whitten, 2016), but also upscale casual and fine dining (Higgins, 2016; Patton, 2016). According to industry consultant Victor Fernandez, as cited in Higgins (2016):

> Consumers are favoring chain restaurants for inexpensive, convenience-driven and on-the-go dining (the vast majority of quick service sales are take-out). On the other end of the spectrum, higher-end, experience-based dining is also strong for chains. Mid-scale spending is where they are having the most trouble.

As one example of a successful US-based QSR chain, Domino's Pizza has seen same-store sales increase for 22 consecutive quarters in the US market (Whitten, 2016), driven largely by its focus on technology and home delivery. In comparison, McDonald's US sales are experiencing same-store declines (Maze, 2017a).

With respect to US independent restaurants, those providing an authentic local experience have reportedly fared well (Bryan, 2016a; 2016b). According to one industry analyst, independents "are attracting consumers with their 'unique offerings, local orientation and strong value propositions'" (Whitten, 2016).

Recently, it has been suggested that there may be some over-supply of restaurants in the "good food revival" space (Alexander, 2016). Restaurants featuring celebrity chefs and innovative menus have revolutionized the importance of the kitchen (the back of house) and the status – and the wages – of its staff. Artistically prepared food and beverage items, made from scratch using local ingredients, require more highly trained kitchen and bar personnel. According to Alexander (2016) given the different cost structure of these types of restaurants, owners are having a hard time making ends meet.

As previously suggested, Amazon recently joined the restaurant industry. In the US, over 3000 restaurants across 19 cities are currently participating in the Amazon program (see https://primenow.amazon.com/restaurants). Using personalized Amazon accounts and Prime Now mobile apps, customers can browse menus, place orders, make payments, and track delivery (Jennings, 2015). Targeting the "food on demand" market,

Gus Lopez, general manager of Amazon's new restaurant division, cites the value proposition for customers and restaurants in Seattle, the first test site for the concept (as cited in Jennings, 2015): "Prime members can now enjoy food from the Seattle restaurants they love without having to drive all over the city. For many of these restaurants, this is the first time they are offering delivery, and we are delighted they have chosen to work with us."

The US Accommodation Industry

According to the American Hotel and Lodging Association (2015), the US is home to over 53 000 hotel properties (representing almost 5 million rooms), of which over 33 000 are considered "small businesses". Together, these properties generate over USD 176 billion in annual sales revenue and employ almost 2 million people, with further growth predicted (American Hotel and Lodging Association, 2015).

Across the US hotel industry, financial results have been robust, with growth in demand outpacing growth in supply every year since 2010. Segments experiencing superior year over year results in occupancy, ADR (average daily rate) and RevPar (revenue per available room) include Independent Chains, Upper Upscale and Luxury (Hotel News Resource, 2016). According to The Global Hotel Industry and Trends for 2016 (Hospitality Net, 2015), the average US occupancy rate was 64.5 percent in 2015 and the average room rate was USD 121.37.

Employment Issues within the US Hospitality Industry

With respect to human resource issues, the US hospitality industry continues to be characterized by high rates of turnover, influenced by poor wages and working conditions. There are, however, some important exceptions, with an increasing number of examples of both restaurant and hotel companies offering an attractive employee value proposition, including competitive wages and benefits, a positive working atmosphere, opportunity for promotion, and values alignment. These issues are explored in brief below.

According to Ruggless (2016), turnover in the foodservices and accommodation sector reached 72.1 percent in 2015, the fifth consecutive year for an increase (up from 66.7 percent in 2014). This figure includes a 50.3 percent "quit rate", 19.5 percent in layoffs and discharges, and 2.3 percent for other separations including retirements, deaths and disabilities. This compares negatively to the national turnover rate of (a still surprisingly high) 45.9 percent for all private sector workers (Ruggless, 2016).

Reporting on this trend, Higgins (2016) offered:

> Turnover has been trending up since 2010 and, particularly for restaurant managers, has reached levels surpassing anything reported for over ten years. In the current environment of falling restaurant sales, this is especially troubling since TDn2K research has continuously shown a relationship between management turnover and a brand's sales and traffic results.

These figures suggest significant mobility and dissatisfaction amongst many Americans, but particularly in hospitality, and therefore difficulties for employers in retaining a qualified and engaged workforce to meet projected increases in consumer demand. This is consistent with the suggestion that a "turnover culture" exists in many hospitality organizations (Iverson and Deery, 1997).

Underscoring the importance of this issue, Enz (2004) determined that "Human resources continues to be the most troubling issue for U.S. restaurant owners and operators" and that "finding and keeping competent employees" is particularly problematic (p. 315). Managers in Enz's study reported inadequacies in: employee skill levels, compensation and benefits, training, and the image of the industry. Enz (2004, p. 330) concluded that the image of the industry was being negatively affected by "The view of employees as costs to be managed rather than key investments for the long-term competitive success of the restaurant". Her study also underscored difficulties in recruitment and retention at all levels (Enz, 2004, p. 319).

> The back-of-house positions, which may require less skill than do those in the front of the house, pose special challenges because managers often rely on recent immigrants to fill many kitchen positions. Finding qualified management candidates is equally challenging, with half of the respondents who mentioned recruiting as a problem identifying the hiring of skilled managers as being a constant concern. Some blame the industry's image as a long-hours, low-wage occupation for contributing to the recruitment problem.

Enz's study suggested that improved compensation, including support for minimum wage increases and health care benefits, were particularly important as was "the reduction in excessively long working hours", the redesign of some jobs in order to enhance productivity, and "training, career development and planning for managers" (p. 330). These recommendations were seen as supporting the increased professionalization of the industry and the creation of "employers of choice".

An earlier study by Enz (2001), which focused on the perceptions of managers in the US and European hotel industry, found similar results with several human resource issues being identified as areas of predominant concern, including "attracting, retaining, motivating, training, and developing the industry's work force" (p. 39). An important secondary area of concern pertained to fostering innovative guest experiences. According to Enz (2001, p. 43):

> Foremost, managers worry about attracting and retaining employees, middle managers, and future leaders. At the staff level the concerns are focused on hiring the best people possible and preparing them through careful training to possess the skills necessary to serve guests and operate as effective team players. The problems experienced in attracting talent . . . are due to the industry's notoriously poor wages, long working hours, and seasonality . . . This problem is particularly acute for managers in tourist locations who are unable to hire sufficiently talented people who also embody the local customs and heritage. Once employees are hired, the managers' second concern is the quality and consistency of their training . . . Raising compensation and employee morale was also of greater concern to U.S. managers than those in Europe.

Barriers to dealing effectively with these issues were attributed to a short-term financial orientation and attitudes of traditional senior managers who "undervalue employees and treat them as short-term costs" (Enz, 2001, p. 43). The lack of career opportunity was also raised: "Many felt that management-education and training programs are inadequate in most companies and that the industry had done a poor job of making the case for why a talented individual should remain in the industry" (p. 44).

Suggesting that Enz's (2001, 2004) studies still hold true today, consulting firm Deloitte recently observed (2016) that many tourism and hospitality organizations are "finding it increasingly difficult to recruit and retain individuals with the right blend of interpersonal and technical skills". They suggested that part of the problem was due to the changing nature of some jobs; "jobs in this industry are becoming much more specialized". Also, competition from other industries is also increasing. Citing the industry's high rate of turnover, they suggested that while seasonality and young employees hold part of the explanation, the industry's failure to offer "long-term career prospects" was a significant contributor to the problem.

The tendency of US employers to pay no more than that mandated by minimum wage legislation has also been acknowledged as a contributing factor. Many hospitality workers earn less than what is considered a "living wage", defined as "the minimum employment earnings necessary to meet a family's basic needs while also maintaining self-sufficiency" (Nadeau, 2015, p. 1). According to the Living Wage Calculator, created in 2004 by Dr Amy K. Glasmeier at MIT, in 2015 the average national (US) living wage was USD 15.12 per hour, for a family of two working adults with two children. This is more than double the federal minimum wage of USD 7.25 (last raised in 2009). As a result, families of minimum wage workers struggle considerably. According to Nadeau (2016):

> While the minimum wage sets an earnings threshold under which our society is not willing to let families slip, it fails to approximate the basic expenses of families in 2015. Consequently, many working adults must seek public assistance and/or hold multiple jobs in order to afford to feed, clothe, house, and provide medical care for themselves and their families.

Minimum wage legislation has been an area of significant controversy in the US, including during the US 2016 Presidential election, with both the Republicans and Democrats suggesting that increases were warranted, albeit to different extents. Now with Trump elected, and Fast-Food Executive Andrew Puzder nominated as Labor Secretary, a national increase in the minimum wage looks unlikely. With ongoing political uncertainty at the federal level, 19 states recently committed to raising the minimum wage, beginning in 2017, with targets ranging from USD 12 to USD 15 per hour, to be phased in over the next several years (National Conference of State Legislatures, 2017).

Opponents from the restaurant industry have been particularly vocal, citing: the labor-intensive nature of the industry (labor costs typically range from about 20 to 40 percent of restaurant sales); pre-tax profit margins ranging from as little as 3 to 6 percent; the preponderance of young employees and students (without necessarily having familial obligations); and the potential of tips for servers (which can add an additional USD 12 to USD 17 to hourly wages) (National Restaurant Association, 2014; Weller, 2017).

According to the NRA, due to these issues, faced with a minimum wage hike, "Many restaurateurs would be forced to limit hiring, increase prices, cut employee hours or implement a combination of all three to pay for the wage increase" (National Restaurant Association, 2014). According to Alfonso Amador, Senior Vice President of the NRA (as cited in Gonzalez, 2016), "Not every job is there to sustain a family of four."

Research, however, has found that contrary to this view, "relatively modest mandated increases" over the past twenty years have not significantly reduced employment levels, demand or profitability, rather "there is strong evidence that increases in the minimum wage reduce turnover, and good reason to believe that it may increase employee productivity as well" (Lynn and Boone, 2015, p. 1). As a result, increases in minimum wage legislation – toward a living wage – has the potential to help the industry, by addressing some of the underlying issues that are driving employee turnover and negatively impacting productivity. In the absence of legislated increases, employers that pay above the industry average will be well positioned to attract and retain superior talent.

Suggesting that the employment culture in the US hospitality industry may be changing toward this view, some US hospitality firms are being noted for progressive HR practices. For example, Starbucks ranked first amongst "the best" hospitality employers in a recent poll, and was noted for offering its employees numerous benefits, including "health coverage, store discounts, chances to study and career sabbaticals" (McCarthy, 2015). Starbucks also recently announced its intention to expand its benefits to birth mothers, including six weeks of paid leave for store employees and 18 weeks for district managers, along with other enhanced parental benefits (Ruggless, 2017).

Some restaurants have also experimented with doing away with tipping, to varying degrees of success (Duffy, 2016). One approach has been to build a service charge into menu prices and to divide the additional revenue between all staff, on top of their basic wages. This system can help to address the wage inequality that has historically existed between servers and back-of-house staff, particularly for skilled chefs where skill shortages are resulting in recruitment and retention challenges. Others have adopted attractive salaries for staff, along with "bonuses, health care, shares in the company, and paid vacation" (Duffy, 2016). At one Pittsburgh restaurant that tried this approach, the menu was reworked in order to generate enhanced margins (in order to pay for the higher wages), and a more engaged and passionate staff delivered improved service and financial results; "The results were a resounding success. After the first month, revenues exceeded expectations by 26%, and overhead decreased by 8%." (Duffy, 2016).

Within the hotel industry several hotel companies made Fortune's 2016 "100 best companies to work for" ranking, including: Kimpton Hotels & Restaurants (20th), Hyatt Hotels & Resorts (47th), Hilton Worldwide (56th), Four Seasons Hotels & Resorts (70th) and Marriott International (83rd). Hyatt CEO Mark Hoplamazian was noted for championing "bringing humanity back to hospitality" (Ting, 2016b): "In the past year, the company spent $50,000 to upgrade its employee cafeterias to feel more like restaurants. Its hotel managers also host 'Night Owl Breakfasts' during which managers break bread with night-shift employees."

Another "Best Places to Work" ranking, by online platform Glassdoor (2017), listed several tourism and hospitality businesses. The top ranked foodservice chain in the large employer category was In-N-Out Burger, a privately run, limited menu hamburger chain, with 250 units and 10 000 employees. It received an overall rating of 4.3 out of 5, with 92 percent of respondents saying they would recommend the employer to a friend, and

95 percent approving of the CEO. According to one employee, the advantages the company offers its managers included attractive benefits and a values-driven working environment (Glassdoor, 2017):

> Full medical benefits, paid vacation, 401K plan, paid meals, life insurance, high pay raises and an overall friendly and ethic driven workforce. The ability to move forward in this company is amazing. I'm not at liberty to disclose how much these people make or their managers, but I can tell you it's more than a lawyer in most cases. Getting to work with other great associates and in a awesome family environment. Very communicative and flexible place to work. I learned a ton of values and social responsibility working for this company. All of my management skills stemmed from this job.

The only "con" this employee mentioned was the long working hours, which could exceed 65 per week.

Airbnb was the top ranked accommodation chain, scoring 4.0 out of 5, with 78 percent of respondents saying they would recommend the employer to a friend, and 93 percent approving of the CEO (Glassdoor, 2017). According to one employee, the advantages the company offers include: "Airbnb takes care of their own. Flexible." No cons were listed.

In summary, the US tourism and hospitality industry reflects many of the global trends previously identified. Growth is expected within both quick service and independent restaurants (providing the convenience of delivery service, or authentic local food and ambience), as well as within independent, upper upscale and luxury hotels. This growth will come from both increasing domestic demand, as well as from tourism, including increasing numbers of international travelers. In order to meet this growth, hospitality businesses will require a workforce capable of delivering the value proposition on order, whether convenience, customization, authenticity or upscale service and experience.

The US hospitality industry is a significant employer of young people and those from traditionally marginalized groups. Many people have their first job experience in the industry, and those who stay have the opportunity for promotion. It therefore has a tremendous impact on society. Unfortunately, the industry continues to experience a disproportionately high turnover rate. While some of this may be accounted for as a natural consequence of the number of students moving on to other careers, management turnover is also a significant and growing concern. Issues with compensation continue to plague the industry, supported by resistance from industry groups to increases in the minimum wage. In addition, other issues such as long working hours and a lack of training and development and clear career trajectory have contributed to the industry's ongoing poor reputation as an employer.

That said, there increasingly appear to be exceptions, with both restaurant and hotel companies appearing on various "best employer" lists. Innovations in compensation are appearing, as are opportunities to work in organizations where there is a strong values alignment and positive and supportive culture. These are the employers that will be able to attract and retain the talent they need, in order to capitalize on the forecasted growth.

CONCLUSION

The global travel and hospitality industry is facing a period of growth over the next several years, including within the United States. This presents considerable opportunity for foodservice and accommodation providers. At the same time, the industry is also experiencing considerable disruption, with digital technologies fundamentally changing business practice and contributing to changes in consumer behavior. Driven in part by the growing influence of Millennials, the customer value proposition is also changing, with increasing focus on value, convenience, ethical consumption, and the quality and authenticity of the guest experience. This in turn has profound implications for human resource management, including the type of employees that are needed, the roles they will play, and how they might best be recruited, trained, engaged and retained.

The hospitality industry has long struggled with its approach to human resource management, seeing employees largely as costs to be minimized, rather than as a source of competitive advantage. Characterized by part-time, minimum wage jobs, with inconvenient hours and poor labor practices, the hospitality industry is known for its exceptionally high rates of turnover. Given the sheer size of the industry, the number of people it employs, including the number of young people experiencing paid employment for the first time, the experience of working in the industry is additionally a social concern.

While technological innovation will undoubtedly replace some front-line jobs (due to digital ordering and check-in), the increasing demand for customized service and an enhanced customer experience will inevitably drive the need for more highly engaged and capable employees (front-line staff and managers alike) effectively delivering the differentiated value propositions on offer. In other words, successful firms will offer more sophisticated and customized customer experiences, which in turn will require more highly engaged employees, with enhanced knowledge and skills. Successful organizations will be those that offer effective human resource practices, including providing innovative recruitment and selection formats, competitive wages and benefits, training and career development, values alignment, and fun and novel working environments.

Calls for the hospitality industry to fundamentally change its approach to human resource management have been made for decades. The current disruption may be the impetus that ensures this occurs.

REFERENCES

AccorHotels (2016). DESIGN, FOOD, UX AccorHotels revolutionizes hospitality with its new brand: JO&JOE, 27 September. Accessed 24 January 2017 at: http://pressroom. accorhotels-group.com/design-food-ux-accorhotels-revolutionizes-hospitality-with-its-new-brand-jo-and-joe.

Airbnb (2017). About Us. Accessed 22 January 2017 at: https://www.airbnb.ca/about/about-us.

Alexander, K. (2016). There's a Massive Restaurant Industry Bubble, and it's About to Burst, 30 December. Thrillist.

Allen, A. (2016). 2017 Restaurant Industry Predictions, 13 December. Accessed 23 January 2017 at: https://www.linkedin.com/pulse/2017-restaurant-industry-predictions-aaron-d-allen.

Almquist, E. (2016). The 30 Things Customers Really Value. Harvard Business Review, 11 August. Accessed 2 January 2017 at: https://hbr.org/2016/08/the-30-things-customers-really-value.

Alton, L. (2016). How Purple, Uber and Airbnb Are Disrupting and Redefining Old Industries, 11 April. Accessed 4 January 2017 at: https://www.entrepreneur.com/article/273650.

America Works Here (2017). National Restaurant Association. Accessed 22 January 2017 at: http://www.americaworkshere.org/whereistarted.

American Hotel and Lodging Association (2015). Lodging Industry Trends 2015. Accessed 22 January 2017 at: https://www.ahla.com/sites/default/files/Lodging_Industry_Trends_2015. pdf.

Ashforth, B. and R. Humphrey (1993). Emotional Labor in Service Roles: The Influence of Identity. *The Academy of Management Review*, **18**(1), 88–115.

A&W. Accessed 25 January 2017 at: http://awguarantee.ca/en/chicken/.

B Corp (2017a). What are B Corps? Accessed 25 January 2017 at: https://www.bcorporation. net/what-are-b-corps.

B Corp (2017b). Find a B Corp. Accessed 25 January 2017 at: https://www.bcorporation.net/ community/find-a-b-corp?search=&field_industry=Food+%26+Beverage&field_city= &field_state=&field_country=.

B Corp (2017c). Find a B Corp. Accessed 25 January 2017 at: https://www.bcorporation. net/community/find-a-b-corp?search=&field_industry=Hospitality&field_city=&field_ state=&field_country=.

Bostock, Amy (2016). 2016 Hospitality Market Report: Operators Continue to Struggle for Market Share as Foodservice Sales Growth Remains Flat. *Food Service and Hospitality*, **49**(6). Accessed 3 January 2017 at: https://www.foodserviceandhospitality. com/2016-hospitality-market-report-operators-continue-to-struggle-for-market-share-as-foodservice-sales-growth-remains-flat/.

Bryan, Bob (2016a). A Massive Shift is Underway in the Restaurant Industry. *Business Insider*, 14 December. Accessed 3 January 2017 at: http://www.businessinsider.com/ retail-sales-show-massive-shift-in-restaurant-industry-2016-12.

Bryan, Bob (2016b). Americans are Ditching Giant Restaurant Chains. *Business Insider*, 14 September. Accessed 3 January 2017 at: http://www.businessinsider.com/americans-ditch ing-big-restaurant-chains-and-eating-local-2016-9.

CHD Expert (2016). Foodservice Segmentation: How We Define the Different Segments of the Foodservice Market, 14 November. CHD Experts Food Service Segment Definitions and

Examples. Available at: https://chdexpert.wordpress.com/2012/11/14/foodservice-segmen
tation-how-we-define-the-different-segments-of-the-foodservice-market/.

Christensen, Clayton (2003). *The Innovator's Solution: Creating and Sustaining Successful Growth*. Boston, MA: Harvard Business School Publishing.

Christensen, Clayton (2011). *The Innovator's Dilemma: The Revolutionary Book That Will Change the Way You Do Business*. Boston, MA: Harvard Business School Publishing.

Deloitte (2016). Travel and Hospitality Industry Outlook 2016. Accessed 24 January 2017 at: https://www2.deloitte.com/nl/nl/pages/consumer-industrial-products/articles/travel-and-hospitality-industry-outlook-2016.html.

Duffy, M. (2016). 6 Emerging Restaurant Trends To Watch in 2016. Accessed 25 January 2017 at: http://blog.myameego.com/6-emerging-restaurant-trends-to-watch-in-2016.

Enz, C.A. (2001). What Keeps You Up at Night? Key Issues of Concern for Lodging Managers [Electronic version]. *Cornell Hotel and Restaurant Administration Quarterly*, **42**(2), 38–45. Accessed 22 January 2017 at: http://scholarship.sha.cornell.edu/articles/378.

Enz, C.A. (2004). Issues of Concern for Restaurant Owners and Managers [Electronic version]. *Cornell Hotel and Restaurant Administration Quarterly*, **45**(4), 315–32. Accessed 22 January 2017 at: http://scholarship.sha.cornell.edu/articles/359/.

Euromonitor (2015). A New Era of Growth and Competition: Global Consumer Foodservice in 2015 and Beyond, August. Euromonitor International. Abstract accessed 23 January 2017 at: http://www.euromonitor.com/a-new-era-of-growth-and-competition-global-consumer-foodservice-in-2015-and-beyond/report.

Glassdoor (2017). Best Places to Work 2017. Available at: https://www.glassdoor.com/Award/Best-Places-to-Work-LST_KQ0,19.htm.

Gonzalez, J. (2016). National Restaurant Association Senior VP on Raising Minimum Wage: "Not Every Job is There to Sustain a Family of Four". 16 February. Accessed 22 January 2017 at: http://www.cnsnews.com/news/article/jose-r-gonzalez/natl-restaurant-association-senior-vp-raising-minimum-wage-not-every.

Higgins, S. (2016). Restaurant Job Growth Grinds to a Halt as Sales and Traffic Continue to Fall, 11 November. Accessed 5 January 2017 at: http://www.prweb.com/releases/2016/11/prweb13841883.htm.

Hochschild, A. (1983). Comment on Kemper's "Social Constructionist and Positivist Approaches to the Sociology of Emotions". *American Journal of Sociology*, **89**(2), 432–4.

Holmes, N. (2017). How "Poshtels" Are Reinventing the Budget Accommodation Sector, 5 January, LL Real Views. Available at: https://www.hotelnewsresource.com/article92645.html.

Hospitality Net (2015). The Global Hotel Industry and Trends for 2016. *Industry News*, 18 December. Available at: http://www.hospitalitynet.org/news/4073336.html.

Hospitality Net (2017). Trends to Expect in the Travel Industry in 2017. Available at: http://www.hospitalitynet.org/news/global/154000320/4080188.html.

Hotel News Resource (2016). U.S. Hotel Forecast. Continued Growth Through 2017 Projected for U.S. Hotel Industry. STR, 6 June. Accessed 5 January 2017 at: https://www.hotelnewsresource.com/article89573.html.

Iverson, R.D. and M. Deery (July 1997). Turnover Culture in the Hospitality Industry. *Human Resource Management Journal* **7**(4), 71–82.

Jennings, L. (2015). Amazon Launches Restaurant Delivery in Seattle. *Nation's Restaurant News*, 8 September. Available at: http://www.nrn.com/technology/amazon-launches-restaurant-delivery-seattle.

Lynn, M. and C. Boone (2015). Have Minimum Wage Increases Hurt the Restaurant Industry? The Evidence Says No! *Cornell Hospitality Report*, **15**(22). Accessed 20 January 2017 at: http://scholarship.sha.cornell.edu/cgi/viewcontent.cgi?article=1000&context=chrreports.

Maze, J. (2017a). McDonald's Same-store Sales Fall. *Nation's Restaurant News*, 23 January. Available at: http://www.nrn.com/finance/mcdonald-s-same-store-sales-fall?NL=NRN-0
2_&Issue=NRN-02__20170124_NRN-02__614&sfvc4enews=42&cl=article_1_1&utm_

rid=CPG06000002292495&utm_campaign=14274&utm_medium=email&elq2=c71b2ea6 a6504639ac9db33804e9285c.

Maze, J. (2017b). IFA: Franchise Sector Expected to Grow by $36B in 2017, 24 January. Accessed 25 January 2017 at: http://www.nrn.com/franchising/ifa-franchise-sector-expect ed-grow-36b-2017?NL=NRN-02_&Issue=NRN-02__20170125_NRN-02__822&sfvc4en ews=42&cl=article_1_2&utm_rid=CPG06000002292495&utm_campaign=14210&utm_ medium=email&elq2=50a0ed058f464e1a9c2ddec4f7e0c9e5.

McCarthy, N. (2015). The Best Employers in the U.S. Restaurant Industry, 26 May. Accessed 22 January 2017 at: http://www.forbes.com/sites/niallmccarthy/2015/05/26/the-best-employers-in-the-u-s-restaurant-industry-infographic/#5eab36896543.

Nadeau, C.A. (2015). Living Wage Calculator: User's Guide / Technical Notes. Accessed 21 January 2017 at: http://livingwage.mit.edu/resources/Living-Wage-User-Guide-and-Technical-Notes-2015.pdf.

Nadeau, C.A. (2016). Calculating the Living Wage for U.S. States, Counties and Metro Areas OpenDataNation, 9 August. Accessed 21 January 2017 at: http://livingwage.mit.edu/ articles/19-new-data-calculating-the-living-wage-for-u-s-states-counties-and-metro-areas.

National Conference of State Legislatures (2017). State Minimum Wages | 2017 Minimum Wage by State, 5 January. Accessed 21 January 2017 at: http://www.ncsl.org/research/ labor-and-employment/state-minimum-wage-chart.aspx.

National Restaurant Association (2014). Minimum Wage. National Restaurant Association, November. Accessed 22 January 2017 at: http://www.restaurant.org/Downloads/PDFs/ News-Research/20131112_Min_Wage_Issue_Brief.

National Restaurant Association (2017). Facts at a Glance. Accessed 14 September 2017 at: http://www.restaurant.org/News-Research/Research/Facts-at-a-Glance.

Natividad, A. (2016). Heineken Just Made an HR Campaign That's as Cool as Any Consumer Ads It's Done. *Adweek*, 15 September. Accessed 18 January 2017 at: http:// www.adweek.com/adfreak/heineken-just-made-hr-campaign-thats-cool-any-consumer-ads-its-done-173289.

Patton, L. (2016). Nobody is Eating Out Anymore, They're Just Ordering Pizza, 21 December. Accessed 3 January 2016 at: https://www.bloomberg.com/news/articles/2016-12-21/pizz a-is-king-during-u-s-restaurant-industry-s-2016-slump.

Pine, J. and J. Gilmore (1999). *The Experience Economy: Work is Theatre & Every Business a Stage*. Boston, MA: Harvard Business School Press.

QSR Magazine (2016). Fast Casual is the Fastest Growing Foodservice Segment Globally, 20 April, Industry News. *QSR*. Accessed 23 January 2017 at: https://www.qsrmagazine. com/news/fast-casual-fastest-growing-foodservice-segment-globally.

QSR Magazine (2017). The Global 30. Accessed 22 January 2017 at: https://www.qsrmaga zine.com/content/global-30.

Ruggless, R. (2016). Hospitality Turnover Rose to 72.1% in 2015. *Nation's Restaurant News*, 23 March. Accessed 21 January 2017 at: http://www.nrn.com/blog/hospitality-turnover-ro se-721-rate-2015.

Ruggless, R. (2017). Starbucks Expands Benefits for New Parents. *Nation's Restaurant News*, 20 January. Available at: http://www.nrn.com/workforce/starbucks-expands-bene fits-new-parents.

Schwab, K. (January 11, 2016). *The Fourth Industrial Revolution*. Geneva: World Economic Forum.

Skift Magazine (2016). Mega Trends Defining Travel in 2016. Skift Magazine. Accessed 22 January 2017 at: https://3rxg9qea18zhtl6s2u8jammft-wpengine.netdna-ssl.com/wp-conte nt/uploads/2017/01/Skift-Magazine-2016-Megatrends-DT-1.pdf.

Starkov, M. and M. Safer (2017). The Smart Hotelier's 2017 Top Ten Digital Technology & Marketing Resolutions. Hotel News Resource, 4 January. Accessed 7 January 2017 at: https://www.hotelnewsresource.com/article92631.html.

Tapscott, D. and A. Tapscott (2016). *Blockchain Revolution: How the Technology Behind Bitcoin is Changing Money, Business, and the World*. New York: Portfolio.

Ting, D. (2016a). Marriott CEO Interview: Buying Starwood and its $13 Billion Bet on

Loyalty, 23 September. Accessed 22 January 2017 at: https://skift.com/2016/09/23/marri ott-ceo-interview-buying-starwood-and-its-13-billion-bet-on-loyalty/.

Ting, D. (2016b). These are the Best Hotel Companies to Work for in 2016. Skift, 5 July. Accessed 22 January 2017 at: https://skift.com/2016/07/05/these-are-the-best-hotel-compa nies-to-work-for-in-2016/.

Vend (2017). Retail Trends and Predictions 2017. 12 Forecasts for the Retail Industry in 2017. Accessed 3 January 2017 at: https://www.vendhq.com/university/retail-trends-and-predictions-2017.

Weller, E. (2017). Labor Cost Guidelines for a Restaurant. Accessed 22 January 2017 at: http://smallbusiness.chron.com/labor-cost-guidelines-restaurant-23753.html.

Whitten, S. (2016). These Restaurant Chains Will Drive the Industry's Growth in 2017. Restaurants. 29 December. Accessed 23 January 2017 at: http://www.cnbc.com/2016/12/29/ these-restaurant-chains-will-drive-the-industrys-growth-in-2017.html.

World Travel and Tourism Council (2016a). 2016 Economic Impact Annual Update Summary, March. Accessed 18 January 2017 at: http://www.wttc.org/research/economic-research/economic-impact-analysis/.

World Travel & Tourism Council (2016b). Travel & Tourism: Economic Impact 2016 United States, March. Accessed 22 January 2017 at: http://www.wttc.org/-/media/files/reports/eco nomic-impact-research/countries-2016/unitedstates2016.pdf.

PART II

DEVELOPING A SERVICE QUALITY CULTURE

3. A motivated workforce: the shifting factors that drive people to work in the hospitality industry
William C. Murray

INTRODUCTION

Understanding and maximizing the value of workers has been studied in depth for nearly 100 years, with researchers recognizing that importance of employee actions and believing that 'employee motivation is vital to the success of organizations' (Curtis et al., 2009, p. 264). The high-touch, interpersonal nature of the hospitality industry creates a dynamic in which employees can directly influence the realization of organizational objectives and positive financial outcomes (Kusluvan et al., 2010). They can create a unique competitive advantage (Chiang and Birtch, 2010) that is found not only within their skills, knowledge and abilities, but also in their intentional choice to voluntarily use those talents for the benefit of themselves and their employer. Yet the shifting nature of motives and volition can be difficult to comprehend and take advantage of in the fast-paced day-to-day operations of a business, and too frequently it is the case that employers fail either to properly understand what truly motivates their employees or how to express and satiate unmet needs in a satisfactory manner (Wiley, 1997; Kuo, 2009).

Yet maintaining a strong, well-trained workforce in the hospitality industry continues to be a challenge. Long, non-traditional hours, compensation that is frequently lower than other occupations, and the fluctuations of labour demands due to seasonality (Kusluvan and Kusluvan, 2000) all contribute to making this an industry that faces difficulties finding and keeping great employees (Watkins, 2014). Additionally, as a component of the services field, the hospitality industry has to contend with four unique characteristics: intangibility, heterogeneity, inseparability, and perishability (Zeithaml et al., 1985). Experiences are created through a combination of products and services that are unique each time they are crafted due to the people involved, both customers and employees. These human interactions between workers and customers play a direct role in the intangible characteristic of services, the inseparability of the production and consumption of services, as well as the non-standardized nature of services due to the unique combinations of workers and customers in every interaction (Parasuraman et al., 1991).

Given this multi-faceted and complicated reality, understanding the factors that drive and influence human behaviour provides hospitality operators with a better likelihood of attracting, keeping and maximizing the value of good employees. The desired outcomes, including organizational commitment, customer engagement, customer satisfaction and loyalty are all influenced in some way by happy employees who find their needs satisfied in their chosen jobs.

This chapter starts by looking at some of the most fundamental motivational theories that have been explored to date, going back to when people studied workers in a mechanistic fashion, trying to get the best day's work out of each person through studies of time and motion. Classic concepts of motivation are discussed, looking at theories of why people are driven to perform certain tasks and how those aspects can be best connected to by employers. Following this, studies of employee motivation within the hospitality industry will be explored, highlighting the shifting nature of expressed motivating factors and noting the influences of context, such as of time, gender, geographic and economic conditions. As the chapter concludes, we will see that our knowledge about what motivates employees has grown richly over the years. However, what we know is grounded within the moment of time. Expressed drivers of behaviours that have been gathered through research can only reveal what motivators were valued yesterday. Shifts in context, in demographics, and in the very nature of the services industry mean that continual research will be required if we are to continue understanding why people act in the future.

EARLY METHODS TO MAXIMIZE WORK EFFORTS

The quest to understand motivation in the workplace began as a practical organizational quest, one grounded in a focus of increased output and greater efficiency. Early work in conditioning people to behave in certain ways when presented with a stimulus, whether through a classical Pavlovian innate response or Skinner's more repeatable directed actions (Gomez and Alstrom, 1995), focused primarily on the inputs that were required to control and command behavioural outcomes. The Industrial Revolution brought with it an organizational, productivity-based perspective that had probably not been experienced to that point at a societal level. The organization of resources, from acquiring and processing raw materials, through the increased dependency on machines and the efforts and actions of people, to the production of finished goods and materials, was all about maximizing value for the company. This required the application of new frameworks and techniques, ones that were initially called 'administration' (Witzel and Warner, 2013) but that would quickly become known simply as 'management' (Drucker, 2008). At the time, increased productivity was the driving force, surfacing questions about how to increase output through administrative activities closely associated with Henri Fayol. These activities included planning, organizing, commanding, coordinating and controlling productive operations, particularly focused on the inconsistent behaviours and activities of employees (Witzel and Warner, 2013).

As a way of ordering the activities of people to reach organizational goals, management was approached as a science. Actions were timed and measured in order to discover the best ways to accomplish a task and then explicit instructions about how a task was to be completed by workers were crafted, enacted and monitored. This machine-based perspective about how to best accomplish tasks was the basis of Frederick Taylor's classic management theory (1911). Drucker (1992) noted that there was an underlying belief in Taylor's work, a belief that people naturally lacked the will to be highly productive in a job, perhaps due to an unwillingness to work hard for others, and did not have the requisite ability to properly direct themselves at work. However, Drucker (2008) later claimed that Taylor's intentions in his management design may have been viewed from one perspective as emancipatory in nature and not primarily profit-centric, allowing the worker to increase their productivity and earn a fair living without excessive effort. When looking back at these early styles of management, Morgan (1997) felt that developing structures to control people like machines was, at its core, paradoxical because it failed to take into account any factors that actually drove people to take action. However, the pragmatism of Taylor and Fayol brought forth early development in human resource management, including 'job training, pay-for-performance incentive systems, improved employee selection techniques, and job redesign, including the introduction of ergonomics' (Steers et al., 2004, p. 380).

The efforts of scientific management and the development of systems that sought to remove the unique qualities of human functioning in place of consistent, replicable and efficient processes held for a number of decades. Some believe that these behaviours to treat workers simply as productive units were the precursor to large-scale unionization during the Great Depression (Steers et al., 2004). In his book *Work and Authority in Industry*, Bendix (1956) expressed that the fundamental flaw in these early machine-based philosophies of command and control was that they failed to appreciate and treat workers like human beings. Thus began a quest by social scientists to better understand the human aspects of their workers, exploring the questions both of what drives people to take action, particularly in the context of their work, and how these drivers could be utilized if there was a better understanding between the casual relationships of motivators and productive outputs.

Pushing people to complete tasks and take actions through the use of external influencers makes the assumption that people have little interest in doing things of their own volition. However, this fails to take into consideration agency, or the human aspect of choosing which behaviours to complete and when. The completion of tasks that provide productive outputs has been described as a combination of a person's skill and knowledge in how to complete the tasks along with their volition, or choice, in performing those actions (Lee-Ross, 1999). People work in certain ways based on the blending of ability and willingness. Additionally, human understanding and decision making is not done in isolation, but is rather completed within context of the events and activities of our lives (Simons and Enz, 1995); ability and willingness are heavily influenced by situational constraints (Christensen Hughes, as cited in Lee-Ross, 1999). What results from this is a model of performance behaviour contingent upon ability, volition and environmental context.

These three areas of ability, motivation and context have been quite consistent in motivations research over the last 50 years. Wiley (1997) noted three assumptions that ran throughout much of contemporary research on human motivation. The first assumption identified these three areas, what she called 'a systematic analysis of how personal, task and environmental characteristics influence behaviour and job performance' (1997, p. 263). The second assumption held that motivation is fluid in nature, not a fixed trait, impacted by both personal factors as well as the external situational contexts they are operating within, including but not limited to current economic conditions. As such, motives and drivers can shift based on changes in either personal or situational factors, surfacing some motives as greater, or more prepotent (Maslow, 1943), than others. Finally, motivation affects behaviours, not job performance directly (Nicholson et al., 1995), meaning employers wishing to influence and direct job performance must ensure there is a link between what drives an employee's effort and the desired behaviours related to job performance.

Some of the challenges when trying to understand motivation are that it is not something that can be seen or measured outside of the person within whom it exists; it is described as being internal, invisible, and a hypothetical construct that we have created as a way to better understand what drives people to take action (Pinder, 1998). The behaviours that stem from motivated action are influenced by the context, both internal and

external, and hold three core characteristics: direction, intensity and duration (Pinder, 1998) or persistence (Kanfer, 1990). As such, the quest to
appreciate motivation within the frame of work is to seek an understanding of how and why the behaviours of people are mobilized, directed and
sustained in the interest of achieving organizational goals.

Kanfer (1992) suggested that motivation fell into three related clusters:
personality-based views, cognitive choices, and self-regulation perspectives. The first cluster emphasized the importance of personal characteristics in motivation, or how people were driven to take action. The
latter two clusters focused on frameworks and decision approaches that
assisted people when placing subjective valuation on behaviour options,
or why certain decisions were made. These clusters have been condensed
by some into two groups: content and process theories. Content theories
address why-centric questions, seeking to describe underlying human
needs and 'specific factors that energize, direct, or stop a person's behaviour' (Hellriegel et al., 1998, p. 153). Alternatively, process theories address
how-based questions, exploring how needs interact with personal factors
and mental processes to form behavioural intentions and commitments
(Hellriegel et al., 1998). The following section will explore core theories,
both content and process models.

CLASSIC MOTIVATION THEORIES

The study of motivation has often broken across the line of content and
process models. The former area concentrated on why people are motivated to take action, typically addressing needs-based explorations. The
latter area focused on how people took action to satisfy their unmet needs.
According to Kanfer, 'motivation is not directly observable' (1990, p. 78);
thus, the motivations of others can only be understood through inference
around how internal and external factors might influence behaviour and
by observing subsequent changes in behaviours, attitudes, knowledge and
ability. Content theories seek to surface what the independence variables
are that influence behaviour, while process theories look at how those
variables are enacted to achieve desired effects or changes.

As an early explorer of human motivations, Maslow understood that
'man is a perpetually wanting animal' (1943, p. 370). Theorizing about
what drives people to take actions, he posited that humans were compelled
to satiate unfulfilled needs, and that concepts about human motivation
must be approached differently from previous studies on animals, likely
due to a person's capacity to be self-aware and their ability to interpret
their need requirements within the context they find themselves in. As a

part of his model, he classified needs within five core groups of needs: physiological, safety, love or belonging, esteem, and self-actualization. According to Maslow, physiological needs, in the most classic perspective, included items such as food, drink, sleep and sex, all things that kept the body functioning and complete. The satisfaction of safety needs is actually the quest to remove or minimize dangers, either perceived or real. These could range from extreme physiological dangers, such as assault or exposure, to more modern concerns, such as the lack of job security or the proper amounts of health insurance. The desire for relationships with others and the quest for affection fall into the category of love and belonging. Maslow described this as a reciprocal need, in which fulfilment comes through a combination of both giving and receiving interpersonal affection. Seeking to achieve a high valuation of oneself in the eyes of others is captured within the esteem need category, including the accomplishment of measurable goals and earning the respect of others in an effort to gain prestige and recognition. Turning this valuation inward, the category of self-actualization is fuelled by the need to be self-fulfilled, following one's personal path of development and stretching one's capabilities.

Although seen as one of the most fundamental models of motivation, Maslow considered this less an absolute model and more a heuristic framework that could help explain the drives of people. It was never meant to be the universal hierarchy that it is frequently presented as. Human needs are messy and difficult to contain within such a prescriptive model. The basic tenet of this 'hierarchy' is that lower level needs must be sated before higher level needs surface to become important. However, Maslow stressed a few key caveats. First, he stressed that needs are strongly influenced by context, as revealed when he wrote: 'While behavior is almost always motivated, it is also almost always biologically, culturally and situationally determined as well' (1943, p. 371). Second, needs flow in a prepotent manner, with the need that has the greatest importance to be satisfied in the moment surfacing once the most recent need has been satisfied. This facet counters the idea of a direct and linear hierarchy, opening the potential of movement throughout the five categories to the most pressing at the moment. Third, most behaviours are intricate and multi-motivated, forcing anyone trying to understand motivated actions to embrace these complexities in their explanations. Finally, needs themselves are rarely fully satiated. In his early expression of needs, he provides an example of simple and full satisfaction: 'Just as the sated man no longer feels hungry, a safe man no longer feels endangered' (Maslow, 1943, p. 379). However, this distinction of full satisfaction versus partial satisfaction of need is more carefully explained further in his writing, wherein he infers that there is simply a higher level of satisfaction of some needs over others, allowing for more prepotent needs to surface as the scales of needs satisfaction shift.

Naturally, in the context of business outputs, the quest to understand what drives people to take action is directly related to achieving the effect of increasing economic outputs. Operators want to understand how they might tap into the motivations of their employees to increase job performance, whether this is through increased revenue generation or more efficient work efforts and, consequently, do so at a reduced cost. Herzberg addressed the question of how to get employees to perform desired tasks directly, grounded in the proposition that the sole way to motivate an employee 'is to give him challenging work in which he can assume responsibility' (Herzberg, 1968, p. 53). This idea was centred in his exploration of work attitudes of employees that revealed various factors that led to either feelings of satisfaction or dissatisfaction. His theories around motivation came from 12 different studies that sampled over 1685 employees, exploring job attitudes across a wide range of industries. One of the more interesting ideas that emerged from his exploration was the complete separation of factors that led to either satisfaction or dissatis- faction. Herzberg concluded that satisfaction and dissatisfaction are not the opposite characteristics that many people assumed them to be, but in fact were two distinct states, and the opposite state was the absence of the original state. In simple terms, this meant that the opposite of satisfaction is no satisfaction while the opposite of dissatisfaction is no dissatisfaction. Two groupings of job-based factors emerged which fell either into the sat- isfaction classification or the dissatisfaction classification. The first group he classified as hygiene factors, which included pay, security, work condi- tions and relationships. When these factors were absent, job dissatisfac- tion was expressed, yet when they were present in sufficient measures, job dissatisfaction disappeared. Herzberg found that over 69 per cent of the elements that contributed to job dissatisfaction were hygiene issues. The second group he classified as motivator factors, including achievement, recognition, responsibility, advancement and growth. When these factors were absent, job satisfaction failed to emerge, yet when they were present in sufficient measure, job satisfaction was expressed. Like the hygiene factors, Herzberg found that 81 per cent of the factors that contributed to job satisfaction were motivators.

Frederick Herzberg believed in two key ideas. First, managers often forget about the importance of hygiene factors when attempting to remove job dissatisfaction. Secondly, there exists a myth around management that external forces and stimulation placed upon an individual will lead to motivation. To the former, he contends that satisfaction and dissatisfac- tion, being distinct entities, must be addressed separately; as so, hygiene factors warrant appropriate attention to stem employee dissatisfaction. With the latter issue, he asserted that external forces, whether positive or negative, do not lead to motivated behaviour but only to simple movement; negative pressures push people while positive external forces pull them, but neither produced an internal drive. As he summarized, 'I can charge a man's battery, and then recharge it, and recharge it again. But it is only when he has his own generator that we can talk about motivation. He then needs no outside stimulation. He wants to do it' (Herzberg, 1968, p. 55).

Other theorists have adapted some of these early ideas, condensing the number of categories while also highlighting differences in needs between survival needs, connection needs and growth needs. In his conceptualization of what drives people to take action, David McClelland (1965) appeared to be more influenced by Herzberg's hygiene-motivator theory, specifically focusing on the motivator side. His motivational triad includes achievement, power and affiliation categories. Much like Maslow, McClelland asserted that these need-based activities were strongly influenced by contextual factors, including culture. People seeking to satisfy their affiliation-based needs seek to build strong, positive relationships with others and maintain healthy companionship. Those influenced by power-based needs feel compelled to control and influence the behaviours of others, whether through influence of authority and status. McClelland saw this need also as one in which the people desired to be responsible for others and make positive impacts in their circle of influence. People motivated by the need for achievement also felt a sense of responsibility, were interested in taking on challenging but achievable goals and taking calculated risks to either gain external recognition or simply to satisfy their internal quest to complete something difficult. The gap in McClelland's construct surrounds the more basic needs at existence level.

Clayton Alderfer (1972) conceptualized a theory grounded in the ideas of Maslow that was a more parsimonious concept of motivation which focused on three core needs. First, existence needs concentrated around physical requirements and comforts, such as food and safety. In a working environment, these translated to the resources to satisfy those requirements, including salary, benefits and working conditions. Second, relationships needs, both professional and personal, encompassed the desire to be connected with others in a positive manner. Finally, the needs to develop, contribute, achieve and gain recognition for those accomplishments were collected within the classification of growth needs. As a model of understanding the motivations of people, these three categories of existence, relatedness and growth (or ERG) of Alderfer appear to condense Maslow's idea of physiological and safety needs as existence-based and the categories of esteem and self-actualization into growth-based needs. In a similar attempt to condense various theories of motivation, Mullins (2002) offered a slightly reworded but none-the-less comparable three-fold classification model, including economic, social and intrinsic rewards.

Within the realm of being motivated at work, Douglas McGregor (1960) expressed a binary belief that has existed in management theory for some time. Either people were indifferent to work and lacked ambition or people had an internal desire to perform and satisfy certain internal needs. If people were naturally lazy, they would require external motivators, what he called KITAs (or 'kicks in the arse'). If people naturally desired to work hard, they would be propelled more by internal motivators. The former state became known as his Theory X and the latter Theory Y. Content theories of motivation appear to have left behind the idea that workers are inherently lazy, focusing instead on two ideas. First, what motivates workers is highly contextually influenced. Second, humans have free will and, therefore, have the ability to enact volition. Volition, or the choices made by workers to act in certain ways within a particular environment, has surfaced frequently in the literature. Some have referred to volition as 'the forces acting on or within a person that cause the person to behave in a specific, goal-directed manner' (Hellriegel et al., 1998, p. 149); others have called it more of a 'willingness to do something and is conditioned by (an) action's ability to satisfy some need for the individual' (Robbins, 2005, p. 48).

Although the core of understanding motivation is grounded in the desire for people to satisfy their unmet needs, a number of theorists have pivoted away from the search for understanding the exact unmet needs that influence the volition to take action. Instead, they have explored how those unmet needs might be triggers to influence actions in certain, directed ways. Victor Vroom (1964) appreciated the importance of volition in motivation, theorizing that people made deliberate choices in their actions in order to achieve outcomes they value. These choices were predicated on three characteristics: expectancy, instrumentality and valence. First, people had to expect that putting forth effort in a particular direction would result in a positive performance of the sought-after action. Secondly, they had to believe that performing well would have a positive, instrumental impact towards their desired outcome or reward. Finally, the rewards available had to have sufficient value so that people would consciously choose to put forth effort to achieve the outcomes sought by the organization. As a process-based theory, Vroom conceptualized that in order to increase motivation, managers could increase expectancies through greater training and education, elevate feelings of instrumentality through recognition and feedback programmes, and/or better align reward valence so that they were contextually meaningful to individuals.

The level of the meaningfulness of a motivational factor has been explored on multiple levels. In their exploration of self-determination theory, Richard Ryan and Edward Deci (2000) teased apart the idea that all outcomes must have instrumental value. They suggested that there were two different types of motivations that produced actions, each grounded in reasons of importance to the people involved. Extrinsic motivations were connected to actions instigated so that someone could gain a particular outcome they valued. Working to gain a positive outcome, such as receiving pay for performance or an external reward for performing a behaviour, or the avoidance of a negative outcome, such as sanctions or punishments, are both examples of extrinsic rewards. The importance is that the outcome, whether positive or negative, must have value to the individual so that the person being motivated acts with volition, willingly accepting and endorsing the behaviour. Should the proposed motivational outcome have no value, people may display resentment and actively resist behaving in a certain way.

Intrinsic motivations, on the other hand, were linked to the performance of behaviours that were inherently interesting, enjoyable and stimulating. People often received no instrumental value at all from these actions beyond the satisfaction that came from the behaviour itself; these activities existed in a harmonious place that Ryan and Deci called 'the nexus between a person and a task' (2000, p.56). Some people seem to enjoy voluntarily participating in work that is fascinating and challenging, that provides opportunities for the development of skills, knowledge and abilities, and that satisfies needs of autonomy, control and self-determination. This is especially important for those desiring greater agency in their work and feelings of self-efficacy. The distinction between extrinsic and intrinsic motivators within self-determination theory wasn't presented as exclusive, but more nuanced as a blending of factors. People could be predominantly driven by intrinsic motivators, yet even those who are intrinsically connected to their work expect reasonable compensation and recognition. This suggests a consistency in self-determination theory that is reflective of Herzberg's hygiene-motivator theory.

From an organizational perspective, understanding the why-centric questions of content and the how-based questions of process serves the purpose of identifying needs of employees and then putting into place appropriate reward-based systems, intrinsic and extrinsic, along with job designs and processes in which employees can expect actions to lead towards outcomes of valence. Having a good idea of what drives people and aligning an environment to this creates a likelihood that employees will choose to act in ways that simultaneously satisfy their needs and those of the organization. The alignments that can be seen across numerous theoretical perspectives suggest that:

> once employee needs are identified, and organisational objectives are defined, the next step is to determine rewards and link these to behaviours that both serve the organisational objectives and also satisfy employee needs. If these are well aligned, high motivation will result; if poorly aligned, then low motivation will be the outcome.' (Bassett-Jones and Lloyd, 2005, p. 932)

APPLIED RESEARCH

About the same time as Maslow and others were developing models of needs-based motivation, industry was also curious about what compelled their employees to work. There are two fundamental ways in which to explore what motivates people: watch them under varying conditions or ask them to articulate it for themselves. In 1946, The Labor Relations Institute (LRI) in New York designed a simple survey for employees to fill out in which they were asked to force-rank 10 different job reward factors to represent what the worker felt was more important to them in the context of their working life (Hersey and Blanchard, 1969). Factors on this list included good wages, interesting work, job security, good working conditions, tactful discipline, full appreciation of work done, available help with personal problems from supervisors, personal loyalty of the organization to employees, opportunities for promotion and growth, and feelings of being included in things. In the year of its development, the survey was administered to industrial workers by Hersey and Blanchard, revealing the top five motivations of employees, at that time, to be appreciated for work done, being in on things (inclusion), help with personal problems, job security, and good wages. At the same time, supervisors were provided with the same list of job rewards and asked to rank them in the way they believed would represent their workers. Supervisors felt that good wages and job security were the two most important reward factors for workers, revealing a large disconnect between what employees said they felt was most important and what supervisors believed was important to their workers.

This method of exploring motivations of employees, which became known as the Ten Factor Model, has become a cornerstone of workplace studies over the last 30 years, with over a dozen studies completed or in progress since 1986 (Kovach, 1987; Charles and Marshall, 1992; Simons and Enz, 1995; Breiter et al., 2002; DiPietro et al., 2014). Its adoption is due to a number of factors. First, the data is self-reported and force-ranked directly by employees, providing more direct insight into the physiological motives of employees that can be quite challenging to assess by outside observation alone. Secondly, although self-reported data can face questions of validity, particularly around biases of social desirability or people answering in a way they believe others want them to, a confidential and anonymous collection process can mitigate these challenges. Moreover, the tendency for self-reported data to overly emphasize the respondents' individual feelings can be viewed positively when seeking to unpack preferred motivational factors. Thirdly, the compact nature of ten factors creates a relatively parsimonious model that is simultaneously easy to facilitate while being rich enough to align with multiple existing motivational theories. Finally, these factors translate easily across cultures.

Kovach (1987) was the first to resurface the LRI exploration of motivational job reward factors and has become so synonymous with the Ten Factor Model that some often credit him with its inception and call it the Kovach model (Breiter et al., 2002). Hershey, Blanchard and Kovach all focused their research on the industrial sector. However, Kovach's addition to the original LRI study included capturing key demographic factors such as gender, age, income level and organizational level. This allowed Kovach to highlight key differences between employee groups, as well as to compare perceived motivations between employees and their supervisor. In his findings, employees ranked interesting work, full appreciation of work done, and feelings of being in on things as their top three job rewards. However, supervisors ranked good wages, job security, promotion and growth in the organization as what they believed to be the top three rewards for their employees, again highlighting a fundamental disconnect between employees' self-perceptions of their own motivators and the factors supervisors were gravitating towards when attempting to motivate them. According to Kovach, 'managers seem to operate under a self-reference system; they rank rewards as they would want them for themselves and assume that their employees would subscribe to the same rewards' (1987, p. 63). Differences were also found between gender, age, income levels and the level within the organization in which people worked.

Following Kovach's application of the Ten Factor Model in the industrial field, Silverthorne (1992) uncovered further differences across cultures. Tapping into a cross-sector of both public and private organizations, Silverthorne surveyed managers and employees (from the same organizations) in the United States of America, Russia and Taiwan. Comparing across cultures, his results revealed strong differences in preferred job reward factors. The top three reported preferences for American workers were job security, full appreciation of work done, and interesting work. In Taiwan, the top three reported preferences were full appreciation of work done, interesting work, and feelings of being included in things within the organization. However, in Russia, sympathetic help with personal problems, personal loyalty to employees, and good working conditions represented the top three job factors desired by employees. Also interesting in Silverthorne's work was the discovery of some alignments between the factors that employees identified as valuable and those that supervisors believed were important to their employees. American managers had a strong, positive and significant alignment to the preferences of their workers. Taiwanese managers had a positive alignment, although it was not found to be significant. However, Russian managers showed a strong and negative alignment, indicating they are unclear about the important drivers of their workers and likely misaligning the offered job rewards to their employees.

THE ADOPTION OF THE TEN FACTOR MODEL IN HOSPITALITY RESEARCH

Kovach's application of the Ten Factor Model and the data it produced grabbed the attention of researchers in the hospitality field. Perhaps this came during a period in the mid-1990s when economies were struggling and hospitality organizations, which are highly labour dependent, sought to better understand their workers. Or perhaps it came from work like Silverthorne's that reinforced the highly contextual nature of motivation. Or perhaps it was the inclusion of Kovach's studies in human resource management textbooks written for the hospitality industry (Drummond, 1990; Tanke, 1990). Whatever the reason, many studies followed exploring different aspects of the hospitality industry in varying geographic regions.

Charles and Marshall (1992) used the Ten Factor Model to uncover job reward factors for hotel workers in the Caribbean, something that had not been explored in prior research studies. In their context, good wages, working conditions, appreciation for work done, and interesting work surfaced respectively as the top four job factors. However, they discovered a number of demographical differences. First, the importance of good wages was significantly more important to male workers than female workers. This meshed with Kovach's (1987) earlier findings that female employees may put greater importance on interpersonal relationships. Secondly, job security became significantly more important as workers got older, perhaps reflective of the greater financial and familial responsibilities that come with age. Finally, older workers had significantly lower needs to receive tactful discipline and loyalty from their supervisors, likely due to both their higher job levels and to age and experience. Their study indicated that the importance of any motivational factor for an individual was impacts both by the pressures faced by unmet needs, such as financial means, as well as the rational choice, or volition, of the person involved, such as the desire to form strong interpersonal relationships at work.

Similar studies using the Ten Factor Theory focused on the hotel workers in North America (Simons and Enz, 1995), blending the theoretical constructs of Herzberg's intrinsic and extrinsic needs with Vroom's idea of valence of job factors to employees. The results presented by Simon and Enz revealed somewhat different findings from Charles and Marshall. For North American employees, good wages surfaced at the top of these job reward rankings; however, job security and opportunities for promotion and growth within the hospitality organization rounded out the top three. Simons and Enz saw, for the first time, the rise of existence needs as the most prominent unmet and thereby most valued job reward factor. As well, they found a strong misalignment between how supervisors and managers ranked motives of their employees.

Later in the 1990s, two additional studies based in China utilized the Ten Factor Model. Fisher and Yuan (1998) noted that hotel workers at a major international hotel in Shanghai ranked good wages, good working conditions, and an organization's personal loyalty to their employees as their top three factors, rankings that aligned with how supervisors perceived employees to be motivated. Wong et al. (1999) attempted to find more explicit connections between the job factor model and Herzberg's motivational model of intrinsic and extrinsic factors. They included 72 Hong Kong hotels in their study. Their results showed finding opportunities for promotion, personal loyalty to employees, and good wages to be the top three motivators. Wong et al. discovered few differences between employees when they rank extrinsic motivators, such as wages, job security and working conditions. However, differences in the importance of intrinsic motivators, specifically, interesting work, opportunities for advancement, and feelings of being included and involved at work, varied significantly among employees of differing genders, marital status, educational levels and income. Their work stressed the importance of focusing on intrinsic work factors to increase motivation and job satisfaction of workers, highlighting the shifting nature of motives based on context, not only culturally but also on personal characteristics.

A few years later, Breiter et al. (2002) published their findings using the Ten Factor Model in the lodging industry in the south-east region of the United States, being specifically interested in exploring the influence of demographic diversity on espoused motivational factors. Their overall results revealed good wages, job security and good working conditions as the top three job motivation factors. Their top four factors mirrored the North American results that Simons and Enz published seven years prior. Although Breiter et al. failed to uncover any significant differences based on gender, they did find that immigrant workers valued inclusive, relational job factors (feelings of being in on things, tactful discipline, and sympathetic help with personal problems) significantly higher than US-born employees. Yet these more interpersonal factors were among the bottom five for both domestic and immigrant employees. Two distinct studies of hotel workers in North America reveal a strong, significant priority towards extrinsic factors, clearly showing areas of unfulfilled needs for these workers.

Near the end of the decade, a longitudinal study was completed in the lodging industry in Canada (Murray, 2009) exploring the motivational factors of employees within the same organization over two separate periods over seven years. The early study in 2000 revealed that good working conditions, interesting work and appreciation of the work done resided as the top three job factors of importance. These results were supported by the significant importance expressed for growth factors that was uncovered in a concurrent application of Alderfer's ERG model. By 2007, results from the same organization had shifted to good wages, appreciation of the work done, and opportunities for promotion and growth. Although growth needs, as an aggregate, still surfaced as most important, the later data showed strong movement towards existence needs, moving this category into the second position of three and establishing it as only mildly distinct from growth needs. Discussion around these results identified two key factors: the differences in which rewards are valued and to what extent between Generation X and the Millennial generation (Strauss and Howe, 1992), and the shift in economic conditions in the two periods, from one of strength in 2000 to the recessionary period leading up to and including 2007 (Statistics Canada, 2009).

Recently, DiPietro et al. (2014) published their examination of hotel employees in Aruba, a similar Caribbean location that had been explored by Charles and Marshall over 20 years earlier. Aruba was particularly interesting to DiPietro et al. for two particular reasons. First, tourism was relatively young in Aruba, and not considered an important economic instrument for the island prior to the closing of the oil refinery in 1985. Secondly, by 2010 tourism had become a dominant industry, employing over 16 per cent of Aruba's population. Similarly to the previous study in the Caribbean, DiPietro and her colleagues found full appreciation of work done, wages and working conditions to be the top three job rewards, identifying a strong preference for existence-related needs to be satisfied.

All of these research studies in Table 3.1 applied the Ten Factor Model

of job factor preferences to uniquely showcase contextual difference, whether cultural or demographic. Recently, an additional application within the Canadian hotel marketplace (Murray, 2016) has shown initial results from a longitudinal project to indicate that the economic conditions that exist when respondents answer the survey also seem to serve as a contextual influence for the espoused job reward preferences. Using Alderfer's ERG theory as a parsimonious model in which to collapse the ten job rewards, this study over three time periods in a 16-year timeframe infers that growth-related needs appear to rise to the forefront of preferred job rewards during periods in which the national economy is strong and employment is plentiful, while existence-related needs come to the top when the economy is uncertain and moves through recessionary periods. Although still in development, this work continues to demonstrate the impact that context plays in shifting desired motivators of individuals, reaffirming the need to continually engage with workers about what is important to them.

EMPLOYEE MOTIVATION: THE KEY TO KEEPING GREAT PEOPLE AND PROVIDING GREAT EXPERIENCES

Comprehending and satisfying the preferred motivational factors of employees is not simply important for altruistic reasons. Certainly it appears to be the right thing to do at face value, but if this were the sole driving force, it would be reasonable to assume that organizations would have already invested the requisite time and resources to address these issues. However, the contextual nature of motivation along with the insatiable, ongoing nature of human desires means that the challenge to meet human needs appears less like a destination and more a moving target. For organizations in the hospitality field, the values that come from satiating employees, or the negative impacts that arise from the alterative situation, are important to understand.

Employment characteristics in the hospitality industry remain extremely problematic, including finding and keeping talented workers (Watkins, 2014) within an industry facing an ongoing labour shortage and suffering from turnover rates that greatly exceed overall industry norms (CTHRC, 2012). People have always been at the core of the hospitality industry but now they are demanding full attention. Failing to address employee interests has multiple consequences. In a recent study of the restaurant industry, it was concluded that 'a lack of employee motivation may cause organizational problems in turnover, retention, morale, and poor productivity' (Curtis et al., 2009, p. 264). Labour shortages mean choice and opportunity for employees in the hospitality industry; they have the ability to find workplaces that meet their needs, and highly qualified workers are finding themselves actively recruited. Employers who are failing to meet the needs of value to their employees may find those who remain with them producing at a suboptimal level. Conversely, when an organization is aware and attempts to align job reward factors offered with those valued by workers, they can create a 'sticky' working environment that is attractive for employees (Cardy and Lengnick-Hall, 2011). According to Salleh et al., 'having a good work motivation among employees may contribute to a full commitment of working as employees feel they are part of an organization' (2016, p. 142).

From a cost perspective, increasing retention and organizational commitment are extremely attractive outcomes that can flow from the improved satisfaction of motivational factors valued by staff members. However, the hospitality industry is one grounded in interpersonal interactions that blend products and services into experiences (Parasuraman, 1987). A major benefit to the satisfaction of employee needs includes the potentially positive interactions that customers can experience. In a recent study, data from employees and customers showed that the relationship between employees who possess customer service orientations and the interaction quality they provide to their guests is strongly and positively impacted by both how well an employee is satisfied and how deeply they are committed to their job (Gazzoli et al., 2013). This, in turn, was found to be a powerful force in providing high quality service and achieving customer satisfaction. Alignment to employee needs and the ability to appropriately satisfy them is paramount to increased organizational commitment. Evidence around the impact of employees' desire to contribute to guests, their volition to provide fantastic customer experiences, appears to reside in the domain of intrinsic drivers. Workers like to get more from their work than a simple pay cheque; pride, a personal sense of accomplishment, and feeling valued all appear to influence whether or not an employee is putting their best talents to use. In his research unpacking employee and customer satisfaction, Garlick states that when workers felt they were not doing meaningful work, they frequently demonstrated disengagement from customers, whereas 'employees who felt they were truly making a difference and using their best talents effectively were the most likely to enjoy their interactions with customers' (2010, p. 305).

What remains clear is that the studying of employee motivation is far from over. Research to date has shown some consistent trends, typically surfacing growth-based/intrinsic needs and existence-based/economic needs as most important. Depending on the time and location of the studies conducted, these groupings shift in relative importance, particularly during recessionary periods and due to the relatively lower wage structure of the hospitality industry itself (Kusluvan and Kusluvan, 2000). Researchers need to continually revisit their measures of employee job reward preferences, not only to push forward theory but to make serious, positive contributions to the tourism field. Motivation theories alone are lenses through which to make sense of human behaviour, particularly content-based ideas. When placed close together, we can see incremental advancements over time. Yet they have as much, if not more, in common than they differ. The application of theory, be it through the use of the Ten Factor Model or another measurement tool, provides rich insight into the changing, shifting, messy nature of human drivers.

REFERENCES

Alderfer, C.P. (1972), *Existence, Relatedness, and Growth: Human Needs in Organizational Settings*, New York: The Free Press/Collier-Macmillan.

Bassett-Jones, N. and Lloyd, G.C. (2005), 'Does Herzberg's motivation theory have staying power?', *Journal of Management Development*, **24** (10), 929–43.

Bendix, R. (1956), *Work and Authority in Industry*, New York: Wiley.

Breiter, D., Tesone, D., Van Leeuwen, D. and Rue, V. (2002), 'An analysis of hotel employees' motivation using Kovach's Ten Factor Model', *Journal of Human Resources in Hospitality & Tourism*, **1** (4), 63–78.

Cardy, R.L. and Lengnick-Hall, M.L. (2011), 'Will they stay or will they go? Exploring a customer-oriented approach to employee retention', *Journal of Business Psychology*, **26**, 213–17.

Charles, K.R. and Marshall, L.H. (1992), 'Motivational preferences of Caribbean hotel workers: An exploratory study', *International Journal of Contemporary Hospitality Management*, **4**, 25–9.

Chiang, F.F.T. and Birtch, T.A. (2010), 'Pay for performance and work attitudes: The mediating role of employee–organization service value congruence', *International Journal of Hospitality Management*, **29**, 632–40.

CTHRC (2012), *The Future of Canada's Tourism Sector*, Ottawa, ON: Canadian Tourism Research Institute and the Conference Board of Canada.

Curtis, C.R., Upchurch, R.S. and Severt, D.E. (2009), 'Employee motivation and organizational commitment: A comparison of tipped and nontipped restaurant employees', *International Journal of Hospitality & Tourism Administration*, **10** (3), 253–69.

DiPietro, R.B., Kline, S.F. and Nierop, T. (2014), 'Motivation and satisfaction of lodging employees: An exploratory study of Aruba', *Journal of Human Resources in Hospitality & Tourism*, **13**, 253–76.

Drucker, P. (1992), *Managing for the Future: The 1990's and Beyond*, New York: Plume / Penguin Books.

Drucker, P. (2008), *Management* (rev. edn), New York: HarperCollins.

Drummond, K.E. (1990), *Human Resource Management for the Hospitality Industry*. New York: Van Nostrand Reinhold.

Fisher, C.D. and Yuan, X.Y. (1998), 'What motivates employees? A comparison of US and Chinese responses', *International Journal of Human Resource Management*, **9** (3), 516–28.

Garlick, R. (2010), 'Do happy employees really mean happy customers? Or is there more to the equation?', *Cornell Hospitality Quarterly*, **51** (3), 304–307.

Gazzoli, G., Hancer, M. and Kim, B. (2013), 'Explaining why employee–customer orientation influences customers' perceptions of the service encounter', *Journal of Service Management*, **24** (4), 382–400.

Gomez, A.V. and Alstrom, P. (1995), 'Adaptive performance and the mechanisms of behavior: Pavlov's dog, the Skinner box, and the balancing act', *Chaos, Solutions, and Fractals*, **5** (8), 1439–46.

Hellriegel, D., Slocum Jr, J.W., Woodman, R.W. and Bruning, N.S. (1998), *Organizational Behaviour* (8th edn), Toronto: Thompson Nelson.

Hersey, P. and Blanchard, K. (1969), *Management of Organizational Behaviour*, Englewood Cliffs, NJ: Prentice Hall.

Herzberg, F. (1968), 'One more time: How do you motivate employees?', *Harvard Business Review*, September–October, 53–62.

Kanfer, R. (1990), 'Motivation theory and industrial and organizational psychology', *Handbook of Industrial and Organizational Psychology – Theory in Industrial and Organizational Psychology* (Vol. 1), California: Consulting Psychologists Press, pp. 75–170.

Kanfer, R. (1992), 'Work motivation: New directions in theory and research', in C.L. Cooper and I.T. Robertson (eds), *International Review of Industrial and Organizational Psychology* (Vol. 7), London: Wiley.

Kovach, K.A. (1987), 'What motivates employees? Workers and supervisors give different answers', *Business Horizons*, **30**, 58–65.

Kuo, C.M. (2009), 'The managerial implications of an analysis of tourist profiles and international hotel employee service attitudes', *International Journal of Hospitality Management*, **28**, 302–309.

Kusluvan, S. and Kusluvan, Z. (2000), 'Perceptions and attitudes of undergraduate tourism students towards working in the tourism industry', *Tourism Management*, **21** (3), 251–69.

Kusluvan, S., Kusluvan, Z., Ilhan, I. and Buyruk, L. (2010), 'The human dimension: A review of human resources management issues in the tourism and hospitality industry', *Cornell Hospitality Quarterly*, **51** (2), 171–214.

Lee-Ross, D. (1999), *HRM in Tourism and Hospitality: International Perspectives on Small to Medium-Sized Enterprises*, London: Cassell.

Maslow, A. (1943), 'A theory of human motivation', *Psychological Review*, **50**, 370–96.

McClelland, D.C. (1965), 'Toward a theory of motive acquisition', *American Psychologist*, **20** (5), 321–33.

McGregor, D.H. (1960), *The Human Side of Enterprise*, New York: McGraw-Hill.

Morgan, G. (1997), *Images of Organization* (2nd edn), Thousand Oaks, CA: SAGE Publications.

Mullins, L.J. (2002), *Management and Organizational Behaviour* (6th edn), UK: Financial Times Prentice Hall.

Murray, W.C. (2009), 'The winds of change: A longitudinal examination of motivational factors and job rewards in the hospitality sector', Proceedings of the 39th Atlantic Schools of Business Conference, Moncton, NB, 2–4 October.

Murray, W.C. (2016), 'Exploring self-perceptions of motivations in the hospitality industry', Visual Presentation at the Travel and Tourism Research Association International Conference, Vail, Colorado. Accessed at http://scholarworks.umass.edu/ttra/2016/Academic_Papers_Visual/20/.

Nicholson, N., Schuler, R.S., Van de Ven, A.H., Cooper, C. and Argyris, C. (eds) (1995), *Encyclopedic Dictionary of Organizational Behaviour*, Oxford: Blackwell Publishing.

Parasuraman, A. (1987), 'Customer-oriented corporate cultures are crucial to service', *The Journal of Services Marketing*, **1**, 39–46.

Parasuraman, A., Berry, L.L. and Zeithaml, V.A. (1991), 'Understanding customer expectations of service', *Sloan Management Review*, **32**, 39–48.

Pinder, C. (1998), *Work Motivation in Organizational Behavior*, Upper Saddle River, NJ: Prentice Hall.

Robbins, S.P. (2005), *Essentials of Organizational Behavior* (8th edn), Upper Saddle River, NJ: Prentice Hall.

Ryan, R.M. and Deci, E.L. (2000), 'Intrinsic and extrinsic motivations: Classic definitions and new directions', *Contemporary Education Psychology*, **25**, 54–67.

Salleh, S.M., Zahari, A.S.M., Said, N.S.M. and Ali, S.R.O. (2016), 'The influence of work motivation on organizational commitment in the workplace', *Journal of Applied Environmental and Biological Sciences*, **6** (5S), 139–43.

Silverthorne, D. (1992), 'Work motivation in the United States, Russia, and the Republic of China (Taiwan): A comparison', *Journal of Applied Social Psychology*, **22** (20), 1631–9.

Simons, T. and Enz, C. (1995), 'Motivating hotel employees: Beyond the carrot and the stick', *Cornell Hotel and Restaurant Administration Quarterly*, **36** (1), 20–27.

Statistics Canada (2009), www.statscan.ca.

Steers, R.M., Mowday, R.T. and Shapiro, D.L. (2004), 'The future of work motivation theory', *The Academy of Management Review*, **29**, 379–87.

Strauss, W. and Howe, N. (1992), *Generations*, New York: Harper Perennial.

Tanke, M.L. (1990), *Human Resource Management for the Hospitality Industry*, New York: Delmar.

Taylor, F.W. (1911), *The Principles of Scientific Management*, New York: W.W. Norton.

Vroom, V.H. (1964), *Work and Motivation*, New York: Wiley.

Watkins, E. (2014), 'The biggest challenge facing hoteliers', *Hotel News Now*, 15 July. Accessed at http://hotelnewsnow.com/article/14068/the-biggest-challenge-facing-hoteliers.

Wiley, C. (1997), 'What motivates employees according to over 40 years of motivation surveys', *International Journal of Manpower*, **18** (3), 263–80.

Witzel, M. and Warner, M. (eds) (2013), *The Oxford Handbook of Management Theorists*, Oxford: Oxford University Press.

Wong, S., Siu, V. and Tsang, N. (1999), 'The impact of demographic factors on Hong Kong hotel employees' choice of job-related motivators', *International Journal of Contemporary Hospitality Management*, **11** (5), 230–41.

Zeithaml, V.A., Parasuraman, A. and Berry, L.L. (1985), 'Problems and strategies in services marketing', *Journal of Marketing*, **49** (2), 33–46.

4. The talent agenda in hospitality and tourism

William J. Pallett

I'm often asked how I lead a major Canadian hotel company to receive the *50 Best Employers in Canada* award for more than 14 consecutive years. In reflection there are several reasons, and I hope to share them with you in the various stories and ideas in this chapter.

Many companies say that "people" are their most valuable asset, yet very few follow through in terms of their everyday behavior, values and actions. Much of the work that is done with regard to the talent agenda in today's organizations can be seen as *reactive* and not *strategic.* Companies spend valuable resources, such as time and capital, implementing disparate programs, systems and the latest talent "fads" but with no real strategic initiatives that are aligned and support either their Strategic Plan and/or their Value Proposition! It is for this very reason that many Chief Executive Officers have questioned the value of Human Resources management in the past few years, in organizations large and small.

If an organization wants to ensure they have a human capital component that will drive and support the Company's strategy and get a good Return On Investment (ROI), it only makes sense then that a Talent Strategy must be developed with a robust and thorough focus on research, data and strategic plan development process to meet the needs of all phases in the Talent Life Cycle (see Figure 4.1).

Figure 4.1 outlines the Talent Life Cycle as it related to Delta Hotels and Resorts in the years between mid-2010 and 2015. The "PR Core Process" refers to the vital few or key human resources (called People Resources at

Figure 4.1   Talent Life Cycle

the time in Delta) that are the "input" for the cycle and resulting in key outcomes or "output" of engagement and retention.

The first step in developing a Talent Strategy will be to identify the Critical Success Factors. The most critical determinants of project success will be an inclusive process within the organization and the creation of buy-in from key stakeholders. You can craft an exceptional go-forward plan but if leadership is not committed to its implementation with the same zeal that they would use when introducing other more client-centric or financially oriented initiatives, then we will have wasted time and money. You need therefore to develop a plan that sequences and builds their engagement in a practical and meaningful way.

PHASE I: PROJECT PLANNING AND ORIENTATION

Phase I is the project kick-off. In advance of the first meeting, you should gather background material on the company that is available to bring you up to speed on the organization's Strategic Plan, branding initiatives, previous human resources planning and so on.

Subsequently you will need to meet with your team (who will constitute the Working Group for this project) for a half day to accomplish four key objectives:

1. Develop a deeper understanding of the information that is available to you and your team and reach agreement on:

    i   *What information do we need to review and analyze?* This will be information that is readily available within the company, for example the various Human Resources reports noted above, some of the key outputs of the recent strategic planning such as the SWOT analysis and the environmental scan, marketing information that highlights the customer perception of employee behavior and where there may be gaps between the old and new company brand. (The latter will be an important filter for your planning.)

    ii *What information do we need to purchase and for what purpose?* This is information that could provide insight into trends or practices that can impact the company's ability to attract, retain and engage critical talent, for example the detailed Aon Hewitt "Best Practices" report, conference board reports.

    iii *What information do we need to collect over and above (i) and (ii),* for example, specific external benchmarking data.

2. Confirm key stakeholders and influencers who should be engaged in the process to build support and momentum for implementation of the Talent Plan. Your corporate office team will constitute the Working Group. You may, however, decide that the scope of the work or the need to secure buy-in necessitates the involvement of a broader group such as several Human Resources Directors (HRDs). You will also need to reach agreement on attendees for the Phase VI Workshop, and set a date to ensure availability.
3. Finalize a project work plan, timelines and responsibilities. For each phase in the project, you will have the option of multiple meetings over several days to allow participants to effectively prepare and assimilate the information *or* to conduct a focused intensive session over a couple of days. You will also need to agree on accountabilities for analysis of the available information.
4. Agree on a format for the final Strategic Talent Plan. You will need to summarize your meeting outcomes to share with the group.

PHASE II: DATA GATHERING AND ANALYSIS

The objective of phases II to V is to gather and analyze the information that will enable your team to identify the most important issues the organization needs to address in the Strategic Talent Plan Workshop in Phase VI.

In Phase II, you will review and analyze all available information with the objective of identifying key trends that will have implications for the development of the Strategic Talent Plan. It is expected that each of the Working Group members will take the lead in analyzing several reports for presentation for the group. You should prepare a template and be available to provide support to ensure a consistent reporting format that will allow the group to readily identify common themes, connections and issues as well as information gaps. My experience is that a Human Resources "War Room" where you can post these findings will be helpful in enabling your team to continue to surface connections, challenges and potential solutions beyond your meetings.

In addition to the review of available surveys, it will also be critical to review any of your hotel/restaurant Human Resource Plans including relevant metrics, for example employee retention and employee satisfaction to identify common issues or concerns. One of the Working Group members will need to take on this assignment.

PHASE III: SUMMARY OF FINDINGS IN CONTEXT OF HUMAN RESOURCES MISSION AND VISION

It is usually the case that there may not be a clear, concise, shared mission and vision for the Human Resources function. I believe that there is value in clarifying both as they can become the "terms" of your work with the respective hotels. Consequently, I recommend that you develop "straw models" at this juncture to frame your discussions.

I anticipate that you will need the equivalent of two days as a team to review the findings of Phase II and to reach agreement on a straw model for a Human Resources Mission and Vision. This review can be scheduled for two consecutive days; alternatively, you can meet for four separate half days.

In addition to a straw model for a Mission and Vision, the deliverable of these meetings will be a summary of common themes including clear strengths and successes, issues, challenges as well as their relative ranking. You will also identify critical information gaps – areas for which you need to collect additional data in order to complete your analysis and move forward to priority setting. Should additional information be required, you will assign accountability and time frames at that time.

Finally, you will also identify those subject areas that will be the target of your external benchmarking efforts. Focused benchmarking on priority areas has proven to be a cost-effective and valuable use of resources.

PHASE IV: FIELD INPUT

It may be unclear at this point whether your Phase II review will provide sufficiently robust information to help your team understand what talent issues are "keeping the General Managers up at night". It has been my experience that you need to address those issues in the short term to enable the General Managers to give time and attention to the broader agenda.

I recommend that you formally reach out to the General Managers to learn more about their talent issues and to solicit feedback on the perceived effectiveness and value of core Human Resources processes/ programs. You will need to work with the Working Group to determine which processes your team would like to include. You may need to prepare an interview guide. The interview guide will include the requirement to "rate" or "prioritize" items so that your team can have a meaningful quantification of the urgency of the issues.

Subsequently, you or a member of the Working Group team will need to conduct a 45-minute telephone interview with each General Manager to develop a deeper understanding of their most pressing people issues as well as their views of the effectiveness of current Human Resources initiatives. This will also be an opportunity to:

- test ideas or concepts that may have surfaced in Phase II;
- build support for the resulting plan as all the General Managers will have been part of the process;
- identify any road bumps that you need to be aware of for implementation.

Finally, it may be appropriate to include the hotel HRDs in these calls so that they also feel engaged in the process. Alternatively, you could develop a short survey for them to complete.

You will need to summarize the feedback to provide to the Working Group. These findings will also be presented more formally in Phase V.

PHASE V: EXTERNAL BENCHMARKING

Based on the list of priorities you identified in Phase II, you will work together to identify the selection criteria for target benchmark organizations. You will also identify the target organizations and assign responsibilities for securing the data.

I envision that the Working Group will contact 4–6 relevant organizations in this phase. You will need to prepare a format for collecting benchmark data. You will also need to consolidate and summarize the findings collected by the Working Group for review in Phase IV.

PHASE VI: TALENT PLAN WORKSHOP

You will need to develop a two-day workshop to be attended by the Working Group and key stakeholders. I anticipate the group will be in the range of 15–20 attendees. The objective of the workshop will be to:

1. Review findings of internal and external information analyses, benchmarking and field survey work.
2. Reach agreement on a Mission and Vision for the Human Resources Group.
3. Identify priorities for action for the Human Resources Strategic Talent Plan.

4. Develop preliminary action items with accountabilities and timelines.
5. Develop metrics to track progress for the Human Resources Group and the organization in general. You will also develop hotel-specific metrics to assess progress over the duration of the plan.

PHASE VII: FINALIZATION OF PLAN

You will work with the members of your Working Group to fine-tune the Talent Plan following the meeting. You will then need to meet as a group for two hours to finalize the plan and to develop a communication strategy for securing broader commitment and submission of your Talent Plan for approval.

AFTER THE TALENT STRATEGY HAS BEEN DEVELOPED AND DEPLOYED

While the development and deployment of your well-researched Talent Strategy is a "first step" to ensuring you have a solid foundation for your company's human resources initiatives, work needs to commence on ensuring you can now be successful in meeting the requirements of the first phase of the Talent Life Cycle: acquisition of your talent.

Acquisition

Many companies fail to address the first component of acquiring talent: the need to develop their Employee Value Proposition (EVP). In other words they need to answer the question that many new potential employees will ask: "Why should I work for your company as opposed to other companies in this industry?"

Your Employee Value Proposition needs to state clearly the key positive attributes of working within your organization. The EVP is a unique set of offerings, associations and values to positively influence target candidates and employees. This is especially important in terms of attracting the Millennial demographic group, which will soon comprise upwards of 50 percent of our workforce in North America.

A company needs a unique employee offer. The EVP gives current and future employees a reason to work for an employer and reflects the company's competitive advantage. Employers that manage their EVP effectively benefit from an increase in their talent pool and employee engagement. Typically, less attractive employers need to pay a wage premium to get

Figure 4.2   Employee Value Proposition

top talent whereas attractive employers do not. The example in Figure 4.2 outlines a typical EVP!

To some leaders the EVP is sometimes used and thought of as an advertising "tag line"; however, properly researched and developed, the EVP can be used for several purposes beyond talent attraction and talent advertising.

The EVP assists the organization in staying true to what it offers employees in terms of benefits, rewards, recognition, training, development and career opportunities by acting as a compass ensuring that as programs, processes and policies are developed, they are fully aligned to what is stated in the value proposition. Often when an organization is developing a program it looks back to the EVP to ensure the new program's intent and purpose is fully aligned to what it has "promised" to deliver to its employees.

Once talent has been "attracted" to the company, the recruitment process will determine which candidates are ideally suited for the company's culture and the role. Much has been written about the actual recruitment process but a key factor in the process will be determining "fit" and "skill level". Several steps in the process will help to narrow the pool of candidates to the one candidate who is best suited for the role; however, it will be important to ensure your process is efficient and not overly cumbersome for both parties. Top talent wants to experience an efficient recruitment process that is not too long. Lengthy delays moving from one stage of the interview process to the other are frustrating and tend to "turn off" a candidate's motivation and enthusiasm for the opportunity!

Two key components of the recruitment process will be to ensure your applicant pre-screening tools are appropriate and that senior leadership is prepared to meet with all final candidates, if only for a few minutes. Having the senior leader meet with a candidate sends a strong message that no matter where an individual is within the organization, their role is so important that senior leadership wants to meet with them! This step alone, should the candidate be hired, sets a strong level of engagement in motion before the onboarding process begins!

In a majority of situations companies today prefer to hire for attitude or personality, knowing they can train for the technical skills. The real issue will be to determine if the candidate is customer- and service-centric, able to solve problems on their own and take initiative in organizations that are increasingly empowering their employees to do what is needed to develop loyal customers.

Onboarding: Celebrating and Making Them Feel Welcome

The next critical phase in the Talent Life Cycle is onboarding.

Research tells us that new employees usually decide within the first six to eight months if they intend to stay with the company. Their initial experience of onboarding, or as some organizations still refer to it, orientation, is crucial to their retention. A poor onboarding experience which fails to deliver on the EVP results in a disgruntled employee who immediately begins to question whether they've made the right choice for employment and usually results in their decision to begin the search for alternative employment and thus in their not concentrating on their current role. As a result the organization loses productivity and the engagement of a new employee. Of course the reverse is true should the employee have a positive onboarding experience.

Onboarding requires the organization to be fully prepared with training checklists and a robust schedule of learning activities for the new employee. Included in this process are regular "check-ins" with the employee to determine their satisfaction with the onboarding process and to elicit any areas of concern or questions from the new team member.

Job standards should be up to date and fully explained to the new recruit, and a designated trainer in the employee's department or functional area of responsibility should be assigned for the onboarding period.

Onboarding should also include a thorough orientation and familiarization of the organization's Vision, Mission and Values, as well as key processes and business strategy. If employees are to contribute to the company's overall success they need to clearly understand the goals going forward and how their role contributes to the achievement of the key objectives in the company's business plan. Too often employees receive the training necessary to carry out their role but they lack the understanding of how their role contributes to the company's success and thus the opportunity to fully engage them is a lost opportunity!

Enable: a Crucial Phase

A key component of the Talent Life Cycle, and crucial to ensuring employee retention rates are strong is the Enable phase. It is here that many companies fail in attaining high engagement and productivity levels. Often an organization will onboard an employee and then fail to continue to develop their skill set.

Enabling an employee goes far beyond the training of immediate skill requirements. Learning should be immediate and accessible. Learning leaders agree that continuing the process of training an employee is like a dripping tap of water, it should be in small, digestible amounts and continuous! In fact the trend today is towards micro learning, which is accessible, on-demand, with real-life performance scenarios, which are self-paced and directed using various technology platforms for their deployment. Millennials in particular are comfortable with and prefer to use technology for their learning and development whenever possible. A company that does not ensure that its learning initiatives use technology wherever possible risks losing the interest and tenure of this growing demographic in the workplace.

Employees should have access to development opportunities that enable them not only to perform their current roles, but also to provide them with an opportunity to develop, grow and compete for other career opportunities within the organization. Evidence is clear that growth and career opportunities are a leading driver of employee engagement and attract talent to your organization.

While an organization may not be able to provide all learning opportunities internally, there are so many external organizations offering a variety of learning and development programs that it would make sense to ensure, as a minimum, that organizations today have a policy, such as tuition reimbursement, that provides resources for high potential employees to secure the training they require in order to develop and grow.

As part of the development process, organizations should ensure that in coaching and performance management discussions an employee's key competencies and skill-up opportunities are identified and addressed. Knowing one's key strengths and areas for development is essential to an employee's ongoing development improvement plan and engagement.

These approaches, when properly deployed, will ensure an organization's employee retention and engagement levels are strong and provide a good return on investment.

Enabling employees requires a broad perspective on key elements that will ensure employees can continue to grow both personally and professionally. Learning opportunities may not always be directed towards the current role but focus on skills and competencies that may be required for future roles or continued personal success. One example that has worked well for one organization includes hosting a workshop for line-level employees on "managing finances" to better understand budgeting for future purchases. While some managers may have argued that line employees didn't require this skill for their current job, employees realized the need and appreciated the organization's support of the workshop and giving them the time to attend in-house.

Of course the first requirement for any "learning" organization is to ensure that it has fully developed its competency framework for all the roles within the company. Competency frameworks need to be customized to the strategic direction and culture of the organization: these are the competencies leaders in the organization must possess in order to be truly successful. Rather than referring to specific skills, competencies provide a broader directional focus such as problem solving, fostering teamwork and listening openly. Some competencies would include:

- working across boundaries: fostering teamwork, embracing differences and developing relationships;
- taking action: communicating effectively, listening openly, and initiating action and empowerment;
- demonstrating resilience: knowing and managing yourself, coping with ambiguity, and demonstrating agility and adaptability;
- acting with integrity: making ethical judgments, demonstrating personal responsibility;
- creating a vision: thinking strategically, learning to listen, developing creative solutions.

Competency models are more flexible and encompassing than job descriptions and are fast becoming the standard in many companies as they describe behaviors required to be successful rather than specific skills, which may become outdated before some job descriptions are even published!

It may be necessary to create competency models for various levels within the organization but it may eliminate the need for job descriptions for all roles.

Once a competency framework for each level has been developed, more productive coaching and performance management discussions can occur, thus giving the employee a clearer focus on their strengths and opportunities for development.

A company's Competency Framework has several primary uses:

- credentials, assessment tools, e.g. diagnostic, formative, summative;
- career guidance, e.g. information, articulation career paths, career development plans, job search tools;
- curriculum, training, education, courses, e.g. certificates, diplomas, degrees, corporate programs;
- learner and worker mobility, e.g. recognition of prior learning, credit transfer, credential reciprocity, program articulation, qualifications frameworks;
- organizational development, change management, e.g. job role definitions, organizational charts, succession planning, labor agreements, labor market plans;
- HR practices, workforce planning, e.g. job ads, career planning and progression, interview guides, job descriptions, onboard checklists, learning and development plans, recognition and reward programs, assessment;
- labor market intelligence, e.g. supply and demand projections; identification of education, qualifications, training and skills; current and future demand and supply of labor and jobs; labor market conditions; demographic information; trends (e.g. social, political, historical, economic, regulatory, ecological, or technological factors).

My experience has confirmed that to make any substantial impact on a company's culture you need to ensure that your leadership learning and development initiatives are targeted and encompass all of your business units (hotels/restaurants/outlets) to have any meaningful impact. This also provides a "trickle down" effect. Remember, employees don't quit the brand, they quit their manager!

Focusing only on one or two business units will create the "have" and "have-nots" and exacerbate confusion within the teams. This requires, therefore, a strategic and consistent approach to scheduling and deployment of your learning and development (L&D) activities and may require a re-think on channels and platforms for these programs. In some cases e-learning will be the best methodology to use, while other subject matter will require in-house workshops. Your L&D strategy, within the Talent Strategy, should detail the approaches, timelines and recipients.

Enrich: a Key Ingredient to Retention

Enriching employees is key to *retaining* employees in the hospitality business and a vital metric! It is easier if you can link your brand to a greater good of social commitment to the community. It's also been my experience that employees who work directly with and for a brand, versus a franchise operator of a brand, are usually easier to engage as they feel a direct "link" to the brand – in fact, properly trained, they see themselves "as the brand".

A key position in retaining employees will be to adopt the philosophy and vision that you will need to challenge and develop your organization's people management practices, every single day.

It will also be crucial to instill a commitment, amongst all of your leaders or managers, to working towards managing people in an innovative and sometimes disruptive way. I believe this is the way we can improve and develop people's working environment in the future, whilst improving an organization's standards and values.

The workplace today is more diverse and demographically complex than ever before. Millennials now make up almost 50 percent of the workforce in many industrialized nations. Yet workplaces continue to have other generations, such as Baby boomers, within their workforce. This has given organizations additional challenges in providing an enriched and engaging work environment over the long term, which in turn impacts their ability to retain talent. It certainly adds credibility to the saying that "one size fits all" doesn't work any more. Simply deploying an "Employee of the Month" program and expecting it to engage all levels of employees for the long term will no longer succeed at keeping them within the organization! While it may work for some employees, others will simply see this as a political façade for the "favorites" to be rewarded by their managers.

There are many tools, programs, workplace committees and processes that should be in place to ensure a workplace culture that enriches the employee's work experience, such as:

- reward and recognition programs;
- health and wellness policy, programs and wellness fairs;
- embracing diversity;
- comprehensive and flexible benefit programs;
- Employee Assistance Program (EAP);
- complete employee communication strategy including, but not limited to regular:

  - townhall meetings in which to review company performance and new developments
  - one-on-one meetings with immediate manager
  - festive celebrations;

- Community Social Responsibility (CSR) program(s);
- employee representative committee;
- employee information and communication portal.

A good approach to ensure that your organization has fully deployed all of the programs and processes is to create an HR Audit Checklist similar to the example in Table 4.1. This will ensure consistency throughout the many business units in a multi-unit or multi-department organization.

While having all of these tools, policies, programs and processes in place will ensure a robust Human Resources function in your organization, the final tool to ensure you are achieving your Talent Strategy goals and providing a good ROI will be to use HR Analytics and an HR Dashboard (scoreboard). This will allow you to review data, make better informed decisions and communicate to various stakeholders within the organization and externally, such as your Board of Directors or investors, the value of this important function within the enterprise.

An example of one component of using human resources analytics and communicating them via an HR Dashboard is outlined in Table 4.2 for those metrics relating to a company's:

- employee engagement score;
- positioning within a national Employee Engagement Survey;
- employee turnover;
- accident and lost time.

Other metrics which can be tracked and trended on the dashboard are, but are not limited to:

- time to hire;
- best sources of recruitment (channels);
- leadership bench strength.

Human resources management is now being seen as a key driver of success in the hospitality and tourism industry. While technology has eliminated many jobs within the industry as it strives to improve and meet the changing demands of the consumer, one component that research continues to show is that the human interaction and personalization of the guest experience remains key to a brand's success and therefore the reliance on a well-trained and engaged labor force will be essential for any organization to succeed in the future.

As one hospitality leader reminded his leadership, "people are our most important asset. You can acquire money, machinery and physical product, but people are free to go at any time". In other words, remember that a company does not "own" its people and when deploying its talent strategy, an organization that keeps that prophetic saying in its philosophy will always succeed when it comes to managing the talent life cycle.

Table 4.1   Human Resources Audit Checklist

	Department Meetings	Frequency
		Minuted
	Mid-Management Meetings	Frequency
		Minuted
	Community Gatherings	Frequency
		Agenda
	Bulletin Boards	Mandatory information posted (Career Ops, Code of Ethics, Colleague Referral, and Health and Wellness)
		My Development Poster posted
		Service Guarantee Poster in place
		Information is up to date and well displayed
D. EMPLOYEE RELATIONS & COMMUNICATIONS (ENRICH)		Bulletin board in each department
		Department bulletin board has appropriate postings (Key services, Community Codes, Schedules, and WHIMIS)
		Department Union Bulletin Boards (unionized hotel)
	Locker Rooms	Cleanliness
		Sufficient Amenities
	Heartland	Menus are posted and rotated
		Menus are nutritious and provide options for dietary preferences
		Special menus or theme days provided regularly
		Room is clean and tastefully decorated

Table 4.1 (continued)

Employee Events	Type and frequency	
Employee Representative Committee (ERC)	Meeting frequency	
	Agenda items	
	Selection process for ERC	
	Who attends ERC	
	Agenda items addressed	
	Selection process for H&W Committee	
Health & Wellness	Meeting frequency and follow-up mechanism	
	Meetings attended by the Leadership Team	
	Meeting issues addressed	
	Wellness fairs conducted annually	
Reward & Recognition Program	Approach used to increase employee participation	
	Results tracked	
	Alternative R&R approaches	
Employee Newsletter	Method by which newsletter is distributed	
Diversity	Type of activities (i.e. alternative recruitment sources, respect in the workplace, guest speakers)	
Employee Handbook	Revisions (Frequency of latest revision; Who was involved with the change)	

Table 4.2   HR Metrics Dashboard

	PR METRICS		
	2010	2011	2012
Overall			
E.E.S	85	87	(76) 87
50 Best	14	9	23
Turnover	27.33%	25.93%	25.14%
Accident rate	342	291	312
– Frequency rate*	43.69	41.74	49.17
– Severity**	95.33	112.41	209.63

Notes:
* Frequency calculates the average number of accidents/hotel.
** Severity calculates the average number of days lost/hotel.

5. How to develop hotel brand internalization among hotel employees
Catherine Cheung and Tom Baum

INTRODUCTION

Service branding topics have given much attention over the past decade to integrating employees' behaviors into the branding process, especially for the hotel industry (Leong, 2007; Vallaster and De Chernatony, 2005). This is mainly because employees play a vital role in delivering the service in which customers' expectations are met. In particular, for a dynamic industry like hotels, organizations rely heavily on employees' abilities and intentions to carry out the required brand initiatives (King, 2010). Furthermore, customers' experiences with the hotel brand are very much dependent upon employees' service performances (Tsang et al., 2011). As employees can form a strong and close connection between a hotel brand and its customers, Harris and De Chernatony (2001) assert the importance of considering internal branding management or brand internalization, with employees portrayed at the center of brand development. Cheung et al. (2014), in a survey of hotel managers in mainland China, found that internal branding significantly affected brand performance. In recent years, hotels have been treating internal brand management as equally important as external brand management.

Previous literature on brand internalization has focused on employees' commitment (e.g. Little and Dean, 2006), customers' perceptions on employees' behaviors (e.g. Burmann and Zeplin, 2005; King and Grace, 2008), the role of leadership (e.g. Morhart et al., 2007), and employees' perception on brand equity-related topics (e.g. Miles and Mangold, 2004; 2005; Punjaisri et al., 2009). Little research work has explored factors of hotel brand internalization despite its crucial function in instilling the required brand promises and messages into employees' actual behaviors. It is necessary to research this area since only when employees can align their knowledge and actions with the espoused brand messages can the brand be 'lived' and the organizational brand management be truly effective (King and Grace, 2008).

The present study provides an in-depth examination of employees' perception of brand internalization, mainly to identify factors that affect the brand internalization process. Drawing on the findings of this research, a conceptual model and a measurement scale are developed for the future study of hotel brand internalization.

LITERATURE REVIEW

Definition of Service Brand and Internal Branding

According to the American Marketing Association (2011), a brand is defined as a name, term, design, symbol or any other feature where goods (tangible) and service (intangible) of unique characteristics can be distinguished from the products of other sellers. It stands out as representing the corporation concerned and an exclusive trademark. Branding theory originally was a substantial part of promotion retrieved from the four P's classification of marketing mix theory (McCarthy, 1960). The nature of marketing or promoting a brand of a service organization requires development of customers' brand association with the actual service instead of with any tangible goods (Goldstein et al., 2002). Hence, in the service industry, the interaction between customers and employees becomes critical in determining the customers' perceptions of the brand experienced (Harris, 2007). The maintenance of service interactions that can keep up with brand promises is sometimes difficult for employees as complex human nature is hard to control (Punjaisri et al., 2009). In this regard, the concept of internal branding management has been introduced to reduce negative service interactions as well as to refine employees' behaviors towards management's expectations.

Internalization can be defined as "an individual's acceptance of a group's values as part of their value system" (De Chernatony and Harris, 2000, pp. 270–71). The concept of internalization is embedded in the internal branding management process. Internal branding management is defined as a process for management to constantly deliver the brand messages to employees at all levels of the organization; these employees are then expected to consistently transform and infuse the espoused messages into their work behavior (Bergstrom et al., 2002; Ind, 2007; Mitchell, 2002; Miles and Mangold, 2004; Punjaisri et al., 2009). Many scholars share very similar views on the value of internal branding management. For instance, Berry (2000) presents four approaches for service companies to cultivate a strong brand, and one of the approaches is to internalize the brand. In his later study, the author further emphasizes that service employees are more likely to perform their roles consistently and effectively when they internalize the brand concept and values (Berry and Lampo, 2004). Vallaster and De Chernatony (2005) use a similar definition of internal branding management, and also identify an association of leadership action and corporate structure with internal branding management. Steinmetz (2004) confirms that leadership participation is one of the keys to the success of internal branding.

The roles played by employees in the internal branding process are identified in the existing literature. Harquail (2006) highlights that employees should match brand attributes associated with the organization and that they should always be "wearing the brand". Some scholars recognize employees as the "brand ambassador" (e.g. Gotsi and Wilson, 2001). The roles played by employees have imbued them with great responsibilities and suggest that employees are representatives of a brand. A number of researchers have echoed that employees' interface between internal branding and external branding environments creates a tremendous impact on the consumers' perceptions of the brand and the organization as a whole (Balmer and Wilkinson, 1991; Schneider and Bowen, 1985). Employees are key figures in the process of brand building. They can either reinforce a brand's advertised values or ruin the credibility of the advertised messages partly conveyed through their personal behavior and their attitude and manner when they serve the customers (Harris and De Chernatony, 2001). Moreover, Cai and Hobson's (2004) research findings revealed that employees do not only represent the brand, according to the customers they interviewed: employees should become the brand. In other words, employees can help the organization to project the desired organizational brand image.

Brand Internalization Strategies

Organizations therefore attempt to make employees become the brand or to project the brand by using the brand internalization process. For instance, they use strategies such as explaining and selling the brand to employees; sharing the strategy behind the presented brand; creatively communicating the brand; training employees in brand-strengthening behaviors; rewarding employees whose actions support the brand; and most importantly, educating employees in caring about and nurturing the brand (Berry and Parasuraman, 1991). De Chernatony and Harris (2000) write that brand reputation relates to brand internalization in terms of reinforcing the brand identity. Leadership, as discussed by Miles and Mangold (2004), has an impact on employees' brand internalization as well. According to their study, to make brand internalization effective, employees have to understand customers' needs and expectations along with organizations' branding strategies. Later, Miles and Mangold (2007) proposed that the delivery of formal messages from management can promote brand knowledge and understanding of the desired brand. In addition, informal messages from word-of-mouth of co-workers, managers and customers can help to reinforce the organization's values and desired brand image.

Managers should place confidence in their subordinates, empower them to be more proactive when implementing the brand delivery programs, coach them to understand that brand values are not confined to the organization's desired behaviors only, they also encompass the initiatives to provide quality customer services (Henkel et al., 2007). Whenever stronger consumer bonds are established with the corporate brand during the course of personalized customer services, managers should exhibit good practice as examples to other employees so that they are able to consider and formulate their own acts within the bounds of the brand's values to excel (De Chernatony and Cottam, 2006). In this way, it is definitely the organization as a whole that is the ultimate beneficiary.

Problems at the level of the organization and with employees can exist in the brand internalization process. Employees can associate their superficial behavior with the brand messages without accepting these behaviors as being "part of them"; it becomes burdensome to apply a psychological internalization when there is a conflict between employees' own identity and a brand's identity (Harquail, 2007; Punjaisri and Wilson, 2007). Moreover, the diverse backgrounds of employees may lead to different interpretations of brand messages. This will affect the degree of brand internalization acquired among all levels of employees within the international hotel setting. While ingraining brand messages into the minds of employees can encourage brand internalization, some initiatives need to be implemented with the right messages from the right channels and the right receivers in order to ensure future success. In other words, it is important that the brand messages conveyed in the employees' training and development process be consistent with those conveyed in the other human resources processes, just as for both internal marketing and external marketing processes (Miles and Mangold, 2004).

A recent study that attempted to develop a Service Brand Internalization Concept Model for four different service industries in managing brands internally, explored five major factors (Bai et al., 2006). The five factors are the role of leadership; brand organization; employee involvement; internal communication of brand; and coherence of corporate culture and brand value. Their study used only a single hotel as a case study, which is not able to cover the international hotel internalization brand process in detail. The present research makes reference to this model and further examines service brand internalization by revealing the potential factors influencing the service brand internalization in the context of international branded hotels in Hong Kong.

METHODOLOGY

Sample

A qualitative research approach was used to seek a detailed and rich understanding of the dimensions and factors that influence hotel employees' perceptions of brand internalization. The sample of this study was targeted at functional-level hotel employees working in international hotel brands. As this study mainly revolves around the concept of brands and branding, only those hotels which have gained international recognition were targeted for the selection of samples. Functional-level hotel employees are the direct members of service delivery. The manner, dress code and the way they speak represent the hotels' brand promise to customers, which makes a significant impact on the brand perception and ultimately on corporate success (Bai et al., 2006). Zucker (2002) echoed that the front line staff who play customer-facing roles deserve specific attention. Although functional-level hotel employees are not directly involved with the initiation of branding activities, they are involved with the progress and the course of the brand internalization process. Thus, their responses are deemed to be valuable information for managers and executive members alike when assessing internal branding.

Semi-structured In-depth Interviews

The development of a measurement scale for brand internalization is one of the main purposes of this study. As recommended by Ap and Crompton (1998), conducting personal interviews with knowledgeable participants on the aspect under investigation is an appropriate procedure for generating an initial pool of scale items. Hence, a semi-structured in-depth interview with a purposive sampling method was adopted, involving hotel employees of major divisions among 10 international branded hotels. Patton (1990, p. 184) indicated that "there are no rules for sample size in qualitative inquiry". Sampling proceeds of a qualitative study should end when the information shared by participants has become repetitive (Lincoln and Guba, 1985). The researchers found that information provided by the last three participants (P10, P11 and P12) no longer added new information to the concepts of brand internalization. Therefore, the data collection process was then completed, with a total of 12 participants,

Table 5.1   Selected interview questions

---

1   How do you learn about your hotel brand?
2   How do you and your colleagues represent the hotel brand?
3   How confident are you in representing the hotel brand?
4   What affects your feelings/ experience towards the hotel brand?
5   Do your personalities fit the values of the hotel brand? Why?
6   How does your hotel ensure consistency between the brand promise and the
    actual service delivery?

---

when the data being collected reached saturation point (Norwood, 2000; Sandelowski, 1995).

In-depth interviews have been defined as repeated face-to-face encounters between the researcher and participant (Minichiello et al., 1990). This provides an opportunity for thorough investigation into each participant's perspective and experience, and an in-depth understanding of the personal context within which the research phenomenon is found (Creswell, 2003; Minichiello et al., 1990). Open-ended questions were used with a view to initiate discussion during interviews and to try to eliminate interview bias. Neuman (1997) emphasized the best way to realize the mindset of a respondent and what is indeed important to him/her can be revealed through open-ended comments. In order to acquire more details and achieve a complete explanation and clarification regarding the primary questions, probing questions were also put forward by the researchers (Minichiello et al., 1990). Table 5.1 lists the selected open-ended questions used for guiding each interview discussion.

The interview questions used in this study were framed after a panel discussion with several academic professionals in the hospitality field as well as hotel students who had working experience in hotels. The reason for arranging the panel discussion is to rule out and revise the misleading and inappropriate interview questions in order to ensure their validity.

Data Collection

Data collection took place in Hong Kong, with a total of 12 semi-structured in-depth interviews conducted with four males and eight females whose age ranged from 21 to 28. All interviewees were under 30; they are representative of employees in most of the Hong Kong international hotels. This is because the age of almost half of the guest contact functional-level hotel employees (50 percent) in Hong Kong are in the age range of 18–30 (Vocational Training Council, 2010). Lincoln and Guba

Table 5.2   Profile of interview participants

Participant	Hotel	Division	Gender	Age	Year(s) of employment
P1	A	Other	Male	28	5
P2	B	Sales and Marketing	Female	23	1
P3	C	Front Office	Female	22	1
P4	A	Other	Male	25	2
P5	D	Front Office	Male	26	4
P6	A	Other	Female	24	3
P7	E	Food and Beverage	Female	21	1
P8	F	Human Resources	Female	25	1
P9	G	Reservations	Female	26	3
P10	H	Human Resources	Male	25	1
P11	I	Marketing	Female	25	1.5
P12	J	Front Office	Female	27	1.5

(1985) asserted that this could enhance the credibility and trustworthiness of findings and interpretations for qualitative research. In addition, the interviewees attended the interviews on a voluntary basis and with the full endorsement of their organizations. The diverse perspectives of functional-level employees were able to be collected as the interviewees worked in different departments such as front office, reservations, food and beverage, sales and marketing, and others. The average length of employment was 2.1 years, with the shortest being 1 year and the longest being 5 years. Table 5.2 presents the profile of the interview participants.

At the beginning of each interview, the purpose of this study was briefly explained to the interviewee to give them a clear picture of the information being requested. Each interview was concluded by the researchers summarizing the main points of the interview content and giving a brief synopsis to each interviewee to ensure content validity. The duration of each interview was approximately 30 to 45 minutes and the interviews were recorded and notes taken. Interviewees' significant facial expressions and gestures were also recorded to register emphasis, implications or hidden meanings in their conversations (Minichiello et al., 1990). Since interviews were conducted in Chinese, the transcript was then translated verbatim into English.

Data coding and analysis of the audio recordings and notes were then carried out, from which the researchers were able to locate similar phrases, patterns, relationships, commonalities and disparities (Miles and Huberman, 1994). Clusters of key words, phrases and themes which revolved around important issues could be identified (Gursoy et al., 2008).

Frequently mentioned factors were then converted into statements to be included in the item pool. Three researchers participated to ensure objectivity and high credibility of the process and interpretation. Thorough discussions among the researchers were held to identify representative categorizations. Significant themes and initial scale items for each aspect were generated. These were also used to compare and contrast with previous hotel branding literature. The following section presents the findings and the discussion drawn from the collected qualitative data.

FINDINGS AND DISCUSSION

The use of content analysis in this study identified five key themes that coincide with Berry and Parasuraman's (1991) definition of brand internalization. The findings provided support for the five variables in the formation of brand internalization, which are: explaining the brand knowledge to employees; associating employees with the desired brand image; communicating the brand messages via various information channels; strengthening employees' brand awareness; and also rewarding employees' behavior, which supports brand delivery.

Explaining the Brand Knowledge

The consensus of opinion of the interviewees was that when brand knowledge was explained clearly to employees, it made a distinctive difference to their working behavior. In particular, they considered that job requirements should contain the brand information that hotels would expect them to understand and deliver to the customers. There is a very close connection between the brand and image in their daily work. Hence, accuracy and practicality of the espoused brand information were the top concern of hotel employees.

Job requirements
Most interviewees revealed that the hotel brand can be represented by their job performance. "I guess I present it through my daily work, from my daily rotations . . . So I'm representing the company through delivering the services that my company offers", as one interviewee (P1) explained. All interviewees understood that they play a role in representing the hotel brand as the job requires. In their understanding, carrying out what is stated by the hotel would be their way to walk the talk. However, it is not compulsory to follow some of the policy statements, "as long [as it] is stated out then an employee has to show this to the other customer. . ."

(P2). Five interviewees interpreted that they should carry out the organization's required work behaviors and actions; to them this represents "professionalism", even though sometimes they do not have the confidence to carry out what is required. By fulfilling their job requirements, they believe that brand promises are delivered and professionalism can be achieved. Employees should always follow the credo of the organization. P7 remarked, "When you are in uniform, people will see you as part of the hotel brand, so you must possess certain characteristics to fit the brand [in order] not to negatively affect people's perception of the luxurious hotel brand. . ."

An exception to this was when P6 mentioned that she did not understand clearly what her responsibility was in representing the hotel brand. She expressed her own knowledge on how the hotel should deliver brand messages to customers. This implies that either her job description did not clearly and thoroughly define employees' roles in portraying the brand, or that the communication of brand meaning failed to reach front-level employees. In addition, interviewees pointed out difficulties when carrying out their job requirements. When their jobs were overloaded with many tasks, employees had low energy, which negatively affected their attitude towards performing their job responsibilities. Hence, job requirements largely influenced brand internalization in terms of providing comprehensive and yet feasible instructions to guide hotel employees' service behavior.

Acquired brand knowledge
While many interviewees recognized that brand values and knowledge can be communicated by their working hotels, P2 raised her concern: "Sometimes I doubt if what I am doing is what the hotel really wants me to do". Her uncertainty revealed ineffective communications. P11, on the other hand, accused the hotel of offering exaggerated brand promises that it was not feasible to implement: "But then sometimes it [delivering what the hotel asks] is quite hard because there are so many things that a hotel brand asks you to do . . . I think as long as you try your best, that would be pretty good already". Along with several other interviewees, P2 suggested that acquiring more accurate, updated and practical brand knowledge would help her gain confidence in representing the hotel brand. Similarly, P3 affirmed that "if we are not updated, every colleague would have their own ways". The knowledge of the customers' needs and expectations as well as the employees' understanding of their responsibility to deliver the brand promise can ensure employees' consistency in work and can avoid misunderstandings and frustration. An example was provided by P1 that:

we have a lot of information from our hotel management. They bring you a lot [of] updates or any news happening during the monthly training or special trainings. . . . if anything comes new, they will send the email and you can read about it. . . . so this is something very important and it really makes a big difference for those people who are willing to go with the company ahead.

This implies that employees who acquire up-to-date brand knowledge can be more committed to the company.

Associating with the Brand Image

With acquired brand information, interviewees more or less associated received brand messages with their personal attributes. It seems that such an association could to some extent generate a stronger image towards the brand. A few interviewees who possessed a stronger brand image expressed a stronger intention to deliver the brand promise. The most frequently mentioned issues with which these participants connected brand knowledge were identified as Personality Fit, Cultural Impact, and Employees' Commitment.

Personality fit

All interviewees were able to reflect two or more of their personality characteristics on the company values. When personality fits were found, employees were more likely to feel a sense of belonging and greater sense of satisfaction towards their job: "this is what I like about the company. It goes with my character" (P10). Whilst many of the personality characteristics identified were deemed to fit in with the company's working environment, such as improving and challenging oneself or being creative and cheerful, others, such as discouraging scolding and shouting, were related to the brand culture value. For instance:

I am naturally a cheerful person . . . when I am interacting with my colleagues, my cheerfulness could encourage a more harmonious working atmosphere and strengthen [the spirit of] teamwork. . . (P5)

In this Hotel B, the brand does not embrace the bad norm of scolding or shouting at each other. I personally think I quite fit [with] this value because I don't like arguing. . . (P2)

Despite fitting certain characteristics with company values, P7 commented that fitting in with the brand could turn a person into a nicer and more caring person, even though it might not be in their nature. This suggested a personality misfit in nature but one that could temporarily transform one's character to fit what the brand stands for. The nature of the hotel industry requires service hotel employees to perform emotional labor. Whether or not the personality characteristics of a hotel employee fit with the company's values could determine whether the brand internalization process is positively or negatively implemented. If there is a fit between employees' characteristics and company values, this will encourage employees to follow brand internalization processes. Conversely, a misfit will hinder the process because those employees would need to mask their true feelings before continuing such a process. With a hint of disappointment, P3 noted as follows: "So yes, I do feel I fit the values [of the] brand but then sometimes, when you go into reality [at work], it (the heavy workload) sometimes can make you depressed." This illustrates that P3 feels her character fits well with the brand value but her true feeling was daunted by the heavy workload. Work stress can be an impediment to employees' work performances as well as to the fulfillment of the brand delivery requirement. The belief that P3 has of her personality matching the brand could fade away eventually if the heavy workload continues to distract her from picturing the desired brand image.

Cultural impact

When answering various interview questions, some participants frequently associated their answers with culture at both national and organizational levels. For national culture, P1 who has more than five years' hotel working experiences shared his view: "The brand is the same [as] the promises, [and] the values. It is more of the hotels that [are] different which can actually influence my impression of the brand . . . I would say probably because of the culture and the mix of the people."

Although this interviewee did not provide differences in detail among hotels under the same brand name that operate in different countries, it can be speculated that national culture will influence the differences in the interpretation of brand values and promises. Management style and employees' working manner to fulfill the brand promises are very likely to be affected by national culture. Hofstede's (2001) study explains this argument as national cultures were found to have considerable differences in values in different national subsidiaries. As an example given by P6, employees who are non-locals act quite differently from their Hong Kong local counterparts: "maybe [it is] the kind of culture, when they were raised with as when they were kids. . .". In general, people tend to share similar values/norms/behavior if growing up in the same nation; it is very likely that these shared values will be different from those from another nation. In this case, having different employees' cultural backgrounds encompassed in a hotel will affect the overall effectiveness of brand internalization.

The possible impact of organizational culture was found when a few interviewees acknowledged getting brand knowledge but saw that little action was taken accordingly. They argued that their feelings towards delivering the brand promises would be affected if the majority of other employees did not carry out the required actions. Since organizational culture is often defined as "a collective programming of the mind [that] distinguishes members of one organization from another" (Hofstede, 2001, p. 393), employees' shared attitude largely forms one of the aspects of organizational culture. In the context of hotel branding described by the interviewees, organizational culture refers to the phenomenon that a large group of employees refuse to perform required brand delivery. Consequently, other employees would be discouraged to take appropriate actions disregarding the extensive brand knowledge received. "So I think this is the real culture instead of writing down on paper or book and then nobody follows it", as P4 stated. Therefore, organizational culture affects the success of brand internalization according to interviewees' opinions.

Employees' commitment
Employees' commitment was remarked upon when referring to brand delivery. The right attitude and appropriate behavior were deemed important, although this was not always the case in reality. Employees could choose not to associate with the desired brand image or could even act against expectations if they did not care. The following statement illustrates the phenomenon: "Whether that employee really has the heart to perform his/her job or whether he/she just wants to earn money from the job . . . that brings quite a difference in delivering the service" (P11).

Therefore, employees' commitment would weaken brand internalization such that internalizing brand values would not be realized unless employees made a personal commitment. Only when employees recognized the importance of adopting brand internalization would they actively participate in the process.

Communicating the Brand

Hotels apply various media to communicate to their employees the importance of the brand promises, messages and values. Among the different sources referred to by the interviewees, the organizational information channel was frequently emphasized.

Organizational information channel
Organizational information channels transformed brand knowledge to various departments within an organization, and most interviewees were

able to list a number of ways of accessing brand knowledge. Knowledge was mostly gained through orientation, corporate and departmental training, daily briefings, booklets, notice boards, email, meetings, memos and the internet. Mass media was mentioned by participants a few times, which generally refers to news reports and advertisements.

The management in the hotel often make a big impact and can fully demonstrate what a brand stands for and what aspects of the brand need to be fulfilled. "We also hear from our big boss, Mr. X, about his values and his stories", commented P4. Hearing managers' real stories would fix their perceived brand values in employees' minds and transfer knowledge directly. Hotel guests' perception of a specific hotel brand could bring additional insight to employees' understanding of the brand messages they are delivering. For instance, P5 noted "even the guests themselves when you talk to them, they sometimes tell you a lot [of] information about the brand that you can learn from". It is not only managers and guests providing different views about the hotel brand who form information channels. Some interviewees thought that colleagues could also offer valuable information, especially those who had a longer working history in the hotel, as P8 revealed: "It is really from the contact I have with my colleagues or associates because some of them have worked in the hotel for quite a long time. So by seeing them and maybe talking to them, I guess more or less you will learn more about the brand."

Various interviewees reflected on their own working experiences as an information channel through which to gain brand knowledge. In particular, learning from mistakes helped them to become more aware of the brand values and promises, as illustrated in the following comments:

> I learned the brand by words but I think how I really learned about the brand is through my everyday work. It's like the incident that I'd mentioned [earlier], it's really when you make mistakes, when you listen to the guests' complaints, when you are doing . . . although this is like a role play, but you really carry out the action, then you really learn about the brand. (P3)

Through word-of-mouth from friends, colleagues, guests and mass media, employees could receive information regarding a hotel brand and learn more about the hotel brand from different perspectives. Once they acquired a comprehensive knowledge, employees could indirectly bridge their connections with the hotel's brand. Positive reviews and comments about the brand would increase employees' acceptance of what brand messages they are required to deliver. Additionally, it could boost employees' sense of pride, as one interviewee stated: "I am proud to work at Hotel A because of the positive reviews and comments from our guests and people who have heard about Hotel A" (P10).

Strengthening Brand Awareness

Brand internalization should be constantly reinforced to gain maximum benefit from its application. Interviewees believed their work and brand experiences would keep them learning about the brand. The physical environment could have an impact on employees' brand awareness, whilst management style could strengthen employees' willingness to accept brand internalization.

Brand and work experience

Employees' experiences with their hotel brand and their work could have an effect on their knowledge of the hotel brand, their intention to work for and their confidence in representing that hotel brand. Hotel brand experience referred to the familiarity employees have with the brand they are working for. The diverse information channels available, such as training, newsletters, brochures and so on, provide more opportunities for employees to familiarize themselves with the brand. Subsequently, practicing what has been learned from the information obtained could keep the brand alive: "If you work longer there, you know more about the brand and their operations. You become more efficient in solving problems and getting things done nicely" (P7).

Nevertheless, employees' working experiences can also have some negative impacts on brand internalization. Interviewees pointed out that their work values, behavior and style acquired from previous jobs were brought to their current jobs to a certain extent. This would affect their feelings towards the brand of the hotel where they were currently working. Moreover, senior staff were seen to behave more according to the written documents whilst junior staff did not seem to pay much attention to the brand values. This might be because the relatively longer length of service in the same position or job enabled senior staff to fully familiarize themselves with the desired brand promises as well as enabling them to practice them in their daily work: "the senior staff is promoted internally so they have a longer working history with the hotel . . . compared to the junior staff who has just graduated from school or just joined from another company, they may not really know the values of the brand" (P12).

Employees with different lengths of service in a hotel approached the brand internalization process at a different pace. The consistency of understanding the brand messages that are delivered via brand internalization could be compromised unless different brand internalization approaches are applied to the different senior and junior groups.

Physical environment

The physical environment, extracted from the interviewees' comments, indicates employees' uniform, hotel facilities and surrounding areas. The hotel's surroundings were also spotted by P11 as: "the building next to our hotel is having a construction project which would cause negative image of our hotel". The guests' image of the hotel also has a certain impact on employees' experience with the brand.

Hotel facilities such as hotel rooms and uniforms made employees feel good about the hotel brand, according to P9. Uniforms helped employees represent the brand but it did not make P8 and P5 feel proud of their hotels. In most of the cases, hotels' hardware supported employees in performing tasks and delivering services. The likability and usefulness of the hardware would elevate employees' vigor and exceed guests' expectations. Moreover, "the expanding number of hotels joining the group is a positive influence", as P4 stated. The nature of the physical environment may psychologically influence employees' perception of the hotel brand. Brand internalization is thus affected collaterally.

The work environment, on the other hand, did not greatly affect the interviewees' feelings towards the brand. Since P2 and P5 believed that sitting in the same office every day resulted in little interaction with their working environment, they paid little attention on it.

Management style

All 12 interviewees made comments regarding management style, which covered a wide range of aspects under management discipline. For instance, offering personal development opportunities reinforced employees' relationship with the hotel brand. The way management treated their employees immediately affected their relationship with employees. If social responsibility to the community were considered it would encourage employees to commit more: "Most voluntary charity work would be visiting the elderly or children or go out to teach children cooking or craft making. These would also make me feel [having] a stronger sense of commitment to the hotel and a closer relationship with the management" (P12).

Despite the variety of management aspects that were discovered, the three that stood out for the authors were communication style, empowerment and leadership style. To most interviewees, empowerment was the key to delivering the desired brand messages to hotel guests: "I think empowerment is quite helpful in delivering the services or the brand promises" (P5). They believed that when they were empowered, they could proactively deliver brand promises to guests, and achieve greater effectiveness. P3 noted, "in case they empower me and they do not challenge me, and I am supported to delight the guests, I would do more next time". Among these interviewees, some were empowered to create a variety of experiences that employees identified as best brand practice, such as: "It [empowerment] enhances our knowledge about the brand because we are able to do different things to gain understanding of certain things which may not have been possible if we were not empowered" (P11).

Managers who permit empowerment enable their employees to creatively deliver brand messages in their own way. When this situation occurs, brand internalization will become more dynamic, with employees' own interpretation embedded. Empowerment could enrich the power of brand internalization and allow employees to actually turn the espoused brand message into their own practice. However, not all of the employees will fully understand the required brand promise. Hence, empowerment failures happen when the empowered employees are not capable of handling what is being asked from them.

Internal communication channels were seen as important. Interviewees felt that they were being respected and their voices were taken seriously through different channels such as the bottom-up channel (e.g. suggestion box); the top-down channel (e.g. management questionnaire); and open communication. They felt connected with the management: "I deliver that message to my upper management and the management takes notes on that ... and they don't just leave it for later but they do really help ... So when they really do that, it strengthens me, my connections to the brand" (P1). Internal communication channels would not only strengthen the interviewees' connection to the brand, but also open doors for brand internalization to take place. The more closely employees are connected with their management, the more trust is developed and the more easily can brand messages be transferred into employees' minds.

Leaders with good leadership skills can recognize and appreciate employees who perform well, which can motivate employees to do better. Specifically, many interviewees pointed out the importance of building a harmonious and fun-filled working environment, in which there is a low hierarchy among the different ranks. P2 gave an example that "he did not really treat himself as someone up in the management level but treated everybody fairly and nicely and would greet you whoever you are". Leaders do not just leave the brand internalization process to their subordinates. They carry it out themselves and set an appropriate environment for their employees to see the value of doing so. Thus, leadership has an impact on the way the brand internalization process is conducted.

Rewarding Brand Delivery

Some interviewees emphasized the value of acknowledging employees' actions that support the brand promises. They considered the chance of being recognized as a motivation to further carrying out the encouraged actions. Additionally, a few interviewees preferred to participate in delivering brand promises only if they were satisfied with their colleagues and management who walk the talk.

Recognition

Recognition was repeated many times by the participants to be a positive reinforcement for delivering brand messages. Employees are motivated to repeat an action when they receive appreciation or recognition for it, as the following statement shows: "If you finish your task and the manager say 'good job', even if it's just a simple sentence you will feel good after what you have done. So next time I would do the same" (P9).

Staff and guests' satisfaction

Several interviewees observed that satisfaction with both their job and colleagues would affect their commitment to strengthen brand delivery. Overall job satisfaction would enable employees to trust their employers and subsequently would encourage employees to engage further. Likewise, when other colleagues carried out the brand promise, it would drive these interviewees to actively participate in it. Examples are as follows:

> If I like the company, I work happily and I would feel more committed to the company and I would try to live up to the brand. (P3)

> the same like me, [if] they also perform according to the values, it would make me to take the initiative to participate in that brand as well. (P7)

Hotel guests' satisfaction with service is also regarded as an influential factor affecting service delivery. Guests' positive responses motivated employees to deliver the brand promise proactively and effectively. P4 declared that "I am also happy when I see them smile. Therefore, I try my best to make them happy, to exceed their expectations".

Brand internalization becomes easier to adopt when employees are happy and committed to their jobs. However, satisfaction does not necessarily drive the success of brand internalization since employees can always fake their emotions when carrying out their duties.

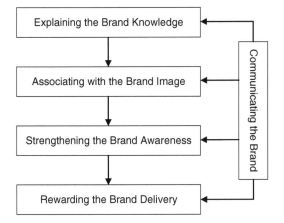

Figure 5.1   Hotel brand internalization process

Hotel Brand Internalization Processes

The findings from this study offer an insight into brand internalization from the hotel employees' perspective. By analyzing, consolidating and integrating the qualitative evidence from the interviews, it is possible to create a clear concept of hotel brand internalization and its components. Figure 5.1 illustrates the process of hotel brand internalization, which comprises all essential variables that have been extracted from the findings.

The entire process starts by providing a thorough explanation of the accurate and up-to-date brand knowledge to employees by branded hotels. Employees are likely to associate the acquired brand knowledge with their own beliefs, personality characteristics, as well as the norms adopted within an organization to picture an image of the brand. Hence, hotels can encourage employees to positively associate their understanding of the brand with the desired brand image. Furthermore, hotels attempted to influence employees in terms of internalizing the brand image by utilizing physical hardware and software to constantly remind employees of the hotel brand. Subsequently, brand awareness was strengthened by recognizing and acknowledging employees' brand delivery performance. The power of rewarding brand delivery would not only affirm employees' commitment but also testify to the performance of the brand internalization process. The influences of the variable communicating the brand co-exist with all the other variables. Different channels are required to deliver brand information, to reinforce the brand image, to create brand awareness, and to reward brand delivery. This stage penetrates the whole process and helps hotel brand internalization to take place.

The above model is the first attempt to describe the hotel brand internalization process, and contributes theoretically to the study of hotel internal branding. To practically utilize the concepts identified, the qualitative data collected were used to construct a solid measurement scale. Table 5.3 displays the developed measurement items of the five core variables.

This newly generated list of items can further enrich the literature on brand internalization. The suggestion of educating employees in caring for and nurturing the brand (Berry and Parasuraman, 1991) is not found in the item list. It can be argued that hotel employees in Hong Kong have less training in particular in caring for and nurturing the brand. In recent years, branded hotels have integrated the brand internalization process with other company initiatives, such as corporate social responsibility; hotel management may have spread the brand caring messages via actual organizational practices, consistent communications, and experienced by employees in many tangible ways (Blomqvist and Posner, 2004). Employees who are aware of these initiatives will have a positive company-related association, and will have a greater commitment to the success of the hotel (Sen et al., 2006). Yet they may not realize that the true value of nurturing the brand underlies their actions. By allowing the message to penetrate everyday practice will bolster trust in the company more effectively. Despite little factual evidence in pursuing employees' care for and nurture of the brand, the findings of this study offer valuable insights into what brand internalization becomes and how it can function in the hotel industry.

The study results were different from Bai et al.'s (2006) study, which generated key factors that influence the hotel brand internalization process; it also initiated the process that hotel brand internalization should follow. Furthermore, a few components in their proposed service brand internalization concept, such as the role of leadership, employee involvement, internal communication and coherence of culture, were not found in our current study. The physical environment was mentioned several times by the interviewees but was only briefly discussed in Bai et al.'s (2006) study. This can be attributed to the fact that the study is focused on hotels only and more fundamental groundwork was sought in this current research. Some significant viewpoints were specifically disclosed in this study; for example, employees' personality fit, employees' working experience and guests' satisfaction were all found to have an impact on the internalization of brand image. Our study did not examine the service brand as a whole; it attempted to explore hotel brand internalization to focus more comprehensively on how brand internalization proceeds from hotel employees' perspective.

Table 5.3   Brand internalization measurement items (developed by the authors)

Measurement Items

Explaining the brand knowledge
1. This hotel explains brand information in the job description.
2. This hotel explains my role in representing the hotel brand.
3. This hotel provides accurate brand information for me to understand.
4. This hotel provides up-to-date brand information for me to understand.
5. This hotel provides practical brand information for me to deliver to guests.
6. This hotel sets out reasonable job tasks for me to perform the brand message.
7. I understand that my daily job performance represents the hotel brand.
8. I understand that brand promises are delivered by fulfilling my job requirement.

Associating with the brand image
1. My personality characteristics fit in with the hotel brand values.
2. My personality characteristics change when associating with the brand image.
3. Employees with different national backgrounds interpret brand promises differently.
4. Other employees' reaction towards delivering brand promises will have an influence on me.
5. Employees act as if they are following specific rules though not written down in the hotel brand information.
6. I recognize the importance of understanding the brand knowledge.
7. I am willing to carry out the brand promises.
8. I am willing to associate brand values with my job.

Communicating the brand
1. This hotel provides job orientation for me to obtain brand knowledge.
2. This hotel provides a training program for me to obtain brand knowledge.
3. This hotel provides a daily briefing for me to obtain brand knowledge
4. This hotel holds meetings for me to obtain brand knowledge.
5. This hotel provides brand knowledge to me through email.
6. This hotel provides brand knowledge to me through memos and notice boards.
7. This hotel provides brand knowledge to me through the hotel's website.
8. This hotel provides brand knowledge to me via public mass media.
9. I can obtain brand knowledge from hotel managers.
10. I can obtain brand knowledge from my colleagues.
11. I can obtain brand knowledge from hotel guests.
12. I can obtain brand knowledge by learning from mistakes at work.

Table 5.3   (continued)

Measurement Items

Strengthening the brand awareness
1. I feel that my daily work experience helps me understand the hotel brand better.
2. I feel that I am more familiar with the brand after working there longer.
3. I feel that my previous work experience has enhanced my understanding of the current hotel brand.
4. I feel that I have a better understanding of the brand values than junior employees in this hotel.
5. I feel that my uniform helps me represent the hotel brand better.
6. I feel that the hotel's hardware benefits me in associating more with the hotel brand.
7. I feel that the personal development opportunity provided by the hotel reinforces my relationship with the hotel brand.
8. I feel that the hotel's social responsibility increases my understanding of the hotel brand.
9. I feel that the hotel's management style helps me understand more about the hotel brand.
10. I feel that empowerment helps me deliver the brand promises.
11. The leaders are role models reminding me what the hotel brand stands for.
12. This hotel offers open communication channels to receive employees' feedback about the hotel brand values.

Rewarding the brand delivery
1. I feel that my work performance is recognized by the manager.
2. I feel that I am motivated to deliver the brand message when it is appreciated by the manager.
3. I feel a strong commitment to deliver brand promises since I am satisfied with my job.
4. I feel that I can actively participate in brand delivery when observing other colleagues doing the same thing.
5. I feel that I am motivated to deliver the brand message when hotel guests are satisfied with my services.

CONCLUSIONS AND RECOMMENDATIONS

The newly developed hotel brand internalization conceptual model and the measurement scale provide references to hotel managers to identify practical elements that influence their employees' perception of brand internalization. When hotel managers enhance their capabilities in these five dimensions, employees become devoted to brand internalization spontaneously, eventually making brand delivery effortless. However, our study has some limitations. The sample conducted in this exploratory study was limited to international branded hotels located in Hong Kong only. It is suggested that future research should make use of the conceptual model established to conduct a larger scale study and to empirically test the model by adopting a quantitative approach to confirm the hotel brand internalization process. Besides, the items generated in the measurement scale have to be proven to be valid and reliable in the hotel context. All the key factors identified in this study should be further reconfirmed to have an influence on hotel employees' perception of brand internalization.

Future studies should consider expanding the findings of this study. For example, the incorporation of brand knowledge, values, promises and messages into the job requirement would ensure that hotel employees gradually come to fully understand the meaning and requirements of the brand. The following research questions could be generated: what kind of knowledge/value/message would contribute to employees' understanding of the brand? Are there any significant differences between those employees who had brand knowledge incorporated in their job requirement and those who didn't? How often would it be deemed appropriate for employees to acquire an accurate and up-to-date brand strategy in order to avoid confusion?

Hotel employees' personality is seen as an important factor in the present study outcomes. It would be interesting to find out if a relationship exists between personality and brand internalization. The assumption is that acknowledging and celebrating employees' various personality characteristics which fit with the brand would motivate employees' willingness to adopt brand internalization. Empirical tests could be useful to examine whether this assumption is true.

Culture at both national and organizational levels can be connected to hotel branding. It would be difficult to separate brand values from culture values or to detach brand experience from the cultural practice in a hotel. The challenge also lies in the inconsistency derived from the cultural diversity of employees in their interpretation of brand promise and message. National and organizational cultures may hinder employees' desire to deliver brand promise. Hence, maintaining congruence between brand values, employees' values and organizations' espoused values could establish a strong brand which is genuinely "lived" by employees (Bai et al., 2006). In sum, would culture have a positive or negative influence on brand internalization? What role does culture play in internalizing brand knowledge/value into employees' mindset?

Flexible communication channels between managers and employees were highly recommended by the participants as a means of enhancing their awareness of the brand meaning and of stimulating them in building up the hotel's brand. Future studies could investigate means of communication in some of the best hotel groups or other organizations for designating best practices of brand communications. Furthermore, the use of technology is proven to improve hotel management and communications: how would technology ease the communication channel for effective brand internalization?

This study has also revealed the significance of leaders' role as they can initiate and facilitate changes to enable brand-supportive behavior (Bai et al., 2006). Leaders' attitude and behavior towards brand internalization have an exemplary role which correspondingly affects the attitude and behavior of their subordinates. Thus, it is in the best interest of hotels to explore whether senior leadership participation and involvement would be consistent and effective throughout the five stages of the brand internalization process proposed in the model of this study. Last but not least, empowerment, training and recognition and reward factors have been suggested to motivate employees to be committed to their work along with actions supporting the desired brand. However, to what extent should empowerment engage in the brand internalization process? In addition, how should recognition and reward be addressed to employees so as to make a difference to their willingness to adopt brand internalization? Finally, based on the study, the implications for managers lead to suggest useful research topics to investigate the field of brand internalization to offer a profound theoretical foundation and useful practical solutions.

REFERENCES

American Marketing Association (2011). *Dictionary*. Accessed 7 March 2012 at http://www.marketingpower.com/_layouts/Dictionary.aspx?dLetter=B.

Ap, J. and Crompton, J. (1998). Developing and testing a tourism impact scale. *Journal of Travel Research*, **37**(2), 120–30.

Bai, C., Chen, Y. and Qiu, W. (2006). Service brand internalization: A concept model and its marketing implications. *Proceedings of the 2006 International Conference on Service Systems and Service Management* (pp. 750–57). Troyes.

Balmer, J.M.T. and Wilkinson, A. (1991). Building societies: Change, strategy and corporate identity. *Journal of General Management*, **17**(2), 20–33.

Bergstrom, A., Blumenthal, D. and Crothers, S. (2002). Why internal branding matters: The case of Saab. *Corporate Reputation Review*, **5**(2/3), 133–42.

Berry, L.L. (2000). Cultivating service brand equity. *Journal of the Academy of Marketing Science*, **28**(1), 128–37.

Berry, L.L. and Lampo, S.S. (2004). Branding labour-intensive services. *Business Strategy Review*, **15**(1), 18–25.

Berry, L.L. and Parasuraman, A. (1991). *Marketing services: Competing through quality*. New York: Free Press.

Blomqvist, K.H. and Posner, S. (2004). Three strategies for integrating CSR with brand marketing. *Market Leader*, Summer, pp. 33–6.

Burmann, C. and Zeplin, S. (2005). Building brand commitment: A behavioural approach to internal brand management. *The Journal of Brand Management*, **12**(4), 279–300.

Cai, L.A. and Hobson, J. (2004). Making hotel brands work in a competitive environment. *Journal of Vacation Marketing*, **10**(3), 197–208.

Cheung, C., Song, H. and Kong, H. (2014). How to influence hospitality employee perceptions on hotel brand performance? *International Journal of Contemporary Hospitality Management*, **26**(8), 1162–78.

Creswell, J.W. (2003). *Research design: Qualitative, quantitative, and mixed methods approaches* (2nd edn). Thousand Oaks, CA: Sage Publications.

De Chernatony, L. and Cottam, S. (2006). Internal brand factors driving successful financial services brands. *European Journal of Marketing*, **40**(5/6), 611–33.

De Chernatony, L. and Harris, F. (2000). Developing corporate brands through considering internal and external stakeholders. *Corporate Reputation Review*, **3**(3), 268–74.

Goldstein, S.M., Johnston, R., Duffy, J. and Rao, J. (2002). The service concept: The missing link in service design research? *Journal of Operations Management*, **20**(2), 121–34.

Gotsi, M. and Wilson, A. (2001). Corporate reputation management: "Living the brand". *Management Decision*, **39**(2), 99–104.

Gursoy, D., Maier, T.A. and Chi, C.G. (2008). Generational differences: An examination of work values and generational gaps in the hospitality workforce. *International Journal of Hospitality Management*, **27**(3), 458–88.

Harquail, C.V. (2006). Employees as animate artifacts: Employee branding by "wearing the brand". In A. Rafaeli and M.G. Pratt (eds), *Artifacts and Organization: Beyond Mere Symbolism* (pp.161–80). Mahwah, NJ: Lawrence Erlbaum Associates.

Harquail, C.V. (2007). *Employee branding: Enterprising selves in the service of the brand.* Accessed 7 March 2012 at http://authenticorganizations.com/wp-content/uploads/2008/03/employee-branding-online.pdf.

Harris, F. and De Chernatony, L. (2001). Corporate branding and corporate brand performance. *European Journal of Marketing*, **35**(3/4), 441–57.

Harris, P. (2007). We the people: The importance of employees in the process of building customer experience. *Journal of Brand Management*, **15**(2), 102–14.

Henkel, S., Tomczak, T., Heitmann, M. and Herrmann, A. (2007). Managing brand consistent employee behaviour: Relevance and managerial control of behavioural branding. *Journal of Product & Brand Management*, **16**(5), 310–20.

Hofstede, G. (2001). *Culture's consequences: Comparing values, behaviours, institutions, and organizations across nations* (2nd edn). Thousand Oaks, CA: Sage Publications.

Ind, N. (2007). *Living the brand: How to transform every member of your organization into a brand champion* (3rd edn). London: Kogan Page.

King, C. (2010). "One size doesn't fit all": Tourism and hospitality employees' response to internal brand management. *International Journal of Contemporary Hospitality Management*, **22**(4), 517–34.

King, C. and Grace, D. (2008). Internal branding: Exploring the employee's perspective. *Journal of Brand Management*, **15**(5), 358–72.

Leong, C.C. (2007). Managing change of hotel brand name: Managerial roles and employees' concerns. *Asia Pacific Journal of Tourism Research*, **12**(1), 19–20.

Lincoln, Y. and Guba, E. (1985). *Naturalistic enquiry.* London: Sage Publications.

Little, M.M. and Dean, A.M. (2006). Links between service climate, employee commitment and employees' service quality capability. *Managing Service Quality*, **16**(5), 460–76.

McCarthy, E. Jerome (1960). *Basic marketing: A managerial approach.* Homewood, IL: Richard D. Irwin.

Miles, M.B. and Huberman, A.M. (1994). *Qualitative data analysis: An expanded sourcebook* (2nd edn). Thousand Oaks, CA: Sage Publications.

Miles, S.J. and Mangold, W.G. (2004). A conceptualization of the employee branding process. *Journal of Relationship Marketing*, **3**(2/3), 65–87.

Miles, S.J. and Mangold, W.G. (2005). Positioning Southwest Airlines through employee branding. *Business Horizons*, **48**(6), 535–45.

Miles, S.J. and Mangold, W.G. (2007). The employee brand: Is yours an all-star? *Business Horizon*, **50**(6), 423–33.
Minichiello, V., Aroni, R., Timewell, E. and Alexander, L. (1990). *In-depth interviewing: Researching people*. Melbourne: Longman Cheshire.
Mitchell, C. (2002). Selling the brand inside. *Harvard Business Review*, **80**(1), 99–105.
Morhart, F., Herzog, W. and Tomczak, T. (2007). The impact of brand-specific transactional and transformational leadership on front-line employees' brand-building behavior. *Proceedings of the 2007 AMA Educators' Conference on Enhancing Knowledge Development in Marketing* (pp.161–2). Chicago, IL: American Marketing Association.
Neuman, W.L. (1997). *Social research methods, qualitative and quantitative approaches* (3rd edn). Boston, MA: Allyn and Bacon.
Norwood, D.L. (2000). *Research strategies for advanced practice nurses*. Upper Saddle River, NJ: Prentice Hall.
Patton, M.Q. (1990). *Qualitative evaluation and research methods*. Thousand Oaks, CA: Sage Publications.
Punjaisri, K. and Wilson, A. (2007). The role of internal branding in the delivery of employee brand promise. *Journal of Brand Management*, **15**(1), 57–70.
Punjaisri, K., Evanschitzky, H. and Wilson, A. (2009). Internal branding: An enabler of employees' brand-supporting behaviours. *Journal of Service Management*, **20**(2), 209–26.
Sandelowski, M. (1995). Sample size in qualitative research. *Research in Nursing and Health*, **18**(2), 179–83.
Schneider, B. and Bowen, D. (1985). Employee and customer perceptions of service in banks: Replication and extension. *Journal of Applied Psychology*, **70**(3), 423–33.
Sen, S., Bhattacharya, C.B. and Korschun, D. (2006). The role of corporate social responsibility in strengthening multiple stakeholder relationships: A field experiment. *Journal of the Academy of Marketing Science*, **34**(2), 158–66.
Steinmetz, A. (2004). Internal branding blueprint. *B to B*, **89**(10), 9.
Tsang, N.K.F., Lee, L.Y.S. and Li, F.X.H. (2011). An examination of the relationship between employee perception and hotel brand equity. *Journal of Travel & Tourism Marketing*, **28**(5), 481–97.
Vallaster, C. and De Chernatony, L. (2005). Internationalization of services brands: The role of leadership during the internal brand building process. *Journal of Marketing Management*, **21**(1), 181–203.
Vocational Training Council (2010). *2009 Manpower Survey Report: Hotel Industry.* Hong Kong SAR, China: Vocational Training Council.
Zucker, R. (2002). More than a name change – Internal branding at Pearl. *Strategic Communication Management*, **6**(4), 24–7.

6. Leadership in hospitality organizations: achieving competitive advantage
Ronald J. Burke

Leadership is obviously one important element in the creation of a service quality culture. Considerable research on the influence of various leadership concepts and approaches has been undertaken. Several studies have considered the role that leadership plays in the delivery of high quality service and a variety of other important work and organizational outcomes in the hospitality and tourism industry. Connell (2001) showed that effective leadership increased the skills of front-line employees. Simons and Robertson (2003) concluded that managers who were perceived to be fairer with others were associated with more favorable organizational outcomes. Finally, Tracey and Hinkin (1994) highlight the association of higher levels of leader transformational leadership and valued organizational outcomes. This chapter considers two approaches to leadership, servant leadership and empowering leadership, in the hospitality and tourism sector. This literature will be briefly reviewed as research evidence on the benefits of both leadership approaches in a variety of industrial sectors that has been published, and the results of studies of both approaches that have been carried out in hospitality and tourism organizations in Turkey will be presented. Finally, implications of this work for practice in hospitality organizations will be offered.

Interestingly, leadership and human resource management policies and practices may even play a larger role in the performance of hospitality organizations given both the negative images and the negative realities of working in this sector such as low pay, emotional labor, work–family conflicts, routine jobs, long work hours, uncaring supervision, unpleasant working conditions, limited career advancement, and high levels of staff turnover (Ayupp and Chung, 2010; Baum, 2007; Kusluvan et al., 2010). In addition, the industry is facing challenges in adopting the latest technologies, dealing with a more diverse workforce whose older members have different values, catering for more culturally and ethnically diverse customers, dealing with firms becoming larger and increasingly internationalized, and global economic changes. Recent economic factors have posed challenges for Greece and Italy; social unrest has limited tourism to Egypt.

This is unfortunate since front-line service workers play a key role in the delivery of high quality service. Service is basically an interpersonal transaction between a service provider and a service consumer. These employees have frequent contact with guests and represent the organization to guests. The quality and tenor of these interactions are influenced by the attitudes, skills, knowledge levels and behaviors of front-line service providers and these reflect, in turn, the expectations and behaviors of supervisors and senior managers, the organizational culture and climate for service, and human resource management practices and strategies of the organization.

There is considerable writing (see Kusluvan et al., 2010; Kusluvan, 2003, for a review) to support evidence that ways front-line workers are managed and led contributes to organizational performance and success. The management and motivation of front-line service workers are significant factors in hotels' effectiveness and success (Hoque, 1999; Kusluvan, 2003; Kusluvan et al., 2010).

LEADERSHIP RESEARCH IN HOSPITALITY ORGANIZATIONS

Most leadership research in general has considered transformational and transactional leadership styles; this is also the case in leadership research in the hospitality and tourism sector (Tracey and Hinkin, 1994). Transformational leadership (Bass, 1985; 1998) consists of four factors: *idealized influence* – followers see leaders as role models having high ethical standards and having a vision for their organization or unit; *individual consideration* – leader listens to staff, serves as a mentor and coach, engages with staff as unique individuals, delegates to staff to develop them; *inspirational motivators* – inspires staff by having high performance expectations for them, creates team excitement and enthusiasm; *intellectual stimulation* – encourages staff to be creative, to try new ways of doing things, encourages staff participation in problem solving.

Transactional leadership contains three elements: *contingent reward* – leader offers recognition and rewards for achieving performance goals, with no recognition or rewards for falling short; *active management by exception* – leader monitors ongoing performance and corrects mistakes as they occur; *passive management by exception or laissez-faire leadership* – leader intervenes after mistakes have occurred.

Leaders can exhibit both transformational and transactional behaviors and styles. There is considerable support for the positive effects of transformational leadership with desired employee and organizational outcomes; use of transactional behaviors or styles has more often been associated with less favorable employee behaviors and organizational outcomes. In addition, these results have been found in different industries and in various countries, suggesting cross-organizational industry and cross-national boundary effects (Bass, 1998).

Here is a sample of research findings involving transformational and transactional leadership in the hospitality and tourism sector. Erkutlu (2008) examined, in a sample of 60 managers and 662 non-managers from boutique hotels in Turkey, the relationship of transformational and transactional leadership styles and both job satisfaction and organizational commitment. Transformational leadership behaviors were associated with higher levels of both job satisfaction and organizational commitment. Laissez-faire leadership behavior was associated with lower levels of job satisfaction; management by exception was associated with less satisfaction with supervision and organizational commitment. Finally, use of contingent reward behaviors was associated with less satisfaction with supervision.

Gill et al. (2010), in a study of hospitality workers in India and Canada (n = 204), found that employees' perceptions of managers' levels of transformational leadership were associated with greater employee desire for empowerment, *and* using their initiative and judgment.

Clarke et al. (2009), using data from 236 General Managers and 561 customer contact employees from 279 different mid-level US hotels, studied the relationship of three leadership styles – Directive, Participative and Empowering – with role clarity (these were measured using items from transformational and transactional leadership), having shared values, job satisfaction, and employee commitment to service quality. In addition they considered a possible relationship of perceptions of commitment to service quality as a predictor of choice of leadership style. Level of perceived management commitment to service quality emerged as a predictor of leadership style. Higher levels of perceived management commitment to service quality were associated with less use of directive leadership but greater use of both participative and empowering leadership styles. Empowering leadership style was related to greater shared values and then to higher levels of both job satisfaction and employee commitment to quality service. Participative leadership was also related to greater shared values and to both job satisfaction and employee commitment to service quality. Directive leadership was found to have no effects on other study variables.

Zopiatis and Constanti (2010) studied the relationship of transformational, transactional and laissez-faire leadership and burnout (emotional exhaustion, depersonalization, lack of personal accomplishment) in a sample of 131 managers in the hospitality sector in Cyprus. Higher levels of transformational leadership were associated with higher levels of personal accomplishment and lower levels of both emotional exhaustion and depersonalization. Higher levels of transactional leadership were associated with greater emotional exhaustion and depersonalization, while higher levels of laissez-faire leadership behaviors were associated with greater emotional exhaustion and depersonalization.

Gill et al. (2006), in a sample of 137 supervisory and non-supervisory customer contact service employees, considered the relationship of transformational leadership and both job stress and burnout. Respondents perceiving higher levels of transformational leadership also indicated lower levels of both job stress and burnout.

The benefits of transformational leadership in hospitality organizations and service settings have also been documented by Liaw et al. (2010), Chuang et al. (2012) and Liao and Chuang (2007). Research evidence suggests that executives in the sector believe that transformational leadership is more likely to yield valued outcomes than transactional leadership (Cichy and Schmidgall, 1996; Greger and Peterson, 2000) though Bond (1998) argued that both are needed.

But transformational and transactional leadership may not be an either-or proposition. Dai et al. (2013) demonstrated the benefits of transformational and transactional leadership among 358 employees of tourist hotels in Taipei China and concluded that both were important. They suggest that managers can use both leadership styles interchangeably. Their findings may reflect the cultural setting in which their research was undertaken, however.

In this chapter we consider the potential benefits of two less researched leadership styles, servant leadership and empowering leadership, likely to be positively related and included under transformational leadership behaviors.

SERVANT LEADERSHIP

Greenleaf (1977) introduced the concept of servant leadership in his essay *The Servant as Leader*, published in 1970. Servant leadership, according to Greenleaf, is "a philosophy and set of practices that enriches the lives of individuals, builds better organizations and a more caring world.... It begins with the natural feeling that one wants to serve, to serve first. Then conscious choice brings one to aspire to lead." In Greenleaf's view, servant leaders place the needs of employees before their own and help them develop and reach their maximum potential and achieve optimal organizational and career success. Therefore, servant leadership is different from traditional leadership; servant leaders "want their employees to improve for their own good, and view the development of followers as an end, in and of itself, not merely a means to reach the leader's or organization's goals" (Ehrhart, 2004, p. 69).

Servant leadership emerged as a potentially important leadership concept in the late 1990s and early 2000s (Greenleaf, 1977; George, 2003; Boyatzis and McKee, 2005). It emerged as a response to the dysfunctional, greedy and self-serving and failing leadership exhibited during this time. Servant leadership focuses on serving the needs of employees and larger communities inside and outside an organization (Hunter, 2004; Badaracco, 2002; Badaracco and Ellsworth, 1993). And unlike more traditional leadership approaches, servant leadership can extend outside the organization to wider communities and society at large.

Servant leaders encourage, motivate, inspire and enable their employees to achieve service excellence (Fletcher, 1999; Berry et al., 1994; Church, 1995; Hallowell et al., 1996). They teach employees the right ways to provide better service and guide them by their own behavior. Thus, employees receiving servant leadership from their manager/supervisor provide better service to customers.

SERVANT LEADERSHIP AND SERVICE QUALITY

Berry et al. (1994) suggested that delivering excellent service requires a special form of leadership called "servant leadership". Because servant leaders believe in their employees, they coach, teach, inspire and listen to them. Thus, servant leaders show employees suitable ways to provide excellent service. Berry et al. (1994) interviewed staff of a medical center and reported the importance of servant leadership in service quality. They observed that servant leadership that offered direction, inspiration and support, was associated with higher levels of service.

Wu et al. (2013), using 304 manager–employee pairs, examined servant leadership and hotel employees' "servant behavior" represented by customer-related organizational citizenship behaviors. Data were collected in hotels in China. Servant leadership positively influenced employees' customer-oriented organizational citizenship behaviors.

A SERVANT LEADERSHIP STUDY

This research examines the relationship of servant leadership and the provision of high quality service by employees to clients in the tourism and hospitality sector (Koyuncu et al., 2014). The general hypothesis underlying this research was that hotel employees perceiving higher levels of servant leadership being provided by their supervisors/managers would rate the quality of service being provided to clients at a higher level. Data were collected from men and women working in 4- and 5-star hotels in Nevsehir, Turkey using anonymously completed questionnaires between April and July 2012. Hotel managers were contacted and asked for help in the distribution and administration of the questionnaires. A total of 600 questionnaires were delivered to 14 hotel managers who agreed to take part. A total of 221 questionnaires were received, a response rate of 37 percent. All held front-line service jobs in these properties.

Slightly over half of the respondents were male (60 percent), most were 27 years of age or younger (56 percent), most had 5 years or less of organizational tenure (74 percent), most had a high school education (53 percent), most worked in the food and beverage department (36 percent), and respondents were equally divided into 4- and 5-star hotels (53 percent and 47 percent, respectively). There was a slightly higher percentage of males in Front Office and Food and Beverage departments and a slightly lower percentage of males in Accounting and Housekeeping, and a slightly lower percentage of males working in 5-star hotels than in the sample as a whole.

A number of measures were included: six personal and work situation characteristics were assessed by single items. These were: gender, age, level of education, organizational tenure, department, and whether respondents worked in a 4- or 5-star hotel.

Servant leadership was measured by a 28-item scale developed by Liden et al. (2008). This scale had seven dimensions: Conceptual skills; Empowering; Helping subordinates grow and succeed; Putting subordinates first; Behaving ethically; Emotional healing; and Creating value for the community. Each scale had four items. In addition, a four-item measure of Role modeling was created specifically for this study; role modeling being an additional way of guiding employees. A composite measure based on the eight dimensions had a reliability of .91. Scores on the eight dimensions were all positively and significantly inter-correlated.

Perceptions of the quality of service provided by the hotel to clients was measured by a 22-item instrument, SERVQUAL, developed by Parasuraman et al. (1998). This measure had five dimensions: Tangibles (physical facilities, equipment, appearance of staff); Reliability (provide promised service, dependable and accountable); Responsiveness (willingness to help clients and providing prompt service); Assurance (knowledgeable and courteous staff able to inspire trust and confidence);

and Empathy (individual and caring attention to clients). The total SERVQUAL scale contained 22 items.

Let us now consider some of our findings. First, employees assessed levels of servant leadership provided to them by their supervisors/managers as fairly high. The modal response on a five-point scale was 4 (Agree), with the mean response being 3.5, s.d. = .70. Employees also rated the quality of service provided to clients in their hotels as also fairly high, mean ratings being 3.9, s.d. = .62 (4 = Agree). Second, considering personal demographic and work situation characteristics relationships with servant leadership dimensions and their composite measure, Gender, Age and Level of education had no relationship with these. Longer tenured respondents rated levels of servant leadership lower on Conceptual skills, Empowering, Helping employees grow and develop, Putting employees first, and Role modeling, as well as on the composite score. In addition respondents working in 5-star hotels rated servant leadership lower on Emotional healing, Creating value for the community, Conceptual skills, Empowering, Helping employees grow and develop, Putting employees first, Behaving ethically, Role modeling, and on the composite measure. Third, considering relationships with perceptions of SERVQUAL, level of education and star rating had no relationship with these perceptions. Older respondents rated level of Empathy lower ($r = -.16$; longer tenured employees also rated level of empathy lower, as well as having lower ratings on the composite measure of SERVQUAL; and males rated both Reliability and Responsiveness lower than females did. Finally, levels of servant leadership were found to be associated with some dimensions of service quality (e.g., Tangibles, Reliability, Assurance) and with the composite SERVQUAL measure. Each dimension of servant leadership was significantly and positively correlated with each dimension of SERVQUAL, and the total scores of the two composites were correlated .61, $p < .001$, $n = 212$). Respondents reporting receiving higher levels of servant leadership from their supervisors/managers indicated they provided higher levels of service quality to their customers. Thus supervisors/managers interested in improving the quality of service provided to customers should consider the merits of servant leadership in motivating and engaging employees on the provision of higher quality service.

Several practical implications follow from these findings. First, organizations could select individuals exhibiting higher levels of servant leadership potential using indications that these individuals are interested in developing long-term relationships with potential subordinates and co-workers and in helping others become more skilled in doing their jobs. In addition, selection can be augmented by servant leadership training (Fulmer and Conger, 2004). Supervisors/managers could also be coached in servant leadership values and skills to help them develop their staff and support their goals to help them fill and satisfy their unique needs (Raelin, 2003). Finally, workplace cultural values supportive of both servant leadership and service quality can be identified, modeled by senior level executives, supported and rewarded. Since the majority of our respondents were relatively young, hospitality organizations that provide higher levels of servant leadership are more likely to have positive effects on absenteeism and turnover by providing a fulfilling work experience.

ELEMENTS OF AN EMPOWERING WORKPLACE

Bowen and Lawler (1992) offered four factors: sharing of information with employees about the organization's performance; rewarding employees based on their performance and their performance improvements; giving employees the power to make or challenge decisions; and providing them with the knowledge and skills so employees can contribute to organizational performance. Seibert et al. (2011) developed a model based on meta-analysis that included antecedents and consequences of psychological and team empowerment. Four contextual factors were associated with higher levels of psychological empowerment: high performance management characteristics; social-political support; leadership behaviors; and job/work characteristics. Individual characteristics (for example, self-confidence, self-efficacy) also were related to levels of psychological empowerment. Psychological empowerment, in turn, was positively associated with job satisfaction, organizational commitment, and job and contextual performance. These findings existed at both individual and team levels of analysis.

EMPOWERING SUPERVISORS, PSYCHOLOGICAL EMPOWERMENT AND PERFORMANCE BENEFITS

We undertook two studies of potential benefits of empowering supervisors in hospitality organizations. Herrenkohl et al. (1999, p. 375) define empowerment as "a set of dimensions that characterize an environment's interaction with persons in it so as to encourage their taking initiative to improve processes and to take action". Thus empowerment exists at two levels (Spreitzer, 1997): macro – the organizational context that enhances levels of employee empowerment (for example, structure, policies, approach to decision making, centralized versus decentralized control) and micro – employees' feelings of empowerment, being encouraged to take risks, supported in showing initiative, having information about organizational priorities. Individuals differ, so some employees are more likely to embrace empowerment than others (for example, they are more educated, more committed to their profession, at higher organizational levels, and have more self-efficacy).

Not surprisingly then, measures of empowerment have addressed both organizational and individual levels. Matthews et al. (2003) created and validated a measure of organizational empowerment that included three dimensions: control of workplace decisions – level of employee input and involvement in decisions and policy making; dynamic structural framework – organizational guidelines indicating potential levels of employee input to decision making and control of their workplace; and fluidity in information sharing – employees are provided with all information on company objectives, rewards, and clients/customers. Arnold et al. (2000) created a measure of leader empowerment behaviors that included five dimensions: Leading by example; Informing employees; Coaching employees; Showing concern for the welfare of employees and interacting with them; and using Participative decision making. Spreitzer (1996, 1995) created and validated a measure of personal or psychological empowerment that had four dimensions: Meaning; Competence; Self-determination; and Impact. There are predictable links between macro- and micro-level indicators with organizational-level factors increasing individual-level responses. Employee feelings of empowerment would also be reflected in more favorable work and well-being outcomes.

These measures have been employed in studies carried out in the hospitality sector. Kazlauskaite et al. (2012), using the Matthews et al. (2003) measure of organizational-level empowerment and the Spreitzer (1995) measure of psychological empowerment, examined the role of both levels of empowerment in the HRM–performance linkage. They collected data from 211 front-line service employees at 30 upscale hotels in Lithuania. They reported that organizational empowerment was positively related to psychological empowerment, job satisfaction and affective commitment. In addition, psychological empowerment and affective commitment mediated the relationship of organizational empowerment on self-reported quality of service. Dewettinck and Van Ameijde (2011) used the Arnold et al. (2000) measure in a study of 381 front-line employees working in four service organizations and found that leadership empowerment behaviors increased levels of both job satisfaction and affective commitment, with psychological empowerment partially mediating these relationships.

ORGANIZATIONAL AND PSYCHOLOGICAL EMPOWERMENT IN THE HOSPITALITY SECTOR

Lawler et al. (2001) suggest that over 70 percent of workplaces have initiated some type of empowerment effort in at least part of their workforce. Since the empowerment concept seems to be a good fit for organizations in the hospitality sector, studies on the potential benefits of empowerment have been reported. Peccei and Rosenthal (2001), using a sample of 717 employees (54 supervisors, 663 general staff) from the third largest supermarket in Britain, assessed an intervention to improve service quality. The intervention was intended to increase supportive and participatory managerial behaviors, role modeling by supervisors, the use of job redesign to increase discretion of front-line workers, and improved customer service training. These changes were targeted at increasing levels of psychological empowerment. Respondents with more favorable views of management behaviors and of their participation in customer service value training also reported higher levels of psychological empowerment; psychological empowerment, in turn, was positively related to higher levels of customer-oriented behaviors.

Raub and Robert (2012), based on data from 440 front-line employees and their supervisors from 16 hotels in the Middle East and Pacific Region, found that empowering leadership increased employee feelings of psychological empowerment, which in turn increased employee organizational commitment and their engaging in voice behaviors (identifying problems and suggesting solutions).

Pelit et al. (2011) investigated the relationship of employee empowerment and job satisfaction in a sample of 1854 employees of 5-star hotels in Turkey, reporting that employee feelings of psychological empowerment were associated with higher levels of job satisfaction.

Chiang and Jang (2008), using data from 159 employees from seven hotels in Taiwan, reported that supervisory leadership had a positive and direct effect on trust and organizational culture, which in turn increased levels of psychological empowerment, the latter being associated with higher levels of job satisfaction.

Kazlauskaite et al. (2012) studied organizational and psychological empowerment in the HRM–performance linkage. They collected data questionnaire data from 211 front-line service employees at 30 upscale hotels in Lithuania. They found that organizational empowerment was positively related to psychological empowerment, job satisfaction and affective commitment. Both psychological empowerment and affective commitment mediated the effects of organizational empowerment on quality of service self-reported to guests and customers.

Hechanova et al. (2006) collected data from 954 employees and supervisors in five different service sectors (including hotels) in the Philippines, examining the relationship of psychological empowerment with both job satisfaction and job performance. Psychological empowerment was positively related to both.

Cacioppe (1998) described the introduction of a structured empowerment project at the Burswood Resort Hotel in Australia, its evaluation, and lessons learned. The program had three key broad elements: management commitment and support of the empowerment concept, and training of department heads to bring this about; a flexible system with guidance to support employee outcomes; and training of staff so that they could provide solutions to customer problems. Not surprisingly they identified some challenges including some department heads and middle managers who did not understand, embrace and encourage empowerment.

Thus empowerment has been shown to have potential benefits within this sector. Empowerment benefits were present in studies carried out in several different cultures and countries, suggesting that empowerment benefits transcended national boundaries.

EMPOWERING LEADERSHIP

Let us now consider two studies we carried out on potential benefits of empowering leadership. The first study (Burke et al., 2015) examined the relationship of supervisor/leader empowerment practices, employee feelings of psychological empowerment, key work outcomes, and perceptions of service quality being provided by front-line service workers from 5-star hotels in Turkey. In the first study, we considered the relationship of employee perceptions of supervisor/leader empowerment behaviors, levels of felt psychological empowerment, important work outcomes (job satisfaction, affective organizational commitment, work engagement, engaging in voice behavior, intent to quit), and assessments of quality of service provided to guests and clients.

Data were collected in eight 5-star hotels in Belek, in the prime tourist region of Antalya Turkey, using anonymously completed questionnaires. Members of the research team had personal contacts in these properties, making it easier to enlist their cooperation and participation. These hotels operate on a year round basis with between 400 and 500 employees, these numbers increasing during peak tourist seasons. Hotel contacts were given 50 surveys each and were asked to have a random sample of employees complete them. A total of 242 fully completed surveys were returned to the research team, a 62 percent response rate. While this response rate is typical for organizational surveys and acceptable for analysis, the length of the survey and the time of data collection (during the busy periods of May and June 2014) probably limited employee participation.

Most respondents were male (58 percent), worked full time (88 percent), were 30 years of age or younger (68 percent), were single (58 percent), without children (58 percent), had high school educations (50 percent), worked in their present jobs and worked for their present hotels for two years or less (61 percent and 51 percent respectively), held non-management positions (87 percent), had no supervisory responsibilities (54 percent), worked between 41 and 50 hours per week (74 percent), and worked in a variety of departments.

Again, a number of measures were included. Personal and work setting characteristics were assessed by a number of single items. The former included: gender, age, current work status, current marital and parental status, and level of education. The latter included hours worked per week, organizational level, job tenure, organizational tenure, and whether the respondent had supervisory duties.

Self-efficacy, a stable individual difference characteristic, was measured by a ten-item scale developed and validated by Schwarzer and Jerusalem (1995).

Supervisory empowerment behaviors were obviously an important variable in the study. Arnold et al. (2000) developed and validated a measure of empowering leader behaviors. They ended up with five factors: Coaching; Informing; Leading by example; Participative decision making; and Showing concern/Interacting with their team, each measured by five items. Respondents indicated how frequently their supervisor exhibited each behavior on a five-point Likert scale.

Psychological or personal feelings of empowerment were measured by a 12-item scale developed and validated by Spreitzer (1995; 1996). This measure tapped into four dimensions: Meaning; Competence; Self-determination; and Impact.

Five work outcomes were included. Job satisfaction was assessed by a seven-item scale developed and validated by Taylor and Bowers (1972). Affective commitment was measured by a six-item scale developed and validated by Meyer and Allen (1997). Three aspects of work engagement were assessed using measures created by Schaufeli et al. (2002): Dedication; Vigor; and Absorption. Employee voice behaviors were measured by a six-item scale developed by Van Dyne and LePine (1998). Intent to quit was measured by two items (Burke, 1991).

Finally, quality of service provided by respondents to guests or clients was assessed by a six-item scale developed and validated by Peccei and Rosenthal (2001).

PERSONAL AND WORK SITUATION CHARACTERISTICS AND EMPOWERMENT

First, considering perceptions of supervisory/leader empowerment behaviors, respondents working fewer hours, who were single and more highly educated reported higher levels of perceived supervisory/leader empowerment behaviors. Considering self-reported levels of psychological empowerment, respondents who were more highly educated, at higher organizational levels, working fewer hours, and who were single reported higher levels of personal empowerment. Finally, respondents reporting higher levels of personal efficacy also indicated higher levels of psychological empowerment.

SUPERVISORY EMPOWERMENT BEHAVIORS AND FEELINGS OF EMPOWERMENT

All correlations (n = 20) between the five supervisory empowerment behaviors and the four indicators of psychological empowerment were significantly and positively correlated; the mean inter-correlation was .47 (p < .001).

PSYCHOLOGICAL EMPOWERMENT AND WORK OUTCOMES

All correlations between the four psychological empowerment dimensions and the five work outcomes were positive and statistically significant (p < .05). The psychological empowerment composite measure was positively and significantly correlated with three of the four work outcomes (not service quality).

SUPERVISOR EMPOWERMENT BEHAVIORS, PSYCHOLOGICAL EMPOWERMENT AND WORK OUTCOMES

A summary of these findings follows. First, none of the predictors accounted for a significant amount or increment in explained variance on Intent to quit. Intent to quit was generally very low in this sample, which was likely to be reflecting the relatively short job tenures of many front-line service workers and the potential difficulty in finding other employment that might be better. Second, both perceptions of supervisor/ leader empowerment behaviors and personal levels of psychological empowerment accounted for significant increments in explained variance on all six work outcomes (job satisfaction; organizational commitment; work engagement; voice behaviors; intent to quit; and quality of service). Third, the measure of personal efficacy accounted for a significant increment in explained variance on four of the size work outcomes considered (not intent to quit and job satisfaction).

BENEFITS OF SUPERVISORY EMPOWERMENT BEHAVIORS: A REPLICATION

Let us now consider our second study (Burke et al., 2016) on the potential benefits of supervisor empowerment behaviors, essentially attempting to replicate the study just reviewed. Data were collected in eight 5-star hotels in Belek, in the prime tourist region of Antalya, Turkey, using anonymously completed questionnaires. These hotels operate on a year round basis with between 400 and 500 employees, with these numbers increasing during peak tourist seasons. A total of 242 fully completed surveys were returned to the research team, a 62 percent response rate. Again, most respondents were male (58 percent), worked full time (88 percent), were 30 years of age or younger (68 percent), were single (58 percent), without children (58 percent), had high school educations (50 percent), had worked in their present jobs and for their present hotels for two years or less (61 percent and 51 percent respectively), held non-management positions (87 percent), had no supervisory responsibilities (54 percent), worked between 41 and 50 hours per week (74 percent), and worked in a variety of departments. Other measures used in this replication study were those described in the previous investigation. These were personal and work situation characteristics; self-efficacy; supervisor empowerment behaviors; feelings of psychological empowerment; five work outcomes and the assessment of service quality.

   The following comments summarize the results of the personal demographic and work situation characteristics and the other measures in the study. First, respondents at higher organizational levels and those having more education indicated higher levels of psychological empowerment. Second, respondents reporting higher levels of supervisory/leader empowerment behaviors also indicated greater psychological empowerment. Finally, respondents reporting higher levels of personal efficacy also indicated higher levels of psychological empowerment. Interestingly, respondents working longer hours had lower reports of both supervisory/

leader empowerment behaviors and levels of psychological empowerment. This probably reflects the facts that these individuals also were at lower levels in the organization and held more routine jobs.

Let us now consider the relationship of supervisor empowerment behaviors, psychological empowerment and the various work outcomes. Most of the results from this study were consistent with those obtained in the earlier study. First, none of the predictors accounted for a significant amount or increment in explained variance on Intent to quit. Intent to quit was generally very low in this sample, which was likely to be reflecting the relatively short job tenures of many front-line service workers and potential difficulty in finding other employment that might be better. Second, both perceptions of supervisor/leader empowerment behaviors and personal levels of psychological empowerment accounted for significant increments in explained variance on all six work outcomes (job satisfaction; organizational commitment; work engagement; voice behaviors; intent to quit; and quality of service). Third, the measure of personal efficacy accounted for a significant increment in explained variance on four of the six work outcomes considered (not Intent to quit or Job satisfaction).

Some practical implications can also be drawn from these findings. Self-efficacy emerged as an important individual difference characteristic associated with the two empowerment measures. This suggested that individual attitudes, skills and feelings of personal confidence made employees more amenable and embracing of empowerment practices and were more likely to take advantage of the opportunity extended to them by higher levels of supervision and leadership.

Quinn and Spreitzer (1997) emphasize important leader behaviors including becoming empowered oneself; clarifying directions for one's own staff; involving staff by encouraging their participation; clarifying expectations of staff, work roles, and lines of accountability; and offering opportunities for development. It is difficult for managers to empower others if they find no meaning in their work, have no impact, influence or power at work, do not feel confident and competent in doing their jobs, or have no sense of self-determination at work.

Lashley (1995) advocates increasing participation – delegating decision making to front-line staff; involvement – getting ideas, feedback, information and suggestions from front-line workers; increasing employee commitment – to the organization's goals, employees take more responsibility for their job performance and job performance improvements; and delayering – reducing levels of hierarchy to keep managers closer to their customers.

Fracard (2006) suggests targeting three elements of empowerment: increasing verbal empowerment – offering ideas while taking part in decision making; increasing behavioral empowerment – working in teams to identify and solve work-related problems; and increasing outcome empowerment – identifying and solving problems affecting important outcomes.

Nichols (1995) makes the case for a three-stage training framework to develop employee empowerment. In the first stage, managers use the current capabilities of staff more fully, empowering them in their current jobs through giving them more responsibilities and freedom. In the second stage, managers coach employees to increase their capabilities (high performance expectations, use of praise), and in the third stage, managers delegate more power to employees beyond their current jobs, extending this to work teams (see Kirkman and Rosen, 1999 and Kirkman et al., 2004 for evidence on the benefits of team empowerment).

Efforts to increase feelings of empowerment often fall short or fail outright. Characteristics of empowerment efforts that have been shown to have a higher probability of success include the following. Organizations need to increase decision-making opportunities within employees' jobs, to provide more information to employees on both big picture matters (for example, their roles and how they make valued contributions to the organization, work unit and organizational objectives, challenges facing the organization, and potential upcoming changes) and small picture matters (work unit and personal job performance objectives, feedback on one's job performance, available training and educational opportunities). They also need to support employees' voice, their participation in and solicitation of their views and ideas on workplace practices and concerns, giving them some elbow room to "job craft", to change their jobs to make them more meaningful and impactful, and training supervisors in what employee empowerment is, why it matters, and how it can be enhanced.

INCREASING EMPLOYEE FEELINGS OF EMPOWERMENT – MISSION POSSIBLE?

Implementing empowerment practices is a difficult challenge (Ahearne et al., 2005). There is typically conflict between management's desire for control and employee feelings of empowerment. There is also a discrepancy between managers' opinions of levels of employee empowerment and employee feelings of empowerment (Greasley et al., 2005; Hales, 2000; Hales and Klidas, 1998; Harley, 1999). Implementing an empowerment initiative represents a major organizational change, and as with all major organizational change efforts, many efforts here fail or fall short.

Based on our work and the work of others (see Spreitzer, 2008 for a review), we conclude that empowerment practices will enhance the delivery of high quality service in the hospitality sector. In addition, several ways to increase levels of empowerment of both front-line employees and managers have been identified. These include increasing employee participation in decision making, delegating authority and control to these employees, creating more challenging work roles through job redesign, leaders sharing more information, and leaders providing more coaching and mentoring to their staff. At the micro level, increasing levels of employee self-efficacy through training and more effective use of their work experiences will increase personal empowerment and improve work outcomes (Maddux, 2002). Getting value from these initiatives comes down to effective change implementation in the end (Cacioppe, 1998; Jones et al., 1997; Hales, 2000; Hales and Klidas, 1998).

IMPLICATIONS

- Validated measures of both servant and empowering leadership are available.
- Training programs for both servant and empowering leadership have been advanced.
- But bringing about cultural change in hospitality organizations (and all organizations) takes time and resources, is difficult to bring about, and is as likely to fall short as succeed based on past history.
- There is a need to introduce these concepts in depth in university and college courses in hospitality management and in hospitality organization training programs.
- It is important to use these concepts in employee selection, orientation and performance management exercises.
- There is a need to focus on general managerial competencies as much as on technical competencies.
- And a need to also focus as much on future-oriented training requirements as on the immediate training needs.

CONCLUSIONS

Leadership emerges as a vital element in successful performance of individuals, work teams and organizations (Barling, 2014). Leadership makes a difference. However, there is no one best leadership approach. We are not advocating the use of servant or empowering leadership styles per se. Instead there are common behaviors, values and attitudes across a range of leadership styles that prove to be effective. Common behaviors include providing support to staff, recognizing and rewarding good performance, clarifying expectations, investing in staff development, being ethical, having some fun, and meeting the needs of one's staff.

REFERENCES

Ahearne, M., Mathieu, J. and Rapp, A. (2005) To empower or not to empower your sales force? An empirical examination of the influence of leadership empowerment behavior in customer satisfaction and performance. *Journal of Applied Psychology*, **90**, 945–55.

Arnold, J.A., Arad, S., Rhoades, J.A. and Drasgow, F. (2000) The empowering leadership questionnaire: The construction and validation of a new scale for measuring leader behavior. *Journal of Organizational Behavior*, **21**, 249–69.

Ayupp, K. and Chung, T.H. (2010) Empowerment: Hotel employees' perspective. *Journal of Industrial Engineering and Management*, **3**, 561–75.

Badaracco, J.L. (2002) *Leading quietly: An unorthodox guide to doing the right thing.* Boston, MA: Harvard Business School Press.

Badaracco, J.L. and Ellsworth, R.R. (1993) *Leadership and the quest for integrity.* Boston, MA: Harvard Business School Press.

Barling, J. (2014) *The science of leadership: Lessons from research for organizational leaders.* Oxford: Oxford University Press.

Bass, B.M. (1985) *Leadership and performance beyond expectations.* New York: Free Press.

Bass, B.M. (1998) *Transformational leadership: Industrial, military and educational impact.* Mahwah, NJ: Lawrence Erlbaum.

Baum, T. (2007) Human resources in tourism: Still waiting for change. *Tourism Management*, **28**, 1383–99.

Berry, L.L., Parasuraman, A. and Zeithaml, V.A. (1994) Improving service quality in America: Lessons learned. *The Academy of Management Executive*, **8**(2), 32–52.

Bond, H. (1998) Lodging's new breed of leader. *Hotel and Motel Management*, **21**, 1104–107.

Bowen, D.E. and Lawler, E.E. (1992) The empowerment of service workers: What, why, how and when. *Sloan Management Review*, **33**, 31–40.

Boyatzis, R.E. and McKee, A. (2005) *Resonant leadership: Renewing yourself and connecting with others through mindfulness, hope, and compassion.* Cambridge, MA: Harvard University Press.

Burke, R.J. (1991) Early work experiences of female and male managers and professionals: Reasons for optimism? *Canadian Journal of Administrative Sciences*, **8**, 224–30.

Burke, R.J., Koyuncu, M., Wolpin, J., Yirik, S. and Koyuncu, K. (2015) Organizational empowerment practices, psychological empowerment and work outcomes among frontline service employees in five-star Turkish Hotels. *Effective Executive*, **18**, 42–65.

Burke, R., Koyuncu, J.M., Wolpin, J., Yirik, S. and Koyuncu, K. (2016) Supervisory empowerment behaviors, psychological empowerment and work outcomes among frontline service employees in five-star Turkish hotel: A replication. Manuscript under editorial review.

Cacioppe, B. (1998) Structured empowerment: An award-winning program at the Burswood Resort Hotel. *Leadership and Organizational Development Journal*, **19**, 264–74.

Chiang, C-F. and Jang, S.C. (2008) The antecedents and consequences of psychological empowerment: The case of Taiwan's hotel companies. *Journal of Hospitality and Tourism Research*, **32**, 40–61.

Chuang, A., Judge, T.A. and Liaw, Y.J. (2012) Transformational leadership and customer service: A moderated mediator model of negative affectivity and emotion regulation. *European Journal of Work and Organizational Psychology*, **21**, 28–56.

Church, A.H. (1995) Linking leadership behaviors to service performance: Do managers make a difference? *Managing Service Quality*, **5**(6), 26–31.

Cichy, R. and Schmidgall, R.S. (1996) Leadership qualities of financial executives in the U.S. lodging industry. *Cornell Hotel and Restaurant Administration Quarterly*, **37**, 46–56.

Clark, R.A., Hartline, M.D. and Jones, K.C. (2009) The effects of leadership styles on hotel employees' commitment to service quality. *Cornell Hospitality Quarterly*, **50**, 209–31.

Connell, J. (2001) Growing the right skills through five-star management. *Australian Journal of Hospitality Management*, **8**, 1–14.

Dai, Y-D., Dai, Y-Y., Chen, K-Y. and Wu, H-C. (2013) Transformational vs. transactional leadership: Which is better? *International Journal of Contemporary Hospitality Management*, **25**, 760–78.

Dewettnick, I. and Van Ameijde, M. (2011) Linking leadership empowerment behavior to employee attitudes and behavioral intentions. *Personnel Review*, **40**, 284–305.

Ehrhart, M.G. (2004) Leadership and procedural justice climate as antecedents of unit level organizational citizenship behavior. *Personnel Psychology*, **57**, 61–94.

Erkutlu, H. (2008) The impact of transformational leadership on organizational and leadership effectiveness: The Turkish case. *Journal of Management Development*, **27**, 708–26.

Fletcher, M. (1999) The effects of international communication, leadership and team performance on successful service quality implementation: A South African perspective. *Team Performance Management: An International Journal*, **5**(5), 150–63.

Fracard, K. (2006) The real meaning of empowerment. *Contract Management*, **15**, 1–7.

Fulmer, R.M. and Conger, J.A. (2004) *Growing your company's leaders*. New York: AMACON.

George, W. (2003) *Authentic leadership: Rediscovering the secrets to creating lasting value*. San Francisco, CA: Jossey-Bass.

Gill, A.S., Flaschner, A.B. and Shachar, M. (2006) Mitigating stress and burnout by implementing transformational leadership. *International Journal of Contemporary Hospitality Management*, **18**, 469–81.

Gill, A., Fitzgerald, S., Bhutani, S., Mand, H. and Sharma, S. (2010) The relationship between transformational leadership and employee desire for empowerment. *International Journal of Contemporary Hospitality Management*, **22**, 263–73.

Greasley, K., Bryman, A., Dainty, A., Price, A., Soetanto, R. and King, N. (2005) Employee perceptions of empowerment. *Employee Relations*, **27**, 354–68.

Greenleaf, R.K. (1977) *Servant leadership: A journey into the nature of legitimate power and greatness*. New York: Paulist Press.

Greger, K.R. and Peterson, J.S. (2000) Leadership profiles for the new millennium. *Cornell Hotel and Restaurant Administration Quarterly*, **41**, 16–29.

Hales, C. (2000) Management and empowerment programs. *Work, Employment and Society*, **14**, 501–19.

Hales, C. and Klidas, A. (1998) Empowerment in five star hotels: Choice, voice or rhetoric? *International Journal of Contemporary Hospitality Management*, **10**, 88–95.

Hallowell, R., Schlesinger, L.A. and Zornitsky, J. (1996). Internal service quality, customer and job satisfaction: Linkages and implications for management. *HR, Human Resource Planning*, **19**(2), 20–31.

Harley, B. (1999) The myth of empowerment: Work organization, hierarchy and employee autonomy in contemporary Australian workplaces. *Work, Employment and Society*, **13**, 41–66.

Hechanova, R.M., Alampay, R.D. and Franco, E.P. (2006) Psychological empowerment, job satisfaction and performance among Filipino service workers. *Asian Journal of Social Psychology*, **9**, 72–8.

Herrenkohl, R.C., Judson, G.T. and Heffner, J.A. (1999) Defining and measuring employee empowerment. *Journal of Applied Behavioral Science*, **35**, 373–89.

Hoque, K. (1999) Human resource management and performance in the UK hotel industry. *British Journal of Industrial Relations*, **37**, 419–43.

Hunter, J.C. (2004) *The world's most powerful leadership principle: How to become a servant leader.* New York: Crown Business.

Jones, C., Taylor, G. and Nickson, D. (1997) Whatever it takes? Managing "empowered" employees and the service encounter in an international hotel chain. *Work, Employment and Society*, **12**, 135–57.

Kazlauskaite, R., Buciuniene, I. and Turauskas, L. (2012) Organizational and psychological empowerment in the HRM–performance linkage. *Employee Relations*, **34**, 138–58.

Kirkman, B.L. and Rosen, B. (1999) Beyond self-management: Antecedents and consequences of team empowerment. *Academy of Management Journal*, **42**, 58–74.

Kirkman, B.L., Rosen, B., Tesluk, P.E. and Gibson, C.B. (2004) The impact of team empowerment on virtual team performance: The moderating role of face-to-face interaction. *Academy of Management Journal*, **47**, 175–92.

Koyuncu, M., Burke, R.J., Ashtakova, M., Eren, D. and Cetin, H. (2014) Servant leadership and perceptions of service quality provided by front-line service workers in four- and five-star hotels in Turkey: Achieving competitive advantage. *International Journal of Contemporary Hospitality Management*, **26**, 1083–99.

Kusluvan, S. (2003) *Managing employee attitudes and behaviors in the tourism and hospitality sector.* New York: Nova Science.

Kusluvan, S., Kusluvan, Z., Ilhan, I. and Buyruk, L. (2010) A review of human resources management issues in the tourism and hospitality industry. *Cornell Hospitality Quarterly*, **51**, 171–214.

Lashley, C. (1995) Towards an understanding of employee empowerment in hospitality services. *International Journal of Contemporary Hospitality Management*, **7**, 27–32.

Lawler, E.E., Mohrman, S.A. and Benson, G. (2001) *Organizing for higher performance: Employee involvement, TQM, reengineering, and knowledge management in the Fortune 1000.* San Francisco, CA: Jossey-Bass.

Liao, H. and Chuang, A. (2007) Transforming employees and climate: A multilevel, multisource examination of transformational leadership in building long-term service relationships. *Journal of Applied Psychology*, **92**, 1016–19.

Liaw, Y., Chi, N. and Chuang, A. (2010) Examining the mechanisms linking transformational leadership, employee customer orientation, and service performance: The mediating roles of perceived supervisor and coworker support. *Journal of Business and Psychology*, **25**, 477–92.

Liden, R.C., Wayne, S.J., Zhao, H. and Henderson, D. (2008) Servant leadership: Development of a multidimensional measure and multi-level assessment. *Leadership Quarterly*, **19**, 161–77.

Maddux, J.E. (2002) Self-efficacy: The power of believing you can. In C.R. Snyder and S.J. Lopez (eds) *Handbook of positive psychology.* New York: Oxford University Press, pp. 227–87.

Matthews, R.A., Diaz, W.M. and Cole, S.G. (2003) The organizational empowerment scale. *Personnel Review*, **32**, 297–318.

Meyer, J. and Allen, N. (1997) *Commitment in the workplace: Theory, research, and applications.* Thousand Oaks, CA: Sage Publications.

Nichols, J. (1995) Getting empowerment into perspective: A three stage training framework. *Empowerment in Organizations*, **3**, 5–10.

Parasuraman, A., Zeithaml, V.A. and Berry, L. (1998) SERVQUAL: A multi-item scale for measuring consumer perceptions of service quality. *Journal of Retailing*, **64**, 12–40.

Peccei, R. and Rosenthal, P. (2001) Delivering customer-oriented behavior through empowerment: An empirical test of HRM assumptions. *Journal of Management Studies*, **38**, 833–57.

Pelit, E., Ozturk, Y. and Arslanturk, Y. (2011) The effects of employee empowerment on employee job satisfaction: A study of hotels in Turkey. *International Journal of Contemporary Hospitality Management*, **23**, 784–802.

Quinn, R.E. and Spreitzer, G.M. (1997) The road to empowerment: Seven questions every leader should consider. *Organizational Dynamics*, **26**, 37–49.

Raelin, J.A. (2003) *Creating leaderful organizations: How to bring out leadership in everyone.* San Francisco: Berrett-Koehler.

Raub, S. and Robert, C. (2012) Empowerment, organizational commitment, and voice behavior in the hospitality industry: Evidence from a multinational sample. *Cornell Hospitality Quarterly*, **54**, 136–48.

Schaufeli, W.B., Salanova, A.M., Gonzalez-Roma, V. and Bakker, A.B. (2002) The measurement of engagement and burnout: A two sample confirmatory factor analysis approach. *Journal of Happiness Studies*, **3**, 71–92.

Schwarzer, R. and Jerusalem, M. (1995) Generalized self-efficacy scale. In J. Weinman, S. Wright and M. Johnston (eds) *Measures in health psychology: a user's portfolio. Causal and control beliefs.* Windsor: NFER-Nelson, pp. 35–7.

Seibert, S.E., Wang, G. and Courtright, S.H. (2011) Antecedents and consequences of psychological and team empowerment in organizations. A meta-analytic review. *Journal of Applied Psychology*, **96**, 981–1003.

Simons, T. and Robertson, Q. (2003) Why managers should care about fairness: The effects of aggregate justice perceptions on organizational outcomes. *Journal of Applied Psychology*, **88**, 432–43.

Spreitzer, G.M. (1995) Psychological empowerment in the workplace: Dimensions, measurement, and validation. *Academy of Management Journal*, **38**, 1442–65.

Spreitzer, G.M. (1996) Social structural characteristics of psychological empowerment. *Academy of Management Journal*, **39**, 483–504.

Spreitzer, G.M. (1997) Toward a common ground in defining empowerment. *Research in Organizational Change and Development*, **10**, 31–62.

Spreitzer, G.M. (2008) Taking stock: A review of more than twenty years of research on empowerment. In J. Barling, C.L. Cooper and S.R. Clegg (eds) *The Sage Handbook of organizational behavior.* London: Sage Publications, pp. 54–72.

Taylor, J.C. and Bowers, D. (1972) *Survey of organizations: A machine-scored standardized questionnaire instrument.* Ann Arbor, MI: Institute for Social Research.

Tracey, J.B. and Hinkin, T.R. (1994) Transformational leaders in the hospital industry. *Cornell Hotel and Restaurant Administration Quarterly*, **35**, 18–24.

Van Dyne, L. and LePine, J.A. (1998) Helping and voice extra-role behaviors: Evidence of construct and predictive validity. *Academy of Management Journal*, **41**, 108–19.

Wu, L-Z., Tse, E.C-Y., Fu, P., Kwan, H.K. and Liu, J. (2013) The impact of servant leadership on hotel employees' "servant behavior". *Cornell Hospitality Quarterly*, **54**, 383–95.

Zopiatis, A. and Constanti, P. (2010) Leadership styles and burnout: Is there an association? *International Journal of Contemporary Hospitality Management*, **22**, 300–20.

PART III

DEVELOPING HUMAN CAPITAL

7. Evolving conceptions of talent management: a roadmap for hospitality and tourism
Julia Christensen Hughes and William C. Murray

Talent management has received significant and increasing attention in both management and academic arenas since its introduction by a team of McKinsey consultants in 1997, twenty years ago (Michaels et al., 2001). Positioned predominantly as a strategy for achieving sustainable competitive advantage, and despite some questions about its effectiveness in practice (Cappelli, 2008), talent management remains a popular undertaking for organizational leaders and management consultants alike. Within the hospitality and tourism industry, which is notorious for its struggle to attract and retain 'talented' employees, and where the quality of the front-line customer experience can have an inordinate impact on business outcomes, it has been suggested that talent management holds particular promise, especially in large multinationals (Christensen Hughes and Rog, 2008).

Talent management has been enthusiastically embraced by many leading hotel and restaurant chains, as evidenced by the appointment of VPs of the same name (for example, Vice President, Talent & Learning, FRHI Hotels & Resorts; Vice President Talent Development, Kempinski Hotels; VP Talent Acquisition & Development, HMS Host). Within academe, however, considerable energy has gone into investigating whether talent management is more than simply hype or a euphemism for human resource management (HRM) (Lewis and Heckman, 2006), and if it is, how so? How is it defined, what are its theoretical underpinnings and what is it meant to achieve? A number of comprehensive reviews have recently explored these questions, including a special issue of the *International Journal of Contemporary Hospitality Management* (2008) as well as the *Human Resource Management Review* (2013; 2015), the *Journal of World Business* (2014) and *Employee Relations* (2016).

Contributors to these special issues have concluded that the field has moved out of its infancy and entered a new stage (Gallardo-Gallardo et al., 2015, p.275). Conceptual and empirical contributions have grown considerably and there has been some convergence on a few key theories and definitions. Increasingly, pluralistic frameworks have been advanced (see for example, Meyers and van Woerkom, 2014; Nijs et al., 2014) and boundaries have been pushed. Calls for additional research have focused on the need to study talent management in situ – within particular industries, types of firms and geographies. According to Sparrow and Makram (2015, p. 249) 'context is everything'. Others have suggested that the views of multiple stakeholders are badly needed, recognizing that much of the work to date has reflected 'a largely managerialist and performative agenda' (Collings et al., 2015).

Given its roots in management practice, some have suggested that rather than a field of study, talent management might best be understood as a 'phenomenon' (Dries, 2013, p. 273; Gallardo-Gallardo et al., 2015, p. 275). Others have suggested that it be considered a 'bridge field', a novel interdisciplinary undertaking that has the potential to play an integrating role across several theoretical perspectives (Sparrow and Makram, 2015, p. 249).

Regardless of perspective, hospitality researchers can make a substantial contribution to furthering understanding of talent management. Research within both large multinationals and small and medium-sized enterprises (SMEs) is needed, from those who wear the title, as well as from diverse front-line managers and hourly employees. Empirical research is needed that tests propositions concerning the relationship between talent management philosophies and practices (the SHRM architecture), and with respect to employee and organizational-level outcomes.

Talent management should also be explored with respect to changing environmental conditions. It is routinely said that we are living in a time of profound disruption, with automation and artificial intelligence poised to increasingly replace both manual and knowledge-based tasks. In this brave new world, assumptions of talent scarcity (a central tenet of talent management) may no longer hold true.

The aim of this chapter is to provide a roadmap for understanding the conceptual development of talent management, both within the hospitality literature and beyond. We seek to shed light on its theoretical underpinnings, evolving definitions and intended outcomes. We begin by revisiting the original contribution made by Michaels et al. (2001). This is followed by a synopsis of the seminal contributions by Lewis and Heckman (2006) and Collings and Mellahi (2009), two of the most cited papers in the field (Gallardo-Gallardo et al., 2015, p. 269). Then each of the contributions from the special issue of the *International Journal of Contemporary Hospitality Management* (2008) are briefly summarized, in order to present perspectives on talent management from hospitality and tourism researchers.

We then synthesize contributions from review articles in mainstream management journals. Our organizing framework is theoretical underpinnings; definitions, tensions and propositions; talent management practices; intended outcomes; and opportunities for further research, including with respect to changes occurring in the employment environment. We conclude with implications for the study of talent management from the perspective of the hospitality and tourism industry. As an industry that has long struggled to attract and retain talent, talent management holds particular promise for extending understanding (and hopefully managerial success) of this important concept.

EARLY SEMINAL CONTRIBUTIONS

Revisiting the *War for Talent*

In 2001, McKinsey consultants Michaels et al. (2001) published *The War for Talent*, bringing focused attention to the concept of talent management. They argued that a battle for talent was being waged due to the increasing need for strategic leaders and sophisticated managerial talent, including 'risk takers, global entrepreneurs and techno-savvy managers (p. 4), as well as growing employee mobility (making talent once found, difficult to keep). Michaels et al. argued that a new organizational paradigm had arrived in which human talent was recognized as a significant source of competitive advantage.

The McKinsey team's insights were based on surveys of managers and senior executives working for predominantly large US businesses, along with in-depth case studies of organizations considered to be 'high performing'. In their conclusions, they emphasized the importance of senior leadership (Michaels et al., 2001, p. x, emphasis in original): 'It wasn't better HR *processes* that made the difference. Rather, it was the *mindset* of leaders throughout the organization. . .What distinguished the high-performing companies [was] the fundamental belief in the importance of talent.'

Interestingly, both time and the courts have judged some of the study's companies more harshly than did the McKinsey team. For example, Enron was one of the companies selected for inclusion as a case study (see Michaels et al., 2001, p. xx). While Enron was named 'America's Most Innovative Company' by *Fortune* magazine six times between 1996 and 2001 (during the time the McKinsey study was conducted), it declared bankruptcy shortly thereafter, amidst scandal and criminal convictions for some senior executives. Many employees, who had been strongly encouraged to invest in Enron stock, lost their life savings. Also included was a case study on Wells Fargo, which has recently seen over five thousand employees (including senior executives) fired for fabricating millions of unauthorized customer accounts in order to meet aggressive sales targets. This occurred despite the existence of a corporate values document expressing values-based aspirations (Wells Fargo, 2016, pp. 5–6):

> We value and support our team members as a competitive advantage. We strive to attract, develop, retain, and motivate the most talented, caring team members ... We strive to be recognized by our stakeholders as setting the standard among the world's great companies for integrity and principled performance ... Everything we do is built on trust.

The Enron and Wells Fargo examples are important reminders that organizations can proclaim certain values, including a commitment to talent, without necessarily living them.

According to Michaels et al. (2001), talent includes both character and the ability to deliver results, defining it as (p. xii): 'the sum of a person's abilities – his or her intrinsic gifts, skills, knowledge, experience, intelligence, judgement, attitude, character and drive. It also includes his or her ability to learn and grow.' With respect to managerial talent, Michaels et al. (2001, p. xiii) proposed: 'Managerial talent is some combination of a sharp strategic mind, leadership ability, emotional maturity, communications skills, the ability to attract and inspire other talented people, entrepreneurial instincts, functional skills, and the ability to deliver results.'

Delving further, Michaels et al. (2001) shared that in ancient times the word 'talent' meant 'a unit of weight' which was used to determine the monetary value of precious metals. Over time, talent became associated with wealth, as revealed in the *Parable of the Talents* (Matthew 25:14–30), in which two servants who put their talents to good use were heralded, while a third servant, who buried his 'talent' in the ground, was banished for allowing his talent to languish. Michaels et al. suggested that it was Martin Luther's interpretation of this parable that gave rise to the Protestant work ethic: 'people should exercise their innate talents through hard work' (p. xiii). Drawing this history together, they advised that organizations 'that multiply their human talents will prosper. Companies that don't will struggle' (p. xiv).

Discovering that many organizations do not manage talent effectively, Michaels et al. (2001) advocated for a 'fundamentally new way of managing talent', including (pp. 11–14): 'Embrace a talent mindset'; 'Craft a winning employee value proposition'; 'Rebuild your recruiting strategy'; 'Weave development into your organization'; and 'Differentiate and affirm your people'. Emphasizing this latter point, they advised that better companies 'reward their best performers with fast-track growth and pay them substantially more than their average performers' (p. 15), observing 'Talented managers want exciting challenges and great development opportunities.' They also emphasized the importance of financial compensation; 'You can't make a great value proposition with money alone, but you can break one if the money isn't in the ballpark' (p. 12). Michaels et al. (2001) claimed that winning the war for talent could bring significant organizational benefit including reduced attrition and improved performance.

Critiques and Contributions from the Academic Literature

Following the *War for Talent* (Michaels et al., 2001), much was written on talent management, particularly in trade publications, with management consultants and organizational leaders exhorting its promise. Lewis and Heckman (2006) provided a critical early review, producing what has become one of the most cited papers in the field (Gallardo-Gallardo et al., 2015, p. 269). Lewis and Heckman suggested that while there was a 'disturbing lack of clarity regarding the definition, scope and overall goals' (p. 139) of talent management, three distinct conceptions arguably existed.

The first viewed talent management as a collection of practices pertaining to the recruitment, selection and development of people, typically carried out by a human resource department on behalf of the organization, potentially supported by an enterprise-wide human resource information system (HRIS). From this perspective, 'talent' is positioned as little more than a euphemism for 'people' and 'talent management' is 'superfluous' or a simple 'rebranding' of HR practices (Lewis and Heckman, 2006, p. 141). Lewis and Heckman (2006, p. 141) suggested that while such a rebranding might help to keep HR practices 'seemingly new and fresh . . . it does not advance our understanding of the strategic and effective management of talent'.

Their second perspective positioned talent management as more akin to succession or human resource planning (HRP). Here, talent management practices included tracking turnover and anticipating growth, creating talent pools and managing the flow of people, in order to meet future operational needs. Lewis and Heckman (2006) suggested that such an approach, while not novel theoretically, could benefit from a closer alignment with the management sciences literature in order to enhance predictive ability and planning.

Lewis and Heckman's (2006) third view highlighted two distinct and still unresolved tensions in the field. One perspective viewed talent as a select or elite group of people – employees assessed as being 'high performers' or 'high potential' workers – to whom differential investments are made (in development and compensation). Clearly, this is what was proposed by Michaels et al. (2001). The second view – the undifferentiated view – holds that all employees have talent and that talent management is about realizing human potential or developing 'the talent in each person, one individual at a time' (Buckingham and Vosburgh, 2001, p. 17).

Lewis and Heckman (2006, p. 142) argued that these various perspectives lacked a theoretical framework and empirical evidence, suggesting that much of the interest in talent management was 'rooted in exhortation and anecdote rather than data and builds an argument based [on] the selective self-reports of executives.' They concluded their review with the observation that talent management 'is not well grounded in research, not distinct from traditional HR practices or disciplines, and is supported mainly by anecdote' (p. 143).

Building on Lewis and Heckman's (2006) contribution, Collings and Mellahi (2009) similarly observed 'despite the growing popularity of talent management and over a decade of debate and hype, the concept of talent management remains unclear' (2009, p. 304). To address this deficit, they explicitly linked talent management to the strategic human resource management (SHRM) literature (drawing on contributions, for example, from Becker and Huselid, 2006; Boxall and Purcell, 2008; Delery and Doty, 1995; Huselid et al., 1997; Huselid et al., 2005; Lepak and Snell, 1999; Pfeffer, 1994; 1998; and Schuler and Jackson, 1987).

Collings and Mellahi (2009) positioned talent management as identifying 'strategic human capital' and ensuring 'that its contribution is maximised' (p. 307). Accordingly, they proposed a definition, below (p. 304), that has become one of the most cited (Gallardo-Gallardo et al., 2015, p. 269), if not most 'ponderous' (Ariss et al., 2014, p. 174) in the field:

> We define strategic talent management as activities and processes that involve the systematic identification of key positions which differentially contribute to the organization's sustainable competitive advantage, the development of a talent pool of high potential and high performing incumbents to fill these roles, and the development of a differentiated human resource architecture to facilitate filling these positions with competent incumbents and to ensure their continued commitment to the organisation.

Explicitly referencing Lewis and Heckman's (2006) three-fold conception, Collings and Mellahi (2009) suggested that their definition represented a fourth categorization, given its focus on differentially strategic positions (potentially at all levels of the organization), filled with differentially talented people. More specifically, drawing on Lepak and Snell (1999), they suggested that employees be assessed on the basis of their value and uniqueness ('A performers'). And, drawing on Huselid et al. (2005), they suggested that positions be assessed on the basis of their strategic importance ('A positions'). Pulling these concepts together, they argued (p. 306):

> It is neither practical nor desirable to fill all positions in an organisation with A performers. This would result in an over-investment in non-pivotal roles . . . Similarly, we posit that the focus of talent management systems should be on high potential and higher performing employees operating in key roles and not all employees in the organisation.

In developing this perspective, rather than a 'best practice' or universal approach to SHRM (Pfeffer, 1994; 1998), or a 'best fit' or contingent approach (Boxall and Purcell, 2008), they argued for what they referred to as a 'differentiated HR architecture', in which 'A' level people in 'A' level positions are managed through a customized approach.

Collings and Mellahi (2009) also referenced the work of Boudreau and Ramstad (2007), who suggested that talent management should be viewed as a new paradigm – 'talentship' – theoretically grounded in the decision sciences. A decision science, they argued, would support evidence-informed decisions about investments in human capital. As one example, they cited training street sweepers at Disney in customer service, who could have an unexpected and disproportionate impact on the guest experience.

In theorizing the relationship between talent management and firm performance, Collings and Mellahi (2009) suggested revisiting the AMO framework (Boselie et al., 2005), whereby 'performance (P) is a function of the employee's ability (A), motivation (M) and opportunity (O) to perform' (p. 310). They suggested that within a talent management framework, talented employees carefully recruited and placed in strategic positions should have the ability and opportunity to perform, leaving motivation, organizational commitment and extra-role performance as key mediating variables, with respect to organizational outcomes. Linking their argument to organizational citizenship behaviour (OCB), they suggested that extra-role performance could lead to 'tolerance of less than ideal working conditions, participation in organisational decision making, increase[d] concern for the success and well being of the organisation, and assistance and mentoring of colleagues/co-workers (Organ, 1988)' (Collings and Mellahi, 2009, p. 311). As such, they argued that extra-role behaviour could have a direct and positive effect on organizational effectiveness, work group cohesiveness, and retention (p. 311). They concluded by encouraging researchers to empirically test their proposed model.

PERSPECTIVES FROM HOSPITALITY AND TOURISM

Guest editors of the special issue of the *International Journal of Contemporary Hospitality Management* sought to answer 'What are the contemporary human resource issues of talent management in hospitality and tourism?' They positioned talent management as a 'pressing consideration' (p. 718) given its potential for competitive advantage, but also due to significant environmental challenges, such as 'worldwide skills shortages and labour market changes' (p. 718). Each of the papers from this issue is briefly summarized below.

Baum (2008) suggested that talent management might not mean the same thing in hospitality and tourism as it does in other sectors, due to unusual 'talent' requirements and poorly developed HRM cultural norms and practices. He posited that hospitality skill sets uniquely include 'emotional, aesthetic and informational processing and analysis dimensions with a strong focus on the delivery of service to diverse consumers' (p. 720). Further, drawing on the work of Riley (1996), he suggested that talent management was complicated by the industry's 'complex, weak labour market' (2008, p. 727), characterized by (p. 723): 'unspecified hiring standards', 'no on-the-job training', 'flexible roles/responsibilities', and the use of 'part-time, casual or outsource staff'. Given these factors, Baum (2008) advised that talent management within hospitality organizations should assume an inclusive approach 'which provides opportunities for all staff to participate and enhance their skills and knowledge sets' (p. 727).

Drawing on the work of Lewis and Heckman (2006), Christensen Hughes and Rog (2008) emphasized the role that 'talent management' could potentially play in elevating strategic human resource management (SHRM) as an organizational priority – in an industry not noted for its progressive HRM practices. Potential outcomes, they suggested, could include increased employee retention and engagement, and bottom line results. They also underscored that its effective implementation would require a deeply embedded cultural belief (a talent mindset) that employees are truly a source of competitive advantage.

Acknowledging lack of agreement on what talent management means, Christensen Hughes and Rog (2008) proposed the following definition (p. 746):

> Talent management is ... both a philosophy and a practice. It is both an espoused and enacted commitment – shared at the highest levels and throughout the organization by all those in managerial and supervisory positions – to implement an integrated, strategic and technology enabled approach to HRM, with a particular focus on human resource planning, including employee recruitment, retention, development and succession practices, ideally for all employees but especially for those identified as having high potential or in key positions.

Drawing on Morton (2005), Christensen Hughes and Rog (2008, pp. 751–2) advised interested organizations to: clearly define what is meant by talent management, including its objectives; explicitly align talent management with the strategic business goals of the organization; ensure CEO commitment; enhance HR planning and analysis skills; develop a broad-based implementation plan with clear line management accountability; align HRM policies and practices with evidence-based best practice; develop an effective employer brand and employee value proposition (Dell and Hickey, 2002); and ensure managers at all levels of the organization (including front-line supervisors) have the requisite skills and attitudes to retain and engage valued employee talent.

Two contributors to the special issue focused on the experience of graduates from hospitality programmes – a key source of 'high potential' talent for the industry. Barron (2008) drew attention to the high rates of attrition of recent hospitality graduates, criticizing both hospitality education (as being too theoretical) and the industry (as not providing sufficiently interesting work or career development opportunities). He suggested more effectively integrating work experience within education curricula.

Scott and Revis (2008) similarly focused on the experience of recent hospitality graduates. Underscoring the challenge in meeting increasingly complex customer expectations, they argued that talent management should apply to front-line employees as well as organizational leaders: 'it is often the lowest paid and perhaps least valued positions, which effectively deliver the service to the consumer-face' (Scott and Revis, 2008, p. 785).

Drawing on the work of Gandz (2006), they recommended the establishment of an integrated 'talent development system' (p. 786). They also underscored the advantage held by large multinational employers in providing exciting career paths to recent graduates. As one example, they cited the Hilton Group's elevator programme, which aims to select 'graduate trainees of the highest quality to become hotel general managers in a short period' (Scott and Revis, 2008, p. 782).

Watson's (2008) focus was on challenges in recruitment and development given the need for increasingly sophisticated managerial talent, particularly with respect to: leadership and interpersonal skills; global experience; a customer service orientation; competence in a range of managerial functions including strategy, finance, marketing, HRM; and personal skills, such as resilience. Watson concluded by suggesting that management development 'is an integral, but complex component of talent management' and that the industry would be wise to work at enhancing its image and working conditions in general (p. 775). Like Barron (2008), she called for greater strategic alignment between hospitality educators and organizations, in researching, developing and delivering experiential management development programmes. She also explicitly recognized the challenge faced by SMEs in this regard, recommending the establishment of development networks for the industry.

Deery's (2008) contribution focused on the industry's high turnover rate, claiming 'the excessively long hours, style of management and conflict between work and family life, present barriers to making the tourism work environment an attractive and stable one' (p. 794). Based on her review of empirical research, Deery (2008) concluded that more effective and equitable scheduling, improved training and mentorship, and stress mitigation strategies (such as more effective breaks) may lead to increased job satisfaction, organizational commitment and employee retention. She advised the consideration of 'family friendly start and finishing times'; 'flexible work arrangements'; training during work time; adequate resources, staffing levels and breaks; innovative leaves (such as sabbaticals), performance-based rewards, 'staff functions that involve families', 'health and well-being' benefits (such as gym memberships), and 'encouraging sound management practices' (p. 804).

D'Annunzio-Green (2008) presented the results of an empirical study that explored the perspectives of senior hospitality managers. Participants were provided with definitions of talent and talent management and then asked a series of questions. Here (p. 808), talent was defined as 'those individuals who can make a difference to organisational performance, either through their immediate contribution or in the longer term by demonstrating the highest levels of potential'. Talent management was defined as 'the systematic attraction, identification, development, engagement, retention and deployment of those individuals with high potential who are of particular value to an organisation'.

Participants responded favourably to the terminology, suggesting that 'talent management' sounded more dynamic and strategic than some human resource practices such as 'appraisal'. Comments included: 'it might help generate some new life back into our process'; 'it is about having that strategic view – where will we be in the next 2 years, what talent do we need to get there?' (p. 813). Participants also noted barriers to talent management, with some acknowledging the need to develop an attractive brand and employee value proposition, but also the challenge in doing so, given compensation restraints. They spoke of the need to emphasize other opportunities, such as career progression, a team culture and attractive benefits (such as free meals and accommodation).

Participants also shared perspectives on 'Generation Y', citing their interest in continuous development and proclivity to change jobs regularly. One respondent emphasized the need to focus on retention as well as recruitment, noting 'we risk seeing our investment walk out of the door into the hands of our competition' (p. 815). Recommended retention strategies included collecting turnover data, analysing why employees leave, and holding managers accountable for retention targets. One participant shared that such an analysis had led to the realization that many of the reasons employees gave for leaving the organization could have been addressed.

While the interviewees understood the need for development, they also acknowledged organizational barriers, including the lack of management time. One participant shared that responsibility for development had consequently been delegated to a team of employees. In another organization, employees were encouraged to proactively take responsibility for their own development (p. 816); 'tell us what your development needs are; tell us about the skills that you have and how we can develop them to the mutual benefit of the business and yourselves and we will do our best to support you.'

Some respondents also identified difficulties in transitioning from one level of management to another, particularly from middle to senior management. They suggested that employees were promoted before they were ready or without adequate support (p. 818): 'we react to vacancies when they arise and fill them with good internal people'; 'we just don't have the management time to support and coach these individuals – we are setting them up to fail'; 'We underestimate the demands on people with no managerial or supervisory experience – they may have lots of talent but they don't have the right amount of experience or confidence to manage teams of people. This is symptomatic of our sector.' Challenges with performance reviews were also acknowledged (p. 818): 'our appraisal process is a bit outdated and laborious. We have got a very lengthy appraisal that takes about two days to complete'; 'Managers tick the boxes but I am not convinced that the process is as rewarding as it could be for employees.'

D'Annunzio-Green's (2008) contribution highlighted the industry's cultural norms that are antithetical to talent management, including inadequate compensation, lack of turnover data and management accountability, reactionary managerial practices, lack of managerial time for engaging in HRM activities, lack of support for those transitioning to new levels of responsibility and inadequate processes for assessing performance.

The final paper in the collection was by Maxwell and MacLean (2008), which similarly centred on perceptions of hospitality and tourism managers. Participants perceived the importance of talent management, but expressed discomfort with the overt recognition of 'rising stars', arguing that all employees should be developed for the benefit of the industry. They also acknowledged that industry norms hampered their ability to attract and retain good people. Particular mention was made of the lack of pride in service work and problems with work–life balance. The suggestion was made that talent management requires senior management support and that external labour pressures will help to bring about change within the industry. The term 'talent management' was also viewed positively, given its potential to generate 'positive buzz'.

In summarizing this special issue, D'Annunzio-Green et al. (2008,

p. 836) offered: 'talent management is a complex multi-dimensional concept that cannot be ignored by industry, educators or individual managers if the tourism industry is to compete for and retain good employees.' Their contribution underscored the importance of understanding talent management in situ – from the perspective of a particular industry, with its attendant strategic opportunities and competitive dynamics, cultural norms and practices, skill requirements and labour market challenges – and from the perspective of managers, struggling with its implementation.

While this work remains the major contribution on talent management from the perspective of the hospitality and tourism industry to date, Deery and Jago (2015) provided an update, based on empirical research published between 2009 and 2013, with a particular focus on work–life balance (WLB). They found excessive levels of stress and exhaustion, as well as increased interest in studying WLB; 'WLB has either become a larger issue within the industry or . . . hospitality researches have perceived it as a more pressing issue' (p. 464). Identifying such issues as 'long and invasive working hours, sacrificing employees' private life and a decreased social and family life', they advocated for the establishment of a 'WLB culture', including policies that 'discourage work–family spillover, especially for women, so that job satisfaction is higher and stress is lower' (p. 464). They also identified some new concerns, such as alcohol and substance abuse by front-line workers, as well as heightened support for recommendations for engaging and retaining talent, including the provision of meaningful work, better training and development, better pay, and better career opportunities.

Deery and Jago (2015) concluded that 'WLB has been identified as essential to retaining staff, especially the more talented' (p. 467). They offered, 'there is still much to be done to assess the relative importance of various strategies that can be implemented to reduce WLB problems'. They advised, 'it is critical that organisations introduce workplace policies that are strongly endorsed by staff if retention rates are to be increased' and that 'managers regularly monitor the levels of WLB being experienced by staff' (p. 467).

In summary, the hospitality industry provides an important context for studying talent management, given evolving customer expectations and the demand for unique and increasingly sophisticated employee and managerial skill sets, alongside a weak labour market. Talent management arguably holds promise as an approach for challenging longstanding industry norms (such as unsocial work hours, poor work–life balance, low pay, and lack of career development and promotion support) which contribute to the industry's poor reputation and turnover culture. Suggestions from the literature include embracing a talent mindset, establishing effective partnerships with educational programmes and adopting evidence-based HRM practices, including: creatively using benefits to ensure an attractive value proposition; adopting work–life balance friendly policies; providing quality training and development programmes; being explicit with respect to career progression and mentorship opportunities; and holding managers accountable for the effective implementation of such practices, including the achievement of retention targets. The lack of managerial time stood out as a particularly important challenge, suggesting that talent management has either not been perceived as a priority and/or there is a lack of sufficient managerial resources, to support its effective implementation. As a result, in many cases talent management may be little more than window dressing; an effort to encourage managers to adopt progressive HR practices, without providing them with the resources to do so.

CONTRIBUTIONS FROM THE MANAGEMENT LITERATURE

Since Lewis and Heckman's (2006) and Collings and Mellahi's (2009) seminal contributions, many conceptual and empirical studies have been undertaken within the generic management domain, culminating in a number of special issues in a variety of journals, including *Human Resource Management Review* (2013; 2015), the *Journal of World Business* (2014) and *Employee Relations* (2016). The articles within these journals clearly demonstrate that talent management continues to generate significant interest and debate, with some convergence beginning to emerge. Various perspectives pertaining to talent management's theoretical underpinnings; definitions, tensions and propositions; practice and purpose are summarized below.

Theoretical Underpinnings

Extensive reviews of the talent management literature have generally found either a lack of theory, a lack of theorizing or a lack of agreement on which theories are most relevant to its study. Gallardo-Gallardo and Thunnissen (2016), for example, found that 38 per cent of authors in their study used no theoretical framework, while 62 per cent used one or more. Of the latter, many were found to have drawn on theory to justify their own positions, rather than contribute to theory building. Suggesting considerable theoretical divergence, Gallardo-Gallardo and Thunnissen identified a total of 57 distinct theoretical concepts in use, with 40 mentioned in just one article of the articles they reviewed.

Despite this lack of convergence, reviewers have identified some theoretical commonalities, in particular HRM, SHRM and the resource-based view of the firm (RBV) (see for example, Dries, 2013; Gallardo-Gallardo et al., 2015; Gallardo-Gallardo and Thunnissen, 2016; Thunnissen et al., 2013). Given the influence of Lewis and Heckman (2006) and Collings and Mellahi (2009), this should not be surprising.

In their review, Gallardo-Gallardo et al. (2015) found that 'by far, the resource-based view was the dominant theoretical framework' (p. 270), which has been closely associated with SHRM. Wright et al. (2001), for example, suggested that while SHRM 'was not directly born of the resource-based view (RBV), it has clearly been instrumental to its development' (p. 702). From this perspective, organizations are seen as being comprised of a number of capital resources – physical, organizational and human – which provide sustainable competitive advantage to the extent that such resources are 'valuable, rare, imperfectly imitable and non-substitutable' (Barney, 1991, p. 116). Human capital resources include the 'training, experience, judgement, intelligence, relationships, and insights of individual managers and workers in a firm' (Barney, 1991, p. 101). Such resources provide competitive advantage on the basis that they have the potential to 'conceive of or implement strategies that improve [a firm's] efficiency and effectiveness' and 'exploit opportunities and neutralize threats in a firm's environment' (p. 106). Sustainable advantage is achieved, as unique human talent cannot be easily replicated (Iles, 1997).

Other theoretical frameworks associated with talent management that have been acknowledged as gaining in use, include international HRM, knowledge management, organizational behaviour, psychological contract theory, employee assessment, careers management and institutionalism (including how national and organizational cultures shape talent management policies and practices) (see for example, Ariss et al., 2014; Gallardo-Gallardo et al., 2015; Gallardo-Gallardo and Thunnissen, 2016; Nijs et al., 2014; Thunnissen et al., 2013).

While concern was initially expressed about the lack of theoretical clarity (Lewis and Heckman, 2006), more recently scholars have supported this diversity, suggesting that as a growing 'phenomenon' (Dries, 2013, p. 273; Gallardo-Gallardo et al., 2015, p. 264) or a 'bridge field' (Sparrow and Makram, 2015, p. 249), a pluralistic approach may be most appropriate.

In keeping with this direction, Dries (2013, p. 276) advocated for additional theoretical views from psychology, including I/O psychology, educational psychology, vocational psychology, positive psychology and social psychology, arguing that psychological theory is the 'missing link' between 'HRM strategy and organizational performance', suggesting that 'employee perceptions, attitudes, and attributions' can serve as critical mediators.

Thunnissen et al. (2013) similarly called for additional focus on the employee work experience (that can help or hinder performance), including the nature of the actual work performed, the opportunity to engage with questions of importance, and the climate and the values of the organization including the dominant approach to leadership, culture and communication. 'The talent management literature thus consistently overestimates the importance of human capital, or talents, and the potential impact of a narrow set of employment practices' (Thunnissen et al., 2013, p. 328).

Further, Thunnissen et al. (2013), as did Collings et al. (2015), argued that much of the literature has viewed talent management as a managerial tool – from an 'instrumental and rational point of view' – for helping to secure and manage talent in order to meet financial and shareholder targets (p. 329). They suggested that research has inappropriately positioned the organization as a 'unified actor' (2013, p. 328). Instead, they advocated for a pluralistic approach to more 'fully understand the nuances and complexity' of the concept (p. 329). More specifically, they suggested conceptualizing talent management as having multiple goals, including an employment relationship that values employee well-being (meaningful and challenging work, positive social interaction, and just and fair treatment) as well as societal well-being (concern for corporate social responsibility, sustainability, diversity, and human rights) (Boudreau and Ramstad, 2005; Boxall and Purcell, 2011, p. 31).

Clearly, while SHRM and RBV have emerged as relatively dominant theoretical frameworks, calls for additional – more critical – perspectives exist. Gallardo-Gallardo and Thunnissen (2016) advised that rather than seeking agreement, 'it is more important that scholars make deliberate choices in terms of theoretical framing and apply these consistently within the project' (p. 48).

Understanding Talent: Definitions, Tensions and Propositions

Given the variety of theoretical perspectives, it should not be surprising that no single, agreed-upon definition of talent has emerged. In fact, Gallardo-Gallardo and Thunnissen (2016) observed that empirical talent management scholars are 'rarely precise about what they mean by talent' (p. 46). When talent is defined, Michaels et al.'s (2001) definition tends to be one of those offered.

Where the literature has made a contribution, it is with respect to the identification of a number of dimensions or 'tensions' in how talent might be defined (see for example, Gallardo-Gallardo et al. 2013; Thunnissen et al., 2013). These include: talent as object (a characteristic of a person) versus talent as subject (a particular person); talent as input (an ability) versus talent as output (actual performance); talent as a transferable skill versus talent as context-dependent; talent as innate (natural) versus talent as acquired (learned); and finally talent as pertaining to all people (inclusive) or talent pertaining to just a select few (exclusive). These distinctions are important, as they have significant implications for the study and practice of talent management.

The latter two of these dimensions have been a point of particular debate. After an extensive review of the nature–nurture literature, Meyers et al. (2013) concluded: 'as there is insufficient evidence supporting any position on the innate-acquired continuum, we do not presume to offer advice about the one best position on it.' (p. 314). Rather, they suggested that the assumptions an organization makes about whether talent is largely innate, largely acquired, or largely the result of nature–nurture interactions, can have a significant impact on the design of talent management practices (and whether the focus is on talent acquisition or development).

With respect to exclusivity, Meyers and van Woerkom (2014) observed that while according to some scholars 'only few employees are talented (Becker et al., 2009), others propose that every employee has specific talents that can be productively applied in organizations (e.g., Buckingham & Vosburgh, 2001)' (p. 192). Much of the talent management literature reflects an exclusive perspective, with a focus on the identification and retention of 'high performers' or 'high potential' employees (Collings and Mellahi, 2009; Gallardo-Gallardo and Thunnissen, 2016). Indeed, this is what was advocated by Michaels et al. (2001). Organizations in practice, however, reportedly might use either or both approaches, with some preference for exclusivity. According to the Chartered Institute of Personnel and Development (CIPD, 2012), three-fifths of organizations report adopting an exclusive approach. This does not mean, however, that such an approach is best in every context. According to Gallardo-Gallardo et al. (2013, p. 295):

> Especially in the services industry, the whole business model is defined by and around the people employed – and thus, defining talent as the entire workforce is not such a far stretch. In companies such as luxury hotels, for instance, front-line and behind the scenes employees play an equally important role in delivering the high-quality service expected of this type of company.

In challenging the exclusive approach, Nijs et al. (2014) suggested it does not adequately 'capture the psychological mechanisms that come into play when managing individuals' (p. 181). Accordingly, they suggested that all individuals possess both strengths and shortcomings, and 'we should provide all people with the opportunities, resources, and encouragement necessary to achieve their full potential' (p. 184). They also argued that talents must be nurtured and practised, in order to result in excellent performance, and that the work environment can influence 'motivation to invest' (p. 183). Accordingly, they proposed the following definition of talent (p. 182):

> Talent refers to systematically developed innate abilities of individuals that are deployed in activities they like, find important, and in which they want to invest energy. It enables individuals to perform excellently in one or more domains of human functioning, operationalized as performing better than other individuals of the same age or experience, or as performing consistently at their personal best.

In an effort to resolve these tensions, Meyers and van Woerkom (2014, p. 200) proposed a 2 × 2 typology of talent, with exclusiveness/inclusiveness on one dimension and enduring/potential on the other. Taken together, these tensions produced four distinct philosophical positions: exclusive and stable (star 'A' players blessed with rare, innate ability); exclusive and developable (potential latent talent that can be developed into 'A' players); inclusive and stable (every employee possesses positive qualities that need to be harnessed); and inclusive and developable ('ordinary employees can be developed into extraordinary performers') (p. 198). Based on these four philosophies, Meyers and van Woerkom (2014, p. 200) developed a number of propositions (explored further in the section that follows), relating each to specific management practices and organizational opportunities and challenges.

In summary, while a clear definition of talent remains elusive, a number of 'tensions' have been identified, as have a number of philosophical positions and propositions for how these various perspectives might influence the practice of talent management. According to Dries (2013), 'no single perspective on talent is objectively better than another (Boudreau and Ramstad, 2005)'; rather, she suggested, it is the question of 'fit': 'fit with strategic objectives, organizational culture, HR practices and policies, and organizational capacity' (p. 283).

Talent Management in Practice

Given the difficulty in defining 'talent', it should not be surprising that defining 'talent management' has proven equally challenging, but in this instance, this is due to an abundance of suggestions. Most academic papers reference Lewis and Heckman's (2006) critique, agreeing that talent management lacks clarity, and supporting their three-fold classification. Responding to the challenge that talent management may simply be a fad or rhetoric, numerous definitions have been offered, with an accompanying argument as to how the concept is distinct. Largely this has been achieved by referencing an exclusive or differentiated approach. Dries (2013, p. 274) presented a broad collection of definitions, some of which are shared below, using the categorization provided by Lewis and Heckman (2006):

> SHRM: 'an integrated set of processes, programs, and cultural norms in an organization designed and implemented to attract, develop, deploy, and retain talent to achieve strategic objectives and meet future business needs' (Silzer and Dowell, 2010, p. 18).

> Succession/Human Resource Planning: 'managing the supply, demand, and flow of talent through the human capital engine' (Pascal, 2004, p. 9); 'anticipating the need for human capital and setting out a plan to meet it' (Cappelli, 2008, p. 1).

> Managing Talent (Exclusive): 'the process by which an organization identifies and develops employees who are potentially able to move into leadership roles sometime in the future' (Jerusalim and Hausdorf, 2007, p. 934).

> Managing Talent (Inclusive): 'it aspires to yield enhanced performance among all levels in the workforce, thus allowing everyone to reach his/her potential, no matter what that might be' (Ashton and Morton, 2005, p. 30)

As previously discussed, Collings and Mellahi (2009) suggested that their definition – which advocated for the identification of strategically important positions, the development of talent pools, and the creation of a differentiated architecture – should be viewed as a fourth possibility.

Gallardo-Gallardo and Thunnissen (2016, pp. 43–5) also provided a comprehensive summary of talent management definitions. As one example, they cited a definition provided by Lockwood (2006), which also emphasized changes to the HRM system (p. 43): 'the implementation of integrated strategies or systems designed to increase workplace productivity by developing improved processes for attracting, developing, retaining and utilizing people with the required skills and aptitudes to meet current and future business needs.'

Drawing on this view, Gallardo-Gallardo and Thunnissen (2016, p. 50) advanced the following definition: 'TM is aimed at the systematic attraction, identification, development, engagement/retention and deployment of high potential and high performing employees, to fill in key positions, which have significant influence on organization's sustainable competitive advantage.'

Other researchers have expanded the definition of talent management to include its role in specific contexts, such as global talent management (GTM) (Vaiman et al., 2012). According to McNulty and de Cieri (2016, p. 9), GTM is the 'strategic integration of high-performing and high-potential employees on a global scale that includes their proactive identification, development, deployment and retention (Collings and Scullion, 2008; Farndale et al., 2010).' Others, such as Khilji et al. (2015), have suggested that GTM additionally concerns itself with a human development agenda (p. 243). Here, talent management is seen to include concern for enterprise-wide HRM practices along with macro-level issues, such as 'economic development, competitiveness and innovation at the firm and national levels' (Khilji et al., 2015, p. 242).

While each of these definitions may be considered helpful (indeed essential) in clarifying how a particular researcher intends to operationalize talent management in support of its study, as previously suggested, for the field in general, a pluralistic perspective has been called for. As such, the typology presented by Meyers and van Woerkom (2014) (introduced in the previous section) is particularly helpful. They suggested that an organization's approach to talent management would necessarily reflect 'the fundamental assumptions and beliefs about the nature, value, and instrumentality of talent that are held by a firm's key decision makers' (p. 192). Accordingly, they defined talent management as (p. 192): 'The systematic utilization of human resource management (HRM) activities to develop and implement effective talent-management programs to identify, develop, and retain individuals who are considered to be "talented" (in practice, this often means the high-potential employees, the strategically important employees, or employees in key positions).'

Drawing on their four-fold typology, they proposed that if talent is considered stable and exclusive, talent management would focus on policies and practices associated with the acquisition and retention of top talent. Talent management from this perspective might arguably involve the development of an attractive employer brand and value proposition, innovative recruitment techniques, differential rewards, and rigorous performance assessment, potentially including the forced ranking of employees through performance appraisal, in support of internal promotion decisions. Meyers and van Woerkom (2014) criticized this approach on several counts. For example, they questioned the ability of managers to assess employee talent accurately. They also questioned assumptions pertaining to the innate nature of talent (suggesting that talent development is in fact possible). They also argued that this approach would be ineffective for organizations struggling to attract talent, such as has been the case for multinationals operating in emerging markets. Finally, they suggested that there may be significant unintended negative consequences, pertaining to employees who are not identified as top 'talent', but who serve the organization in numerous important ways (this point is explored more in the next section).

While this critique is well taken, elements of such a strategy may have benefit for the hospitality industry. One example of differential treatment for top performers that is already commonly practised is preferred scheduling. Top restaurant servers (those who consistently rank high on sales and customer satisfaction) are often assigned what are considered to be 'premium shifts' as well as the 'best sections'. This provides valued front-line staff with the opportunity to maximize their earnings, while achieving the organization's customer service goals. Good servers are highly mobile and practices such as this are thought to help with retention.

With respect to exclusive/developable talent, the challenge here is to identify 'high potential' employees and to provide them with strategic developmental opportunities (typically through special assignments and customized training opportunities). Meyers and van Woerkom (2014) criticized this approach on the basis that talent can be hard to assess and that the talent needs of organizations are dynamic. They also suggested that this approach can lead to organizations overlooking internal talent, on the basis that 'more people than commonly presumed possess talent (Gladwell, 2008)' (p. 196).

An example of this approach within the hospitality industry pertains to the apprenticeship of cooks aspiring to become chefs, or front-desk clerks being provided with 'stretch' assignments. This approach is also reflected in the creation of special 'co-op' positions for hospitality students, or fast tracking recent graduates through successive short-term job assignments and career development opportunities, culminating in their placement in prime managerial roles, such as through Hilton's Elevator programme.

With respect to inclusive/stable talent, Meyers and van Woerkom (2014) suggested that from this perspective the role of the organization is to identify and capitalize on the talents inherent in each employee, and then by matching talents to assigned tasks, providing employees with the opportunity to capitalize on their strengths. This approach is thought to be conducive to creating cohesive, interdependent teams, with employees differentially contributing, depending upon their skills. Meyers and van Woerkom (2014) reported that research on this approach has found enhancements in employee 'well-being and happiness' as well as 'higher levels of in-role and extra-role performance' (p. 197). They suggested that employees are more likely to feel supported and valued. One drawback of this approach is that talent that is truly in short supply might not feel sufficiently 'special' to be attracted to or retained within the organization.

An example of this approach in the hospitality industry is providing employees with job rotation opportunities, helping them to identify where they most want to contribute. Another example would be the career planning support provided in some hotel and restaurant chains to help employees assess their strengths and interests, and charting their career paths accordingly.

Finally, Meyers and van Woerkom (2014, p. 198) suggested that the inclusive/developable talent approach is reflective of the assumption that employees have both the capacity and the need to grow. This position reflects the contribution of Dweck (2006; 2012) who proposed the existence of a 'growth mindset'. From this perspective, the role of the organization is to help employees achieve their potential through training and development. Organizations adopting this approach are characterized by cultures that emphasize continuous learning and HR practices that emphasize development 'stretch assignments, mentoring, networking, individual development plans, feedback, and reflection (Yost & Chang, 2009)' (Meyers and van Woerkom, 2014, p. 199). Potential benefits of the inclusive/developable approach include: improved employee performance; enhanced ability to respond to changing talent needs; and the ability to overcome scarcity by 'growing your own'. Critics cite the costs of such an approach as well as the fact that sustained practice is required to develop new skills, which some employees might resist.

One example of this approach in the hospitality industry is often found in large multinational fast food chains, such as McDonald's, who have developed highly structured, comprehensive, mandatory training programmes, premised on the assumption that for many employees it is their first paid job. At the management level, such a philosophy is reflected in the existence of comprehensive in-house management development programmes, corporate universities, and generous educational benefits that cover tuition fees, allowing employees to pursue a college or university degree in an area related to their job.

Meyers and van Woerkom (2014, p. 201) concluded by suggesting that due to the 'global scarcity of talent' and the 'highly dynamic environment organizations operate in', talent management will likely 'shift toward more inclusive philosophies in the future'.

Nijs et al. (2014) similarly presented a number of propositions linking conceptions of talent (or in this case 'excellence') to the practice of talent management, two of which are included below for illustrative purposes (p. 184):

Proposition 5. Organizational decision makers who operationalize excellence as performing better than other individuals of the same age or experience in a specific domain of human functioning are more likely to adopt talent-management practices in which there is differential investment – i.e., orientation of a select group of high performers toward activities they like, find important and in which they want to invest energy.

Proposition 6. Organizational decision makers who operationalize excellence as performing consistently at one's personal best, are more likely to adopt talent management practices in which there is egalitarian investment – i.e., orientation of all employees toward activities they like, find important and in which they want to invest energy.

This is another helpful contribution, as it further underscores the importance of researchers specifying the hypothesized relationships between how talent is understood and how talent management is operationalized, in particular contexts and by different stakeholders.

In summary, many definitions of talent management have been proposed, reflecting various philosophical and theoretical positions. Many have been closely associated with strategic HRM and HR planning perspectives. More recently, typologies of talent management have been suggested, based on the explicit recognition that talent may be perceived in a variety of ways, particularly with respect to whether an exclusive or inclusive approach is taken, and whether talent is assumed to be innate or developable. Such philosophical positions can be influenced by a host of contextual variables, including the nature of the work in question, the perceived scarcity of talent, and dynamism within the external environment.

Purpose: What is Talent Management meant to Achieve?

Given the diversity of theories, philosophies and definitions of talent management reviewed, it is perhaps surprising that there appears to be some agreement on what it is ultimately meant to achieve. This is arguably due to the lack of theorizing in general, along with the domination of SHRM and assumptions aligned with a managerial orientation. Articles claiming the importance of talent management typically reference Michaels et al. (2001), who suggested that talent management provides organizations with a sustainable competitive advantage. While outside of an SHRM framework, other potential outcomes – such as employee or social well-being or national development – might be the focus, for the purposes of this chapter we are interested in identifying outcomes that may help to clarify the proposed link between talent management and the achievement of sustainable competitive advantage. To this end, we have synthesized elements of the previously reviewed literature below.

Sustainable competitive advantage has been hypothesized to occur through the timely acquisition and retention of valuable and unique/scarce human capital placed in strategically important positions (see for example, Dries, 2013; Collings and Mellahi, 2009; Thunnissen et al., 2013), thus narrowing the organization's 'supply–demand gap' (Thunnissen et al., 2013, p. 327). The mechanism by which the gap is narrowed is an improved HR 'architecture' (Collings and Mellahi, 2009; Gallardo-Gallardo and Thunnissen, 2016; Lockwood, 2006).

Some scholars have theorized the relationship between these processes and employee-level outcomes. For example, Smart (2005) suggested that high performers contribute to organizational performance in a variety of ways, including demonstrating greater innovation, resourcefulness, initiative, passion, teamwork, and getting the job done for less (as cited in Gallardo-Gallardo et al., 2013, p. 296). Collings and Mellahi (2009) suggested that talent management results in enhanced employee ability and opportunity, which can lead to improved organizational performance, moderated by employee motivation, commitment and extra-role performance. Michaels et al. (2001) also identified the importance of senior leadership support or an organizational 'talent mindset'.

In their extensive discussion on the pros and cons of an exclusive approach to talent management, Gallardo-Gallardo et al. (2013, p. 296) referenced the potential for a Pygmalion effect, 'whereby expectations of performance (high or low) determine actual performance'. Empirical research on talent pool membership has found a range of employee-level benefits for those designated as talent, including greater commitment to performance demands, skill development and organizational priorities (see for example, Bjorkman et al., 2013). Gallardo-Gallardo et al. (2013, p. 296) also suggested that exclusive programmes can result in negative effects, including damage to morale, resentment and undermining teamwork. This point was made by Pfeffer (2001) who concluded that 'fighting the war for talent can readily create self-fulfilling prophecies that leave a large proportion of the workforce demotivated or ready to quit' (p. 258). In their study, Swailes and Blackburn (2016) suggested that top talent can experience negative effects from poor implementation; 'the threat in elite talent programmes may be less that of a disaffected majority and more that of a disenchanted critical minority if talent programmes do not live-up to expectations' (p. 123).

From these various contributions, talent management (if well-implemented) has clearly been associated with a number of important outcomes, at multiple levels. At an organizational level, it has been associated with a talent mindset or organizational culture and an improved HRM architecture, leading to the enhanced ability to reduce the organization's talent supply–demand gap. Additional outcomes include improved placement of valued/unique talent in key positions (in the case of an exclusive approach) or enhanced employee growth (in the case of an inclusive approach).

Positive employee-level outcomes from these practices potentially include improvements in employee ability and opportunity to perform, as well as enhanced motivation, commitment and extra-role performance. These outcomes in turn may result in enhanced employee innovativeness, resourcefulness and initiative. Finally, employee behaviours drive organizational performance, potentially including improved employee retention, customer satisfaction and profitability.

WHERE TO FROM HERE?

Calls for Additional Research

According to an extensive review by Gallardo-Gallardo and Thunnissen (2016), empirical research on talent management has largely investigated its conceptualization and perceived value, as well as particular HRM practices. Research methods have included both quantitative (web-based surveys) and qualitative approaches (semi-structured interviews, focus groups, review of archival data), with the majority (63 per cent) of articles based on descriptive research (p. 39). Level of analysis has tended to focus on the organization (42 per cent), but with an increasing interest (23 per cent) in employee-level issues (p. 40). Senior and/or middle managers and HR representatives have been the most common subjects (p. 40). Geographic focus has been diverse, with considerable activity in Europe and Asia (p. 42). The organizations studied have tended to be large (29 per cent) and multinational (31 per cent), with little participation by smaller, private firms operating in a single country.

Calls for additional research have highlighted the need for research that explicitly studies talent management in context, and considers how its conceptualization, practice and outcomes might vary by organizational size, industry or geography. The need for research that considers the perspective of multiple stakeholders – diverse employees situated in a range of positions and organizational levels – has also been noted. Nijs et al. (2014), for example, called for more research that investigates how 'organizational characteristics (e.g., size, sector, culture) relate to a certain definition and operationalization of talent' (p. 187). Gallardo-Gallardo and Thunnissen (2016) suggested that more work needs to be done within SMEs and that participants should include employees working in a variety of roles, including line managers, given their responsibility for implementing HR practices and policies.

Ariss et al. (2014) additionally suggested studying talent management as a 'relational construct' and seeking to understand the connections between 'individual, organizational, institutional, and national/international contexts' (p. 176). For example, 'the subjective experience' of talent management by an individual might be influenced by gender or race (Ng and Burke, 2005), organizational culture and HR practices, or national policies pertaining to education or employment. As one example, Ariss et al. (2014)

encouraged studying talent management in the developing world, suggesting that within that context a commitment to corporate social responsibility can be effective, as it 'creates a sense of pride in the company and helps managers and HR professionals to make effective use of their talents' (p. 177).

Ariss et al. (2014) concluded their contribution by suggesting that the practice of talent management will likely change significantly in the near future, due to a number of environmental factors including technological advances, globalization and the changing nature of work. In contrast to the scarcity of talent identified in the *War for Talent* (Michaels et al., 2001), they argued that on a global basis, there may actually be an abundance of talent and that LinkedIn and other social media platforms are now providing organizations with the means to locate it. The nature of employment is also changing; talent can be more easily, more cheaply and more temporarily acquired through people brokering their own talent on a limited-contract basis. The increasing rise of contract labour and its social consequences has been well-documented in the book *The Precariat – The New Dangerous Class* by Guy Standing (2014). Standing suggested that the precariat (who he identified as a new social class characterized by the precarious nature of its members' employment) is growing, dramatically. Ariss et al. (2014, p. 178) similarly suggested that in the future many organizations will be comprised of just 'a small group of core employees' and that talent management practices may increasingly include sourcing 'talent on demand'. Research that explores how conceptions of talent management are changing, given these environmental shifts, is clearly needed.

With respect to methods, Gallardo-Gallardo et al. (2015) suggested that 'TM scholars need to invest more effort into developing methodologically and statistically rigorous research designs' (p. 276). Consistent with this advice, Meyers and van Woerkom (2014) suggested testing their propositions via discourse analysis with talent managers, as well as through the review of archival data and conducting cross-cultural comparisons. Nijs et al. (2014) presented a comprehensive summary of various instruments available for assessing innate ability, knowledge and skill development, motivation, interpersonal strengths and interests (p. 186). Nijs et al. (2014) also called for research that 'explicitly investigates attitudinal and behavioral reactions to (not) being identified as talent' (p. 187) as well as how talent manifests itself in team settings (p. 188).

In summary, additional research on talent management is needed with respect to myriad factors, including organizational and national context and culture, the views and experience of multiple stakeholders, environmental shifts (such as the role of technology), and the interaction between these various components. More research is also needed that explicitly bridges theoretical domains, develops and tests propositions, helps the field to advance and supports management practice in new, evidence-informed ways.

The Potential for Research within the Hospitality and Tourism Context

Hospitality researchers can potentially make a substantial contribution with respect to all of these opportunities for further research. The hospitality and tourism industry provides a unique and important context, given deeply embedded industry norms, its weak labour market, and the need to meet increasingly complex and demanding customer expectations. While it has been suggested that, given these factors, an inclusive approach to talent management might be most appropriate for this industry, we suspect a hybrid approach to be the answer. Identifying components of such strategies and comparing their effectiveness in use would make a significant contribution to the literature.

Another recommended avenue for further research is the exploration of talent management philosophies, practices and outcomes within 'high performing' multinational hotel and restaurant chains or tourism enterprises. Many of these organizations have formalized senior talent management positions with links to educational programmes. Some are also routinely recognized as employers of choice (Aon Canada, 2017). Talent management could be explored from the perspective of organizations recognized as talent management leaders, as well as from different national contexts (potentially exploring the impact of differences in educational policies, employment legislation and economic factors on the talent supply–demand gap), as well as the efficacy of various GTM practices. Research is also needed from the perspective of employees in different types of positions (front of house, back of house), and organizational levels (front line, front-line supervisor, middle management, senior management), as well as with respect to various demographic factors (gender, race, age).

Research that seeks to identify elements of a successful SRHM architecture within hospitality and tourism operations is needed, with respect to the acquisition, retention and engagement of both core and contingent employees. A typology of SHRM architectures could be developed on the basis of the customer value proposition on offer, whether the focus of the organization is largely on the delivery of a high quality, customized service experience (such as in a luxury hotel or restaurant), or in the consistent delivery of a commodity (such as in a fast food restaurant chain or budget hotel).

Similar research could be conducted within successful SMEs, including independents and national or regional chains noted for their innovation, positive employer brands, and reputations for delivering exceptional customer service and/or products. The identification of components within a successful employee value proposition could help to assess the extent to which inadequate compensation (the lack of a living wage) is contributing to the industry's HRM problems. It could also help to identify the perceived value of other more progressive elements (reportedly of interest to Millennials), such as corporate social responsibility objectives (including, for example, an organization's commitment to sustainable environmental practices and fair trade across the supply chain).

As previously suggested, research is also needed on the impact of automation and artificial intelligence. One recent study (Frey and Osborne, 2013, p. 38) concluded that '47 percent of total US employment' is at 'high risk' of being automated over the next several years. Of the 702 jobs categorized, Frey and Osborne positioned 'lodging managers' as one of the jobs least susceptible to automation. That said, they ranked many hospitality and tourism jobs in the high-risk category, suggesting the industry might be more susceptible to automation than most. Job categories assigned a greater than 90 per cent probability of being replaced included: 'Dining Room and Cafeteria Attendants and Bartender Helpers; Food Prep and Serving Workers; Short Order Cooks; Hotel, Motel and Resort Desk Clerks; First-Line Supervisors of Housekeeping and Janitorial Workers; Counter Attendants, Cafeteria, Food Concession & Coffee Shop; Restaurant Cooks; and Host and Hostesses'.

A more recent study by McKinsey consultants Manyika et al. (2017) challenged the Frey and Osborne (2013) study, suggesting that few jobs have ever actually disappeared as a result of automation. Rather, automation is more likely to augment work tasks and create new, more knowledge-intensive jobs. That said, the McKinsey analysis similarly placed jobs in the 'accommodation and foodservices' sector at the top of their list of where they perceived the most potential for automation (p. 7). Given this brave new world, the hospitality and tourism industry provides an ideal context for studying the impact of automation on talent management, in terms of its conception and associated management practices.

CONCLUSION

'Talent management' has received considerable attention within organizations, and increasingly within academe, since its introduction as a source of sustainable competitive advantage 20 years ago. Yet debate continues as to what talent management actually means, including its underlying theory, definition, practice and intent. This chapter has provided a roadmap to the evolving understandings of talent management within the hospitality and tourism field, but also within the management literature more generally. While talent management has largely had its roots in SHRM and RBV, reflecting a managerialist perspective, it has increasingly been acknowledged as a pluralistic concept, one that is both relational and context-dependent, one that has the potential to bridge various theoretical traditions and play an integrating role in advancing new understanding. The hospitality industry presents an ideal opportunity for contributing to this task.

Our understanding of talent management would benefit substantially from research on its implementation within large multinationals as well as SMEs, and from the perspective of multiple stakeholders (including front-line employees and managers, as well as senior staff). The study of talent management in situ holds great promise for developing a typology of strategic HRM practices that could help inform the development of a strategic talent management architecture, including the identification of successful SHRM practices. Investigations that explore the link between elements of the HR architecture and employee behaviours and attitudes could help to inform organizational priorities and managerial practice. For example, the industry has long struggled with the impact of its low compensation levels and other negative workplace practices. It would be interesting to explore the impact (or return on investment) of a living wage and commitment to work–life balance, on employee retention, customer satisfaction and organizational performance. Research is also needed that explicitly links all of the above to the broader environment and changes that are occurring with respect to automation and labour scarcity. One central premise of the talent management literature is that talent is scarce. Given pending automation, it is unclear to what extent this will continue to be the case and what the implications of a significantly altered labour market might have for talent management. Clearly, there is no shortage of fascinating and important research questions; we encourage hospitality researchers to participate in their exploration and in advancing the field.

REFERENCES

Aon Canada (2017), *Aon Best Employers in Canada 2017*, accessed 22 March 2017 at: www.aon.com/canada/products-services/human-capital-consulting/consulting/best_employers/Winners.html.
Ariss, A.A., W.F. Cascio and J. Paauwe (2014), 'Talent management: current theories and future research directions', *Journal of World Business*, **49**, 173–9.
Ashton, C. and L. Morton (2005), 'Managing talent for competitive advantage', *Strategic HR Review*, **4** (5), 28–31.
Barney, J.B. (1991), 'Firm resources and sustained competitive advantage', *Journal of Management*, **17**, 99–120.

Barron, P. (2008), 'Education and talent management: implications for the hospitality industry', *International Journal of Contemporary Hospitality Management*, **20** (7), 730–42.

Baum, T. (2008), 'Implications of hospitality and tourism labour markets for talent management strategies', *International Journal of Contemporary Hospitality Management*, **20** (7), 720–29.

Becker, B.E. and M.A. Huselid (2006), 'Strategic human resource management: where do we go from here?', *Journal of Management*, **32** (6), 898–925.

Becker, B.E., M.A. Huselid and R.W. Beatty (2009), *The Differentiated Workforce: Transforming Talent into Strategic Impact*, Boston, MA: Harvard Business Press.

Bjorkman, I., M. Ehrnrooth, K. Makela, A. Smale and J. Sumelius (2013), 'Talent or not? Employee reactions to talent identification', *Human Resource Management*, **52** (2), 195–214.

Boselie, P., G. Dietz and C. Boon (2005), 'Commonalities and contradictions in HRM and performance research', *Human Resource Management Journal*, **15** (3), 67–94.

Boudreau, J.W. and P.M. Ramstad (2005), 'Talentship, talent segmentation, and sustainability: a new HR decision science paradigm for a new strategy definition', *Human Resource Management*, **44** (7), 129–36.

Boudreau, J.W. and P.M. Ramstad (2007), *Beyond HR: The New Science of Human Capital*, Boston, MA: Harvard Business School Press.

Boxall, P. and J. Purcell (2008), *Strategy and Human Resource Management*, second edn, Basingstoke: Palgrave Macmillan.

Buckingham, M. and R.M. Vosburgh (2001), 'The 21st century human resources function: it's the talent, stupid!', *Human Resource Planning*, **24**, 17–23.

Cappelli, P. (2008), 'Talent management for the twenty-first century', *Harvard Business Review*, accessed 22 March 2017 at: http://hosteddocs.toolbox.com/talent%20manage ment%20for%20the%2021st%20century.pdf.

Christensen Hughes, J. and E. Rog (2008), 'Talent management: a strategy for improving employee recruitment, retention and engagement within hospitality organizations', *International Journal of Contemporary Hospitality Management*, **20** (7), 743–57.

CIPD (2012), *Learning and Talent Development Report*, accessed 23 March 2017 at: www. digitalopinion.co.uk/files/documents/CIPD_2012_LTD_Report.pdf.

Collings, D.G. and K. Mellahi (2009), 'Strategic talent management: a review and research agenda', *Human Resource Management Review*, **19** (4), 304–13.

Collings, D. and H. Scullion (2008), 'Resourcing international assignees', in M. Dickmann, C. Brewster and P. Sparrow (eds), *International Human Resource Management: A European Perspective*, Abingdon: Routledge, pp. 87–106.

Collings, D.G., H. Scullion and V. Vaiman (2015), 'Talent management: progress and prospects', *Human Resource Management Review*, **25**, 233–5.

D'Annunzio-Green, N. (2008), 'Managing the talent management pipeline: towards a greater understanding of senior managers' perspectives in the hospitality and tourism sector', *International Journal of Contemporary Hospitality Management*, **20** (7), 807–19.

D'Annunzio-Green, N., G. Maxwell and W. Watson (2008), 'Concluding commentary on the contemporary human resource issues for talent management in hospitality and tourism', *International Journal of Contemporary Hospitality Management*, **20** (7).

Deery, M. (2008), 'Talent management, work–life balance and retention strategies', *International Journal of Contemporary Hospitality Management*, **20** (7), 792–806.

Deery, M. and L. Jago (2015), 'Revisiting talent management, work–life balance and retention strategies', *Journal of Contemporary Hospitality Management*, **27** (3), 453–72.

Delery, J.E. and D.H. Doty (1995), 'Modes of theorizing in strategic human resource management: tests of universalistic, contingency and configurational performance prediction', *Academy of Management Journal*, **39** (4), 802–35.

Dell, D. and J. Hickey (2002), 'Sustaining the talent quest: getting and keeping the best people in volatile times', *Research Report 1318*, Ottawa, ON: Conference Board of Canada.

Dries, N. (2013), 'The psychology of talent management: a review and research agenda', *Human Resource Management Review*, **23** (4), 272–85.

Dweck, C.S. (2006), *Mindset: The New Psychology of Success*, New York: Random House.

Dweck, C.S. (2012), 'Mindsets and human nature: promoting change in the Middle East, the schoolyard, the racial divide and willpower', *The American Psychologist*, **67**, 614–22.

Employee Relations (2016), *Employee Relations*, Special issue: Strategic Talent Management, **38** (1).

Farndale, H., P. Scullion and P. Sparrow (2010), 'The role of the corporate HR function in global talent management', *Journal of World Business*, **45** (2), 161–8.

Frey, C. and M. Osborne (2013), 'The future of employment: how susceptible are jobs to computerisation?', *Oxford Martin School*, accessed 4 March 2017 at: www.oxfordmartin.ox.ac.uk/downloads/academic/The_Future_of_Employment.pdf.

Gallardo-Gallardo, E. and M. Thunnissen (2016), 'Standing on the shoulders of giants? A critical review of empirical talent management research', *Employee Relations*, **38** (1), 31–56.

Gallardo-Gallardo, E., N. Dries and T.F. Gonzalez-Cruz (2013), 'What is the meaning of "talent" in the world of work?', *Human Resource Management Review*, **23** (4), 290–300.

Gallardo-Gallardo, E., S. Nijs, N. Dries and P. Gallo (2015), 'Towards an understanding of talent management as a phenomenon-driven field using bibliometric and content analysis', *Human Resource Management Review*, **25** (3), 264–79.

Gandz, J. (2006), 'Talent development: the architecture of a talent pipeline that works', *Ivey Business Journal*, **70** (5), 1–4.

Gladwell, M. (2008), *Outliers: The Story of Success*, London: Penguin Books.

Human Resource Management Review (2013), Dries, N. (ed.) **23** (4). Elsevier.

Human Resource Management Review (2015), Collings, D.G., H. Scullion and V. Vaiman (eds) **25** (3). Elsevier.

Huselid, M.A., R.W. Beatty and B.E. Becker (2005), '"A players" or "A positions"? The strategic logic of workforce management', *Harvard Business Review*, **83** (12), 110–117.

Huselid, M.A., S.E. Jackson and R.S. Schuler (1997), 'Technical and strategic human resource management effectiveness determinates of firm performance', *Academy of Management Journal*, **40**, 171–88.

Iles, P. (1997), 'Sustainable high potential career development: a resource-based view', *Career Development International*, **2** (7), 347–53.

Jerusalim, R.S. and P.A. Hausdorf (2007), 'Managers' justice perceptions of high potential identification practices', *The Journal of Management Development*, **26** (10), 933–50.

Journal of World Business (2014), Ariss, A.A., W.F. Cascio and J. Paauwe (eds), **49**.

Khilji, S.E., I. Tarique and R.S. Schuler (2015), 'Incorporating the macro view in global talent management', *Human Resource Management Review*, **25** (3), 236–48.

Lepak, D.P. and S.A. Snell (1999), 'The human resource architecture: toward a theory of human capital allocation and development', *Academy of Management Review*, **24** (1), 31–48.

Lewis, R.E. and R.J. Heckman (2006), 'Talent management: a critical review', *Human Resource Management Review*, **16** (2), 139–54.

Lockwood, N.R. (2006), 'Talent management: driver for organizational success', *HR Magazine*, **51** (6), (June), S1:S11.

Manyika, J., M. Chui, M. Miremadi, J. Bughin, K. George, P. Willmott and M. Dewhurst (2017), 'A future that works: automation, employment, and productivity', *McKinsey Global Institute*, accessed 10 March 2017 at: www.google.ca/search?q=Mckinsey+job+automation&ie=utf-8&oe=utf-8&gws_rd=cr&ei=wb3JWI7ELIysjwTD4p74Ag.

Matthew 25:14–30, *Parable of the talents*, accessed 23 March 2017 at: www.theologyofwork.org/new-testament/matthew/living-in-the-new-kingdom-matthew-18-25/the-parable-of-the-talents-matthew-2514-30/.

Maxwell, G.A. and S. MacLean (2008), 'Talent management in hospitality and tourism in Scotland: operational implications and strategic actions', *International Journal of Contemporary Hospitality Management*, **20** (7), 820–30.

McNulty, Y. and H. de Cieri (2016), 'Linking global mobility and global talent management: the role of ROI', *Employee Relations*, **38** (1), 8–30.

Meyers, M.C. and M. van Woerkom (2014), 'The influence of underlying philosophies on talent management: theory, implications for practice, and research agenda', *Journal of World Business*, **49** (2), 192–203.

Meyers, M.C., M. van Woerkom and N. Dries (2013), 'Talent–innate or acquired? Theoretical considerations and their implications for talent management', *Human Resource Management Review*, **24** (4), 305–321.

Michaels, E., H. Handfield-Jones and B. Axelrod (2001), *The War for Talent*, Boston, MA: Harvard Business School Press.

Morton, L. (2005), 'Talent management value imperatives: strategies for successful execution', *Research Report R-1360-05-RR*, Conference Board of Canada.

Ng, E.S.W. and R.J. Burke (2005), 'Person–organization fit and the war for talent: does diversity management make a difference?', *International Journal of Human Resource Management*, **16** (7), 1195–210.

Nijs, S., E. Gallardo-Gallardo, N. Dries and L. Sels (2014), 'A multidisciplinary review into the definition, operationalization, and measurement of talent', *Journal of World Business*, **49**, 180–91.

Organ, D.W. (1988), *Organizational Citizenship Behaviour: The Good Soldier Syndrome*, Lexington, MA: Lexington Books.

Pascal, C. (2004), 'Foreword', in A. Schweyer (ed.), *Talent Management Systems: Best Practices in Technology Solutions for Recruitment, Retention, and Workforce Planning*, Canada: Wiley.

Pfeffer, J. (1994), *Competitive Advantage Through People. Unleashing the Power of the Workforce*, Boston, MA: Harvard Business School Press.

Pfeffer, J. (1998), *The Human Equation: Building Profits by Putting People First*, Boston, MA: Harvard Business School Press.

Pfeffer, J. (2001), 'Fighting the war for talent is hazardous to your organization's health', *Organizational Dynamics*, **29** (4), 248–59.

Riley, M. (1996), *Human Resource Management in the Hospitality and Tourism Industry*, Oxford: Butterworth-Heinemann.

Schuler, R.S. and S.E. Jackson (1987), 'Linking competitive strategies and human resource management practices', *Academy of Management Executive*, **1** (3), 207–19.

Scott, B. and S. Revis (2008), 'Talent management in hospitality: graduate career success and strategies', *International Journal of Contemporary Hospitality Management*, **20** (7), 781–91.

Silzer, R. and B.E. Dowell (2010), 'Strategic talent management matters', in R. Silzer and B.E. Dowell (eds), *Strategy-driven Talent Management: A Leadership Imperative*, San Francisco, CA: Jossey-Bass, pp. 3–72.

Smart, B.D. (2005), *Topgrading: How Leading Companies Win by Hiring, Coaching and Keeping the Best People* (rev. edn), New York: Portfolio (Penguin Group).

Sparrow, P.R. and H. Makram (2015), 'What is the value of talent management? Building value-driven processes within a talent management architecture', *Human Resource Management Review*, **25** (3), 249–63.

Standing, G. (2014), *The Precariat: The New Dangerous Class*, New York: Bloomsbury Academic.

Swailes, S. and M. Blackburn (2016), 'Employee reactions to talent pool membership', *Employee Relations*, **38** (1), 112–28.

Thunnissen, M., P. Boselie and B. Fruytier (2013), 'Talent management and the relevance of context: towards a pluralistic approach', *Human Resource Management Review*, **23**, 326–36.

Vaiman, V., H. Scullion and D. Collings (2012), 'Talent management decision making', *Management Decision*, **50** (5), 925–41.

Watson, S. (2008), 'Where are we now? A review of management development issues in the hospitality and tourism sector', *International Journal of Contemporary Hospitality Management*, **20** (7), 758–80.

Wells Fargo (2016), *The Vision and Values of Wells Fargo*. Accessed 24 February 2017 at: www08.wellsfargomedia.com/assets/pdf/about/corporate/vision-and-values.pdf.

Wright, P.M., B.B. Dunford and S.A. Snell (2001), 'Human resources and the resource based view of the firm', *Journal of Management*, **27** (6), 701–21.

Yost, P.R. and G. Chang (2009), 'Everyone is equal, but some are more equal than others', *Industrial and Organizational Psychology*, **2** (4), 442–5.

8. Jobs for the girls? Women's employment and career progression in the hospitality industry

Shelagh Mooney

1. INTRODUCTION

The hospitality industry is widely considered to be female dominated; however, many women's employment opportunities appear to be at the lower levels of hospitality work. When examining why men occupy senior management positions in hospitality in greater proportions than women (Boone et al., 2013; Santero-Sanchez et al., 2015), this chapter takes the perspective that the vast majority of hospitality and tourism workforce studies have focused on the individual and organizational level, without looking at the myriad of contextual relationships that influence the agency of women within hospitality organizations across diverse contexts and locations. Sectoral employment studies would benefit from exploring the nuanced linkages that exist within and between the micro/meso/macro levels of hospitality and tourism work as suggested by Baum et al. (2016a). The intersectional approach taken in this chapter captures the complex interactions between women (micro-level); their employing organizations (meso-level); and state/societal institutions and structures (macro-level) in a specific context. These connections are significant, as Powell and Butterfield (2015) consider it is the combination of factors at all three levels that hinders women's advancement and keeps them in low quality jobs. At organizational level in the hospitality sector, 'resource based' human resource management (HRM) policies (Hughes, 2008) do not appear to further women's interests. The view of human resource as cost, rather than investment, has led to many of the circumstances that are both cause and effect of the prevailing high turnover in the sector.

The chapter is structured as follows. First, the meaning(s) attached to gender are explained, before the context of women's employment in hospitality at the societal, organizational and individual levels is outlined. A brief review of HRM practices in the industry is included in this overview. The chapter concludes with a list of recommendations that will benefit not only women's advancement possibilities but additionally, by increasing individual job quality across organizations, will help to increase retention in the sector for all employees, not only women. Generally, the term 'gender' is commonly only associated with women. Men are not perceived to have 'gender' and the word tends to be associated with biological factors (Lewis and Simpson, 2010). It is significant that successful men rarely question the various nuances of gender. However, gendered processes affect both men and women in the workplace and it is essential to consider local, organizational and industrial context (Hyde, 2005) as the workplace experiences of women can vary according to where they are located, even within the same country. For example, in Turkey, women working in city hotels are more highly educated and more satisfied with their working conditions than their counterparts working in isolated resort areas (Okumus et al., 2010). The perspective about gender taken in this chapter is that gender is socially constructed. Particular social assumptions are associated with gendered roles; there are conscious and unconscious expectations that men and women will play specific roles in the workplace (Lewis and Simpson, 2010). There are implications for how gendered processes reinforce power and inequality in hospitality organizations, for example, dictating who does the 'dirty work' of housekeeping; therefore, gender is seen as embodied in doing and performativity. Individuals may subvert their gendered identities in order to fit in with organizational norms that mould and change their behaviour, whether they realize it or not (Martin, 2003). Dominant forms of masculinity associated with strategic HRM have been implicated in the 'promotion of hetero-normativity and the corresponding subordination of feminine attributes and non-hegemonic masculinities' (Broadbridge and Simpson, 2011, p.474). Gendered identities are expressed in symbols or entrenched beliefs that workers use to represent embedded workplace norms, for example, the belief that hard work is recognized (Mooney et al., 2016). Sexual orientation is seen as another aspect of performance in the workplace; hetero-normativity is the prevailing societal expression of a heterosexual and 'obvious' norm (Winker and Degele, 2011, p.55). It explains why men who may appear to be homosexual may be subject to sexual harassment in masculine areas in hospitality (see Ineson et al., 2013).

2. THE MACRO CONTEXT OF EMPLOYMENT IN HOSPITALITY AND TOURISM

Hospitality work provides significant employment opportunities: one in eleven jobs is provided by the global tourism industry (World Travel and Tourism Council (WTTC), 2016). Although globalization has led to increased diversity in the scale of operation, as well as diversity of guests and employees (Riley and Szivas, 2009; Testa, 2009), the hospitality industry continues to be highly vulnerable to economic pressures because of inconsistent demand (Yu et al., 2014); individual sectors offer unpredictable and seasonal financial disparities and return on investment (WTTC, 2016). Market-led economic forces at macro-level have led to significant changes in international internal and external labour markets, reflected in hospitality employment patterns (McDowell et al., 2009). Globally, to decrease costs, hospitality organizations have flattened their organizational structures, removed tiers of middle management, outsourced departments such as housekeeping and 'casualized' much of their workforce (Knox, 2014; Lai et al., 2008).

As the sector remains labour intensive, there is a constant search to reduce labour costs and increase productivity. This has resulted in the wide-scale adoption of flexible work practices and use of technology and automation across the sector (Davidson et al., 2011; Hinkin and Tracey, 2000; Kusluvan et al., 2010). However, technical advances have had variable impact on a largely skills-based industry; many jobs are physically demanding, essentially requiring some degree of emotional, social, technical and physical skill (Bernhardt et al., 2003; Furunes and Mykletun, 2005; Powell, 2002). Low entry barriers (Baum, 2007) have led to the misperception that hospitality jobs are temporary stopgaps. A majority of hospitality workers, many women, are engaged in poorly paid casual jobs (Baum, 2013; McIntosh and Harris, 2012; Zampoukos and Ioannides, 2011). Such non-standard work, associated with low quality jobs and precarious employment (Acker, 2006), has evolved into the concept of a 'zero-hours contract', where the worker is tied to one employer with no guaranteed minimum hours of work (McDowell et al., 2014). Offe and Standing (2011) refer to those without formal employment contracts as a new marginalized underclass, bereft of a work identity or job security.

Women's traditional 'homemaker' role has also changed, however, the considerable societal expectations about the domestic responsibilities of women have failed to keep pace with the social role demands of women in the workforce. There are now a higher proportion of women than previously in paid employment, and in Western economies dual career families at all levels of society are the rule (Cha, 2013; Clevenger and Singh, 2013; Strachan, 2010). Gender equality in the workplace has yet to be achieved and women are disadvantaged by being placed in certain sectors of the labour market, which 'ghettoize them' (Anthias, 2001, p. 383), such as hospitality work. The combination of factors that retain women in less privileged positions than men is known as the glass ceiling (Williams, 2013). Broadbridge and Mavin's (2016) editorial, which sought advances beyond the glass ceiling metaphor, cited more recent iterations, including Ashcraft's (2013) 'glass slipper' metaphor and Simpson and Kumra's (2016) 'Teflon effect', which explain why merit does not 'stick' to talented women who seek advancement to senior management. Globally women hold jobs with lower prestige and pay than men (Anderson et al., 2010; Williams, 2013), which are seen as commensurate with the domestic skills that they are presumed to possess. Bourdieu (2001) theorized that the restriction of career opportunities for women is associated with a lack of value placed on their activities, in either the home or workplace. Correspondingly, there is a lower proportion of women than men in senior leadership positions across many societies (Broadbridge and Mavin, 2016; Burke, 2014).

Structurally at macro level, there are common barriers that hinder women's ability to advance or earn equal pay to men, even in societies that appear to have powerful Equal Employment Opportunity (EEO) legislation. For instance, a review of women's participation in hospitality management in the United States indicates that at governmental level, there is 'inadequate reporting and publicising of information relevant to glass ceiling issues' (Clevenger and Singh, 2013, p. 389). There is considerable work–life conflict in the hospitality sector due to the unpredictable nature of business levels (Burke et al., 2011; Cleveland et al., 2007), and the workplace requirement that managers be visible for guests and employees (Guerrier, 1986; O'Neill, 2012). For women managers, work–life conflict is exacerbated by the societal expectation that women will take care of older dependents (to a greater or lesser extent depending on the culture), household management and childcare generally (Lan and Wang Leung, 2001). Women's equal participation in hospitality management appears to reduce at department head level (Mooney and Ryan, 2009; Riley, 1990), suggesting that gender intersects with age/life stage in hospitality careers. Although both men and women experience difficulty in reconciling home and work life (Kesting and Harris, 2009), women continue to experience the greater share of the domestic burden. Cha (2013) argues that women who work in excess of 50 hours a week (commonplace in hospitality management roles) find it practically impossible to meet the competing 'greedy' demands of workplaces and family: the result of trying to conform leads to overwork and exhaustion for the majority of women.

3. MESO LEVEL: WORK AT HOSPITALITY ORGANIZATIONAL LEVEL

Due to the macro financial and operational stressors influencing HRM practices in the sector, the hospitality working environment reflects both the fragmentation of the industry, seasonality and unpredictability of demand. The tendency for hospitality organizations to see their employees as costs rather than assets, creates a negative work environment (Baum, 2007; Davidson and Wang, 2011; Hughes, 2008). In the 24/7 industry, there is a common perception of long hours (Altman and Brothers, 2013), low pay and precarious work (Janta et al., 2011). The poor pay and conditions are a source of dissatisfaction for many hospitality workers and contribute to high turnover (Hinkin and Tracey, 2000; Kuria et al., 2012); other contributors are poor human resource management practices (Kusluvan et al., 2010), high vocational mobility (Baum, 2007) and seasonality (Chalkiti and Sigala, 2010). Regrettably, the high turnover is accepted by managers as an inevitable aspect of the industry in a variety of diverse hospitality environments (for example, see Anvari and Seliman, 2010; Lub et al., 2012). Negative repercussions are the associated tangible and intangible costs, such as losses in productivity and guest loyalty (Deery, 2002; Lashley, 2001; Michel et al., 2013). It is unsurprising that talent shortfall is cited as a major human resource problem in hospitality (Enz, 2009; Enz and Siguaw, 2000; Song et al., 2015).

Unsurprisingly, low levels of job satisfaction, motivation and engagement are revealed in audits of HRM practices in the hospitality industry (Hughes, 2008; Kusluvan et al., 2010). In hotels, for instance, poor HRM practices are visible in many Western contexts, such as the United Kingdom (Knox and Walsh, 2005) and the United States (Hinkin and Tracey, 2000). In Spain, many hotels practise a 'hard' HRM approach that focuses on minimizing labour costs, as opposed to a more humanistic human resources approach emphasizing team work and employee commitment (Marco-Lajara and Úbeda-García, 2013). The side-effect of such practices is work intensification, reduced job security and little time for workplace socializing (Yamashita and Uenoyama, 2006). In Western countries, attention paid to diversity matters is inconsistent; some global organizations in the United States, such as Sodexo and Starwood, have developed diversity management strategies, but others appear to demonstrate few initiatives (Clevenger and Singh, 2013). In developing countries, attention paid to such HRM practices that encourage employee commitment and engagement is variable. Some state-run hotels in China (Kong et al., 2010) show advanced human resources management practices; however, in other developing countries such as the Cameroons (Karatepe, 2012) and Turkey (Pinar et al., 2011), the hospitality industry focuses on minimizing labour costs rather than employee satisfaction. These issues affect women's job quality and career opportunities.

3.1 Organizational Norms for Hospitality Careers

The majority of hospitality career studies take a gender-neutral perspective that is somewhat at odds with what the literature tells us about women's inferior positioning in hospitality employment, compared with men. Gender tends to be generally noted as a mere demographic descriptor, and the majority of hospitality studies do not consider how gender influences hospitality career patterns in various cultural contexts, for example, China (Kong et al., 2010; 2011; 2012), Japan (Yamashita and Uenoyama, 2006), or Zimbabwe (Mkono, 2010). There are, of course, exceptions: Okumus et al.'s (2010) study of Turkish women employees, Ng and Pine's (2003) research into gender in Hong Kong hotels, Lan and Wang Leung's (2001) exploration of career challenges facing Asian women and Adler and Adler's (2004) in-depth sociological examination of hospitality work in Hawaii. A further difficulty in understanding how women's careers in hospitality play out is the absence of a common hospitality career construct due to the varying contexts of hospitality employment and the seasonality aspects of the sector; therefore, many understandings of hospitality careers are based on hotel studies. It appears that the contemporary vision of the hotel/hospitality manager has moved beyond an earlier focus on technical competencies (Beck and Lopa, 2001; Nebel et al., 1994), to an appreciation that advanced social skills and attitudes are an essential component of career success (Akrivos et al., 2007; Mkono, 2010). Geographical and functional mobility are encouraged by hospitality organizations, leading employees to higher positions and increased pay (Ayres, 2006; Houran et al., 2012), thus a 'butterfly' or boundaryless career pattern is frequently demonstrated by managers, who gain human capital from strategic moves across different organizations (McCabe and Savery, 2007). In order for individuals to achieve career success in hospitality management, complex competencies are required, including career development, career adjustment and control, communication/networking skills and the ability to manage work–life balance at different life stages (Wang, 2013).

In contrast to the linear trajectory of 'career managers', the hospitality sector also attracts many workers who do not necessarily intend to have a career in hospitality, for example, migrants, students and women seeking part-time work who enter the sector because of flexible work shifts and low entry barriers (Baum, 2015; McPhail et al., 2015). Mooney et al.'s (2016) detailed analysis of hospitality career patterns among long-term hospitality workers covers both career options, breaking careers into three phases. In Phase 1, the absence of skill or qualification requirements at entry level makes it a convenient option particularly for women seeking part-time work in housekeeping or service roles. In Phase 2, career enablers and boundaries regulate career development and progression. Barriers are lack of training opportunities and the absence of influential mentors. Where these are lacking, senior managers can block development opportunities and fail to facilitate geographical development for competent individuals. Fixed location creates a further boundary in isolated (and seasonal) areas, as there are fewer promotional opportunities than in urban centres. In Phase 3, hospitality workers accept their career and do not necessarily seek changes in position for promotional reasons; however, they may change location or function for lifestyle reasons. Factors that retain them in long-term hospitality careers are the perception of close social bonds; a professional identity; autonomy and their belief, *at whatever level in the hierarchy*, that their jobs hold variety and challenge.

Taking the level playing field approach adopted by the hospitality career literature, it appears that women have access to the same career opportunities to achieve senior executive positions as men, yet this is clearly not the case. In a larger scale study of American lodging establishments, Woods and Viehland (2000) concluded that women were occupationally segregated into 'pink ghettoes', for example, the conference and housekeeping departments, earning less and with limited promotional prospects. Rather optimistically, the authors concluded that ultimately force of numbers, due to women's majority in most hospitality management courses, would ensure that women would predominate at the senior levels in future years. It is dismaying to see that this has not happened; in many countries women remain concentrated at the lower levels of hospitality work; for example, Spain (Santero-Sanchez et al., 2015), the United States (Clevenger and Singh, 2013) and New Zealand (Baum et al., 2016b) and/or excluded from career ladders. Meanwhile, gender in hospitality work remains under-researched by the hospitality and tourism academy (Figueroa-Domecq et al., 2015).

The literature paints a disturbing picture about women's lack of participation in senior leadership roles. Horizontal and vertical segregation is clearly illustrated in the hierarchical structures of hotels globally (Baum, 2013), for example, in Hong Kong (Ng and Pine, 2003), New Zealand (Mooney and Ryan, 2009), Australia (Knox, 2008) and the United Kingdom (Guerrier, 2008; Guerrier and Adib, 2002). In Wang's (2013) study, at entry-level managerial positions women comprised 54.5 per cent of the total; by middle managerial level, the proportion of men had grown to 68.4 per cent, compared to 31.6 per cent women. It is not clear what happened to the women, if they left or were not promoted. Other studies suggest that at organizational level, the causes of women's failure to achieve senior management positions range from occupational sex stereotyping, exclusion from common male networking venues by the old boy's network (Brownell, 1994; Clevenger and Singh, 2013; Ng and Pine, 2003; Patwardhan et al., 2014) compounded by a lack of visible (or realistic) female role models and mentors and the requirement to move geographically for promotional or developmental opportunities (Mooney and Ryan, 2009). Boone et al. (2013, p. 236) suggest that the barriers to women's advancement are 'self-imposed and largely involve choices they make about family and household'. In some regards this 'insight' is on a par with what Caproni (2004) suggests is the organizational orientation of blaming employees with a heavy workload for their failure to achieve work–life balance. Boone et al. (2013) temper their observation by noting that organizations must take responsibility for failing to provide mentoring or career development plans for women that contribute to these barriers. However, this caveat does not reflect the profound ways that organizational norms penalize ambitious women. Age and ethnicity also intersect with gender to inhibit women's career progression in hospitality; the possibility that women may bear children or being a woman of minority ethnicity forms a further career barrier (Mooney et al., 2017a).

3.2 Masculine Organizational Norms: Occupational Sex Stereotyping

Embedded occupational stereotyping throughout the industry shapes expectations of men's and women's roles and careers in hospitality organizations. Occupational gender stereotyping is complex and contextual; both gender and race affect perceptions about women's suitability for managerial positions (Booysen and Nkomo, 2010; Elsaid and Elsaid, 2012). In the hospitality sector, Adib and Guerrier (2003) observed that too little consideration has been given to how individual aspects of ethnicity or class identity affect women's and men's career experiences. Yet it appears that pronounced hetero-normativity norms prevail in hospitality organizations that limit women's suitability for promotion, segregating them in female-only areas with their very limited career advancement possibilities (Mooney et al., 2017a).

Hospitality work appears to be perceived as 'feminized' work, a logical extension of women's reproductive work (Harris et al., 2011; Heimtun, 2012). Studies note women's concentration in the lower paid hospitality jobs, such as housekeeping (for instance, Campos-Soria et al., 2009). From an emotional labour perspective, women are viewed as more suitable for service work due to their innate nurturing characteristics (Zampoukos and Ioannides, 2011) and more favoured for customer interactions (Kara et al., 2013) yet receive fewer opportunities to supervise others in Jamaica (Spencer and Bean, 2011) and the United States (Lee and Way, 2010). A masculine orientation influences perceptions about what work is skilled or unskilled; jobs considered as 'women's work' are frequently considered as unskilled (Powell, 2002) or 'dirty'. Dirty work positions its workers so that they are seen as of lesser social value (Simpson et al., 2012) and women in particular are engaged in the 'dirty jobs' of housekeeping (Harris et al., 2011). Jobs in housekeeping may be perceived as morally tainted and further stigma attaches to handling bodily fluids (Ashforth and Kreiner, 2013). The devaluation of women's roles in tandem with occupational sex stereotyping means that women may be discouraged from straying into areas regarded as masculine, for example, management (Burke, 2014; Mooney and Ryan, 2009). Associations with dirty work or non-suitability for managerial jobs is referred to as the 'sticky floor' in the women in management literature, which retains women in lower positions; the 'glass slipper' metaphor (Ashcraft, 2013) suggests that women must 'fit' the social identity associated with a specific job. Merit that leads to promotion is associated with male symbols or male identity characteristics (Gherardi, 2014) in hospitality management, yet is positioned as objective and unchanging. Simpson and Kumra (2016) suggest that the 'Teflon effect' explains how merit (including the right skills, qualifications and appearance) does not 'stick' to women whose gender(ed), or race(d) or class(ed) identities do not fit the image of the ideal manager for a defined position. A powerful and depressing example of the sector's assumption that hospitality leaders are, and will continue to be, male, is embedded in Houran et al.'s (2012) article in the influential *Cornell Hospitality Quarterly* that *only* (author's italics) refers to male management careers. Women hospitality executives must be exceptionally able to combat the organizational merit (think career privilege) that automatically adheres to their male peers.

3.3   The Norm of Sexual Harassment

Sexual harassment is another facet of discrimination experienced by women in the workplace. Regrettably, the hospitality sector has the highest level of reported incidents of sexual harassment of any industry sector, according to Ram et al. (2016). They argue that the lack of attention paid to resolving the issue is symptomatic of the truth barriers that appear to discourage studies about unpalatable topics, which have the potential to disrupt tourism businesses (Veijola et al., 2014). In the hospitality context sexual harassment is difficult to define and Aksonnit's (2014, p. 8) definition given here is based on a wide review of hospitality-specific literature and the Equal Employment Opportunity Commission (EEOC) perspective:

> Sexual harassment is any unwanted, unwelcome or uninvited verbal, visual, written, or physical conduct based on sex or of a sexual nature, which occurs

with the purpose or effect of violating the dignity of a person, which makes a person feel hostile, degraded, humiliated, intimidated or offended and unreasonably interferes with an individual's work performance, or, which constitutes an abuse of authority.

Poulston (2008b) and Wijesinghe (2017) consider that the origins of sexual harassment lie in antiquity, when extending hospitality included offering the sexual services of the women of the household; wives, sisters, servants or slaves. The residue of the objectification and commodification of women's sexuality still appears to taint women's employment experiences in hospitality settings. The power imbalance in the server–customer relationship, which ensures 'the customer is king' in service interactions (Korczynski, 2002), makes women vulnerable to sexual harassment. Such harassment is compounded by the intersection of gender with age, and gender with occupational class, as youth is easier to manipulate or bully by virtue of the higher status held by older workers or managers (Dagsland et al., 2015; Mooney, 2016). The occupational sex segregation in hospitality, which reproduces wider societal norms, where women's work is valued less than men's work (Calás et al., 2014; Holvino, 2010) adds further layers of disadvantage for women. It is no surprise that women working in housekeeping experience high levels of sexual harassment (Kensbock et al., 2015). As observed previously, men as well as women suffer from sexual harassment; workers in male-dominated areas may be pressured into conforming to male behavioural norms (Ashforth and Kreiner, 2013; Simpson, 2014). The male-dominated kitchen area is a case in point: the presence of women and men who do not behave like 'real men' undermines the essential maleness of this masculine preserve; young women or young men deemed to be homosexual report repeated and significant incidences of sexual harassment (Ineson et al., 2013).

The norm of sexual harassment appears to be embedded in hospitality workplaces. Poulston's New Zealand research (2008b) into sexual harassment indicated that sexual banter was part and parcel of hospitality work, enjoyed by some workers adept with coping with sexual advances in customer facing environments such as bars and nightclubs. Waudby (2012), when researching female bar workers' attitudes towards sexual harassment, suggests that younger women go through a form of induction (or desensitization) into social norms where they gradually learn to protect themselves at work. It is not only in bars and places where alcohol is consumed that women are at risk. Kensbock et al. (2015, p. 36) found 'guest-initiated sexual harassment to be pervasive and normalized within the hotel workplace' for housekeeping staff. Organizational factors contributing to the high incidence were the isolated bedroom settings, the sexualized uniform that indicated power differentials, and management's lack of attention to harassment of their staff by guests. There is evidence of under-recording in diverse hospitality environments, such as cruise ships (Klein and Poulston, 2011). Effective sexual harassment strategies are persistently absent across the sector; for example, in Thai hotels, staff 'did not want to report the incidents to the management because they perceived that doing so was useless' (Aksonnit, 2014, p.427). Theocharous and Philaretou (2009), in their study of sexual harassment in the Cypriot hospitality industry, listed the significant and severe consequences for victims, both short and long term, including loss of employment, social, physical, psychological and emotional harm. Although these authors suggest the most effective way to combat sexual harassment is by preventative training, disturbingly, they argue: 'The victim must also take responsibility for stopping or containing the harassing behavior by developing and/or sharpening her detection skills in immediately identifying sexually harassing behavior from a fellow co-worker' (p.301).

Such unenlightened perspectives confirm that throughout the hospitality industry, dealing with sexual attention is a matter *to be dealt with by individuals* (authors' italics), rather than the responsibility of management and owners. It is further justification of management's unwillingness to handle the 'messy' aspects of the guest–owner or management relationship, particularly if it may potentially damage the business relationship (Mooney et al., 2017b). The effects of sexual discrimination are severe and the following section discusses how structural and organization factors profoundly influence individual women's career options and choices.

4.   INDIVIDUAL EFFECTS ON WOMEN: MICRO LEVEL

At first glance, a hospitality management career appears conducive to ambitious individuals regardless of their sex or ethnicity. As indicated previously, strong social competencies are necessary for a successful hospitality career and one would imagine women's strengths in social skills and participative leadership (Anderson et al., 2010; Hochschild, 1983; Singh et al., 2002) should designate them for a successful hospitality career. Women form a majority of undergraduates in hospitality-specific degree courses (Chuang and Dellmann-Jenkins, 2010; Pizam, 2006); female graduates feel their personalities and attributes draw them to hospitality (Chuang and Dellmann-Jenkins, 2010). However, research shows that women are inclined to leave the hotel industry earlier than men (see

Garavan et al., 2006). Possibly this is because women in Western countries, who often belong to ethnic minority groups, continue to dominate the lowest-quality positions with poorest job security, pay, working conditions and developmental opportunities in the hospitality sector (Santero-Sanchez et al., 2015).

When we look to career theory for an explanation, it appears that theories frequently fail to reflect the reality of women's working lives (Sullivan and Baruch, 2009). Earlier career models referred (only) to male careers, although there were later attempts to update them to reflect women's career patterns (for example, Levinson, 1986). Although Sabelis and Schilling (2013, p. 128) consider the disruption of linear career paths as normal, women generally experience more disruption and penalties from 'frayed careers' than men, due to their biological childbearing role. Burke and Mattois (2005) suggest women adapt their roles and relationships to accommodate their most immediate priorities, which shift with life stage. Convenience in dealing with the competing demands of work and family is primarily sought by women because of the greater share of family responsibilities they bear (Raley et al., 2012). As observed previously, it is logistically more difficult for women with children to combine career and family, and specific career theories, such as the Kaleidoscope theory, describe the relational, rather than linear models that encompass their women's family and career orientations (Mainiero and Sullivan, 2005).

Mooney et al.'s (2017a) intersectional career analyses, which compared men and women's hospitality careers, indicated there were two different hospitality career pathways: a managerial path (mainly for men, or women who assumed male norms) through Food and Beverage or Front Office Administration, and a more limited career path for women in housekeeping. Being a New Zealand male with European origins appeared to be a 'marker' for a managerial career, due to the gendered, classed and racialized norms within hospitality organizational cultures, which restricted opportunities available to women and minority groups. Research in the United Kingdom reveals that women start from lower ranked jobs at the beginning and are willing to take risks and move to new employers to gain promotion (Hicks, 1990; Purcell, 1996; 1997). Highly educated female alumni tracked in a European study also tended primarily to leave their hotel employers for promotional reasons, in contrast to men (Blomme et al., 2010). These decisions made by women to 'jump ship' suggest that women may have no option but to move for promotion; Hausknecht et al. (2009) observe that high performers, especially at senior positions in the hierarchy, stay with their employers if there are no financial or status advantages to be gained from moving.

Thus, it can be seen that the women transcend the organizational barriers (masculine culture and the necessity to move geographically) in unsympathetic organizations by moving to competitor organizations. In Mooney's (2014, p. 181) hospitality career study, one female General Manager commented that women grew tired of fighting the system and left their employer for better opportunities: 'Quite often, and particularly with women they will say – oh yes, I'm leaving because of family or whatever and then three months later they're working for another hotel chain in a senior management role'. It is worth considering the other side of the coin: a counter-force may retain women managers who start a family, with their current organization, as the organizational and social capital they have already built up can enable them to negotiate more flexible working hours than would be possible with a new employer (Mooney, 2009).

The rewards of a managerial career are obvious in hospitality: high social status, superior financial rewards and benefits, autonomy, complex competitive roles and wide industry social connections and respect. In contrast, many women in seasonal, contingent work have a succession of low paid hospitality jobs that do not lead to higher ranked jobs in the hierarchy (Heimtun, 2012; Rydzik et al., 2012). Such careers, for example the careers of room attendants, appear not to be visualized as careers in their own right, yet women on a non-managerial career path can have fulfilling careers without seeking further advancement. Where working conditions are good and positive relationships exist in the workplace, there is every reason to remain within the employing organization (Robinson et al., 2014). However, viewing women's hospitality careers through the 'Teflon effect' lens, it appears obvious that many women in hospitality choose not to challenge masculine progression norms as successful female hospitality executives are frequently single and without children (Clevenger and Singh, 2013). Women may actively choose not to 'fight' for a management career, if they judge the unpredictable hours associated with a supervisory role are incompatible with their family responsibilities (Mooney et al., 2017a). Rather than this choice being 'self-imposed', as argued by Boone et al. (2013), male privilege dictates whose ideal (gendered, body-aged and raced) embodiment best fits a managerial position, with its associated 'organizational man' (Houran et al., 2012; Randall, 1987) working practices geared to the primary allegiance to organizational goals.

Sexual harassment, another form of gendered discrimination, also influences women's decisions to stay working in the sector. Several studies (for example, Ineson et al., 2013; Maxwell and Broadbridge, 2014) suggest that young women rethink their choice of hospitality as a career and leave the industry after negative experiences of being sexually harassed in the initial work experience placements. Again, here gender interacts with youth; Dagsland et al.'s (2015) study of young Norwegian kitchen apprentices showed that initial work experiences were so negative that many consequently decided against pursuing a career in the hospitality sector.

4.1 Summary of Interactions between Macro, Meso and Micro Level

The interactions between the macro–meso–micro effects on women's employment in hospitality are portrayed in Figure 8.1. At macro level, the hospitality sector has low entry barriers, which make it easy for women to find lower level work, particularly as room attendants in accommodation premises. The structural features of the industry, which offer flexible and diverse career paths, *should* enable qualified workers to rise to senior levels regardless of gender but hospitality management career frameworks appear to display a traditional linear pattern globally, and gendered organizational norms appear to limit women's career choices. Women are segregated into feminized areas that have little career progression, and in areas such as the kitchen or management, where men predominate generally, women are subject to sexual harassment, which is another form of gender discrimination. It can be argued that gendered role associations form the nexus of women's failure to thrive in hospitality sectors, such as hotels (Mooney et al., 2017a). Therefore, at the micro level, many women appear to prioritize career or family. If they are career focused they may move from one organization to another to avoid the geographical moves that are necessary for promotion if they stay with one organization. Or they may decide not to seek promotion, as the unpredictability of hours associated with a supervisory role makes it difficult to manage family life.

It is clear from the foregoing section that many factors contribute to women's employment quality in the sector and Table 8.1 lays out the various barriers for women at macro/meso and micro levels. Yet, as can be seen from the actions in the fourth column, the way forward, there is hope for the future as women demonstrate their own agency in their employment decisions. Enlightened HRM policies can ensure that women enjoy the same entitlement to a fulfilling career without sacrificing their rights to enjoy a satisfying family life.

5. CONCLUSION AND RECOMMENDATIONS

Hospitality work offers many advantages to those seeking a flexible, exciting career involving travel and the opportunity to meet and work alongside people from different cultures. It offers strong social connectivity; a variety of occupational pathways; flexible work options; and career development and advancement opportunities (McPhail et al., 2015; Mooney et

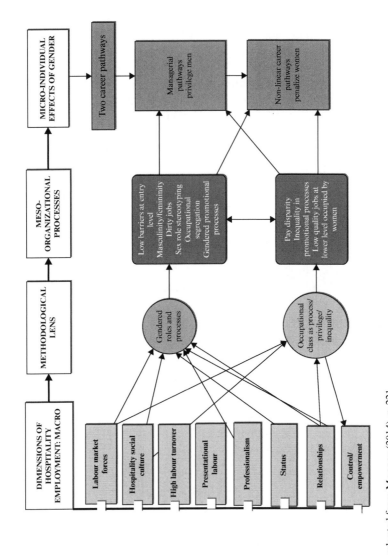

Source: adapted from Mooney (2014), p. 221.

Figure 8.1   Interactions between macro–meso–micro effects on women's employment in hospitality

Table 8.1 Macro, meso and micro factors influencing women's careers in hospitality

Macro: sectoral and societal factors influencing women's careers in hospitality	Meso: organizational processes affecting women	Micro: individual effects on women	Way forward
Economic Globalization Impact of Global financial crisis (GFC) Neo-liberal policies	Focus on labour cost cutting Zero hours contracts Flattening of organizational structures Fewer opportunities for management development, due to fewer assistant manager roles	Lower quality jobs High turnover Disadvantages for society and, therefore, individual	Employ full-time workers rather than casual workers at lower level jobs Instigate interdepartmental and intra departmental team building exercises Instigate good socialization practices Train managers in how to build positive workplace relationships (including equity training) Instigate mentoring programmes for women and minorities
Sectoral Massive growth in tourism sector Seasonal nature of tourism employment	24-hour industry Easy entry sector: few qualifications required at entry level Skills shortages Many opportunities for women at lower levels in feminized areas Casualized, seasonal, precarious work	Women seeking part-time work disadvantaged Women concentrated in feminized departments with few career advancement possibilities	
Societal Changing working norms in global north: dual career families	Norm of occupational segregation: managerial spaces reserved for men: few women leaders	In dual career families, women use their agency to stay at lower level jobs	Set organizational wide ambitious targets for managers to increase women in senior leadership positions

Table 8.1 (continued)

Macro: sectoral and societal factors influencing women's careers in hospitality	Meso: organizational processes affecting women	Micro: individual effects on women	Way forward
Gendered societal norms in employment: women have greater share of aged care, childcare and domestic responsibilities Societal undervaluation of what are perceived to be 'feminized' skills Lack of women's participation at senior management level and board level Gendered pay gap	Biologically perceived norms linking with age and life stage disadvantage women Masculine workplace norms disadvantage women, e.g. norm of geographical mobility Power imbalances disadvantage younger women in managerial interactions and in guest interactions: sexual harassment Work–life balance issues affect women more than men Workaholism: the 'facetime' pervasive throughout the industry disadvantages men and women but more detrimental for women with caregiving commitments Sector-wide high levels of sexual discrimination and sexual harassment	Women frequently leave current employers for promotion Lack of effective harassment policies at organizational level are detrimental to individual women Women may leave the sector or suffer ill effects from harassment	Family-friendly working policies Development of individual succession plans for workers that do not involve geographical moves Implement strict policies for dealing with sexual harassment

al., 2016; Santero-Sanchez et al., 2015). Theoretically, there should be no problem retaining the women who commence working in the sector. As governments generally have Equal Employment Opportunity legislation in place, it would appear that many of the problems occur at societal level, reflecting widely prevalent patriarchal attitudes that question women's ability to combine work with family life and additionally at organizational level. It is beyond the remit of this chapter to suggest measures that may help at the macro or global level; however, at the organizational level it is clear that enlightened HRM policies can do a great deal to redress the balance for women. Without progress in this area, hospitality management will lack equal gender participation in the layers of middle management coming through in the future. This is concerning, as the talent pool will not reflect the diversity of customers or employees. Significantly, however, it is of vital importance for HR managers to be mindful that while career advancement is of critical importance, a large majority of women are engaged in long-term careers at the lowest levels of hospitality work, whose entitlement to high quality work is not reflected in HRM policies and practices in hospitality organizations.

Organizational loyalty appears to be low throughout the hospitality industry. At the lower levels, the 'easy in, easy out' nature of hospitality jobs means that women change employers frequently (see Rydzik et al., 2012, p.137). At managerial level, due to the culture of forced transition (Mooney et al., 2016), management turnover rates are as high, if not higher, than entry-level jobs (Davidson et al., 2010). Unfortunately, the widespread practice of utilizing an hourly paid labour force does not encourage a positive psychological contract. Buonocore's (2010) Italian hotel study highlighted that part-time hotel workers felt like outsiders, with no attachment to their individual property. She concluded that an HRM approach that does not discriminate between full-time and part-time workers is likely to lessen workers' sense of alienation. Although HRM strategies designed to encourage employee engagement and higher productivity will not necessarily retain workers, organizational support such as good management and supervision practices increase employees' propensity to remain in hospitality organizations (Cho et al., 2009; Song et al., 2015; Yang, 2010). Gender influences job satisfaction; women experience more job role ambiguity and role-related stress than men (Kim et al., 2009), which good supervision and training can reduce (Karatepe and Aleshinloye, 2009). At individual level, women's life stage affects their perception of work–life balance and thus their organizational commitment. The issue of work–life balance surfaces in all hospitality employment contexts, for example, in Australia (Deery and Jago, 2009; 2015), Switzerland (Lewis, 2010) and China (Zhao et al., 2011). It is regarded as particularly problematic for women trying to balance family needs with work in the sector (Baum, 2013; Okumus et al., 2010; O'Leary and Deegan, 2005; Pinar et al., 2011). Unfortunately, throughout the sector, there is a lack of flexible work practices that enable women (and men) in dual career families to combine work and caregiving commitments (Baum et al., 2016b; Deery and Jago, 2015). Therefore, ambitious measures are required to produce a sustainable labour force and the following recommendations are designed to facilitate women's full participation in the hospitality and tourism workforce.

5.1 Set Organization-wide Ambitious Targets for Managers to Increase Women in Senior Leadership Positions

The literature indicates that for progress to be made in increasing women's participation at senior levels, positive actions need to be taken. The previous section reveals the persistence of the old boy's networks, which preserve the male career privilege in hospitality organizations (Ayres, 2006; Clevenger and Singh, 2013; Guerrier, 1986; Mooney et al., 2017a). For change to be successful, it needs the commitment of leadership, as most men do not consider 'the advancement of women to be very important' (Burke, 2014, p. 387) and it appears unlikely that women's participation in senior management will occur without affirmative action in favour of women. Although quotas have mixed appeal, they prove effective in releasing unrealized female talent (Tatli et al., 2013) in environments such as hospitality. The elements of an effective quota system incorporate many features recommended by Hughes and Rog (2008) for an effective talent management system. The first step should be an organization-wide audit of promotional processes and an inventory of women and minorities occupying each position. Strategic targets should be set for a proportional increase of women (especially minority women) for senior positions. The targets can then be linked to management and hotel performance goals and bonuses for senior executives and corporate vice presidents. Succession planning, development programmes and personalized development plans may form part of the annual plan. Independent monitoring should take place on a six-monthly basis and HRM teams should receive professional training from specialized organizations, such as the Simmons Center for Gender in Organizations in Boston, USA, on how to design gender-neutral 'merit'-based evaluation systems (Simpson and Kumra, 2016).

5.2 Train Managers in How to Build Positive Workplace Relationships (Including Equity Training)

Constructive supervisory relationships can ameliorate the effects of stressful working conditions across different cultural and hospitality work settings. Employee-focused HRM practices increase workers' motivation to remain with the organization (Cho et al., 2009; Karatepe, 2012; Kim and Jogaratnam, 2010; Yang, 2010). Positive relationships between co-workers and supervisors are linked with greater organizational commitment, thus increasing job quality and retaining women. Although the constituents of a good supervisory or management relationship may vary, good interpersonal relations are based on the employee's perception of fair treatment from supervisors (Poulston, 2009; Upchurch et al., 2010). The reverse is also true; conflict between management and staff contributes to role stress and high staff turnover (Yang, 2010). The authoritarian relationships frequently demonstrated in female-dominated housekeeping departments not only put a strain on relationships between workers and management (Kensbock et al., 2013; OnsØyen et al., 2009), but fuel individual women's intentions to leave their employer for a more positive working environment.

5.3 Instigate Interdepartmental and Intra-departmental Team Building Exercises

An additional benefit of a positive workplace culture is that close personal relationships with co-workers can help women to overcome the stigma of dirty jobs in hospitality (McDowell et al., 2007; OnsØyen et al., 2009; Wildes, 2005). Ashforth and Kreiner (2013) observe how the negative self-perception of those engaged in 'dirty work' can be transformed by the positive feeling of solidarity and collegiality with fellow workers. Korczynski (2002) also explains how close attachment networks among service workers enable them to surmount unreasonable treatment from customers. In Japanese hotels, intensive work practices have led to cold, impersonal working relationships and deterioration of loyalty to the individual employer. Therefore, enlightened HRM ensures that altruism and loyalty is given to the organization rather than to the collective group, as occurs in housekeeping departments suffering from oppressive supervision (OnsØyen et al., 2009).

5.4   Employ Full-time Workers rather than Casual Workers at Lower Level Jobs

Hospitality Human Resource departments should carefully consider the hidden costs of relying on a casual labour force. The ongoing drive to casualize the labour force further reinforces the outsider status and job security of temporary or part-time workers (many of whom are women) in hospitality (Buonocore, 2010). In addition to the loss of productivity associated with short-term labour practices (Chikwe, 2009; Davidson et al., 2010; Yang, 2010), strong social connection within a stable workforce ensures greater job satisfaction (linked to higher productivity), reduced requirements for close supervision, a higher standard of work and flexibility from colleagues when staff are absent (Mooney et al., 2016). Hospitality employers, where possible, should move away from a casual labour model and instead focus on realistic alternatives, such as permanent part-time contracts, where flexibility is required.

5.5   Instigate Mentoring Programmes for Women and Minorities

Hospitality organizations need to look at better ways to engage all their workers, such as mentoring schemes for women and minorities. Career success in hospitality is linked with the availability of mentors (Kong et al., 2012), who help with the development of career competencies (Burke, 2014; Wang, 2013). Mentors are particularly important for women's careers (Clevenger and Singh, 2013; Mooney et al., 2017a) and the lack of suitable mentors is a particular problem for women and minority groups (Ayres, 2006; Mooney and Ryan, 2009). International hotel groups, such as Hyatt and IHG, have recognized the importance of mentors by introducing official mentoring programmes. Although such formal mentoring plans are viewed as less effective than those which develop naturally (Chuang and Dellmann-Jenkins, 2010; Yamashita and Uenoyama, 2006), by introducing programmes that include a high proportion of women and minorities, HR managers can help less privileged groups to gain a critical mass. If the mentoring programmes are successful they can be extended to all employees.

5.6   Instigate Good Socialization Practices for All Employees

It is essential that new employees develop a close social connection to their work colleagues within a short timeframe to encourage them to remain within the industry (Wan et al., 2014). Regrettably, training and induction programmes are widely regarded as inconsistent (Kusluvan et al., 2010; Poulston, 2008a). Many hospitality undergraduates explore hospitality employment as casual workers or interns and look for alternative careers in other industries if their early experiences are unfavourable. Realistic induction, coupled with mentorship from experienced employees (Chuang and Dellmann-Jenkins, 2010; Ineson et al., 2013; Maxwell and Broadbridge, 2014) and effective team building practices, reduce bullying and harassment. It can, therefore, be seen that measures that would improve job quality for women will also benefit other oppressed groups, such as young people. For example, in kitchens, skills shortages are pronounced, sexual harassment is rife and turnover is exceptionally high (Dagsland et al., 2011; 2015; Young and Corsun, 2010). If women and young people were warmly welcomed into this environment, rather than being asked to survive what, at times, is a harsh initiation, the current negative situation could be reversed.

5.7 Instigate Family-friendly Working Policies

Although the hospitality industry is perceived as a long hours industry (Cleveland et al., 2007), it is not the number of hours worked, but the perception of balance that contributes to hospitality workers' job satisfaction (Burke et al., 2011; Lewis, 2010). The hospitality industry needs to focus on family-friendly working policies for both women and men in order to retain its workers (Deery and Jago, 2015). Women will reject promotion in order to retain control over their working hours and shifts and the hospitality industry generally does not encourage off-site working, even for functions such as HRM or sales where it is logistically viable (Mooney, 2009). If human resource managers introduce accessible family-friendly policies for men and women, then a higher proportion of workers will be empowered to realize their full potential by availing themselves of promotional opportunities. However, managers must remain vigilant to ensure that employees who avail themselves of such policies are not discriminated against by appearing to put personal before organizational goals. In the legal profession, for example, frequently young ambitious women's experience with discrimination occurred only when they became pregnant (Lyng, 2010) and in the financial services sector, women (or men) were regarded as uncommitted to management careers, by betraying 'weakness' when they accessed family flexibility policies (Liff and Ward, 2001).

5.8 Prepare Succession Plans for Workers that Do Not Involve Geographical Moves

Global hospitality organizations, particularly hotels, which tradition-ally give promotions through transfer opportunities away from the current location (Kong et al., 2010; Mooney et al., 2016; Yamashita and Uenoyama, 2006), should abandon the necessity for employees to move geographically for career progression. The necessity to move for promo-tion is a profound disincentive for women to build careers in the industry. Further, exploratory research based on interviews with global senior hospitality executives also indicates that men in dual career relationships are not as willing as previous generations to move country to further their careers (Mooney, 2017). As Hausknecht et al.'s (2009) research reveals, executives will remain with their employing organisations if conditions are suitable and there are career development possibilities, therefore, 'staying local' may be an important consideration.

5.9 Implement a Cohesive Policy and Code of Practice for Sexual Harassment

It is important to note that sexual harassment has been recognized by the United Nations as a form of discrimination and violence against women (UN Women, 2012). International statements of law and principle provide an important starting point in drafting legislation that prohibits sexual harassment. The ILO, while acknowledging that individuals may take individual actions to protect themselves, places the responsibility of pro-tecting its employees on employing organizations (Women Watch China and ILO, 2010). The following are the recommended steps in a set of issued guidelines for the hospitality industry:

1. Establish specific bylaws on the prevention of sexual harassment in the workplace, with protection from retaliation and obligations for supervisors and managers.
2. Set up a dedicated organization or department and specify its duties, including zero tolerance, reporting of sexual harassment, protection of individuals' privacy and maintenance of a just and fair attitude to sexual harassment issues.
3. Have regular education and training campaigns on the prevention of sexual harassment, including what constitutes sexual harassment and its effects. They should not only take place for employees but man-agement should receive additional training on how to deal with and investigate reports.

4. Deal with irregularities in a timely and appropriate manner.
5. Establish measures to prevent sexual harassment by customers, including a corporate policy in notices and contracts, publicly posted warnings and proactive encouragement of staff to make complaints.
6. Establish other measures such as including the prohibition of sexual harassment in individual contracts or collective employments agreements.

CLOSING THOUGHTS

In conclusion, organizations that follow the above recommendations, and many may already have such measures in place, will go a long way to reducing the high turnover rate in their own properties and ultimately across the hospitality sector. Measures to support women are generally more favourably received when they are aimed at all employees rather than singling out women. This is a double-edged sword, however, as the dual standards and discrimination suffered by women in hospitality workplaces are so engrained they are normalized – affirmative action will be required to redress the balance. Therefore, the improvements in working conditions that facilitate women's equal opportunities to gain high quality jobs and to advance to senior levels in the organizational hierarchy will ultimately benefit not just women, but all workers in hospitality organizations.

REFERENCES

Acker, J. (2006). *Class questions: Feminist answers*. Lanham, MD: Rowman & Littlefield Publishers.

Adib, A. and Guerrier, Y. (2003). The interlocking of gender with nationality, race, ethnicity and class: The narratives of women in hotel work. *Gender, Work and Organisation*, **10**(4), 413–32.

Adler, P.A. and Adler, P.H. (2004). *Paradise laborers: Hotel work in the global economy*. Ithaca, NY: Cornell University Press.

Akrivos, C., Ladkin, A. and Reklitis, P. (2007). Hotel managers' career strategies for success. *International Journal of Contemporary Hospitality Management*, **19**(2), 107–19.

Aksonnit, P. (2014). *Sexual harassment by hotel customers: Impacts on workers, and reactions from management: A Thailand study*. University of Waikato. Accessed at: http://research commons.waikato.ac.nz/handle/10289/8851.

Altman, L.A. and Brothers, L.R. (2013). Career longevity of hospitality graduates. *Hospitality Review*, **13**(2), 9.

Anderson, D., Vinnicombe, S. and Singh, V. (2010). Women partners leaving the firm: Choice, what choice? *Gender in Management: An International Journal*, **25**(3), 170–83.

Anthias, F. (2001). The material and the symbolic in theorizing social stratification: Issues of gender, ethnicity and class. *The British Journal of Sociology*, **52**(3), 367–90.

Anvari, R. and Seliman, S. (2010). Personal needs assessment approach in strategic training and affective commitment. *International Journal of Business and Management*, **5**(7), 144–57.

Ashcraft, K.L. (2013). The glass slipper: 'Incorporating' occupational identity in management studies. *Academy of Management Review*, **38**(1), 6–31.

Ashforth, B. and Kreiner, G. (2013). Dirty work and dirtier work: Differences in countering physical, social, and moral stigma. *Management and Organization Review*, **10**(1), 81–108.

Ayres, H. (2006). Career development in tourism and leisure: An exploratory study of the influence of mobility and mentoring. *Journal of Hospitality and Tourism Management*, **13**(2), 113–23.

Baum, T. (2007). Human resources in tourism: Still waiting for change. *Tourism Management*, **28**(6), 1383–99.

Baum, T. (2013). International perspectives on women and work in hotels, catering and tourism. Working Paper No. 1/2013. Geneva: International Labour Organization.

Baum, T. (2015). Human resources in tourism: Still waiting for change? – A 2015 reprise. *Tourism Management*, **50**, 204–12.

Baum, T., Kralj, A., Robinson, R. and Solnet, D. (2016a). Tourism workforce research: A review, taxonomy and agenda. *Annals of Tourism Research*, **60**, 1–22.

Baum, T., Cheung, C., Kong, H., Kralj, A., Mooney, S., Nguyễn Thị Thanh, H., Ramachandran, S. et al. (2016b). Sustainability and the tourism and hospitality workforce: A thematic analysis. *Sustainability*, **8**(8), 809–830.

Beck, J. and Lopa, J. (2001). An exploratory application of Schein's career anchors inventory to hotel executive operating committee members. *International Journal of Hospitality Management*, **20**(1), 15–28.

Bernhardt, A., Dresser, L. and Hatton, E. (2003). The coffee pot wars: Unions and firm restructuring in the hotel industry. In E. Appelbaum, A. Bernhardt and R. Murnane (eds), *Low wage-America: How employers are reshaping opportunity in the workplace* (pp. 33–76). New York: Russell Sage Foundation.

Blomme, R., Van Rheede, A. and Tromp, D. (2010). Work–family conflict as a cause for turnover intentions in the hospitality industry. *Tourism and Hospitality Research*, **10**(4), 269–85.

Boone, J., Veller, T., Nikolaeva, K., Keith, M., Kefgen, K. and Houran, J. (2013). Rethinking a glass ceiling in the hospitality industry. *Cornell Hospitality Quarterly*, **54**(3), 230–39.

Booysen, L. and Nkomo, S. (2010). Gender role stereotypes and requisite management characteristics: The case of South Africa. *Gender in Management: An International Journal*, **25**(4), 285–300.

Bourdieu, P. (2001). *Masculine domination*. California: Stanford University Press.

Broadbridge, A. and Mavin, S. (2016). Editorial. *Gender in Management: An International Journal*, **31**(8), 502–13.

Broadbridge, A. and Simpson, R. (2011). 25 years on: Reflecting on the past and looking to the future in gender and management research. *British Journal of Management*, **22**(3), 470–83.

Brownell, J. (1994). Women in hospitality management: General managers' perceptions of factors related to career development. *International Journal of Hospitality Management*, **13**(2), 52–61.

Buonocore, F. (2010). Contingent work in the hospitality industry: A mediating model of organizational attitudes. *Tourism Management*, **31**(3), 378–85.

Burke, R.J. (2014). Organisational culture, work investments, and the careers of men: Disadvantages to women? In S. Kumra, R. Simpson and R.J. Burke (eds), *The Oxford handbook of gender in organizations* (pp. 371–93). Oxford: Oxford University Press.

Burke, R.J. and Mattois, C. (2005). *Supporting women's career advancement, challenges and opportunities*. Cheltenham, UK and Northampton, MA, USA: Edward Elgar Publishing.

Burke, R.J., Jeng, W., Koyuncu, M. and Fiksenbau, L. (2011). Work motivations, satisfaction and well-being among hotel managers in China: Passion versus addiction. *Interdisciplinary Journal of Research in Business*, **1**(1), 21–34.

Calás, M., Smircich, L. and Holvino, E. (2014). Theorizing gender-and-organization: Changing times, changing theories. In S. Kumra, R. Simpson and R.J. Burke (eds), *The Oxford handbook of gender in organizations* (pp. 17–52). Oxford: Oxford University Press.

Campos-Soria, J.A., Ortega-Aguaza, B. and Ropero-García, M.A. (2009). Gender segregation and wage difference in the hospitality industry. *Tourism Economics*, **15**(4), 847–66.

Caproni, P.J. (2004). Work/life balance: You can't get there from here. *The Journal of Applied Behavioral Science*, **40**(2), 208–18.

Cha, Y. (2013). Overwork and the persistence of gender segregation in occupations. *Gender & Society*, **27**(2), 158–84.

Chalkiti, K. and Sigala, M. (2010). Staff turnover in the Greek tourism industry: A comparison between insular and peninsular regions. *International Journal of Contemporary Hospitality Management*, **22**(3), 335–59.

Chikwe, A.C. (2009). The impact of employee turnover: The case of leisure, tourism and hospitality industry. *Consortium Journal of Hospitality & Tourism*, **14**(1), 43–56.

Cho, S., Johanson, M.M. and Guchait, P. (2009). Employees intent to leave: A comparison of determinants of intent to leave versus intent to stay. *International Journal of Hospitality Management*, **28**(3), 374–81.

Chuang, N-K. and Dellmann-Jenkins, M. (2010). Career decision making and intention: A study of hospitality undergraduate students. *Journal of Hospitality & Tourism Research*, **34**(4), 512–30.

Cleveland, J., O'Neill, J., Himelright, J., Harrison, M., Crouter, A. and Drago, R. (2007). Work and family issues in the hospitality industry: Perspectives of entrants, managers, and spouses. *Journal of Hospitality & Tourism Research*, **31**(3), 275–98.

Clevenger, L. and Singh, N. (2013). Exploring barriers that lead to the glass ceiling effect for women in the U.S. hospitality industry. *Journal of Human Resources in Hospitality & Tourism*, **12**(4), 376–99.

Dagsland, Å.-H., Mykletun, R. and Einarsen, S. (2011). Apprentices' expectations and experiences in the socialisation process in their meeting with the hospitality industry. *Scandinavian Journal of Hospitality and Tourism*, **11**(4), 395–415.

Dagsland, Å.-H., Mykletun, R. and Einarsen, S. (2015). 'We're not slaves – we are actually the future!' A follow-up study of apprentices' experiences in the Norwegian hospitality industry. *Journal of Vocational Education & Training*, **67**(4), 460–81.

Davidson, M. and Wang, Y. (2011). Sustainable labor practices? Hotel human resource managers' views on turnover and skill shortages. *Journal of Human Resources in Hospitality & Tourism*, **10**(3), 235–53.

Davidson, M., McPhail, R. and Barry, S. (2011). Hospitality HRM: Past, present and the future. *International Journal of Contemporary Hospitality Management*, **23**(4), 498–516.

Davidson, M., Timo, N. and Wang, Y. (2010). How much does labour turnover cost?: A case study of Australian four- and five-star hotels. *International Journal of Contemporary Hospitality Management*, **22**(4), 451–66.

Deery, M. (2002). Labour turnover in international hospitality and tourism. In N. D'Annunzio-Green, G.A. Maxwell and S. Watson (eds), *Human resource management: International perspectives in hospitality and tourism* (pp. 51–63). London: Continuum Books.

Deery, M. and Jago, L. (2009). A framework for work–life balance practices: Addressing the needs of the tourism industry. *Tourism and Hospitality Research*, **9**(2), 97–108.

Deery, M. and Jago, L. (2015). Revisiting talent management, work–life balance and retention strategies. *International Journal of Contemporary Hospitality Management*, **27**(3), 453–72.

Elsaid, A.M. and Elsaid, E. (2012). Sex stereotyping managerial positions: A cross-cultural comparison between Egypt and the USA. *Gender in Management: An International Journal*, **27**(2), 81–99.

Enz, C. (2009). Human resource management: A troubling issue for the global hotel industry. *Cornell Hospitality Quarterly*, **50**(4), 578–83.

Enz, C. and Siguaw, J. (2000). Best practices in human resources. *Cornell Hotel and Restaurant Adminisration Quarterly*, **41**(48), 48–61.

Figueroa-Domecq, C., Pritchard, A., Segovia-Pérez, M., Morgan, N. and Villacé-Molinero, T. (2015). Tourism gender research: A critical accounting. *Annals of Tourism Research*, **52**, 87–103.

Furunes, T. and Mykletun, R.J. (2005). Age management in Norwegian hospitality businesses. *Scandinavian Journal of Hospitality and Tourism*, **5**(2), 116–34.

Garavan, T., O'Brien, F. and O'Hanlon, D. (2006). Career advancement of hotel managers since graduation: A comparative study. *Personnel Review*, **35**(3), 252–80.

Gherardi, S. (2014). Organisations as symbolic gendered orders. In S. Kumra, R. Simpson and R.J. Burke (eds), *The Oxford handbook of gender in organizations* (pp.76–106). Oxford: Oxford University Press.

Guerrier, Y. (1986). Hotel management: An unsuitable job for a woman? *Service Industries Journal*, **6**, 227–40.

Guerrier, Y. (2008). Organisational studies and hospitality management. In B. Brotherton and R. Wood (eds), *The Sage handbook of hospitality management* (pp.257–73). London: Sage Publications.

Guerrier, Y. and Adib, A. (2002). Working in the hospitality industry. In C. Lashley and A. Morrison (eds), *In search of hospitality* (pp.255–75). Oxford: Butterworth Heinemann.

Harris, C., Tregidga, H. and Williamson, D. (2011). Cinderella in Babylon: The representation of housekeeping and housekeepers in the UK television series Hotel Babylon. *Hospitality & Society*, **1**(1), 47–66.

Hausknecht, J.P., Rodda, J. and Howard, M.J. (2009). Targeted employee retention: Performance-based and job-related differences in reported reasons for staying. *Human Resource Management*, **48**(2), 269–88.

Heimtun, B. (2012). Life in the bubble: The leisure experiences of female Swedish seasonal hospitality workers in Nordkapp, Norway. *Hospitality & Society*, **2**(2), 159–78.

Hicks, L. (1990). Excluded women: How can this happen in the hotel world? *The Service Industries Journal*, **10**(2), 348–63.

Hinkin, T.R. and Tracey, J.B. (2000). The cost of turnover. *Cornell Hospitality Hotel and Restaurant Administration Quarterly*, **41**, 14–22.

Hochschild, A. (1983). *The managed heart: Commercialization of human feeling*. Berkeley, CA: University of California Press.

Holvino, E. (2010). Intersections: The simultaneity of race, gender and class in organization studies. *Gender, Work & Organization*, **17**(3), 248–77.

Houran, J., Lange, R. and Kefgen, K. (2012). Industry trends: Fascinating rhythms in the career paths of hospitality executives. *Cornell Hospitality Quarterly*, **54**(1), 6–9.

Hughes, J. (2008). Human resource management in the hospitality industry. In B. Brotherton and R. Wood (eds), *The Sage handbook of hospitality management* (pp.273–301). London: Sage Publications.

Hughes, J.C. and Rog, E. (2008). Talent management: A strategy for improving employee recruitment, retention and engagement within hospitality organizations. *International Journal of Contemporary Hospitality Management*, **20**(7), 743–57.

Hyde, J.S. (2005). The gender similarities hypothesis. *The American Psychologist*, **60**(6), 581–92.

Ineson, E.M., Yap, M.H.T. and Whiting, G. (2013). Sexual discrimination and harassment in the hospitality industry. *International Journal of Hospitality Management*, **35**, 1–9.

Janta, H., Brown, L., Lugosi, P. and Ladkin, A. (2011). Migrant relationships and tourism employment. *Annals of Tourism Research*, **38**(4), 1322–43.

Kara, A., Andaleeb, S., Turan, M. and Cabuk, S. (2013). An examination of the effects of adaptive selling behavior and customer orientation on performance of pharmaceutical salespeople in an emerging market. *Journal of Medical Marketing: Device, Diagnostic and Pharmaceutical Marketing*, **13**(2), 102–14.

Karatepe, O.M. (2012). Perceived organizational support, career satisfaction, and performance outcomes: A study of hotel employees in Cameroon. *International Journal of Contemporary Hospitality Management*, **24**(5), 735–52.

Karatepe, O.M. and Aleshinloye, K.D. (2009). Emotional dissonance and emotional exhaustion among hotel employees in Nigeria. *International Journal of Hospitality Management*, **28**(3), 349–58.

Kensbock, S., Bailey, J., Jennings, G. and Patiar, A. (2015). Sexual harassment of women working as room attendants within 5-star hotels. *Gender, Work & Organization*, **22**(1), 36–50.

Kensbock, S., Jennings, G., Bailey, J. and Patiar, A. (2013). 'The lowest rung': Women room attendants' perceptions of five star hotels' operational hierarchies. *International Journal of Hospitality Management*, **35**, 360–68.

Kesting, K. and Harris, C. (2009). Providing a theoretical foundation for work–life balance – Sen's capability approach. *New Zealand Journal of Employment Relations*, **34**(1), 47–61.

Kim, B., Murrmann, S. and Lee, G. (2009). Moderating effects of gender and organizational level between role stress and job satisfaction among hotel employees. *International Journal of Hospitality Management*, **28**(4), 612–19.

Kim, K. and Jogaratnam, G. (2010). Effects of individual and organizational factors on job satisfaction and intent to stay in the hotel and restaurant industry. *Journal of Human Resources in Hospitality & Tourism*, **9**(3), 318–39.

Klein, R. and Poulston, J. (2011). Sex at sea: Sexual crimes aboard cruise ships. *Tourism in Marine Environments*, **7**(2), 67–80.

Knox, A. (2008). Gender desegregation and equal employment opportunity in Australian luxury hotels: Are we there yet? *Asia Pacific Journal of Human Resources*, **46**(2), 153–72.

Knox, A. (2014). Human resource management (HRM) in temporary work agencies: Evidence from the hospitality industry. *The Economic and Labour Relations Review*, **25**(1), 81–98.

Knox, A. and Walsh, J. (2005). Organisational flexibility and HRM in the hotel industry: Evidence from Australia. *Human Resources Management Journal*, **15**(1), 57–75.

Kong, H., Cheung, C. and Song, H. (2011). Hotel career management in China: Developing a measurement scale. *International Journal of Hospitality Management*, **30**(1), 112–18.

Kong, H., Cheung, C. and Song, H. (2012). From hotel career management to employees' career satisfaction: The mediating effect of career competency. *International Journal of Hospitality Management*, **31**(1), 76–85.

Kong, H., Cheung, C. and Zhang, H.Q. (2010). Career management systems: What are China's state-owned hotels practising? *International Journal of Contemporary Hospitality Management*, **22**(4), 467–82.

Korczynski, M. (2002). *Human resource management in service work*. London: Palgrave.

Kuria, K.S., Wanderi, M.P. and Ondigi, A. (2012). Hotel employment in Kenya: Contingent work or professional career? *International Journal of Academic Research in Business and Social Sciences*, **2**(7), 394–404.

Kusluvan, S., Kusluvan, Z., Ilhan, I. and Buyruk, L. (2010). The human dimension: A review of human resources management issues in the tourism and hospitality industry. *Cornell Hospitality Quarterly*, **51**(2), 171–214.

Lai, P-C., Soltani, E. and Baum, T. (2008). Distancing flexibility in the hotel industry: The role of employment agencies as labour suppliers. *The International Journal of Human Resource Management*, **19**(1), 132–52.

Lan, L. and Wang Leung, R. (2001). Female managers in Asian hotels: Profile and career challenges. *International Journal of Contemporary Hospitality Management*, **13**(4), 189–96.

Lashley, C. (2001). Costing staff turnover in hospitality service organisations. *Journal of Services Research*, **1**(2), 3–24.

Lee, C. and Way, K. (2010). Individual employment characteristics of hotel employees that play a role in employee satisfaction and work retention. *International Journal of Hospitality Management*, **29**(3), 344–53.

Levinson, D. (1986). A conception of adult development. *American Psychologist*, **41**(1), 3–13.

Lewis, P. and Simpson, R. (2010). *Revealing and concealing gender: Issues of visibility in organization research*. Basingstoke: Palgrave Macmillan.

Lewis, R. (2010). Work–life balance in hospitality: Experiences from a Geneva-based hotel. *International Journal of Management & Information Systems*, **14**(5), 99–106.

Liff, S. and Ward, K. (2001). Distorted views through the glass ceiling: The construction of women's understanding of promotion and senior management positions. *Gender, Work and Organisation*, **8**(1), 19–36.

Lub, X., Bijvank, M., Bal, M., Blomme, R. and Schalk, R. (2012). Different or alike? Exploring the psychological contract and commitment of different generations of hospitality workers. *International Journal of Contemporary Hospitality Management*, **24**(4), 553–73.

Lyng, S. (2010). 'Mothered' and othered. In P. Lewis and P. Simpson (eds), *Revealing and concealing gender: Issues of visibility in organisations* (pp. 77–99). Basingstoke: Palgrave Macmillan.

Mainiero, L.A. and Sullivan, S.E. (2005). Kaleidoscope careers: An alternate explanation for the 'opt-out' revolution. *The Academy of Management Executive (1993–2005)*, **19**(1), 106–23.

Marco-Lajara, B. and Úbeda-García, M. (2013). Human resource management approaches in Spanish hotels: An introductory analysis. *International Journal of Hospitality Management*, **35**, 339–47.

Martin, P. (2003). 'Said and done' versus 'saying and doing': Gendering practices, practicing gender at work. *Gender & Society*, **17**(3), 342–66.

Maxwell, G.A. and Broadbridge, A. (2014). Generation Y graduates and career transition: Perspectives by gender. *European Management Journal*, **32**(4), 547–53.

McCabe, V. and Savery, L. (2007). 'Butterflying' a new career pattern for Australia? Empirical evidence. *Journal of Management Development*, **26**(2), 103–16.

McDowell, L., Batnitzky, A. and Dyer, S. (2007). Division, segmentation and interpellation: The embodied labors of migrant workers in a Greater London hotel. *Economic Geography*, **83**(1), 1–25.

McDowell, L., Batnitzky, A. and Dyer, S. (2009). Precarious work and economic migration: Emerging immigrant divisions of labour in Greater London's service sector. *International Journal of Urban and Regional Research*, **33**(1), 3–25.

McDowell, L., Rootham, E. and Hardgrove, A. (2014). Precarious work, protest masculinity and communal regulation: South Asian young men in Luton, UK. *Work, Employment & Society*, **28**(6), 847–64.

McIntosh, A. and Harris, C. (2012). Critical hospitality and work: (In)hospitable employment in the hospitality industry. *Hospitality & Society*, **2**(2), 129–35.

McPhail, R., Patiar, A., Herington, C., Creed, P. and Davidson, M. (2015). Development and initial validation of a hospitality employees' job satisfaction index: Evidence from Australia. *International Journal of Contemporary Hospitality Management*, **27**(8), 1814–38.

Michel, J.W., Kavanagh, M.J. and Tracey, J.B. (2013). Got support? The impact of supportive work practices on the perceptions, motivation, and behavior of customer-contact employees. *Cornell Hospitality Quarterly*, **54**(2), 161–73.

Mkono, M. (2010). In defence of hospitality careers: Perspectives of Zimbabwean hotel managers. *International Journal of Contemporary Hospitality Management*, **22**(6), 858–70.

Mooney, S. (2009). Children and a career: Yeah right! Barriers to women managers' career progression in hotels. *New Zealand Journal of Human Resources Management, Special Issue 3: Work, Family & Gender*.

Mooney, S. (2014). *How the intersections of age, gender, ethnicity and class influence the longevity of a hospitality career in New Zealand* (Thesis). Auckland University of Technology. Accessed at: http://aut.researchgateway.ac.nz/handle/10292/7486.

Mooney, S. (2016). Wasted youth in the hospitality industry: Older workers' perceptions and misperceptions about younger workers. *Hospitality & Society*, **6**(1), 9–30.

Mooney, S. (2017). Caught between a rock and an inhospitable place: How should hospitality students negotiate the changed employment landscape? In *CTS 2017 – Critical Tourism Studies Conference VII Book of Abstracts* (p. 184). Majorca, Spain: University de les Iles Balears, Copenhagen Business School and Thompson Rivers University. Retrieved from https://www.criticaltourismstudies.info/book-of-abstracts.

Mooney, S. and Ryan, I. (2009). A woman's place in hotel management: Upstairs or downstairs? *Gender in Management: An International Journal*, **24**(3), 195–210.

Mooney, S., Harris, C. and Ryan, I. (2016). Long hospitality careers – a contradiction in terms? *International Journal of Contemporary Hospitality Management*, **28**(11), 2589–608.

Mooney, S., Ryan, I. and Harris, C. (2017a). The intersections of gender with age and ethnicity in hotel careers: Still the same old privileges? *Gender, Work & Organization*, **24**(4), 360–75.

Mooney, S., Schänzel, H. and Poulston, J. (2017b). Illuminating the blind spots. *Hospitality & Society*, **7**(2), 105–13.

Nebel, E., Braunlich, C. and Yihong, Z. (1994). Career paths in American luxury hotels: Hotel food and beverage directors. *International Journal of Contemporary Hospitality Management*, **6**(6), 3–9.

Ng, C. and Pine, R. (2003). Women and men in Hong Kong: Perceptions of gender and career development issues. *International Journal of Hospitality Management*, **22**(1), 85–102.

Offe, C. and Standing, G. (2011). The Precariat: The new dangerous class. *Archives Européennes de Sociologie*, **52**(3), 466–74.

Okumus, F., Sariisik, M. and Naipaul, S. (2010). Understanding why women work in five-star hotels in a developing country and their work-related problems. *International Journal of Hospitality & Tourism Administration*, **11**(1), 76–105.

O'Leary, S. and Deegan, J. (2005). Career progression of Irish tourism and hospitality management graduates. *International Journal of Contemporary Hospitality Management*, **17**(4/5), 421–33.

O'Neill, J.W. (2012). Face time in the hotel industry: An exploration of what it is and why it happens. *Journal of Hospitality & Tourism Research*, **36**(4), 478–94.

OnsØyen, L.E., Mykletun, R.J. and Steiro, T.J. (2009). Silenced and invisible: The work-experience of room-attendants in Norwegian hotels. *Scandinavian Journal of Hospitality and Tourism*, **9**(1), 81–102.

Patwardhan, V., Mayya, S. and Joshi, H.G. (2014). Research on career management of women managers in hospitality industry: A review and analysis of journal publications of twenty years. *Human Resource Reflection: An International Refereed Journal of HR and OB*. Accessed at: http://eprints.manipal.edu/140780/.

Pinar, M., McCuddy, M.K., Birkan, I. and Kozak, M. (2011). Gender diversity in the hospitality industry: An empirical study in Turkey. *International Journal of Hospitality Management*, **30**(1), 73–81.

Pizam, A. (2006). Editorial: The new gender gap. *International Journal of Contemporary Hospitality Management*, **25**(4), 533–5.

Poulston, J. (2008a). Hospitality workplace problems and poor training: A close relationship. *International Journal of Contemporary Hospitality Management*, **20**(4), 412–27.

Poulston, J. (2008b). Metamorphosis in hospitality: A tradition of sexual harassment. *International Journal of Hospitality Management*, **27**(2), 232–40.

Poulston, J. (2009). Working conditions in hospitality: Employees' views of the dissatisfactory hygiene factors. *Journal of Quality Assurance in Hospitality & Tourism*, **10**(1), 23–43.

Powell, G. and Butterfield, D.A. (2015). The preference to work for a man or a woman: A matter of sex and gender? *Journal of Vocational Behavior*, **86**, 28–37.

Powell, P. (2002). *Service unseen: A study of hotel accommodation workers*. Milton Keynes: Open University.

Purcell, K. (1996). The relationship between career and job opportunities: Women's employment in the hospitality industry as a microcosm of women's employment. *Women in Management Review*, **11**(5), 17–24.

Purcell, K. (1997). Women's employment in UK tourism. In M. Thea Sinclear (ed.), *Gender, work and tourism* (pp. 33–57). London: Routledge.

Raley, S., Bianchi, S.M. and Wang, W. (2012). When do fathers care? Mothers' economic contribution and fathers' involvement in child care. *American Journal of Sociology*, **117**(5), 1422–59.

Ram, Y., Tribe, J. and Biran, A. (2016). Sexual harassment: Overlooked and under-researched. *International Journal of Contemporary Hospitality Management*, **28**(10), 2110–31.

Randall, D.M. (1987). Commitment and the organization: The organization man revisited. *The Academy of Management Review*, **12**(3), 460–71.

Riley, M. (1990). Role of age distributions in career path analysis. *Tourism Management*, **11**(1), 38–44.

Riley, M. and Szivas, E. (2009). Tourism employment and poverty: Revisiting the supply curve. *Tourism Economics*, **15**(2), 297–305.

Robinson, R., Kralj, A., Solnet, D., Goh, E. and Callan, V. (2014). Thinking job embeddedness not turnover: Towards a better understanding of frontline hotel worker retention. *International Journal of Hospitality Management*, **36**, 101–109.

Rydzik, A., Pritchard, A., Morgan, N. and Sedgley, D. (2012). Mobility, migration and hospitality employment: Voices of Central and Eastern European women. *Hospitality & Society*, **2**(2), 137–57.

Sabelis, I. and Schilling, E. (2013). Editorial: Frayed careers: Exploring rhythms of working lives. *Gender, Work & Organization*, **20**(2), 127–32.

Santero-Sanchez, R., Segovia-Pérez, M., Castro-Nuñez, B., Figueroa-Domecq, C. and Talón-Ballestero, P. (2015). Gender differences in the hospitality industry: A job quality index. *Tourism Management*, **51**, 234–46.

Simpson, R. (2014). Doing gender differently: Men in caring occupations. In S. Kumra, R. Simpson and R.J. Burke (eds), *The Oxford handbook of gender in organizations* (pp.480–99). Oxford: Oxford University Press.

Simpson, R. and Kumra, S. (2016). The Teflon effect: When the glass slipper meets merit. *Gender in Management: An International Journal*, **31**(8), 562–76.

Simpson, R., Slutskaya, N., Lewis, P. and Höpfl, H. (2012). *Dirty work: Concepts and identities*. Basingstoke: Palgrave Macmillan.

Singh, V., Kumra, S. and Vinnicombe, S. (2002). Gender and impression management: Playing the promotion game. *Journal of Business Ethics*, **37**(1), 77–89.

Song, Z., Chon, K., Ding, G. and Gu, C. (2015). Impact of organizational socialization tactics on newcomer job satisfaction and engagement: Core self-evaluations as moderators. *International Journal of Hospitality Management*, **46**, 180–89.

Spencer, J. and Bean, D. (2011). 'Sex matters': Differences in the perceptions of male and female line level employees about their work in the hospitality industry in Jamaica. *International Journal of Arts and Sciences*, **4**(9), 413–25.

Strachan, G. (2010). Still working for the man? Women's employment experiences in Australia since 1950. *Australian Journal of Social Issues*, **45**(1), 117–30.

Sullivan, S. and Baruch, Y. (2009). Advances in career theory and research: A critical review and agenda for future exploration. *Journal of Management*, **35**(6), 1542–71.

Tatli, A., Vassilopoulou, J. and Özbilgin, M. (2013). An unrequited affinity between talent shortages and untapped female potential: The relevance of gender quotas for talent management in high growth potential economies of the Asia Pacific region. *International Business Review*, **22**(3), 539–53.

Testa, M. (2009). National culture, leadership and citizenship: Implications for cross cultural management. *International Journal of Hospitality Management*, **28**, 78–85.

Theocharous, A. and Philaretou, A. (2009). Sexual harassment in the hospitality industry in the Republic of Cyprus: Theory and prevention. *Journal of Teaching in Travel & Tourism*, **9**(3–4), 288–304.

UN Women (2012). Sources of international law related to sexual harassment [United Nations Entity for Gender Equality and the Empowerment of Women]. Accessed 3 January 2017 at: http://www.endvawnow.org/en/articles/492-sources-of-international-law-related-to-sexual-harassment.html?next=493.

Upchurch, R.S., DiPietro, R.B., Curtis, C. and Hahm, J. (2010). Research note: Organizational commitment in the restaurant industry. *Journal of Foodservice Business Research*, **13**(2), 127–43.

Veijola, S., Molz, J., Pyyhtinen, O., Höckert, E. and Grit, A. (2014). *Disruptive tourism and its untidy guests: Alternative ontologies for future hospitalities*. London: Springer.

Wan, Y.K., Wong, I.A. and Kong, W.H. (2014). Student career prospect and industry commitment: The roles of industry attitude, perceived social status, and salary expectations. *Tourism Management*, **40**, 1–14.

Wang, Y-F. (2013). Constructing career competency model of hospitality industry employees for career success. *International Journal of Contemporary Hospitality Management*, **25**(7), 994–1016.

Waudby, B. (2012). *Employee experiences and perceptions of sexual harassment in hospitality: An exploratory study* (Thesis). Auckland University of Technology. Retrieved from http://aut.researchgateway.ac.nz/handle/10292/5522.

Wijesinghe, G. (2017). Editorial to the special issue: Illuminating the blind spots – Challenging dominant thinking about hospitality work and encounters. *Hospitality & Society*.

Wildes, V. (2005). Stigma in food service work: How it affects restaurant servers' intention to stay in the business or recommend a job to another. *Tourism and Hospitality Research*, **5**(3), 213–33.

Williams, C. (2013). The glass escalator, revisited: Gender inequality in neoliberal times. *Gender & Society*, **27**(5), 609–29.

Winker, G. and Degele, N. (2011). Intersectionality as multi-level analysis: Dealing with social inequality. *European Journal of Women's Studies*, **18**(1), 51–66.

Women Watch China and ILO (2010). *Guide on prevention of sexual harassment in the workplace*. Beijing: Beijing Zhongze Women's Legal Consultation and Service Center – Women Watch China and ILO.

Woods, R. and Viehland, D. (2000). Women in hotel management. *Cornell Hotel and Restaurant Administration Quarterly*, **41**(5), 51–4.

World Travel and Tourism Council (2016). *World travel and tourism economic impact*. London: World Travel and Tourism Council.

Yamashita, M. and Uenoyama, T. (2006). Boundaryless career and adaptive HR practices in Japan's hotel industry. *Career Development International*, **11**(3), 230–42.

Yang, J. (2010). Antecedents and consequences of job satisfaction in the hotel industry. *International Journal of Hospitality Management*, **29**(4), 609–19.

Young, C. and Corsun, D. (2010). Burned! The impact of work aspects, injury, and job satisfaction on unionized cooks' intentions to leave the cooking occupation. *Journal of Hospitality & Tourism Research*, **34**(1), 78–102.

Yu, Y., Byun, W-H. and Lee, T.J. (2014). Critical issues of globalisation in the international hotel industry. *Current Issues in Tourism*, **17**(2), 114–18.

Zampoukos, K. and Ioannides, D. (2011). The tourism labour conundrum: Agenda for new research in the geography of hospitality workers. *Hospitality & Society*, **1**(1), 25–45.

Zhao, X., Qu, H. and Ghiselli, R. (2011). Examining the relationship of work–family conflict to job and life satisfaction: A case of hotel sales managers. *International Journal of Hospitality Management*, **30**(1), 46–54.

9. Ageism and age discrimination in hospitality employment: issues, challenges and remedies

Andrew Jenkins

1. INTRODUCTION

The hospitality industry has traditionally relied on younger workers (Poulston and Jenkins, 2016). A research insight report entitled 'Will recruiting younger workers become a thing of the past?' from People 1st (2014) reveals that the hospitality industry in the UK relies on young workers, with 34 per cent of employees aged under 25, compared to 12 per cent in the economy as a whole. In particular, pubs, bars, clubs and restaurants attract a younger workforce, with 66 per cent of waiting staff and 60 per cent of bar staff aged under 25 (People 1st, 2014). However, as a result of increasing longevity and declining fertility rates (Sargeant, 2016), resulting in a smaller pool of younger people in the labour market, the number of older workers will increase significantly over the next 20 years (Chartered Institute of Personnel and Development, 2016). Hospitality employers will need to focus on the employment of older workers. Recruiting, retaining and developing older workers is a key employment issue facing hospitality businesses (Jenkins and Poulston, 2014). In order to address this issue, hospitality employers will need to confront workplace inequality faced by older workers and develop policies and practices to promote the health and well-being of their older workers. Negative stereotypical attitudes towards older workers, such as resistance to change, inability to assimilate technological developments and physical and cognitive decline, need to be challenged. These stereotypes can hinder the older people seeking employment and negatively affect the employment opportunities of those older people in employment (Carmichael et al., 2011).

This chapter examines the barriers facing older employees in the hospitality industry. These barriers are to be found outside, as well as inside hospitality workplaces, and, therefore, ageism and age discrimination and the treatment of older people in society first need to be considered. Thereafter, the role of employers in relation to age discrimination will be examined. Selected countries and supranational organizations' initiatives and legislation concerning age discrimination will subsequently be discussed. This discussion will focus on the USA, Canada, Australia, the UK, the European Union and the United Nations. Whilst it would undoubtedly be of interest to establish the nature of legislation protecting older workers from discrimination in a number of other countries, it is not within the scope of this chapter to undertake such an activity. The health and well-being of older workers will thereafter be examined and the chapter will conclude by assessing organizational responses to ageism and age discrimination.

2.   CONCEPTS OF AGE AND AGEING

Age is a complicated phenomenon. It is socially constructed (Wilson, 2000) and represents complex socio-cultural formations (Hardy, 1997). Age represents physiological ageing, social and economic change, and membership of a generation or cohort (Arber et al., 2003). It constitutes a dimension of social structure used to allocate opportunities, power and privilege (Thompson, 2006). Age is a pervasive and complex discourse, 'cutting across diverse organizations, institutions and societies, and producing significant material effects' (Thomas et al., 2014, p. 1570). Age, and the process of ageing, are phenomena which are biological in nature but their meanings are socially and culturally constructed (Wilson, 2000).

A limitation of research on older workers is that they are treated as a homogeneous group (Taylor et al., 2016). However, experiences of ageing will be radically influenced by gender, class and race (Biggs, 1993). Indeed, differences according to class will invariably persist into old age and may increase (Blaikie, 1999). Ageing involves both psychological and biological changes (Doering et al., 1983). It is, however, important to remember that both ageism and old age are ideas and ways of thinking, reflecting cultural forces which are very powerful (Bytheway, 1995). In order to study ageism, the way in which age is measured is crucial. This measurement usually corresponds to chronological age. However, it is important to remember that, for some people, a clear boundary into old age does not exist (Wilson, 2000). In the literature on ageism in the workplace, there is a lack of general agreement in what constitutes old age, with 'old age seemingly representing a potentially wide and ever changing age range' (Macdonald and Levy, 2016).

In any discussion on age, it is important to consider the words used to describe phenomena, processes and situations and, if possible, to use relative rather than absolute terms. Ageist language should be avoided, especially the word 'elderly' (Bytheway, 1995). In relation to ageing, it may be useful to consider stages of life rather than chronological age. This approach would involve viewing ageing as a process involving change during a person's life course (Harris, 1990). However, this approach also has its limitations because the stages of life may form a rigid basis for expectations regarding behaviour and appearance (Bytheway, 1995)

It is difficult to establish the moment at which a person becomes old as old age is affected by socially constructed practices (Mullan, 2002). Old age is an imprecise term and there is no fixed moment in an individual's life when they become old (Minois, 1989). One way of defining 'old' is to ask the person concerned whether they think of themselves as old (Hazan, 1994). Whether the system used to define age is scientific, bureaucratic, socially constructed or by the individual concerned, any theoretical constructs about ageing are 'replete with contradictions, conflicts, and paradoxes originating in our cultural system' (Hazan, 1994, p. 17).

Being 'older' is heavily related to the social context, including the industry, organizational context and organizational culture (Riach, 2011). In some industries, such as parts of the Hospitality Industry that rely on aesthetic labour, an 'older worker' may represent an individual in his or her thirties, whereas in other industries, such as medicine, an 'older worker' may represent an employee in his or her sixties. Similarly, within the same industry, one firm may rely on older workers whereas another may focus more on recruiting and retaining younger workers. Furthermore, many workplaces are highly gendered. Some rely overwhelmingly on female workers, and older women will experience differences in terms of the type of work undertaken, the amount of work done, the level of remuneration and motivation to continue working (Loretto and Vickerstaff, 2011).

As discussed, there are many different ways of conceptualizing 'age'. Pitt-Catsouphes et al. (2011) identify ten 'prisms of age' (as established by the Sloan Centre of Ageing at Boston College, Massachusetts). These are: physical-cognitive, socio-emotional, subjective, social, generational, relative, normative, life events, occupational/career and organizational. Table 9.1 outlines the key characteristics of each of these.

It is evident from Table 9.1 that there are many different perspectives of age. Indeed, the concept of age is multifaceted and multidimensional (Aaltio et al., 2014). Managers need to consider these because policies and programmes designed to reflect variations in chronological age may be quite different from policies and programmes developed to respond to other age-related factors (Pitt-Catsouphes et al., 2011). Perceptions of age and ageing can affect the working environment, affecting job satisfaction, work commitment and employee engagement (Macdonald and Levy, 2016).

Table 9.1   Perspectives/prisms of age

Type of age	Characteristics
Physical-cognitive	The changes to human development throughout our lives. This can be positive as well as negative and will depend on the individual's capacities, the tasks to be undertaken and the supports and demands in relation to the work environment.
Socio-emotional	The developmental tasks that gain importance during our life.
Subjective	The employee's overall feeling about their life stage (e.g. young at heart).
Social	The age attributed to us by other people.
Generational	The use of generational labels such as 'mature workers' or 'older employees'.
Relative	The person's age relative to a referent group such as a work group.
Normative	The expectations about age-appropriate activities.
Life events	The importance of life-course events (such as marriage/civil partnership, having children and caring for ageing parents).
Occupational/Career	The assumptions that jobs provide opportunities for employees to develop.
Organizational	The tenure (length of time) that the employee has worked for the organization.

3.   AGEISM AND AGE DISCRIMINATION

Ageism is not a new phenomenon (Vasconcelos, 2015). Older people have experienced extremes of treatment throughout history, ranging from ridicule to respect (Kingston, 1999). Butler and Lewis (1973, p. 127) developed one of the earliest definitions of ageism, stating that it represents 'the prejudices and stereotypes that are applied to older people sheerly on the basis of their age'. Ageism limits an older person's life chances due to restrictions being placed on them as a result of stereotypical assumptions about their role and abilities (Thompson, 2003). Much ageism and age discrimination is indirect. It is subtle and those affected may be unaware that they are being discriminated against (Carmichael et al., 2011). Ageism and age discrimination are closely related. Indeed, the terms are often used interchangeably (Rippon et al., 2014). However, Sargeant (2016) states that age discrimination represents a practical manifestation of ageism. According to Palmore (1999), ageism stems from prejudice, based on a person's beliefs and attitudes, and actions constitute discrimination.

220 Handbook of HRM in the tourism and hospitality industries

Age discrimination can affect people of all ages and now affects individuals in their thirties and forties (Wersley, 1996). Age discrimination sets older people apart as being different in a generalized and oversimplified way and is a set of social relations which is used to discriminate against older people (Minichiello et al., 2000). According to Thompson (2003) there are eight processes which are closely associated with inequality, discrimination and oppression, these being stereotyping, marginalization, invisibilization, infantilization, welfarism, medicalization, dehumanization and trivialization. In turn, these processes will result in different categories of discrimination (for example based on age), leading to a form of oppression (for example ageism) (Thompson, 2003). Similarly, Thompson and Thompson (2001) consider that older people represent an oppressed group due to discrimination, marginalization and dehumanization. Thus, Thompson (2006) argues, older people are assigned lower status in the labour market because they are viewed as marginal to the labour market.

Age discrimination in employment principally concerns professional encounters, that is, encounters in the workplace. However, these will be affected by the social construction of ageing which, in turn, will be influenced by wider political, economic, socio-cultural and technological factors (Lucas, 2004). As a result of actual or perceived age discrimination, policies will be developed by the government of the country concerned or by a supranational organization such as the United Nations or the European Union. At the organizational level, policies and practices may be developed to address age discrimination.

Within an organization, discrimination can take one of three forms: individual discrimination, structural discrimination or organizational discrimination (Hollinshead et al., 2003). Individual discrimination concerns prejudice demonstrated by one individual against another; structural discrimination results in certain groups being excluded due to certain practices (for example requirements for promotion); and organizational discrimination reflects commonly held beliefs about the suitability of certain groups for certain jobs (Hollinshead et al., 2003).

Hollinshead et al. (2003) propose three economic explanations for discrimination: human capital theory, segmented labour market theory and reserve army of labour theory. According to human capital theory, there is a positive correlation between education, level of skills and earnings (Bae and Patterson, 2014). In relation to segmented labour market theory, differences in wages between individuals are not the result of differences in skills but institutional roles and social influences (Leontaridi, 1998). Finally, the reserve army of labour theory is based on the writings of Marx, who saw the reserve army being employed when conditions were right or being repelled from the labour market at other times (Hollinshead et al., 2003).

According to Thompson (2003), discrimination operates at three levels. First, at the personal level discrimination manifests itself as prejudice, which may be explicit or implicit (Thompson, 2003). Secondly, at the cultural level discrimination can be used to exclude other groups, it can create beliefs of superiority and assumptions which lead to discrimination (Thompson, 2003). Thirdly, at the structural level, discrimination includes political, social and economic factors and inequalities which are embedded in the social order and play an important role in maintaining this order (Thompson, 2003).

All organizations discriminate in that they have to choose between individuals when recruiting, selecting and promoting (Newell, 1995). If undertaken with care, this would constitute fair discrimination. Unfair discrimination takes place when non-relevant criteria are used, such as the colour of a person's skin, the individual's gender or their age (Newell, 1995). Discrimination in employment concerns the inequitable treatment of some employees, irrespective of their skills, knowledge and abilities (Rose, 2001).

Discrimination can be direct or indirect (Tomei, 2003). Direct discrimination takes place where an employee is treated less favourably on the grounds of age, gender, race, etc. than an employee of a different age, gender, race, etc. (Daniels, 2004). However, being treated differently does not necessarily mean that the person is treated less favourably (Daniels and Macdonald, 2005). Indirect discrimination takes place when an employer applies an unjustifiable criterion to different groups (for example, based on age, gender and race) which adversely affects one group, resulting in a person from the disadvantaged group being unable to comply with the criterion (Daniels, 2004). Direct discrimination is easier to uncover than indirect discrimination (Tomei, 2003). A similar concept to indirect discrimination is the concept of adverse impact, which refers to a 'substantially different rate of selection in hiring, promotion or other employment decision which works to the disadvantage of members of a race, sex or ethnic group' (Biddle, 2006, p. 1). Unlike direct or indirect discrimination, however, adverse impact is not a legal term (Biddle, 2006).

4.   AGE DISCRIMINATION AND EMPLOYERS

Employment opportunities for older workers are largely determined by employers (OECD, 2006). These opportunities will be affected by discriminatory policies and practices. Thus, employers' attitudes and discriminatory practices are pivotal to understanding inequalities based on a person's age (Canduela et al., 2012). Age discrimination in the workplace takes place when 'Decisions made by an employer, about an individual, are based on an individual's chronological age' (Sargeant, 2001, p. 141). Age discrimination may also result from an employer's attitude about an employee's perceived age (Glover and Branine, 2001).

Age discrimination appears to be deeply embedded in the policies, practices and cultures of many organizations (Hollywood et al., 2003). Kirton and Greene (2000) claim that employers are the main barrier to the employment of older workers, with their attitudes towards older workers being rooted in myths and stereotypes. In a review of ageing and employment policies in OECD countries, stereotypical attitudes of older workers were found to be widespread (OECD, 2006). Some employers believe older workers to be incompetent and untrainable (Nelson, 2016). Appelbaum et al. (2016) state that there are a number of common negative stereotypical beliefs about older workers: they are reluctant to change because they are set in their ways; they are slow to learn; they have poor health; they are more costly; they are less motivated; they are less innovative; and they are less productive. De Beauvoir (1996) claims that employers dislike the very idea of employing older people.

Organizations are major sites of power conflict and the employment of older people may be affected by formal and informal power relations between the organization, groups and individuals (Thompson, 2003). In order to understand and eliminate age discrimination it is necessary to understand these power relations (Thompson, 2003). Discrimination will be strongest where relatively powerful groups are able to systematically discriminate against relatively less powerful groups (Thompson, 2006).

According to Blakemore and Boneham (1994) thoughts about ageing are permeated by myths and stereotypes. These stereotypes are not limited to the workplace. They reflect widespread stereotypes of older people in society (McCann and Giles, 2004). Employers' stereotypes of older workers are likely to lead to fewer older workers being promoted, fewer being trained and may lead to lower pay (Wersley, 1996). According to the OECD (2006), negative perceptions held by employers about the characteristics of older workers translate into lower recruitment levels and retention rates, which fall dramatically when a person reaches their fifties.

Discrimination against older people in employment is not just about individual prejudice; it is a social construct. It is institutionalized in social, economic and employment systems (Taylor and Walker, 1998). Moreover, it is not just employers who are discriminatory towards older people, as the state, unions and works councils have conspired to provide opportunities for younger workers by removing older people from the labour force (Institute of Personnel Management, 1993).

Some employers have recognized· the benefits of employing older workers. For example, in 1989 B&Q opened a store in Macclesfield, UK which was staffed entirely by workers over the age of 50. This initiative worked very well and the company began encouraging applications from older people (Department for Education and Employment, 1999). David Fairhurst, from McDonald's UK and Northern Europe, has commented that 'It might surprise people to learn that at McDonald's we employ over 1,000 people aged 60 and above. These employees play an important role in our business and, as the research shows, they make a huge impact on customer satisfaction' (Department for Work and Pensions, 2013a, p. 4). Research by Lancaster University Management School on the performance of more than 400 McDonald's restaurants across the UK found that employees aged 60 and above helped deliver a significant boost to the business (Department for Work and Pensions, 2013b). The study further revealed that customer satisfaction was, on average, 20 per cent higher in restaurants that employ employees aged 60 and above as part of a mixed-age workforce.

5.   AGE DISCRIMINATION AND THE LAW IN SELECTED COUNTRIES AND REGIONS

From an American legal perspective, there are two forms of age discrimination: animus discrimination and statistical discrimination (Posner, 1999). Animus discrimination is a 'systematic undervaluation, motivated by ignorance, viciousness, or irrationality, of the value of older people in the workplace' (Sargeant, 2001, p. 141) whereas statistical discrimination refers to the 'Failure or refusal, normally motivated by the costs of information, to distinguish a particular member of a group from the average member' (Sargeant, 2001, p. 142). In the USA the Age Discrimination in Employment Act (ADEA) of 1967 protects people over 40 years of age from discrimination in relation to employment (Nazarov and Von Schrader, 2016). This Act has been successful in greatly increasing the employment of workers aged over 40 (Adams, 2004). The ADEA prohibits age discrimination in almost all areas of employment including recruitment, retention, training and compensation (Peng and Kleiner, 1999). Before the ADEA came into existence, many US states already had laws regarding age discrimination. Colorado was the first state in the US to have such a law. This law, passed in 1903, covered the 18–60 age group (Adams, 2004).

In Canada, age discrimination measures are provided at the federal level and at the province/territory level (Sargeant, 2016). In addition, the Canadian Charter of Rights and Freedoms, adopted in 1982, regulates discrimination issues in the government and public sector (Sargeant, 2016).

Employment can be terminated if a person has reached the maximum age applied to employment by law or when the person has reached the 'normal' age of retirement, although some provinces, such as Ontario, have abolished the compulsory retirement age (Filinson, 2008). Like Canada, Australia also has a federal and state (provincial) structure and measures to alleviate age discrimination have traditionally been developed at the state level (Sargeant, 2016). According to McGann et al. (2016, p. 375), 'successive Australian governments have implemented policies aimed at extending working lives and increasing older employment'. In 2004, the federal government of Australia adopted the Age Discrimination Act, which covers employment, access to goods and services, education, transport, federal laws and programmes, accommodation and land (Sargeant, 2016).

In 2010, the Equality Act came into effect in the UK. This Act was designed to bring a more uniform approach to equality legislation in the UK. It addresses unlawful discrimination in terms of employment and the provision of facilities, goods and services (Sargeant and Lewis, 2014). The Act protects 'older' and 'younger' people against discrimination, although no specific chronological age is stated in the Act (Foot et al., 2016). Although the Equality Act 2010 affects all aspects of the employment relationship, the immediate impact has been on recruitment and selection (Foot et al., 2016). In 2011, the UK Conservative–Liberal Coalition Government further strengthened the age discrimination provisions by abolishing the default retirement age (Sargeant and Lewis, 2014). Blackham (2016), having reviewed the impact of the Equality Act 2010 on age equality measures in organizations, concluded that age discrimination legislation in the UK had a limited impact on organizational practices, with organizational measures largely focusing on formal equality policies rather than practical measures to achieve change.

At a supranational level, the European Union has been instrumental in establishing a general framework for the equal treatment of older people in employment. Article 13 of the Amsterdam Treaty of 1999 enables the Council 'to take appropriate action to combat discrimination based on sex, racial or ethnic origin, religion or belief, disability, age or sexual orientation' (Caracciolo, 2001). Following on from the Treaty of Amsterdam, EU Directive, 2000/43/EC, although dealing primarily with the principle of equal treatment between persons of racial or ethnic origin, states that 'The right to equality before the law and protection against discrimination for all persons constitutes a universal right' (http://europa.eu.int). The Council Directive 2000/78/EC, issued on the 27 November 2000, refers specifically to 'older people', stating that 'The Community Charter of the Fundamental Social Rights of Workers recognises the importance of combating every form of discrimination, including the need to take appropriate action for the social and economic integration of elderly and disabled people' (point 6, page 1) and 'The prohibition of age discrimination is an essential part of meeting the aims set out in the European Guidelines and encouraging diversity in the workforce' (point 25, page 2). In 2006, the Employment Equality (Age) Regulations (SI 2006/1031) were passed by the European Union (Herring, 2011). EU law on age discrimination provides 'a broader range of exceptions to the principle of equal treatment than is permitted in connection with any other protected characteristic' (O'Dempsey and Beale, 2011, p. 5).

The United Nations has also been preoccupied with the problem of age discrimination in employment. In a report of the Second World Assembly on Ageing in Madrid, 8–12 April 2002, Article 12 states that 'Older persons should have the opportunity to work for as long as they wish and are able to, in satisfying and productive work, continuing to have access to education and training programmes' (United Nations, 2002a, p. 3). In terms of recommendations for action, the Second World Assembly on Ageing identified a number of initiatives which needed to be taken. These include promoting a favourable attitude towards older workers amongst employers, increasing the awareness of the benefits of an ageing workforce, paying special attention to ageism and women's employment, making appropriate adjustments to workplace environments, increasing labour-market participation of older people, promoting self-employment for older persons and developing a more flexible approach to retirement (United Nations, 2002a). Following on from the Second World Assembly in Madrid, the Economic and Social Council of the United Nations held a meeting about ageism in society and employment at the UNECE Ministerial Conference on Ageing, Berlin, 11–13 September 2002. The report states that 'Older persons are a valuable resource and make an essential contribution to society' (United Nations, 2002b, p.1) and that priority should be given to 'encouraging labour markets to respond to ageing and take advantage of the potential of older persons' (United Nations, 2002b, p. 2). The UN continues to advocate for the rights of older people and is working towards a UN convention on the rights of older persons (United Nations, 2010).

6.   THE HEALTH AND WELL-BEING OF OLDER WORKERS

The concept of wellness has grown in importance in twenty-first-century society and a culture of 'wellness' is affecting every aspect of modern day living (Walsh, 2015). The aim of workplace health and wellness pro-grammes is to continually engage workers with the intention of making a positive and sustainable change in terms of lifestyle choices (Arena et al., 2013). Whilst health and wellness programmes differ according to organization and country, common goals of such programmes typically include raising awareness, reinforcing positive behaviour and helping people develop tools to engender positive change (Joslin et al., 2006). According to Linde (2015), there are two types of wellness in relation to work: employee wellness and relational wellness. The former refers to the individual worker, focusing on such issues as job satisfaction, job insecurity and the psychological contract, whereas the latter concerns the collective relationship in the workplace and focuses on employee relations, employment relations and labour relations.

There are many benefits of workplace health and wellness initiatives such as better health for workers, greater productivity and lower medical costs (Liu et al., 2014). Other benefits include improved employee engagement, lower levels of absenteeism and fewer work-related accidents (Ingham and Norris, 2007). In particular, an all-inclusive approach to older-worker wellness can enhance the working lives of older people. As Isaac and Ratzan (2013) noted, successful health and wellness programmes should incorporate a holistic view of health that includes 'physical, occupational, intellectual, social/spiritual, and emotional components because there's a clear connection between wellness, productivity and competitiveness' (pp. 301–302). According to Shephard (2000), wellness programmes in the workplace have changed from a simple focus on fitness classes to a more modular structure, encompassing many aspects of health. After studying 277 older working residents of Pennsylvania, USA, Crowne (2013) sug-gested that managers consider providing an environment that benefits older workers' health. Once again, this would entail not just providing fitness facilities, for example, but focusing on broader aspects of health and well-being.

In a longitudinal study of well-being in older workers and retirees, Potočnik and Sonnentag (2013) found four mechanisms relating to better well-being: the achievement of personal goals in undertaking a particular activity; the opportunity to socialize as a result of an active lifestyle; providing a time structure and generativity through activities outside the workplace; and engaging in physical activities improving health and well-being. However, the same authors also recognize that there are activities that can have a detrimental effect on the health and well-being of older workers such as (for example) their caring responsibilities.

Despite the fact that workplaces can potentially be effective vehicles for health and wellness promotion, resulting in improved productivity and reduced healthcare costs, Elliot et al. (2012) claimed that occupational health and wellness programmes have not yet penetrated many workplaces.

7. ORGANIZATIONAL AND INSTITUTIONAL RESPONSES TO AGEISM AND AGE DISCRIMINATION

In examining the barriers to the employment of older workers in the hospitality industry, Poulston and Jenkins (2016) recommend addressing discriminatory, ageist attitudes in hospitality education. As hospitality moves to become an industry where degree-level qualifications become commonplace and, perhaps, the norm, it is incumbent on hospitality educators to teach students about equality and diversity, confronting the stereotypical views held about older workers. Indeed, the need to focus on understanding older workers and age diversity in higher education was revealed in the findings of Hertzman and Zhong's (2016) research into the attitudes of hospitality students from five US universities. Poulston and Jenkins (2016) further suggest that hospitality employers need to address the apparent disconnect between older and younger workers, both in relation to current and potential employees. Specific actions to remedy this problem include using older workers to mentor younger workers, combining older and younger workers in work teams and the use of in-house training programmes to help educate employees about the benefits of having a diverse workforce.

Research by Poulston and Jenkins (2013) on older workers in the hospitality industry in New Zealand found that a barrier to the employment of older workers stemmed from negative stereotypes about older employees. The authors recommend that employers move away from the view of youth as the major labour source and, instead, focus on the skills and attributes of individuals. Research on managers' perceptions of older workers in British hotels by Jenkins and Poulston (2014) revealed that managers were generally positive about older workers yet older workers remained under-represented. A possible explanation for this under-representation is 'new ageism' where employers use the rhetoric of equality whilst continuing to marginalize older workers. Jenkins and Poulston (2014) state that hospitality employers should focus on the knowledge, skills and capabilities of the worker rather than focusing on his or her chronological age. Furthermore, the authors recommend that hotel management undertake a number of activities:

- challenge negative stereotypical views held of older workers;
- assess if older workers have equal access to training;
- employ a greater number of older workers to reflect the demographic composition of the population;
- introduce flexible employment practices (these would benefit all workers, whatever their age);
- where necessary, make modifications to the job to address specific health and safety needs.

Line managers play an important role with respect to the recruitment, selection, training and development of older workers yet a survey undertaken by the Chartered Institute of Personnel and Development and the Chartered Management Institute in 2010 on managing an ageing workforce revealed that only 7 per cent of organizations provided training for line managers with respect to managing older workers. The same survey revealed that only 14 per cent of managers and HR managers considered their organization very well prepared to cope with the issues caused by an ageing workforce. In order to encourage the employment of older workers, hospitality organizations need to prepare for population ageing. It is essential that support for older workers is provided by senior management and training be provided for line managers because line managers play a front-line role in the delivery and achievement of the organization's objectives, including its Human Resource, Equal Opportunity and Diversity Management objectives (Foot et al., 2016).

8. CONCLUSION

This chapter has focused on older workers in the hospitality industry. Despite the obvious advantages of employing older employees, they remain under-represented and marginalized. This is at least partly due to negative stereotypical views about them. Demographic changes mean that the industry's traditional reliance on younger workers is unsustainable. Older workers have much to offer, such as experience, wisdom and patience (although it would be a generalization to suggest that older people necessarily possess these qualities where younger people do not).

Increasingly, employers are being influenced by the business case for effective age management policies that can help facilitate cooperation amongst different generations of employees, transfer of knowledge and succession planning (MacDermott, 2014). Moreover, as the population ages, there will be a greater number of older customers, and older workers should be well placed to understand the needs and wants of their peers.

There is also an ethical argument to employing older workers. Current and potential employees should be chosen because of their skills and knowledge, not their age.

People should not be discriminated against because of a particular demographic characteristic (such as age). Although the focus of this chapter has been on older workers, it is important to remember that workers from different generational cohorts have different qualities and, therefore, an age-diverse workforce may offer the organization an optimal mix of experience, knowledge, skills and enthusiasm. As population ageing continues to gather pace, hospitality businesses need to examine their traditional reliance on younger workers. An ageing population is one of the biggest issues facing our planet. It brings about challenges but also opportunities.

REFERENCES

Aaltio, I., Maria Salminen, H. and Koponen, S. (2014). Ageing employees and human resource management – evidence of gender-sensitivity? *Equality, Diversity and Inclusion: An International Journal*, **33**(2), 160–76.

Adams, S. (2004). Age discrimination legislation and the employment of older workers. *Labour Economics*, **11**(2), 219–41.

Appelbaum, S.H., Wenger, R., Pachon Buitrago, C. and Kaur, R. (2016), The effects of old-age stereotypes on organizational productivity (Part one). *Industrial and Commercial Training*, **48**(4), 181–8.

Arber, S., Davidson, K. and Ginn, J. (eds) (2003). *Gender and Ageing: Changing Roles and Relationships*. Maidenhead: Open University Press.

Arena, R., Guazzi, M., Briggs, P.D., Cahalin, L.P., Myers, J., Kaminsky, L.A. and Lavie, C.J. (2013). Promoting health and wellness in the workplace: A unique opportunity to establish primary and extended secondary cardiovascular risk reduction programs. *Mayo Clinic Proceedings*, **88**(6), 605–17.

Bae, S. and Patterson, L. (2014). Comparison and implications of human capital theory at the individual, organization, and country levels. *Journal of Organizational Culture, Communications and Conflict*, **18**(1), 11–28.

Biddle, D. (2006). *Adverse Impact and Test Validation: A Practitioner's Guide to Valid and Desirable Employment Testing*. Aldershot: Gower Publishing.

Biggs, S. (1993). *Understanding Ageing: Images, Attitudes and Professional Practice*. Buckingham: Open University Press.

Blackham, A. (2016). Reflexive change? A quantitative review of the impact of the Equality Act 2010 on age equality measures in organizations. *International Journal of Discrimination and the Law*, **16**(2/3), 122–42.

Blaikie, A. (1999). *Ageing and Popular Culture*. Cambridge: Cambridge University Press.

Blakemore, K. and Boneham, M. (1994). *Age, Race and Ethnicity: A Comparative Approach*. Buckingham: Open University Press.

Butler, R. and Lewis, M. (1973). *Aging and Mental Health: Positive Psychological Approaches*. Saint Louis, MO: C.V. Mosby Press.

Bytheway, B. (1995). *Ageism*. Buckingham: Open University Press.

Canduela, J., Dutton, M., Johnson, S., Lindsay, C., McQuaid, R.W. and Raeside, R. (2012). Ageing, skills and participation in work-related training in Britain: Assessing the position of older workers. *Work, Employment & Society*, **26**(1), 42–60.

Caracciolo, E. (2001). The family-friendly workplace: The EC position. *The International Journal of Comparative Labour Law and Industrial Relations*, Autumn, 325–44.
Carmichael, F., Hulme, C., Porcellato, L., Ingham, B. and Prashar, A. (2011). Ageism and age discrimination: The experiences and perceptions of older employees. In: E. Parry and S. Tyson (eds), *Managing an Age Diverse Workforce*. Basingstoke: Palgrave Macmillan, pp. 115–28.
Chartered Institute of Personnel and Development and Chartered Management Institute (2010). *Managing an Ageing Workforce: How Employers are Adapting to an Older Labour Market*. London: CIPD.
Chartered Institute of Personnel and Development (2016). *Factsheet: Age and Employment*. Accessed 6 January 2017 at: www.cipd.co.uk.
Crowne, K.A. (2013). Developing a better understanding of the older worker. *The Journal of Applied Business and Economics*, **15**(1), 54–63.
Daniels, K. (2004). *Employment Law for HR and Business Students*. London: CIPD.
Daniels, K. and Macdonald, L. (2005). *Equality, Diversity and Discrimination: A Student Text*. London: CIPD.
De Beauvoir, S. (1996). *The Coming of Age*. London: W.W. Norton & Company.
Department for Education and Employment (1999). *Age Diversity in Employment: Guidance and Case Studies*. Nottingham: DfEE Publications.
Department for Work and Pensions (2013a). *Employing Older Workers: An Employer's Guide to Today's Multi-generational Workforce*. London: DWP.
Department for Work and Pensions (2013b). *Employer Case Studies: Employing Older Workers for an Effective Multi-generational Workforce*. London: DWP.
Doering, M., Rhodes, S. and Schuster, M. (1983). *The Aging Worker*. London: Sage.
Elliot, D.L., MacKinnon, D.P., Mabry, L., Kisbu-Sakarya, Y., DeFrancesco, C.A., Coxe, S.J. and Favorite, K.C. (2012). Worksite wellness program implementation: A model of translational effectiveness. *Translational Behavioral Medicine*, **2**(2), 228–35.
Filinson, R. (2008). Age discrimination legislation in the UK: A comparative and geronto-logical analysis. *Journal of Cross-Cultural Gerontology*, **23**(3), 225–37.
Foot, M., Hook, C. and Jenkins, A. (2016). *Introducing Human Resource Management*. Harlow: Pearson Education.
Glover, I. and Branine, M. (2001). Ageism and the labour process: Towards a research agenda. *Personnel Review*, **26**(4), 274–92.
Hardy, M. (ed.) (1997). *Studying Ageing and Social Change: Conceptual and Methodological Issues*. London: Sage.
Harris, D.K. (1990). *Sociology of Ageing*. London: Harper and Row.
Hazan, H. (1994). *Old Age Constructions and Deconstructions*. Cambridge: Cambridge University Press.
Herring, J. (2011). Age discrimination and the law: Forging the way ahead. In: E. Parry and S. Tyson (eds), *Managing an Age Diverse Workforce*. Basingstoke: Palgrave Macmillan, pp. 24–42.
Hertzman, J. and Zhong, Y. (2016). A model of hospitality students' attitude toward and willingness to work with older adults. *International Journal of Contemporary Hospitality Management*, **28**(4), 681–99.
Hollinshead, G., Nicholls, P. and Tailby, S. (2003). *Employee Relations*. Harlow: Prentice Hall.
Hollywood, E., Brown, R., Danson, M. and McQuaid, R. (2003), *Older Workers in the Scottish Labour Market: A New Agenda*. Stirling: Scotecon.
Ingham, J. and Norris, A. (2007). Health and wellness programs help manage human capital. *Strategic HR Review*, **6**(3), 10–11.
Institute of Personnel Management (1993). *Age and Employment; Policies, Attitudes and Practice*. London: IPM.
Isaac, F. and Ratzan, S. (2013). Corporate wellness programs: Why investing in employee health and well-being is an investment in the health of the company. In: Cary L. Cooper and Ronald Burke (eds), *The Fulfilling Workplace: The Organization's Role in Achieving Individual and Organizational Health*. Aldershot: Gower Publishing, pp. 301–14.

Jenkins, A. and Poulston, J. (2014). Managers' perceptions of older workers in British hotels. *Equality, Diversity and Inclusion: An International Journal*, **33**(1), 54–72.

Joslin, B., Lowe, J.B. and Peterson, N.A. (2006). Employee characteristics and participation in a worksite wellness programme. *Health Education Journal*, **65**(4), 308–19.

Kingston, P. (1999). *Ageism in History*. Nursing Times Monographs No. 28. London: NT Books.

Kirton, G. and Greene, A. (2000). *The Dynamics of Managing Diversity: A Critical Approach*. Oxford: Butterworth Heinemann.

Leontaridi, M. (1998). Segmented labour markets: Theory and evidence. *Journal of Economic Surveys*, **12**(1), 63–101.

Linde, B. (2015). *The Value of Wellness in the Workplace: A Perspective of the Employee–Organisation Relationship in the South African Labour Market*. Singapore: Springer.

Liu, H., Mattke, S., Harris, K.M., Weinberger, S., Serxner, S., Caloyeras, J.P. and Exum, E. (2014). Do workplace wellness programs reduce medical costs? Evidence from a Fortune 500 company. *Inquiry*, **50**(2), 150–58.

Loretto, W. and Vickerstaff, S. (2011). *The Relationship between Gender and Age*. In: E. Parry and S. Tyson (eds), *Managing an Age Diverse Workforce*. Basingstoke: Palgrave Macmillan, pp.59–79.

Lucas, R. (2004). *Employment Relations in the Hospitality and Tourism Industries*. London: Routledge.

MacDermott, T. (2014). Older workers and extended workforce participation: Moving beyond the 'barriers to work' approach. *International Journal of Discrimination and the Law*, **14**(2), 83–98.

Macdonald, J.L. and Levy, S.R. (2016). Ageism in the workplace: The role of psychosocial factors in predicting job satisfaction, commitment, and engagement. *Journal of Social Issues*, **72**(1), 169–90.

McCann, R. and Giles, H. (2004). Ageism in the workplace: A communication perspective. In: T.D. Nelson (ed.), *Ageism: Stereotyping and Prejudice Against Older Persons*. Cambridge, MA: MIT Press, pp.163–99.

McGann, M., Ong, R., Bowman, D., Duncan, A., Kimberley, H. and Biggs, S. (2016). Gendered ageism in Australia: Changing perceptions of age discrimination among older men and women. *Economic Papers: A Journal of Applied Economics and Policy*, **35**(4), 375–88.

Minichiello, V., Browne, J. and Kendig, H. (2000). Perceptions and consequences of ageism: Views of older people. *Ageing and Society*, **20**, 253–78.

Minois, G. (1989). *History of Old Age: From Antiquity to the Renaissance*. Chicago, IL: The University of Chicago Press.

Mullan, P. (2002). *The Imaginary Time Bomb: Why an Ageing Population is not a Social Problem*. London: I.B. Tauris and Co.

Nazarov, Z.E. and Von Schrader, S. (2016). Trends and patterns in Age Discrimination in Employment Act. *Research on Aging*, **38**(5), 580–601.

Nelson, T.D. (2016). The age of ageism. *Journal of Social Issues*, **72**(1), 191–8.

Newell, S. (1995). *The Healthy Organization: Fairness, Ethics and Effective Management*. London: Routledge.

O'Dempsey, D. and Beale, A. (2011). *Age and Employment*. Luxemburg: European Commission.

OECD (2006). *Live Longer, Work Longer: A Synthesis Report*. Paris: OECD.

Palmore, E. (1999). *Ageism: Negative and Positive*. New York: Springer Publishing Company.

Peng, B. and Kleiner, B. (1999). New developments in age discrimination. *Equal Opportunities International*, **18**(2/3/4), 72–5.

People 1st (2014). 'Will recruiting younger workers become a thing of the past?' (online), Accessed 5 September 2016 at: www.people1st.co.uk.

Pitt-Catsouphes, M., Matz-Costa, C. and Brown, M. (2011). *The Prism of Age: Managing Age Diversity in the Twenty-First Century Workplace*. In: E. Parry and S. Tyson (eds), *Managing an Age Diverse Workforce*. Basingstoke: Palgrave Macmillan, pp.80–94.

Posner, R. (1999). Employment discrimination: Age discrimination and sexual harassment. *International Review of Law and Economics*, **19**, 421–46.

Potočnik, K. and Sonnentag, S. (2013). A longitudinal study of well-being in older workers and retirees: The role of engaging in different types of activities. *Journal of Occupational and Organizational Psychology*, **86**(4), 497–521.

Poulston, J. and Jenkins, A. (2013). The persistent paradigm: Older worker stereotypes in the New Zealand hotel industry. *Journal of Human Resources in Hospitality & Tourism*, **12**(1), 1–25.

Poulston, J. and Jenkins, A. (2016). Barriers to the employment of older hotel workers in New Zealand. *Journal of Human Resources in Hospitality & Tourism*, **15**(1), 45–68.

Riach, K. (2011). Situating age (in)equality within the paradigm and practices of diversity management. In: E. Parry and S. Tyson (eds), *Managing an Age Diverse Workforce*. Basingstoke: Palgrave Macmillan, pp. 43–58.

Rippon, I., Kneale, D., De Oliveira, C., Demakakos, P. and Steptoe, A. (2014). Perceived age discrimination in older adults. *Age and Ageing*, **43**(3), 379–86.

Rose, E. (2001). *Employment Relations*. Harlow: Pearson Education.

Sargeant, M. (2001). Lifelong learning and age discrimination in employment. *Education and the Law*, **13**(2), 141–54.

Sargeant, M. (2016). *Age Discrimination: Ageism in Employment and Service Provision*. Aldershot: Gower Publishing.

Sargeant, M. and Lewis, D. (2014). *Employment Law*. Harlow: Pearson Education.

Shephard, R.J. (2000). Worksite health promotion and the older worker. *International Journal of Industrial Ergonomics*, **25**(5), 465–75.

Taylor, P. and Walker, A. (1998). Policies and practices towards older workers: A framework for comparative research. *Human Resource Management Journal*, **8**(3), 61–76.

Taylor, P., Loretto, W., Marshall, V., Earl, C. and Phillipson, C. (2016). The older worker: Identifying a critical research agenda. *Social Policy and Society*, **15**(4), 675–89.

Thomas, R., Hardy, C., Cutcher, L. and Ainsworth, S. (2014). What's age got to do with it? On the critical analysis of age and organizations. *Organization Studies*, **35**(11), 1569–84.

Thompson, N. (2003). *Promoting Equality: Challenging Discrimination and Oppression*. Basingstoke: Palgrave Macmillan.

Thompson, N. (2006). *Anti-discriminatory Practice*. Basingstoke: Palgrave Macmillan.

Thompson, N. and Thompson, S. (2001). Empowering older people: Beyond the care model. *Journal of Social Work*, **1**(1), 61–76.

Tomei, M. (2003). Discrimination and equality at work: A review of the concepts. *International Labour Review*, **142**(4), 401–18.

United Nations (2002a). *Report of the Second World Assembly on Ageing*. New York: UN.

United Nations (2002b). *Berlin Ministerial Declaration: A Society for all Ages in the UNECE Region*. New York: UN.

United Nations (2010). *Strengthening Older People's Rights: Towards a UN Convention*. New York: UN.

Vasconcelos, A.F. (2015). Older workers: Some critical societal and organizational challenges. *Journal of Management Development*, **34**(3), 352–72.

Walsh, B. (2015). America's evolution toward wellness. *Generations*, **39**(1), 23–29.

Wersley, R. (1996). *Age and Employment: Why Employers Should Think Again about Older Workers*. London: Age Concern England.

Wilson, G. (2000). *Understanding Old Age: Critical and Global Perspectives*. London: Sage.

PART IV

CRITICAL EMPLOYEE AND ORGANIZATION OUTCOMES

10. Advancing engagement: debates in the field and proposed directions for hospitality and tourism research and practice
Julia Christensen Hughes

Academic interest in 'employee engagement' has grown considerably over the past several years. While ten years ago scholars routinely commented on the 'surprising dearth of empirical research on employee engagement in the academic literature' (Saks, 2006, p. 600), a growing body of work suggests this is no longer the case. Meta-analyses in the extant literature have identified numerous antecedents and outcomes, with significant implications for management practice, employee well-being and organizational effectiveness.

Employee engagement may be especially important within service organizations, where front-line staff are responsible for enacting the organization's customer value proposition, affecting the quality of the customer experience as well as customer intention to return (Berezan et al., 2013). In addition, in countries where hospitality and tourism comprise a significant proportion of the economy, employee engagement can influence the success of national tourism branding strategies and economic development agendas (Karatepe et al., 2010; Pienaar and Willemse, 2008).

Achieving a consistently high level of employee engagement in any industry may be challenging, but perhaps particularly so in hospitality and tourism, given unique job demands within the work environment. Hospitality employees can be exposed to substantial stress and poor working conditions (Pienaar and Willemse, 2008), including 'emotionally challenging service encounters' as well as 'long work hours and unstable shift work, working on weekends and holidays, low wages, and lack of employment stability' (Lee and Ok, 2015, p. 85). Scholars have highlighted the prevalence of work overload (for both managers and hourly employees), and the consequences of 'emotional labour' (Hochschild, 1983a) including high rates of turnover and emotional exhaustion (Karatepe and Olugbade, 2009).

These types of pressures may only increase in the future. The hospitality and tourism industry is undergoing considerable disruption,

236 Handbook of HRM in the tourism and hospitality industries

with profound implications for the human resource function and the employees who work within it (see Christensen Hughes, Chapter 2, this volume). Consumer expectations are increasing, whether the focus is on value and convenience, local food, sustainability and integrity across the supply chain, or the provision of unique social and cultural experiences. In keeping with the rise of the 'experience economy' (Pine and Gilmore, 1999), employees with the capacity for orchestrating authentic guest experiences will become increasingly essential. Arguably, the industry will be well served to the extent that these employees are fully 'engaged' with their roles. Accordingly, this chapter provides an overview of the conceptual development of employee engagement, introduces the main debates concerning its evolution, and identifies implications for further research as well as management practice within hospitality and tourism enterprises.

The chapter begins by revisiting Kahn's (1990) original conception of personal engagement. Kahn proposed that employees bring their physical, cognitive and emotional selves to their employment tasks based in part on the extent to which they find their jobs psychologically meaningful. Next, more recent contributions to the extant literature are summarized. This includes Bakker et al. (2014), who provided a critical review and update of definitions, theory and empirical findings; Schaufeli et al. (2006), who reviewed employee engagement measures and proposed a new, nine-item scale; Saks and Gruman (2014), who proposed a new integrative model and suggested that a new valid measure of engagement (conceptually distinct from burnout) is warranted; and Knight et al. (2016), who conducted a meta-analysis of emerging research on workplace engagement interventions.

Following this, a brief summary of perspectives on engagement from the consulting industry, including Aon Hewitt, Willis Towers Watson and Psychometrics is offered. Finally, empirical research on engagement from the hospitality and tourism industries is summarized. The chapter concludes with practical advice for organizations and implications for further research.

THE SEMINAL CONTRIBUTION OF WILLIAM KAHN

William Kahn (1990) developed the originating theory of personal engagement over 25 years ago. In reflecting on his work, Kahn offered, 'The engagement concept was developed based on the premise that individuals can make real choices about how much of their real, personal selves they would reveal and express in their work. That premise was radically different than the operating assumptions of the time' (Burjeck, 2015).

Kahn's (1990) work was based on an ethnographic study of employees at two distinct research sites: an elite summer camp (where Kahn was a counsellor) and a renowned US architectural firm. Kahn concluded that engaged individuals brought their physical, cognitive and emotional selves to the performance of their work. More recently – and more commonly – this has been expressed as 'hands, head and heart' (Rich et al., 2010, p. 619).

Kahn's theory of engagement integrated a number of existing conceptual frameworks into two primary notions. The first was that the 'psychological experience of work' can significantly affect employee attitudes and behaviours, including 'effort (Hackman and Oldham, 1980), involvement (Lawler and Hall, 1970), flow (Csikszentmihalyi, 1982), mindfulness (Langer, 1989), and intrinsic motivation (Deci, 1975)' (Kahn, 1990, p. 700). The second notion, drawing on the work of Alderfer (1985), was that interpersonal and organizational factors can influence these psychological experiences, enhancing or undermining 'people's motivation and sense of meaning at work' (p. 694).

Also, drawing on the work of Goffman (1959; 1961), Kahn (1990) placed particular emphasis on the notion of 'role performance', suggesting that people bring varying degrees of themselves to the roles they perform; 'Presumably, the more people draw on their selves to perform their roles within those boundaries, the more stirring are their performances and the more content they are with the fit of the costumes they don' (p. 692).

Accordingly, Kahn (1990, p. 700) defined personal engagement as 'the simultaneous employment and expression of a person's "preferred self" in task behaviors that promote connections to work and to others, personal presence (physical, cognitive, and emotional), and active, full role performances.' Kahn (1990) also explored the notion of disengagement, which he defined as the (p. 701): 'simultaneous withdrawal and defense of a person's preferred self in behaviors that promote a lack of connections, physical, cognitive, and emotional absence, and passive, incomplete role performances.' Disengaged employees, he suggested, might be variously described as robotic, burned out, or detached, having become 'physically uninvolved in tasks, cognitively unvigilant, and emotionally disconnected from others' (p. 702).

Another important aspect of Kahn's (1990) work is the idea that rather than being an enduring trait, engagement may be task or context-dependent. Kahn suggested that employees are psychologically present (attentive, connected, integrated and focused) during 'moments in time', alternately engaging (moving towards) and disengaging (pulling away from) their work tasks, and that such 'pulls and pushes are people's calibrations of self-in-role, enabling them to cope with both internal ambivalences and external conditions' (p. 694).

Reflecting Hackman and Oldham's (1980) position that certain psychological factors can influence employee motivation, Kahn proposed three conditions of engagement: psychological meaningfulness, psychological safety and psychological availability. These three dimensions may have particular relevance for hospitality and tourism and are elaborated below (see Kahn, 1990, p. 705 for an overview).

- Psychological meaningfulness: Kahn (1990) suggested that people invest themselves in tasks and roles where they perceive an adequate return, such as feeling useful and valued. Kahn identified relevant job-based factors as including: 'task characteristics' (appropriate challenge, variety, creativity, autonomy, and goal clarity); 'role characteristics' including role identity (status, centrality, power/ influence); and 'work interactions' including the extent to which interactions with colleagues and customers meet relatedness needs (Alderfer, 1972). Kahn (1990) noted that such interactions can involve 'mutual appreciation, respect and positive feedback' and promote 'dignity, self-appreciation, and a sense of worthwhileness' (p. 707).
- Psychological safety: Kahn (1990) suggested that engagement is enhanced in the absence of 'fear of negative consequence to self-image, status or career' and where 'situations are trustworthy, secure, predictable, and clear in terms of behavioral consequences' (p. 703). Elements of social systems that impact perceptions of safety include: interpersonal relationships (trust and support); informal group and intergroup roles and dynamics; management and leader behaviours ('supportive, resilient and clarifying' as opposed to 'unpredictable, inconsistent, or hypocritical') (p. 711); and organizational norms (the extent to which roles reflect shared expectations for behaviours and emotions and leave 'room for investment of self during role performance' (p. 711).
- Psychological availability: Kahn (1990) identified the importance of employees 'having the physical, emotional, or psychological resources to personally engage at a particular moment' (p. 714). He proposed four potential detractors to psychological availability including: depletion of physical energy; depletion of emotional energy; individual insecurity (anxiety, confidence, self-consciousness, ambivalence about fit with the organization and its purpose); and issues in people's outside lives or personal preoccupa-

tions, including intimate work relationships, 'that leave them more or less available for investments of self during role performances' (p. 703). According to Kahn (1990, p. 703) engaged individuals have the necessary energy and feel 'capable of driving physical, intellectual, and emotional energies into role performance.'

From this perspective, hospitality employers who provide their employees with: autonomy through empowered decision-making; a sense of dignity, by treating all employees with respect; protection from sexual harassment from customers and co-workers; and supporting work–life balance, through appropriate scheduling and health benefits, would be in partial alignment with what Kahn proposed.

Also, explicitly recognizing the role of emotional labour in engagement processes, Kahn (1990) offered: 'employing and expressing the self in tasks requiring emotional labor takes a certain level of emotionality that personally disengaging does not' (Hochschild, 1983a) (p. 715). He suggested that psychological availability can be enhanced, through mitigating feelings of insecurity and self-consciousness, when organizations exhibit a 'stage-like' quality on which the performance occurs (p. 716). One explicit example of this is Disney, where employees take on the roles of particular characters. Less obvious may be a performance that occurs in a restaurant or hotel lobby, involving a deliberately 'staged' environment, through lighting, decor, music, costumes (uniforms) and perhaps even an employee 'script'. In restaurants and bars when the doors unlock, welcoming the first customers of the night, it can literally be 'show time'. Seymour (2000) also found that in fast food environments, scripts can help employees cope with ambiguous guest interactions.

Finally, Kahn also brought attention to the potential impact of the goals or purpose of the organization. According to Kahn (1990, p. 716):

> People struggling with their desires to contribute to the end goals of their systems became less able or willing – less available – to do so. It is difficult for people to engage personally in fulfilling work processes when organizational ends do not fit their own values, as research on organizational commitment has suggested (Mowday et al., 1982).

This idea is also reflected in the self-efficacy literature. Self-efficacy is defined as 'people's beliefs in their capabilities to mobilize the motivation, cognitive resources and courses of action needed to exercise control over events in their lives' (Wood and Bandura, 1989, p. 364). According to Bandura (1986, p. 348), once the condition of self-efficacy is met, engagement may be a choice: 'people do not care much how they do in activities that have little or no significance for them, and they expend little effort on devalued activities'. Citing laboratory studies in which people were paid to sacrifice quality for quantity, Bandura found that people who subscribed to high standards continued to emphasize quality, despite disincentives to do so: 'there is no punishment more devastating than self-contempt' (p. 374). More recently, this idea has been reflected in the popular management literature as 'know your why' (Sinek, 2009), with organizations being encouraged to engage both customers and employees through an appeal to a higher and compelling purpose.

Bandura's work on self-efficacy was applied to a fourfold typology of empowerment strategies developed through a grounded study of empowerment in the hospitality industry (Christensen Hughes, 1999). From one perspective, empowerment was positioned as a motivational construct with the objective of achieving enhanced organizational effectiveness through increased self-efficacy belief. Bandura (1977; 1986) suggested that self-efficacy could be enhanced through: 'enactive attainment' – successful task completion; 'vicarious experience' – observing others in successful task completion; 'verbal persuasion' – encouragement and positive feedback by supervisors; and avoidance of a negative 'emotional arousal state' – removing 'stress and fear through such techniques as generating a supportive and trusting group atmosphere, and avoiding both information and task overload'.

Conger and Kanungo (1988) identified contextual factors that could undermine the achievement of such outcomes, including: organizational factors (such as impersonal bureaucratic climate, poor communication); supervisory style (authoritarian, negativism); reward systems (lack of competence-based rewards); and job design (unrealistic goals, lack of appropriate authority, high rule structure, lack of meaningful goals).

Despite the importance of Kahn's (1990) seminal contribution and these associated concepts, in their comprehensive review of the literature, Saks and Gruman (2014) found that only one empirical study had actually tested its underlying propositions. May et al. (2004) developed a 13-item scale based on Kahn's propositions and found support for a number of them (Saks and Gruman, 2014, pp. 160–61):

> meaningfulness, safety, and availability were significantly related to engagement ... job enrichment and role fit were positively related to meaningfulness; rewarding coworker and supportive supervisor relations were positively related to safety while adherence to coworker norms and self-consciousness were negatively related; and resources available were positively related to psychological availability while participation in outside activities was negatively related.

Support therefore exists for Kahn's perspective that employees are more likely to be engaged at work if they feel useful and valued, are appropriately challenged, have meaningful social interactions, are treated with dignity and respect, feel supported by their managers and encounter reasonable workload expectations. Additionally, it may be the case that where 'performance' is required, organizations that support their employees through appropriate 'staging' will see positive engagement effects, as well as organizations that embody an inspiring purpose.

It is interesting to reflect on the extent to which hospitality and tourism employers may or may not be providing their employees with work dimensions conducive to engagement, as defined above. Certainly, research has suggested that the industry suffers from a host of employment challenges. In his extensive contribution, Kusluvan (2003) characterized the industry as being highly labour-intensive, with a preponderance of unskilled and semi-skilled, low status jobs, and unprofessional, autocratic, impulsive management practices. Employees, he suggested, tended to be from marginalized groups, including women and migrants. Working conditions were described as poor and unstable, encompassing low pay and high stress, including harassment and bullying, and even violence in the workplace. HR practices were viewed as unprofessional and informal, with little in the way of employee training or opportunities for career development. One contributor to Kusluvan's volume drew particular attention to the industry's poor compensation practices (Wood, 2003, p. 63):

> until employers, especially in the hospitality sector, are prepared to tackle the question of remuneration and working practices, employment in the industry will always be perceived as possessing more disadvantages than advantages. The tendency for operational employment in the tourism sector to be viewed as a last resort, rather than work of first choice, persists.

In her investigation of the link between turnover and work–life balance (including research on employee burnout), Deery (2008, p. 794) also highlighted the industry's poor employment conditions: 'the pressures that hospitality and tourism employees are under appears to significantly contribute to employee turnover and the lack of staff retention. The excessively long hours, style of management and conflict between work and family life, present barriers to making the tourism work environment an attractive and stable one.'

Hence, rather than having established a reputation for positive employee engagement practices, the industry has been described as ripe for disengagement, having poor work–life balance (Deery, 2008), a 'weak labour market' (Baum, 2008; Riley, 1996) and a 'turnover culture' (Iverson and Deery, 1997).

ENGAGEMENT (AND BURNOUT): A SYNOPSIS OF CRITICAL REVIEWS AND SUGGESTIONS FOR ADVANCING THE FIELD

Definition, Conceptualization and Measurement

Bakker et al. (2014) provided a critical review of the burnout and engagement literatures; 'two core concepts in the field of organizational psychology and organizational behavior' (p. 390). They presented definitions and constructs, antecedents and consequences (from a number of meta-reviews) and suggested future research directions.

Bakker et al. (2014) credited Freudenberger (1974) with being the first to introduce the concept of burnout, having defined it as 'a state of mental and physical exhaustion caused by one's professional life' (in Bakker et al., 2014, p. 390). Maslach and Jackson (1981) later positioned burnout as a syndrome characterized by three distinct elements: 'emotional exhaustion, depersonalization, and lack of personal accomplishment' (in Bakker et al., 2014, p. 390). Maslach and Leiter (1997) suggested that engagement was the opposite of burnout, characterized by energy, involvement and efficacy. Bakker et al. observed that most early empirical research on engagement adopted this perspective.

The Maslach Burnout Inventory-General Survey (MBI-GS) (Schaufeli et al., 1996) resulted from this conceptualization, consisting of three subscales: exhaustion (5 items), cynicism (5 items), and professional efficacy (6 items). Respective statements included: 'feel used up by the end of a work day'; 'doubt the significance of my work' and 'I can effectively solve the problems that arise in my work'.

Engagement has also been conceptualized as a related but distinct concept. The seminal work by Schaufeli et al. (2002), and in the tradition of Positive Psychology, defined engagement as a 'positive, fulfilling, work-related state of mind that is characterized by vigor, dedication, and absorption' (p. 74). Schaufeli et al. (2006), drawing on the work of Maslach et al. (2001), suggested that while vigour and dedication could be considered the counterpoints of exhaustion and cynicism, their proposed third dimension of professional efficacy (for burnout) and absorption (for engagement) served to differentiate the two concepts. Meta-analyses of empirical studies that have used this measure have led to the claim that 'burnout and work engagement are definitely not redundant concepts' (Bakker et al., 2014, p. 402).

Schaufeli et al. (2002) defined each of engagement's three proposed dimensions as follows: vigour – 'high levels of energy and mental resilience while working, the willingness to invest energy in one's work, and persistence even in the face of difficulties' (p. 74); dedication – 'a sense of significance, enthusiasm, inspiration, pride and challenge' (p. 74); and, absorption – 'being fully concentrated and deeply engrossed in one's work, whereby time passes quickly and one has difficulties with detaching oneself from work' (p. 75). In contrast with Kahn, Schaufeli et al. (2006) suggested that 'rather than a momentary and specific state, engagement refers to a more persistent and pervasive affective-cognitive state that is not focused on any particular object, event, individual or behavior' (p. 702).

Measuring Engagement

Much of the recent empirical research investigating the antecedents and consequences of employee engagement has adopted the 17-item Utrecht Work Engagement Scale (UWES-17) (Schaufeli et al., 2002), which provides items for measuring each of the three factors (vigour: VI; dedication: DE; and absorption: AB), using a 7-point frequency scale ranging from 0 (never) to 6 (always).

Schaufeli et al. (2006) reported on the results of a meta-review of studies using the UWES-17. With respect to demographic variables, they found engagement was weakly and positively related to age, with older workers reporting slightly greater engagement. Results for gender were weak and equivocal. In three countries (Australia, Canada, France), no gender differences were found. In four countries (Belgium, Germany, Finland and Norway), men scored higher; in one country (South Africa) women scored higher. The most robust differences were found with respect to occupational group. Here, significant differences were found with respect to all three dimensions (VI, DE and AB). Mean scores for vigour ranged from 3.47 (blue collar workers) to 4.41 (educators); dedication scores ranged from 3.4 (blue collar workers) to 4.55 (police officers); and absorption scores ranged from 2.74 (blue collar workers) to 4.05 (police officers). 'Managers' were part of the 'top three' highest scoring occupations, reporting significantly higher levels of engagement overall than blue collar workers.

Schaufeli et al. (2006) also proposed a shorter, one-factor model (UWES-9), reporting high internal consistency (p. 712). In comparing the two scales, Schaufeli et al. (2006) reported that while confirmatory factor analysis found the three-factor (VI, DE, AB) structure to be superior, 'this result was not unequivocal' (p. 712). Consequently they advised: 'practically speaking, rather than computing three different scores for VI, DE and AB, researchers might consider using the total nine-item score as an indicator of work engagement' (p. 712). At the same time, they also advised that 'future research should uncover whether VI, DE and AB have different causes and consequences so that instead of a single score, a differentiation between the three aspects would be preferred' (p. 712).

With respect to the relationship between burnout (MBI-GS) and engagement (UWES-9), they found a negative relationship, particularly between vigour and exhaustion (as expected). Professional efficacy was also strongly rated to all three engagement dimensions. They concluded that exhaustion and cynicism were core to burnout, while vigour, dedication, absorption and professional efficacy represented an 'extended engagement factor' (p. 712), and that 'professional efficacy might be considered a consequence (or an antecedent) of engagement' (p. 713). The items for the UWES-9 are listed below:

1. At my work, I feel bursting with energy (VI1).
2. At my job, I feel strong and vigorous (VI2).
3. I am enthusiastic about my job (DE1).
4. My job inspires me (DE2).
5. When I get up in the morning, I feel like going to work (VI3).
6. I feel happy when I am working intensely (AB1).
7. I am proud of the work that I do (DE3).
8. I am immersed in my work (AB2).
9. I get carried away when I am working (AB3).

Theoretical Foundation

The dominant theory underlying much of the current work on burnout and engagement is the Job Demands-Resources Theory (JD-R) (Bakker and Demerouti, 2007; 2008). JD-R divides work characteristics into two general categories: job demands and job resources. Job demands (such as workload, working conditions and role stress) generally predict burnout, defined as 'aspects of the job that require sustained physical, emotional or cognitive effort' (Bakker et al., 2014, p. 392). Job resources (such as task significance, autonomy and social support) generally predict engagement, defined as 'those aspects of the job that help to achieve work goals, reduce job demands, or stimulate personal growth' (Bakker et al., 2014, p. 393).

Associated with JD-R is Conservation of Resources Theory (COR) (Hobfoll, 1989; 2001). According to Hobfoll (2001), COR is 'an integrative stress theory that considers both environmental and internal processes with relatively equal measure' (p. 338). Its underlying premise is that 'individuals strive to obtain, retain, protect and foster those things they value', including 'object, condition, personal characteristic, and energy resources' (p. 341). Further, Hobfoll (2001) proposed that psychological stress will occur when resources are threatened, lost, or when an adequate return on invested resources is not achieved. Hobfoll (2001, p. 342) presented a list of 74 resources that were found to have validity in Western contexts. These included, for example, feeling successful, time for sleep, personal health, status, stable employment, help with tasks at work, retirement security and help with child care. Many of these 'resources' contain elements that are consistent with Kahn's meaningfulness dimensions (particularly psychological availability).

Hobfoll (2001) also advanced a number of principles and corollaries: (1) 'resource loss is disproportionally more salient than resource gain' (p. 343); (2) 'people must invest resources to protect against resource loss' (p. 349); (3) 'those who lack resources are not only more vulnerable to resource loss, but that initial loss begets future loss' (p. 354); (4) 'those who possess resources are more capable of gain' (p. 355); (5) 'those who lack resources are likely to adopt a defensive posture to conserve their resources' (p. 356). Hobfoll's views may be particularly salient to understanding psychological availability deficits in hospitality employees, particularly those who have had challenging personal life experiences that may compromise resource availability (whether sleep, health, safety or financial security).

Another related, but distinct theory is Core Self-Evaluation (CSE) theory (Judge et al., 1997), which refers to the 'core self-valuations' or 'bottom-line evaluations that individuals hold about themselves' (Judge and Bono, 2001, p. 80). CSE (also referred to as 'positive self-concept') is defined as a 'broad dispositional trait that is indicated by four more specific traits – self-esteem, generalized self-efficacy, locus of control, and emotional stability (low neuroticism)' (Judge and Bono, 2001, p. 80). Judge et al. (1997) originally proposed CSE as an explanatory variable for job satisfaction, but later added motivation and job performance. The results of a meta-analysis of 274 correlations suggested that 'these traits are among the best dispositional predictors of job satisfaction and job performance' (p. 80).

Bakker et al. (2014) drew on both theories in their discussion of 'personal resources', which they suggested was an 'important extension of the original JD-R model' (p. 401). Drawing on Hobfoll et al. (2003) they stated that 'personal resources are positive self-evaluations that are linked to resiliency'. Drawing on Judge et al. (2004; 2005) they suggested that positive self-evaluations predict a number of outcomes, such as 'motivation, performance, and job and life satisfaction' (p. 401). As an example, of the importance of considering personal resources, they cited the work of Xanthopoulou et al. (2007), who studied the effect of self-efficacy, organizationally based self-esteem, and optimism on engagement and exhaustion. They found that personal resources mediated the relationship between job resources and work engagement.

Antecedents and Consequences of Engagement

Bakker et al. (2014) drew on a number of meta-analyses in summarizing the antecedents and consequences that have been found to be associated with burnout and engagement. Antecedents included both situational factors (job demands and job resources) and individual factors (personality). Consequences included health/motivational outcomes and job-related outcomes.

For example, Lee and Ashforth (1996) found that job demands (particularly 'role ambiguity, role conflict, role stress, stressful events, workload and work pressure') were a more important predictor of burnout than a lack of job resources (Bakker et al., 2014, p. 392). However, job resources were found to mitigate the impact of job demands on engagement, particularly when job demands were high: 'Employees who have many job resources available can cope better with their daily job demands' (Bakker et al., 2014, p. 400). Studying employees in a higher education setting, Bakker et al. (2005) found that excessive work demands did not result in burnout if 'employees experienced autonomy, received feedback, had social support or had a high-quality relationship with their supervisors' (as cited in Bakker et al., 2014, p. 400).

This observation may have particular relevance for the hospitality industry. It suggests that while some negative aspects of the working environment may be difficult, if not impossible, to change (such as high stress, frequent guest interaction, emotional labour and unsocial working hours), these factors may be buffered to the extent that employees have mitigating resources available to them.

With respect to personal resources, Alarcon et al. (2009) found that four of the Big Five personality factors (emotional stability, extraversion, conscientiousness and agreeableness) were 'consistently negatively related to each of the three dimensions of burnout', with emotional stability being 'the most important predictor of exhaustion and depersonalization'; and extraversion being 'the most important predictor of personal accomplishment' (Bakker et al., 2014, p. 393). In addition, lower-order factors such as 'self-esteem, self-efficacy, locus of control, positive affectivity, negative affectivity, optimism, proactive personality, and hardiness each had a significant relationship with burnout' (p. 393).

In terms of consequences, burnout has been associated with various psychological and physical health outcomes, including depression, anxiety, sleep disturbance, memory impairment, headaches, infections and alcohol dependence, with physical exercise providing a moderating effect in some instances (Bakker et al., 2014, pp. 395–6). The most significant job-related outcome of burnout is 'in role performance', measured primarily through self-reports, but also through objective performance measures by supervisors, colleagues and customers (Taris, 2006). Specific performance outcomes found to be associated with burnout include reduced sales levels and financial results, and increased sick days and absence duration (Bakker et al., 2014).

In contrast, in studies of engagement, 'job resources' rather than 'job demands' have been found to be the strongest predictor. In their meta-analysis, Christian et al. (2011) found that 'task variety, task significance, autonomy, feedback, social support from colleagues, a high quality relationship with the supervisor, and transformational leadership' were important predictors of employee engagement (Bakker et al., 2014, p. 393).

Research on the 'Big Five' personality factors has found that three dimensions consistently predict work engagement: 'emotional stability, extraversion, and conscientiousness' (Makikangas et al., 2013, as cited in Bakker et al., 2014, p. 394). In addition, lower-order individual factors have also been found to have a positive effect, particularly optimism, self-efficacy, self-esteem and proactive personality (Bakker et al., 2014; Halbesleben, 2010; Makikangas et al., 2013). In reference to the latter, Bakker et al. (2012) found that employees with proactive personalities 'craft their jobs', helping to change expectations or enhance their resources (by asking for support for example).

Empirical studies on the consequences of engagement have tended to focus on motivational outcomes. The extant literature has reported positive associations between engagement and employee happiness, openness to new experiences, willingness to learn new things and initiative (Bakker et al., 2014). Job-related outcomes have included higher in-role and extra-role performance ratings, including citizenship behaviour (both self-reported and supervisor and co-worker assessed). A meta-analysis by Harter et al. (2002) linked engagement to higher profitability, with business unit outcomes including higher customer satisfaction, customer loyalty, profitability, productivity and safety, and reduced employee turnover (Harter et al., 2002).

A Critique and Proposed Integrative Model

In an invited feature article to *Human Resource Development Quarterly*, Saks and Gruman (2014) remarked on the 'explosion of research activity and heightened interest in employee engagement among consultants, organizations, and management scholars' (p. 155). Challenging the extent to which engagement has been lauded as the 'key to an organization's success and competitiveness' (p. 156), they questioned 'what do we really know about employee engagement?' (p. 155). In particular, they raised concerns about 'meaning, measurement, and theory' (p. 178), suggesting that research has been impeded by several factors, including 'lack of agreement and consensus on what engagement actually means', 'the validity of existing measures' and the lack of a 'generally accepted theory of employee engagement' (p. 156).

More specifically, they challenged the construct validity of the UWES, suggesting that some scale items may actually duplicate items in more established constructs, hypothesized to be either antecedents or outcomes of engagement (such as autonomy, task significance, job satisfaction, commitment and involvement) (Cole et al., 2012; Saks, 2006; Shuck et al., 2012). They also argued that its close association with burnout was problematic. Here, they referenced the work of Cole et al. (2012), suggesting that 'there is mounting evidence that the UWES measure of work engagement is a positive representation of burnout and its dimensions resulting in conceptual overlap and redundancy' (Saks and Gruman, 2014, p. 178). In this regard, studies on engagement that shorten the scale and only measure vigour and dedication are arguably measuring burnout. Similarly, studies that only find positive effects for vigour and dedication may only be identifying antecedents and consequences of burnout. Saks and Gruman (2014) emphasized that Kahn (1990) intended engagement to mean so much more than employees energetically performing their tasks, but rather it involves 'bringing one's complete and true self to the performance' (p. 167). In support of measuring the 'right' construct, they acknowledged a number of alternative scales, such as the one by May et al. (2004) that was developed to test Kahn's propositions, but they also noted that most had only been used in one study. Such is their critique of the UWES, however, that they advised researchers to 'move away from reliance on the UWES as a measure of engagement and begin to use measures that are more in line with Kahn's (1990; 1992) original conceptualization' (p. 167).

Saks and Gruman (2014) also challenged the extent to which correlational data has been used to infer causation (p. 171):

> for all of the hoopla about how to 'drive' employee engagement and its consequences, we have very little evidence that demonstrates a change and improvement in employee engagement from one time period to another or its causal effect on outcomes. Thus, at best, we can simply say that a number of known factors in the work environment are positively related to engagement . . . We know that there are positive relationships between employee engagement and work outcomes; however we are not in a position to say that employee engagement causes a particular outcome, nor can we even be sure of the direction of causality . . . Thus engagement might lead to greater social support or autonomy and higher performers might become more engaged.

Finally, they expressed concern about the extent to which the concept of 'work' engagement has pervaded much of the engagement literature. They suggested that in addition to being engaged with an assigned work role or task, employee engagement may encompass additional domains, such as engagement with one's work colleagues or team, occupation or professional role, or the organization itself. In addition they suggested that rather than a pervasive concept, the degree of engagement might vary between these domains. Indeed, a study by Saks (2006) found 'a significant and meaningful difference between job and organization engagement and differences with respect to the antecedents of job and organizational engagement' (p. 174).

In proposing a new model of engagement, Saks and Gruman (2014) suggested that Kahn's (1990) original work on psychological dimensions warranted inclusion alongside JD-R. Drawing on Pratt and Ashforth (2003), they distinguished between two types of meaningfulness: 'meaningfulness in work' that is derived from intrinsic motivation in one's tasks as well as perceived 'return on investment' with respect to personal resources employed; and 'meaningfulness at work' which comes from organizational-level factors, such as perceptions of procedural justice (Saks and Gruman, 2014, p. 175).

They also proposed that 'three types of leadership (transformational, empowering, and leader–member exchange)' be included in the model, as leadership can influence engagement through the provision or withholding of 'job resources, job demands and the psychological conditions' (Saks and Gruman, 2014, p. 176). Accordingly, Saks and Gruman (2014) proposed a new model that integrated JD-R, Kahn's psychological conditions (meaningfulness, safety and resource availability) and 'transformational, leader–member exchange and empowering leadership' (Saks and Gruman, 2014, p. 173). They concluded by calling for the development of a valid measure of engagement, suggesting that further empirical research doesn't make much sense until this occurs.

Workplace Interventions

In contrast to the advice of Saks and Gruman (2014), others have endorsed the continuation of the current trajectory and using longitudinal and experimental research methods to test the efficacy of existing models and measures through workplace interventions. Bakker et al. (2014, p. 402) proposed three types of interventions: 'optimizing job demands' (such as reducing role ambiguity); 'increasing job resources' (such as providing enhanced 'social support and performance feedback ... by redesigning the work environment or through training'); and fostering personal resources (such as 'training for optimism, resilience and self-efficacy'), which research suggests 'can be taught' (Demerouti et al., 2011; Luthans et al., 2006 as cited in Bakker et al., 2014, p. 403).

Consistent with this advice, Knight et al. (2016) provided a meta-analysis of 14 empirical studies of engagement interventions, published between 2009 and 2015. The studies took place in a variety of countries (primarily Western) and industries (primarily services – police, fire, financial, nursing, welfare, but none in hospitality). They proposed four categories of interventions: personal resource building interventions (developing self-efficacy, resilience or optimism); job resource building interventions (enhanced autonomy, social support and feedback); leadership training interventions (knowledge and skill-building workshops for managers); and health promotion interventions (encouraging healthy lifestyles). They identified studies in each of these categories and reported small but reliable effects.

In considering the above contributions, it appears that the field is truly at a crossroads. While Saks and Gruman (2014) have called for a fundamental reconsideration of the theory and measurement of engagement, others such as Bakker et al. (2014) and Knight et al. (2016) have suggested that the time is right to study workplace interventions. Progress mirroring both of these suggestions is occurring simultaneously, as the original JD-R model has evolved to include personal resources and other constructs such as leadership, while research on engagement interventions within oganizations is also underway.

PERSPECTIVES FROM THE MANAGEMENT CONSULTING INDUSTRY

While academic scholars have been engaged in analysis and debate over theory and measurement issues, management consultants have been assessing the engagement (using their own definitions) of millions of employees and proclaiming annual increases or decreases in the extent to which the world's employees are engaged.

As one example, Aon Hewitt produces annual national engagement rankings (as well as weekly email blasts), identifying top firms, by organizational size, based upon their employee engagement scores. Hospitality firms that have consistently ranked in the top tier of engaged firms in the Aon Hewitt study include Keg Restaurants and Marriott Hotels of Canada (for examples, see Aon, 2017).

Participating organizations are assessed through surveys and focus groups on the concepts of 'say, stay and strive', the extent to which employees 'speak positively about their employer to others, are committed to staying with their current employer and are motivated by their organization's leaders and culture to go above and beyond to contribute to business success' (Aon, 2016a). According to Aon (2016a), 'Engaged employees deliver greater productivity, better customer service, superior quality products and services, and more innovative solutions'.

Aon (2016b) also recently published a report comparing levels of engagement around the world (from surveys conducted in 2014 and 2015, involving more than 7 million responses from 60 industries). They found that while on a global scale, overall engagement had increased, with 25 per cent of employees in their surveys considered 'highly engaged' and 40 per cent 'moderately engaged', there were important variations by continent. The most significant increases in engagement over the prior year's report occurred in Asia, with China and India leading the way. The highest overall rates of engagement were found in Latin America.

In comparing the scores of employees who participated in both the 2014 and 2015 surveys, they noted that almost half (46 per cent) moved at least one category, with 14 per cent becoming less engaged and 11 per cent becoming more engaged. It was not clear from the report what accounted for these changes, but the suggestion was made that external forces (political and economic volatility) might have had an effect.

Aon's model (2016b, p. 3) consists of six 'engagement drivers', divided into three 'differentiators' and three 'foundational' elements. Differentiators include: brand (reputation, employee value proposition, corporate responsibility); leadership (corporate and business unit); and performance (career opportunities, learning and development, performance management, people management and rewards and recognition). Foundational components include: company practices (communication, customer focus, diversity and inclusion, enabling infrastructure, and talent and staffing); the basics (benefits, job security, safety, work environment and work–life balance) and the work (collaboration, empowerment/ autonomy and work tasks) (Aon, 2016b, p. 3). The report stated that these dimensions were found to be associated with higher levels of employee engagement as well as valued outcomes, including improved retention of talent and reduced absenteeism; improved operational productivity; greater customer satisfaction and retention; and improved business performance (including increases in revenue/sales, operating income/margin, total shareholder return).

Another consulting group, Willis Towers Watson, has suggested that the conception of employee engagement is evolving to include a stronger focus on employee wellness (Free et al., 2015). They introduced the notion of 'sustainable engagement', suggesting that it additionally includes measures of physical and mental wellness as well as the quality of employee professional, social and family life. They suggested that measurement of employee well-being will eventually become more important than engagement.

Finally, Psychometrics (2010) conducted a study of 368 Canadian HR professionals working in a variety of organizations. They found that the majority of respondents (69 per cent) felt that engagement was a problem in their organizations. Workplace benefits of engagement were perceived to include: 'willingness to do more than expected (39%), higher productivity (27%), better working relationships (13%) and more satisfied customers (10%)' (p. 4). Rather than quitting, disengaged employees were found to contribute to organizational dysfunction. The dominant view (84 per cent) was that senior leaders and managers were responsible for employee engagement. In terms of specific opportunities, the HR managers felt that organizational leaders and managers could do more to 'communicate clear expectations, listen to employees' opinions and give recognition' (p. 5). The consultants also advised providing engagement training, having found a strong correlation between companies who offered training and their overall engagement scores.

From a consulting perspective, engagement is seen as an important, multi-faceted concept that requires vision and leadership as well as effective HR policies and practices. It has also been associated with employee well-being. Some large chain-based hospitality organizations (such as Keg Restaurants and Marriot Hotels Canada), have consistently scored near the top of a national engagement ranking.

THE STUDY OF EMPLOYEE ENGAGEMENT WITHIN HOSPITALITY AND TOURISM: FUTURE DIRECTIONS

While some hospitality and tourism scholars continue to claim a dearth of empirical research on employee engagement (particularly in non-Western contexts), this no longer appears to be the case. Paek et al. (2015) summarized an extensive review of 16 empirical studies published between 2005 and 2014. This work was undertaken in 13 different countries, predominantly outside the US and Europe. The vast majority of studies took place in hotels, with data collected from front-line (high customer contact) employees. This focus should not be surprising. As Karatepe and Olugbade (2009, p. 505) observed, customer contact employees 'are the main actors in the delivery of service quality (Bettencourt and Brown, 2003) and are at the heart of effective service recovery efforts (Tax and Brown, 1998)'. As such, they represent the organization 'in the customer's eyes', serving as 'marketers' and defining the organization's brand (Zeithaml et al., 1988 as cited in Slatten and Mehmetoglu, 2011, p. 94). Paek et al. (2015) similarly argued that in creating a positive service climate, front-line employees 'exert a critical influence on performance, outcomes and customer satisfaction' (p. 10).

In synthesizing their review's main findings, Paek et al. (2015, pp. 13–14) reported that statistically significant relationships were found between engagement and many proposed antecedents and outcomes, including for example, job autonomy and high-performance work practices on the one hand, and enhanced job satisfaction and organizational performance on the other.

In 2017, I sought to build upon Paek et al.'s (2015) approach. I was interested in identifying the underlying theory and measures used, as well as the main results. Eighteen articles published between 2005 and 2017 were reviewed in detail, including seven from Paek's original study. A synopsis of each of these articles and a summary table is included in Christensen Hughes, Chapter 11, this volume. A brief summary is included below.

A Summary of Engagement Research in Hospitality Contexts

The dominant approach taken in the reviewed articles was to survey front-line hotel employees (13 studies), such as front-desk clerks, wait staff and bartenders, with respect to their perceptions of themselves and their work. Only three studies additionally included back of house employees (Lee and Ok, 2015; 2016; Rigg et al., 2013). One study focused exclusively on managers (Burke et al., 2009). The focus on front-line workers is understandable. Karatepe et al. (2010) shared that 'in today's turbulent and rapidly changing market environment, it is of paramount importance to acquire and retain a pool of employees in frontline service jobs who have the personality traits needed to perform effectively in the workplace' (p. 62).

The research sites included: 13 hotels, two restaurants and three mixed settings. The studies all collected data from multiple restaurant unit and hotel sites, including 3-, 4- and 5-star hotels, with one project differentiating between 'sun and sand' and 'conference' properties (Carrasco et al., 2014). One study mentioned that the hotels were part of a large international hotel chain (Karatepe and Demir, 2014). The geographic context was diverse, with six studies having taken place in the Middle East; three in Asia; three in North America; two in Europe; and one in each of Africa, the Caribbean and South Africa.

In terms of theory, as previously suggested JD-R was reflected to some extent in every study. While there were varying degrees of theorizing, JD-R was the dominant theory in use. Other theories were used to hypothesize relationships with additional antecedents or consequences of engagement. The most common theoretical frameworks, in addition to JD-R, were COR theory (Hobfoll, 1989; 2001) which was referenced in six studies, as well as Core self-evaluations theory (Judge et al., 1997), Job characteristics theory (Hackman and Oldham, 1980), Self-regulation theory (Hochschild, 1983a) and Social exchange theory (Blau, 1964) (which were referenced twice each). Nine other theories were mentioned once each.

All of the studies collected confidential survey data. Most used a pen and paper approach, onsite in the work environment; one explicitly used an online survey tool (Liu et al., 2017). Some collected data at two points in time (Karatepe and Demir, 2014), from supervisors (Karatepe et al., 2014) or from customers (Salanova et al., 2005; Yagil, 2012), in order to help deal with common-methods bias. A number of well-established scales (or elements of scales) were employed, with most of the published articles including a detailed list of constructs and items. All of the studies used some version of the UWES: eight used the UWES-17 (Schaufeli et al., 2002); eight used the UWES-9 (Schaufeli et al., 2006); one used six items from the UWES-9 (Schaufeli et al., 2006); and one used 11 items from the UWES-17 (Carrasco et al., 2014).

It was interesting to note that while earlier studies (pre-2013) tended to use the UWES-17 and hypothesized relationships for each of the three factors of engagement (vigour: VI; dedication: DE; and absorption: AB), more recent studies have tended to treat engagement as a single construct. Also, while not every study published mean engagement scores; those that were published ranged from 3.13 for the single item vigour (Karatepe et al., 2010) to 5.56 for a composite measure of UWES-9 (Lee and Ok, 2015; 2016).

Some modest differences were found on the basis of demographics. As an example, Karatepe and Demir (2014) found education to be negatively related to engagement. In explanation, they observed, 'what is available in frontline service jobs does not seem to be attractive for better educated employees' (p. 315). Karatepe and Olugbade (2009) also found differences for tenure, with longer-serving employees reporting lower levels of vigour. Suan and Nasurdin (2016) found gender to be a moderating variable between supervisor support and engagement, with a positive effect for male employees and negative for females. Burke et al. (2013) reported that 'married, frontline employees indicated higher levels of vigor and dedication' (p. 197), while 'older frontline workers and males indicated higher levels of absorption'. Also, males, front-line employees who were parents, and those reporting lower dedication, had greater intention to quit, while front-line employees working in larger properties, indicating higher engagement, reported higher job satisfaction.

In their extensive review of the extant literature, as previously suggested, Schaufeli et al. (2006) found that engagement scores were weakly related to age, with older workers reporting slightly greater engagement. Results for gender were described as 'weak and equivocal', with women in some countries scoring higher than men, and in others scoring lower. The most robust differences they found pertained to occupation, with mean scores for blue collar workers being 3.47, 3.4 and 2.74 respectively. For professional service workers (educators and police officers), mean scores were 4.41, 4.55 and 4.05. This suggests that studies involving more occupational types and organizational levels should reasonably expect more variation in engagement scores. It would also be interesting to identify an 'expected range' of engagement scores for the hospitality industry (perhaps by organizational type/size), to assist in benchmarking.

Statistically significant results were found for many of the hypothesized relationships. Select findings are organized below, using the framework proposed by Bakker et al. (2014) including: situational factors (job demands and job resources); individual factors (personality); and consequences (health/motivational outcomes and job-related outcomes).

Situational Factors: Job Demands

Job demands, as previously suggested, are 'aspects of the job that require sustained physical, emotional, or cognitive effort (Demerouti et al., 2001)' and can include 'role ambiguity, role conflict, role stress, stressful events, workload, and work pressure' (Bakker et al., 2014, p.392). Only a few of the studies explicitly included job demand factors. Karatepe et al. (2013) found an association between engagement and polychronicity (task switching) (Bluedorn et al., 1999), and Karatepe et al. (2014) found an association with challenge stressors (work overload and high job responsibility). In both cases, higher levels of engagement were reported, suggesting that a certain degree of pressure can be engaging. Drawing on self-regulation theory (Hochschild, 1983a), Yagil (2012) found 'deep acting' to be associated with higher levels of engagement (and 'surface acting' to be associated with burnout). Emotional dissonance was negatively associated with engagement (Carrasco et al., 2014).

Situational Factors: Job Resources

Job resources, as previously suggested, are 'those aspects of the job that help to achieve work goals, reduce job demands, or stimulate personal growth' (Bakker et al., 2014, p.393) and can include support from colleagues, high quality employee–supervisor relationships and transformational leadership, as well as particular job attributes (such as variety, autonomy and significance). Drawing on role theory (Sieber, 1974), Slatten and Mehmetoglu (2011) found a positive association between engagement and perceived role benefit, job autonomy and strategic attention (the latter defined as the 'degree of implementation of a firm's strategy in a specific work role') (p. 94). Burke et al. (2013) found a positive association between engagement and employee voice (the inclination of employees to speak up and share ideas) (Van Dyne and LePine, 1998). Carrasco et al. (2014) found a positive relationship with service climate (defined as 'employee perceptions of the practices, procedures and behaviours rewarded, supported and expected with regard to customer service quality' (p. 950). Positive associations were also found with: Psychological Service Climate (PSC) (customer orientation, managerial support, internal service and information/communication) (Lee and Ok, 2015); intrinsic rewards and quality of leader–member exchange (mutual trust, respect and obligation) (Lee and Ok, 2016); supervisory support (Suan and Nasurdin, 2016); 'perceived organizational support' (POS) (Liu et al., 2017); and co-worker support (with vigour only) (Karatepe et al., 2010). Karatepe and Demir (2014) also found a positive association between engagement and work–family facilitation (WFF) and family–work facilitation (FWF), suggesting that work and family circumstances can be mutually beneficial; WFF/FWF was defined as 'the extent to which participation at work (or home) is made easier by virtue of the experiences, skills, and opportunities gained or developed at home (or work)' (p. 308).

Personal Resources: Personality

Personality is considered an important personal resource, as employees with particular personalities 'may be better able to mobilize job resources' (Bakker et al., 2014, p. 394). Karatepe and Olugbade (2009) found a positive association between trait competitiveness and engagement (VI, DE and AB) and between self-efficacy and absorption (AB). Karatepe et al. (2010) found a positive association between CSEs (self-esteem, generalized self-efficacy, locus of control, and emotional stability–low neuroticism) and engagement (VI and DE). Karatepe and Demir (2014) found CSEs to be associated with engagement, as did Lee and Ok (2015). Paek et al. (2015) found that PsyCap factors (optimism, self-efficacy, hope and resilience) were associated with engagement.

Consequences of Engagement: Health and Motivational Outcomes

Burke et al. (2009) found associations between engagement and well-being. Managers with higher levels of dedication reported lower levels of exhaustion, psychosomatic symptoms and work–family conflict. Engagement was also associated with greater: job satisfaction (VI, DE), career satisfaction (DE) and intention to stay (DE). Absorption, however, was associated with higher levels of stress, exhaustion, psychosomatic symptoms and work–family conflict. Burke et al. (2013) found a positive association between engagement and job satisfaction, intention to stay and reduced work–family and family–work conflict (WFC/FWC). Absorption, once again, however, was associated with greater WFC/FWC. Rigg et al. (2013) found a positive association between engagement and job satisfaction and intention to stay. Paek et al. (2015) found engagement to be positively associated with job satisfaction and commitment, as did Lee and Ok (2016). Pienaar and Willemse (2008) found a significant relationship between engagement (DE) and health, mediated by coping strategies and symptom reduction.

Consequences of Engagement: Job-related Outcomes (Performance)

Engagement was found to be associated with a number of important job-related outcomes, including: innovative behaviour (Slatten and Mehmetoglu, 2011); job performance and extra-role customer service behaviour (Karatepe et al., 2013) and organizational commitment and job performance (Karatepe et al., 2014). Engagement was also found to fully mediate the relationship between challenge stressors and job outcomes (Karatepe et al., 2014). In addition, Yagil (2012) found engagement fully mediated the relationship between deep acting and customer satisfaction and loyalty.

Reflecting the complexity of the relationships found in a number of these studies, Salanova et al. (2005) described a 'cycle of success spiral', in which service climate was found to fully mediate the relationship between organizational resources and work engagement, and between organizational resources and employee performance and customer loyalty.

Discussion

Higher levels of engagement were found to be associated with a variety of important dimensions, including job demands, job resources, personal resources, health/motivational outcomes and job-related outcomes, either directly or through a mediating function. While we do not know the direction of these effects (as suggested by Saks and Gruman, 2014), it does appear that a positive 'cycle of success' is at play (Salanova et al., 2005).

Many managerial implications were suggested by the scholars who conducted these studies, in support of enhanced employee engagement, including: creating a service climate and supportive work atmosphere (including family-friendly scheduling and benefits); using standardized personality tests to select, develop and retain engaged employees; providing jobs with autonomy, empowerment, and meaning; developing supervisor–subordinate relationships characterized by respect, appreciation, trust and effective two-way communication (assess supervisor leadership capability as part of performance reviews); involving employees in strategy development; providing employees with stress reduction and assertiveness training (including deep acting and multi-tasking); training managers in how to support self-efficacy development in others, and in developing empathy and listening skills; providing differential rewards and career opportunities to engaged employees; and investing in high-performance work practices.

While these suggestions may arguably read much like a table of contents of an introductory human resource management textbook, confirmation of their importance is useful, particularly given the industry's reputation for not embracing progressive human resource management practices. Further, in combining these results with the literature previously reviewed, additional management advice can be offered. For example, recruitment activity might begin with the development of an employee value proposition, one that speaks to the vision of the organization, its commitment to the guest experience, as well as its more socially significant aspirations. Employees also need to understand the career opportunities and development support available to them, as well as what they can expect in terms of general working conditions. An audit of the organization's job design and work scheduling practices might help to identify opportunities for more healthy and more family-friendly practices. Selection, as previously suggested, might include standardized assessments for measuring lower-order personality factors, such as optimism, self-efficacy, hope and resilience. Training, rather than simply focusing on particular job tasks, should reinforce the purpose of the organization, its brand promise, service climate and the importance of the employee's role in contributing to organizational success. Management and supervisory training might focus on approaches for fostering employee self-efficacy, drawing on Bandura's (1977; 1986) fourfold model of enactive attainment, vicarious experience, verbal persuasion and positive arousal state. And, given all of the suggestions made about differential treatment (attention, rewards and career development) for the most highly engaged employees, a talent management strategy should potentially be considered.

In terms of opportunities for further research on engagement in hospitality and tourism contexts, given all of the research that has taken place over the last decade, a comprehensive meta-analysis is needed. This will help to identify key gaps and focus future effort. From the current limited review, one potential consideration for future research is increasing the variety of research settings. For example, given the predominance of hotels in the current study, new research sites might include restaurants, cruise ships, airlines, travel agencies and tourist attractions. Additional variety in geographic location is also important, as the effectiveness of managerial interventions may vary by culture or local economic conditions. Organizational governance and organizational size are other variables of potential interest. For example, there may be differences in how engagement is approached and experienced, depending on whether the business is part of a large international chain, with a sophisticated human resources management function and multiple layers of policies and people; operated by a government office, with considerable bureaucracy; or whether it is a small single unit operation, managed and owned by a local independent.

While differences in employee demographic factors have largely not been found to predict engagement, occupation did (Schaufeli et al., 2006). As previously suggested, studies might therefore consider different roles and organizational levels, such as back of house, part-time or seasonal employees, unit managers and corporate staff. This could aid in the development of mean employee engagement scores for the industry, by position and country, for benchmarking purposes (as is available to organizations who participate in engagement ranking studies with consulting firms). Two other potentially important demographic variables are education and career aspiration. As explained by role theory (Sieber, 1974), if an employee is working in a front-line position as a stepping stone to a career (either within the industry or outside of it), their level of engagement may be quite different from someone who is either content where they are, or is working because they feel they have 'no other option'.

In terms of antecedents, more research is needed on *job demands*. Given all that has been said about the challenging working conditions in the industry, it is surprising that more studies didn't include measures for workload, emotional labour and task-switching, for example. For *job resources*, and at the organizational level, more research is needed that explores the influence of leader–member exchange (and other leadership attributes) and organizational culture, including service climate and psychological climate (customer orientation, managerial support, internal service and communication), as well as 'perceptions of organizational politics' (Paek et al., 2015, p. 24). These factors need to be assessed at both the business unit and organizational level, and in the case of a hotel or restaurant chain, ideally also at corporate office (to account for cultural and other differences by unit). This is consistent with Saks and Gruman's (2014) observation that there may be several distinct engagement domains (task, workgroup and organization). An employee may be highly engaged with his or her workgroup but disrespect the organization (and hence resist implementing corporate directives, for example).

More attention also needs to be paid to the purpose of the organization, its stated values and priorities. This is consistent with Kahn's (1990) psychological availability dimension, which includes 'ambivalence about fit with the organization and its purpose' as a key potential detractor. Similarly, as previously noted, Bandura (1986, p. 348) suggested that employees 'expend little effort on devalued activities'. In the developing world, hospitality and tourism ventures may be viewed either positively or not, depending upon the perceived costs and benefits to local stakeholders, including social, environmental and economic factors. Where an exploitive business model is in place, employees may feel more resentful than engaged. Where significant economic gaps exist between local economies and foreign guests, this dynamic may be particularly acute, revealing itself through employee theft or disengagement, for example.

Finally, while engagement is largely assumed to be associated with intrinsic motivation (with Lee and Ok (2016) drawing on Herzberg et al.'s (1959) two-factor theory, finding a positive association), it might be instructive to test the association between engagement and the extent to which employees perceive their compensation to be adequate, in meeting their basic physiological and safety needs (Maslow, 1943), or perceptions of fairness (equity theory; Adams, 1963). This suggestion is made due to the notoriously low wages of many front-line hospitality workers, and debates over the necessity of providing a living wage (see Christensen Hughes, Chapter 2, this volume). The argument is that if employees are unable to provide for themselves and their families, it is doubtful they will be engaged (fair and reasonable compensation may be a necessary but not sufficient condition of engagement). Theoretically, this would also link to COR theory (Hobfoll, 2001, p. 342), where a number of financially dependent personal resources were identified, including: 'personal transportation (car, truck etc.)', 'housing that suits my needs', 'providing children's essentials', 'adequate food', 'money for extras', 'savings or emergency money', 'adequate financial credit', 'financial assets (stocks, property, etc.)', 'financial stability', 'medical insurance', and 'retirement security (financial)'. In comparison to this list, in the development of research instruments, COR has largely been associated with two or three psychological factors, making its practice (if not its underlying theory) largely redundant with the inclusion of CSE theory.

With respect to outcomes, Paek et al. (2015) suggested more work on innovation and creativity, which may become increasingly important due to changing consumer demands and an increasingly competitive landscape. More input from customers may be helpful in this regard. More work is also needed on longer-term organizational outcomes (such as sales and profitability), which longitudinal research will be needed to support.

With respect to the measurement of engagement itself, as previously suggested there have been considerable debates, with Schaufeli et al. (2006) pointing to meta-reviews that attest to its internal consistency and validity, and Cole et al. (2012) and Saks and Gruman (2014) suggesting the opposite. Certainly, Saks and Gruman's concern about the distinction between vigour and dedication on the one hand (as the antipode of burnout) and absorption on the other, was reflected in some of the studies reviewed, with positive associations found for one or two factors of engagement and not for the others, with differences in direction noted as well. Due to these differences, Burke et al. (2009; 2013) suggested, for example, additional research on the potential 'dark side' of absorption. I agree with Saks and Gruman (2014) that in looking at each of the nine statements that comprise the UWES-9, it is not clear how they would collectively measure Kahn's (1990) concern with the extent to which employees 'bring their physical, cognitive and emotional selves to their employment tasks based in part on the extent to which they find their jobs psychologically meaningful'. Therefore, researchers who draw on Kahn (1990) in their conceptualization of engagement need to find a new measurement tool. Developing one specifically for service contexts is recommended.

Methodologically, collecting self-report data from front-line employees at one point in time has been the dominant approach. Future studies should consider collecting data at multiple points of time, from multiple sources (for example, co-workers, supervisors, customers) as well as through multiple methods (diaries, participant observation, interviews and focus groups). If a new measure is to be developed, it could begin with in-depth interviews of employees identified by their organizations as being highly engaged.

WHERE TO FROM HERE?

In integrating the various components of this chapter, several observations and recommendations can be made. First, as previously suggested, the field appears to be at a crossroads. Given the current appetite for empirical studies on engagement (and the considerable convenience of existing scales), it is unlikely that there will be a self-imposed moratorium until the theoretical debates are sorted and measurement consensus is achieved. Rather, an incremental approach to changing the model and accompanying scales will likely unfold (for better or worse), with most scholars continuing to build on the dominant theoretical framework (JD-R) (Bakker and Demerouti, 2007; 2008), by adding additional constructs and scale items, as occurred with the inclusion of 'personal resources' and the integration of COR and CSE theory, with respect to measures of self-efficacy and optimism, for example.

As was found within this review, to a certain extent this is already occurring. Empirical studies in hospitality and tourism were found to have incorporated additional theoretical frameworks and constructs, including service climate, psychological climate and leadership, for example. In this way, over time, while new insights and evidence supporting 'best practice' may be gleaned, an unwieldy patchwork may emerge, with more and more theories and constructs being added, and all found to be associated in some way with 'engagement'. To this end, I do agree that Saks and Gruman's (2014) proposed model holds promise, as a more comprehensive organizing framework.

Given this complexity, however, I wonder if over time engagement may be come to be thought of as an integrating theoretical device that connects a number of well-established constructs, including: strategic factors (vision, culture, leadership); job demands (physical environment, general working conditions, workload, emotional labour); job factors (job design, rewards, meaningful goals); group factors (team dynamics, interpersonal relationships); and personal factors (personality, personal goals and obligations). To some extent, this is consistent with AON's model (2016b, p. 3) that consisted of differentiators (brand, leadership and performance) and foundational components (company practices, enabling infrastructure, the basics, and the work).

All of these factors arguably come together through a kaleidoscope of interaction, each influencing the other, potentially in unexpected ways and directions, and producing a lived experience in a moment of time, complete with observable behaviour (performance, social exchange) and psychological affect (motivation, commitment, burnout). Whether 'engagement' belongs beside burnout, as an additional independent psychological construct, or whether it is the kaleidoscope itself that connects the dots, is the question. In reflecting on this possibility, I was reminded of the garbage can theory of decision-making (Cohen et al., 1972), whereby organizations are seen to consist of 'a collection of choices looking for problems, issues and feelings looking for decision situations in which they might be aired, solutions looking for issues to which they might be the answer, and decision makers looking for work'. It may be that engagement is looking for a theory, definition, antecedents and outcomes, and that they are all in the mix together.

Finally, Bakker et al. (2014) and Knight et al. (2016) suggested that the time is right to move beyond correlational studies and start testing interventions. I also agree with this recommendation, despite some of the conceptual and methodological confusion. Research in hospitality and tourism studies could benefit from longitudinal and experimental designs. Applying Knight's fourfold intervention model, the following types of interventions might be tested: *personal resource building interventions* (introduce psychological assessment as part of selection procedures); *job resource building interventions* (redesign jobs to include enhanced autonomy); *leadership training interventions* (train supervisors and managers in how to support the development of self-efficacy belief); and *health promotion interventions* (implement a programme to encourage employee fitness). The question of what the dependent variable should be, and how it should be measured remains.

BIBLIOGRAPHY

Abraham, R. (1998), 'Emotional dissonance in organizations: antecedents, consequence, and moderators', *Psychology Monographs*, **124**, 229–246.

Adams, J.S. (1963), 'Toward an understanding of inequity', *Journal of Abnormal and Social Psychology*, **67**, 422–436.

Alarcon, G., K.J. Eschleman and N.A. Bowling (2009), 'Relationships between personality variables and burnout: a meta-analysis', *Work Stress*, **23**, 244–263.

Alderfer, C.P. (1972), *Human Needs in Organizational Settings*, New York, NY: Free Press of Glencoe.

Alderfer, C.P. (1985), 'An intergroup perspective on group dynamics', in J. Lorsch (ed.), *Handbook of Organizational Behavior* (pp. 190–222), Englewood Cliffs, NJ: Prentice Hall.

Allen, N.J. and J.P. Meyer (1990), 'The measurement and antecedents of affective, continuance, and normative commitment to the organization', *Journal of Occupational Psychology*, **63** (1), 1–18.

Amenumey, E.K. and A. Lockwood (2008), 'Psychological climate and psychological empowerment: an exploration in a luxury UK hotel group', *Tourism and Hospitality Research*, **8**, 265–281.

Aon (2016a), *Employee Engagement*, accessed 25 March 2017 at: www.aon.com/unitedking dom/trp/talent/predictive-talent-analytics/employee-engagement.jsp.

Aon (2016b), *Trends in Global Employee Engagement*, accessed 9 January 2017 at: www.modernsurvey.com/wp-content/uploads/2016/05/2016-Trends-in-Global-Employee-Engagement.pdf.

Aon (2017), *Aon Best Employers 2017*, accessed 11 January 2017 at: www.aon.com/canada/products-services/human-capital-consulting/consulting/best_employers/Winners.html.

Ashforth, B. and R. Humphrey (1993), 'Emotional labor in service rules: the influence of identity', *Academy of Management Review*, **18** (1), 88–115.

Avey, J.B., F. Luthans and S.M. Jensen (2009), 'Psychological capital: a positive resource for combatting employee stress and turnover', *Human Resource Management*, **48** (5), 677–693.

Babakus, E., U. Yavas and N.J. Ashill (2009), 'The role of customer orientation as a moderator of the job demand–burnout–performance relationship: A surface-level trait perspective', *Journal of Retailing*, **85** (4), 480–492.

Babin, B. and J.S. Boles (1998), 'Employee behavior in a service environment: a model and test of potential differences between men and women', *Journal of Marketing*, **62** (2), 77–91.

Bakker, A.B. and E. Demerouti (2007), 'The job demands-resources model: state of the art', *Journal of Management Psychology*, **22**, 309–328.

Bakker, A.B. and E. Demerouti (2008), 'Towards a model of work engagement', *Career Development International*, **13** (3), 209–223.

Bakker, A.B. and E. Heuven (2006), 'Emotional dissonance, burnout, and in-role performance among nurses and police officers', *International Journal of Stress Management*, **13**, 423–440.

Bakker, A.B., E. Demerouti and M.C. Euwema (2005), 'Job resources buffer the impact of job demands on burnout', *Journal of Occupational Health Psychology*, **10**, 170–180.

Bakker, A.B., E. Demerouti and A.A. Sanz-Vergel (2014), 'Burnout and work engagement: the JD-R approach', *The Annual Review of Organizational Psychology and Organizational Behavior*, **1**, 389–411.

Bakker, A.B., M. Tims and D. Derks (2012), 'Proactive personality and job performance: the role of job crating and work engagement', *Human Relations*, **65**, 1359–1378.

Bandura, A. (1977), 'Self-efficacy: toward a unifying theory of behavioral change', *Psychological Review*, **84** (2), 191–215.

Bandura, A. (1986), *Social Foundations of Thought and Action: A Social-Cognitive View*, Englewood Cliffs, NJ: Prentice Hall.

Baum, T. (2008), 'Implications of hospitality and tourism labour markets for talent management strategies', *International Journal of Contemporary Hospitality Management*, **20** (7), 720–729.

Beehr, T.A., L.A. King and D.W. King (1990), 'Social support and occupational stress: talking to supervisors', *Journal of Vocational Behavior*, **36** (1), 61–81.

Berezan, O., C. Raab, Y. Myongjee and L. Curtis (2013), 'Sustainable hotel practices and nationality: the impact on guest satisfaction and guest intention to return', *International Journal of Hospitality Management*, **34** (1), 227–233.

Bettencourt, L.A. and S.W. Brown (1997), 'Contact employees: relationships among workplace fairness, job satisfaction and prosocial service behaviors', *Journal of Retailing*, **73** (1), 39–61.

Bettencourt, L.A. and S.W. Brown (2003), 'Role stressors and customer-oriented boundary-spanning behaviors in service organizations', *Journal of the Academy of Marketing Science*, **31** (4), 394–408.

Blau, P.M. (1964), *Exchange and Power in Social Life*, New York, NY: Wiley.

Bluedorn, A.C., T.J. Kalliath, M.J. Strube and G.D. Martin (1999), 'Polychronicity and the inventory of polychromic values (IPV): the development of an instrument to measure a fundamental dimension of organizational culture', *Journal of Managerial Psychology*, **14** (3/4), 205–230.

Brotheridge, C.M. and R.T. Lee (2003), 'Development and validation of the emotional labour scale', *Journal of Occupational and Organization Psychology*, **76**, 365–379.

Brown, K. and T.R. Mitchell (1991), 'A comparison of just-in-time and batch manufacturing: the role of performance obstacles', *Academy of Management Journal*, **34**, 906–917.

Brown, S.P., W.L. Cron and J.S. Slocum Jr. (1998), 'Effects of trait competiveness and perceived intraorganizational competition on salesperson goal setting and performance', *Journal of Marketing*, **62** (October), 88–98.

Burjeck, A. (14 December 2015). *Re-engaging with William Kahn 25 years After he Coined Term Employee Engagement*, accessed 25 January 2017 at: www.workforce.com/2015/12/14/re-engaging-with-william-kahn-25-years-after-he-coined-term-employee-engagement/.

Burke, R.J. (1991), 'Early work and career experiences of female and male managers and professionals: reasons for optimism?' *Canadian Journal of Administrative Sciences*, **8**, 224–230.

Burke, R.J., M. Koyuncu, L. Fiksenbaum and Y. Tekin (2013), 'Antecedents and consequences of work engagement among frontline employees in Turkish hotels', *Journal of Transnational Management*, **18**, 191–203.

Burke, R.J., M. Koyuncu, W. Jing and L. Fiksenbaum (2009), 'Work engagement among hotel managers in Beijing, China: potential antecedents and consequences', *Tourism Review*, **64** (3), 4–18.

Cammann, C., M. Fichman, D. Henkins and J. Klesh (1979), *The Michigan Organizational Assessment Questionnaire*, (unpublished manuscript), University of Michigan at Ann Arbor.

Carlson, D., J. Kacmar and L. Williams (2000), 'Construction and initial validation of a multidimensional measure of work–family conflict', *Journal of Vocational Behavior*, **56**, 249–276.

Carrasco, H., V. Martinez-Tur, C. Moliner, J.M. Peiro and C. Ramis (2014), 'Linking emotional dissonance and service climate to well-being at work: a cross-level analysis', *Universitas Psychologica*, **13** (3), 947–960.

Carter, K.L. (1997), *Why Workers won't Work: The Worker in a Developing Economy, a Case Study of Jamaica*, London: Macmillan.

Chen, C.-Y., C.-H. Yen and F.C. Tsai (2014), 'Job crafting and job engagement: the mediating role of person-job fit', *International Journal of Hospitality Management*, **37** (February), 21–28.

Chen, M., X. Gao, H. Zheng and B. Ran (2015), 'A review of psychological safety: concepts, measurements, antecedents, and consequences variables', *International Conference on Social Sciences and Technology Education* (January).

Christensen Hughes, J.M. (1999), 'Organizational empowerment: a historical perspective and conceptual framework', in J.J. Quinn and P. Davies (eds), *Ethics and Empowerment* (115–146), London, UK: Macmillan Business Press.

Christensen Hughes, J. (2018), 'The changing tourism and hospitality context: implications for human resource management in an age of disruption and growth', in R. Burke and J. Christensen Hughes (eds), *Handbook of HRM in the Tourism and Hospitality Industries*, Cheltenham, UK: Edward Elgar Publishing.

Christensen Hughes, J. (2018), 'Synopses of empirical studies on engagement in hospitality and tourism research', in R. Burke and J. Christensen Hughes (eds), *Handbook of HRM in the Tourism and Hospitality Industries*, Cheltenham, UK: Edward Elgar Publishing.

Christensen Hughes, J. and W. Murray (2018), 'Evolving conceptions of talent management: a roadmap for hospitality and tourism', in R. Burke and J. Christensen Hughes (eds), *Handbook of HRM in the Tourism and Hospitality Industries*, Cheltenham, UK: Edward Elgar Publishing.

Christian, M.S., A.S. Garza and J.E. Slaughter (2011), 'Work engagement: a quantitative review and test of its relations with task and contextual performance', *Personal Psychology*, **64**, 89–136.

Cohen, M.D., J.G. March and J.P. Olsen (1972), 'A garbage can model of organizational choice', *Administrative Science Quarterly*, **17** (1), 1–25.

Colarelli, S.M. (1984), 'Methods of communication and mediating processes in realistic job previews, *Journal of Applied Psychology*, **69** (4), 633–642.

Cole, M.S., F. Walter, A.G. Bedeian and E.H. O'Boyle (2012), 'Job burnout and employee engagement: a meta-analytic examination of construct proliferation', *Journal of Management*, **38** (5), 1550–1581.

Conger, J.A. and R.N. Kanungo (1988), 'The empowerment process: integrating theory and practice', *Academy of Management Review*, **13** (3), 471–482.

Csikszentmihalyi, M. (1982), *Beyond Boredom and Anxiety*, San Francisco, CA: Jossey-Bass.

Deci, E.L. (1975), *Intrinsic Motivation*, New York, NY: Plenum Press.

Deery, M. (2008), 'Talent management, work–life balance and retention strategies', *International Journal of Contemporary Hospitality Management*, **20** (7), 792–806.

Demerouti, E., A.B. Bakker, F. Nachreiner and W.B. Schaufeli (2001), 'The job demands-resources model of burnout', *Journal of Applied Psychology*, **86**, 499–512.

Demerouti, E., E. Van Eeuwijk, M. Snelder and U. Wild (2011), 'Assessing the effect of a "personal effectiveness" training on psychological capital, assertiveness and self-awareness using self–other agreement', *Career Development International*, **16**, 60–81.

Dietz, J., S.D. Pugh and J.W. Wiley (2004), 'Service climate effects on customer attitudes: an examination of boundary conditions', *Academy of Management Journal*, **47**, 81–92.

Eisenberger, R., R. Huntington, S. Hutchison and D. Sowa (1986), 'Perceived organizational support', *Journal of Applied Psychology*, **71** (3), 500–507.

Free, C., C. Hathaway, N. Lynn and A. Paul (March 2015), *How do you Engage and Retain Employees in the Battle for Top Talent?*, accessed 1 April 2017 at: https://www.towers watson.com/en/Insights/IC-Types/Ad-hoc-Point-of-View/2015/03/Viewpoint-Strategies-for-engaging-and-retaining-top-talent.

Freudenberger, H.J. (1974), 'Staff burn-out', *Journal of Social Issues*, **30** (1), 159–165.

Frey, C. and M. Osborne (2013), 'The future of employment: how susceptible are jobs to computerisation?', *Oxford Martin School*, accessed 4 March 2017 at: www.oxfordmartin. ox.ac.uk/downloads/academic/The_Future_of_Employment.pdf.

Goffman, E. (1959), *The Presentation of Self in Everyday Life*, New York, NY: Doubleday Anchor.

Goffman, E. (1961), *Encounters: Two Studies in the Sociology of Interaction*, Indianapolis: Bobbs-Merrill Co.

Goldberg, D. (1979), *Manual of the General Health Questionnaire*, London: NFER Nelson.

Grandey, A.A. (2000), 'Emotion regulation in the workplace: a new way to conceptualize emotional labor', *Journal of Occupational Health Psychology*, **5** (1), 95–110.

Gremler, D.D. and K.P. Gwinner (2000), 'Customer–employee rapport in service relationships', *Journal of Service Research*, **3**, 82–104.

Gruman, J.A. and A.M. Saks (2011), 'Performance management and employee engagement', *Human Resource Management Review*, **21**, 123–136.

Grzywacz, J.G. and N.F. Marks (2000), 'Reconceptualizing the work–family interface: an ecological perspective on the correlates of positive and negative spillover between work and family', *Journal of Occupational Health Psychology*, **5** (1), 111–126.

Hackman, J.R. and G.R. Oldham (1975), 'Development of the job diagnostic survey', *Journal of Applied Psychology*, **60** (2), 159–170.

Hackman, J.R. and G.R. Oldham (1980), *Work Redesign*, Reading, MA: Addison-Wesley.

Halbesleben, J.R.B. (2010), 'A meta-analysis of work engagement: relationship with burnout demands, resources and consequences', in A.B. Bakker and M.P. Leiter (eds), *Work Engagement: A Handbook of Essential Theory and Research* (pp. 102–111), New York: Psychological Press.

Hammer, T.H., P.O. Saksvik, K. Nytro, H. Torvatn and M. Bayazit (2004), 'Expanding the psychosocial work environment: workplace norms and work–family conflict as correlates of stress and health', *Journal of Occupational Health Psychology*, **9** (1), 83–97.

Harter, J.K., G.L. Schmidt and T.L. Hayes (2002), 'Business-unit-level relationship between employee satisfaction, employee engagement and business outcomes: a meta-analysis', *Journal of Applied Psychology*, **87**, 268–279.

Hartline, M.D., J.G. Maxham and D.O. McKee (2000), 'Corridors of influence in the dissemination of customer-oriented strategy to customer contact device employees', *Journal of Marketing*, **64** (April), 52–70.

Herzberg, F., B. Mausner and B. Snyderman (1959), *The Motivation to Work*, New York, NY: Wiley.

Hobfoll, S.E. (1989), 'Conservation of resources: a new attempt at conceptualizing stress', *American Psychologist*, **44** (3), 513–524.

Hobfoll, S.E. (2001), 'The influence or culture, community, and the nested-self in the stress process: advancing conservation of resources theory', *Applied Psychology: An International Review*, **50**, 337–370.

Hobfoll, S.E., R.J. Johnson, N. Ennis and A.P. Jackson (2003), 'Resource loss, resource gain, and emotional outcomes among inner city women', *Journal of Personality and Social Psychology*, **84**, 632–643.

Hochschild, A.R. (1983a), *The Managed Heart: Commercialization of Human Feeling*, Berkeley, CA: University of California Press.

Hochschild, A.R. (1983b), 'Comment on Kemper's "social constructionist and positivist approaches to the sociology of emotions"', *American Journal of Sociology*, **89** (2), 432–434.

Iverson, R.D. and M. Deery (1997), 'Turnover culture in the hospitality industry', *Human Resource Management Journal*, **7** (4), 71–82.

James, L.R. and L.E. Tetrick (1986), 'Confirmatory analytic test of three causal models relating job perceptions to job satisfaction', *Journal of Applied Psychology*, **71**, 77–82.

Janssen, O. (2000), 'Job demands, perceptions of effort-reward fairness and innovative work behaviour', *Journal of Occupational and Organizational Psychology*, **73**, 287–302.

Jones, C.R. (1986), 'Socialization tactics, self-efficacy, and newcomers' adjustments to organizations', *Academy of Management Journal*, **29** (2), 262–279.

Judge, T.A. and J.E. Bono (2001), 'Relationship of core self-evaluations traits—self-esteem, generalized self-efficacy, locus of control, and emotional stability—with job satisfaction and job performance: a meta-analysis', *Journal of Applied Psychology*, **86** (1), 80–92.

Judge, T.A., J.E. Bono, A. Erez and E.A. Locke (2005), 'Core self-evaluations and job and life satisfaction: the role of self-concordance and goal attainment', *Journal of Applied Psychology*, **90** (2), 257–268.

Judge, T.A., A. Erez, J.E. Bono and C.J. Thoresen (2003), 'The core self-evaluations scale: development of a measure', *Personnel Psychology*, **56** (2), 303–331.

Judge, T.A., E.A. Locke and C.C. Durham (1997), 'The dispositional causes of job satisfaction: a core evaluations approach', *Research in Organizational Behavior*, **19**, 151–188.

Judge, T.A., E.A. Locke, C.C. Durham and A.N. Kluger (1998), 'Dispositional effects on job and life satisfaction: the role of core evaluations', *Journal of Applied Psychology*, **83** (10), 17–34.

Judge, T.A., A.E.M. Van Vianen and I.E. De Pater (2004), 'Emotional stability, core self-valuations, and job outcomes: a review of the evidence and an agenda for future research', *Human Performance*, **17**, 325–346.

Kahn, W.A. (1990), 'Psychological conditions of personal engagement and disengagement at work', *Academy of Management Journal*, **33** (4), 692–724.

Kahn, W.A. (1992), 'To be fully there: psychological presence at work', *Human Relations*, **45**, 321–349.

Karatepe, O.M. (2013), 'High-performance work practices and hotel employee performance: the mediation of work engagement', *International Journal of Hospitality Management*, **32** (1), 132–140.

Karatepe, O.M. (2013a), 'Perceptions of organizational politics and hotel employee outcomes: the mediating role of work engagement', *International Journal of Contemporary Hospitality Management*, **25** (1), 82–104.

Karatepe, O.M. and E. Demir (2014), 'Linking core self-evaluations and work engagement to work–family facilitation: a study in the hotel industry', *International Journal of Contemporary Hospitality Management*, **26** (2), 307–323.

Karatepe, O.M. and O.A. Olugbade (2009), 'The effects of job and personal resources on hotel employees' work engagement', *International Journal of Hospitality Management*, **28**, 504–512.

Karatepe, O.M., E. Beirami, M. Bouzari and H.P. Safavi (2014), 'Does work engagement mediate the effects of challenge stressors on job outcomes? Evidence from the hotel industry', *International Journal of Hospitality Management*, **36**, 14–22.

Karatepe, O.M., G. Karadas, A.K. Azar and N. Naderiadib (2013), 'Does work engagement mediate the effect of polychronicity on performance outcomes? A study in the hospitality industry in Northern Cyprus', *Journal of Human Resources in Hospitality & Tourism*, **12**, 52–70.

☙

☙

☙

☙

☙

☙

☙

☙

Karatepe, O.M., S. Keshavarz and S. Nejati (2010), 'Do core self-evaluations mediate the effect of coworker support on work engagement? A study of hotel employees in Iran', *Journal of Hospitality and Tourism Management*, 17, 62–71. DOI 10.1375/jhtm.17.1.62.

Keaveney, S.M. and J.E. Nelson (1993), 'Coping with organizational role stress: intrinsic motivation orientation, perceived role benefit, and psychological withdrawal', *Journal of Academy of Marketing Science*, 21 (2), 113–124.

Kim, H.J., K.H. Shin and N. Swanger (2009), 'Burnout and engagement: a comparative analysis using the Big Five personality dimensions', *International Journal of Hospitality Management*, 28 (1), 96–104.

Knight, C., M. Patterson and J. Dawson (2016), 'Building work engagement: a systematic review and meta-analysis investigating the effectiveness of work engagement interventions', *Journal of Organizational Behavior*, Wiley Online Library (wileyonlinelibrary.com) DOI: 10.1002/job.2167.

Kofodimos, J. (1993), *Balancing Act*, San Francisco, CA: Jossey-Bass.

Kusluvan, S. (2003), 'Characteristics of employment and human resource management in the tourism and hospitality industry', in S. Kusluvan (ed.), *Managing Employee Attitudes and Behaviors in the Tourism and Hospitality Industry* (pp. 3–24), Hauppauge, NY: Nova Science Publishers.

Langer, E.J. (1989), *Mindfulness*, Reading, MA: Addison-Wesley.

Lawler, E.E., and D.T. Hall (1970), 'Relationship of job characteristics to job involvement, satisfaction, and intrinsic motivation', *Journal of Applied Psychology*, 54, 305–312.

Lazarus, R.S. and S. Folkman (1984), *Psychological Stress and the Coping Process*, New York: Springer.

Lee, J. and C. Ok (2015), 'Drivers of work engagement: an examination of core self-evaluations and psychological climate among hotel employees', *International Journal of Hospitality Management*, 44, 84–98.

Lee, J. and C. Ok (2016), 'Hotel employee work engagement and its consequences', *Journal of Hospitality Marketing & Management*, 25, 133–166.

Lee, R.T. and B.E. Ashforth (1996), 'A meta-analytic examination of the correlates of the three dimensions of job burnout', *Journal of Applied Psychology*, 8, 123–133.

LePine, J.A., N.P. Podsakoff and M.A. LePine (2005), 'A meta-analytic test of the challenge stressor–hindrance stressor framework: an explanation for inconsistent relationships among stressors and performance', *Academy of Management Journal*, 48 (5), 764–775.

Liu, C.M. (2006), 'The effect of organizational vision on service quality delivery', *The Service Industries Journal*, 26 (8), 849–859.

Liu, J., S. Cho and E.D. Putra (2017), 'The moderating effect of self-efficacy and gender on work engagement for restaurant employees in the United States', *International Journal of Contemporary Hospitality Management*, 29 (1), 624–642.

Locke, E.A. (1976), 'The nature and causes of job satisfaction', in M.D. Dunnette (ed.), *Handbook of Industrial and Organizational Psychology* (pp. 1297–1349), Chicago, IL: Rand McNally College Publishing.

Luthans, F. and C.M. Youssef (2007), 'Emerging positive organizational behavior', *Journal of Management*, 33 (3), 321–349.

Luthans, F., J.B. Avey, B.J. Avolio, S.M. Norman and G.J. Combs (2006), 'Psychological capital development: toward a micro-intervention', *Journal of Organizational Behavior*, 27, 387–393.

Luthans, F., C.M. Youssef and B.J. Avolio (2007), *Psychological Capital: Developing the Human Competitive Edge*, Oxford, UK: Oxford University Press.

Macey, W.H., B. Schneider, K.M. Barbera and S.A. Young (2009), *Employee Engagement: Tools for Analysis, Practice, and Competitive Advantage*, Malden, MA: Wiley-Blackwell.

Makikangas, A., T. Feldt, U. Kinnunen and S. Mauno (2013), 'Does personality matter? Research on individual differences in occupational well-being', in A.B. Bakker (ed.), *Advances in Positive Organizational Psychology* (pp. 107–143), Bingley, UK: Emerald.

Manyika, J., M. Chui, M. Miremadi, J. Bughin, K. George, P. Willmott and M. Dewhurst

(2017), 'A future that works: automation, employment, and productivity', *McKinsey Global Institute*, accessed 10 March 2017 at: www.google.ca/search?q=Mckinsey+job+automatio n&ie=utf-8&oe=utf-8&gws_rd=cr&ei=wb3JWI7ELIysjwTD4p74Ag.

Martinez-Tur, V., J. Ramos, J.M. Peiro and E. Buades (2001), 'Relationships among perceived justice, customers' satisfaction, and behavioral intentions: the moderating role of gender', *Psychological Reports*, **88**, 805–811.

Maslach, C. and S. Jackson (1981), 'The measurement of experienced burnout', *Journal of Organizational Behavior*, **2** (2), 99–113.

Maslach, C. and S.E. Jackson (1984), 'Burnout in organizational settings', *Applied Social Psychology Annual*, 5, 133–153.

Maslach, C. and S.E. Jackson (1986), *The Maslach Burnout Inventory* (2nd ed.), Palo Alto, CA: Consulting Psychologist Press.

Maslach, C. and M.P. Leiter (1997), *The Truth About Burnout: How Organizations Cause Personal Stress and What To Do About It*, San Francisco: Jossey-Bass.

Maslach, C., W.B. Schaufeli and M.P. Leiter (2001), 'Job burnout', *Annual Review of Psychology*, **52**, 397–422.

Maslow, A.H. (1943), 'A theory of human motivation', *Psychological Review*, **50** (4): 370–396.

May, D.R., R.L. Gilson and L.M. Harter (2004), 'The psychological conditions of meaningfulness, safety and availability and the engagement of the human spirit at work', *Journal of Occupational and Organizational Psychology*, **77**, 11–37.

Meyer, J.P., N.J. Allen and C.A. Smith (1993), 'Commitment to organizations and occupations: extension and test of a three-component conceptualization', *Journal of Applied Psychology*, **78**, 538–551.

Miles, L. (2000), 'Services innovation: coming of age in the knowledge-based economy', *International Journal of Innovation Management*, **4** (4), 371–389.

Mowday, R.T., L.W. Porter and R.M. Steers (1982), *Employee–organization Linkages: The Psychology of Commitment, Absenteeism, and Turnover*, New York, NY: Academic Press.

Mowday, R.T., R.M. Steers and L.W. Porter (1979), 'The measurement of organizational commitment', *Journal of Vocational Behavior*, **14** (2), 224–247.

Nelson, D. and C.L. Cooper (2007), *Positive Organizational Behaviour: Accentuating the Positive at Work*, Thousand Oaks, CA: Sage Publications.

Paek, S., M. Schuckert, T.T. Kim and G. Lee (2015), 'Why is hospitality employees' psychological capital important? The effects of psychological capital on work engagement and employee morale', *International Journal of Hospitality Management*, **50**, 9–26.

Parasuraman, A., V.A. Zeithaml and L.L. Berry (1988), 'SERVQUAL: a multiple-item scale for measuring consumer perceptions of service quality', *Journal of Retailing*, **64**, 12–40.

Park, J. and D. Gursoy (2012), 'Generational effects on work engagement among U.S. hotel employees', *International Journal of Hospitality Management*, **31**, 1195–1202.

Peterson, D. and M. Seligman (2004), *Character Strengths and Virtues: A Handbook and Classification*, New York, NY: Oxford University Press.

Pienaar, J. and S.A. Willemse (2008), 'Burnout, engagement, coping and general health of service employees in the hospitality industry', *Tourism Management*, **29**, 1053–1063.

Pine, J. and J. Gilmore (1999), *The Experience Economy: Work is Theatre & Every Business a Stage*, Boston, MA: Harvard Business School Press.

Pratt, M.G. and B.E. Ashforth (2003), 'Fostering meaningfulness in working and at work', in K.S. Cameron, J.E. Dutton and R.E. Quinn (eds), *Positive Organizational Scholarship: Foundations of a New Discipline* (pp. 309–327), San Francisco, CA: Berrett-Koehler.

Price, J.L (2001), 'Reflection on the determinants of voluntary turnover', *International Journal of Manpower*, **22** (7), 600–624.

Psychometrics (2010), 'Control, opportunity & leadership: a study of employee engagement in the Canadian workplace', *Engagement Study*, Psychometrics Canada, accessed 6 April 2017 at: https://www.psychometrics.com/wp-content/uploads/2015/04/engagement_study.pdf

Rich, B.L., J.A. Lepine and E.R. Crawford (2010), 'Job engagement: antecedents and effects on job performance', *Academy of Management Journal*, **53** (3), 617–635.

Richman, A. (2006), 'Everyone wants an engaged workforce: how can you create it?', *Workspan*, **49**, 36–39.

Rigg, J., J. Day and H. Adler (2013), 'An empirical analysis of Jamaican hotel employees' engagement, job satisfaction, and quitting intentions', *Consortium Journal of Hospitality and Tourism*, **18** (2), 17–33.

Riley, M. (1996), *Human Resource Management in the Hospitality and Tourism Industry*, Oxford: Butterworth-Heinemann.

Saks, A.M. (2006), 'Antecedents and consequences of employee engagement', *Journal of Managerial Psychology*, **21**, 600–619.

Saks, A.M. and J.A. Gruman (2014), 'What do we really know about employee engagement?', *Human Resource Development Quarterly*, **25** (2), 155–182.

Salanova, M., S. Agut and J.M. Peiro (2005), 'Linking organizational resources and work engagement to employee performance and customer loyalty: the mediation of service climate', *Journal of Applied Psychology*, **90** (6), 1217–1227.

Schaufeli, W.B. and A.B. Bakker (2003), *UWES-Utrecht Work Engagement Scale: Test Manual*. Utrecht University, Department of Psychology.

Schaufeli, W.B., A.B Bakker and M. Salanova (2006), 'Measurement of work engagement with a short questionnaire: a cross-national study', *Educational and Psychological Measurement*, **66** (4), 701–716.

Schaufeli, W.B., M.P. Leiter, C. Maslach and S.E. Jackson (1996), 'The Maslach Burnout Inventory–General Survey', in C. Maslach, S.E. Jackson and M.P. Leiter (eds), *Maslach Burnout Inventory—Test Manual* (3rd edn) (pp.19–26), Palo Alto, CA: Consulting Psychologists Press.

Schaufeli, W.B., M. Salanova, V. Gonzales-Roma and A.B. Bakker (2002), 'The measurement of engagement and burnout: a two-sample confirmatory factor-analytic approach', *Journal of Happiness Studies*, **3**, 71–92.

Schaufeli, W.B., T. Taris, P. Le Blanc, M. Peeters, A. Bakker and J. De Jonge (2001), 'Can work produce health? The quest for the engaged worker', *Psychology*, **36**, 422–428.

Schneider, B., S.S. White and M.C. Paul (1998), 'Linking service climate and customer perceptions of service quality: tests of a causal model', *Journal of Applied Psychology*, **83** (2), 150–163.

Schwarzer, R., J. Babler, J. Kwiatek, P. Schroder and J. Zhang (1997), 'The assessment of optimistic self-beliefs: comparison of the German, Spanish, and Chinese version of the general self-efficacy scale', *Applied Psychology*, **46** (1), 69–88.

Seymour, D. (2000), 'Emotional labour: a comparison between fast food and traditional service work', *Hospitality Management*, **19**, 159–171.

Shuck, B., R. Ghosh, D. Zigarmi and K. Nimon (2012), 'The jingle jangle of employee engagement: further exploration of the emerging construct and implications for workplace learning and performance', *Human Resource Development Review*, **12**, 11–35.

Sieber, S.D. (1974), 'Toward a theory of role accumulation', *American Sociological Review*, **39**, 567–578.

Sinek, S. (2009), 'How great leaders inspire action', *TED Ideas Worth Spreading*, 28 March 2017, accessed at: www.ted.com/talks/simon_sinek_how_great_leaders_inspire_action.

Slatten, T. and J. Mehmetoglu (2011), 'Antecedents and effects of engaged frontline employees: a study from the hospitality industry', *Managing Service Quality*, **21** (1), 88–107.

Suan, C.L. and A.M. Nasurdin (2016), 'Supervisor support and work engagement of hotel employees in Malaysia: is it different for men and women?', *Gender in Management: An International Journal*, **31** (1), 2–18.

Susskind, A.M., K.M. Kacmar and C.P. Borchgrevink (2003), 'Customer service providers' attitudes relating to customer service and customer satisfaction in the custom–service exchange', *Journal of Applied Psychology*, **8** (1), 179–187.

Swan, J.E. and R.L. Oliver (1989), 'Post purchase communications by consumer', *Journal of Retailing*, **65**, 516–533.

Sweetman, D. and F. Luthans (2010), 'The power of positive psychology: psychological capital and work engagement', in A.B. Bakker and M.P. Leiter (eds), *Work Engagement: A Handbook of Essential Theory and Research* (pp. 54–68), New York, NY: Psychology Press.

Taris, T.W. (2006), 'Is there a relationship between burnout and objective performance? A critical review of 16 studies', *Work Stress*, **20**, 316–334.

Tax, S. and S. Brown (1998), 'Recovering and learning from service failure', *Sloan Management Review*, **40** (1), 75–88.

Towers Watson (2015), 'Top management's role in driving employee engagement', *Towers Watson study*, accessed 1 April 2017 at: https://www.towerswatson.com/en/Press/2015/12/Towers-Watson-Employee-Engagement-in-India.

Tsui, A.S., J.L. Pearce, L.W. Porter and A.M. Tripoli (1993), 'Alternative approaches to the employee–organization relationship: does investment in employees pay off?', *Academy of Management Journal*, **40** (5), 1089–1121.

Van Dyne, L. and J.A. LePine (1998), 'Helping and voice extra-role behaviors: evidence of construct and predictive validity', *Academy of Management Journal*, **41**, 108–119.

Wood, R. (2003), 'The status of tourism employment', in S. Kusluvan (ed.), *Managing Employee Attitudes and Behaviors in the Tourism and Hospitality Industry* (pp. 53–65), Hauppauge, NY: Nova Science Publishers.

Wood, R. and A. Bandura (1989), 'Social cognitive theory of organizational management', *Academy of Management Review*, **14** (3), 361–384.

Xanthopoulou, D., A.B. Bakker, E. Demerouti and W.B. Schaufeli (2007), 'The role of personal resources in the job demands-resources model', *International Journal of Stress Management*, **14**, 121–141.

Xanthopoulou, D., A.B. Bakker, E. Demerouti and W.B. Schaufeli (2009), 'Reciprocal relationships between job resources, personal resources, and work engagement', *Journal of Vocational Behavior*, **74**, 235–244.

Xanthopoulou, D., A.B. Bakker, E. Heuven, E. Demerouti and W.B. Schaufeli (2008), 'Working in the sky: a diary study on work engagement among flight attendants', *Journal of Occupational Health Psychology*, **13** (4), 345–356.

Yagil, D. (2012), 'The mediating role of engagement and burnout in the relationship between employees' emotion regulation strategies and customer outcomes', *European Journal of Work and Organizational Psychology*, **21** (1), 150–168.

Zapf, D. (2002), 'Emotion work and psychological well-being: a review of the literature and some conceptual considerations', *Human Resource Management Review*, **12** (2), 237–268.

Zapf, D., C. Vogt, C. Seifert, H. Mertini and A. Isic (1999), 'Emotional work as a source of stress: the concept and development of an instrument', *European Journal of Work and Organizational Psychology*, **8** (3), 371–400.

Zeithaml, V.A., L.L. Berry and A. Parasuraman (1988), 'Communication and control processes in the delivery of service quality', *Journal of Marketing*, **52**, 35–48.

Zeithaml, V.A., M.J. Bitner and D.D. Greemier (2013), *Services Marketing: Integrating Customer Focus Across the Firm*, New York: McGraw-Hill.

11. Synopses of empirical studies on engagement in hospitality and tourism research

Julia Christensen Hughes

This chapter presents selected studies on employee engagement published in the hospitality and tourism literature between 2008 and 2017. Each publication is summarized with respect to the context of the study, the underlying theory, methods (including instruments) and key findings. The chapter concludes with a brief synthesis of key findings. This chapter complements Chapter 10, which provides an overview of the conceptual and theoretical development of the field and suggests implications for management practice and further research.

METHOD

A 2017 inquiry via the University of Guelph Library's online journal resource 'Primo', using the terms 'employee, engagement and hospitality', ranked 863 peer-reviewed, empirically based academic journal articles. Osman Karatepe, from the Faculty of Tourism at Eastern Mediterranean University in Turkey, was identified as the most prolific contributor to the collection. Articles included in a recent review by Paek et al. (2015) were also reviewed. Google Scholar was consulted for citation counts.

Ultimately, seven articles from Paek et al.'s (2015) review were selected, along with eleven others, based on a combination of factors, including rankings in online searches, citations, the novelty of items included in the study, and the publication date (in order to include recent work). Rather than a systematic meta-review, these articles represent a range of studies, each having been assessed as having made a unique contribution to the literature. A summary table is included in Appendix 11A.1.

Empirical Studies on Engagement

The eighteen articles are presented below, in order of publication date, with a brief summary of the context, theoretical foundation, methods and findings of each. With respect to theory, each of these studies arguably draws, to some extent, on job, demands, resources (JD-R) theory (Bakker and Demerouti, 2007; 2008), given that every study uses some form of the Utrecht Work Engagement Score (UWES) (Schaufeli and Bakker, 2003; Schaufeli et al., 2002; 2006). The UWES was developed from the foundation of JD-R theory (Schaufeli et al., 2006). Hence, only where additional theory is explicitly mentioned by the authors, is it included in the summary chart. With respect to the UWES, distinction is made between the UWES-17, a 3-factor model that separately measures vigour, dedication and absorption (VDA) (Schaufeli et al., 2002), and the UWES-9, a 1-factor model (see Schaufeli et al., 2006 for a comprehensive discussion of these measures).

Organizational Resources and Service Climate

One of the earliest empirical studies that considered work engagement in the hospitality industry, by Salanova et al. (2005), explored the relationships between organizational resources (training, autonomy and technology), work engagement, service climate (Schneider et al., 1998), employee performance and customer loyalty. Drawing from Schneider et al. (1998), service climate was defined as 'employees' shared perceptions of the practices, procedures, and behaviours that are rewarded, supported and expected by the organization with regard to customer service and customer service quality'.

Theoretical constructs included job characteristics theory (JCT) (Hackman and Oldham, 1980) and conservation of resources theory (CRT) (Hobfoll, 2001). The study took place in Spain and involved 114 service units (58 hotels and 56 restaurants), with three randomly selected employees and ten customers from each service unit surveyed.

Survey questions were drawn from a number of standard instruments (see Salanova et al., 2005, p. 1227 for the final versions of the scales and items). The Organizational Resources Scale (Brown and Mitchell, 1991) was used for assessing perceptions of training, autonomy and technology. Survey participants were asked to respond to statements about each resource; for example, 'Training was practical', 'Autonomy to choose what tasks to perform' and 'Technology is available'. Engagement was assessed using the UWES-17 (Schaufeli et al., 2002); for example, 'At work, I feel full of energy'. Service Climate was assessed using the Global Service Climate Scale (Schneider et al., 1998); for example, 'The overall quality of service provided by our organization to customers is excellent'. Employee performance as perceived by customers was assessed with respect to both empathy (SERVQUAL Empathy Scale, Parasuraman et al., 1988) and excellence (Service Provider Excellence Scale, Price et al., 1995). Statements included, for example, 'Employees understand specific needs of customers' (empathy) and 'Employees do more than usual for customers' (excellent performance). Customer service was also assessed from the perspective of customers with respect to intention to return and positive word-of-mouth behaviours (Martinez-Tur et al., 2001; Swan and Oliver, 1989); for example, 'If possible, I will return to this hotel/restaurant in the future' and 'I will recommend this hotel/restaurant to other people' (Salanova et al., 2005, p. 1227).

The results partially supported the hypotheses, in that engagement was found to fully mediate the relationship between organizational resources and service climate. Service climate was also associated with customer loyalty, mediated by performance. In terms of practical implications, the authors advised providing work units with resources sufficient to foster employee engagement in order to build and sustain a positive service climate and produce desired customer effects.

Assertiveness, Stress-reduction Training and Employee Health

Pienaar and Willemse (2008) explored the impact of coping strategies on the general health of front-line food and beverage workers in 16 restaurants and coffee shops in South Africa. Standardized instruments included: the 22-item MBI-HSS (Maslach and Jackson, 1986); the UWES-17 (Schaufeli et al., 2002); the Cybernetic Coping Scale (CSS) (Edwards, 1988; 1992; Edwards and Cooper, 1988), which, based on 'Edwards' Cybernetic theory of stress, coping and well-being', measures five distinct coping mechanisms: changing, accommodating, devaluing, avoiding and symptom reduction; and the General Health Questionnaire (GHQ) (Goldberg, 1979), which measures general mental health.

They found that the 'core dimensions' of burnout (exhaustion and depersonalization) and engagement (vigour and dedication) were strongly and negatively associated. Also the professional efficacy dimension of burnout was positively associated with engagement (p. 1060). In terms of main effects, 28 per cent of the variance in employee health was predicted by 'burnout and coping, with significant effects for emotional exhaustion, personal accomplishment, and having a coping strategy of avoidance or symptom reduction' (p. 1058). Engagement (dedication only) was positively associated with health, mediated by coping strategies (avoidance and symptom reduction). In terms of managerial implications, they suggested that 'especially for new employees, some assertiveness training or even information on basic ideas of emotional labour could be helpful in maintaining general health, while remaining sensitive to customers' needs' (p. 1061). Also, in underscoring the conceptual distinctiveness between engagement and burnout, they found that coping strategies for reducing burnout did not contribute to higher levels of engagement.

The Experience of Hotel Managers

Burke et al. (2009) focused on the experience of 309 managers working in 19 (3-, 4- and 5-star) hotels in China. Their study noted the mounting challenges in finding skilled workers with the right attitude for the industry, particularly at managerial and executive levels. Measures included Work Engagement UWES-17 items (Schaufeli et al., 2002). Work Outcomes included: job satisfaction (Kofodimos, 1993); career satisfaction (Greenhaus et al., 1990); job stress (Spence and Robbins, 1992); and intention to quit (Burke, 1991). Psychological well-being was measured by psychosomatic symptoms (Quinn and Shepard, 1974); emotional exhaustion (Maslach et al., 1996); and work–family conflict (Carlson et al., 2000) plus family–work conflict (nine items).

Results found work engagement to be a significant predictor of work and personal outcomes. Dedication, in particular, was found to be more strongly and consistently associated with job satisfaction, career satisfaction, lower stress, less likelihood to quit, lower levels of exhaustion, and less family conflict. Absorption, on the other hand, was found to be associated with higher levels of stress, exhaustion, psychosomatic symptoms and work–family conflict. Further research on each of the components of engagement is clearly needed.

Some interesting associations were also found for some of the demographic variables. For example, job tenure was associated with greater stress and psychosomatic symptoms. Managers with children reported higher levels of exhaustion. In addition, gender (males) and education were associated with greater work–family conflict.

They suggested that organizations should work to foster work engagement in order to benefit from greater work outcomes and employee well-being, but that they should be wary of the potential negative effects of absorption.

Trait Competitiveness and Supervisor Support

Karatepe and Olugbade (2009) investigated the link between supervisor support, self-efficacy, trait competitiveness and engagement. Building on the work of Xanthopoulou et al. (2007; 2008), who found a relationship between self-efficacy and the engagement of front-line hospitality and tourism workers, Karatepe and Olugbade theoretically grounded their work in Conservation of Resources (COR) theory (Hobfoll, 1989; 2001).

Also, noting that much of the extant literature had been based on studies in Western countries, their study took place in Nigeria. Participants were 130 full-time, front-line hotel employees, working in one of four hotels (one 4-star, three 5-star), licensed by the Nigerian Tourism Development Corporation.

Items from standard instruments were used to measure the hypothesized antecedents, including (p. 509): supervisor support (Beehr et al., 1990), for example, 'My supervisor is easy to talk to'; trait competitiveness (Brown et al., 1998), for example, 'It is important to me to perform better than others on a task'; and self-efficacy (Jones, 1986), for example, 'I did not experience any problems in adjusting to work in this hotel'. Engagement was measured using the UWES-17 (Schaufeli et al., 2002).

As hypothesized, supervisor support and trait competitiveness were both positively associated with self-efficacy. While supervisor support was not found to be associated with engagement (vigour, dedication and absorption), trait competitiveness was. A significant and positive relationship was also found between self-efficacy and absorption.

This work underscored the importance of supervisor support in prompting self-efficacy and further that employees with strongly held self-efficacy belief are more likely to be fully absorbed in their work. Also, trait competitiveness was identified as a particularly important employee attribute, given its association with all three engagement components. In exploring demographic differences, Karatepe and Olugbade (2009, p. 510) reported differences by gender and seniority; 'female frontline employees need less support from their supervisors. Employees with longer tenure report lower feelings of vigor'. In commenting on their results, Karatepe and Olugbade (2009) cautioned that the relationship between supervisor support and engagement could vary by country.

In terms of managerial implications, they emphasized the importance of creating a supportive work environment, with good working relationships between supervisors and employees, and where supervisors are actively engaged in supporting the self-efficacy development of subordinates. They also advised endeavouring to retain employees who demonstrate strong self-efficacy and trait competitiveness, through differential rewards (promotion and career opportunities).

Core Self-evaluations and the Importance of Co-worker Support

Karatepe et al. (2010) introduced the importance of Core Self-evaluations (CSE) to the study of engagement within hospitality contexts. CSEs are comparable to 'personal resources' in the extant literature (p. 62) and draw from JD-R (Bakker and Demerouti, 2008). CSEs include assumptions people hold concerning their own worthiness and capability, including 'self-esteem, generalized self-efficacy, locus of control and emotional stability' (Judge et al., 1998; 2005). Karatepe et al. called attention to the lack of 'empirical evidence regarding the mediating roles of personal resources on the relationship between job resources and work engagement' (p. 68), as well as more specifically within hospitality contexts and beyond Western borders. Accordingly, they investigated the moderating influence of personal resources (optimism and generalized self-efficacy), on the relationship between job resources (co-worker support) and work engagement, using data collected from 100 front-line, full-time employees ('front desk agents, food servers, guest relationship representatives and reservations agents') in two 4-star and one 5-star hotels in Iran (p. 65).

Scale items (p. 67) included: Co-worker support (CS), measured with five items from Hammer et al. (2004), for example, 'I feel I am accepted in my work group'; CSE was measured drawing on 12 items from Judge et al. (2003), for example, 'When I try, I generally succeed'; and engagement was measured using the UWES-17 (Schaufeli et al., 2002).

They found that co-worker support was positively associated with core-self evaluations, as well as vigour. Core-self evaluations were positively associated with vigour and dedication, and also partially mediated the effect of co-worker support on vigour and fully on dedication. Neither co-worker support nor core self-evaluation was significantly associated with absorption. In terms of demographics, interestingly, less educated frontline employees reported more positive core self-evaluations, while more educated employees reported greater rates of absorption.

In terms of managerial implications, they suggested that managers should seek to 'acquire and retain frontline employees with positive core self-evaluations' by using 'objective and standard tests to screen candidates' as well as by providing 'attractive career and promotional opportunities' for select employees (p. 69). They also suggested that training could be used to help develop social support.

Strategic Intention and Innovation

Slatten and Mehmetoglu (2011) surveyed 279 front-desk staff in hotels and restaurants in Southern Norway. Drawing on role theory, they sought to explore the effect of boundary-spanning roles (Bateson, 1989) and the potential 'role benefit' provided through 'role accumulation' (Sieber, 1974). An example of role benefit is a position that may serve as a 'springboard to a career' or an opportunity for profile. Within the hotel industry, the front desk is often perceived as such a position, with it being well-recognized as a training ground for future managers. Slatten and Mehmetoglu (2011, p. 92) were particularly interested in perceived 'status enhancement' through 'perceptions of career opportunities and professional visibility'. They also drew on Hackman and Oldham's (1980), Job Characteristics theory, focusing on 'autonomy'. They hypothesized a relationship between role benefit and engagement, and between role autonomy and engagement.

They also uniquely introduced the concept of 'strategic attention', defining it as the 'degree of implementation of a firm's strategy in a specific work role' (p. 94). They suggested that the extent to which an employee 'perceives a match between the strategy and his or her own contribution', the more engaged the employee will be (p. 94). In terms of the consequence of engagement, they focused on innovation, suggesting its study in service organizations has been 'neglected and marginal' (Miles, 2000, p. 371), while being important to the customization of the service experience.

Slatten and Mehmetoglu (2011, p. 98) developed a structured survey consisting of 13 statements modified from a number of instruments, including: role benefit (Keaveney and Nelson, 1993), for example, 'the job gives me an opportunity to show my skills'; autonomy (Babakus et al., 2003), for example, 'I have a great deal of freedom for how I can go about doing my job'; strategic attention (Liu, 2006), for example, 'The management has informed [me] about the company's vision and aim'; engagement (Schaufeli et al., 2002), for example, 'I view my job as being meaningful'; and innovation (Janssen, 2000), for example, 'I always try out innovative ideas at my work'.

Statistically significant associations were found for all three hypothesized antecedents of engagement – role benefit, autonomy and strategic attention – collectively explaining '45.2 percent of the variance in employee engagement' (p. 101), with perceived role benefit being the most important of the three. They also found that 'engagement alone explained [almost] 40 percent of the variance of innovative behavior' (p. 99).

This study underscored the importance of providing career paths – so employees can see personal benefit to their engagement – as well as supporting employees with respect to their development. The importance of providing employees with autonomy ('the necessary freedom, flexibility, independence and discretion') was also emphasized (p. 102). Further, they suggested that managers should seek to assess employee perceptions of the extent to which autonomy is being provided. With respect to strategy, they recommended involving employees in strategy development activities and explicitly linking strategic priorities to employee roles, as well as training employees on how to achieve strategic aims. For example, if enhanced customer service is a strategic objective, employees should be trained on what exactly that means, and how they might accomplish it.

Emotional Regulation (Deep and Surface Acting)

Yagil (2012) focused on employee emotional regulation. Her study involved data collected from 135 employee–customer dyads in various service-oriented businesses, including hotels (26 per cent of the participant pool), in Israel. Yagil studied the effects of employees' emotional regulation strategies (deep acting and surface acting) on customer outcomes (satisfaction and loyalty intentions), mediated by engagement and burnout. Drawing on the work of Hochschild (1983a), she suggested that surface acting involves employees displaying organizationally required emotions (such as happiness or enthusiasm), without internalizing or actually experiencing them, which can cause a number of negative outcomes, including stress, the depersonalization of customers (Grandey, 2000) or emotional dissonance (Abraham, 1998). Deep acting, on the other hand, involves internal transformation, such that the displayed emotions are actually felt (at least for the duration of the performance). Accordingly, deep acting may promote greater feelings of authenticity and motivation (Deci and Ryan, 1985).

Yagil (2012) hypothesized surface acting would be associated with burnout; deep acting with engagement; and that burnout would mediate the relationship between surface acting and customer outcomes and that engagement would mediate the relationship between deep acting and customer outcomes. The study used a number of well-established scales. Employee scales included: burnout, 22-item MBI (Maslach and Jackson, 1984); engagement, UWES-9 (Schaufeli et al., 2006); and emotion regulation, six items (Brotheridge and Lee, 2003), with three items measuring surface acting (for example, 'I pretend to have emotions that I don't really have') and three items measuring deep acting (for example, 'I try to actually experience the emotions that I must show') (Yagil, 2012, p. 158). Customer scales included a 7-item customer satisfaction survey (Dietz et al., 2004), including, for example, 'how satisfied are you with the service you received from that employee in terms of courtesy and friendliness?' (Yagil, 2012, pp. 158–9). Loyalty intentions included three statements (Gremler and Gwinner, 2000), such as 'I intend to continue doing business with this hotel over the next few years'.

Following an observed service interaction, the customer and service provider were approached and asked if they would be willing to participate in the study. If they were, they were each provided with a confidential survey and asked to focus their responses on the specific interaction. Surveys took approximately 15 to 20 minutes to complete.

The results showed a positive relationship between surface acting and burnout, and deep acting and engagement. Further, engagement was found to fully mediate the relationship between deep acting and customer outcomes, while burnout partially mediated the relationship between surface acting and customer outcomes. Yagil (2012) suggested that future research should replicate the study with a larger sample in order to allow for cross-industry comparisons. While she did not address organizational implications specifically, she did suggest that 'service employees may engage in deep acting by adopting an empathetic view of customers, reminding themselves of the meaning of their job, or recalling positive experiences.' Accordingly, employee training or coaching might support such dimensions.

Personal Demographic and Work Situation Characteristics

Burke et al.'s (2013) exploratory study involved 549 front-line employees working at fifteen 4- and 5-star hotels in Turkey. They suggested that personal demographic factors (such as gender) and work situation characteristics (such as organizational level) might predict engagement, as 'more men occupy supervisor and managerial jobs than women and women tend to be congregated in particular functions' (p. 193). They hypothesized that work engagement is associated with intention to quit (QT), job satisfaction (JS), employee voice (EV), work–family conflict (WFC) and family–work conflict (FWC).

Measures included the UWES-17 (Schaufeli et al., 2002); two-item intention to quit (Burke, 1991), for example, 'Are you currently looking for a different job in a different organization?'; 7-item job satisfaction (Kofodimos, 1993), for example, 'I feel challenged by my work'. In addition, work–family/family–work conflict was measured by 'a composite 9-item family–work conflict score' which combined three subscales (Carlson et al., 2000), for example, 'My work keeps me from my family activities more than I would like' and 'Tensions and anxiety from my family life often weaken my ability to do my job' (p. 196). Other measures included: 5-item scale for organizational support (Thompson et al., 1999), for example, 'In general, managers in this organization are quite accommodating for family-related needs'; 8-item descriptive scale for supervisor behaviour, for example, 'My supervisor spends time teaching and coaching his or her staff'; and 6-item scale for employee voice (adapted from Van Dyne and LePine, 1998), for example, 'I speak up in my workplace with ideas for new projects or changes in the way we do things'.

Burke et al. (2013) found that while, in general, personal demographic factors and work situation characteristics were weakly and inconsistently related with engagement, some unanticipated relationships were found. For example, 'married, frontline employees indicated higher levels of

Synopses of empirical studies 281

vigor and dedication' (p. 197). Also, 'older frontline workers and males indicated higher levels of absorption'.

In terms of outcomes, 'employees reporting higher levels of work engagement were generally more work satisfied, engaged in more empowered voice behavior, and were less likely to quit, and indicated lower levels of work–family and family–work conflict. Thus, work engagement was associated with more favourable individual and organizational outcomes' (p. 199). More specifically (pp. 198–9), males, front-line employees who were parents, and those reporting lower dedication, had greater intention to quit; front-line employees working in larger properties, indicating higher engagement, reported higher job satisfaction; front-line employees who supervised others and worked in larger properties, and indicated higher levels of vigour, reported greater employee voice; front-line employees who supervised others, occupied upper organizational levels, and displayed higher vigour, indicated less work–family conflict; front-line employees showing higher absorption indicated greater work–family conflict; front-line employees who supervised others, occupied upper organizational levels, worked in larger properties, and indicated higher levels of vigour reported lower levels of family–work conflict; front-line workers reporting higher level of absorption, indicated greater family–work conflict.

Interestingly, employees who supervised others, and who were situated at higher organizational levels or larger properties, indicated more favourable work outcomes, while front-line employees high in absorption reported greater conflict. Burke et al. (2013) suggested a potential 'dark side' to engagement and encouraged its further exploration.

Polychronicity and Person–Environment Fit

Karatepe et al. (2013) investigated the relationships between 'polychronicity', work engagement and job performance. Polychronicity refers to the extent to which people engage in 'multi-tasking' (performing more than one task at a time) or 'task-switching' (moving between tasks at distinct moments in time). They hypothesized a relationship between person–environment fit (Kristof-Brown et al., 2005), represented by polychronicity (task-switching) and engagement, as well as between engagement and performance outcomes. Drawing from Babin and Boles (1998, p. 82), they defined job performance as 'the level of productivity of an individual employee, relative to his or her peers, on several job-related behaviors and outcomes'. Extra-role performance was assessed as 'discretionary behaviors of contact employees in serving customers that extend beyond formal role requirements' (Bettencourt and Brown, 1997, p. 41).

Their study was based on the opinions of 185 front-line employees working at eleven 5-star hotels in Northern Cyprus ('front desk agents, door attendants, wait staff, bell attendants, concierges, and guest relations representatives') (p. 58). Polychronicity was operationalized using the 10-item Inventory of Polychronic Values (Bluedorn et al., 1999), for example, 'I like to juggle several activities at the same time' (Karatepe et al., 2013, p. 59). Engagement was measured using the UWES-9 (Schaufeli et al., 2006); for example, 'I am enthusiastic about my job'. Job performance was operationalized by five items from Babin and Boles (1998), for example, 'I get along better with customers than do others'. Extra-role performance was measured by five items from Bettencourt and Brown (1997); for example, 'I voluntarily assist customers even if it means going beyond job requirements' (Karatepe et al., 2013, p. 60).

Composite scores were tabulated for each variable, by averaging scores across items. The results supported the hypothesized relationships. Polychronicity was found to be positively and significantly associated with engagement. In addition, work engagement was positively and significantly associated with job performance and extra-role behaviour. However, the results explained less than 10 per cent of the variance in any one construct.

The findings reinforced the importance of hiring and retaining employees with the right 'person–job fit'. In the case of polychronicity, training programmes that help to build multi-tasking and task-switching skills may be of benefit.

Context: Back of House and Long-tenured Employees

Rigg et al. (2013) studied engagement in the Caribbean, where the lodging industry faces considerable employment challenges with respect to employee morale, productivity and absenteeism (Carter, 1997). They hypothesized a significant positive relationship between engagement and job satisfaction, and a negative relationship between both employee engagement and employee satisfaction, with intention to quit.

Their sample included 290 non-supervisory employees, from eight departments within nine mid-upper-scale hotels. Measures included the UWES-17 (Schaufeli et al., 2002). Job satisfaction was measured by a single item: 'Overall how satisfied are you with your organization as a place of work?' Intention to quit was measured by three items, adapted from Colarelli (1984); for example 'I frequently think of quitting my job' (p. 24). The hypotheses were supported. In analysing demographic variables, they found that employees who had no or low guest contact were less satisfied with their jobs and were more likely to want to quit their jobs.

Also, the longer employees had been at the hotel, the higher their intention was of quitting.

In terms of managerial implications, they suggested more attention needs to be paid to the experience of employees with no or little guest contact, such as the initiation of a rewards programme as well as improved management attitudes towards back of house employees. Long-tenured employees should be supported by additional development and career progression opportunities.

Emotional Dissonance, Service Climate and Well-being at Work

Carrasco et al. (2014) focused on emotional dissonance (Ashforth and Humphrey, 1993), service climate (Schneider et al., 1998), and employee well-being. Drawing on self-regulation theory (Babakus et al., 2009; Hochschild, 1983b) and COR theory (Hobfoll, 1988; 1989), they hypothesized a positive relationship between emotional dissonance (where emotions are acted rather than felt) with increased burnout and reduced engagement. Emotional dissonance was positioned as a consequence of 'surface' as opposed to 'deep acting' (Grandey, 2000) in the delivery of 'emotional labour' (Hochschild, 1983b; Zapf, 2002). Service climate (Schneider et al., 1998), positioned here as 'job resources' was hypothesized to be associated with 'well-being', including enhanced engagement and reduced burnout. Drawing from Schneider et al. (1998), service climate was defined as 'employee perceptions of the practices, procedures and behaviors rewarded, supported and expected with regard to customer service quality' (Carrasco et al., 2014, p. 950).

Their study included 512 employees (receptionists and waiters) working in 152 work units across 3- and 4-star hotels in Spain. Each property was designated as either a predominantly 'sun and sand' or 'conference' property. Measures included three items on emotional dissonance, FEWS scale (Zapf et al., 1999), for example, 'in your job, how often do you have to display positive emotions that do not correspond to what you feel in this situation?'; four items on service climate (Global Service Climate Scale) (Schneider et al., 1998), for example, 'Employees receive recognition and rewards for the delivery of superior work and service'; ten items on burnout (MBI-GS) (Schaufeli et al., 1996), including five items on exhaustion, for example 'I feel burnt out by my work' and five on cynicism, for example, 'I have become more cynical about whether my work contributes anything'; 11 items on engagement (adapted from UWES-17), including six items on vigour, for example, 'When I wake up in the morning, I feel like going to work' and five items on dedication, for example 'I am enthusiastic about my job' (p. 952).

Significant relationships were found as predicted. Service climate was found to be negatively related to burnout and positively to engagement, while emotional dissonance (an individual measure) was positively related to burnout and negatively to engagement. Of the two, work-unit service climate was the most important predictor.

These relationships were tested using an additive model that considered both an internal-individual construct (emotional dissonance) as well as a group-level construct (service climate). The authors concluded, 'emotional dissonance and service climate are additive significant predictors of burnout and engagement, describing two independent corridors' (p. 957). The managerial implications include: service climate informs employees about what is valued and can impact their well-being. Managers should support employees by contributing to the development of a positive service climate.

Work–Family Influence

Karatepe and Demir (2014) explored the relationship between work engagement, core self-evaluations (CSEs) (self-esteem, generalized self-efficacy, internal locus of control, and emotional stability) and work–family interactions. Specifically, they focused on work–family facilitation (WFF) and family–work facilitation (FWF), suggesting that work and family circumstances can be mutually beneficial; 'the extent to which participation at work (or home) is made easier by virtue of the experiences, skills, and opportunities gained or developed at home (or work)' (p. 308). They hypothesized that CSEs are positively related to work engagement, engagement is positively related to WFF and FWF, and that work engagement mediates the relationship between CSEs and WFF and FWF.

Karatepe and Demir (2014) collected usable data from 211 front-line hotel employees (front-desk agents, reservation agents, waiters/waitresses, bartenders, door attendants, guest relations representatives, bell attendants) working at eight international chain-based, 5-star hotels in Turkey, using a two-week delay to minimize common method bias (Buckley et al., 1990).

Measures included: 12 items, CSEs (Judge et al., 2003), for example, 'When I try, I generally succeed' and URES-9 (Schaufeli et al., 2006), for example, 'At my work, I feel bursting with energy'. WFF and FWF were measured with four items each (Grzywacz and Marks, 2000), for example, 'The things you do at work help you deal with personal and practical issues at home' and 'Talking with someone at home helps you deal with problems at work'.

Karatepe and Demir (2014) found significant results for all hypothesized relationships, noting that CSEs stimulate work engagement and support the effective integration of work and family roles. In addition, they also reported that married employees reported higher WFF and FWF. Age (older) and tenure (longer) were also associated with higher rates of WFF. Education was negatively associated with work engagement.

This work highlighted the importance of CSEs and the work–family dynamic. In terms of implications, the results underscored the importance of hiring and retaining the right people – in particular those high in CSEs (for which standardized assessments exist). For retention, they suggested investing in high-performance work practices (including financial incentives as well as training, job empowerment, job security and enhanced career opportunities) (pp. 319–20). Finally, and perhaps most uniquely, they recommended establishing a 'family-supportive work environment' potentially including mentorship for dealing with work–family nexus issues, life insurance support and 'on-site child care services, family leave, flexible work schedules' (p. 320).

The Positive Side of Challenge Stressors (When Mediated by Engagement)

Drawing from the transactional theory of stress (Lazarus and Folkman, 1984), Karatepe et al. (2014) hypothesized engagement as a mediating variable between challenge stressors (work overload and job responsibility) and valued job outcomes (affective organizational commitment and job performance). They suggested that challenge stressors could result in positive outcomes, due to enhanced employee motivation (LePine et al., 2005). Participants included 195 front-line hotel employees (including front-desk agents, guest relations representatives, food servers, bartenders, and bell attendants) from twelve 5-star hotels in Cyprus. Self-report employee data were collected with a two-week time lag, to protect from common method bias (Buckley et al., 1990). At time 1, demographic factors as well as work overload, job responsibility and work engagement data were assessed. At time 2, affective organizational commitment was measured. Supervisors additionally assessed job performance for each employee.

'Challenge stressors' was operationalized by four items for work overload (Price, 2001), such as 'my workload is heavy on my job' and four items for job responsibility (Hackman and Oldham, 1975), such as 'I feel a very high degree of personal responsibility for the work I do on this job'. Engagement was measured using the UWES-9 (Schaufeli et al., 2006). Organizational commitment was measured by five items from Mowday et al. (1979), such as 'I feel happy when I am working intensely' and job performance was measured by five items adapted from Babin and Boles (1998), such as 'this employee gets along better with customers than do others'. Karatepe et al. (2014) found support for all of their hypothesized relationships, reporting that employees who experience high rates of work overload and job responsibility are 'engaged in their work, and therefore, display positive job outcomes' (p. 14). More specifically, challenge stressors (work overload and job responsibility) were positively associated with work engagement. Also, work engagement was found to be positively associated with job outcomes (organizational commitment and job performance). In addition, job engagement was found to fully mediate the relationship between challenge stressors and job outcomes.

This research underscores the point that not all stress is bad. Workplace stressors may have a positive effect on employee engagement, performance outcomes and organizational commitment. They observed, 'that challenge stressors enhance work engagement suggests that employees who try to perform multiple tasks concurrently and have a considerable amount of personal responsibility on the job feel energetic, are proud of their work that is done, and are immersed in their work' (p. 19). They also suggested that job characteristics represented in the JD-R model could be classified into 'challenge stressors, hindrance stressors, and job resources' (p. 20). Their incorporation of supervisor ratings additionally addressed common method bias.

In terms of managerial implications, they advised that managers should provide employees with self-regulation training in order to help them deal with anxiety effectively, as well as empowerment and support ensuring 'the fulfillment of tasks successfully during busy times' (p. 21) and so that guest encounters are positive. Finally, they suggested pre-screening job candidates via standardized tests, in order to help select those with the abilities and skills to meet the demands of front-line work.

Psychological Factors: Employee Self-efficacy, Optimism, Resilience and Hope

Paek et al. (2015) suggested that Psychological Capital theory (PsyCap) (Luthans and Youssef, 2007; Nelson and Cooper, 2007; Sweetman and Luthans, 2010) was relevant to the study of employee engagement, along with COR (Hobfoll, 1989; 2001) and JD-R (Bakker and Demerouti, 2007; 2008). PsyCap has been theorized to consist of four constructs: self-efficacy, optimism, hope and resilience (Luthans et al., 2007). A 24-item PsyCap measure was developed by Luthans et al. (2007), with six items for each of the four factors (see Paek et al., 2015, p. 19). For example: self-efficacy, 'I feel confident analyzing a long-term problem to find a solution'; optimism, 'When things are uncertain for me at work I usually expect the best'; hope, 'If I find myself in a jam at work, I can think of many ways to get out of it'; and resilience, 'When I have a setback at work, I have trouble recovering from it and moving on'. Empirical research has found PsyCap to be associated with numerous personal and organizational outcomes, including work attitudes, job satisfaction, organizational commitment, trust and citizenship behaviour (see Paek et al., 2015, pp. 11–12).

Paek et al. (2015) surveyed 312 front-line employees across fifteen 5-star hotels in Korea, using a two-wave data collection protocol. Measures included UWES-9 (Schaufeli et al., 2002) and the 24-item PsyCap instrument. Morale was operationalized as job satisfaction ('the positive emotional state resulting from the appraisal of one's job or job experiences (Locke, 1976, p. 1300)' (p. 12), and organizational commitment was operationalized as 'an affective or emotional attachment to the organization such that the strongly committed individual identifies with, is involved, in and enjoys membership in the organization (Allen and Meyer, 1990, p. 2)' (p. 12). Job satisfaction was measured through eight items from Hartline and Ferrell (1996). Respondents were asked to assess their satisfaction with their job, co-workers, supervisor, hotel policies and support provided. Organizational commitment was assessed via an adaption of Allen and Meyer's (1990) 8-item scale, for example, 'I would be very happy to spend the rest of my career with this hotel' (Paek et al., 2015, p. 15). Paek et al. hypothesized direct positive effects between PsyCap and engagement, engagement and morale, and PsyCap and morale. They also suggested that engagement may play a mediating role between PsyCap and morale.

In terms of main effects, Paek et al. (2015) found a significant and positive relationship between PsyCap and work engagement, with PsyCap explaining 71.5 per cent of the variance in work engagement. Also, PsyCap and engagement both had a significant and positive impact on job satisfaction, jointly explaining 63.1 per cent of the variance. Similarly, PsyCap and engagement both had a significant and positive impact on affective organizational commitment, jointly explaining 70.1 per cent of the variance. With respect to mediating effects, they found that engagement significantly mediated the effects of PsyCap on both job satisfaction and commitment.

In other words, service employees with higher levels of self-efficacy, optimism, hope and resilience had higher levels of work engagement. They also reported higher levels of job satisfaction and commitment (but with commitment relying more on work engagement than did satisfaction). In terms of practical implications, Paek et al. (2015) advised developing selection and training programmes that might positively influence PsyCap factors. According to Avey et al. (2009), self-efficacy, hope, optimism and resilience can be enhanced through short training interventions. They also advocated for 'high-performance work practices', including empowerment and rewards, which have been found to support engagement (Karatepe, 2013). Such practices, they suggested, could support enhanced employee satisfaction and commitment.

Psychological Climate: Customer Orientation, Managerial Support, Internal Service and Communication

Lee and Ok's 2015 and 2016 studies were based on the same data set, 394 entry-level employees, supervisors and managers working in the US hotel industry across four areas of operation: rooms, food and beverage, sales and marketing, and administration. Participants were contacted via LinkedIn or by regional professional directories. Data were collected via an online survey.

For their 2015 study, Lee and Ok drew on Kahn (1990), COR (Hobfoll, 1989; 2001) and JD-R (Bakker and Demerouti, 2007; 2008). They adopted the UWES-9 (Schaufeli et al., 2002), and hypothesized a relationship between employee engagement with core self-evaluations (CSEs) (self-esteem, generalized self-efficacy, locus of control and emotional stability or neuroticism) and with psychological climate (PSC), defined below. They also hypothesized that psychological climate would moderate the relationship between core self-evaluations and engagement.

For scales (see p. 92), they used the 12-item Core self-evaluation scale (CSE) (Judge et al., 2003). A sample statement includes, 'I am capable of coping with most of my problems'. Psychological climate pertains to assumptions people make about their organization's practices (James and Tetrick, 1986). A PSC measurement instrument has been developed specifically for the hospitality industry, with 13 items pertaining to four dimensions: 'customer orientation, managerial support, internal service and information and communication' (Amenumey and Lockwood, 2008 as cited in Lee and Ok, 2015, p. 88). A sample statement for each of the four dimensions includes: 'My organization does a good job of keeping customers informed of changes that affect them'; 'Managers in my organization recognize and appreciate high quality work and service'; 'Other departments provide quality service to your unit'; and 'I have access to strategic information I need to do my job well' (p. 92).

Lee and Ok (2015) reported that psychometric assessment supported using engagement as a single-factor model. Of the demographic variables, only age was found to be significant in predicting engagement. Lee and Ok (2015) found support for their hypothesized relationship between engagement and CSE and between engagement and PSC (but not for the interaction effect). CSEs were found to predict 26 per cent of the variance in engagement. All four PSC dimensions also significantly related to engagement, increasing explained variance by another 16 per cent.

In terms of managerial implications, Lee and Ok (2015) suggested measuring CSE as part of employee selection procedures. Management practices that reinforce perceptions of self-esteem or self-efficacy (through encouragement, role modelling or the assignment of special projects) may help to strengthen the CSE of existing employees. Other implications include providing employees with empowered jobs, treating employees with respect, embracing two-way communication and showing appreciation. Lee and Ok (2015) also underscored the importance of providing employees with 'worthwhile jobs that add value to the organization' (p. 95).

Leadership Quality: Building Trusting Supervisor/Subordinate Relationships

Lee and Ok (2016, p. 135) drew on Herzberg et al.'s (1959) two-factor motivation theory and Blau's social exchange theory (1964) in hypothesizing a relationship between employee engagement and intrinsic rewards, the quality of leader–member exchange (Graen and Cashman, 1975), job satisfaction and affective organization commitment. Leader–member exchange (LMX) theory posits that leaders interact with subordinates differentially, on the basis of experiences over time, in which mutual trust, respect and obligation are developed, or not. In high quality relationships, subordinates perform well and leaders provide valued resources such as information, influence, autonomy and support. LMX was measured with a seven-item scale (Graen and Cashman, 1975), for example, 'My supervisor recognizes my potential'. In addition, the UWES-9 (Schaufeli and Bakker, 2003) was used, as well as: intrinsic rewards, four items (Lawler and Hall, 1970), for example, 'I feel a great sense of personal satisfaction when I do my job well'; job satisfaction, three items (Cammann et al., 1979), for example, 'In general, I like working at my organization'; and affective organizational commitment, six items (Affective Commitment Scale) (Meyer et al., 1993), for example 'I feel personally attached to my work organization' (p. 146).

Lee and Ok (2016) found significant positive associations as hypothesized, between engagement and job satisfaction, intrinsic rewards, organizational commitment and LMX quality, respectively, and further, between LMX quality and job satisfaction, and LMX quality and organizational commitment. In fact, over 70 per cent 'of variance in job satisfaction was explained by employee engagement and LMX quality' (p. 150). In addition, 'employee engagement, job satisfaction, and LMX quality together explained 66.99 percent of total variance in affective organizational commitment' (p. 150). From these results, the authors concluded that 'a good manager/employee relationship leads to job satisfaction' (p. 149) and 'employees satisfied with their job are likely to feel committed to their organization' (p. 149). No relationship was found between intrinsic rewards and job satisfaction when engagement was included in the model, suggesting that 'what accounts for job satisfaction may not be intrinsic rewards, but engaging in the job itself' (p. 157). Linking their results to other studies that have shown positive organizational impacts resulting from LMX quality, job satisfaction and organizational commitment, such as employee service behaviour, they concluded that 'employee engagement is a good way to manage employee service behaviors' (p. 157). More specifically, they recommended cultivating and supporting engagement by 'encouraging supervisors to establish and maintain a trust-based relationship with engaged employees' (p. 158). In support of the latter, they advised that the quality of supervisor/employee relationships should be included in performance reviews.

Supervisor Support and the Role of Gender

Suan and Nasurdin (2016) explored the role of supervisor support in enhancing employee engagement amongst 438 hotel employees in thirty-four 4- and 5-star hotels in Malaysia. They hypothesized a relationship between supervisor support and work engagement, with gender serving as a moderator (stronger for female employees). Measures included: Supervisor Support, four items (adapted from Susskind et al., 2003), for example, 'I can rely on my supervisor to serve customers in the appropriate manner' (p. 7). Work engagement was measured using the UWES-9 (Schaufeli et al., 2006).

Results found a significant relationship between supervisor support and engagement. In terms of gender, the results were the reverse of what was predicted, with the relationship between supervisor support and engagement being stronger for male employees (explaining 14 per cent of the variance). The researchers suggested that given the preponderance of male supervisors in Malaysian hotels, a male–female dynamic might be at play, with achievement-oriented supervisors overwhelming female subordinates who were perceived as more social.

The authors suggested training and mentoring programmes that help employees to more easily receive guidance and feedback from their supervisors, as well as training for the supervisors, in terms of empathy and listening skills. Finally, they recommended the implementation of employee-centred HR practices, such as flexible working hours and a compressed work week, to signal that management cares about employee well-being. They also recommended further sub-group analysis, assessing group level engagement.

Perceived Organizational Support (POS)

Liu et al. (2017) explored the effect of gender and self-efficacy on work engagement, as well as 'perceived organizational support' (POS) (Eisenberger et al., 1986). POS, explained by social exchange theory (Blau, 1964), refers to employee perceptions about the extent to which their employers are 'concerned with their well-being and value their contributions' (Eisenberger et al., 1986 as cited in Liu et al., 2017, p. 626). Their sample consisted of 149 surveys collected from 105 restaurants in a Midwest American town. Participants included both managers and non-managerial employees.

Liu et al. (2017) hypothesized a positive relationship between POS and work engagement (H1) and a negative relationship between engagement and employee intention to leave (H2). Drawing on Bandura (1986), they also suggested that self-efficacy would moderate the relationship between POS and engagement (H3); and between POS and intent to leave (H4), with the interaction effect of self-efficacy being stronger for women in both cases (H5). Measures included the 17-item UWES (Schaufeli et al., 2001); eight-item Global POS Scale (Eisenberger et al., 1986); 10-item General Self-Efficacy Scale (Schwarzer et al., 1997) and three-item intent to leave (Tsui et al., 1997).

They found support for H1, H3 and H5, with self-efficacy moderating the relationship between POS and engagement, only for women with low self-efficacy. H4 and H6 were rejected. There was no difference found between managers and non-managers. The authors concluded that employers should work to increase the self-efficacy of female employees (through verbal persuasion and vicarious experience). Further, they concluded that by working to increase employee engagement, turnover intention may be reduced.

FINDINGS

The research sites included: 13 hotels; two restaurants; and three mixed settings. The studies all collected data from multiple sites, including 3-, 4- and 5-star hotels and with one project differentiating between 'sun and sand' and 'conference' properties' (Carrasco et al., 2014). One study mentioned that the hotels in their study were part of a large international hotel chain (Karatepe and Demir, 2014). The geographic context was diverse, with six studies taking place in the Middle East; three in Asia; three in North America; two in Europe; and one in each of Africa, the Caribbean and South Africa.

The most common theoretical framework, in addition to JD-R, was COR theory (Hobfoll, 1989; 2001). Other theories, mentioned twice each, included: Core self-evaluations theory (Judge et al., 1997), Job characteristics theory (Hackman and Oldham, 1980), Self-regulation theory (Hochschild, 1983a) and Social exchange theory (Blau, 1964). Nine other theories were mentioned once. The dominant method was pen and paper surveys of front-line hotel employees (13 studies). Other studies included back of house employees, supervisors and customers. One study focused exclusively on managers (Burke et al., 2009). All of the studies used some version of the UWES: eight used the UWES-17 (Schaufeli et al., 2002); eight used the UWES-9 (Schaufeli et al., 2006); one used six items from the UWES-9 (Schaufeli et al., 2006); and one used 11 items from the UWES-17 (Schaufeli et al., 2002).

Statistically significant results were found for many, if not most, of the hypotheses. Job resources found to be significantly associated with engagement included role benefit, job autonomy and strategic attention (Slatten and Mehmetoglu, 2011; V&D only); employee voice (Burke et al., 2013); service climate (Carrasco et al., 2014); Psychological Service Climate (PSC) (Lee and Ok, 2015); intrinsic rewards and leader–member exchange (Lee and Ok, 2016); supervisor support (Suan and Nasurdin, 2016); and perceived organizational support (POS) (Liu et al., 2017). Various psychological dimensions were also found to be associated with engagement, including trait competitiveness (Karatepe and Olugbade, 2009); CSEs (Karatepe and Demir, 2014; Lee and Ok, 2015), and PsyCap factors (Paek et al., 2015).

In terms of consequences, support for health, employee motivational outcomes and organizational outcomes were found. For example, Burke et al. (2009) found that managers with higher levels of dedication reported lower levels of exhaustion, psychosomatic symptoms and work–family conflict, while engaged employees reported greater: job satisfaction (V,D), career satisfaction (D) and intention to stay (D). Absorption, however, was associated with higher levels of stress, exhaustion, psychosomatic symptoms and work–family conflict. Engagement was also found to be associated with innovative behaviour (Slatten and Mehmetoglu, 2011); job performance and extra-role customer service behaviour (Karatepe et al., 2013) and organizational commitment and job performance (Karatepe et al., 2014).

DISCUSSION

On the basis of this review, employee engagement has been found to be associated with a number of important factors, some specific to individual employees, others specific to the nature of the job, to the climate of the organization or the quality of the leadership. Associated outcomes included enhanced job satisfaction, employee performance and customer loyalty.

Recommended organizational strategies for enhancing employee engagement include screening prospective employees for relevant personality factors, providing meaningful, autonomous jobs and supportive leadership.

Future research should introduce additional contextual variety (geography and type of business) as well as greater participant variety (back of house employees, managers, customers). More research is needed that explores the effect of leadership and climate, as well as job demands. The industry was characterized in many of the studies reviewed as having particularly negative working conditions and poor compensation practices. The potential impact of these factors needs to be better understood. Research on the 'dark side' of absorption was also suggested (Burke et al., 2009).

Methodologically, collecting self-report data from front-line employees at one point in time has been the dominant approach. Future studies should consider collecting longitudinal data (in order to test causal effects) as well as revisiting the UWES in order to ensure it is representative of the underlying conceptualizing of the construct. A grounded theory approach could help to develop an instrument specifically for assessing engagement in hospitality and tourism contexts.

REFERENCES

Abraham, R. (1998), 'Emotional dissonance in organizations: antecedents, consequences and moderators', *Psychology Monographs*, **124**, 229–46.

Allen, N.J. and J.P. Meyer (1990), 'The measurement and antecedents of affective, continuance, and normative commitment to the organization', *Journal of Occupational Psychology*, **63** (1), 1–18.

Amenumey, E.K. and A. Lockwood (2008), 'Psychological climate and psychological empowerment: an exploration in a luxury UK hotel group', *Tourism and Hospitality Research*, **8**, 265–81.

Ashforth, B. and R. Humphrey (1993), 'Emotional labor in service rules: the influence of identity', *The Academy of Management Review*, **18** (1), 88–115.

Avey, J.B., F. Luthans and S.M. Jensen (2009), 'Psychological capital: a positive resource for combating employee stress and turnover', *Human Resource Management*, **48** (5), 677–93.

Babakus, E., U. Yavas and N.J. Ashill (2009), 'The role of customer orientation as a

294 Handbook of HRM in the tourism and hospitality industries

moderator of the job demand–burnout–performance relationship: a surface-level trait perspective', *Journal of Retailing*, **85** (4), 480–92.

Babakus, E., U. Yavas, O.M. Karatepe and T. Avci (2003), 'The effect of management commitment to service quality in employees' affective and performance outcomes,' *Journal of the Academy of Marketing Science*, **31** (3), 272–86.

Babin, B. and J.S. Boles (1998), 'Employee behavior in a service environment: a model and test of potential differences between men and women', *Journal of Marketing*, **62** (2), 77–91.

Bakker, A.B. and E. Demerouti (2007), 'The job demands-resources model: state of the art', *Journal of Management Psychology*, **22**, 309–28.

Bakker, A.B. and E. Demerouti (2008), 'Towards a model of work engagement', *Career Development International*, **13** (3), 209–23.

Bandura, A. (1986), *Social Foundations of Thought and Action*, Englewood Cliffs, NJ: Prentice Hall.

Bateson, J.E.G. (1989), *Managing Services Marketing: Text and Reading*, Chicago: Dryden.

Beehr, T.A., L.A. King and D.W. King (1990), 'Social support and occupational stress: talking to supervisors', *Journal of Vocational Behavior*, **36** (1), 61–81.

Bettencourt, L.A. and S.W. Brown (1997), 'Contact employees: relationships among workplace fairness, job satisfaction and prosocial service behaviors', *Journal of Retailing*, **73** (1), 39–61.

Blau, P.M. (1964), *Exchange and Power in Social Life*, New York: Wiley.

Bluedorn, A.C., T.J. Kalliath, M.J. Strube and G.D. Martin (1999), 'Polychronicity and the inventory of polychromic values (IPV): the development of an instrument to measure a fundamental dimension of organizational culture', *Journal of Managerial Psychology*, **14** (3/4), 205–30.

Brotheridge, C.M. and R.T. Lee (2003), 'Development and validation of the emotional labour scale', *Journal of Occupational and Organization Psychology*, **76**, 365–79.

Brown, K. and T.R. Mitchell (1988), 'Performance obstacles for direct and indirect labour in high technology manufacturing', *International Journal of Production Research*, **26**, 1819–32.

Brown, K. and T.R. Mitchell (1991), 'A comparison of just-in-time and batch manufacturing: the role of performance obstacles', *Academy of Management Journal*, **34**, 906–17.

Brown, S.P., W.L. Cron and J.S. Slocum, Jr (1998), 'Effects of trait competitiveness and perceived intraorganizational competition on salesperson goal setting and performance', *Journal of Marketing*, **62** (October), 88–98.

Buckley, M.R., J.A Cote and S.M. Comstock (1990), 'Measurement errors in behavioral sciences: the case of personality/attitude research', *Educational Psychology Measures*, **50** (3), 447–74.

Burke, R.J. (1991), 'Early work and career experiences of female and male managers and professionals: reasons for optimism?', *Canadian Journal of Administrative Sciences*, **8** (4), 224–30.

Burke, R., J. Koyuncu, L. Fiksenbaum and Y. Tekin (2013), 'Antecedents and consequences of work engagement among frontline employees in Turkish hotels', *Journal of Transnational Management*, **18**, 191–203.

Burke, R.J., M. Koyuncu, W. Jing and L. Fiksenbaum (2009), 'Work engagement among hotel managers in Beijing, China: antecedents and consequences', *Tourism Review*, **64** (3), 4–18.

Cammann, C., M. Fichman, D. Henkins and J. Klesh (1979), *The Michigan Organizational Assessment Questionnaire* (unpublished manuscript), Ann Arbor, MI: University of Michigan.

Carlson, D., J. Kacmar and L. Williams (2000), 'Construction and initial validation of a multidimensional measure of work–family conflict', *Journal of Vocational Behavior*, **56**, 249–76.

Carrasco, H., V. Martinez-Tur, C. Moliner, J.M. Peiro and C. Ramis (2014), 'Linking emotional dissonance and service climate to well-being at work: a cross-level analysis', *Universitas Psychologica*, **13** (3), 947–60.

Carter, K.L. (1997), *Why Workers Won't Work: The Worker in a Developing Economy: A Case Study of Jamaica*, London: Macmillan.

Colarelli, S.M. (1984), 'Methods of communication and mediating processes in realistic job previews', *Journal of Applied Psychology*, **69** (4), 633–42.

Deci, E.L. and R.M. Ryan (1985), 'The general causality orientations scale: self-determination in personality', *Journal of Research in Personality*, **19**, 109–34.

Dietz, J., S.D. Pugh and J.W. Wiley (2004), 'Service climate effects on customer attitudes: an examination of boundary conditions', *Academy of Management Journal*, **47**, 81–92.

Edwards, J.R. (1988), 'The determinants and consequences of coping with stress', in C.L. Cooper and R. Payne (eds), *Causes, Coping and Consequences of Stress at Work* (pp. 233–63), New York: Wiley.

Edwards, J.R. (1992), 'A cybernetic theory of stress, coping, and well-being in organizations', *Academy of Management Review*, **17**, 238–74.

Edwards, J.R. and C.L. Cooper (1988), 'The impacts of positive psychological states on physical health: a review and theoretical framework', *Social Science and Medicine*, **27**, 1447–59.

Eisenberger, R., R. Huntington, S. Hutchison and D. Sowa (1986), 'Perceived organizational support', *Journal of Applied Psychology*, **71** (3), 500–507.

Goldberg, D. (1979), *Manual of the General Health Questionnaire*, London: NFER Nelson.

Graen, G.B. and J.F. Cashman (1975), 'A role-making model in formal organizations: a developmental approach', in J.G. Hunt and L.L. Larson (eds), *Leadership Frontiers* (pp. 143–65), Kent, OH: Kent State University Press.

Grandey, A.A. (2000), 'Emotion regulation in the workplace: a new way to conceptualize emotional labor', *Journal of Occupational Health Psychology*, **5** (1), 95–110.

Greenhaus, J.J., S. Parasuraman and W. Wormley (1990), 'Organizational experiences and career success of black and white managers', *Academy of Management Journal*, **33** (1), 64–86.

Gremler, D.D. and K.P. Gwinner (2000), 'Customer–employee rapport in service relationships', *Journal of Service Research*, **3**, 82–104.

Grzywacz, J.G. and N.F. Marks (2000), 'Reconceptualizing the work–family interface: an ecological perspective on the correlates of positive and negative spillover between work and family', *Journal of Occupational Health Psychology*, **5** (1), 111–26.

Hackman, J.R. and G.R. Oldham (1975), 'Development of the job diagnostic survey', *Journal of Applied Psychology*, **60** (2), 159–70.

Hackman, J.R. and G.R. Oldham (1980), *Work Redesign*, Reading, MA: Addison-Wesley.

Hammer, T.H., P.O. Saksvik, K. Nytro, H. Torvatn and M. Bayazit (2004), 'Expanding the psychosocial work environment: workplace norms and work–family conflict as correlates of stress and health', *Journal of Occupational Health Psychology*, **9** (1), 83–97.

Hartline, M.D. and O.C. Ferrell (1996), 'The management of customer-contact service employees: an empirical investigation', *Journal of Marketing*, **60** (4), 52–70.

Herzberg, F., B. Mausner and B. Snyderman (1959), *The Motivation to Work*, New York: Wiley.

Hobfoll, S.E. (1988), *The Ecology of Stress*, New York: Hemisphere.

Hobfoll, S.E. (1989), 'Conservation of resources: a new attempt at conceptualizing stress', *American Psychologist*, **44** (3), 513–24.

Hobfoll, S.E. (2001), 'The influence or culture, community, and the nested-self in the stress process: advancing conservation of resources theory', *Applied Psychology: An International Review*, **50**, 337–70.

Hochschild, A.R. (1983a)/(2003), *The Managed Heart: Commercialization of Human Feeling*, Berkeley, CA: University of California Press.

Hochschild, A.R. (1983b), 'Comment on Kemper's "social constructionist and positivist approaches to the sociology of emotions"', *American Journal of Sociology*, **89** (2), 432–4.

James, L.R. and L.E. Tetrick (1986), 'Confirmatory analytic test of three causal models relating job perceptions to job satisfaction', *Journal of Applied Psychology*, **71**, 77–82.

Janssen, O. (2000), 'Job demands, perceptions of effort-reward fairness and innovative work behaviour', *Journal of Occupational and Organizational Psychology*, **73**, 287–302.

Jones, C.R. (1986), 'Socialization tactics, self-efficacy, and newcomers' adjustments to organizations', *Academy of Management Journal*, **29** (2), 262–79.

Judge, T.A. (2009), 'Core self-evaluations and work success', *Current Directions in Psychological Science*, **18** (1), 58–62.

Judge, T.A., E.A. Locke and C.C. Durham (1997), 'The dispositional causes of job satisfaction: a core evaluations approach', *Research in Organizational Behavior*, **19**, 151–88.

Judge, T.A., J.E. Bono, A. Erez and E.A. Locke (2005), 'Core self-evaluations and job and life satisfaction: the role of self-concordance and goal attainment', *Journal of Applied Psychology*, **90** (2), 257–68.

Judge, T.A., A. Erez, J.E. Bono and C.J. Thoresen (2003), 'The core self-evaluations scale: development of a measure', *Personnel Psychology*, **56** (2), 303–31.

Judge, T.A., E.A. Locke, C.C. Durham and A.N. Kluger (1998), 'Dispositional effects on job and life satisfaction: the role of core evaluations', *Journal of Applied Psychology*, **83** (10), 17–34.

Kahn, W.A. (1990), 'Psychological conditions of personal engagement and disengagement at work', *Academy of Management Journal*, **33** (4), 692–724.

Karatepe, O.M. (2013), 'High-performance work practices and hotel employee performance: the mediation of work engagement', *International Journal of Hospitality Management*, **32** (1), 132–40.

Karatepe, O.M. and E. Demir (2014), 'Linking core self-evaluations and work engagement to work–family facilitation: a study in the hotel industry', *International Journal of Contemporary Hospitality Management*, **26** (2), 307–23.

Karatepe, O.M. and O.A. Olugbade (2009), 'The effects of job and personal resources on hotel employees' work engagement', *International Journal of Hospitality Management*, **28**, 504–12.

Karatepe, O.M., S. Keshavarz and S. Nejati (2010), 'Do core self-evaluations mediate the effect of coworker support on work engagement? A study of hotel employees in Iran', *Journal of Hospitality and Tourism Management*, **17**, 62–71.

Karatepe, O.M., E. Beirami, M. Bouzari and H.P. Safavi (2014), 'Does work engagement mediate the effects of challenge stressors on job outcomes? Evidence from the hotel industry', *International Journal of Hospitality Management*, **36**, 14–22.

Karatepe, O.M., G. Karadas, A.K. Azar and N. Naderiadib (2013), 'Does work engagement mediate the effect of polychronicity on performance outcomes? A study in the hospitality industry in Northern Cyprus', *Journal of Human Resources in Hospitality & Tourism*, **12**, 52–70.

Katz, D. and R.L. Kahn (1978), *The Social Psychology of Organizations*, New York: John Wiley & Sons.

Keaveney, S.M. and J.E. Nelson (1993), 'Coping with organizational role stress: intrinsic motivation orientation, perceived role benefit, and psychological withdrawal', *Journal of Academy of Marketing Science*, **21** (2), 113–24.

Kofodimos, J. (1993), *Balancing Act*, San Francisco, CA: Jossey-Bass.

Kristof-Brown, A.L., R.D. Zimmerman and E.C. Johnson (2005), 'Consequences of individuals' fit at work: a meta-analysis of person–job, person–organization, person–group, and person–supervisor fit', *Personnel Psychology*, **58** (2), 281–342.

Lawler, E.E. and D.T. Hall (1970), 'Relationship of job characteristics to job involvement, satisfaction, and intrinsic motivation', *Journal of Applied Psychology*, **54**, 305–12.

Lazarus, R.S. and S. Folkman (1984), *Psychological Stress and the Coping Process*, New York: Springer.

Lee, J. and C. Ok (2015), 'Drivers of work engagement: an examination of core self-evaluations and psychological climate among hotel employees', *International Journal of Hospitality Management*, **44**, 84–98.

Lee, J. and C. Ok (2016), 'Hotel employee work engagement and its consequences', *Journal of Hospitality Marketing & Management*, **25**, 133–66.

LePine, J.A., N.P. Podsakoff and M.A. LePine (2005), 'A meta-analytic test of the challenge stressor–hindrance stressor framework: an explanation for inconsistent relationships among stressors and performance', *Academy of Management Journal*, **48** (5), 764–75.

Liu, C.M. (2006), 'The effect of organizational vision on service quality delivery', *The Service Industries Journal*, **26** (8), 849–59.

Liu, J., S. Cho and E.D. Putra (2017), 'The moderating effect of self-efficacy and gender on work engagement for restaurant employees in the United States', *International Journal of Contemporary Hospitality Management*, **29** (1), 624–42.

Locke, E.A. (1976), 'The nature and causes of job satisfaction', in M.D. Dunnette (ed.), *Handbook of Industrial and Organizational Psychology* (pp. 1297–349), Chicago, IL: Rand McNally College Publishing.

Luthans, F. and C.M. Youssef (2007), 'Emerging positive organizational behavior', *Journal of Management*, **33** (3), 321–49.

Luthans, F., B.J. Avolio, J.B. Avey and S.M. Norman (2007), 'Positive psychological capital: measurement and relationship with perfomance and satisfaction', *Personnel Psychology*, **60** (3), 541–72.

Martinez-Tur, V., J. Ramos, J.M. Peiro and E. Buades (2001), 'Relationships among perceived justice, customers' satisfaction, and behavioral intentions: the moderating role of gender', *Psychological Reports*, **88**, 805–11.

Maslach, C. and S.E. Jackson (1984), 'Burnout in organizational settings', *Applied Social Psychology Annual*, **5**, 133–53.

Maslach, C. and S.E. Jackson (1986), *The Maslach Burnout Inventory* (2nd edn), Palo Alto, CA: Consulting Psychologists Press.

Maslach, C., S.E. Jackson and M.P. Leiter (1996), *The Maslach Burnout Inventory* (3rd edn), Palo Alto, CA: Consulting Psychologists Press.

Meyer, J.P., N.J. Allen and C.A. Smith (1993), 'Commitment to organizations and occupations: extension and test of a three-component conceptualization', *Journal of Applied Psychology*, **78**, 538–51.

Miles, L. (2000), 'Services innovation: coming of age in the knowledge-based economy', *International Journal of innovation Management*, **4** (4), 371–89.

Mowday, R.T., R.M. Steers and L.W. Porter (1979), 'The measurement of organizational commitment', *Journal of Vocational Behavior*, **14** (2), 224–47.

Nelson, D. and C.L. Cooper (2007), *Positive Organizational Behaviour: Accentuating the Positive at Work*, Thousand Oaks, CA: Sage Publications.

Paek, S., M. Schuckert, T.T. Kim and G. Lee (2015), 'Why is hospitality employees' psychological capital important? The effects of psychological capital on work engagement and employee morale', *International Journal of Hospitality Management*, **50**, 9–26.

Parasuraman, A., V.A. Zeithaml and L.L. Berry (1988), 'SERVQUAL: a multiple-item scale for measuring consumer perceptions of service quality', *Journal of Retailing*, **64**, 12–40.

Peterson, D. and M. Seligman (2004), *Character Strengths and Virtues: A Handbook and Classification*, New York: Oxford University Press.

Pienaar, J. and S.A. Willemse (2008), 'Burnout, engagement, coping and general health of service employees in the hospitality industry', *Tourism Management*, **29**, 1053–63.

Price, J.L. (2001), 'Reflection on the determinants of voluntary turnover', *International Journal of Manpower*, **22** (7), 600–24.

Price, L.L., E.J. Arnould and P. Tiemey (1995), 'Going to extremes: managing service encounters and assessing provide performance', *Journal of Marketing*, **59**, 83–97.

Quinn, R.P. and L.J. Shepard (1974), *The 1972–73 Quality of Employment Survey*, Institute of Social Research, University of Michigan, Ann Arbor, MI.

Rigg, J., J. Day and H. Adler (2013), 'An empirical analysis of Jamaican hotel employees' engagement, job satisfaction, and quitting intentions', *Consortium Journal of Hospitality and Tourism*, **18** (2), 17–33.

Salanova, M., S. Agut and J.M. Peiro (2005), 'Linking organizational resources and work engagement to employee performance and customer loyalty: the mediation of service climate', *Journal of Applied Psychology*, **90** (6), 1217–27.

Schaufeli, W.B. and A.B. Bakker (2003), *UWES-Utrecht Work Engagement Scale: Test Manual*, Utrecht University, Department of Psychology.
Schaufeli, W.B., A.B. Bakker and M. Salanova (2006), 'Measurement of work engagement with a short questionnaire: a cross-national study', *Educational and Psychological Measurement*, **66** (4), 701–16.
Schaufeli, W.B., M.P. Leiter, C. Maslach and S.E. Jackson (1996), 'The Maslach Burnout Inventory – General Survey', in C. Maslach, S.E. Jackson and M.P. Leiter (eds), *Maslach Burnout Inventory — Test Manual* (3rd edn) (pp. 19–26), Palo Alto, CA: Consulting Psychologists Press.
Schaufeli, W.B., M. Salanova, V. Gonzales-Roma and A.B. Bakker (2002), 'The measurement of engagement and burnout: a two-sample confirmatory factor-analytic approach', *Journal of Happiness Studies*, **3**, 71–92.
Schaufeli, W.B., R. Taris, P. Le Blanc, M. Peetrs, A. Bakke and J. De Jonge (2001), 'Can work produce health? The quest for the engaged worker', *Psychology*, **36**, 422–8.
Schneider, B., S.S. White and M.C. Paul (1998), 'Linking service climate and customer perceptions of service quality: tests of a causal model', *Journal of Applied Psychology*, **83** (2), 150–63.
Schwarzer, R., J. Babler, J. Kwiatek, P. Schroder and J. Zhang (1997), 'The assessment of optimistic self-beliefs: comparison of the German, Spanish, and Chinese version of the general self-efficacy scale', *Applied Psychology*, **46** (1), 69–88.
Sieber, S.D. (1974), 'Toward a theory of role accumulation', *American Sociological Review*, **39**, 567–78.
Slatten, T. and J. Mehmetoglu (2011), 'Antecedents and effects of engaged frontline employees: a study from the hospitality industry', *Managing Service Quality*, **21** (1), 88–107.
Spence, J.T. and A.S. Robbins (1992), 'Workaholism: definition, measurement, and preliminary results', *Journal of Personality Assessment*, **58** (1), 160–78.
Suan, C.L. and A.M. Nasurdin (2016), 'Supervisor support and work engagement of hotel employees in Malaysia: is it different for men and women?', *Gender in Management: An International Journal*, **31** (1), 2–18.
Susskind, A.M., K.M. Kacmar and C.P. Borchgrevink (2003), 'Customer service providers' attitudes relating to customer service and customer satisfaction in the custom–service exchange', *Journal of Applied Psychology*, **8** (1), 179–87.
Swan, J.E. and R.L. Oliver (1989), 'Post purchase communications by consumer', *Journal of Retailing*, **65**, 516–33.
Sweetman, D. and F. Luthans (2010), 'The power of positive psychology: psychological capital and work engagement', in A.B. Bakker and M.P. Leiter (eds), *Work Engagement: A Handbook of Essential Theory and Research* (pp. 54–68), New York: Psychology Press.
Thompson, C., L.L. Beuvais and K.S. Lyness (1999), 'When work-family benefits are not enough: the influence of work-family culture in benefit utilization, organizational attachment and work-family conflict', *Journal of Vocational Behavior*, **54**, 392–415.
Tsui, A.S., J.L. Pearce, L.W. Porter and A.M. Tripoli (1997), 'Alternative approaches to the employee–organization relationship: does investment in employees pay off?', *Academy of Management Journal*, **40** (5), 1089–121.
Van Dyne, L. and J.A. LePine (1998), 'Helping and voice extra-role behaviors: evidence of construct and predictive validity', *Academy of Management Journal*, **41**, 108–19.
Wanous, J.P., A.E. Reichers and M.J. Hudy (1997), 'Overall job satisfaction: how good are single-item measures?', *Journal of Applied Psychology*, **82** (2), 247–52.
Xanthopoulou, D., A.B. Bakker, E. Demerouti and W.B. Schaufeli (2007), 'The role of personal resources in the job demands-resources model', *International Journal of Stress Management*, **14**, 121–41.
Xanthopoulou, D., A.B. Bakker, E. Heuven, E. Demerouti and W.B. Schaufeli (2008), 'Working in the sky: a diary study on work engagement among flight attendants', *Journal of Occupational Health Psychology*, **13** (4), 345–56.
Yagil, D. (2012), 'The mediating role of engagement and burnout in the relationship between

employees' emotion regulation strategies and customer outcomes', *European Journal of Work and Organizational Psychology*, **21** (1), 150–68.

Zapf, D. (2002), 'Emotion work and psychological well-being: a review of the literature and some conceptual considerations', *Human Resource Management Review*, **12** (2), 237–68.

Zapf, D., C. Vogt, C. Seifert, H. Mertini and A. Isic (1999), 'Emotional work as a source of stress: the concept and development of an instrument', *European Journal of Work and Organizational Psychology*, **8** (3), 371–400.

APPENDIX

Table 11A.1 Summary of selected empirical research on engagement in hospitality and tourism (2007–17)

Author (Year)	Sample (FL=Front-Line)	Theory (in addition to JD-R)	Scales/Measures	Proposed Relationships	Findings and Implications Vi= Vigour; De=Dedication; Ab=Absorption
Salanova et al. (2005)	Spain; 114 service units (58 hotels, 56 restaurants); 342 FL employees; 1140 customers	Job characteristics theory (Hackman and Oldham, 1980); COR theory (Hobfoll, 2001)	Organizational Resources Scale (Brown and Mitchell, 1988, 1991); Global Service Climate Scale (Schneider et al., 1998); SERVQUAL Empathy Scale (Parasuraman et al., 1988); Service Provider Excellence Scale (Price et al., 1995); Customer intention to return (Martinez-Tur et al., 2001; Swan and Oliver, 1989); **UWES-17 (Schaufeli et al., 2002)**	A = Organizational resources (OR) (training, autonomy and technology) M = Work engagement (WE) M = Service climate (SC) M = Employee performance (EP) C = Customer loyalty (CL)	Mean engagement scores: Vi, 5.28; De, 4.43 and Ab, 4.02 Hypotheses largely supported: WE fully mediated OR & SC; EP fully mediated SC & CL Implications: Provide resources; build and sustain a service climate
Pienaar and Willemse (2008)	South Africa 16 restaurants & coffee shops; 150 FL employees	Emotional labour (Hochschild, 1983a/2003); Burnout (Maslach and Jackson, 1984);	MBI-HSS (Maslach & Jackson, 1986); Cybernetic Coping Scale (CSS) (Edwards, 1988); General Health Questionnaire (GHQ) (Goldberg, 1979); **UWES-17 (Schaufeli et al., 2002)**	A = Psychological well-being, Burnout and Engagement M = Coping strategies (CS) C = General health (GH)	Mean engagement scores: Vi, 4.15; De, 4.03; Ab, 3.5 Hypotheses partially supported: 28% of variance in GH predicted by burnout & CS Implications: Provided employee stress reduction & assertiveness training

		Theory	Measures	Variables	Findings
Burke et al. (2009)	Beijing China; 309 managers working in 19 hotels (3-, 4- and 5-star)	Cybernetic theory of stress, coping and well-being (Edwards, 1988)	UWES-17 (**Schaufeli et al., 2002**)	Work engagement (WE) C1 = Work outcomes (WO): job satisfaction (JS), career satisfaction (CS), job stress (ST) and intention to quit (QT); C2 = Psychological well-being (PWB): psychosomatic symptoms (PS), emotional exhaustion (EX); C3 = Work–family and family–work conflict (WFC/FWC); C4 = Life satisfaction (LS)	WE was sig. predictor for all four WOs (JS, CS, ST, QT): De & Vi, greater JS; De & Vi, less QT; De greater JS, PWB less < ST & EX; Ab greater ST&PS&WFC&QT; WE was a stronger predictor of WO than PWB; Implications: Foster WE for greater work outcomes and personal well-being, but be wary of 'absorption' (potential negative effects)
Karatepe and Olugbade (2009)	Nigeria; 4 hotels (1, 4-star; 3, 5-star); 130 full-time, FL employees	COR theory (Hobfoll, 1989, 2001);	Supervisor support (Behr et al., 1990); Trait competitiveness (Brown et al., 1998); Self-efficacy (Jones, 1986); UWES-17 (**Schaufeli et al., 2002**)	A1 =Job resources (supervisor support – SS); Personal resources (trait competitiveness – TC); A2 = Personal resources (Self-efficacy – SE); C = work engagement (WE)	Hypotheses partially supported: SS & TC +ve SE; TC +ve WE; SE +ve Ab; Differences by gender and seniority: females less SS; longer tenure less Vi

Table 11A.1 (continued)

Author (Year)	Sample (FL=Front-Line)	Theory (in addition to JD-R)	Scales/Measures	Proposed Relationships	Findings and Implications Vi= Vigour; De=Dedication; Ab=Absorption
					Implications: Create a supportive work environment, support self-efficacy development; retain employees who demonstrate self-efficacy and trait competitiveness, through differential rewards (promotion and career opportunities)
Karatepe et al. (2010)	Iran; 2, 4-star & 1, 5-star hotels; 100 full-time, FL employees	Core self-evaluations theory (CSE) (Judge et al., 1997, 2005);	Co-worker support (CS), (Hammer et al., 2004); CSE (Judge et al., 2003); UWES-17 (**Schaufeli et al., 2002**)	A = Job resources (co-worker support) (CS) M = Personal resources (CSEs) (optimism and generalized self-efficacy) C = Work engagement	Mean engagement scores: Vi, 3.13; De, 3.33; Ab, 3.14 CS +ve CSEs & Vi; CSEs +ve Vi & De Neither CS nor CSEs were significantly associated with Ab. < educated employees +ve CSEs; > educated employees +ve Ab Implications: Acquire and retain employees with +ve CSEs by using standard tests and providing career and promotional opportunities; use training to develop social support amongst co-workers

Study	Location/sample	Theory	Scales/measures	Variables	Results/implications
Slatten and Mehmetoglu (2011)	Norway; Hotels and restaurants; 279 FL employees	Role Theory (Katz and Kahn, 1978); Job Characteristics theory (Hackman and Oldham, 1980)	Role benefit (Keaveney and Nelson, 1993); Autonomy (Babakus et al., 2003); Strategic attention (Liu, 2006); Innovation (Janssen, 2000); UWES-6 (adapted from Schaufeli et al., 2002)	Work engagement (WE) A1 = Role benefit (RB) A2 = Job autonomy (AU) A3 = Strategic attention (SA) C2 = Innovative behaviour (IB)	RB, AU & SA all +ve with WE, explaining approx. 45% of variance WE, with RB being most important; WE +ve IB, explaining approx. 40% of variance. Implications: Provide career paths, development and autonomy; assess employee perceptions; involve employees in strategy development; explicitly link goals to employee roles; train employees on how to achieve strategic aims.
Yagil (2012)	Israel; 135 FL employee–customer dyads in various service businesses, (26% hotels)	Emotional regulation (deep & surface acting) (Hochschild 1983a; Emotional dissonance (Abraham, 1998); Motivation theory (Deci and Ryan, 1985)	Employee scales: MBI-HSS (Maslach and Jackson, 1984); UWES-9 (Schaufeli et al., 2006); emotional regulation (Brotheridge and Lee, 2003) Customer scales: customer satisfaction (Dietz et al., 2004); customer loyalty (Gremler and Gwinner, 2000)	A = Emotional regulation: surface acting (SA) and deep acting (DA) M1 = Work engagement (WE) M2 = Burnout (BO) CO = Customer outcomes: satisfaction and loyalty intentions	Mean engagement score: 4.83 SA +ve BO; DA +ve WE; BO partially mediated relationships between SA & CO (satisfaction and loyalty); WE fully mediated relationship between DA & CO (satisfaction and loyalty) Implications: Employees should be trained and supported in deep acting

Table 114.1 (continued)

Author (Year)	Sample (FL=Front-Line)	Theory (in addition to JD-R)	Scales/Measures	Proposed Relationships	Findings and Implications Vi= Vigour; De=Dedication; Ab=Absorption
Burke et al. (2013)	Turkey; 15, 4- and 5-star hotels; 549 FL employees		**UWES-17 (Schaufeli et al. 2002);** Intention to quit/stay (Burke, 1991); Job satisfaction (Kofodimos, 1993); family–work conflict (Carlson et al., 2000); Organizational support (Thompson et al., 1999); Supervisor behaviour; Employee voice (adapted from Van Dyne and LePine, 1998)	Work engagement (WE)– A = Personal demographics (PD); A = Work situation characteristics (WSC) C = Work outcomes: Intent to quit (QT); Job satisfaction (JS); Employee voice (EV) Work–family & family–work conflict (WFC/ FWC)	Mean engagement scores: Vi, 3.9; De, 3.7; Ab, 3.0 WE generally +ve JS & EV WE generally –ve QT & WFC/FWC. PD & WSCs had weak relationships with WE: Greater supervision, org level, property size +ve WO; Front-line employees: A +ve WFC/ FWC. Implication: More study on 'dark side' of Ab is needed.
Karatepe et al. (2013)	Northern Cyprus; 11, 5-star hotels; 185 FL employees	Person–environment fit (Kristof-Brown et al., 2005)	Inventory of Polychronic Values (Bluedorn et al., 1999); **UWES-9 (Schaufeli et al., 2006);** Job performance (Babin and Boles, 1998); Extra-role performance (Bettencourt and Brown, 1997)	Work engagement (WE) A = Polychronicity (PO) C1 = Job performance (JP) C2 = Extra-role customer service behaviour (ERB)	Mean engagement score: 4.71 PO +ve WE; WE +ve JP & ERB However, results explained less than 10 per cent of the variance in any one construct. Implications: Hire & retain employees with 'person–job fit'; training programmes that help to build multi-tasking & task-switching skills.

Study	Sample	Theory	Measures	Variables/Model	Findings
Rigg et al. (2013)	Caribbean; 9 mid-upper scale hotels; 8 departments; 290 non-supervisory (front of house and back of house employees)		**17-item UWES (Schaufeli et al. 2002)**; Job satisfaction (JS) (Wanous et al., 1997); Intention to quit (adapted from Colarelli, 1984)	Engagement (WE) C1 = Job satisfaction (JS) C2 = Intention to quit (QT)	Mean engagement score: 3.95 WE +ve JS; WE –ve QT no or low guest contact employees: -ve JS; +ve QT; job tenure +ve QT Implication: More focus on back of house & LT employees (rewards, +ve supervisor attitudes, development and career progression opportunities).
Carrasco et al. (2014)	Spain; 3- and 4-star hotels ('sun and sand' & 'conference'); 152 work units; 512 FL employees	Self-regulation theory (Babakus et al., 2009); Emotional labour (Hochschild, 1983a/2003); COR theory (Hobfoll, 1988, 1989)	Emotional dissonance FEWS scale (Zapf et al., 1999); Service climate (Global Service Climate Scale) (Schneider et al., 1998; Burnout (MBI-GS) (Schaufeli et al., 1996), **UWES-11 (Schaufeli et al., 2002); V&D only**	Emotional dissonance (ED) & Service climate (SC) as independent predictors of Burnout (BO) & Engagement (WE) Additive model	Mean engagement score: 4.6 SC –ve BO; SC +ve WE ED +ve BO; ED –ve WE SC most important predictor. Implications: Service climate informs employees about what is valued and can impact their well-being; support employees by creating +ve service climate.
Karatepe and Demir (2014)	Turkey, 8 (5-star), international hotels; 211 FL employees	Core Self-Evaluations (CSE) (Judge, 2009; Judge et al., 2003)	CSEs (Judge et al., 2003); **UWES-9 (Schaufeli, et al., 2006);** WFF/FWF (Grzywacz and Marks, 2000) Two-week data collection lag to minimize common method bias.	A = CSEs M = Work engagement C = WFF and FWF	Mean engagement score: 4.81 CSEs +ve WE (explaining 15% of the variance); WE +ve WFF/FWF, and WE mediates CSEs with WFF/FWF. Married employees greater WFF/FWF; Age (older) and tenure (longer) greater WFF. Education –ve WE.

Table 11A.1 (continued)

Author (Year)	Sample (FL=Front-Line)	Theory (in addition to JD-R)	Scales/Measures	Proposed Relationships	Findings and Implications Vi= Vigour; De=Dedication; Ab=Absorption
					Implications: Hire and retain people high in CSEs; invest in high-performance work practices; establish a 'family-supportive work environment'.
Karatepe et al. (2014)	Cyprus; 12, 5-star hotels; 195 FL hotel employees Supervisors assessed employee performance	Transactional theory of stress (Lazarus and Folkman, 1984); Employee motivation (LePine et al., 2005)	Challenge stressors: work overload (Price, 2001); job responsibility (Hackman and Oldham, 1975); UWES-9 (Schaufeli et al., 2006); Organizational commitment (Mowday et al., 1979); Job performance (Babin and Boles, 1998) Two-week data collection lag	A = challenge stressors: work overload (WO); job responsibility (JR) M = engagement (WE) O = job outcomes: organizational commitment (OC) and job performance (JP)	Mean engagement score: 4.37 Support for all hypothesized relationships: Results explain 64% of variance in challenge stressors, 30% in work engagement, 27% in affective organizational commitment, and 3% in job performance. Implications: 'not all stressors are bad'; provide self-regulation training to help employees deal with anxiety; provide empowerment and support. Pre-screen job candidates via standardized tests, to identify ability to meet the demands of front-line work.

Study	Context/Sample	Theory	Measures	Variables	Findings/Implications
Paek et al., (2015)	South Korea 15 5-star hotels; 312 FL staff	COR (Hobfoll, 1989; 2001); PsyCap (Luthans and Youssef, 2007; Nelson and Cooper, 2007; Peterson and Seligman, 2004)	(UWES-9) (Schaufeli et al., 2002); PsyCap (Luthans et al., 2007); Morale/job satisfaction (Hartline and Ferrel, 1996; Locke, 1976, p. 1300); Organizational commitment (Allen and Meyer, 1990)	A = PsyCap (self-efficacy, optimism, hope and resilience) M = Engagement (WE) C = Employee morale (JS) C2 = Organizational commitment (OC)	Mean engagement score: 4.09 Main effects: PsyCap +ve WE; explaining 71.5% of variance. PsyCap & WE +ve JS, jointly explaining 63.1% of variance. PsyCap & WE +ve OC, jointly explaining 70.1% of the variance. Mediating effects: WE mediated PsyCap on JS & OC. Implications: Develop selection and training programmes that influence PsyCap factors; enhance 'high-performance work practices', including empowerment and rewards.
Lee and Ok (2015)	US hotel industry; 394 entry-level employees, supervisors and managers	Psychological condition theory (Kahn, 1990) COR (Hobfoll, 1989; 2001)	(UWES-9) (Schaufeli et al., 2002); Core self-evaluation scale (CSE) (Judge et al., 2003); PSC scale (customer orientation, managerial support, internal service, and information/ communication), (James and Tetrick, 1986; Amenumey and Lockwood, 2008)	A = Core self-evaluations (CSEs) M = Psychological climate (PSC) C = Engagement Single fit measure of engagement	CSEs +ve WE, predicted 26% of variance in WE; 4 dimensions of PSC +ve WE, increased explained variance by another 16%. None of the interactions between CSEs and PSCs were significant. Implications: Measure CSE as part of employee selection procedures; adopt mgmt. practices that reinforce perceptions of self-esteem or self-efficacy: provide employees with empowered jobs, treat employees with respect, embrace two-way communication and show appreciation. Provide employees with worthwhile jobs that add value.

Table 11A.1 (continued)

Author (Year)	Sample (FL=Front-Line)	Theory (in addition to JD-R)	Scales/Measures	Proposed Relationships	Findings and Implications Vi= Vigour; De=Dedication; Ab=Absorption
Lee and Ok (2016)	US hotel industry; 394 entry-level employees, supervisors and managers	Organizational behaviour, Herzberg et al.'s two-factor motivation theory (1959); Blau's social exchange theory (1964)	(UWES-9) **(Schaufeli and Bakker, 2003)**; quality of leader–member exchange (LMX) (Graen and Cashman, 1975); intrinsic rewards (Lawler and Hall, 1970); job satisfaction (Cammann et al., 1979); Affective Commitment Scale (Meyer et al., 1993)	A = Work engagement (WE) M1 = Intrinsic rewards (IR) M2 = LMX C1 = Job satisfaction (JS) C2 = Organizational commitment (OC)	Mean engagement score: 5.56 WE +ve with each of IR, LMX, JS and OC; LMX +ve JS; LMX +ve OC. Over 70% of variance in JS explained by WE and LMX. And, WE, JS and LMX together explained 66.99% of total variance in OC. Implications: Strong associations between engagement, leadership, satisfaction and commitment. Cultivate and support WE by 'encouraging supervisors to establish and maintain a trust-based relationship with engaged employees' (p.158). Assess quality of supervisor–employee relationships in performance reviews.
Suan and Nasurdin (2016)	Malaysia 34, 4- and 5-star hotels; 438 FL employees	COR (Hobfoll, 1989, 2001)	Supervisor support (adapted from Susskind et al., 2003); Work engagement UWES-9 **(Schaufeli et al., 2006)**	A = Supervisor support (SS) M = Gender C = Work engagement (WE)	Mean engagement score: Men (5.03) Women (5.09) SS +ve WE Mediating effect: relationship between SS and WE, stronger for men (Gender explained 14% of variance).

| Liu et al. (2017) | USA – Midwest; 105 restaurants; 149 managers and non-managerial employees | Social exchange theory (Blau, 1964); Self-efficacy (Bandura, 1986) | UWES-17 (**Schaufeli et al., 2001**); Global POS Scale (Eisenberger et al., 1986); General Self-Efficacy Scale (Schwarzer et al., 1997) and Intent to leave (Tsui et al., 1997) | A = Perceived organizational support (POS) M = Self-efficacy (SE) C1 = Engagement (WE) C2 = Intent to leave (TO) (H1) POS +ve WE (H2) WE –ve TO (H3) SE moderates POS on WE (H4) SE moderates WE on TO (H5) H3 is stronger for women (H6) H4 is stronger for women | Implications: Training and mentoring programmes to help employees more easily receive guidance and feedback from supervisors; supervisor training in empathy and listening skills. Implement +ve HR practices (flexible working hours, compressed work week) to signal that management cares about employees. Assess group level engagement. H1, H3 and H5 were supported Self-efficacy significantly moderated the relationship between POS and WE for women. H4 and H6 were rejected. Implications: Employers should work to increase the self-efficacy of female employees (through verbal persuasion and vicarious experience). By increasing engagement, turnover intention may be reduced. |

12. Security and safety: an internal customer perspective
Alfred Ogle

PROLOGUE

The Ritz-Carlton is a multi-award-winning luxury hotel chain which vigorously upholds its motto 'We are Ladies and Gentlemen serving Ladies and Gentlemen'. A two time recipient of the coveted Malcolm Baldrige National Quality Award[1] in the Service Company category, it is the only hotel company to be awarded since the inception of the award in 1987.

What distinguishes this hospitality enterprise, a fervent champion of service excellence and consistent winner of major hospitality industry and leading consumer organization awards? Perhaps an answer can be offered by way of the Internal Marketing (IM) concept; 'The employee promise' of the Ritz-Carlton Hotel Company states:

> At The Ritz-Carlton, our Ladies and Gentlemen are the most important resource in our service commitment to our guests.
>
> By applying the principles of trust, honesty, respect, integrity and commitment, we nurture and maximize talent to the benefit of each individual and the company.
>
> The Ritz-Carlton fosters a work environment where diversity is valued, quality of life is enhanced, individual aspirations are fulfilled, and The Ritz-Carlton Mystique is strengthened. (The Ritz-Carlton Hotel Company, 2016)

THE HOSPITALITY HUMAN RESOURCE (INTERNAL CUSTOMER)

Hospitality and tourism ostensibly are people's industries (Craik, 1995; Faulkner and Patiar, 1997; Kusluvan et al., 2010) wherein people are often lauded as the most valuable asset. Many companies allude to this value in their mission statements (Solnet et al., 2014). As successful delivery of the hospitality and tourism products is attributed to people (Baum, 2007; Yang, 2010), it would stand to reason that these 'deliverers' would be highly valued and greatly appreciated. Indeed, Hoque (2013) noted that hotel companies extol the virtues of their Human Resources (HR) more frequently than their manufacturing counterparts.

While many hotel mission statements ring true under scrutiny, some sound hollow and disingenuous. For example, Leong (2001) found that only three of the 11 Singaporean hotels' mission statements in his study fulfilled all the criteria of an effective mission statement. Some mission statements liberally proclaim 'green' credentials without disclosing any sustainability reporting practices to support those claims (Halbe, 2013).

Sufi and Lyons' (2003) content analysis of 30 large hospitality firms' mission statements revealed the preponderance of attention is on guests. Their findings suggest that, while care for employees featured in 23 of the 30 mission statements, the primary focus of virtually all those hospitality firms (95 per cent) was on their external customers ($n = 29$). Upon drilling down on the statement content, Sufi and Lyons (2003) isolated 28 separate descriptive components. These components crystallize the range of hospitality enterprises' core purpose and focus, which communicate organizational priority, audience and modus operandi.

On the premise that hospitality enterprises genuinely extol their employees, IM, which originates from the marketing literature (Berry et al., 1976; Greene et al., 1994) and is defined as 'the philosophy of treating employees as customers and it is the strategy of shaping job-products to fit human needs' (Berry and Parasuraman, 1991, p. 151), could be expected to be clearly evident in amongst those 28 components. The key element in IM is the notion of the Internal Customer (IC), which Berry (1981, p. 34) succinctly describes as 'the customer (who) is inside the organization', viz. the employee.

Notwithstanding reservations about the practicality of the 'employees as customers' concept (Hales, 1994; Mudie, 2003; Rafiq and Ahmed, 1993), this characterization is credible as even its detractors subsumed it in the first element of their reading of IM:

1. Employee motivation and satisfaction.
2. Customer orientation and customer satisfaction.
3. Inter-functional coordination and integration.
4. Marketing-like approach to the above.
5. Implementation of specific corporate or functional strategies.

(Rafiq and Ahmed, 2000, p. 453)

Therefore, the definition of IM is open to interpretation and implementation; however, the core concept of IC stands evidenced by Hwang and Der-Jang's (2005) alternative categorization of IM streams:

1. Treating the Employee as an Internal Customer.
2. Developing Employee Orientated Behavior.

3.   Human Resource Management (HRM) orientation.
4.   Internal Exchange.

Similarly, the IC concept is central to Abdullah and Rozario's (2009) study on employee satisfaction of their staff cafeteria, and Sufi and Lyons' (2003) analysis of hospitality companies' mission statements.

Table 12.1 shows the 28 components identified by Sufi and Lyons (2003) as categorized by the author according to customer alignment (internal, external or both).

The tabulation would suggest that the external customer was the primary focus of organizational objectives and that ICs, specifically direct employees, were noticeably ignored. Sufi and Lyons (2003, p. 260) opined that the variables identified were indicative of a design problem. 'It is too easy to construct a good-looking mission statement from this heterogeneous list, yet real commitment to a component is not always easy to achieve. There is a hierarchy of components, some of which relate to overall business activities and others which pragmatically relate to particular business functions.'

It is interesting to note that because Ritz-Carlton properties differ on account of geographic locality and guest mix, each hotel is permitted to tailor its own mission statement within the parameters of the corporate mission (Jones and Kahaner, 2011). This strategy resonates with the assertions of Dickson et al. (2006) that successful organizations are able to align their missions with the external environment as well as all the factors internal to the organization. Furthermore, Kotler et al. (2006) affirm that a mission statement, apart from identifying a business's goals and philosophy, defines the industry, products and applications, competencies, market segment, vertical integration and geographical coverage.

INTERNAL CUSTOMERS: WHAT ABOUT THEM?

The notion that IC service quality is very positively related to IC satisfaction is widely documented (see De Ruyter et al., 1997; Finn et al., 1996; Jun and Cai, 2010; Wisner and Stanley, 1999), and also that it in turn 'is a driving force to achieve external customer satisfaction, which is critical to the long-term success of any organisation' (Jun and Cai, 2010, p. 219). Thus, the well-being of the IC (employee) elicits satisfaction in the external customer (guest/customer) (Berry, 1981), which in turn engenders organizations that are sustainable both in the HR and finance dimensions (Organizational Success). Organizational Success is typically measured

Table 12.1 *The internal/external customer alignment of mission statements*

Internal Customer	Internal & External Customer		External Customer	
3. best employer	6.	investor in technology and innovation	1.	best company
10. empower through training and accountability	11.	improve the balanced scorecard	2.	best provider of customer service
22. provide a great work environment	12.	recognize the values	4.	deliverer of operational excellence
	15.	achieve consistent excellence	5.	achieve profitable growth
	16.	satisfy internal and external customers	7.	seeker of new markets
	17.	serve all the stakeholders	8.	strengthen the brand
	19.	build on strengths	9.	exceed the expectations
	23.	treat each other with respect and dignity	13.	quality leader
	24.	embrace diversity	14.	use freshly made products
	26.	environmental responsibility	18.	maximize the value of each shareholder
	28.	easiest company to do business with	20.	enrich the lifestyles
			21.	anticipate the needs
			25.	contribute positively to customers
			27.	provide a memorable experience

Source: Based on Sufi and Lyons (2003, p. 260).

by profitability for shareholders/owners. This relationship is illustrated in Figure 12.1.

This relationship fulfils the characterization of the hotel industry being made up of three principal parties, that is, customers, employees and owners (Medlik and Ingram, 2000). Figure 12.2 depicts this tripartite relationship incorporating the Internal Customer nomenclature.

Source: Author.

Figure 12.1   *The relationship between internal customer service quality, internal customer satisfaction, external customer satisfaction and organizational success*

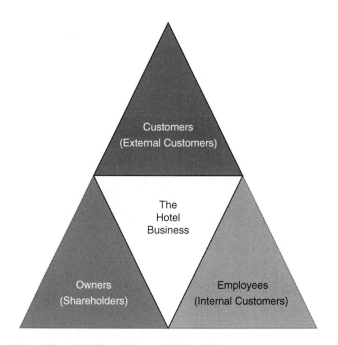

Source: Adapted from Medlik and Ingram (2000, p. 27).

Figure 12.2   *The hotel business tripartite relationship*

INTERNAL CUSTOMER SECURITY

Kusluvan et al.'s (2010) review of Human Resources Management (HRM) issues in the hospitality and tourism industries acknowledges that health and safety were a function of HRM. Their extensive review, however, revealed only one reference to health and safety which was related to

HR practices of Total Quality Management (TQM) hotels (Partlow, 1996). Partlow (1996, p. 75) noted that 'companies reaffirm the value of their employees in creating a TQM culture by providing a safe and healthy work environment'. The TQM hotels in his survey employed a 'prevention-oriented approach to safety and health', exemplified by one hotel hosting a resort-wide health fair, another availing its employees of an onsite counselling department, and widespread availability of employee assistance programmes.

> With respect to promoting a safe work environment, each of the hotels surveyed has a safety program in which committees or teams address issues related to guest and employee safety. For instance, Bergstrom's safety program, called 'zero-accident culture,' or ZAC, requires that every job-related accident be investigated, even if no work time is lost. The ZAC team makes regular job-safety observations, such as checking to see how a housekeeper flips a mattress, and every two months the team conducts safety audits of the entire hotel. Any department that goes accident-free for a full 30 days receives scratch-off 'lottery tickets' for each of its employees. Prizes on the tickets range from a dinner for two to a cruise on the company's executive yacht.
>
> Treasure Island Inn's safety program is headed up by the 'Keepers of Property and Security' (KOPS) team, which recently completed a comprehensive hurricane plan for the safe evacuation of employees and guests. (Partlow, 1996, p. 75)

The initiatives described by Partlow (1996) might come across as being unexceptional, even flippant, given the gravity of the health and well-being of the industry's purportedly most valuable asset, the employee. The acknowledgement by both properties of both IC and external customer, however, is significant. Findlay et al.'s (2017) observation of the fact that employers are forcibly coerced by legislation and regulatory interventions by quasi-government agencies to affect occupational health and safety standards in the workplace, further suggests that there has been minimal advancement in attitudes towards the IC. Safety and security standards are legislated and typically set quality standards benchmarks (Eraqi, 2006, p. 478). This view, however, points to a reactive mindset contrary to the prevention-oriented approach to safety and health evident in Partlow's (1996) study. Furthermore, Madera et al.'s (2017) review of the hospitality and tourism industries' strategic HRM (SHRM) research literature showed a tendency to focus on (external) customer service as a measure of firm performance. Hotels continually upgrade their guestroom product to meet the rising expectations of guests while overlooking the additional workload and physical stress being borne by housekeeping staff as a consequence (Trotto, 2015). Such accounts are symptoms of organizational myopia as IC satisfaction clearly has been overlooked.

Baum (2015) observed how the expanding nature of tourism has significantly changed the historically discrete scope of employees, resulting in hybridized work that has created HR challenges, including health and safety. In comparison to his 2007 assessment of the role and management of HR in tourism, however, he noted the changes to be marginal compared to the ever evolving tourism and allied industries. Indeed, a ten-year comparative review of tourism stakeholder assessments of workforce issues in Scotland and Australia showed only minimal progress in HRM innovation (Solnet et al., 2014). Kusluvan et al. (2010) summarized the then prevailing argument that employees engender organizational performance via strategic HRM in a model: A Basic Model of the Strategic Role of Human Resources for Organizational Performance displayed the antecedent elements of the SHRM stratagem (Human Capital Stock, Human Resource Management Systems and Practices, Internal Marketing, Organizational Culture and Climate, Business and HRM Strategy). While IM is included as an antecedent element, the model when juxtaposed with Figure 12.1 exemplifies the diminished role of the IC concept (as a subset of IM) in contemporary hospitality HR practices.

SAFETY AND SECURITY, AND THE INTERNAL CUSTOMER

Parasuraman et al. (1985, p. 46), in their seminal article in which they introduced their seminal conceptual model of Service Quality, identified security as one of the 10 key categories of 'service quality determinants'. They defined security as 'the freedom from danger, risk, or doubt' and that it involves physical safety, financial security, and confidentiality (Parasuraman et al., 1985, p. 47). Their definition broadly extends to, and applies to, both IC and external customers. Besides physical safety, service quality determination involves assessing other intangible/subjective sensory attributes (Ogle, 2009). Ambient noise, however, is difficult to measure accurately and typically is described in lay terms that the individual customer relates to (Benítez et al., 2004). Safety, one of those attributes, is defined by the American Society for Industrial Security (ASIS, 2000) (as cited in Brooks, 2010, p. 232) as 'theories, principles, concepts and practices that consider a process for a safe and healthy work environment'. Here, security is lent an objective framework which is very IC specific.

However, when the term 'security' is used without context, it becomes ambiguous. Davidson (2005) asserts that security presents different meanings to different people depending on time, place and context. The ASIS definition referred to earlier would explicitly refer to Workplace Health

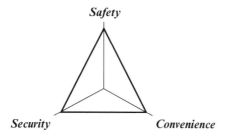

Safety

Security   Convenience

Source: Ogle and Moreira (2002, p.438).

Figure 12.3 Safety, Security and Convenience Model

and Safety (WHS), sometimes referred to as Occupational Health and Safety (OH&S), not necessarily the provision of safety provided by the function of security (Brooks, 2010). Similarly Belilos (2001) delineates security from safety with the former referring to the protection of property and assets, and the preservation of life while the latter refers to structural elements such as installations and fixtures. Coursen (2014) illustrates the relationship of security and safety with the former as an umbrella which shelters the latter. He asserts that safety, which consists of emotional and physical attributes, is protected by security thereby suggesting that safety and security are interdependent. Parasuraman et al. (1985) alluded to the concept that security is the antecedent of guests' physical safety. Ogle and Moreira's (2002) Safety, Security and Convenience Model (Figure 12.3) suggests that effective protection of a hotel guest is underpinned by measures taken by the hotel which incorporate those three discrete elements in equilibrium.

Three-quarters of the 3 million workplace injuries reported in the US in 2014 occurred in service industries, which includes hotels, restaurants and bars (Quezada, 2016). Statistically, hotel workers in the US are 40 per cent more likely to be injured on the job than all other service sector workers, and sustain comparatively more severe injuries compared to their hospitality industry counterparts (Buchanan et al., 2010). Similarly in Australia, the accommodation and food services industry's rate of injuries and diseases in 2013 to 2014 was 38 per cent higher than the rate for the whole Australian workforce (Safe Work Australia, 2015). This high rate of injuries could be a consequence of deficiencies in the security coverage using Coursen's (2014) umbrella metaphor.

Australian business owners are legally bound to assess and mitigate risks that may impact the health, safety or welfare of those at the workplace. The coverage is inclusive, as can be seen below:

This may include the health and safety of your customers, employees, visitors, contractors, volunteers and suppliers.

Creating a safe work environment is a legal requirement and critical to the long-term success of your business.

It can:

- help you retain staff
- maximise employee productivity
- minimise injury and illness in the workplace
- reduce the costs of injury and workers' compensation
- ensure you meet your legal obligations and employee responsibilities.

(Workplace Health & Safety, 2017)

The criticality of staff retention cannot be overstated. Vogt (2017) asserts that whilst talent retention is a concern all businesses face, it is particularly challenging for the leisure and hospitality industry as it has seen the highest workforce turnover rate in comparison to other private sector industries (US Bureau of Labor Statistics, 2014).

IMPACT OF EMPLOYEE HEALTH AND SAFETY ON HRM

Hayes and Ninemeier (2008) exhort the criticality of IM and IC within hospitality industry HRM:

> most managers would agree that their employees are the most important asset, and their protection must receive the highest priority. Effective hospitality managers carefully enact programs designed to help ensure the long-term care and protection of physical assets, such as their buildings, equipment, and cash. In a similar manner, it makes sense for these managers to just as carefully design and implement those programs that will help ensure the safety and protection of their workers.
>
> While it is certainly good business for managers to ensure the health and safety of workers, it is also a legal requirement that they do so. The hospitality industry includes job positions that, if not properly structured, may be quite dangerous or threatening. Legislation has been enacted to guide managers in addressing these concerns. It is the responsibility of HR managers to prevent employees from working in unhealthy or threatening environments because healthy workers are more productive than those who are not. In addition, from an ethical perspective, employers should want to ensure the safety of their workers simply because it is the right thing to do. (Hayes and Ninemeier, 2008, p. 332)

Source: Photograph provided by the author.

Figure 12.4   *Air sampling apparatus on casino premises (A) (Macau SAR, November 2016)*

SMOKING IN CASINOS IS AN HR ISSUE

The genesis of this chapter was the experience I had as an external customer during a research trip to the Macau SAR in 2016. My research was unrelated to casinos per se; however, as the majority of prestigious casinos in Macau are housed within Integrated Resorts (IR), often I had to transverse the casinos to get to various parts of the properties for my data collection activities. I was intrigued to see two arrays of air quality sampling apparatus at a separate location in a newly opened luxury casino (Figure 12.4) and my interest was further piqued when I subsequently encountered another air monitoring device

Source: Photograph provided by the author.

*Figure 12.5   Air sampling apparatus in corridor outside casino (B)
(Macau SAR, November 2016)*

outside the casino of another luxury property in the near vicinity
(Figure 12.5).

The motivation to address smoking in casinos crystallized when I was
enveloped in tobacco smoke while walking in the corridor on a subsequent
visit to the first casino. The odour was overwhelming and disconcerting.
It immediately dawned on me why the air sampling devices had been
deployed. Upon investigation, I discovered that the source of the smoke
was a high roller salon adjoining the corridor. The salon was screened
from the corridor by an open wooden latticework. The smoke could therefore freely travel out of that smoking area which was located adjacent to a
restaurant in the middle of the casino complex.

Employees and guests smoking in the workplace is an important HR issue, one that escalates with the introduction of stringent, smoke-free legislation and the pushback from customers who are habitual smokers (Hayes and Ninemeier, 2008). Given that the literature roundly concurs that tobacco smoking has health implications and that passive smoking (inhalation of second-hand smoke (SHS) or also commonly known as secondary smoke) is injurious,[2] this chapter turns to the implication of gaming customer smoking sections in Macau casinos.

Berman and Post (2007) assert that smoke-free casinos provide significantly healthier and safer working environments for employees. The only way to protect non-smokers is to eliminate the source of SHS created by the burning of tobacco products such as cigarettes, cigars or pipes (Centers for Disease Control and Prevention, 2017). However, in the United States in 2011, 88 per cent of commercial casinos and nearly all tribal casinos allow smoking and therefore pose danger to casino patrons and workers (Myers, 2011). Babb et al. (2015) report that most US casinos continue to allow smoking, thus exposing workers and patrons to the hazards of SHS. The continued availability of working environments where smoking is permissible has been attributed to various factors, one being lobbying by special interest groups.

Delays and weakness in legislation to separate gambling and smoking have been influenced by pressure from tobacco interest groups. The tobacco industry has been reported as providing resources to create smoking areas and financial incentives to install tobacco vending machines in licensed venues. The tobacco and gambling industries work together to increase profits from smoking gamblers – as confirmed by Tattersalls-commissioned psychology report describing the 'trance-inducing ritual' of simultaneous gambling and smoking. Problem gamblers are being exploited as more likely to gamble if they can smoke at the same time.

There are two compelling reasons for 100% smoke-free policies covering all gambling areas:

● For the general health of employees and patrons in such settings; and
● As a significant harm reduction measure to reduce problem gambling.
(ASH Australia/SmokeFree Australia Coalition, 2009)

The stereotypical casino is a smoky and dark place, and this conception will probably not disappear anytime soon. Many gamblers smoke (*Las Vegas Sun*, 2010) and therefore the gaming industry continues to accommodate smokers of tobacco products and e-cigarettes. According to Dearlove et al. (2002), the 'accommodation' of smokers in a space shared with non-smokers by the hospitality industry has been instigated by the tobacco industry's posture on solution advocacy and dissemination of pseudo-scientific claims of negative financial impact of going smoke-free. The strategy to 'infiltrate and coopt the hospitality industry to serve the tobacco industry's political needs' (Dearlove et al., 2002, p. 101) used since the 1970s has since waned in impact but its legacy is still clearly felt in the gaming industry. International high rollers visiting casinos expect perks such as smoking while gambling as they are accustomed to a smoking environment in their home countries (Demasi, 2012). Chapman et al. (2016) report that vaping emissions are toxic. Consequently, the consumption of e-cigarettes creates airborne pollution and therefore is not a benign alternative to tobacco smoke.

Smoking is commonplace in Macau and historically smoking in public places has been widely tolerated. Smoking is permitted in its casinos, resulting in smoky indoor environments for both casino workers and their clients. McCartney (2016) noted that the legislation to prohibit smoking in casino VIP rooms and the airport-style smoking lounges on the mass gaming floors floundered in the face of concerted opposition by the casino industry to what they considered to be overly harsh restrictions and a significant disincentive to gaming patronage. Until the deadlock is resolved, smoking continues unabated as casinos claim that casino ventilation systems do protect non-smoking employees and visitors from SHS (Tasker, 2016). This uneasy truce is what I had experienced during my visit to Macau. Macau legislators are reportedly in consultation with lobby groups while collecting more economic data regarding the impact of the proposed legislation to extend the ban on smoking inside the city's casinos to include smoking lounges and VIP areas (GGRAsia, 2016). Ironically, a survey undertaken by Macau's gaming operators reported that 66 per cent of the 34 000 casino worker respondents were in favour of the retention and development of casino smoking lounges (GGRAsia, 2015). This contradicts the stand of the Professional for Gaming of New Macau, a gaming labour activist group which opposes any deviation from the government's original plan to implement a zero-smoking regime (GGRAsia, 2017).

The reason for the conspicuous air quality sampling is crystal clear. Despite ventilation manufacturer claims of their product efficacy, ventilation systems do not fully eliminate SHS (Butler, 2013). Dearlove et al. (2002) note that the tobacco industry does not explicitly claim that ventilation eliminates health dangers associated with SHS. In addition, Zhou et al. (2016) found that SHS migrates rapidly and contaminates adjacent non-smoking areas. They ascertained that casino ventilation systems did not fully eliminate SHS and concluded that a completely smoke-free casino is the only way to fully protect non-smoking patrons and employees from the dangers of SHS. Shamo et al.'s (2015) research on the effects of smoke-free law enforcement in Michigan restaurants showed very high efficacy in SHS exposure reduction where complete cessation of smoking was enforced. In contrast, the casinos, which were exempted from the ruling, continued to have to experience unhealthy air quality. Furthermore, the ventilation solution has had limited uptake and success in the US (Drope et al., 2004), thereby further negating its utility.

Exemption from smoking restriction in public places is observed in Australian casinos. The 'high-roller' rooms at Crown Casino in Melbourne remain the last places in Victoria where indoor workers in licensed premises are exposed to SHS (Quit, 2016). The Crown Perth Casino's International Room is the only exception to the Tobacco Products Control Act 2006 (Healthy WA, n.d.). In New South Wales, Sydney's casinos enjoy exemptions from smoke-free laws (Rooke, 2016), thereby in effect circumventing laws designed:

(a) to reduce the incidence of illness and death related to the use of tobacco products by:

1 prohibiting the supply of tobacco products and smoking implements to young persons
2 discouraging the use of tobacco products
3 restricting the promotion of tobacco products and smoking generally
4 reducing the exposure of people to tobacco smoke from tobacco products that are smoked by other people.

(b) to promote good health and activities which encourage healthy lifestyles.
(Tobacco Products Control Act 2006, 2006)

The pervasive indoor SHS poses an even graver health threat to casino workers (Myers, 2011). Any amount of exposure to SHS increases the risk of lung cancer, other respiratory diseases and heart disease. Studies have shown that even low levels of SHS exposure can be harmful. The only way to fully protect non-smokers from SHS exposure is to completely eliminate smoking in indoor spaces (CDC, 2016). Quit Victoria, Cancer Council Victoria, the Heart Foundation (Victoria) and AMA Victoria (Quit Victoria, 2016), in their joint position statement on smoke-free outdoor dining and drinking areas in Victoria, assert that only totally smoke-free work and public spaces can adequately protect non-smokers from exposure to SHS.

What recourse does a casino employee have, if any? Achutan et al. (2009) recommend employees to stop smoking, seek medical attention if they have any health concerns or symptoms, and to get involved in the work of casino health and safety committees. Based on this recommendation, casino employees already impacted by SHS appear to have negligible recourse. The question that arises is whether the hospitality industry's internal customers in general and its casino employees, in particular, are valued HR assets. On the premise that the lofty HRM principles and service quality aspirations are sound, why do casino employees confront 'danger' at their workplace? Are hospitality enterprise mission statements merely an exercise in smoke and mirrors? A major Australian gaming and entertainment group's proclamation of its value proposition to future employees reads:

VALUES

(Our) vision is simple – to create a world-leading entertainment precinct. Our valued employees are fundamental to helping us achieve this vision. We strive to create enjoyment for every customer, every time, under the guidance of our four key values:

- We are friendly
- We aim higher
- We do the right thing
- We work together

EPILOGUE

As hospitality industry HR practitioners operate in an ever morphing industry and labour market, it would perhaps be timely to revisit Collins and Payne's (1991) article that advocated a marketing approach in HRM manifested in IM. Their article features an illustration which alludes to the irrelevance of IC safety to HR practitioners in the late 1980s. Depicting an HRM practitioner supermarket, the Safety product is to be found in an Out of Date barrel. Fast forwarding to 2017, safety appears still to be elusive, at least for those ICs of casinos.

The traditional inputs into a typical business were capital, raw materials, and production and non-production workers. These inputs shaped traditional HRM into a principally administrative function. The advent of resource-based view (RBV) influence on HRM spawned the field of SHRM (Wright et al., 2001) with three new categories of input: hardware, software and wetware. Wetware refers to people as opposed to hardware and software, and with reference to Collins and Payne's (2001) 'Internal Supermarket' illustration, increases the range and scope of items available and to choose from. The wider range of HRM 'products' available makes for either a more satisfying or confounding 'shopping' experience, depending on who the shopper is (personality and competency), and also the peculiar purpose of the shopping activity. This profusion of variables further confounds the choices that HR practitioners who operate in a highly heterogeneous hospitality industry cultural servicescape have (Davidson et al., 2011).

Nyberg and Ulrich (2015, p.415) refer to the new skills that HR professionals need to acquire in order to deliver 'strategies and solutions to better align the most important resource – human capital – with the organizations goals' as 'Renaissance HR'. One of the 13 roles that HR professionals have to uptake and master is that of the marketer.

> Customers are the focus of marketers. Marketers must understand who their customers are, what their customers need, how their organization can meet those needs, and how to communicate this with customers. HR must act similarly. HR serves a number of internal customers, and must be able to effectively identify their needs and communicate how the tools, processes, and programs HR offers can meet those needs. HR must also understand outside customers in order to know how best to develop the personnel to meet those customers' needs. (Nyberg and Ulrich, 2015, pp. 417–18)

The concept is not a new one. However, despite IM and IC concepts having been readily availed to HRM practitioners in the hospitality and tourism industries, the reference to renaissance by Nyberg and Ulrich (2015) insinuates hitherto lacklustre or declining uptake. Given Tom Baum's (2015) recurring question about whether changes in HRM practices in the hospitality and tourism industries are afoot, unless there is a definitive answer a second reprisal can be anticipated.

CONCLUDING THOUGHTS

This chapter is not meant as an indictment of the state of HRM in the hospitality and tourism industry. It serves to spark discussion as to why there has only been one hospitality enterprise to have ever won a Malcolm Baldrige Award. Such a discussion might precipitate greater representation in the future underpinned by SHRM. At the very least, the hospitality and tourism industry can anticipate sharing a collective sense of pride in the event of a Ritz-Carlton 'three-peat', an occasion that would be contingent of it honouring its lofty Employee Promise: 'At The Ritz-Carlton, our Ladies and Gentlemen are the most important resource in our service commitment to our guests'.

FUTURE RESEARCH

Underpinned by the following question:

1. Is the people asset relegated in role?
2. Will automated decision making outweigh augmented decision

making? In other words, will the hospitality industry become more reliant on automation?

The following research direction is proposed:

1. Content analysis of hotel chains' mission statements to determine the posture vis-à-vis IC.
2. The extent of SHS-related safety incidences at the workplace.

NOTES

1. An award established by the US Congress in 1987 to raise awareness of quality management and recognize US companies that have implemented successful quality management systems. Awards can be given annually in six categories: manufacturing, service, small business, education, healthcare and non-profit. The award is named after the late Secretary of Commerce Malcolm Baldrige, a proponent of quality management. The US Commerce Department's National Institute of Standards and Technology manages the award, and ASQ (2016) administers it (http://asq.org/learn-about-quality/malcolm-baldrige-award/overview/overview.html).
2. Whilst a 2013 study did not definitively prove a clear link between passive smoking and lung cancer (Peres, 2013), the probability of a causal linkage was not discounted.

REFERENCES

Abdullah, D. and Rozario, F. (2009). Influence of service and product quality towards customer satisfaction: A case study at the staff cafeteria in the hotel industry. *World Academy of Science, Engineering and Technology*, **53**, 185–90.

Achutan, C., West, C., Mueller, C., Boudreau, Y. and Mead, K. (2009). Health hazard evaluation report: Environmental and biological assessment of environmental tobacco smoke exposure among casino dealers. Las Vegas, NV: *National Institute for Occupational Safety and Health*, NIOSH HETA, (2005-0076), 2005-0201.

ASH Australia/SmokeFree Australia Coalition (2009). The case for 100% smokefree gambling areas. Accessed at www.pc.gov.au/inquiries/completed/gambling-2009/submissions/subdr304.pdf

ASIS (2000). Paper presented at the 2000 Academic/Practitioner Symposium, Oklahoma.

ASQ (2016). Malcolm Baldridge National Quality Award (MBNAQ). Accessed at http://asq.org/learn-about-quality/malcolm-baldrige-award/overview/overview.html

Babb, S., McNeil, C., Kruger, J. and Tynan, M.A. (2015). Secondhand smoke and smoking restrictions in casinos: A review of the evidence. *Tobacco Control*, **24**(1), 11–17.

Baum, T. (2007). Human resources in tourism: Still waiting for change. *Tourism Management*, **28**(6), 1383–99.

Baum, T. (2015). Human resources in tourism: Still waiting for change? A 2015 reprise. *Tourism Management*, **50**, 204–12.

Belilos, C. (2001). Safety and Security in the Workplace. *Hotel Online*. Accessed at www.hotelonline.com/Neo/News/PR2001_4th/Nov01_SafetySecurity.html

Benítez, J., Martin, J. and Roman, C. (2004). Using stated preferences for measuring quality of service in the hotel industry. *Resuscitation*, **1**, 2.

Berman, M.L. and Post, C. (2007). Secondhand smoke and casinos. *Legal Studies Research Paper Series, Paper No. 80.*

Berry, L.L. (1981). The employee as customer. *Journal of Retail Banking*, **3**(1), 33–40.

Berry, L. and Parasuraman, A. (1991). *Marketing Services: Competing Through Quality.* New York: The Free Press.

Berry, L.L., Hensel, J.S. and Burke, M.C. (1976). Improving retailer capability for effective consumerism response. *Journal of Retailing*, **52**(3), 3–14.

Brooks, D.J. (2010). What is security: Definition through knowledge categorization. *Security Journal*, **23**(3), 225–39.

Buchanan, S., Vossenas, P., Krause, N., Moriarty, J., Frumin, E., Shimek, J.A.M., Mirer, F. et al. (2010). Occupational injury disparities in the US hotel industry. *American Journal of Industrial Medicine*, **53**(2), 116–25.

Butler, B. (2013). Crown 'putting profits before health' at casino. *The Sydney Morning Herald*, 9 July. Accessed at http://www.smh.com.au/business/crown-putting-profits-before-health-at-casino-20130708-2pmaq.html

CDC (2016). Ventilation does not effectively protect nonsmokers from secondhand smoke. Accessed at https://www.cdc.gov/tobacco/data_statistics/fact_sheets/secondhand_smoke/protection/ventilation/

Centers for Disease Control and Prevention (2017). Secondhand smoke (SHS) facts. Accessed at https://www.cdc.gov/tobacco/data_statistics/fact_sheets/secondhand_smoke/general_facts/

Chapman, S., Daube, M. and Maziak, W. (2016). Should e-cigarette use be permitted in smoke-free public places? No. *Tobacco Control*, 7 November, tobaccocontrol-2016-053359.

Collins, B. and Payne, A. (1991). Internal marketing: A new perspective for HRM. *European Management Journal*, **9**(3), 261–70.

Coursen, S. (2014). Safety vs. security: Understanding the difference may soon save lives. Accessed at https://safetymadesimple.wordpress.com/2014/08/31/understanding-the-difference-may-soon-save-lives-safety-vs-security-spencer-coursen/

Craik, J. (1995). Are there cultural limits to tourism? *Journal of Sustainable Tourism*, **3**(2), 87–98.

Davidson, M. (2005). A matter of degrees: A look at homeland security programs on college and university campuses. *Security Management*, **49**(12), 72.

Davidson, M.C.G., McPhail, R. and Barry, S. (2011). Hospitality HRM: Past, present and the future. *International Journal of Contemporary Hospitality Management*, **23**(4), 498–516.

De Ruyter, K.D., Bloemer, J. and Peeters, P. (1997). Merging service quality and service satisfaction. An empirical test of an integrative model. *Journal of Economic Psychology*, **18**(4), 387–406.

Dearlove, J.V., Bialous, S.A. and Glantz, S.A. (2002). Tobacco industry manipulation of the hospitality industry to maintain smoking in public places. *Tobacco Control*, **11**(2), 94–104.

Demasi, J. (2012). Crown staff forced to passively smoke. *WAtoday*. Accessed at http://www.watoday.com.au/wa-news/crown-staff-forced-to-passively-smoke-20121126-2a4ew.html

Dickson, D.R., Ford, R.C. and Upchurch, R. (2006). A case study in hotel organizational alignment. *International Journal of Hospitality Management*, **25**(3), 463–77.

Drope, J., Bialous, S. and Glantz, S.A. (2004). Tobacco industry efforts to present ventilation as an alternative to smoke-free environments in North America. *Tobacco Control*, **13**(suppl. 1), i41–i47.

Eraqi, M.I. (2006). Tourism services quality (TourServQual) in Egypt: The viewpoints of external and internal customers. *Benchmarking: An International Journal*, **13**(4), 469–92.

Faulkner, B. and Patiar, A. (1997). Workplace induced stress among operational staff in the hotel industry. *International Journal of Hospitality Management*, **16**(1), 99–117.

Findlay, P., Warhurst, C., Keep, E. and Lloyd, C. (2017). Opportunity knocks? The possibilities and levers for improving job quality. *Work and Occupations*, **44**(1), 3–22.

Finn, D.W., Baker, J., Marshall, G.W. and Anderson, R. (1996). Total quality management and internal customers: Measuring internal service quality. *Journal of Marketing Theory and Practice*, **4**(3), 36–51.

GGRAsia (2015). Most Macau casino staff ok with smoking lounges: Poll. Accessed at http://www.ggrasia.com/most-macau-casino-staff-ok-with-smoking-lounges-study/

GGRAsia (2016). Macau smoke ban final vote date uncertain: Legislator. Accessed at http://www.ggrasia.com/macau-smoke-ban-final-vote-date-uncertain-legislator/

GGRAsia (2017). Labour group petitions against smoking lounges in Macau. Accessed at http://www.ggrasia.com/gaming-labour-group-petitions-against-smoking-lounges/

Greene, W.E., Walls, G.D. and Schrest, L.J. (1994). Internal marketing: The key to external marketing success. *Journal of Services Marketing*, **8**(4), 5–13.

Halbe, A. (2013). *Green Energy Initiatives in the Hotel Industry: Factors Influencing Adoption Decisions* (Master of Environmental Studies in Geography), The University of Waterloo.

Hales, C. (1994). 'Internal Marketing' as an approach to human resource management: A new perspective or a metaphor too far? *Human Resource Management Journal*, **5**(1), 50–71.

Hayes, D.K. and Ninemeier, J.D. (2008). *Human Resources Management in the Hospitality Industry*. Hoboken, NJ: John Wiley & Sons.

Healthy WA (n.d.). Smoking in public places. Accessed at http://healthywa.wa.gov.au/Articles/S_T/Smoking-in-public-places

Hoque, K. (2013). *Human Resource Management in the Hotel Industry: Strategy, Innovation and Performance*. London: Routledge.

Hwang, S. and Der-Jang, C. (2005). Relationships among internal marketing, employee job satisfaction and international hotel performance: An empirical study. *International Journal of Management*, **22**(2), 285–93.

Jones, P. and Kahaner, L. (2011). *Say it and Live it: The 50 Corporate Mission Statements that Hit the Mark*. New York: Crown Business.

Jun, M. and Cai, S. (2010). Examining the relationships between internal service quality and its dimensions, and internal customer satisfaction. *Total Quality Management*, **21**(2), 205–23.

Kotler, P., Bowen, J.T. and Makens, J.C. (2006). *Marketing for Hospitality and Tourism*. Frenchs Forest: Pearson Education.

Kusluvan, S., Kusluvan, Z., Ilhan, I. and Buyruk, L. (2010). The human dimension: A review of human resources management issues in the tourism and hospitality industry. *Cornell Hospitality Quarterly*, **51**(2), 171–214.

Las Vegas Sun (2010). Despite health risks, casino dealers still exposed to cigarette smoke. *Las Vegas Sun*. Accessed at https://lasvegassun.com/news/2010/feb/14/smoky-casino-good-business/

Leong, C-C. (2001). Marketing practices and internet marketing: A study of hotels in Singapore. *Journal of Vacation Marketing*, **7**(2), 179–87.

Madera, J.M., Dawson, M., Guchait, P. and Belarmino, A.M. (2017). Strategic human resources management research in hospitality and tourism: A review of current literature and suggestions for the future. *International Journal of Contemporary Hospitality Management*, **29**(1), 48–67.

McCartney, G. (2016). How much to a puff? Macao's casino smoking ban debate and the implications for mainland Chinese visitation. *Gaming Law Review and Economics*, **20**(7), 571–9.

Medlik, S. and Ingram, H. (2000). *The Business of Hotels*. London: Routledge.

Mudie, P. (2003). Internal customer: By design or by default. *European Journal of Marketing*, **37**(9), 1261–76.

Myers, N. (2011). Secondhand smoke raises the stakes in America's casinos. *Stanford Report*, 25 March. Accessed at http://news.stanford.edu/news/2011/march/casino-secondhand-smoke-032511.html

Nyberg, A.J. and Ulrich, M.D. (2015). Renaissance HR. In D. Ulrich, W.A. Schiemann and L. Sartain (eds), *The Rise of HR: Wisdom From 73 Thought Leaders* (pp.415–20). Alexandria, VA: HR Certification Institute.

Ogle, A. (2009). Making sense of the hotel guestroom. *Journal of Retail & Leisure Property*, **8**(3), 159–72.

Ogle, A. and Moreira, P. (2002). Attuning managers' decisions to customer satisfaction:

An introductory study on the evolutionary trend of a 'key' component of hotel service in the Macao SAR (South China). Proceedings from the 'Tourism in Asia: Development, Marketing and Sustainability' Conference, Hong Kong SAR, PR China, organized by the Hong Kong Polytechnic University, Hong Kong SAR, PR China, the University of Houston, Houston, United States of America, and the University of Angers, Angers, France.

Parasuraman, A., Zeithaml, V.A. and Berry, L.L. (1985). A conceptual model of service quality and its implications for future research. *The Journal of Marketing*, **49**(4), 41–50.

Partlow, C.G. (1996). Human-resources practices of TQM hotels. *The Cornell Hotel and Restaurant Administration Quarterly*, **37**(5), 67–77.

Peres, J. (2013). No clear link between passive smoking and lung cancer. *Journal of the National Cancer Institute*, **105**(24), 1844–6.

Quezada, D. (2016). Keeping Hotel Staff Safe. *Hotel Business Review*. Accessed at http://hotelexecutive.com/business_review/5016/keeping-hotel-staff-safe

Quit (2016). Diseases related to secondhand smoke. Accessed at http://www.quit.org.au/about/frequently-asked-questions/faqs-passive-smoking/diseases-secondhand-smoke.html

Quit Victoria (2016). Smokefree outdoor dining and drinking in Victoria. (Position Statements: Quit Resource Centre). Accessed at http://www.quit.org.au/downloads/resource/policy-advocacy/position-statements/smokefree-outdoor-dining-drinking-position-statement.pdf

Rafiq, M. and Ahmed, P.K. (1993). The scope of internal marketing: Defining the boundary between marketing and human resource management. *Journal of Marketing Management*, **9**(3), 219–32.

Rafiq, M. and Ahmed, P.K. (2000). Advances in the internal marketing concept: Definition, synthesis and extension. *Journal of Services Marketing*, **14**(6), 449–62.

Rooke, D. (2016). Sydney's casinos escape lockout laws, smoking bans and more. *The Saturday Paper*. Accessed at https://www.thesaturdaypaper.com.au/news/law-crime/2016/03/12/sydneys-casinos-escape-lockout-laws-smoking-bans-and-more/14577012002995

Safe Work Australia (2015). *Work Health and Safety in the Accommodation and Food Services Industry*. Canberra: Safe Work Australia.

Shamo, F., Wilson, T., Kiley, J. and Repace, J. (2015). Assessing the effect of Michigan's smoke-free law on air quality inside restaurants and casinos: A before-and-after observational study. *BMJ Open*, **5**(7).

Solnet, D., Nickson, D., Robinson, R.N., Kralj, A. and Baum, T. (2014). Discourse about workforce development in tourism: An analysis of public policy, planning, and implementation in Australia and Scotland: Hot air or making a difference? *Tourism Analysis*, **19**(5), 609–23.

Sufi, T. and Lyons, H. (2003). Mission statements exposed. *International Journal of Contemporary Hospitality Management*, **15**(5), 255–62.

Tasker, S-J. (2016). Smoking decision helps James Packer's Macau casinos. *The Australian*, 3 June. Accessed at http://www.theaustralian.com.au/business/companies/smoking-decision-helps-james-packers-macau-casinos/news-story/072bd982181db0487c4f00dfe199500c

The Ritz-Carlton Hotel Company (2016). The employee promise. Accessed at http://www.ritzcarlton.com/en/about/gold-standards

Tobacco Products Control Act 2006, 005 of 2006 C.F.R. (2006).

Trotto, S. (2015). Keeping hotel housekeepers safe. *Safety + Health, National Safety Council*. Accessed at http://www.safetyandhealthmagazine.com/articles/13370-keeping-hotel-housekeepers-safe

US Bureau of Labor Statistics (2014). Bureau of Labor Statistics' Job Openings and Labor Turnover (JOLTS), October.

Vogt, B.J. (2017). Keeping your employees safe and productive. *Hotel Business Review*. Accessed at http://hotelexecutive.com/business_review/4339/keeping-your-employees-safe-and-productive

Wisner, J.D. and Stanley, L.L. (1999). Internal relationships and activities associated with high levels of purchasing service quality. *Journal of Supply Chain Management*, **35**(2), 25–32.

Workplace Health & Safety (2017). Benefits of WHS in your business, 24 February. Accessed at https://www.business.gov.au/info/run/workplace-health-and-safety

Wright, P.M., Dunford, B.B. and Snell, S.A. (2001). Human resources and the resource based view of the firm. *Journal of Management*, **27**(6), 701–21.

Yang, J-T. (2010). Antecedents and consequences of job satisfaction in the hotel industry. *International Journal of Hospitality Management*, **29**(4), 609–19.

Zhou, Z., Bohac, D. and Boyle, R.G. (2016). Continuous weeklong measurements of indoor particle levels in a Minnesota Tribal Casino Resort. *BMC Public Health*, **16**(1), 870.

13. Gender differences in burnout perceptions: the case of hotel employees
Derya Kara and Muzaffer Uysal

INTRODUCTION

Over recent years, tourism and hospitality organizations have constantly improved the quality of services to attract new clients, retain current clients and remain competitive, while at the same time trying to offer better working conditions to attract and retain the best employees (Mansour and Tremblay, 2016). Organizations are required to provide customer contact around the clock 7 days a week. Such a work situation has been reported to be stressful for hospitality workers (Kim et al., 2007). Some researchers reported that the hospitality sector is an important economic force and its contributions to the national economy are numerous in providing employment opportunities, alternative and added income for the rural population, and support for the growth of secondary activities such as material and equipment suppliers. The sector also complements the expansion of both domestic and inbound tourism (Patah et al., 2009). For example, Turkish tourism revenues realized at about $31.5 billion in 2015 (Ministry of Culture and Tourism, 2015). These figures emphasize the centrality of the tourism sector to Turkey's economic success and growth but they also have human resource consequences.

Jenaro et al. (2007) reported that according to estimations, 28 percent of European workers suffer from stress and 23 percent already have burnout. Burnout is a type of prolonged response to chronic emotional and interpersonal stressors on the job. It is an individual stress experience embedded in a context of complex social relationships, and it involves the person's conception of both self and others (Maslach and Goldberg, 1998). Employees who work in hotel enterprises frequently suffer from the effects of burnout since they have constant contact with both co-workers and guests. Employee burnout has some extremely serious consequences for employees and employers (Jackson and Schuler, 1983). Maslach and Jackson (1981) claimed that burnout seems to be correlated with various self-reported indices of personal distress, including physical exhaustion, insomnia, increased use of alcohol and drugs, and marital and family problems. Moreover, burnout is associated with decreased job satisfaction and a reduced commitment to the job or the organization (Maslach et al., 2001). While some hospitality employees cope more effectively than others (Hu and Cheng, 2010), if employees feel that work and life are not balanced, they may leave the job and seek 'quality of life' (Wong and Ko, 2009). Therefore, needs and demands of employees are of concern and interest to hotel managers. Individuals in these positions will endeavor to master and overcome any stress they encounter with whatever unique, diverse methods they can employ (Hu and Cheng, 2010). Thus, this study is designed to address the perceptions of burnout of hotel employees using data from 5-star hotels in Turkey.

DEFINITION OF BURNOUT

The use of the term 'burnout' began to appear with some regularity in the 1970s in the United States, especially among people working in the human services (Maslach et al., 2001). Pienaar and Willemse (2008) reported that the term 'burnout' was initially well researched in the so-called 'helping professions', such as primary care nurses or doctors, but also with respect to teachers, who are in constant interpersonal interaction. Maslach and Jackson (1981) defined burnout as a syndrome of emotional exhaustion and cynicism that occurs frequently among individuals who do 'people-work' of some kind. Maslach et al. (2001) claim that burnout is a problem that is specific to the work context, in contrast to depression, which tends to pervade every domain of a person's life.

Burnout is generally characterized by three key dimensions: exhaustion, personal accomplishment/efficacy and depersonalization. Exhaustion represents the basic individual stress dimension of burnout and refers to feelings of being over-extended and having one's emotional and physical resources depleted (Maslach et al., 2001). Employees who are emotionally exhausted typically feel as though they lack adaptive resources and cannot give any more to their job. The energy that they once had to devote to their work is now depleted, leaving them without the resources to perform their work (Halbesleben and Buckley, 2004). Personal accomplishment (also known as personal efficacy in the literature) represents the self-evaluation dimension of burnout. It refers to feelings of incompetence and a lack of achievement and productivity at work (Maslach et al., 2001). Employees perceive that they cannot perform as well at their job as they once could (Halbesleben and Buckley, 2004). It is characterized by a tendency to evaluate oneself negatively. Frequently there is the perception of a lack of progress or even lost ground (Ledgerwood et al., 1998). Depersonalization (also known as cynicism in the literature) represents the interpersonal context dimension of burnout and refers to a negative, callous or excessively detached response to various aspects of the job (Maslach et al., 2001).

Burnout is a particularly tragic endpoint for professionals who entered the job with positive expectations, enthusiasm, and a dedication to helping people (Maslach and Goldberg, 1998). Organizational conditions can potentially cause burnout such as lack of rewards, excessive and outdated policies and procedures, lack of clear-cut expectations and job responsibilities, and the lack of support groups or cohesive work groups (Jackson and Schuler, 1983). Kilic et al. (2011) reported that working environment, working conditions, organizational structure, task uncertainty, task conflict, weak management, weak communication, problematic customers and heavy workload are factors in professional burnout in the accommodation industry. Moreover, several personal characteristics (for example idealistic expectations, idealistic job and career goals, and personal responsibility for low personal accomplishment) usually interact with organizational conditions to actually cause employee burnout (Jackson and Schuler, 1983). Jung and Yoon (2013) found that hotel employees' perception of stress depends more on the particular organization than on individual characteristics. In other words, the source of stress was either the unique rules or the work environment of an organization, but not so much personal characteristics.

The feelings created by burnout can have a significant effect on an employee's ability to deliver quality service (Ledgerwood et al., 1998). Also, burnout appears to be a factor in job turnover, absenteeism, low morale and reduced service quality (Maslach and Jackson, 1981; Singh, 2000; Schaufeli and Bakker, 2004). Choi (2006) reported that the hospitality industry has a higher turnover rate than other industries. Aksu (2004) investigated employee turnover in Turkey using data from 5-star hotels and found that the main reasons for personal turnover are low wages, bad relationships between subordinates and superiors, long working hours, lack of social life and limited job guarantees in Turkey. Lee and Shin (2005) investigated the psychological dimensions such as job burnout, engagement and exhaustion. They found that turnover intention was positively correlated with workload, exhaustion and cynicism. Babakus et al. (2008) investigated effects of job demands, job resources and a personal resource (intrinsic motivation) on emotional exhaustion and turnover intentions. Also they found that job demands (role conflict and role ambiguity) trigger front-line employees' emotional exhaustion and turnover intentions. Jung et al.'s (2012) study investigated interrelationships among culinary employees' perception of role stress, burnout and turnover intention in a deluxe hotel. The results showed a positive relationship between employees' perceptions of role stress and burnout. Participants who reported a high level of burnout were more likely to leave their position. Moreover, burnout is also extremely costly for organizations, with estimates from $500 to $10000 per person in the hotel industry, depending upon the level of the position (Perrewe et al., 1991). Since burnout has important and costly ramifications for organizations and individuals, it is important that management have a clear and accurate understanding of the construct as well as an understanding of the factors and conditions that may contribute to burnout (Ledgerwood et al., 1998).

GENDER DIFFERENCES IN PERCEPTIONS OF BURNOUT

In the developing countries, the tourism sector has grown since the 1950s and has become the area where women are employed the most. Relying on research results, Oktik (2001) states that one in every 15 people in the world works in the tourism sector and half of these are women. Especially in the USA, 52 percent of employees in this sector are women. It is clear that women make up a significant proportion of the labor force in an increasing number of countries. A heightened awareness of the particular factors, which influence women's participation and/or the constraints they may be facing, is increasingly desirable for those who manage these women in the industry (Burrell et al., 1997). According to ILO estimates, the proportion of women in the tourism industry (excluding the informal sector) has risen to 46 percent, while in catering and accommodation they represent over 90 percent of all employees. They occupy the lower levels of the occupational structure in the tourism labor market, with few career development opportunities and low levels of remuneration (some estimates suggest that wages for women are up to 20 percent lower than those for men). The greater incidence of unemployment among women is attributed to their low skill levels and their low social status in many poor countries. They also tend to be the first affected when labor retrenchment occurs as a result of recession or adjustment to new technology. It should also be noted that the majority of workers in subcontracted, temporary, casual or part-time employment are women (ILO, 2001).

Changing gender roles in the last 20 to 25 years have allowed more women to combine domestic responsibilities with paid work outside the home environment. More families are comprised of dual earners where both partners participate in the labor market and are expected to participate in work in the household. Women's traditional caring responsibilities as well as their primary responsibility for housework remain a significant barrier to employment opportunities (Lane, 2008). Doble and Supriya (2010) reported that when work does not permit women to take care of their family, they feel unhappy, disappointed and frustrated. They draw tight boundaries between work and family. Moreover, there is enough evidence to suggest that even if a woman were to gain a position in management, she might not necessarily benefit from equal pay (Skalpe, 2007). Female employees usually are quite powerless to compete with their male counterparts due to several visible or invisible barriers and challenges; these include: forgoing marriage, motherhood, discrimination, and stereotyping. This problem becomes magnified when the operational aspects of hospitality management require long working hours and high degrees of mobility (Pinar et al., 2011).

Results from the literature show that studies about burnout with respect to gender have mixed findings. Some studies show higher burnout for women, some show higher scores for men, and others find no overall differences (Maslach et al., 2001). Civilidag (2014) investigated hotel employees' burnout in Turkey and found that burnout doesn't differ significantly with respect to gender variable. Anitei et al. (2015) investigated gender differences in workload and self-perceived burnout in a multinational company from Bucharest. Their findings showed that there are significant differences between women and men in workload and burnout that show women being characterized by significantly higher levels of burnout and workload than men. Bahar (2006) studied burnout of front-line hotel employees and found that there were significant correlations with respect to gender. Matlin's research (2004) shows that individuals stereotypically assume that women are more susceptible to stress – and by extension to burnout – than men. If managers tend to perceive female employees as disproportionately more susceptible to burnout than male employees, women may have less chance of obtaining challenging assignments and promotions (cited in Purvanova and Muros, 2010). Schwab and Iwanicki (1982) found gender-based feelings of burnout. Male teachers were found to have more negative attitudes toward students than females. Jackson (1993) also found significant differences in levels of burnout with respect to gender variable. Other research done by Cooper and Payne (1992) has shown that gender can moderate the associations between stressors and outcomes such as physical symptoms, job satisfaction, turnover and burnout (cited in O'Neill and Davis, 2011). Study conducted by Michael et al. (2009) examined gender differences in occupational stress and showed that females experience higher levels of occupational stress than males.

In spite of the substantial numbers of female employees in the tourism industry, there are still many barriers that prevent them from reaching senior positions in management. These include compensation and job

hotel, an appropriate number of questionnaires were sent to each hotel manager to distribute. Each hotel property, depending on its employee size, received 50 to 120 questionnaires, and in total around 1200 questionnaires were distributed. The questionnaire was completed by employees in all departments of the hotels selected for this study. After a waiting period of 5 months, 443 usable questionnaires were generated, which provided a response rate of almost 37 percent. To prevent potential language problems, the questionnaire was translated into Turkish by the research team using a back translation method.

The data questionnaire consisted of employees' demographic characteristics such as gender, age, marital status and education level, and employee burnout. Employee burnout was captured using a 22-item measure developed by Maslach and Jackson (1981). The measure involved three dimensions: emotional exhaustion; personal accomplishment; and depersonalization. The coefficient Alpha for the entire list of 22 items was 0.76, which is deemed acceptable. Nine items in the emotional exhaustion subscale described feelings of being emotionally over-extended and exhausted by one's work. Personal accomplishment contained eight items that describe feelings of competence and successful achievement in one's work with people. Five items in the depersonalization subscale described an unfeeling and impersonal response toward recipients of one's care or service.

The data analysis of the study consisted of three steps. First, a descriptive analysis of the characteristics of hotel employees was done. In the second step, independent t-tests were used to examine gender differences regarding burnout dimensions (emotional exhaustion, personal accomplishment and depersonalization). Finally, multivariate analysis of variance and co-variance (MANOVA and MANCOVA) were employed in order to test 'true' gender differences while controlling for other variables such as age, marital status, monthly income level (TL), education level, type of department, type of work (part-time or full-time work), length of time in the organization, and length of time in the tourism sector.

RESULTS

According to the descriptive statistics, the majority of the respondents were male (72.9 percent), 27–42 years old (50.6 percent) and single (61.2 percent). The income distribution of respondents showed that 36.1 percent of employees were between 1501 and 2500 TL and 28.9 percent employees were between 1500 TL and less. In total, 47.9 percent of the respondents had high school education. The distribution of work departments was fairly even: 11.7 percent front office, 14.9 percent food and beverage, 20.8 percent housekeeping, 10.2 percent accounting, 10.4 percent public relations, 7.7 percent sales and marketing, 13.1 percent human resources and 8.6 percent other departments. In terms of the employment status, the majority of the respondents were full-time employees (81.0 percent). Respondents had been working for an average of 1–5 years in their current organization, with 42.4 percent working in the tourism sector.

GENDER DIFFERENCES IN PERCEPTIONS OF EMPLOYEE BURNOUT DIMENSIONS

Table 13.1 reports the t-test results in gender differences in perceptions of employees' burnout dimensions. According to these results, female employees reported significantly different mean scores in 'depersonalization' (Xfemale = 2.8667, Xmale = 2.3697, $p < 0.05$). However; 'emotional exhaustion' and 'personal accomplishment' dimensions were not statistically significant at the 0.05 probability level. There are no differences between the two groups in regard to the rank importance of burnout dimensions. Female employees scored lowest for 'emotional exhaustion' and male employees scored lowest for 'depersonalization'.

In order to shed further light on the issue, MANOVA (A one-way between-group multivariate analysis of variance) was also performed to investigate sex differences in burnout dimensions. Three delineated factors were used: 'emotional exhaustion', 'personal accomplishment' and 'depersonalization' as dependent variables. The independent variable was gender. Preliminary assumptions were evaluated to check for normality, linearity, univariate and multivariate outliers, homogeneity of variance–covariance matrices, and multicollinearity, with no serious violations noted. There was a statistically significant difference between males

Table 13.1   Gender differences in perceptions of employee burnout dimensions

Burnout dimensions	Female	Male	t-value	Sig.
Emotional exhaustion	2.7722 (3)	2.6663 (2)	−1.185	.237
Personal accomplishment	3.0917 (1)	3.2078 (1)	−1.131	.258
Depersonalization	2.8667 (2)	2.3697 (3)	−5.702	.000

Notes:
Scale ratings:1= Always; 2 = Usually; 3 = Sometimes; 4 = Seldom; 5 = Never.
The parentheses beside the mean scores indicate the rank of the main values.

and females on the combined dependent variables, F (3, 439) = 14.302, p = .000; Wilk's Lambda = 0.94; partial eta squared = 0.08. When the results for the dependent variables were considered separately, difference to reach statistical significance, using a Bonferroni adjusted alpha level of 0.067, was observed in depersonalization, F (1, 441) = 32.515, p = .000, partial eta squared = 0.069. An inspection of the mean scores indicated that females reported slightly higher levels of 'depersonalization' (M = 2.867, SD = 0.86824) than males (F = 2.370, SD = 0.79483). Once this was confirmed, then controlling for other variables was also introduced into the analysis of the study.

GENDER DIFFERENCES IN BURNOUT DIMENSIONS CONTROLLING FOR OTHER VARIABLES

MANCOVA was employed to test gender differences while controlling for other variables, such as age, marital status, monthly income level, education, type of department, type of work (part-time or full-time), length of time in the organization, and length of time in the tourism sector. In terms of assumptions, the distribution of data variables was checked for outliers first, and then the box plot and normal Q-Q plot of skewness options of selected variables were examined. It was determined that the data met multivariate normality. The findings indicate that gender differences in perceptions of burnout dimensions (that is, multivariate main effect) exist after controlling for these covariates (see Table 13.2). These findings reveal that male and female respondents, after eliminating the impact of age, marital status, income level, education, type of department, type of work, length of time in the organization, and length of time, show statistically significant variation in burnout perceptions. After controlling for age, the mean score of 'emotional exhaustion', 'personal accomplishment', and 'depersonalization' factors showed a significant change between male and female respondents. When the study controlled monthly income level, type of department, and length of time in the tourism sector the mean score 'personal accomplishment' factor showed a significant change between male and female respondents. After controlling for type of work and length of time in this organization, the mean score of 'emotional exhaustion' and 'depersonalization' factors showed a significant change between male and female respondents.

Table 13.2   Gender differences in burnout dimensions controlling for other variables

Item controlled	Emotional exhaustion (F,p)	Personal accomplishment (F,p)	Depersonalization (F,p)
Age	5.143 (.024)*	15.540 (.000)*	5.566 (.019)*
Marital status	.279 (.598)	.743 (.389)	1.386 (.240)
Monthly income level (TL)	.017 (.896)	14.120 (.000)*	1.080 (.299)
Education level	.449 (.503)	.069 (.793)	.019 (.889)
Type of department	2.570 (.110)	28.541 (.000)*	1.754 (.186)
Type of work	14.731 (.000)*	2.271 (.133)	8.091 (.005)*
Length of time in this organization	5.202 (.023)*	.598 (.440)	6.910 (.009)*
Length of time in tourism sector	1.707 (.192)	42.964 (.000)*	.580 (.447)

Note: Significance levels are indicated in parentheses (*$p < 0.05$); *indicates the significant gender differences in burnout perceptions.

CONCLUSIONS

This study utilized employees in 5-star hotels in Turkey to examine if there are differences between female and male hotel employees with respect to dimensions of burnout. From a theoretical implication perspective, the main contribution of this research is to further examine and reveal evidence for gender differences in perceptions of burnout while controlling select variables in the setting of hospitality employees. From this evaluation, we can reach some conclusions about gender equality and opportunity in the hospitality and tourism sector in Turkey. The results provide information that can be utilized to understand and reduce the burnout levels of both male and female employees.

The findings of this study suggest several practical implications. If employees feel that work and life are not balanced, they may leave their job and seek 'quality of life' (Wong and Ko, 2009). Since burnout has important and costly ramifications for organizations and individuals, it is important that management have a clear and accurate understanding of the construct as well as an understanding of the factors and conditions that contribute to burnout (Ledgerwood et al., 1998). In order to decrease the burnout level of employees, managers should attempt to provide a working environment that is sensitive to the needs of employees and their competency levels. This will help improve the relationship with employees.

Gender differences were first compared using independent t-tests, and according to these results female employees reported significantly different mean scores in 'depersonalization'; however, 'emotional exhaustion' and 'personal accomplishment' dimensions were not statistically significant at the 0.05 probability level. This finding is also consistent with the MANOVA analysis in which the independent variable was gender and the three delineated factors were dependent variables. An inspection of the mean scores indicated that females reported slightly higher levels of 'depersonalization' than males. In a subsequent analysis, MANCOVA was also employed to test the gender differences while controlling for other variables, such as age, marital status, monthly income level, education level, type of department, type of work (part-time or full-time), length of time in the organization, and length of time in the tourism sector (Table 13.2). For example, after controlling for the variable 'age', the mean score of emotional exhaustion, personal accomplishment and depersonalization showed a significant difference between male and female respondents. When the study controlled for monthly income level, the mean score of the 'personal accomplishment' dimension showed a significant difference between male and female respondents. This implies that male employees reported higher burnout in the 'personal accomplishment' dimension than female employees. Type of department shows a difference between male and female respondents for the 'personal accomplishment' dimension. As a result of this analysis, it can be inferred that male employees reported higher burnout in the personal accomplishment dimension. After controlling for the type of work, the mean score of the 'emotional exhaustion' and 'depersonalization' dimensions showed a significant difference between male and female respondents. After controlling for length of time in this, the mean score of the 'emotional exhaustion' and 'depersonalization' dimensions showed a significant difference between male and female respondents. When the study controlled for length of time in the tourism sector, the mean score of the 'personal accomplishment' dimension showed a significant difference between male and female respondents.

The study results can be beneficial for many hospitality employees (especially for many female employees). In order to improve gender equality in the Turkish hospitality industry, an initial remedy could be to offer more employment opportunities for females. This may attract highly skilled female employees, which could positively impact the performance and productivity of the tourism and hospitality industry. A similar sentiment was also echoed by an earlier study that examined gender issues in the hospitality sector in Turkey (Pinar et al., 2011). This study contributes to the literature of human resource practices in tourism and hospitality management in 5-star hotels in Turkey. Research findings shed light on the ways burnout matters could be viewed and improvements can be done. Future studies should also include place- and culture-specific variables as control variables to understand gender differences in burnout perceptions. Future studies need to also consider the role of controlling variables and their moderation influences on the outcome of burnout for the study to provide meaningful and useful implications. Simple comparisons of two gender groups may cancel important information and could also lead to ineffective implications.

REFERENCES

Aksu, A.A. (2004). Turnover cost: Research among five-star hotels in the city of Antalya, Turkey. *Tourism Analysis*, **9**(3), 207–17.

Anitei, M., Chraif, M. and Ioniţa, E. (2015). Gender differences in workload and self-perceived burnout in a multinational company from Bucharest. *Procedia – Social and Behavioral Sciences*, **187**, 733–7.

Babakus, E., Yavas, U. and Karatepe, O.M. (2008). The effects of job demands, job resources and intrinsic motivation on emotional exhaustion and turnover intentions: A study in the Turkish hotel industry. *International Journal of Hospitality & Tourism Administration*, **9**(4), 384–404.

Bahar, E. (2006). Tukenmislik sendromu, otel isletmelerinde on buro calisanlarinda bir uygulama (Unpublished Master's thesis). Adnan Menderes Universitesi Sosyal Bilimler Enstitusu, Turkey.

Bailyn, L., Drago, R. and Kochan, T. (2001). Integrating work and family life: A holistic approach (Report for Alfred P. Sloan Foundation). Washington, DC: Family Policy Network.

Burrell, J., Manfredi, S. and Rollin, H. (1997). Equal opportunities for women employees in the hospitality industry: A comparison between France, Italy, Spain and the UK. *International Journal of Hospitality Management*, **16**(2), 161–79.

Choi, K. (2006). A structural relationship analysis of hotel employees' turnover intention. *Asia Pacific Journal of Tourism Research*, **11**(4), December, 321–37.

Civilidag, A. (2014). Hotel employees' mobbing, burnout, job satisfaction and perceived organizational support: A research on hospitality in Turkey. *European Scientific Journal*, **10**(35), 1–22.

Cooper, C.L. and Payne, R.L. (1992). International perspectives on research into work, well-being, and stress management. In J.C. Quick, L.R. Murphy and J.J. Hurrell Jr. (eds), *Stress and Well-being at Work: Assessments and Interventions for Occupational Mental Health*. Washington, DC: APA, pp. 348–68.

Doble, N. and Supriya, M.V. (2010). Gender differences in the perception of work–life balance. *Management*, **5**(4), 331–42.

Halbesleben, J.R.B. and Buckley, M.R. (2004). Burnout in organizational life. *Journal of Management*, **30**(6), 859–79.

Hu, H-H. and Cheng, C-W. (2010). Job stress, coping strategies, and burnout among hotel industry supervisors in Taiwan. *The International Journal of Human Resource Management*, **21**(8), 1337–50.

ILO (International Labour Organization) (2001). Human resources development, employment and globalization in the hotel, catering and tourism sector. Report for discussion at the Tripartite Meeting on the Human Resources Development, Employment and Globalization in the Hotel, Catering and Tourism Sector. Geneva: International Labour Office.

Jackson, R.A. (1993). An analysis of burnout among School of Pharmacy faculty. *American Journal of Pharmaceutical Education*, **57**(1), 9–17.

Jackson, S.E. and Schuler, R.S. (1983). Preventing employee burnout. *Personnel*, **60**(2), 58–68.

Jenaro, C., Flores, N. and Arias, B. (2007). Burnout and coping in human service practitioners. *Professional Psychology: Research and Practice*, **38**(1), 80–87.

Jung, H. and Yoon, H. (2013). Is the individual or the organization the cause of hotel employees' stress? A longitudinal study on differences in role stress between subjects. *International Journal of Hospitality Management*, **33**, 494–9.

Jung, H.S., Yoon, H.H. and Kim, Y.J. (2012). Effects of culinary employees' role stress on burnout and turnover intention in hotel industry: Moderating effects on employees' tenure. *The Service Industries Journal*, **32**(13), 2145–65.

Kilic, G., Pelit, E. and Selvi, M.S. (2011). The relationship between professional burnout and job satisfaction levels of employee: A study into employees in hotel enterprises. *International Journal of Human Sciences*, **8**(1), 441–63.

Kim, H.J., Shin, K.H. and Umbreit, W.T. (2007). Hotel job burnout: The role of personality characteristics. *International Journal of Hospitality Management*, **26**(2), 421–34.

Lane, L. (2008). Perceived work–life conflict among Swedish women in dual-earner families – a preliminary study. Paper presented at *Fourth Symposium: Gender and Well-being: the Role of Institutions from Past to Present*, June, Madrid.

Ledgerwood, C., Crotts, J. and Everett, A. (1998). Antecedents of employee burnout in the hotel industry. *Progress in Tourism and Hospitality Research*, **4**(1), 31–44.

Lee, K.E. and Shin, K.H. (2005), Job burnout, engagement and turnover intention of dieticians and chefs at a contract foodservice management company. *Journal of Community Nutrition*, **7**(2), 100–106.

Li, L. and Leung, R. (2001). Female managers in Asian hotels: Profile and career challenges. *International Journal of Contemporary Hospitality Management*, **13**(4), 189–96.

Mansour, S. and Tremblay, D.G. (2016). How the need for 'leisure benefit systems' as a 'resource passageways' moderates the effect of work–leisure conflict on job burnout and intention to leave: A study in the hotel industry in Quebec. *Journal of Hospitality and Tourism Management*, **27**, 4–11.

Maslach, C. and Goldberg, J. (1998). Prevention of burnout: New perspectives. *Applied and Preventive Psychology*, **7**(1), 63–74.

Maslach, C. and Jackson, S. (1981). The measurement of experienced burnout. *Journal of Organizational Behavior*, **2**(2), 99–113.

Maslach, C., Schaufeli, W.B. and Leiter, M.P. (2001). Job burnout. *Annual Review of Psychology*, **52**(1), 397–422.

Matlin, M.W. (2004). *The Psychology of Women*, 5th edn. Belmont, CA: Thomson Wadsworth.

Michael, G., Anastasios, S., Helen, K., Catherine, K. and Christine, K. (2009). Gender differences in experiencing occupational stress: The role of age, education, and marital status. *Stress and Health*, **25**(5), 397–404.

Ministry of Culture and Tourism (1989). Hotel and tourism industry labor force survey. Ankara: Ministry of Culture and Tourism.

Ministry of Culture and Tourism (2009). Tourism Statistics. Accessed at http://www.kultur.gov.tr/TR/belge/1-63779/turizm-belgeli-tesisler.html.

Ministry of Culture and Tourism (2015). Tourism statistics. Accessed 20 February 2016 at https://www.kultur.gov.tr/EN,153030/tourism-receipt-expenditure-and-average-expenditure.html.

O'Neill, J.W. and Davis, K. (2011). Work stress and well-being in the hotel industry. *International Journal of Hospitality Management*, **30**(2), 385–90.

Oktik, N. (2001). Turizm sektorunde calisan kadinlarin toplumsal degisime etkileri. *Sosyal ve Beseri Bilimler Araştırmaları Dergisi*, **4**(Spring), 145–51.

Patah, M.O.R.A., Radzi, S.M., Abdullah, R., Adzmy, A., Zain, R.A. and Derani, N. (2009). The influence of psychological empowerment on overall job satisfaction of front office receptionists. *International Journal of Business and Management*, **4**(11), 167–76.

Perrewe, P.L., Brymer, R.A., Stepina, L.P. and Hassell, B.L. (1991). A causal model examining the effects of age discrimination on employee psychological reactions and subsequent turnover intentions. *International Journal of Hospitality Management*, **10**(3), 245–60.

Pienaar, J. and Willemse, S.A. (2008). Burnout, engagement, coping and general health of service employees in the hospitality industry. *Tourism Management*, **29**(6), 1053–63.

Pinar, M., McCuddy, M.K., Birkan, I. and Kozak, M. (2011). Gender diversity in the hospitality industry: An empirical study in Turkey. *International Journal of Hospitality Management*, **30**(1), 73–81.

Purvanova, R.K. and Muros, J.P. (2010). Gender differences in burnout: A meta-analysis. *Journal of Vocational Behavior*, **77**(2), 168–85.

Schaufeli, W.B. and Bakker, A.B. (2004). Job demands, job resources, and their relationship with burnout and engagement: A multi-sample study. *Journal of Organizational Behavior*, **25**(3), 293–315.

Schwab, R.L. and Iwanicki, E.F. (1982). Who are our burned out teachers? *Educational Research Quarterly*, **7**(2), 5–17.

Singh, J. (2000). Performance productivity and quality of frontline employees in service organizations. *Journal of Marketing*, **64**(2), 15–34.

Skalpe, O. (2007). The CEO gender pay gap in the tourism industry – evidence from Norway. *Tourism Management*, **28**(3), 845–53.

Wong, S.C.K. and Ko, A. (2009). Exploratory study of understanding hotel employees' perception on work–life balance issues. *International Journal of Hospitality Management*, **28**(2), 195–203.

Yamane, T. (2001). *Temel Ornekleme Yontemleri* (1st edn). (trans. Alptekin Esin, M. Akif Bakir, Celal Aydin and Esen Gurbuzsel). Istanbul: Literatur Yayincilik.

PART V

HUMAN RESOURCE MANAGEMENT INITIATIVES

14. Diversity training in the hospitality and tourism industry

Juan M. Madera, Camille E. Kapoor and Lindsey Lee

INTRODUCTION

The hospitality and tourism workforce encompasses a diversity of cultures, age groups, racial and ethnic backgrounds, sexual orientations, religions, and disability statuses (Gröschl, 2011; Madera, 2011; Singal, 2014). According the Bureau of Labor Statistics (2015), 52.6 percent of those employed in the Accommodation and Food Services sectors are women, 13.4 percent are Black or African American, 7.2 percent are Asian, and 25.3 percent are Hispanic or Latino. Therefore, women account for more than half of the hospitality industry employees in the US and non-whites account for approximately 45.9 percent (Bureau of Labor Statistics, 2015). While the majority of workplace diversity research has focused on the North American workforce, a diverse workforce is also a global reality (Shen et al., 2009). For example, in most Western countries, including Europe, Australia, New Zealand, Canada and the United States, cultural diversity has been the most studied dimension of diversity due to the large number of immigrants in the workforce. In fact, a search of peer-reviewed journal articles in academic journals since 1990 for the keywords "cultural diversity" resulted in over 18 000 articles in the English language (almost 1000 more articles with these keywords were available in other languages). As a result of such diversity, hospitality and tourism companies have invested in programs that facilitate and create a positive environment for organizational members employed in a diverse workplace (Gröschl, 2011; Madera, 2013).

Diversity training is the most commonly used method to implement and maintain a culture of diversity and inclusion. Although diversity training can vary widely with regard to many characteristics (for example, specific content, trainer characteristics, and delivery methods), they share one common goal, which is to "increase knowledge about diversity, to improve attitudes about diversity, and to develop diversity skills" (Kulik and Roberson, 2008, p. 310). A wide variety of delivery methods are used in diversity training, including online modules, classroom-based training, videos, discussions, role plays, simulations and exercises (Bendick et al., 2001; Pendry et al., 2007). Meta-analytic research illustrates that diversity training is effective in influencing organizational members' behavioral, attitudinal, cognitive and affective learning (Bezrukova et al., 2016; Kalinoski et al., 2013). In fact, Bezrukova et al. (2016) found that diversity training had stable or even increased effects on cognitive learning in the long term. They also found that focusing on diversity skills, as well as awareness, is more effective in diversity training than focusing on either skills or awareness alone (Bezrukova et al., 2016). Kalinoski et al. (2013) found that affective learning may be better enhanced when diversity training uses active training, such as exercises, and occurs face-to-face. Holding longer diversity training sessions was also found to positively impact affective-based outcomes (Kalinoski et al., 2013).

Research on diversity training in the hospitality and tourism industry is sparse; however, this body of literature is consistent with the general management literature, demonstrating the positive effects of diversity training (Madera et al., 2011a; Madera et al., 2013c; Waight and Madera, 2011; Weaver et al., 2003). For example, Reynolds et al. (2014) argue that although little research on diversity training has been conducted in the hospitality industry, the high employment rates of women and minorities in the service sector make diversity training research in this industry especially important.

This chapter will review the reasons why diversity training is important for the hospitality and tourism industry. We will then review the literature on how diversity training is developed and implemented in organizations. Finally, we provide practical suggestions on how hospitality and tourism organizations should implement diversity training.

WHY DIVERSITY TRAINING MATTERS

Defining Diversity

Theoretically, "diversity" can be attached to various meanings, including broad definitions that encompass a variety of demographic dimensions (for example, race, age, gender, ethnicity, disability, sexual orientation) as well as individual dimensions (for example, parental status, learning styles, education level, personality) and narrow definitions of diversity, which may only consider a few demographic dimensions, such as race, gender or age (Roberson et al. 2003). While the decision to define diversity broadly versus narrowly in a diversity training program should be based on the outcome goal for the diversity training, the literature does suggest that a broader definition is more accepted by trainees (Jones et al., 2013). A major reason for this finding is that employees feel that a broad approach is more inclusive and therefore representative of any demographic group, including their own (Roberson et al., 2003). A key distinction in the current understanding of the definition of diversity is a shift toward an overall inclusiveness in how diversity is understood (Kapoor, 2011).

Macro-Level Perspective

The literature on workforce diversity provides macro-level and micro-level understanding of the benefits of diversity training for hospitality and tourism organizations (that is, macro-level perspective) and illustrates why diversity training leads to positive benefits for diverse employees (that is, micro-level perspective). From a macro-level perspective, research in the area of strategic human resource management theory purports that diversity training can be considered a strategic human resource practice that is likely to provide firms with a competitive advantage (Cox and Blake, 1991; McKay et al., 2008; 2009). For example, Richard (2000) suggests that managing diversity programs, such as diversity training, provide organizations with a competitive advantage based on building and maintaining an inimitable, multicultural workforce. Accordingly, a multicultural workforce serves as capital that is valuable for organizational outcomes. In fact, research demonstrates that diversity is positively related to organizational outcomes, such as innovation, financial performance and lower turnover rates (for example, Richard et al., 2004; Richard and Johnson, 1999; Richard et al., 2003).

Following this line of research, Kim (2006) argues that diversity provides hospitality organizations with four broad benefits. These include: (1) providing new and fresh ideas: a diverse workforce can enhance an organization's marketing strategy, because diversity in work groups often leads to diverse ideas and perspectives; (2) improving firm growth through competing effectively in international markets, because a diverse workforce can be leveraged to compete in international markets; (3) enhancing firm image through reducing the chance of negative publicity from discrimination allegations; and (4) creating a pool of valuable human resources, because women and ethnic groups account for the fastest growing group of employees.

Supporting the notion that hospitality organizations benefit from diversity programs, Singal (2014) argues that diversity management and performance influence financial performance. This study examines two hypotheses focusing on diversity management and performance in hospitality firms compared to non-hospitality firms and how investing in diversity management and performance leads to higher business performance. Singal found that hospitality organizations utilize statistically stronger diversity performance and diversity initiatives compared to non-hospitality organizations. Secondly, the study found that although diversity performance influenced financial performance for both hospitality and non-hospitality organizations, the superior nature of hospitality diversity management and performance was mirrored in greater financial performance for hospitality organizations compared to non-hospitality organizations. Most importantly, the findings suggest that continuing to invest in diversity management and improving diversity performance will positively influence financial performance for the future.

Micro-Level Perspective

From a micro-level perspective, social identity theory (Hogg and Terry, 2000; Tajfel and Turner, 1986) provides a theoretical rationale for why diversity training has a positive impact on diverse employees. Social identity theory suggests that individuals perceive themselves as members of a social group using personally meaningful dimensions such as sex, race or age to categorize themselves and others into groups. Accordingly, because part of their self-esteem depends on identifying with a group, individuals tend to express favoritism toward their own group, preferring to interact with members of their own identity group than with members of other groups – leading to in-group solidarity, cooperation and support.

This line of reasoning suggests that having diversity training could send signals to diverse employees about how diversity is valued in the workplace. Past research shows that diverse employees, such as women, ethnic minorities, and sexual-orientation minorities take into account the extent to which organizations have supportive policies and structures when considering job opportunities. For example, Black applicants are attracted to organizations that consciously recruit minorities (Avery, 2003; Avery et al., 2004). Similarly, gay employees have more positive work attitudes and are more likely to be "out" in organizations that have gay-supportive policies than in organizations that do not have such supportive policies (Griffith and Hebl, 2002). Lastly, ethnic minority employees perceive less workplace discrimination, which leads to more job satisfaction and fewer turnover intentions, when their workplace offers diversity training (Waight and Madera, 2011).

Research also shows that diversity training and other diversity management initiatives have a positive impact on diversity climate. Diversity climate is both a shared macro-level climate and an individual-level (that is, psychological) diversity climate, which is based on an employee's observations of his or her organization's policies related to diversity. Both the shared and individual perceptions create a climate that fosters a positive work environment for a multicultural workforce versus a climate that is hostile or indifferent toward a multicultural workforce (Mor Barak et al., 1998). Research has shown that positive diversity climates are related to employee job satisfaction and organizational commitment, and lower turnover intentions (for example, Chen et al., 2012; Kunze et al., 2011; Madera et al., 2013a; McKay et al., 2007; McKay et al., 2011).

Positive diversity climates are also related to lower turnover intentions and higher commitment among managers (Gonzalez and DeNisi, 2009; Kunze et al., 2011; McKay et al., 2007). In a study from the hospitality and tourism industry, Madera et al. (2013a) examined the influence of managers' perceived diversity climate on role ambiguity, role conflict and job satisfaction. The study found that when managers positively perceived a diversity climate they also reported less role ambiguity and role conflict, along with higher job satisfaction. Consequently, in conjunction with previous findings associating perceived diversity climate and commitment, commitment was positively influenced since these job stressors were reduced and job satisfaction increased.

In addition, Madera et al. (2016) support previous findings of psychological diversity climate, organizational justice, and ultimately job satisfaction. The study found that racioethnic minorities experience stronger effects of psychological diversity climate and, by proxy, organizational justice and job satisfaction. Therefore, by influencing organizational justice through racioethnic minority status for managers, the benefits of positive diversity climates can exponentially increase job satisfaction. Influencing managers and managerial decisions through positive diversity climates can help further facilitate the benefits throughout hospitality organizations and organization members.

IMPLEMENTING DIVERSITY TRAINING: A REVIEW OF THE LITERATURE

Diversity training can be implemented as a one-time effort or can be implemented as part of a broader ongoing effort (Bendick et al., 2001). Diversity training programs are implemented in a variety of ways, but a common theme to all diversity training programs is to improve knowledge and attitudes toward diversity and to develop skills related to managing workforce diversity (Kulik and Roberson, 2008). There are also a variety of objectives of diversity training, but the majority are often related to: (1) increasing awareness about diversity issues; (2) reducing discrimination toward minority employees; and (3) attracting and retaining a diverse workforce (Cox, 1991; Chavez and Weisinger, 2008; Wentling and Palma-Rivas, 1999).

With respect to the delivery methods, the most common include traditional classroom-based training, the use of visual stimuli (for example, videos), group and class readings and discussions, role-playing, scenario-based simulations, and exercises (Pendry et al., 2007). While the literature is not clear on which delivery method is the most effective, the literature does suggest that using multiple methods is more effective than using a single method (Bezrukova et al., 2016). Regarding the trainer, Bendick et al. (2001) found that the typical diversity training program involves 1–2 trainers with about 20–30 participants and that the typical diversity training program lasts 4–10 hours. Bendick et al. (2001) also reported that the most common reason for implementing a diversity training program was to decrease discrimination.

Most of the research regarding the outcomes of diversity training relies on Kirkpatrick's (1987) typology of training outcomes: training reactions, learning, behavior and results. For example, attitudes and knowledge regarding diversity are often assessed immediately after training (for example, Holladay et al., 2003; Holladay and Quinones, 2008). Behavioral measures often rely on self-report surveys that include supportive behaviors and intentions (for example, Combs and Luthans, 2007; De Meuse et al., 2007; Madera et al., 2013b). Lastly, the experience of discrimination from minority employees has also been examined as an outcome of diversity training (for example, King et al., 2012; Waight and Madera, 2011).

Diversity Training Research in the Hospitality and Tourism Context

In a study of hospitality and tourism organizations ranked as the best employers for diversity, Madera (2013) found that the majority of these organizations implement diversity training. For example, Starwood Hotels and Resorts Worldwide offered inclusion training to reinforce positive messages about diversity. Similarly, Marriott International encourage their employees to gain cultural competencies by requiring them to take diversity training. The diversity training program at Marriott International teaches employees how to work with diverse customers and diverse employees. MGM Mirage also offers diversity training for both employees and managers. And finally, the Walt Disney Company offers an array of diversity training programs that are customized to meet employee needs. Madera (2013) also found that the majority of these organizations define diversity broadly in their approach to diversity training. By taking a broad approach to diversity training, these organizations were consistent with research-based evidence that shows that employees prefer diversity training that takes a broad approach (Roberson et al., 2003). In doing so, employees feel that every group, whether based on race or age, is represented as diverse, including their own.

Lee and Chon (2000) examined diversity training in regard to training practices and effectiveness in the franchise restaurant industry. Lee and Chon found that awareness of the legal repercussions and management attitudes toward diversity should be emphasized and highlighted. Providing a "big picture" approach to diversity training would help solidify the need for such programs. The results also suggested that companies focused on reactive and result-oriented training goals, and showed communication and diversity sensitivity to be the most useful training content needed for successful diversity programs. Lastly, the results indicated most delivery methods were limited to traditional workshops or seminars and suggested a need for more sophisticated and innovative training media; therefore, utilizing technology and new training techniques could be beneficial. In regard to training effectiveness, diversity programs increased employee interpersonal skills and changed attitudes and perceptions toward diversity, but did not improve job performance. This suggests training is more effective on an individual rather than corporate-level basis. Another significant finding from this study is that employers are reluctant to implement diversity training programs because of the high turnover rate within the restaurant industry. In addition to the cost, time and difficulty in administering such programs, restaurants did not see the value in training employees because turnover is so high in the industry.

Weaver et al. (2003) studied how to maximize the effectiveness and usefulness of diversity training in order to help recruit and retain minority groups. More specifically, their study examined how managers within the hotel and lodging industry could be grouped together based on reported diversity training management initiatives (DMTIs). The findings of this study suggest that DMTIs can be more successfully administered if they cater for different managerial groups. Since diversity training is most effective when perceived to be useful and important, dividing and grouping managers by DMTI importance can help human resource directors educate and highlight diversity training based on similar importance. Consequently, grouping managers with similar perceived DMTI importance and with similar diversity training significance can help streamline diversity efforts and long-term sustainability of diversity management.

Madera et al. (2011a) examined empathy diversity training through perspective-taking training. They conducted an experimental study whereby participants were randomly assigned to groups of three or four, with one participant assigned as "manager" and the other participants in the group assigned as "employees". Managers were provided with a recipe in English while the employees were given non-English recipes. Using the behavioral manipulation of perspective-taking, the participants were required to complete the recipe without speaking and in complete silence. Follow-up questionnaires revealed that the negative attitudes toward non-English-speaking immigrants reported in the pre-questionnaires decreased after the perspective-taking training. Additionally, participants reported feelings of more positive attitudes toward and equality with non-English speakers, irrespective of the controlling factors (that is, gender, race). Their findings suggest that this method of diversity training can successfully change the attitudes and behaviors of out-group members. The mediating effect of empathy was also supported in this study, suggesting both that perspective-taking evokes empathy toward out-group members and that evoking empathy can strengthen the success of perspective-taking and diversity training. Therefore, in order to compete with a diverse and growing hospitality workforce, the need to promote positive attitudes and create communication barriers through diversity training, perspective-taking, and empathy for out-group members is growing and will be a competitive advantage for hospitality organizations.

Waight and Madera (2011) examined differences in organizational attitudes of ethnic minorities based on diversity training. In particular, the study examined the mediating effect of perceived discrimination and job satisfaction between diversity training and turnover intentions. The results showed that diversity training influenced the organizational attitudes of perceived discrimination, job satisfaction and turnover intention. Consequently, diversity training lowered perceived discrimination, raised job satisfaction, and lowered turnover intention for minority participants. Additionally, the results showed that employees who receive diversity training experience less perceived discrimination, which is negatively related to job satisfaction and turnover intentions. Therefore, the findings of this study suggest building positive organizational attitudes within an organization is possible through diversity training.

Lastly, Reynolds et al. (2014) studied how lodging hotel managers perceived diversity training. In particular, the study examined how managers perceived the value of diversity training at a personal, peer, subordinate and corporate level. The authors argue that diversity training is often weighed against the financial cost of employee training in terms of costs and benefits. The managers reported that after diversity training, managers themselves and corporate-level employees created the most value for an organization, as opposed to their peers and subordinates. This suggests that hospitality organizations should focus diversity training on managers and corporate-level employees because of their wide influence on both individual organizations and, in the case of corporate-level employees, companies that oversee multiple organizations. The study also examines how ethnic and gender minorities perceive the value of diversity training and found that neither ethnic nor gender minorities perceived diversity training to be more valuable than their non-minority counterparts. Thus, based on these findings, future diversity training efforts can be concentrated on those organizational members perceived to be adding the most value, managers themselves, and corporate-level employees. An additional consideration is that ethnic and gender minority group status does not influence the value proposition of diversity training.

PRACTICAL IMPLICATIONS FOR IMPLEMENTING DIVERSITY TRAINING

Framing Diversity Training

Despite being the most used method to manage diversity, diversity training programs do not always lead to positive outcomes. Specifically, a growing body of literature has examined the effect of specific programs (for example, diversity training) and has shown that not all have positive attitudes toward diversity training (for example, Herrera et al., 2011; Holladay et al., 2003; Kidder et al., 2004; Sawyerr et al., 2005; Strauss et al., 2003; Williams and Bauer, 1994). In particular, the literature has illustrated that the way in which diversity training is framed can have an impact on the outcomes. For example, if not framed appropriately, diversity training can ironically lead to more expressions of prejudice (Legault et al., 2011). According to Chavez and Weisinger (2008), this type of backlash may occur when diversity training is framed around discovering and pointing out racial differences using "blame and shame" techniques that lead to criticizing majority-group employees (p. 334). This type of framing can often cause participating employees to feel defensive, which may lead to more prejudice rather than promoting cultural diversity. Thus, the framing of a diversity training program needs to be based on reasons that will increase the effectiveness of its outcomes.

Avery's (2011) model of diversity support suggests that there are two general factors why employees would support diversity efforts, including diversity training. The first factor is based on self-interest, because "individuals tend to be motivated to maximize their personal outcomes, which could put them in favor of diversity, depending on the nature of their identity" (p. 242). This first reason suggests that diversity training should be framed around the self-interests of all participants. Using an inclusive framing, such as pointing out that diversity includes all people, makes diversity training programs compatible with the self. In other words, an inclusive framing of diversity training, in which all employees, regardless of race and gender, can benefit from the diversity training, can lead to more perceived compatibility. Thus, employees are more likely to be receptive to diversity training when the diversity training focuses on how all employees are members of many different identity groups (Stewart et al., 2008).

The second factor includes ideological beliefs in intergroup equality. Research shows that employees often think about how they will be treated at work, because all employees strive to work for organizations that care about their treatment and development (Greening and Turban, 2000; Turban and Greening, 1997). That is, employees have implicit expectations that their workplace is fair to all members, including themselves. Employees are accepting of diversity training programs when they are framed as being fair for all members and not just specifically for minorities (Jansen et al., 2015). Diversity training programs can serve as a signal that their organization supports egalitarian values that are compatible with the implicit expectations that the organization will treat all employees fairly. The literature, therefore, suggests that diversity training should also be framed around the expectations that the workplace is fair for all, regardless of their identity group.

Pre- and Post-Training Attitudes and Beliefs

In addition to the framing of diversity training programs, the outcomes of diversity training are also influenced by how open or ready an employee is for the training, as well as their attitudes and beliefs post-training. The general training literature highlights theoretical and empirical evidence with respect to the relationship between employees' pre- and post-training attitudes and beliefs with training outcomes (for example, Alliger et al., 1997; Colquitt et al., 2000; Gully and Chen, 2010; Mathieu and Martineau, 1997; Mathieu et al., 1992; Sitzmann et al., 2008). Regarding diversity training, the research underscores the importance of assessing pre- and post-training attitudes and beliefs toward the training to increase the overall effectiveness of diversity training (Roberson et al., 2013).

The literature also underscores several attitudes and beliefs related to how receptive an employee might be to diversity training before and after the training program. For example, motivation to learn is the extent to which a trainee wants to learn the content presented during the training. Research shows that employees who have low motivation before the training will learn less and be less likely to use what they learned in the future (Mathieu et al., 1992; Tracey et al., 2001; Patrick et al., 2012). Another important attitude is pre-training self-efficacy, which is the extent to which an employee believes he or she can learn and use what is learned in the training (Mathieu et al., 1992). The literature illustrates the importance of pre-training self-efficacy on learning, the transfer of training back to the workplace, and job performance (Colquitt et al., 2000; Tracey et al., 2001).

Another key attitude for the best outcome of diversity training is the perceived utility of training, which is an employee's belief about how useful the training content will be for their job (Colquitt et al., 2000). Employees assigned to training often think about whether the content of training can be useful to their job; the more they perceive a link, the more they are likely to learn during the training than employees who do not find the content useful to their job (Alliger et al., 1997). Post-training perceived utility is also fundamental for the outcomes of training (Ruona et al., 2002). After the training is complete, employees also assess how useful the content is to their job, while also considering the opportunity and support of the organizational environment (Madera et al., 2011b).

The literature also points to an employee's pre-training intention to use training, which is an attitude based on one's intention to use what was learned in the training program (Mathieu and Martineau, 1997; Tracey et al., 2001). The link between pre-training intention to use training and the outcomes of training is based on the theory of planned behavior (Ajzen, 1991), which suggests that the intention to use or apply a given skill or attitude can strongly predict future behavior. By extension, the trainee's intention to use diversity training content can predict whether the trainee learns to perform the specific behaviors on the job or acquires knowledge and skills related to training transfer. Wiethoff (2004) outlines a framework on how the theory of planned behavior can influence the outcomes of diversity training by focusing on how and why an employee is motivated to learn and apply diversity-related behaviors.

Lastly, training fulfillment refers to the extent to which an employee perceives that the training met or fulfilled her or his expectations and desires and has been shown to be related to multiple training outcomes (Tannenbaum et al., 1991). Training fulfillment is low when the training does not meet trainees' expectations and desires, and these unmet expectations can have negative outcomes for the training program. Thus, diversity training is more effective when expectations about the training are communicated realistically.

Who Should Complete Diversity Training?

The outcome of diversity training – the successful management of diversity – should be a corporate core value. Specifically, diversity training should be supported and completed by top management. Without leader buy-in, diversity initiatives may not be modeled, reinforced or rewarded. For example, Marriott International, Starwood Hotels and Walt Disney Company all have formal, corporate positions that are responsible for monitoring diversity management initiatives, including diversity training (Madera, 2013). Top management's attitude toward diversity can have a significant influence on the way managers and their employees experience the culture and climate of the organization. Top management establishes the norms, philosophies and values, including diversity climate. If top management communicates that diversity is an important corporate value, then this serves as a signal to operation managers and their employees that diversity is a core value and not something to check off a list. This becomes common practice, as the ways things are done or viewed "around here" rather than dictated by the corporate office.

Front-line managers play an important role for diversity management. They are the link between organizational policies related to diversity and the front-line employees. Diversity management policies are often related to recruiting, selecting, training, managing and maintaining a diverse workforce (Madera, 2013), which are functions that are mostly carried out by front-line managers. Front-line managers are frequently responsible for selecting, training, appraising and rewarding front-line employees. If front-line managers do not embrace diversity management programs, their negative attitudes can disrupt the efficacy of diversity management programs. Resource-based theory (Barney and Clark, 2007) suggests that diversity management programs can be a source of competitive advantage providing that managers implement the policies and procedures of diversity management programs. Building on the resource-based theory, Yang and Konrad (2011) argued that "differences in managers' views regarding the value of diversity for organizational effectiveness can affect the acceptance of diversity management programs" (p. 21). Thus, the literature underscores the importance of diversity training for managers.

Lastly, new employees should take part in diversity training. Given that the hospitality and tourism workforce encompasses a diversity of cultures, age groups, racial and ethnic backgrounds, sexual orientation, religion, and disability status (Gröschl, 2011; Madera, 2011; Singal, 2014), new employees will have to work with a diverse set of co-workers. Diversity training can give new employees diversity-related knowledge and tools for working with diverse co-workers. Diversity training can also help new employees understand their organization's value regarding diversity. In addition, diversity training can serve as a signal that their organization supports egalitarian values and fulfills implicit expectations of a fair workplace (Greening and Turban, 2000). However, for new employees, diversity training will only be effective if they perceive support from their organization. In fact, the training literature illustrates how perceived organizational support is an important factor that influences numerous training outcomes (Arthur et al., 2003; Broad, 2005; Martin, 2010; Smith-Jentsch et al., 2001; Tracey et al., 2001; Tracey et al., 1995). The characteristics of the work environment, especially differences between the work and training environment, can encourage or discourage trainees to adopt their newly trained methods in the workplace. Thus, organizational support and supportive environments from both managers and co-workers are integral influences on training outcomes (Martin, 2010).

REFERENCES

Ajzen, I. (1991). The theory of planned behavior. *Organizational Behavior and Human Decision Processes*, **50**, 179–211.

Alliger, G.M., Tannenbaum, S.I., Bennett, W. Jr, Traver, H. and Shotland, A. (1997). A meta-analysis of the relations among training criteria. *Personnel Psychology*, **502**, 341–58.

Arthur, W., Bennett, W., Edens, P.S. and Bell, S.T. (2003). Effectiveness of training in organizations: A meta-analysis of design and evaluation features. *Journal of Applied Psychology*, **88**, 234–45.

Avery, D.R. (2003). Reactions to diversity in recruitment advertising: Are differences black and white? *Journal of Applied Psychology*, **88**, 672–9.

Avery, D.R. (2011). Support for diversity in organizations: A theoretical exploration of its origins and offshoots. *Organizational Psychology Review*, **1**(3), 239–56.

Avery, D.R., Hernandez, M. and Hebl, M.R. (2004). Who's watching the race? Racial salience in recruitment advertising. *Journal of Applied Social Psychology*, **34**, 146–61.

Barney, J.B. and Clark, D.N. (2007). *Resource-Based Theory: Creating and Sustaining Competitive Advantage*. New York: Oxford University Press.

Bendick, M. Jr, Egan, M.L. and Lofhjelm, S.M. (2001). Workforce diversity training: From anti-discrimination compliance to organizational development. *Human Resource Planning*, **24**, 10–25.

Bezrukova, K., Spell, C.S., Perry, J.L. and Jehn, K.A. (2016). A meta-analytical integration of over 40 years of research on diversity training evaluation. *Psychological Bulletin*, **142**(11), 1227–74.

Broad, M.L. (2005). *Beyond Transfer of Training: Engaging Systems to Improve Performance*. San Francisco, CA: Pfeiffer.

Bureau of Labor Statistics (2015). Labor force statistics from the current population survey. United States Department of Labor. Accessed 15 January 2017 at: https://www.bls.gov/cps/cpsaat18.htm.

Chavez, C.I. and Weisinger, J.Y. (2008). Beyond diversity training: A social infusion for cultural inclusion. *Human Resource Management*, **47**, 331–50.

Chen, X.P., Liu, D. and Portnoy, R. (2012). A multilevel investigation of motivational cultural intelligence, organizational diversity climate, and cultural sales: Evidence from U.S. real estate firms. *Journal of Applied Psychology*, **97**, 93–106.

Colquitt, J.A., LePine, J.A. and Noe, R.A. (2000). Toward an integrative theory of training motivation: A meta-analytic path analysis of 20 years of research. *Journal of Applied Psychology*, **855**, 678–707.

Combs, G.M. and Luthans, F. (2007). Diversity training: Analysis of the impact of self-efficacy. *Human Resource Development Quarterly*, **18**, 91–120.

Cox, T. (1991). Organizational culture, stress, and stress management. *Work and Stress*, **5**, 1–4.

Cox, T.H. and Blake, S. (1991). Managing cultural diversity: Implications for organizational competitiveness. *Academy of Management Executive*, **5**, 45–56.

De Meuse, K.P., Hostager, T.J. and O'Neill, K.S. (2007). A longitudinal evaluation of senior managers' perceptions and attitudes of a workplace diversity training program. *Human Resource Planning*, **30**, 38–46.

Gonzalez, J.A. and DeNisi, A.S. (2009). Cross-level effects of demography and diversity climate on organizational attachment and firm effectiveness. *Journal of Organizational Behavior*, **30**, 21–40.

Greening, D.W. and Turban, D.B. (2000). Corporate social performance as a competitive advantage in attracting a quality workforce. *Business and Society*, **39**, 254–81.

Griffith, K. and Hebl, M.R. (2002). The disclosure dilemma for gay men and lesbians: "Coming out" at work. *Journal of Applied Psychology*, **87**, 1191–9.

Gröschl, S. (2011). Diversity management strategies of global hotel groups: A corporate web site based exploration. *International Journal of Contemporary Hospitality Management*, **23**(2), 224–40.

Gully, S.M. and Chen, G. (2010). Individual differences, attribute–treatment interactions, and training outcomes. In S.W.J. Kozlowski and E. Salas (eds), *Learning, Training, and Development in Organizations* (pp. 3–64). San Francisco, CA: Jossey-Bass.

Herrera, R., Duncan, P.A., Green, M., Ree, M. and Skaggs, S.L. (2011). The relationship between attitudes toward diversity management in the southwest USA and the GLOBE study cultural preferences. *The International Journal of Human Resource Management*, **22**(12), 2629–46.

Hogg, M.A. and Terry, D.J. (2000). Social identity and self-categorization processes in organizational contexts. *Academy of Management Review*, **25**, 121–40.

Holladay, C.L. and Quinones, M.A. (2008). The influence of training focus and trainer characteristics on diversity training effectiveness. *Academy of Management Learning and Education*, **7**, 343–54.

Holladay, C.L., Knight, J.L., Paige, D.L. and Quinones, M.A. (2003). The influence of framing on attitudes toward diversity training. *Human Resource Development Quarterly*, **14**, 245–63.

Jansen, W.S., Otten, S. and Van der Zee, K.I. (2015). Being part of diversity: The effects of an all-inclusive multicultural diversity approach on majority members' perceived inclusion and support for organizational diversity efforts. *Group Processes & Intergroup Relations*, **18**(6), 817–32.

Jones, K.P., King, E.B., Nelson, J., Geller, D.S. and Bowes-Sperry, L. (2013). Beyond the business case: An ethical perspective of diversity training. *Human Resource Management*, **52**(1), 55–74.

Kalinoski, Z.T., Steele-Johnson, D., Peyton, E.J., Leas, K.A., Steinke, J. and Bowling, N.A. (2013). A meta-analytic evaluation of diversity training outcomes. *Journal of Organizational Behavior*, **34**(8), 1076–104.

Kapoor, C.E. (2011). Defining diversity: The evolution of diversity. *Worldwide Hospitality and Tourism Themes*, **3**(4), 284–93.

Kidder, D.L., Lankau, M.J., Chrobot-Mason, D., Mollica, K.A. and Friedman, R.A. (2004). Backlash toward diversity initiatives: Examining the impact of diversity program justification, personal and group outcomes. *International Journal of Conflict Management*, **15**(1), 77–102.

Kim, Y.B. (2006). Managing workforce diversity: Developing a learning organization. *Journal of Human Resources in Hospitality and Tourism*, **5**(2), 69–90.

King, E.B., Dawson, J.F., Kravitz, D.A. and Gulick, L. (2012). A multilevel study of the relationships between diversity training, ethnic discrimination and satisfaction in organizations. *Journal of Organizational Behavior*, **33**(1), 5–20.

Kirkpatrick, D.L. (1987). Evaluation of training. In R.L. Craig (ed.), *Training and Development Handbook: A Guide to Human Resource Development*, 3rd edn (pp. 301–319). New York: McGraw-Hill.

Kulik, C.T. and Roberson, L. (2008). Common goals and golden opportunities: Evaluations of diversity education in academic and organizational settings. *Academy of Management Learning and Education*, **7**, 309–31.

Kunze, F., Boehm, S.A. and Bruch, H. (2011). Age diversity, age discrimination climate and performance consequences – a cross organizational study. *Journal of Organizational Behavior*, **32**(2), 264–90.

Lee, C. and Chon, K-S. (2000). An investigation of multicultural training practices in the restaurant industry: The training cycle approach. *International Journal of Contemporary Hospitality Management*, **12**(2), 126–34.

Legault, L., Gutsell, J.N. and Inzlicht, M. (2011). Ironic effects of antiprejudice messages: How motivational interventions can reduce (but also increase) prejudice. *Psychological Science*, **22**, 1472–77.

Madera, J.M. (2011). Removing communication barriers at work: What workforce diversity means for the hospitality industry. *Worldwide Hospitality and Tourism Themes*, **3**(4), 377–80.

Madera, J.M. (2013). Best practices in diversity management in customer service organizations: An investigation of top companies cited by Diversity Inc. *Cornell Hospitality Quarterly*, **54**(2), 124–35.

Madera, J.M., Dawson, M. and Guchait, P. (2016). Psychological diversity climate: Justice, racioethnic minority status, and job satisfaction. *International Journal of Contemporary Hospitality Management*, **28**(11), 2514–32.

Madera, J.M., Dawson, M. and Neal, J.A. (2013a). Hotel managers' perceived diversity climate and job satisfaction: The mediating effects of role ambiguity and conflict. *International Journal of Hospitality Management*, **35**, 28–34.

Madera, J.M., King, E.B. and Hebl, M.R. (2013b). Enhancing the effects of sexual orientation diversity training: The effects of setting goals and training mentors on attitudes and behaviors. *Journal of Business and Psychology*, **28**(1), 79–91.

Madera, J.M., Dawson, M., Neal, J.A. and Busch, K. (2013c). Breaking a communication barrier: The effect of visual aids in food preparation on job attitudes and performance. *Journal of Hospitality & Tourism Research*, **37**(2), 262–80.

Madera, J.M., Neal, J.A. and Dawson, M. (2011a). A strategy for diversity training focusing on empathy in the workplace. *Journal of Hospitality & Tourism Research*, **35**(4), 469–87.

Madera, J.M., Steele, S.T. and Beier, M. (2011b). The temporal effect of training utility perceptions on adopting a trained method: The role of perceived organizational support. *Human Resource Development Quarterly*, **22**(1), 69–86.

Martin, H.J. (2010). Workplace climate and peer support as determinants of training transfer. *Human Resource Development Quarterly*, **21**, 87–104.

Mathieu, J.E. and Martineau, J.W. (1997). Individual and situational influences on training motivation. In J.K. Ford, S.W.J. Kozlowski, K. Kraiger, E. Salas and M.S. Teachout (eds), *Improving Training Effectiveness in Work Organizations* (pp. 193–221). Mahwah, NJ: Erlbaum.

Mathieu, J.E., Tannenbaum, S.I. and Salas, E. (1992). Influences of individual and situational characteristics on measures of training effectiveness. *Academy of Management Journal*, **35**, 828–47.

McKay, P.F., Avery, D.R. and Morris, M.A. (2008). Mean racial-ethnic differences in employee sales performance: The moderation role of diversity climate. *Personnel Psychology*, **61**, 349–74.

McKay, P.F., Avery, D.R. and Morris, M.A. (2009). A tale of two climates: Diversity climate from subordinates' and managers' perspectives and their role in store unit sales performance. *Personnel Psychology*, **62**, 767–91.

McKay, P.F., Avery, D.R., Liao, H. and Morris, M.A. (2011). Does diversity climate lead to customer satisfaction? It depends on the service climate and business unit demography. *Organization Science*, **22**(3), 788–803.

McKay, P.F., Avery, D.R., Tonidandel, S., Morris, M.A., Hernandez, M. and Hebl, M.R. (2007). Racial differences in employee retention: Are diversity climate perceptions the key? *Personnel Psychology*, **60**(1), 35–62.

Mor Barak, M.E., Cherin, D.A. and Berkman, S. (1998). Organizational and personal dimensions in diversity climate. *Journal of Applied Behavioral Science*, **34**, 82–104.

Patrick, J., Smy, V., Tombs, M. and Shelton, K. (2012). Being in one's chosen job determines pre-training attitudes and training outcomes. *Journal of Occupational and Organizational Psychology*, **85**, 245–57.

Pendry, L.F., Driscoll, D.M. and Field, S.C.T. (2007). Diversity training: Putting theory into practice. *Journal of Occupational and Organizational Psychology*, **80**, 27–50.

Reynolds, D., Rahman, I. and Bradetich, S. (2014). Hotel managers' perceptions of the value of diversity training: An empirical investigation. *International Journal of Contemporary Hospitality Management*, **26**, 426–46.

Richard, O., Barnett, T., Dwyer, S. and Chadwick, K. (2004). Cultural diversity in management, firm performance, and the moderating role of entrepreneurial orientation dimensions. *Academy of Management Journal*, **47**, 255–66.

Richard, O., McMillan, A., Chadwick, K. and Dwyer, S. (2003). Employing an innovation strategy in racially diverse workforces: Effects on firm performance. *Group & Organization Management*, **28**, 107–26.

Richard, O.C. (2000). Racial diversity, business strategy, and firm performance: A resource-based view. *Academy of Management Journal*, **43**, 164–77.

Richard, O.C. and Johnson, N.B. (1999). Making the connection between formal human diversity practices and organizational effectiveness: Beyond management fashion. *Performance Improvement Quarterly*, **12**, 77–96.

Roberson, L., Kulik, C.T. and Pepper, M.B. (2003). Using needs assessment to resolve controversies in diversity training design. *Group and Organization Management*, **28**, 148–74.

Roberson, L., Kulik, C.T. and Tan, R.Y. (2013). Effective diversity climate. In Q.M. Roberson (ed.), *The Oxford Handbook of Diversity and Work* (pp. 341–65). New York: Oxford University Press.

Ruona, W.E.A., Leimbach, M., Holton III, E.F. and Bates, R.A. (2002). The relationship between learner utility reactions and predictors of learning transfer among trainees. *International Journal of Training and Development*, **6**, 218–28.

Sawyerr, O.O., Strauss, J. and Yan, J. (2005). Individual value structure and diversity attitudes: The moderating effects of age, gender, race, and religiosity. *Journal of Managerial Psychology*, **20**(6), 498–521.

Shen, J., Chanda, A., D'netto, B. and Monga, M. (2009). Managing diversity through human resource management: An international perspective and conceptual framework. *The International Journal of Human Resource Management*, **20**(2), 235–51.

Singal, M. (2014). The business case for diversity management in the hospitality industry. *International Journal of Hospitality Management*, **40**, 10–19.

Sitzmann, T., Brown, K.G., Casper, W.J., Ely, K. and Zimmerman, R.E. (2008). A review and meta-analysis of the nomological network of trainee reactions. *Journal of Applied Psychology*, **93**, 280–95.

Smith-Jentsch, K.A., Salas, E. and Brannick, M.T. (2001). To transfer or not to transfer? Investigating the combined effects of trainee characteristics, team leader support, and team climate. *Journal of Applied Psychology*, **86**, 279–92.

Stewart, M.M., Crary, M. and Humberd, B.K. (2008). Teaching value in diversity: On the folly of espousing inclusion, while practicing exclusion. *Academy of Management Learning & Education*, **7**(3), 374–86.

Strauss, J.P., Connerley, M.L. and Ammermann, P.A. (2003). The "threat hypothesis", personality, and attitudes toward diversity. *The Journal of Applied Behavioral Science*, **39**(1), 32–52.

Tajfel, H. and Turner, J.C. (1986). The social identity theory of intergroup behavior. In S. Worchel and W.G. Austin (eds), *Psychology of Intergroup Relations*, 2nd edn (pp. 7–24). Chicago: Nelson-Hall.

Tannenbaum, S.I., Mathieu, J.E., Salas, E. and Cannon-Bowers, J.A. (1991). Meeting trainees' expectations: The influence of training fulfillment on the development of commitment, self-efficacy, and motivation. *Journal of Applied Psychology*, **76**(6), 759–69.

Tracey, J.B, Tannenbaum, S.I. and Kavanaugh, M.J. (1995). Applying trainee skills on the job: The importance of the work environment. *Journal of Applied Psychology*, **80**, 239–52.

Tracey, J.B., Hinkin, T.R., Tannenbaum, S.I. and Mathieu, J.E. (2001). The influence of individual characteristics and the work environment on varying levels of training outcomes. *Human Resource Development Quarterly*, **12**, 5–23.

Turban, D.B. and Greening, D.W. (1997). Corporate social performance and organizational attractiveness to prospective employees. *Academy of Management Journal*, **40**, 658–72.

Waight, J. and Madera, J.M. (2011). Diversity training: Examining minority employees' organizational attitudes. *Worldwide Hospitality and Tourism Themes*, **3**, 365–76.

Weaver, P., Wilborn, L., McCleary, K. and Lekagul, A. (2003). Diversity training management initiatives in the lodging industry: An exploratory analysis of underlying dimensions. *Journal of Hospitality & Tourism Research*, **27**(2), 237–53.

Wentling, R.M. and Palma-Rivas, N. (1999). Components of effective diversity training programs. *International Journal of Training and Development*, **3**, 215–26.

Wiethoff, C. (2004). Motivation to learn and diversity training: Application of the theory of planned behavior. *Human Resource Development Quarterly*, **15**(3), 263–78.

Williams, M.L. and Bauer, T.N. (1994). The effect of a managing diversity policy on organizational attractiveness. *Group & Organization Management*, **19**(3), 295–308.

Yang, Y. and Konrad, A.M. (2011). Understanding diversity management practices: Implications of institutional theory and resource-based theory. *Group and Organization Management*, **36**, 6–38.

15. The happiest place on earth? A case study of the Disney World employment experience*

Sara L. Mann and Marie-Hélène Budworth

INTRODUCTION

Fortune recently ranked Disney as the fifth most admired company in the world, and first for people management, social responsibility and quality of management. With more than 74 000 workers, approximately $16.2 billion in revenue, and $4709 million in labour costs, Disney World is the largest single-site employer in America, perhaps even the world ("Disney Annual Report", 2016). Understanding Disney's Human Resource Management (HRM) practices and the impact of these practices on its employees is of particular interest given their continued success. However, there is a paucity of scholarly research examining Disney's HRM practices as a case study.

This chapter will use the hospitality and tourism literature to inform an understanding of Disney's Human Resource Management practices. Focus group and survey data collected from UNITE HERE Local 362 (a union representing 29 000 members who work in the Disney theme parks) will provide insight into the employee's perspective on the Disney employment experience. The research presented in this chapter is exploratory in nature, and as such, provides preliminary research findings and suggests avenues for future research.

Hospitality and Tourism

A review of the human resource management literature specific to hospitality and tourism reveals two relevant themes. The first theme is the intensity of human capital in this industry. Human capital in the form of compensation accounts for approximately 70 to 80 per cent of total business costs (Lawler and Mohrman, 2003). Employers in this industry lead through a management culture focused on controlling labour expenditure (Christensen Hughes, 2008).

Second, in order to be competitive, organizations require their employees to provide more than standardized interactions with customers. The main pressure on the industry is that of providing a strong customer experience. Customer service is the "product", underlining the importance of managing human resources such that employees provide the core goods. This is a complex issue given that the service encounter is intangible, heterogeneous and perishable; the production of service cannot be separated from its consumption (Lashley, 2001; Kusluvan, 2003; Christensen Hughes, 2008). In this way, performance expectations rely on displays of emotional labour, or publicly observable displays that enhance service quality (Hochschild, 1983; Lashley, 2001; Christensen Hughes, 2008). There is pressure on the employee to "perform" in all customer interactions.

These themes appear to be in conflict; a need to decrease the cost of labour while motivating front-line employees to provide superior customer service experiences. In this chapter, we focus on the HRM practices that are used in the case study organization as a way of understanding how employers resolve these competing demands, by understanding the experiences of employees within this industry.

Labour Intensity and Labour Costs

The theme park industry has grown rapidly for the past thirty years, with a projection for continued growth despite the global economic uncertainty and the recent recession (Milman, 2010; Milman et al., 2010; Milman and Dickson, 2013). Theme parks, such as Disney World, generate billions of dollars in revenue, have a significant effect on local economies, are a large employer in the service sector of the US and are considered a significant driver of the hospitality and tourism industry (Milman, 2008; Milman et al., 2010).

Walt Disney World Resort is located on 25 000 acres, 22 miles southwest of Orlando, Florida. The state is home to six theme parks and 18 resorts. As stated previously, human capital is a significant percentage of overall costs for theme parks, and Disney is no exception. According to the Orlando Economic Development Commission, in 2016, Walt Disney World Resort employed 74 000 employees, and according to Disney's 2016 annual report, the operating labour costs for the theme parks were $4709 million, or 47 per cent of total operating expenses. When labour comprises such a significant portion of total expenditure, management becomes focused on controlling and reducing labour costs (Christensen Hughes, 2008). Several strategies could be used to reduce labour costs, the main one being shifting from full-time to part-time or casual employment (for example Blyton et al., 2011; Cappelli et al., 1997; Torres, 2012; Zeytinoglu et al., 2016). Alternatively, an organization may alter their compensation practices, as Disney did when it implemented a two-tier wage structure in 1998 (Nissen et al., 2007).

In addition to a focus on reducing labour costs, theme parks also face employment challenges specific to being in a service industry, and more specifically in the amusement and theme park industry. There are four main HRM strategies that help successful theme parks deliver quality customer experiences: (1) hiring the right people; (2) developing people to deliver service quality; (3) providing needed support systems; and (4) retaining the best people (Mayer, 2002; Anh and Kleiner, 2005). However, the need to create economic savings through labour is in conflict with HRM practices more generally and with the overall strategy.

In organizations where service is important, the employees provide the product, the product being personal contact with customers, interactions which dictate the success or failure of the organization (Jerome and Kleiner, 1995). More than anything else, an employer like Disney World requires dedicated and motivated employees who truly enjoy the business of entertaining and bringing happiness to others (Jerome and Kleiner, 1995).

Despite the size and importance of this industry, there is limited empirical research on the HRM practices utilized by theme and amusement parks (Milman and Dickson, 2013). One of the few studies to investigate this population found that theme park hourly employees valued advancement opportunities and humane working conditions (Milman and Dickson, 2013). Specifically, employees were concerned with whether their employer cared about them and whether the daily working experience aligned with the vision and mission of the company. Having a fun and challenging job was the third most important factor for employees in this theme park sample.

Since the mission of any theme park is to impress and delight customers, and superior guest experience brings differentiation and profit, service excellence is paramount. Execution of this strategy relies on the front-line employees who have direct contact with customers (Jerome and Kleiner, 1995). The resulting expectations on front-line employees can lead to high levels of pressure along with the unspoken expectation to go above and beyond their job requirements. In this way, conflicting strategies of lowering labour costs while delivering superior customer service can prove challenging. Little is known of how theme park employees experience the pressure to perform at all times under the working conditions typically found in theme parks. The current case study will examine these themes.

EMOTIONAL LABOUR AND MOTIVATION

In order to perform service work effectively, employees are required to provide customers with a service while creating an interpersonal connection with customers in a time-limited interaction (Albrecht and Zemke, 1985; Gremler and Gwinner, 2000). In this way, service workers in hospitality are expected to display positive emotions even when their feelings are inconsistent with their current emotional experience. This type of work is an example of emotional labour. Emotional labour is a self-regulation strategy that describes the extent to which employees manage emotions with others, typically with customers, as part of their paid work (Hochschild, 1983).

According to theory, employees utilize a range of emotion regulation strategies to maintain positive behavioural displays with customers while performing the duties of their job. These strategies are generally categorized as surface acting and deep acting. When an employee is surface acting, they are "faking" an emotional display, behaving in one way while maintaining conflicting internal feelings. While deep acting, employees change their internal feelings such that they align with organizational expectations, thereby experiencing authentic and genuine emotional displays (Grandey, 2000). Both of these strategies have been shown to moderate the effects of employees' internal feelings and attitudes on interpersonal performance. Engaging in either form of acting can be beneficial if one feels negatively, or can amplify the benefits of positive feelings (Beal et al., 2006; Diefendorff and Gosserand, 2003). In particular, employees who use deep acting tend to be more customer oriented than those who do not (Pugh et al., 2011). In this way, the use of emotional regulation strategies has been linked to increases in both job satisfaction and job performance. However, emotional labour has also been linked to exhaustion, stress and burnout (Pugliesi, 1999). Recent research has suggested that the variability in outcomes following emotional labour is due to the motives that guide behaviour.

Maneotis et al. (2014) have suggested that emotional labour can alter the motivations employees have for the work they perform. In particular, they offer prosocial motivation as a mechanism that can explain the link between emotional labour and performance. Prosocial motivation is the extent to which an employee is working in order to benefit others (Baston, 1987). This theory is particularly relevant to the service industry. Prosocially motivated employees expend a great deal of effort in assisting customers (Grant, 2007). Notably, prosocial work motives are not directly related to service performance outcomes (Grant, 2008; Grant et al., 2009; Grant and Sumanth, 2009). However, Maneotis et al. (2014) found that prosocially motivated individuals tended to use deep acting strategies with their customers. Deep acting can reduce emotional exhaustion and emotional dissonance (Pugh et al., 2011).

Employees who are focused on the customer experience may be motivated through prosocial means. To the extent that an organization can support this focus, service workers could be motivated to engage in emotion regulation that aligns with positive performance outcomes.

EMOTION REGULATION AT WALT DISNEY WORLD

Walt Disney himself developed a corporate strategy rooted in brands and franchises. Todd Zenger later called the model "a corporate theory of sustained growth" (2013). As seen in Mr Disney's chart, the corporation's success is built on the success of theatrical films which create brands that can be marketed through publications, merchandising, television, music and theme park experiences (see Figure 15.1). With regard to their theme parks, the stated purpose is to be "one of the world's leading providers of family travel and leisure experiences, giving millions of guests each year the chance to spend time with their families and friends, making memories that last a lifetime".

The Disney theme parks have a clear mission to create "magic" and to be the "happiest place on earth". Material presented at the Disney Institute indicates that there is a "common goal – we create happiness by providing the finest in entertainment for people of all ages, everywhere". In order to realize this image, Disney requires its employees to present as happy, smiling and helpful. This expectation applies to every customer-facing employee group, including the custodial staff. The strategy and mission are evident in every part of their HR practice. For example, Disney has a unique vocabulary. Employees are "cast members" and when they are in inside the park, they are "onstage". Each employee group goes through two weeks of orientation training where they learn the values of the organization and familiarize themselves with the park (Reyers and Matusitz, 2012). Mr Walt Disney viewed training as an investment in the future rather than as a budget line, and as such is given top priority. The training that new employees are put through before going "onstage" is considered an experience as opposed to a programme at an institution (Reyers and Matusitz, 2012).

The language, stated expectations, and the inculcation into the Disney employment experience prepare employees for the challenge of maintaining a façade at all times while on the job. Disney expects all their

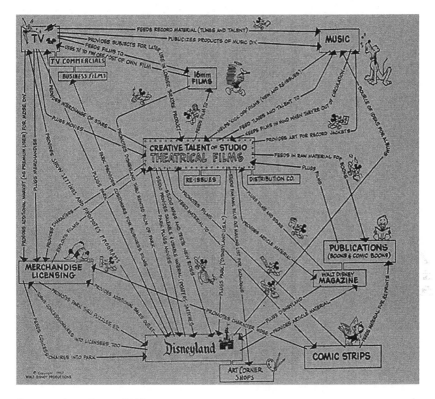

Source: From Zenger (2013).

Figure 15.1   An infographic of Walt Disney's 1957 corporate theory

cast members to maintain and regulate their emotions onstage. Many "onstage" employees at Walt Disney World (WDW) Florida engage in surface acting and suffer high levels of emotional exhaustion (Reyers and Matusitz, 2012).

The limited research available on Disney to date has focused on factors that mitigate emotional exhaustion on the job. This study found that cast members who felt confident in their ability to perform well on the job along with those who enjoyed the support of their managers were better equipped to deal with on-the-job demands (Reyers and Matusitz, 2012).

AESTHETIC LABOUR

Closely related to emotional labour is aesthetic labour, described as the physical attributes that employers seek when hiring employees for customer-facing roles (Tsaur and Tang, 2013). This could include employee dress, physical appearance, as well as grooming and efforts to appear attractive to customers. To the organization, aesthetic presentation represents the corporate image and serves as a competitive advantage (Tsaur and Tang, 2013). While the organization often believes that requiring aesthetic labour has the potential to improve the customer experience, for the employee the result can be unwanted stress. Stress can result from fear of criticism from customers as well as the pressure of surveillance from both co-workers and supervisors (Tsaur and Tang, 2013). For some, there might be a need to constantly conceal something that is a part of their personal image or identity (for example, tattoo, piercings, or religious symbols). The psychological stress increases when disciplinary actions leading up to terminations can occur if there are repeated infringements on the aesthetic policies of the organization (Warhurst and Nickson, 2007).

Disney emphasizes what they refer to as "good stage presence", where they outline the many different aspects of the "look" that they require all employees to maintain (that is, The Disney Look). This ranges from the strict prohibition of visible body modifications to the length and proper cut of hair. These requirements are imposed on both males and females. Employee appearance is used in the selection process and enforced throughout the employment relationship through the use of uniforms, dress codes and grooming policies (Warhurst and Nickson, 2007).

THE DISNEY EXPERIENCE

Data Collection

In 2011 and 2013, interviews, focus groups and a survey study were conducted with union leaders and 22 members of UNITE HERE Local 362, the union representing more than 29 000 Walt Disney World Resort employees. The data collected through these multiple methods provided insights into the relationship between Walt Disney World's HRM practices and the employee experience. Both qualitative and quantitative data collected from the members of UNITE HERE Local 362 will be examined in this chapter. The findings are exploratory in nature and, as such, provide preliminary research findings and suggest avenues for future research.

It is important to highlight the significance of the access through which these data were collected. UNITE HERE Local 362 is the largest union representing Walt Disney World Resort workers. The data were not collected through Disney directly or from members of their management or leadership teams. However, the lead author did attend a training programme at Disney's Institute on People Management in order to better understand the organization's policies and practices. The description of strategy, culture and HR policy comes from formal public documents, the training materials from the Disney Institute, as well as conversations with union members.

Human Resource Management Practices

Disney offers an opportunity for outsiders to understand their management practices through courses offered by the Disney Institute. The following quotes are from the training materials distributed at the Disney Institute course. Disney's HR systems have a strong underlying foundation in the company's "milestones, heritage, traditions and values" (Disney Institute Training Materials, 2011, p. 12). "The key factors of the Disney people management strategy are the following: continuously reinforcing the culture; selecting right-fit talent; training for consistent quality; communicating to inform and inspire; and creating an environment of care" (Disney Institute Training Materials, 2011, p. 3). These are aligned with the four HRM strategies typically employed by theme parks mentioned in the introduction, namely (1) hire the right people; (2) develop people to deliver service quality; (3) provide needed support systems; and (4) retain the best people (Mayer, 2002; Anh and Kleiner, 2005).

HR is based on the premise that "by educating the Cast on the traditions of the past and the priorities of the present, it can maintain its competitive edge in the future" (Disney Institute Training Materials, 2011, p. 11). The company materials are rich with the vocabulary unique to the organization. In the course materials "Cast Members can be part of the memories and dreams for guests and each other" (Disney Institute Training Materials, 2011, p. 12). When hiring employees, the materials refer to "cast members", highlighting that "the casting environment demonstrates the company's reputation for friendliness and fun" (Disney Institute Training Materials, 2011, p. 7) and that "the casting process establishes the importance of people to the company's success" (Disney Institute Training Materials, 2011, p.7). Disney notes that orientation for employees is to "introduce new Cast Members to the foundations of the Disney culture; to perpetuate Disney heritage and traditions, language and symbols, shared values, and traits and behaviors; to generate excitement about working for Disney; to introduce new Cast Members to core safety regulations and ethical expectations at Disney" (Disney Institute Training Materials, 2011, p. 12). The impression given within the Disney Institute is that this is an organization strongly committed to HRM practices that are tied to the organization's strategy. There is also a sense that the organization is committed to the employee experience, encouraging a playful, fun and rewarding opportunity.

The focus groups in this study allowed for a direct comparison between the stated objectives of the organization as represented in the Disney Institute, and the employee experience. Members of UNITE HERE local 362 were asked questions regarding the perceptions of Disney's HRM practices, including types of position, hours of work and procedural fairness. In the sections that follow, we review the working conditions and attitudes reported by UNITE HERE Local 362.

Labour

Disney relies heavily on contingent and part-time employees. They have several categories of part-time employee. "Casual Regulars" are permanent employees who are able to opt into a health insurance plan yet have no guaranteed number of hours. "Casual Temps" work approximately 10 days per week, and have no health insurance or benefits. Students employed through a college programme work approximately 30 hours per week. In recent years, the percentage increase in hiring of part-time and contingent employees has outnumbered the percentage increase in hiring of full-time permanent employees. The perception of current workers is that "the company is bringing in two part-time employees instead of one full-time". Current part-time employees get "right of refusal" for full-time opportunities but union members told us that waiting for an opportunity can take anywhere from nine months to a year.

According to union records, the number of part-time employees has increased. The rate at which part-time casual employees were utilized was 17.1 per cent in 2003, and has increased year over year. In 2009, it was 29.2 per cent, with a total of 43 442 996 full-time hours versus 17 917 765 casual hours. Conversely, according to the union data, full-time hours have been declining. All increases in working hours in 2009 were allocated to casual employees.

Almost all of the union members we interviewed said that they normally work the same number of paid hours per week at their job. Full-time employees reported working an average of 40 hours per week, and at least 6 hours per day, while part-time employees reported hours ranging from 14 to 27 per week. Many of the members interviewed reported working some amount of weekly overtime, with an average of 7 overtime hours per week. Still, almost all would like to work more hours, with a preference for an average of 5 additional hours per week. Union members who were part-time employees reported working between 2 to 4 days per week, while full-time employees worked between 4 to 7 days per week.

While some respondents reported that they appreciated having a consistent schedule, most reported discontent with the many split shifts. Individuals reported opening and closing on some days. Others reported having 8 hours between shifts, not enough time to sleep, eat or do anything meaningful. Respondents reported their perception that extra hours are being filled with part-time employees. The union members articulated their assumption that the company preferred part-time hours since they would only be required to pay an hourly wage without the added expense of benefits. Some remembered a time when they used to work 50 hours per week, before the increased use of casual part-time employees. Some full-time respondents reported working 3 days per week and 6 hours per day. Amongst those interviewed, it was reported that the company regularly scheduled 7 to 8 hours per day so that they only have to offer 30-minute and 15-minute breaks. It was also reported that those with low seniority can have three different times for shifts within one week, while most workplaces would have an employee on straight days, nights or afternoons within any given week.

Respondents also expressed dissatisfaction with their wages. The full-time respondents in this study earned an average of $397 per week after taxes and deductions. The average full-time hourly rate was reported at $11.74 per hour. Almost all of our respondents were unsatisfied with their wages. Another individual expressed concern that "after 22 years, my wage is still only $12.84 per hour, compared to $7.94 when I started". One respondent commented "the pay they receive and how the company treats them makes them feel like they aren't worth it". Another noted that "they make you work too hard and keep every penny they ever make for them". Respondents were concerned about the pension, stating that "after 22 years, it is only $1200 per month".

In summary, the perception of those interviewed and surveyed is that the employer makes labour hiring and scheduling decisions for economic reasons rather than considering the employee's desire for a regular schedule or full-time hours.

Employee Attitudes

Procedural justice is a measure of perceived fairness (Greenberg, 1987). This is an important construct because it predicts outcomes such as job satisfaction, organizational commitment, emotional exhaustion, health, and job performance. In this study, procedural justice was measured and ideas relevant to this construct were explored in the interviews and focus groups. Survey respondents reported a mean of 2.12 out of 5 on a measure of procedural fairness (SD = .68). Interviewees and focus group respondents reported feelings of helpfulness, or lack of input into decision-making. The organization is "unsympathetic to the needs of employees unless it is convenient to them". We "should be more involved in decisions about the job and responsibilities". Finally, one employee noted that "It's all about the shareholders. They can do better with their employees."

Respondents also expressed confusion over what they perceived as a lack of care and respect for the employee. "They don't create consistent guidelines and don't follow their own expectations." "They should show courtesy not only to guests but to workers too." "We work at the happiest place on earth but the company makes very little effort to make the employees the happiest employees on earth." "We promote family but we don't take care of our own family."

In measuring job satisfaction, it was found that full-time individuals within our sample were either "dissatisfied" or "very dissatisfied" with their job (m = 2.96/5; SD = .60). There were also several comments regarding poor working conditions. "It is a high-pressure environment." "Our breakrooms are hot." "Public transportation is awful. I need a car but can't afford one. I have to leave one hour for travel time to work and then 15 minutes to walk in."

With respect to motivation, respondents reported higher prosocial motivation (m = 5.25/7; SD = 1.96) compared to intrinsic motivation (m = 3.97/7; SD = 2.20). When describing the positive aspects of their job, respondents noted: "Interaction with the guests"; "Diverse coworkers"; "See a lot of great shows, fireworks, etc."; "Everything – it is fast paced, fun, cast members are phenomenal". A common narrative is represented by the comment that "Disney does not value me, but I feel like coworkers are family". Similarly, respondents found motivation in providing customers with a good experience (for example, "Rewards from the customer motivate me"). Some even viewed working at Disney as a calling: "Working for Disney is something you really have to want to do".

With respect to engagement and organizational commitment, respondents reported a mean of 3.19 out of 6 on a measure of engagement (SD = 1.00), and 2.64 out of 5 for organizational commitment (SD = .63). In our discussion with respondents, some reported stronger affiliations with the union as compared to the organization. "We are well protected by the union." Respondents also compared themselves to employees of other organizations indicating that their employment situation was fine when compared to others. "We are better off locally, compared to other theme parks or Walmart employees. They are in much worse shape." Finally, as with motivation, many respondents cited their experiences with the customers as being particularly rewarding. "Working with the guests is the only reason we are still here." "We don't mind being treated badly because we love the guests." "We get to see people from all around world." "I love the smile on kids' faces when you do something nice for them." "I like to participate in making magical experiences for the guests." "Interacting with people and get instant feedback in the form of reactions to my performance with them." "I love people!"

On a measure of emotional labour, respondents reported a mean of 3.09 out of 6 (SD = 1.51), with a higher level of surface acting (m = 3.42; SD = 1.62) as compared to deep acting (m = 2.76; SD = 1.49). Respondents also reported a moderate level of importance placed on authentic emotional display (m = 2.97/5; SD = 1.26).

When discussing emotional labour, respondents noted that "The smile is part of the uniform" and there is a need to "control your emotions". Others indicated that the "unbalanced and unrealistic work expectations are emotionally taxing".

The respondents reported concerns regarding aesthetic labour. "There is a mirror at every entrance to the park." "You can only wear one ring, no watch, no hair dye and no ear piercing." "You need to meet the appearance guidelines, even on the first day." "Men were just recently allowed to have a beard." The participants in this sample did report some emotional strain, yet the bulk of their frustration was aimed at the working conditions (for example, scheduling and management practices).

Perhaps one of our most surprising observations was within the focus groups. There were consistent negative opinions of the company's HR practices and general treatment of employees. "Disney can do better. It's not what it used to be." "It's all about the shareholders." However, when the researchers began to comment on their perceptions, or attempted to summarize their thoughts, the respondents became defensive and protective of their employer. The respondents were comfortable speaking negatively about the company, but did not want outsiders to do the same. They would say things like "but we are proud of the company".

DISCUSSION

The results of this study are consistent with the existing research on HR in the service industry. The central themes of the broader literature were evident in this sample, namely the pressure to provide an excellent customer experience while focusing on controlling labour costs, and the stresses of emotional labour inherent in the work. The perceptions of the individuals we surveyed and interviewed, as well as those thoughts of the union leaders, suggested that the company had a focus on controlling labour costs by employing strategies such as favouring part-time over full-time employment, and the implementation of shorter, sometimes split shifts to avoid offering longer breaks and lunches. Our research also found evidence of a workforce that feels the pressure to perform, pressure that is applied by both the organization and by the employee him or herself. This pressure to provide excellent customer experiences resulted in high levels of emotional labour, in particular the prevalence of surface acting or "faking" emotional displays on the job.

This case study was also consistent with the broader literature in that there was alignment with the four HRM strategies typically employed by theme parks, namely: (1) hire the right people; (2) develop people to deliver service quality; (3) provide needed support systems; and (4) retain the best people (Mayer, 2002; Anh and Kleiner, 2005). Our research found that Disney's HR practices, as promoted through its Disney Institute course, emphasized all four of these strategies.

There is a large body of research to suggest that investing in HRM practices leads to positive outcomes (Bowen and Ostroff, 2004; Huselid, 1995). Disney does appear to invest in its management strategies, as evidenced by the policies and practices shared through the Disney Institute. This approach to HRM is strongly linked to the organizations strategy, a focus on the "guest" and the customer experience. To that end, Disney has managed to focus on hiring employees who are committed to providing the Disney experience, and employees who, throughout their employment, are motivated by customer outcomes. Interestingly, individuals in this sample were largely unsatisfied with working conditions such as wages and hours worked. They were also generally critical of management and management practices. Despite all of this, they remained committed to and motivated by Disney as an institution and the customers as individuals. In other words, despite high levels of dissatisfaction among individuals in this sample, they still remained motivated to do their job well for the benefit of the Disney brand and for the experience of the guest.

The union members in this sample articulated elements of prosocial motivation. They appeared to be working for the benefit of others. Many respondents talked about creating a magical experience for the guest. Others described their co-workers as family and felt a desire to contribute to the work of their peers. In this organization where there is a clear higher order goal, employees remained committed to the larger goal despite the presence of hurdles and obstacles.

Interestingly, both survey and focus group results uncovered the prevalent use of surface acting over deep acting strategies. Many individuals were "faking" their smiles rather than attempting to take on the emotions required for the job. This is consistent with the methods advocated by Walt Disney himself who espoused "acting" as the main strategy for emotional regulation (Reyers and Matusitz, 2012). This approach is evident in HR policies and vocabulary, where employees are called "cast members" and told that they are "onstage". Unfortunately, surface acting strategies can be detrimental in the long run. While deep acting can reduce emotional dissonance, surface acting can lead to emotional exhaustion (Pugh et al., 2011).

Although the corporate strategy determines the HRM strategy with the intention of guiding the employee experience, respondents reported a disconnect between the corporate level and execution through HRM practices. From the perspective of those we surveyed and interviewed, the perception is that the corporation's overall strategy and vision drives employee behaviours and the HR function is a subject of distrust. Disney World has successfully managed to motivate its employees, and maintains a high level of customer service by selecting employees who are aligned with the corporate vision and by providing intense training on the vision and mission once hired. However, the day-to-day working conditions are a source of frustration for many employees. Despite this frustration, the employees remain motivated by the corporate vision.

Hospitality and tourism in general, and theme parks in particular, are under unique market pressures to balance labour costs while maintaining a motivated and engaged workforce. In this sample, the employees felt the pressures of cost cutting in employment practices around wages and shift scheduling. At the same time, the workers who felt frustrated about their working conditions expressed commitment to the job and to the organization. HR focused on hiring and training, but exercised cost savings in their scheduling and compensation practices. The HR policies and practices are in conflict, as is the employee experience.

Limitations

The findings from this study need to be understood in context. They were collected from a relatively small sample recruited through the union. All interviews and focus groups took place at the union office. Given these conditions, it is possible that participants were focused on working conditions because of the presence of their union colleagues. In other words, the way in which the participants were recruited may have primed them to give certain issues importance. Despite that limitation, the participants were candid and descriptive in their responses.

Future Research

Given that this study is exploratory in nature, it follows that there are several avenues for future research. There were many constructs explored in this study, namely motivation, emotional labour, procedural justice and job satisfaction. These variables were important to workers and were often identified in the focus groups' discussions. Future research could add to our understanding of how a constellation of HRM practices affects these various outcomes. While there is preliminary evidence that some HR practices outweighed the effects of others, it is not known how these various practices fit together. Similarly, this study focused on the affective experiences of the employee. There is a need to examine consequential outcomes for employees (for example, health, living conditions, career) and the organization (for example, employee performance).

NOTE

*   We would like to acknowledge the contribution by our Research Assistant, Abir Mohammed Hanif Moosa.

REFERENCES

Albrecht, K. and Zemke, R. (1985). Instilling a service mentality: Like teaching an elephant to dance. *International Management*, **40**(11), 61–7.

Anh, N.H and Kleiner, B.H. (2005). Effective Human Resource Management in the entertainment industry. *Management Research News*, **28**(2/3), 100–107.

Baston, C.D. (1987). Prosocial motivation: Is it ever truly altruistic? In L. Berkowitz (ed.), *Advances in Experimental Psychology*, Vol. 20 (pp. 65–122). New York: Academic Press.

Beal, D. J., Trougakos, J.P., Weiss, H.M. and Green, S.G. (2006). Episodic processes in emotional labor: Perceptions of affective delivery and regulation strategies. *Journal of Applied Psychology,* **91**(5), 1053–65.

Blyton, P., Heery, E. and Turnbull, P. (2011). Reassessing the employment relationship: An introduction. In P. Blyton, E. Heery and P. Turnbull (eds), *Reassessing the Employment Relationship* (pp. 1–20). Basingstoke: Palgrave Macmillan.

Bowen, D. and Ostroff, C. (2004). Understanding HRM–firm performance linkages: The role of the "strength" of the HRM system. *Academy of Management Review*, **29**(2), 203–21.

Cappelli, P., Bassi, L., Katz, H., Knoke, D., Osterman, P. and Usem, M. (1997). *Change at Work*. New York: Oxford University Press.

Christensen Hughes, J. (2008). Human Resource Management in the hospitality industry. In B. Brotherton and R.C. Wood (eds), *The Sage Handbook of Hospitality Management* (pp. 273–301). London: Sage.

Diefendorff, J.M. and Gosserand, R.H. (2003). Understanding the emotional labor process: A control theory perspective. *Journal of Organizational Behaviour*, **24**(8), 945–59.

Disney Annual Report (2016, 31 January). Accessed at https://ditm-twdcus.storage.google apis.com/2016-Annual-Report.pdf.

Disney Institute Training Materials (2011). *Disney's Approach to People Management.*

Grandey, A. (2000). Emotion regulation in the workplace: A new way to conceptualize emotional labor. *Journal of Occupational Health Psychology*, **5**, 95–110.

Grant, A.M. (2007). Relational job design and the motivation to make a prosocial difference. *Academy of Management Review*, **32**, 393–417.

Grant, A.M. (2008). Does intrinsic motivation fuel the prosocial fire? Motivational synergy in predicting persistence, performance, and productivity. *Journal of Applied Psychology*, **93**, 48–58.

Grant, A.M. and Sumanth, J.J. (2009). Mission possible? The performance of prosocially motivated employees depends on manager trustworthiness. *Journal of Applied Psychology*, **94**, 927–44.

Grant, A.M., Parker, S. and Collins, C. (2009). Getting credit for proactive behavior: Supervisor reactions depend on what you value and how you feel. *Personnel Psychology*, **62**, 31–55.

Greenberg, J. (1987). A taxonomy of organizational justice theories. *Academy of Management Review*, **12**, 9–22.

Gremler, D. and Gwinner, K.P. (2000). Customer–employee rapport in service relationships. *Journal of Service Research*, **3**(1), 82–104.

Hochschild, A.R. (1983). *The Managed Heart: Commercialization of Human Feeling.* Berkeley, CA: University of California Press.

Huselid, M.A. (1995). The impact of human resource management practices on turnover, productivity, and corporate financial performance. *Academy of Management Journal*, **38**, 635–72.

Jerome, L. and Kleiner, B.H. (1995). Employee morale and its impact on service: What companies do to create a positive service experience. *Managing Service Quality*, **5**(6), 21–5.

Kusluvan, S. (2003). *Managing Employee Attitudes and Behaviors in the Tourism and Hospitality Industry.* New York: Nova Science.

Lashley, C. (2001). *Empowerment: HR Strategies for Service Excellence.* Oxford: Butterworth-Heinemann.

Lawler, E.E. and Mohrman, S.A. (2003). *Creating a Strategic Human Resources Organization: An Assessment of Trends and New Directions.* Stanford, CA: Stanford Business Books.

Maneotis, S.M., Grandey, A.A. and Krauss, A.D. (2014). Understanding the "why" as well as the "how": Service performance is a function of prosocial motives and emotional labor. *Human Performance*, **27**(1), 80–97.

Mayer, K.J. (2002). Human resource practices and service quality in theme parks. *The International Journal of Contemporary Hospitality Management*, **14**(4), 169–75.

Milman, A. (2008). Theme park tourism and management strategy. In A. Woodsie and D. Martin (eds), *Tourism Management* (pp. 218–31). Wallingford: CABI.

Milman, A. (2010). The global theme park industry. *Worldwide Hospitality and Tourism Themes*, **2**(3), 220–37.

Milman, A. and Dickson, D. (2013). Employment characteristics and retention predictors among hourly employees in large US theme parks and attractions. *International Journal of Contemporary Hospitality Management*, **26**(3), 447–69.

Milman, A., Okumus, F. and Dickson, D. (2010). The contribution of theme parks and attractions to the social and economic sustainability of destinations. *Worldwide Hospitality and Tourism*, **2**(3), 338–45.

Nissen, B., Schutz, E. and Zhang, Y. (2007). Walt Disney World's hidden costs: The impact of Disney's wage structure on the Greater Orlando area. Research Report for the Research Institute on Social and Economic Policy, Center for Labor Research and Studies. Miami: Florida International University.

Pugh, S.D., Groth, M. and Hennig-Thurau, T. (2011). Willing and able to fake emotions: A closer examination of the link between emotional dissonance and employee well-being. *The Journal of Applied Psychology*, **96**(2), 377–90.

Pugliesi, K. (1999). The consequences of emotional labor: Effects on work stress, job satisfaction and well-being. *Motivation and Emotion*, **23**(2), 125–54.

Reyers, A. and Matusitz, J. (2012). Emotional regulation at Walt Disney World: An impression management view. *Journal of Workplace Behavioral Health*, **27**(3), 139–59.

Torres, R. (2012). Editorial. In *World of Work Report 2012: Better Jobs for Better Economy: vii=xi*. Geneva: ILO/International Institute for Labour Studies.

Tsaur, S. and Tang, W. (2013). The burden of esthetic labor on front-line employees in hospitality industry. *International Journal of Hospitality Management*, **35**, 19–27.

Warhurst, C. and Nickson, D. (2007). Employee experience of aesthetic labour in retail and hospitality. *Work, Employment & Society*, **21**(1), 103–20.

Zenger, T. (2013). The Disney recipe. *Harvard Business Review*, 28 May. Blog post. Accessed at https://hbr.org/2013/05/what-makes-a-good-corporate-st.

Zeytinoglu, I., Chowhan, J., Cooke, G. and Mann, S. (2016). An ill-informed choice: Empirical evidence of the link between employers' part-time or temporary employment strategies and workplace performance in Canada. *International Journal of Human Resource Management*, 1–25.

16. Benefits of workplace learning in hospitality organizations
Ronald J. Burke

Organizational learning has been identified as a significant factor in organizational performance and success (Denton, 1998; Nonaka, 1991; Salas and Von Glinow, 2008). But organizations themselves do not learn; individuals working in organizations are the agents of all organizational learning and organizational actions (Argyris, 2003; 1997).

Here are two examples of research on learning in the hospitality sector. Li et al. (2013) observed General Managers of hospitality organizations, also analyzing their documents, as they learned how to manage their hotels. Their learning involved experiences through four stages: feeling challenged, seeking information, trying new responses, and observing results. Reflection was central to their learning. A range of challenges, ways to obtain new information, outcomes and tasks, and obtaining data on results were noted.

Magnini (2009) created a model of learning and knowledge transfer in international joint ventures in the hospitality sector. Foreign and domestic partners had knowledge, information and expertise in different areas, which needed to be considered. Individual characteristics (for example, one's learning orientation), relationship characteristics (for example, trust, respect), and organizational-level variables (for example, organizational learning culture) were relevant.

Organizational learning by hospitality firms will become increasingly important as these firms face new challenges requiring new behaviors from organizational leaders. These challenges include the introduction of new technologies, increasing speed of change, greater competitiveness, both unanticipated and expected events, the need to utilize the talents of all employees, and access information from a wider range of sources.

Emerging research evidence in other sectors has shown a relationship between organizational learning and firm financial performance. These have involved Spanish firms (Lopez et al., 2006), manufacturing and wholesale retail operations in Hong Kong (Law and Ngai, 2008), South Korean firms (Park and Jacobs, 2011), and US manufacturing firms (Ellinger et al., 2002).

Organizations that learn have cultures that facilitate learning. Marsick and Watkins (2003) write that workplace learning can take place formally through training and the communication of policies and practices, and informally via communication with others, observation of co-workers, and personal reflection of one's work behaviors and experiences. Learning also occurs at organizational, work unit and individual levels. They suggest that learning cultures contain seven features: creating continuous learning opportunities, promoting inquiry and dialogue, supporting collaboration and team learning, developing systems to retain and disseminate learning, encouraging staff to embrace a common vision, linking the organization to its external environment, and having leaders who themselves exhibit, embrace and encourage learning.

Nikolova et al. (2014) proposed two avenues to work-based learning: interacting with co-workers and supervisors, and through personal exploration and experimentation. Thus four potential avenues for learning emerge: through reflection and experimentation and from interactions with and observation of co-workers and supervisors.

Hicks et al. (2007, p.64) define workplace learning as "a process whereby people, as a function of completing their organizational tasks and roles, acquire knowledge, skills and attitudes that enhance individual and organizational performance".

Individual learning can benefit both learners and their workplaces. New hires can master their jobs more quickly. Individuals can become more engaged at work, more productive employees and more "employable", not only in retaining their present jobs but also in getting other jobs that they might want (De Vos and Van der Heijden, 2015). Workplace learning is also likely to reduce turnover, which is particularly high in the hospitality sector because of the low pay, long work hours, poorly trained supervisors and limited upward mobility. Workplaces have stronger performers and are better able to understand events in their workplaces. Thus supervisors and managers benefit by creating learning cultures and learning opportunities.

Historically, most training and development in the hospitality sector has been formal and teacher-directed (Furunes, 2005; Costen et al., 2010). Yet most learning at work is informal; formal education and formal training make only small contributions here. Informal workplace learning occurs from the challenges in one's job and learning from these. However, workplace learning is not a major objective of organizations; it is usually an afterthought.

Informal learning becomes important in part because employees view some formal training as falling short in terms of quality and requiring improvement (Chiang et al., 2005; Poulston, 2008) and some properties skimp on training investments because of high staff turnover (Gjelsvik,

2002). Chand (2010) suggests that human resource management efforts besides addressing basics such as recruitment, selection and development, should also make efforts to address informal learning.

Although there is little data on the learning opportunities and learning outcomes of women compared to men in the hospitality sector, Fenwick (2004) and Tangaard (2006) noted persistent gender inequalities which limit women's access to training and learning opportunities.

Workplace learning is likely to be facilitated when employees feel free to discuss their work experiences, their successes and difficulties, with others (Burke, 2013; Greenberg and Edwards, 2009). This has been termed engaging in "voice". Argyris and Schon (1978) write about how engaging in voice behaviors can increase individual competence and effectiveness and can enhance individual and organizational learning. Unfortunately, high levels of fear exist in too many organizations, resulting in employees telling their supervisors what the supervisors want to hear, becoming "housebroken" as a result (Burke and Cooper, 2013; Perlow and Williams, 2003). Learning here becomes limited and incomplete.

A number of facilitators of workplace learning have been identified. Crouse et al. (2011) offered nine learning strategies. These included taking courses and programs, doing work and new tasks at work, working with others, e-learning, observing others, engaging in trial and error, reading and undertaking research, reflecting on one's actions, and getting feedback on one's efforts, replicating one's actions, and learning from this effort.

They also identified nine barriers to workplace learning. A barrier to learning (Hicks et al., 2007, p. 64) was "those factors that prevent learning from starting, impede or interrupt learning or result in learning being terminated earlier than it might have been ordinarily". These included resource constraints; lack of access to a range of opportunities (for example, computers, learning resources, challenging work); technological constraints; personal constraints such as fear of failure and loss of motivation; interpersonal constraints such as poor management skills and the reluctance of others to help; structural and cultural constraints that do not support learning; poor or overwhelming course learning content and delivery; power relationships; and work change that is both fast and overwhelming.

Finally, they observed six types of facilitators. These included cultural, structural and managerial support; task and job-related factors; the role of others; efforts that assisted learning such as presence of informal trainers and feedback that helps learning; personal attributes such as asking for help and being open to new ideas; and increased resources such as time and access to technology. Organizations need then to decrease barriers to workplace learning while simultaneously increasing facilitating factors.

Doyle et al. (2012) studied workplace learning by 151 employees, a 20 percent response rate, in eight Canadian hotels in Halifax, Nova Scotia. The sample contained more women (89; 59 percent), more non-managerial employees (97; 64 percent), most in housekeeping and front desk (77; 52 percent) and most were between 19 and 30 years of age (67; 45 percent). The typical respondent was a 19 to 30-year-old woman in a non-managerial job, likely to be working in housekeeping and front desk. Doyle et al. were interested in comparing learning experiences of men and women, and managers and non-managers. Measures of 13 learning strategies, 12 learning facilitators, 19 learning barriers and 11 learning outcomes were used. These were all measured on a five-point scale, with 1 being the least favorable response and 5 the most favorable response. The sample as a whole scored close to 4 on use of various learning strategies, presence of learning facilitators, favorable learning outcomes and about 2 on the presence of learning barriers. Thus the sample as a whole was generally active in informal workplace learning. There were no differences between managers and non-managers on these measures. There were, however, significant gender differences on all four measures. Women scored higher on learning strategies, learning facilitators and learning outcomes and lower on learning barriers. One must treat these conclusions as tentative, given the nature of the sample.

WORKPLACE LEARNING CULTURES, LEARNING POTENTIAL AND IMPORTANT WORKPLACE OUTCOMES

We undertook a study of perceived workplace learning culture, potential workplace learning opportunities, feelings of psychological empowerment, personal self-efficacy, and individual work and well-being outcomes, including self-reported levels of service quality in a sample of 205 supervisors and managers working in 5-star hotels in Turkey (Burke et al., 2016).

Workplace learning is perhaps more important in the hospitality sector than in other sectors as their workforces tend to be young and new to their jobs and workplace learning would help them more quickly perform their jobs adequately, reduce levels of turnover which are very high in this sector because of the long work hours and relatively low pay, and equip employees for potential job advancement.

Data were obtained from 205 supervisors and managers from 12 5-star hotels, a 89 percent response rate (114 males and 91 females). The following measures were included: workplace learning culture (Marsick and Watkins, 2003; Yang et al., 2004); workplace learning potential (Nikolova et al., 2014); psychological empowerment (Spreitzer, 1995); self-efficacy (Schwarzer and Jerusalem, 1995); job satisfaction (Taylor and Bowers, 1972); intent to quit (Burke, 1991); perceived employability (Wittekind et al., 2010); and perceived quality of service (Peccei and Rosenthal, 2001).

Let us consider some of the results. First, managers scoring higher on self-efficacy reported a stronger workplace learning culture, more workplace learning opportunities, higher levels of employability, more psychological empowerment, more job satisfaction, lower intentions to quit and higher perceived quality of service levels.

Second, managers reporting stronger workplace learning cultures and more workplace learning opportunities also indicated higher levels of employability. Managers reporting higher levels of workplace learning cultures also indicated more job satisfaction and more psychological empowerment.

Third, managers reporting higher levels of workplace learning culture and more opportunities for workplace learning also were less likely to intend to quit.

Finally, strength of workplace learning culture, but not opportunities for workplace learning, predicted perceptions of higher levels of service quality.

Several practical implications follow from these findings. First, given the importance of individual self-efficacy in our results, organizations should immediately consider training efforts targeting increasing individual self-efficacy (Maddux, 2002).

In order to increase levels of workplace learning, organizations need to identify this as an important element in their business practices, and then communicate this to all employees. In addition, human resource management policies and practices need to support this priority by providing resources such as places to talk, encouraging reflection, and making technology and information available.

Finally, employees should receive training in the wide variety of informal learning avenues now available to them.

GENDER DIFFERENCES

In addition to our interests in human resource management in the hospitality and tourism sector in Turkey and elsewhere, we have always studied potential gender differences in the work and well-being experiences of women and men where possible. There is considerable evidence that women encounter different workplace challenges than men. These include bias and discrimination; sexual harassment; greater home and family responsibilities; more work–family and family–work conflict; exclusion from the old boy's network; lack of female role models in executive ranks; limited mentoring; hierarchical and gender job segregation; lower levels of pay; and almost no organizational efforts in this sector to support the career aspirations and advancement of qualified women. In addition, women in Turkey face societal values that have more recently become even less supportive of women in the workforce (Burke and Koyuncu, 2013; Kabasakal et al., 2017).

We compared responses of males and females on all measures in this study. Females and males were much more similar than they were different. Consistent with other studies we have carried out in the hospitality sector in Turkey, significant differences were present on some personal and work situation characteristics. In this study, women were older, more likely to be parents, worked more hours per week and had longer job tenures. But there were no gender differences on job satisfaction, learning culture, learning opportunities, self-efficacy, psychological empowerment, perceptions of employability, and intent to quit. We have historically considered the absence of significant gender differences here, and in a host of other studies we have undertaken as "good news" and "signs of progress". We are now beginning to see the absence of gender differences here as worrisome in terms of the promotion of qualified women. If women are performing basically the same as men, why aren't more women represented in the ranks of supervisors and managers?

BENEFITS OF VOICE BEHAVIOR

We undertook a study of antecedents and consequences of employees engaging in voice behaviors in hospitality organizations. Morrison (2011, p.375) defines voice as "discretionary communication of ideas, suggestions, concerns or opinions about work-related issues with the intent to improve organizational and unit functioning". Data were collected from 594 front-line service workers employed in 15 top quality hotels in Alanya, Turkey, a 59 percent response rate. The sample consisted of 371 males and 174 females. The following measures were included: voice (Van Dyne and LePine, 1998); work engagement (Schaufeli et al., 2002); job satisfaction (Kofodimos, 1993); intent to quit (Burke, 1991); organizational support for work–family balance (Thompson et al., 1999); and work–family and family–work conflict (Carlson et al., 2000).

Let us consider some of our results. The sample as a whole reported a generally moderate level of voice behavior. First, hierarchical analyses were undertaken in which the measure of voice was regressed on three blocks of predictor variables: five personal demographic items (for example, age, education level), five work situation characteristics (for example, supervise others, organizational level) and two indicators of workplace culture (support for work–family balance, positive supervisor behaviors). Personal characteristics failed to predict engaging in voice behavior. Work situation characteristics accounted for a significant increment in voice behaviors. Respondents who supervised others, worked in larger properties, and were at higher organizational levels engaged in more voice behavior. Respondents indicating higher levels of positive supervisor behaviors and higher levels of organizational support for work–family balance also reported engaging in more voice behaviors.

Finally, engaging in voice behavior was significantly and positively related to job satisfaction and work engagement, and negatively related to intentions to quit. Engaging in voice behavior was unrelated to levels of work–family or family–work conflict however.

GENDER DIFFERENCES

We compared the responses of 371 males with responses of 174 females. A greater percentage of males worked in food and beverage, technical services and security, while a greater percentage of females worked in housekeeping, accounting and human resources. Females were more likely to be parents, were more highly educated and worked fewer hours than males. Males indicated that they had higher levels of quit intentions and more family–work conflict. But again there were more gender similarities than differences for the remaining measures. Males and females engaged in similar levels of voice behavior, had similar levels of job satisfaction, work engagement, positive supervisor behaviors, and levels of organizational support.

CONCLUSIONS

1. Workplace learning is important for individuals and organizations.
2. Employees use a variety of learning strategies at work, with most being informal. These include learning from one's daily experiences, through reflection and experimentation, learning from observations and discussions with co-workers and supervisors, and from undertaking new tasks and job responsibilities.
3. Informal learning is more effective than formal learning, both leading to somewhat different outcomes.

4. An employee's age, amount of previous work experience, organizational level, and the nature of the demands in their job will affect what needs to be learned, the facilitators and barriers to informal workplace learning in their organization, and which learning strategies are relevant.
5. Workplaces can increase informal learning by providing more space, time, resources and information, and reading materials, and more rewards for learning.
6. Increasing supervisory and managerial skills in coaching and mentoring increases workplace learning.
7. A variety of job experiences, giving employees feedback on their job performance, and increasing interactions between employees and their supervisors increases workplace learning opportunities.
8. Learning is important for employees in each generation (Millennials, Gen Xers, Baby boomers) and across these generations, and at all career stages.

ACKNOWLEDGMENT

Preparation of this manuscript was supported in part by York University. I thank my colleagues Mustafa Koyuncu, Jacob Wolpin, Bekir Esitti and Kadife Koyuncu for their contributions to this research program.

REFERENCES

Argyris, C. (1997) Double loop learning in organizations. *Harvard Business Review*, **55**, 115–24.
Argyris, C. (2003) A life full of learning. *Organizational Studies*, **24**, 1178–97.
Argyris, C. and Schon, D. (1978) *Organizational Learning*. Reading, MA: Addison-Wesley.
Burke, R.J. (1991) Early work and career experiences of female and male managers and professionals: Reasons for optimism? *Canadian Journal of Administrative Sciences*, **8**, 224–30.
Burke, R.J. (2013) Encouraging voice: Why it matters. In R.J. Burke and C.L. Cooper (eds), *Voice and Whistleblowing in Organizations: Overcoming Fear, Fostering Courage and Unleashing Candour*. Cheltenham, UK and Northampton, MA, USA: Edward Elgar Publishing, pp. 3–71.
Burke, R.J. and Cooper, C.L. (2013) *Voice and Whistleblowing in Organizations: Overcoming Fear, Fostering Courage and Unleashing Candour*. Cheltenham, UK and Northampton, MA, USA: Edward Elgar Publishing.
Burke, R.J. and Koyuncu, M. (2013) Women in management in Turkey: Challenges and opportunities. In M.A. Paluidi (ed.), *Women and Management: Global Issues and Promising Solutions*. Santa Barbara, CA: Praeger, pp. 239–53.
Burke, R.J., Koyuncu, M., Wolpin, J., Esitti, B. and Koyuncu, K. (2016) Workplace learning cultures, learning and important work outcomes among managerial employees in five-star Turkish hotels. *Turizam*, **20**, 76–91.

Carlson, D., Kacmar, J. and Williams, L. (2000) Construction and initial validation of a multidimensional measure of work–family conflict. *Journal of Vocational Behavior*, **56**, 249–76.

Chand, M. (2010) The impact of HRM practices on service quality, customer satisfaction and performance in the Indian hotel industry. *Journal of Human Resource Management*, **21**, 551–66.

Chiang, C., Back, K. and Canter, D.D. (2005) The impact of employee training on job satisfaction and intention to stay in the hotel industry. *Journal of Human Resources in Hospitality and Tourism*, **4**, 99–118.

Costen, W.M., Johanson, M.M. and Poisson, D.K. (2010) The development of quality managers in the hospitality industry: Do employee development programs make cents? *Journal of Human Resources in Hospitality and Tourism*, **9**, 131–41.

Crouse, P., Doyle, W. and Young, J.D. (2011) Workplace learning strategies, barriers, facilitators and outcomes: A qualitative study among human resource management professionals. *Human Resource Development International*, **14**, 39–55.

Denton, J.I. (1998) *Organizational Learning and Effectiveness*. London: Routledge.

De Vos, A. and Van der Heijden, B. (2015) *Handbook of Research on Sustainable Careers*. Cheltenham, UK and Northampton, MA, USA: Edward Elgar Publishing.

Doyle, W., Findlay, S. and Young, J.D. (2012) Workplace learning issues of hotel employees: Examining differences across management status and gender. *Journal of Human Resources in Hospitality and Tourism*, **11**, 259–79.

Ellinger, A.D., Ellinger, A.E., Yang, B. and Howton, S.W. (2002) The relationship between the learning organization concept and firms' financial performance: An empirical assessment. *Human Resource Development Quarterly*, **13**, 5–21.

Fenwick, T. (2004) What happens to the girls? Gender, work and learning in Canada's new economy. *Gender and Education*, **16**, 169–85.

Furunes, T. (2005) Training paradox in the hotel industry. *Scandinavian Journal of Hospitality and Tourism*, **5**, 231–48.

Gjelsvik, M. (2002) Hotels as learning arenas. *Scandinavian Journal of Hospitality and Tourism*, **2**, 31–48.

Greenberg, J. and Edwards, M. (2009) *Voice and Silence in Organizations*. Bingley: Emerald Publishing.

Hicks, E., Bagg, R., Doyle, W. and Young, J.D. (2007) Canadian accountants: Examining workplace learning. *Journal of Workplace Learning*, **19**, 61–77.

Kabasakal, H., Karakas, F.J., Maden, C. and Aycan, Z. (2017) Women in management in Turkey. In R.J. Burke and A.M. Richardsen (eds), *Women in Management Worldwide: Signs of Progress*. London: Routledge, pp. 226–46.

Kofodimos, J. (1993) *Balancing Act*. San Francisco: Jossey-Bass.

Law, C.C.H. and Ngai, E.W.T. (2008) An empirical study of the effects of knowledge sharing and learning behaviors on firm performance. *Expert Systems with Applications*, **34**, 2342–9.

Li, L., Gray, D.E., Lockwood, A.J. and Buhalis, D. (2013) Learning about managing the business in the hospitality industry. *Human Resource Development Quarterly*, **24**, 525–59.

Lopez, S.P., Montez Peon, J.M. and Vazquez Ordas, C. (2006) Human resource management as a determining factor in organizational learning. *Management Learning*, **17**, 215–30.

Maddux, J.E. (2002) Self-efficacy: The power of believing you can. In C.R. Snyder and S.J. Lopez (eds), *Handbook of Positive Psychology*. New York: Oxford University Press, pp. 271–87.

Magnini, V.P. (2008) Practicing effective knowledge sharing in international hotel joint ventures. *International Journal of Hospitality Management*, **27**, 249–58.

Magnini, V.P. (2009) An exploratory investigation of the real-time training modes used by hotel expatriates. *International Journal of Hospitality Management*, **28**, 513–18.

Marsick, V.J. and Watkins, K.E. (2003) Demonstrating the value of an organization's learning culture: The dimensions of the learning organization questionnaire. *Advances in Developing Human Resources*, **5**, 132–56.

Morrison, E.W. (2011) Employee voice behavior: Integration and directions for future research. *Academy of Management Annals*, **5**, 373–412.

Nikolova, I., Van Ruysseveldt, J., De Witte, H. and Syroit, J. (2014) Work-based learning: Development and validation of a scale measuring the learning potential of the workplace (LPW). *Journal of Vocational Behavior*, **84**, 1–10.

Nonaka, I. (1991) The knowledge creating company. *Harvard Business Review*, **69**, 96–104.

Park, Y. and Jacobs, R.I. (2011) The influence of investment in workplace learning on learning outcomes and organizational performance. *Human Resource Development Quarterly*, **22**, 437–58.

Peccei, R. and Rosenthal, P. (2001) Delivering customer-oriented behavior through empowerment: An empirical test of HRM assumptions. *Journal of Management Studies*, **38**, 833–57.

Perlow, L. and Williams, S. (2003) Is silence killing your company? *Harvard Business Review*, **81**, 53–8.

Poulston, J. (2008) Hospitality workplace problems and poor training: A close relationship. *International Journal of Contemporary Hospitality Management*, **20**, 412–27.

Salas, S. and Von Glinow, M.A. (2008) Fostering organizational learning: Creating and maintaining a learning culture. In R.J. Burke and C.L. Cooper (eds), *Building More Effective Organizations*. Cambridge: Cambridge University Press, pp. 207–27.

Schaufeli, W.B., Salanova, M., Gonzalez-Roma, V. and Bakker, A.B. (2002) The measurement of engagement and burnout: A two-sample confirmatory factor analytic approach. *Journal of Happiness Studies*, **3**, 71–92.

Schwarzer, R. and Jerusalem, M. (1995) Generalized self-efficacy scale. In J. Weinman, S. Wright and M. Johnston (eds), *Measures in Health Psychology: A User's Portfolio*. Causal and Control Beliefs. Windsor: NFER-Nelson, pp. 35–7.

Spreitzer, G. (1995) Psychological empowerment in the workplace: Dimensions, measurement, and validation. *Academy of Management Journal*, **38**, 1442–65.

Tangaard, L. (2006) Situating gendered learning in the workplace. *Journal of Workplace Learning*, **18**, 220–34.

Taylor, J.C. and Bowers, D. (1972) *Survey of Organizations: A Machine-scored Standardized Questionnaire Instrument*. Ann Arbor, MI: Institute for Social Research.

Thompson, C., Beauvais, L.L. and Lyness, K.S. (1999) When work–family benefits are not enough: The influence of work–family culture, benefit utilization, organizational attachment, and work–family conflict. *Journal of Vocational Behavior*, **54**, 393–419.

Van Dyne, L. and LePine, J. (1998) Helping and voice extra-role behaviors: Evidence of construct and predictive validity. *Academy of Management Journal*, **41**, 108–19.

Wittekind, A., Reader, S. and Grote, G.A. (2010) A longitudinal study of determinants of perceived employability. *Journal of Organizational Behavior*, **31**, 566–86.

Yang, B., Watkins, K.E. and Marsick, V.J. (2004) The construct of the learning organization: Dimensions measurement, and validation. *Human Resources Development Quarterly*, **15**, 31–66.

17. The benefits of high performance human resource practices in the implementation of an artistic strategy in the hotel industry

Ta-Wei Tang, Ya-Yun Tang, Michael Chih-Hung Wang and Tsai-Chiao Wang

1. INTRODUCTION

Recent research has acknowledged artistic strategies as a unique way for hotels to distinguish themselves from their competitors (Akoğlan Kozak and Acar Gürel, 2015; Cheng et al., 2016; Strannegård and Strannegård, 2012). By incorporating performing arts into service design (Swanson and Davis, 2012), hotels can offer a memorable sensory experience (Jones et al., 2013; Barsky and Nash, 2002) to attract customers who seek spiritual satisfaction (Durna et al., 2015; Barsky and Nash, 2002). More specifically, by providing in-depth travel to foreign customers, the local culture and lifestyles can be experienced (Lee, 2011; Chick, 2009).

To fulfill the customers' needs for tourism, international hotels began adapting their servicescape design by exploring and adding some elements with an authentic experience of local lifestyle services (Pizam, 2015; Jones et al., 2013), such as nature, art, performance and local culture (Chang, 2016; Countryman and Jang, 2006). However, not all hotels are able to offer attractive artistic services to their customers. The major barriers to investing in artistic service design or to creating attractive artistic activities concern the high costs and the probability of failure when providing these special service designs (Akoğlan Kozak and Acar Gürel, 2015; Strannegård and Strannegård, 2012). To implement artistic strategies, alternatively, hotels may choose to invest in developing employees' performance abilities, that is, high performance human resource practices (hereafter, HPRPs) (Gannon et al., 2015; Úbeda-García et al., 2014). HPRPs can be defined as an HR system in which service quality is improved by enhancing the abilities, motivation and opportunities of service personnel (Tang and Tang, 2012). By aligning each HR activity, service employees are likely to help hotels not only to achieve their artistic aims but also to reduce the costs of implementing artistic services (Karatepe, 2013; Tang and Tang, 2012).

More importantly, hotels rely on their employees to develop and provide innovative services to meet the service quality required by their customers (Tang, 2016). Despite the fact that employees' capabilities are successfully adapted to develop new services, there has been little to no attention paid to exploring HPRPs with regard to employees' development and implementation of innovative arts performance services in hospitality studies. To fill this gap, a conceptual framework is proposed to explore the linkage between artistic strategy and HPRPs and how this linkage benefits service employee development and implementation of artistic performance (including factors related to capability, motivation and opportunities), which contribute to the hotel's operational performance (including service quality, experience value, service innovation performance, financial performance and competitive advantage) in consequence.

2. LITERATURE REVIEW

2.1 Art as a Competitive Strategy

Art is not only a medium for people to express their spiritual and individual characteristics, convey affection, and experience local nature and cultural authenticity (Chick, 2009), but is also the key to the globalization and localization of service product designs. Artistic strategies in hotel service design express the uniqueness of service products, thus enhancing their experiential value (Akoğlan Kozak and Acar Gürel, 2015; Strannegård and Strannegård, 2012) and creating competitive advantages that help hotels to develop a new profitable market (Cheng et al., 2016; Strannegård and Strannegård, 2012; McCleary et al., 2008).

As experienced consumers seek an emotional experience through service contacts (Barsky and Nash, 2002), such as feeling the hotel's ambience (Weaver, 2009; Heide et al., 2007) and passively engaging in performing arts or artistic services (Swanson and Davis, 2012), they can relieve their stress and enhance their positive emotions, which evokes affective experiences (Addis and Holbrook, 2001; Cheng et al., 2016; Holbrook, 2000). Considering that the creation of compelling customer experiences should be the consequence not only of design choices but also of culture and art (Gruber et al., 2015), international hotels must actively employ unique local culture and art as raw materials for designing service processes and formulating operational strategies (Ryan, 2015). More specifically, by arranging experiential artistic activities, international hotels can appeal clearly to those who are seeking self-realization (McCleary et al., 2008; Rhodes, 1981). An example of this is Leader Village Taroko in the Taroko

National Park in Eastern Taiwan, which used its mountainous environment as a natural entrance, decorating the hotel interior with design elements such as the Taroko rattan and weaving works. To provide customers with an in-depth experience of the indigenous culture, the hotel is also furnished with an installation of art works such as stone and wood sculptures and crescent-shaped room keys (traditionally, the crescent shape serves as a means of repelling evil spirits), all of which contribute to enhancing the hotel's service value.

Previous studies have indicated that adopting cultural resources and creating an artistic climate provide sustainable competitive advantages and contribute to hotel performance (McCleary et al., 2008; Heide et al., 2007). The success of performing arts services was determined by building hotels' abilities to evoke emotional and subjective responses from customers (Swanson and Davis, 2012). In particular, artfulness and authenticity are important factors in evoking emotional responses (Tussyadiah, 2014; Hume et al., 2006). Previous researchers have also noted that authentic cultural elements can evoke emotional responses from the audience (Weaver, 2009).

Furthermore, Magelssen (2003) indicated that using local architecture and handicrafts to maintain and promote traditions enables consumers to experience past lifestyles. From the customer orientation perspective, artistic services should be richly endowed with authentic, local cultural content if hotels want to try to stimulate customers' emotions.

2.2 HPRPs and Service Innovation in the Hospitality Industry

According to the above definition, HPRPs imply individual service provided to employees through complementary, mutually supportive, and mutual human resource activities to improve service-related behaviors, which leads to improvement of service quality (Úbeda-García et al., 2014; Karatepe, 2013; Murphy and Murrmann, 2009). Studies have indicated that HPRPs that include recruitment, training, performance evaluations, rewarding, participation, and empowering allow service employees to enhance their service abilities, increase service motivation, and acquire performance opportunities to aid hotels in improving their operational performance (Karatepe, 2013; Tang and Tang, 2012). In other words, employees who meet hotel requirements (that is, performing arts skills and having service attitudes required for attaining a favorable business performance) are recruited (Swanson and Davis, 2012; Chang et al., 2011) for selective training, not only to improve their performing arts skills but also to enhance their artistic knowledge (Úbeda-García et al., 2014; Chang et al., 2011); this helps hotels control the service process effectively.

Moreover, performance evaluation enables the assessment of the performing arts ability of service employees and provides equivalent rewards to those who perform well in artistic services, thus motivating service employees to actively gain knowledge and skills with regard to culture and art (Chang, 2016; Crick and Spencer, 2011). Therefore, opportunities for improving service quality can be granted to service personnel by empowering them to participate in designing services for performing arts activities, decision-making processes, and in the solving of problems encountered during service contact (Yavas et al., 2010; Ottenbacher and Gnoth, 2005) to respond effectively to unpredictable customer demands (Raub, 2008). Considered together, by using HPRPs, hotels assist their employees' art- and culture-related knowledge, and cultivate their performing arts skills and service behaviors in order to deliver optimal services to customers, thereby achieving their target business performance (Karatepe, 2013).

Moreover, an increasing number of hospitality studies have empirically investigated the relation between HPRPs and service innovation or operational performance (Chang et al., 2011). From the configuration perspective, these studies focus on investigating a combination of HPRP sets in terms of service innovative behavior, firm innovation or hospitality innovation. For instance, studies have found that selective staffing, extensive training, internal mobility, employment security, clear job descriptions, results-oriented appraisal, incentive rewards, participation (Dhar, 2015), selection, training and development, performance management, compensation, information sharing, and participation and mentoring (Fu et al., 2015) are important. From the universalistic perspective, studies have focused on assessing whether some HPRPs are appropriate for hospitality companies' innovation. Chang et al. (2011) focus on two specific HPRP systems, that is, selection and training, which are recognized as determinants of two innovations – incremental and radical innovation in hospitality hotels. Nieves and Quintana (2016) found that recruitment/selection and training/development determine innovation performance in hotels.

However, the study of human resource activities in the field of hospitality needs to be further explored in terms of how human resource activities contribute to assisting managers in implementing the specific business strategies developed by them. The business strategy chosen by the managers requires the support of human resource activities in order to guide the deployment of human resources in the hotel toward this business strategy and ensure the successful implementation of this strategy. To maximize the contribution of such a business strategy and thus contribute to the hotel's financial output, hotel researchers and managers need to focus on the relationship between human resource activities and business strategies and the impact of such a relationship on service employees. Otherwise, the hotel is still unable to gain a competitive advantage if it lacks the ability, motivation and opportunity to implement this strategy, despite the fact that the manager has proposed a unique business strategy.

Therefore, the following research framework and parts of this study will focus on analyzing the support of HPRPs for artistic strategy and the enhancement of collective employees' ability in creating service innovation, motivation and opportunities that ultimately improve the performance of hotel operations.

3.   RESEARCH FRAMEWORK

This study focuses on exploring the key processes that HPRPs can induce service employees to follow and thus support hotels in reaching their goals. With HPRPs as an effective tool, hotels can shape the abilities, motivations and opportunities for employees to engage in arts-related services.

This study recommends that managers enable employees to develop the abilities, motivations and opportunities required to implement the artistic strategies by establishing mutually aligned high performance human resource activities. Through the acquisition or cultivation of human capital required for the implementation of artistic strategy, the organizational climate can be shaped to stimulate service employees' motivation to engage in the development and implementation of artistic services that ultimately allow employees to have the opportunity to perform. Managers can establish human resources conducive to the implementation of artistic strategies to further influence hotels' operational performance.

According to Ostroff and Bowen's (2000) argument, employee attributes play a mediating role in connecting HPRPs and firm performance. Following this logic, this study argues that three interrelated sets of employee attributes influence operational performance: human capital (that is, performing arts capabilities and service innovation/improvement capabilities); organizational climates (that is, innovation climate, service climate, and trust climate); and attitudes and behaviors (that is, performance opportunities and organization support).

This study proposes a model regarding how HPRPs work to create better operational performance. Beginning on the left-hand side of Figure 17.1, the relationship between artistic strategy and HPRPs can maximize the value of human resources, including promoting employees' human capital, shaping the organizational climate and making it conducive to strategy implementation, and encouraging employees to engage in service performance-related attitudes and behaviors so that they have

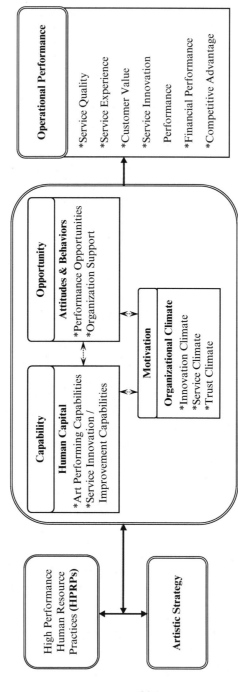

Figure 17.1   The benefits of high performance human resource practices on the operational performance of implementing artistic strategy

the abilities, motivations and opportunities to successfully implement the artistic strategies developed by the hotel. Human capital, organizational climates, and attitudes and behaviors were recognized as key mediating mechanisms linking HPRPs and operational performance. The proposed frameworks are depicted in Figure 17.1.

3.1 The Effects of HPRPs on the Implementation of Artistic Strategies

As mentioned previously, HPRPs refer to an HR system in which service quality is improved by enhancing the abilities, motivation and opportunities of service personnel (Tang and Tang, 2012), including selection policies, training, performance appraisals, compensation, participation and empowerment. Selection policies and training practices emphasize the improvement of employees' artistic service performance competencies. Performance appraisals and compensation practices are mainly implemented to elicit employees' motivation for enhancing their artistic service performance. Participation and empowerment practices provide opportunities for employees to improve or promote their artistic service performance (Tang and Tang, 2012).

3.2 The Effects of HPRPs on Human Capital

Moreover, some studies have also emphasized that HPRPs are a fundamental way for organizations to influence human capital levels (Lepak and Snell, 2002; Yamao et al., 2009; Youndt and Snell, 2004). Studies have highlighted the elements of HPRPs required for improving human capital levels. Selective recruitment practices can help hotels acquire sufficient employees with valuable capabilities (Huselid, 1995). Studies have also shown that selective recruitment practices can help firms to develop human capital (López-Cabrales et al., 2011). In addition, investments in training employees to acquire knowledge and skills encourage them to adjust their knowledge and skills according to organizational needs (López-Cabrales et al., 2011), which may improve human capital levels in the hotel (Liao and Chuang, 2004; Minbaeva et al., 2009). Furthermore, internal promotion policies help in training and motivating employees to develop firm-specific skills and knowledge (Youndt and Snell, 2004), which are also positively related to human capital levels (Yamao et al., 2009; Youndt and Snell, 2004).

3.3   The Effects of HPRPs on Organizational Climate

According to James and Jones (1974), organizational climate refers to a shared perception that individuals attach to particular features of their work environment (Schneider and Reichers, 1983). In this study, organizational climate includes innovation climate, service climate and trust climate. The following review describes the effect of relationships among HPRPs on various climates in hotels. In the hospitality context, HPRPs enable employees to be fairly treated by the employing hotel in various respects, including developing service competence, enhancing service motivation, and enabling them to find opportunities for improving service quality. Several HPRPs that align with each other in hotels are discussed below.

First, innovation is the heart of the success of a hotel to distinguish itself from its competitors (for example, Jones, 1996; Ottenbacher and Gnoth, 2005; Tang, 2016). In this case, the HPRPs are expected to shape innovation climate. Mumford (2000) argued that innovation is based on employees' ability to generate new ideas, which links to creative problem solving. Therefore, by hiring service employees who have the job-relevant knowledge, skills and talents necessary for creative innovation (Mumford, 2000), innovations are likely to be achieved in hotels (Chang et al., 2011; Tang, 2016). Training is recognized as another factor underlying hospitality innovation success (Ottenbacher, 2007) because it increases employees' capability levels (Tracey and Tews, 2004; Roehl and Swerdlow, 1999; Dewar and Dutton, 1986). Training service employees with multiple skills can enhance both incremental and radical innovation among hotels (Chang et al., 2011).

Second, HPRPs can be expected to build and maintain a service climate. As one of the pioneer studies in this field, Schneider et al. (1998) revealed that the elements of HPRPs, including training and decision-making activities, are the fundamental factors that shape service climate (Lin and Liu, 2016). In the hospitality context, hiring service employees through a selection policy can ensure that they have a positive service orientation and empathy (Schneider, 1990), while through training, hotels can help service employees to achieve the standard for hotel performance appraisals, which are likely to trigger them paying more attention to service quality (Chiang and Birch, 2010). Furthermore, rewards and public commendation help to connect with shared interests between employees and hotels, which guide and motivate employees' actions to provide better service with regard to the hotel's service value (Chiang and Birch, 2010). Empowerment and participation practices provide employees with opportunities not only for satisfying distinctive customer needs but also for encouraging them to take non-standardized, customized, adaptable action in immediate response to various customer requests (Batt, 2002; Liao and Chuang, 2004; Ro and Chen, 2011). Therefore, by clarifying organizations' means of support and their expectations and rewards (Bowen and Ostroff, 2004), HPRPs operate to link hotels' goals and service climates.

Third, HPRPs and employees' attitudes and behaviors are bridged by trust (Gould-Williams, 2003), which implies that HPRPs help a trust climate to be established. Unlike the justice and service climates, the association between HPRPs and trust climate is still unclear. According to Tremblay et al. (2010), compared with systems in which only the supervisors judge performance, a performance appraisal system that provides 360-degree feedback instills more trust. Findings in Mayer and Davis (1999) also support this argument by stating that the implementation of a good evaluation system enables employees to build up trust in their supervisors, which may strengthen the shaping of a trust climate. In Whitener's (2001) study, it was observed that internal fair rewards, one of the HPRPs, are significantly linked to trust, whereas findings in other studies revealed that non-monetary rewards positively influenced procedural justice (Tremblay et al., 2010; Meyer and Smith, 2000; Paré and Tremblay, 2007), which may benefit in shaping the trust climate. Moreover, studies also indicated that training opportunities, information sharing and performance-related compensation systems were positively linked to trust (Appelbaum et al., 2000). Therefore, HPRPs can be expected to build a trust climate.

3.4 The Effects of HPRPs on Attitudes and Behaviors

HPRPs recognize employees' contributions and encourage investments in employees, which employees interpret to be a signal of support from the organization (Tremblay et al., 2010). Previous studies have found a link between HPRP policies and a stronger feeling of support (Allen, 1992; Guzzo et al., 1994). Findings in previous studies concluded that HPRPs were associated with perceived organizational support components, including skills development (Allen et al., 2003; Whitener, 2001; Wayne et al., 1997; 2002; Meyer and Smith, 2000), promotion and career development opportunities (Wayne et al., 1997, Meyer and Smith, 2000), formative performance appraisal (Whitener, 2001), and fair rewards (Allen et al., 2003). Moreover, various empirical studies also found that specific elements of HPRPs such as rigorous training (Wayne et al., 1997), appropriate reward policies (Allen et al., 2003), and autonomy and organizational rewards (Rhoades and Eisenberger, 2002) influenced perceived organizational support.

Through HPRPs, managers can inform employees that the hotel offers many sites and opportunities for them to display their talent for artistic performance. They support employees in finding opportunities for performance services that can enhance their self-confidence in their performance abilities. Employees will regard performance services as service activities with a sense of honor. Therefore, they will continue to specialize or refine their own performance abilities to achieve the objectives and expectations of the hotel with an improved artistic performance.

3.5 The Effects of Human Capital on Operational Performance

Human capital, particularly significant in performing activities (Korczynski, 2002; Ployhart et al., 2009), is one of the most important resources in the hospitality industry (Kim et al., 2012; Kumar et al., 2008; Sainaghi et al., 2013) that can be leveraged to achieve sustainable competitive advantage (Nyberg et al., 2014). Human capital refers to the "set of knowledge, skills, and abilities that are embedded in the firms' human resources" (Lado and Wilson, 1994, p. 705). By routinely investing in training and development activities, organizations expect to see an increase in the levels of knowledge, skills and abilities within the organization (Kotey and Folker, 2007; Way, 2002). Since knowledge is intrinsically associated with the level of human capital in the organization, individuals with high levels of knowledge, ability and experience are a source of new ideas for organizations. Hayton and Kelley (2006) indicated that individuals who have more resources to build their cognitive ability, education, training and practical experience are more likely to be innovative. Therefore, the greater the stock of human capital, the greater the opportunities for knowledge exchange and combination processes (Wu, 2004). This leads to innovation activity (Dhanaraj and Parkhe, 2006; Kang et al., 2007; Molina and Martínez, 2010).

Previous empirical studies have indicated how human capital links to various operational performances in the hospitality context. For example, Thornhill (2006) found that enhancing human capital allows organizations to achieve higher, more productive levels of innovation. In the hospitality-related context, Jogaratnam (2017) indicated that human capital was an intangible resource that improved performance (including financial performance and market performance) for independent restaurants. In sum, in the hospitality context, employees who are selected and trained in service talents (that is, HPRPs) may enhance employee human capital for service delivery and subsequently service performance (Liao et al., 2009). From a strategy perspective, human capital is a resource that affects the firm's ability to obtain competitive advantage (Javalgi and Todd, 2011; Nyberg et al., 2014).

3.6 The Effects of Organizational Climate on Operational Performance

Organizational climate is also important in hotels since studies have demonstrated that service climate has a positive relation with customer perceptions of service quality (Schneider, 1990; Schneider et al., 1998), although these perceptions can be attributed to service innovation as well (Liao and Chuang, 2004). The establishment of a service climate helps employees understand the importance of customer service and recognize that their service is supported, expected and rewarded; therefore, service performance is more likely to be enhanced (Lin and Liu, 2016). Employees then realize that high-quality customer service is expected, valued and desired, and they are thus willing to exert efforts to provide that superior service. Therefore, service employees are more likely to read customer needs, which drive them to generate ideas for customer service improvement (Lages and Piercy, 2012). Furthermore, employees consequently provide ideas with regard to innovation service or improved service delivery processes for satisfying customer needs and improving service quality. This can be treated as a customer-oriented service, which is believed to positively affect innovation within hotels (Grissemann et al., 2013). Schneider et al. (1998) argued that a service climate focuses service employee effort and competency on delivering excellent service, which in turn yields positive experiences for customers as well as positive customer perceptions of service quality. Salanova et al. (2015) also found that service climate influences employee performance and then customer loyalty.

3.7 The Effects of Attitudes and Behaviors on Operational Performance

Perceived organizational support (POS) will generate a sense of responsibility for the organization's goals, which translates into concern and assistance in achieving the goal. When employees perceive managers' beneficial treatment, the organization and employees are encouraged to develop a mutually beneficial relationship according to social exchange relationships, thus affecting work results (Yu and Frenkel, 2013). Therefore, when employees receive support for their work performances, they will increase their motivation and willingness to provide better service in response to the organization's beneficial treatment by trying to improve the service process and quality and by providing innovative services to achieve the organization's goals.

Previous studies have shown that HPRPs contribute to increased service quality in hotels, inspiring service employees to enhance their service abilities, increase service motivation, and acquire performance opportunities to aid hotels in improving their business performance (Karatepe, 2013;

Tang and Tang, 2012). Therefore, when employees have the opportunity to show their abilities, they will try to find any possible way to provide better service, thus resulting in service innovations and improvements in business performance (Tang, 2014). Moreover, studies have also found that perceived organizational support positively influences service quality (Garg and Dhar, 2014) and organizational citizenship behavior, which in turn influences job performance (Chiang and Hsieh, 2012).

3.8 Summary

Hotels with HPRPs are helpful for new service developments (NSD), strategic business planning, and changing market needs (Ottenbacher and Gnoth, 2005). This is because HPRPs provide a flexible environment that motivates individuals to dedicate their efforts to both exploitative and exploratory activities (Cordery et al., 1993; Lepak et al., 2003). Since both exploitative and exploratory activities belong to innovation behaviors, HPRP activities may facilitate innovation behaviors.

More specifically, training helps to improve not only front-line employees' expertise in initiating the innovation process (Ottenbacher and Gnoth, 2005) but also employees' instrumental skills with regard to the delivery of new services and the development of their ability to adapt new services (Tang, 2014). In addition, firms' evaluation of their performances depends on whether employees have provided service courteously, resolved consumers' complaints and problems, satisfied consumers' needs, and whether they are committed to both the hotels and their consumers (Ottenbacher and Gnoth, 2005). Therefore, employees can do their best to plan and design better innovation services to help hotels achieve a better operational performance.

3.9 Case Illustrations

In this section, we consider Taiwan's Volando Urai Spring Spa & Resort (Volando) as an illustration to explore how Volando uses high performance human resource practices (HPRPs) to implement artistic strategies. This study considers its HR activities, including how Volando allows service personnel to develop their motivation, capabilities and opportunities to perform the artistic target business strategy developed by hotel managers.

Volando, co-founded by the Japanese and Taiwanese in 2001, is a famous international hot spring hotel located in the north of Taiwan, with 60 employees, revenue of around NT 80 million, and an average of around 6000 guests visiting every year. Volando's strategy focuses on embedding art into service processes for their customers to relieve stress and restore vitality. The hotel combines the natural local beauty and aboriginal culture of Wu Lai (located in the north of Taiwan) as its foundation and incorporates artistic performances with cultural connections to differentiate their service, which helps Volando improve the value of its existing service processes.

With regard to HPRPs, Volando established a collaborative team with its top-level management team (TMT) (including a General Manager, Managing Directors, and an Artistic Director) and an artistic performance team comprising employees who contribute beyond their regular service and management tasks. Accordingly, Volando implements its artistic strategy effectively by integrating HPRPs to achieve an artistic innovation service.

More specifically, the way that Volando added the value of human resource activities will now be explained in detail. First, Volando strengthens the basic artistic skills and inner qualities of the employees to establish the human capital required for the implementation of artistic services. By using selective recruitment, they attract potential candidates with special artistic performance skills (such as drumming) to join the artistic performance activities team. However, when there were no current service employees with the relevant experience, the Artistic Director therefore openly solicited those who wanted to learn drumming from him and then chose those who could act as performers through a drum training process.

Furthermore, Volando emphasizes inner quality training with a series of artistic training courses including three aspects called "body", "mind" and "spirit". For instance, Volando's employees are trained in breathing and relaxation in order to practice the performance skills of the art of Tibetan drumming. Through this process, Volando thus nurtures outstanding employees with altruistic behaviors. An employee working in Volando's spa department said:

> I have been trained in performing art skills and have been involved in performing for three years. During this time, I realized that not only the resonance of voice is beautiful. More importantly, it let me learn how to calm my mind down. This allows me to be calm and focused while working on stressful jobs to successfully resolve customer complaints and improve service quality.

Second, to motivate employees to engage in artistic services, Volando is actively building a beneficial organizational climate. Volando's organizational climate includes innovation, service and trust. What Volando does for its innovation climate is to encourage its employees to combine new ideas to develop higher value-added services that will promote employees as art creators. At Volando, employees can bring any of their ideas about artistic services to the Artistic Director for discussion at any time. These new ideas are then evaluated by the TMT to see if they are feasible. Finally, the Artistic Director will implement the innovative ideas that are highly viable in artistic services. For the service climate, Volando places considerable focus on performance services and the meanings they convey to enrich customers' travel experience through the artistic show. The show tries to build an internal corporate culture, lets employees appreciate it, and conveys the value of performing arts to both employees and clients. Volando uses material and spiritual incentives to encourage employees to demonstrate quality artistic performances so that they can attach importance to artistic performance services and bring value to customers. With regard to material rewards, Volando gives extra bonuses to employees who act as artistic performers, as certified by the Artistic Director. For spiritual rewards, Volando differentiates performance time based on the skill levels of the employees. The ones who have been assessed and certified by the Artistic Director are asked to perform in the afternoon when there are more customers. The ones who are not up to standard perform artistic activities on weekday mornings. Moreover, since employees who perform better receive better performance evaluations and greater remuneration, they may trust the hotel in taking artistic strategic action and are more willing to engage in performance services, which relates to the trust climate.

Third, to develop the quality of artistic services, Volando provides employees with opportunities for artistic performance. In addition to receiving basic training in artistic performance skills, employees of Volando can also opt to participate in training courses for special artistic performance projects. Any performer who chooses to be trained independently for special artistic performances is invited by the general manager to perform solo when his/her ability as a performer is assessed and accredited by the Artistic Director.

To satisfy the employee's desire for self-fulfillment and gratification, he/she can decide on how to present his/her performance. The General Manager said:

> One of the employees in the customer service department was reticent by nature and not good at contacting and communicating with people. At that time, this employee volunteered to learn to play the drum; however, in addition to playing the drums, the performer who can give this artistic performance needs to introduce the connotation and conception of the artistic performance to all customers after drumming. It was a big test for someone who is not good at talking! But after the employee was trained by the Artistic Director and through repeated self-practice for a period of time, I then invited all employees to help him open a special solo concert in the hotel in order to encourage him. This boosted his confidence and opened him up.

Moreover, to create opportunities for employees to conduct performance services at the hotel, the General Manager authorized the Artistic Director to decide on the visual presentation of the hotel and minimized administrative interference in the artistic performances. This shows that Volando not only provides employees with performance opportunities but also supports and encourages them to engage in special artistic performances. Furthermore, more suitable performance space and environments are also provided to show Volando's support for its employees.

The implementation of artistic service innovation strategies can enhance the hotel's business performance. Volando's operating performances can be examined by looking at its financial performance and customer feedback. In the financial performance section, it is divided into total revenue and total number of visitors. In Volando's first official year of operation (2011), its total revenue was about USD 2.6 million. In its third year of implementing the artistic business strategy (2013), its total revenue exceeded USD 3.4 million, with a revenue growth rate of 30.7 percent. Moreover, the total number of visitors in 2011 was about 6000, which subsequently increased by 1000 per year on average. Volando's artistic services are acclaimed by its customers. For example, a spectator at the artistic activities emotionally stated:

> Enjoying afternoon tea in a natural field with green waters under the verdant mountain, watching the changes in water and light. The changing drumbeats and reverberating sound of the gong inspired me with awe in body and mind. I subconsciously stopped all actions at hand and quietly experienced the musical feast. The sweat shed by the performers was enough to illustrate their presentation of the tension in power and beauty. And in an unhurried gentle tone, the performer talked about the implication behind the performance of art that moved me with utter sincerity. In this short hour of performance, it not only touched my vision and hearing, but completely purified my mind and moved me to tears!

Through the above Volando case, this study has suggested that well-developed HPRPs can be seen as a cornerstone for the successful implementation of artistic services in hotels. To implement artistic services or to operate an artistic hotel, hotel operators first need to view art as a primary business strategy and build core HPRPs for implementing artistic strategies. Furthermore, HPRPs can be used to obtain the necessary skills to implement artistic strategies and create an organizational climate motivating employees to engage in artistic performances, as well as to create a self-determined space for employees to enhance their artistic performance opportunities.

Through the aforementioned process, hotel managers can accurately conduct artistic HR arrangements, develop innovative arts services, and improve business performance.

4.   CONCLUSIONS AND IMPLICATIONS

Local arts and traditional culture can easily be used to provide a unique experience for customers. These experiences are key in attracting customers and guiding them to make choices. Although hotels can rely on the investment of hardware equipment to let customers experience different service environments, in order to provide a memorable experience it is necessary and important to create unique values for them through intangible service. Hence, hotels can adopt an artistic strategy to satisfy customers' sensory experience. This study suggests that hotels can cultivate high-quality service employees through the construction of HPRPs and then successfully implement artistic strategies proposed by their managers.

Previous studies have revealed that hotels employ HPRPs to improve the professional skills and behaviors of their service employees so that they can render high-quality services (Karatepe, 2013; Tang and Tang, 2012). The present study confirms that HPRPs enhance service employees' artistic performance knowledge and skills and increase their flexibility in interacting with customers. HPRPs can help hotels perform artistic strategies so that managers can plan their realizable vision and create a unique service experience for customers. Thus, service employees can deliver excellent services to customers and assist in achieving their target operating performance.

The arts can enhance the life experience and enrich the meaning of life. In the past, scholars believed that using art as a management strategy is a source for hotels to obtain sustainable competitive advantages (Akoğlan Kozak and Acar Gürel, 2015; Strannegård and Strannegård, 2012). This study has further concluded that successful implementation of HPRPs is key for artistic hotels in improving their business performance. As HPRPs align HR practices with artistic strategies and each other, they directly implement those HR practices that can stimulate employees' abilities, motivation and opportunities and help them support each other. In particular, only the three-way interaction among three attributes of employees (that is, abilities × motivations × opportunities) in performing artistic services can maximize the contribution of artistic strategies to the hotels. HPRPs cannot achieve the best value of artistic strategies if any one of the employees' abilities, motivations or opportunities in implementing artistic performing service is relatively low. Hence, this study recommends to hotel managers that successful implementation of an artistic strategy requires managers to properly plan and implement HPRPs. Through the implementation of HPRPs, managers can enhance employees' ability to create and perform performance services (e.g., abilities of service innovation and service improvement) in the hotel, strengthen the motivations of employees to engage in artistic services (e.g., service, innovation and trust climate), as well as provide opportunities to implement performance services (e.g., provide performance opportunities and organizational support), and finally, improve operational performance.

This study has suggested that HPRPs are the key to cultivating hotel employees to become valuable resources. Through various mutually aligned HR activities, HPRPs reallocate the talents, tasks and time of each service employee. HPRPs can help managers reconfigure resources to stimulate employees' motivations and provide them with opportunities to develop their abilities. HPRPs are the driver to convert hotel resources in order to implement artistic strategies. More importantly, HPRPs that help with the successful implementation of artistic strategies are the key to increasing the added value of employee services. This strategic HR system can convert some of the employees' inefficient services into high value-added artistic performing services. By adjusting the allocation of human resources, managers can enable employees to provide local and artistic services that are distinct from those of their competitors and thus provide a better experiential value for their customers. HPRPs can help a hotel to maximize the value of its employees, even under limited human resources, by changing the service capabilities of each service employee in a flexible way.

Furthermore, the hotel's business costs can be lowered and its profits can be increased through the manpower required for implementing artistic performing services through HPRPs. Since managers arrange for hotel employees to act as performers for artistic performing services, the hotel could also indirectly reduce its costs for hiring performers and groups externally. This study has recommended that the hotel managers use HPRPs to support the implementation of a special service strategy (that is, artistic strategy). This will not only improve the quality of service and customer value, but also develop the hotel's unique services at the lowest cost.

HPRPs can balance the dilemma between the pursuit of value and cost reduction. Developing artistic service activities is expensive; therefore, implementation costs are a major challenge that hotels must overcome. The results of the present study show that hotels can employ HPRPs to precisely execute their artistic policy objectives. HPRPs ensure that each task accurately implements artistic strategies, and using HPRPs can effectively lower art-associated costs and thus assist the hotel in reaching its operational goals. HPRPs can assist hotels in reaching their target performance and also lower costs. Thus, HPRPs that support and target innovative artistic operational strategies can offset the conflict between business management and artistic values to gain a sustained competitive advantage.

4.1 Future Directions

This study presents the new development orientation and architecture of HPRPs and provides a hotel case for illustration. We call on prospective researchers to conduct qualitative or quantitative studies to examine the theoretical framework presented in this study. Several research directions are presented below for future reference. First, examine the proposed model with regard to the relationship between artistic strategies and HPRPs to influence operational performances. Second, verify the effect of HPRPs on abilities (human capital), motivations (organizational climate), and opportunities (attitudes and behaviors) of employees to implement artistic performance. Third, explore the three-way interaction among the three attributes of employees (that is, abilities × motivations × opportunities) on the performing arts services and operational performance. Last but not least, exploring the contribution of HPRPs to the hotel's management would be informative. Researchers should consider the characteristics of specific research contexts and the key strategies for achieving competitive advantage in this context. In summary, HPRPs can be used as hotel managers' tools to enable hotels to obtain a competitive advantage.

REFERENCES

Addis, M. and Holbrook, M.B. 2001. On the conceptual link between mass customisation and experiential consumption: An explosion of subjectivity. *Journal of Consumer Behaviour*, 1(1), 50–66.
Akoğlan Kozak, M. and Acar Gürel, D. 2015. Service design in hotels: A conceptual review. *Turizam: znanstveno-stručničasopis*, 63(2), 225–40.
Allen, D., Shore, L. and Griffeth, R. 2003. The role of perceived organizational support and supportive human resource practices in the turnover process. *Journal of Management*, 29, 99–118.
Allen, M. 1992. Communication and organizational commitment: Perceived organizational support as a mediating factor. *Communication Quarterly*, 40, 357–67.
Appelbaum, E., Bailey, T., Berg, P. and Kalleberg, A.L. 2000. *Manufacturing Advantage: Why High-performance Work Systems Pay Off*. Ithaca, NY: Cornell University Press.
Barsky, J. and Nash, L. 2002. Evoking emotion: Affective keys to hotel loyalty. *The Cornell Hotel and Restaurant Administration Quarterly*, 43(1), 39–46.
Batt, R. 2002. Managing customer services: Human resources practices, quit rates, and sales growth. *Academy of Management Journal*, 45(3), 587–97.
Bowen, D.E. and Ostroff, C. 2004. Understanding HRM–firm performance linkages: The role of the "strength" of the HRM system. *Academy of Management Review*, 29(2), 203–21.

Chang, K.C. 2016. Effect of servicescape on customer behavioral intentions: Moderating roles of service climate and employee engagement. *International Journal of Hospitality Management*, **53**, 116–28.

Chang, S., Gong, Y. and Shum, C. 2011. Promoting innovation in hospitality companies through human resource management practices. *International Journal of Hospitality Management*, **30**(4), 812–18.

Cheng, J.S., Tang, T.W., Shih, H.Y. and Wang, T.C. 2016. Designing lifestyle hotels. *International Journal of Hospitality Management*, **58**, 95–106.

Chiang, C.F. and Hsieh, T.S. 2012. The impacts of perceived organizational support and psychological empowerment on job performance: The mediating effects of organizational citizenship behavior. *International Journal of Hospitality Management*, **31**(1), 180–90.

Chiang, F.F.T. and Birtch, T.A. 2010. Pay for performance and work attitudes: The mediating role of employee–organization service value congruence. *International Journal of Hospitality Management*, **29**, 632–40.

Chick, G. 2009. Culture as a variable in the study of leisure. *Leisure Sciences*, **31**(3), 305–10.

Cordery, J., Sevastos, P., Mueller, W. and Parker, S. 1993. Correlates of employee attitudes toward functional flexibility. *Human Relations*, **46**(6), 705–23.

Countryman, C.C. and Jang, S. 2006. The effects of atmospheric elements on customer impression: The case of hotel lobbies. *International Journal of Contemporary Hospitality Management*, **18**(7), 534–45.

Crick, A.P. and Spencer, A. 2011. Hospitality quality: New directions and new challenges. *International Journal of Contemporary Hospitality Management*, **23**(4), 463–78.

Dewar, R.D. and Dutton, J.E. 1986. The adoption of radical and incremental innovations: An empirical analysis. *Management Science*, **32**, 1422–33.

Dhanaraj, C. and Parkhe, A. 2006. Orchestrating innovation networks. *Academy Management Review*, **31**(3), 659–69.

Dhar, R.L. 2015. The effects of high performance human resource practices on service innovative behaviour. *International Journal of Hospitality Management*, **51**, 67–75.

Durna, U., Dedeoglu, B.B. and Balikçioglu, S. 2015. The role of servicescape and image perceptions of customers on behavioral intentions in the hotel industry. *International Journal of Contemporary Hospitality Management*, **27**(7), 1728–48.

Fu, N., Flood, P.C., Bosak, J., Morris, T. and O'Regan, R. 2015. How do high performance work systems influence organizational innovation in professional service firms? *Employee Relations*, **37**(2), 209–31.

Gannon, J.M., Roper, A. and Doherty, L. 2015. Strategic human resource management: Insights from the international hotel industry. *International Journal of Hospitality Management*, **47**, 65–75.

Garg, S. and Dhar, R.L. 2014. Effects of stress, LMX and perceived organizational support on service quality: Mediating effects of organizational commitment. *Journal of Hospitality and Tourism Management*, **21**, 64–75.

Gould-Williams, J. 2003. The importance of HR practices and workplace trust in achieving superior performance: A study of public-sector organisations. *International Journal of Human Resource Management*, **14**, 28–54.

Grissemann, U., Plank, A. and Brunner-Sperdin, A. 2013. Enhancing business performance of hotels: The role of innovation and customer orientation. *International Journal of Hospitality Management*, **33**, 347–56.

Gruber, M., De Leon, N., George, G. and Thompson, P. 2015. Managing by design. *Academy of Management Journal*, **58**(1), 1–7.

Guzzo, R., Noonan, K. and Elron, E. 1994. Expatriate managers and the psychological contract. *Journal of Applied Psychology*, **79**, 617–27.

Hayton, J.C. and Kelley, D.J. 2006. A competency-based framework for promoting corporate entrepreneurship. *Human Resource Management*, **45**(3), 407–27.

Heide, M., Lardal, K. and Gronhaug, K. 2007. The design and management of ambience: Implications for hotel architecture and service. *Tourism Management*, **28**, 1315–25.

Holbrook, M.B. 2000. The millennial consumer in the texts of our times: Experience and entertainment. *Journal of Macromarketing*, **20**(2), 178–92.

Hume, M., Mort, G.S., Liesch, P.W. and Winzar, H. 2006. Understanding service experience in non-profit performing arts: Implications for operations and service management. *Journal of Operations Management*, **24**(4), 304–24.

Huselid, M.A. 1995. The impact of human resource management practices on turnover, productivity, and corporate financial performance. *Academy of Management Journal*, **38**, 635–62.

James, L.R. and Jones, A.P. 1974. Organizational climate: A review of theory and research. *Psychological Bulletin*, **81**, 1096–112.

Javalgi, R.R.G. and Todd, P.R. 2011. Entrepreneurial orientation, management commitment, and human capital: The internationalization of SMEs in India. *Journal of Business Research*, **64**(9), 1004–10.

Jogaratnam, G. 2017. The effect of market orientation, entrepreneurial orientation and human capital on positional advantage: Evidence from the restaurant industry. *International Journal of Hospitality Management*, **60**, 104–13.

Jones, D.L., Day, J. and Quadri-Felitti, D. 2013. Emerging definitions of boutique and lifestyle hotels: A Delphi study. *Journal of Travel & Tourism Marketing*, **30**(7), 715–31.

Jones, P. 1996. Managing hospitality innovation. *Cornell Hotel and Restaurant Administration Quarterly*, **37**, 86–95.

Kang, S.C., Morris, S.S. and Snell, S. 2007. Relational archetypes, organizational learning and value creation: Extending the human resource architecture. *Academy of Management Review*, **32**(1), 236–56.

Karatepe, O.M. 2013. High-performance work practices and hotel employee performance: The mediation of work engagement. *International Journal of Hospitality Management*, **32**, 132–40.

Kim, T.T., Kim, W.G., Park, S.S.S., Lee, G. and Jee, B. 2012. Intellectual capital and business performance: What structural relationships do they have in upper-upscale hotels? *International Journal of Tourism Research*, **14**(4), 391–408.

Korczynski, M. 2002. *Human Resource Management in Service Work*. New York: Palgrave.

Kotey, B. and Folker, C. 2007. Employee training in SMEs: Effect of size and firm type – Family and nonfamily. *Journal of Small Business Management*, **45**(2), 214–38.

Kumar, U., Kumar, V. and De Grosbois, D. 2008. Development of technological capability by Cuban hospitality organizations. *International Journal of Hospitality Management*, **27**(1), 12–22.

Lado, A.A. and Wilson, M.C. 1994. Human resource systems and sustained competitive advantage: A competency-based perspective. *Academy of Management Review*, **19**(4), 699–727.

Lages, C.R. and Piercy, N.F. 2012. Key drivers of frontline employee generation of ideas for customer service improvement. *Journal of Service Research*, **15**(2), 215–30.

Lee, T.J. 2011. Role of hotel design in enhancing destination branding. *Annals of Tourism Research*, **38**(2), 708–11.

Lepak, D.P. and Snell, S.A. 2002. Examining the human resource architecture: The relationships among human capital, employment, and human resource configurations. *Journal of Management*, **28**(4), 517–43.

Lepak, D.P., Takeuchi, R. and Snell, S.A. 2003. Employment flexibility and firm performance: Examining the interaction effects of employment mode, environmental dynamism, and technological intensity. *Journal of Management*, **29**(5), 681–703.

Liao, H. and Chuang, A. 2004. A multilevel investigation of factors influencing employee service performance and customer outcomes. *Academy of Management Journal*, **47**(1), 41–58.

Liao, H., Toya, K., Lepak, D.P. and Hong, Y. 2009. Do they see eye to eye? Management and employee perspectives of high-performance work systems and influence processes on service quality. *Journal of Applied Psychology*, **94**(2), 371–91.

Lin, Y.T. and Liu, N.C. 2016. High performance work systems and organizational service performance: The roles of different organizational climates. *International Journal of Hospitality Management*, **55**, 118–28.

López-Cabrales, Á., Real, J.C. and Valle, R. 2011. Relationships between human resource management practices and organizational learning capability: The mediating role of human capital. *Personnel Review*, **40**(3), 344–63.

Magelssen, S. 2003. The staging of history: Theatrical, temporal and economic borders of Historyland. *Visual Communication*, **2**(1), 7–24.

Mayer, R.C. and Davis, J.H. 1999. The effect of the performance appraisal system on trust for management: A field quasi-experiment, *Journal of Applied Psychology*, **84**, 123–36.

McCleary, K.W., Lattimer, C.L., Clemenz, C.E. and Weaver, P.A. 2008. From Broadway to the Bistro: Partnering with the arts to attract upscale customers. *International Journal of Hospitality Management*, **27**(2), 197–203.

Meyer, J.P. and Smith, C.A. 2000. HRM practices and organizational commitment: Test of a mediation model. *Canadian Journal of Administrative Sciences*, **17**, 319–31.

Minbaeva, D., Foss, N. and Snell, S. 2009. Guest editors' introduction: Bringing the knowledge perspective into HRM. *Human Resource Management*, **48**(4), 477–83.

Molina, F.X. and Martínez, M.T. 2010. Social networks: Effects of social capital on firm innovation. *Journal of Small Business Management*, **48**(2), 258–79.

Mumford, M.D. 2000. Managing creative people: Strategies and tactics for innovation. *Human Resource Management Review*, **10**, 313–51.

Murphy, K.S. and Murrmann, S. 2009. The research design used to develop a high performance management system construct for US restaurant managers. *International Journal of Hospitality Management*, **28**(4), 547–55.

Nieves, J. and Quintana, A. 2016. Human resource practices and innovation in the hotel industry: The mediating role of human capital, *Tourism and Hospitality Research* (January).

Nyberg, T.P., Moliterno, D. and Hale, D.P. 2014. Resource-based perspective on unit-level human capital: A review and integration. *Journal of Management*, **40**(1), 316–46.

Ostroff, C. and Bowen, D.E. 2000. Moving HR to a higher level: HR practices and organizational effectiveness. In K.J. Klein and S.W.J. Kozlowski (eds). *Multilevel Theory, Research, and Methods in Organizations: Foundations, Extensions, and New Directions*. San Francisco, CA: Jossey-Bass, pp. 211–66.

Ottenbacher, M.C. 2007. Innovation management in the hospitality industry: Different strategies for achieving success. *Journal of Hospitality & Tourism Research*, **31**(4), 431–54.

Ottenbacher, M. and Gnoth, J. 2005. How to develop successful hospitality innovation. *The Cornell Hotel and Restaurant Administration Quarterly*, **46**(2), 205–22.

Paré, G. and Tremblay, M. 2007. The impact of human resources practices on IT personnel commitment, citizenship behaviors, and turnover intentions. *Group and Organization Management*, **37**(3), 326–57.

Pizam, A. 2015. Lifestyle hotels: Consistency and uniformity vs. individuality and personalization. *International Journal of Hospitality Management*, **46**, 213–14.

Ployhart, R.E., Weekley, J.A. and Ramsey, J. 2009. The consequences of human resource stocks and flows: A longitudinal examination of unit service orientation and unit effectiveness. *Academy of Management Journal*, **52**(5), 996–1015.

Raub, S. 2008. Does bureaucracy kill individual initiative: The impact of structure on organizational citizenship behavior in the hospitality industry. *International Journal of Hospitality Management*, **27**(2), 179–86.

Rhoades, L. and Eisenberger, R. 2002. Perceived organizational support: A review of the literature. *Journal of Applied Psychology*, **87**, 698–714.

Rhodes, D. 1981. The fine art of selecting fine art for hotels. *Cornell Hotel and Restaurant Administration Quarterly*, **22**(3), 62–4.

Ro, H. and Chen, P.J. 2011. Empowerment in hospitality organizations: Customer orientation and organizational support. *International Journal of Hospitality Management*, **30**(2), 422–8.

Roehl, W. and Swerdlow, S. 1999. Training and its impact on organizational commitment among lodging employees. *Journal of Hospitality and Tourism Research*, **23**, 176–94.

Ryan, C. 2015. Trends in hospitality management research: A personal reflection. *International Journal of Contemporary Hospitality Management*, **27**(3), 340–61.

Sainaghi, R., Phillips, P. and Corti, V. 2013. Measuring hotel performance: Using a balanced scorecard perspectives' approach. *International Journal of Hospitality Management*, **34**, 150–59.

Salanova, M., Agut, S. and Peiró, J.M. 2015. Linking organizational resources and work engagement to employee performance and customer loyalty: The mediation of service climate. *Journal of Applied Psychology*, **90**(6), 1217–27.

Schneider, B. 1990. The climate for service: An application of the climate construct. In B. Schneider (ed.). *Organizational Climate and Culture*. San Francisco: Jossey-Bass, pp. 383–412.

Schneider, B. and Reichers, A.E. 1983. On the etiology of climates. *Personnel Psychology*, **36**(1), 19–39.

Schneider, B., White, S.S. and Paul, M. 1998. Linking service climate and customer perceptions of service quality: Test of a causal model. *Journal of Applied Psychology*, **83**(2), 150–63.

Strannegård, L. and Strannegård, M. 2012. Works of art: Aesthetic ambitions in design hotels. *Annals of Tourism Research*, **39**(4), 1995–2012.

Swanson, S.R. and Davis, J.C. 2012. Delight and outrage in the performing arts: A critical incidence analysis. *Journal of Marketing Theory and Practice*, **20**(3), 263–78.

Tang, T.W. 2014. Becoming an ambidextrous hotel: The role of customer orientation. *International Journal of Hospitality Management*, **39**, 1–10.

Tang, T.W. 2016. Making innovation happen through building social capital and scanning environment. *International Journal of Hospitality Management*, **56**, 56–65.

Tang, T.W. and Tang, Y.Y. 2012. Promoting service-oriented organizational citizenship behaviors in hotels: The role of high-performance human resource practices and organizational social climates. *International Journal of Hospitality Management*, **31**(3), 885–95.

Thornhill, S. 2006. Knowledge, innovation and firm performance in high- and low-technology regimes. *Journal of Business Venturing*, **21**(5), 687–703.

Tracey, J.B. and Tews, M.J. 2004. An empirical investigation of the relationships among climate, capabilities, and unit performance. *Journal of Hospitality & Tourism Research*, **28**(3), 298–312.

Tremblay, M., Cloutier, J., Simard, G., Chênevert, D. and Vandenberghe, C. 2010. The role of HRM practices, procedural justice, organizational support and trust in organizational commitment and in-role and extra-role performance. *The International Journal of Human Resource Management*, **21**(3), 405–33.

Tussyadiah, I.P. 2014. Toward a theoretical foundation for experience design in tourism. *Journal of Travel Research*, **53**(5), 543–64.

Úbeda-García, M., Cortés, E.C., Marco-Lajara, B. and Zaragoza-Sáez, P. 2014. Strategy, training and performance fit. *International Journal of Hospitality Management*, **42**, 100–16.

Way, S.A. 2002. High performance work systems and intermediate indicators of firm performance within the US small business sector. *Journal of Management*, **28**(6), 765–85.

Wayne, S.J., Shore, L.M. and Liden, R.C. 1997. Perceived organizational support and leadership–member exchange: A social exchange perspective. *Academy of Management Journal*, **40**, 82–111.

Wayne, S., Shore, L., Bommer, W. and Tetrick, L. 2002. The role of fair treatment and rewards in perception of organizational support and leader–member exchange. *Journal of Applied Psychology*, **87**, 590–98.

Weaver, A. 2009. Tourism and aesthetic design: Enchantment, style, and commerce. *Journal of Tourism and Cultural Change*, **7**(3), 179–89.

Whitener, E. 2001. Do high commitment human resource practices affect employee commitment: A cross-level analysis using hierarchical linear modeling. *Journal of Management*, **27**, 515–37.

Wu, J. 2004. Knowledge stock, search competence and innovation performance in the U.S. electrical medical device industry. Doctoral thesis, Purdue University, West Lafayette.

Yamao, S., De Cieri, H. and Hutchings, K. 2009. Transferring subsidiary knowledge to global headquarters: Subsidiary senior executives' perceptions of the role of HR configurations in the development of knowledge stocks. *Human Resource Management*, **48**(4), 531–54.

Yavas, U., Karatepe, O.M. and Babakus, E. 2010. Relative efficacy of organizational support and personality traits in predicting service recovery and job performances: A study of frontline employees in Turkey. *Tourism Review*, **65**(3), 70–83.

Youndt, M.A. and Snell, S.A. 2004. Human resource configurations, intellectual capital and organizational performance. *Journal of Managerial Issues*, **XVI**(3), 337–60.

Yu, C. and Frenkel, S.J. 2013. Explaining task performance and creativity from perceived organizational support theory: Which mechanisms are more important? *Journal of Organizational Behavior*, **34**(8), 1165–81.

Index